Reference
Does Not Circulate

NOV 12 1996

Contemporary Authors ®
Autobiography Series

ISSN 0748-0636

Contemporary Authors

Autobiography Series

Shelly Andrews
Editor

volume **24**

GALE

DETROIT · NEW YORK · TORONTO · LONDON

EDITORIAL STAFF

Shelly Andrews, *Editor and Desktop Publisher*
Linda R. Andres, *Associate Editor*
Marilyn O'Connell Allen and Sheryl Ciccarelli, *Assistant Editors*
Alan Hedblad, Joanna Brod, Cindy Buck, Charity Anne Dorgan, Mary Gillis, Heidi J. Hagen,
Laurie Collier Hillstrom, Motoko Fujishiro Huthwaite, Carolyn C. March, Tom and Sara Pendergast,
Adele Sarkissian, Diane Telgen, Kathleen Witman, and Lauri Wulf, *Contributing Copyeditors*

Victoria B. Cariappa, *Research Manager*
Corporate Research Information Service, *Research*

Hal May, *Publisher*
Joyce Nakamura, *Managing Editor, Children's and Young Adult Literature*

Mary Beth Trimper, *Production Director*
Deborah Milliken, *Production Assistant*

Barbara Yarrow, *Graphic Services Manager*
C. J. Jonik, *Desktop Publisher (book cover)*
Randy A. Bassett, *Imaging Supervisor*
Robert Duncan, *Imaging Specialist*

Theresa Rocklin, *Manager, Technical Support Services*

Library of Congress Catalog Card Number 86-641293
ISBN 0-8103-9331-X
ISSN 0748-0636

Printed in the United States of America

10 9 8 7 6 5 4 3 2 1

Contents

Preface   vii
Special Thanks   ix
A Brief Sampler   xi
Acknowledgments   xiii

Preface

A Unique Collection of Essays

Each volume in the *Contemporary Authors Autobiography Series (CAAS)* presents an original collection of autobiographical essays written especially for the series by noted writers.

CA Autobiography Series is designed to be a meeting place for writers and readers—a place where writers can present themselves, on their own terms, to their audience; and a place where general readers, students of contemporary literature, teachers and librarians, even aspiring writers can become better acquainted with familiar authors and meet others for the first time.

This is an opportunity for writers who may never write a full-length autobiography to let their readers know how they see themselves and their work, what brought them to this time and place.

Even for those authors who have already published full-length autobiographies, there is the opportunity in *CAAS* to bring their readers "up to date" or perhaps to take a different approach in the essay format. In some instances, previously published material may be reprinted or expanded upon; this fact is always noted at the end of such an essay. Individually, the essays in this series can enhance the reader's understanding of a writer's work; collectively, they are lessons in the creative process and in the discovery of its roots.

CAAS makes no attempt to give a comprehensive overview of authors and their works. That outlook is already well represented in biographies, reviews, and critiques published in a wide variety of sources. Instead, *CAAS* complements that perspective and presents what no other ongoing reference source does: the view of contemporary writers that is shaped by their own choice of materials and their own manner of storytelling.

Who Is Covered?

Like its parent series, *Contemporary Authors*, the *CA Autobiography Series* sets out to meet the needs and interests of a wide range of readers. Each volume includes essays by writers in all genres whose work is being read today. We consider it extraordinary that so many busy authors from throughout the world are able to interrupt their existing writing, teaching, speaking, traveling, and other schedules to converge on a given deadline for any one volume. So it is not always possible that all genres can be equally and uniformly represented from volume to volume, although we strive to include writers working in a variety of categories, including fiction, nonfiction, and poetry. As only a few writers specialize in a single area, the breadth of writings by authors in this volume also encompasses drama, translation, and criticism as well as work for movies, television, radio, newspapers, and journals.

What Each Essay Includes

Authors who contribute to *CAAS* are invited to write a "mini-autobiography" of approximately 10,000 words. In order to give the writer's imagination free rein, we suggest no guidelines or pattern for the essay.

We only ask that each writer tell his or her story in the manner and to the extent that feels most natural and appropriate. In addition, writers are asked to supply a selection of personal photographs showing themselves at various ages, as well as important people and special moments in their lives. Our contributors have responded generously, sharing with us some of their most treasured mementoes. The result is a special blend of text and photographs that will attract even the casual browser. Other features include:

Bibliography at the end of each essay, listing book-length works in chronological order of publication. Each bibliography in this volume was compiled by members of the *CAAS* editorial staff and submitted to the author for review.

Cumulative index in each volume, which cites all the essayists in the series as well as the subjects presented in the essays: personal names, titles of works, geographical names, schools of writing, etc. To ensure ease of use for these cumulating references, the name of the essayist is given before the volume and page number(s) for every reference that appears in more than one essay. In the following example, the entry in the index allows the user to identify the essay writers by name:

> Auden, W.H.
>   Allen **6**:18, 24
>   Ashby **6**:36, 39
>   Bowles **1**:86
>   etc.

For references that appear in only one essay, the volume and page number(s) are given but the name of the essayist is omitted. For example:

> Stieglitz, Alfred **1**:104, 109, 110

CAAS is something more than the sum of its individual essays. At many points the essays touch common ground, and from these intersections emerge new patterns of information and impressions. The index is an important guide to these interconnections.

For Additional Information

For detailed information on awards won, adaptations of works, critical reviews of works, and more, readers are encouraged to consult Gale's *Contemporary Authors* cumulative index for authors' listings in other Gale sources. These include, among others, *Contemporary Authors*, *Contemporary Authors New Revision Series*, *Dictionary of Literary Biography*, and *Contemporary Literary Criticism*. For autobiographical entries written by children and young adult authors see *Something about the Author Autobiography Series*.

Special Thanks

We wish to acknowledge our special gratitude to each of the authors in this volume. They all have been most kind and cooperative in contributing not only their talents but their enthusiasm and encouragement to this project.

We also would like to thank past, current, and future contributors and other individuals who have taken the time to provide feedback and make recommendations for this series.

Ivan Argüelles

Rae Armantrout

Dorothy Bryant

Neeli Cherkovski

Cid Corman

Antonio D'Alfonso

Jack Foley

Reginald Gibbons

Edwin Honig

Norman Levine

Judith Roeke

Craig Tenney

Nanos Valaoritis

Alma Luz Villanueva

Lisa Zeidner

We encourage our readers to explore the whole *CAAS* series. Please write and tell us if we can make *CAAS* more helpful to you. Direct your comments and suggestions to the editor:

MAIL: Shelly Andrews, *Contemporary Authors Autobiography Series*
Gale Research
835 Penobscot Bldg.
645 Griswold St.
Detroit, MI 48226-4094

TELEPHONE: (800) 347-GALE

FAX: (313) 961-6599

E-MAIL: sandrews@Gale.com@Galesmtp

A Brief Sampler

Each essay in the series has a special character and point of view that sets it apart from its companions. A small sampler of anecdotes and musings from the essays in this volume hint at the unique perspective of these life stories.

Rick DeMarinis: "There was a family summer house on Staten Island. My father was given the job of entertaining some men who had just arrived from Sicily. He brought me and my mother, as well as my grandmother and Aunt Mildred, to the house. It was billed as a vacation. The men from Sicily were very polite and helpful. They did most of the cooking, sang songs, played with me, and in general charmed everyone with their good manners and high spirits. They charmed everyone except my grandmother, who did not trust Sicilians. 'Killers!' My grandmother muttered. 'Assassins!' And of course they *were*. Their services had been solicited by the mob and they had come to New York to rub someone out. It was a job they were obviously comfortable with and consequently they were not the grimacing hoodlums Hollywood in the 1930s liked to portray, but fine, jovial, life-loving fellows who really knew how to cook."

Vincent Ferrini: "I had already seen Edmund Sullivan's show of sculptures, drawings, paintings, when he asked me what I liked best, and I said that self-portrait. And John Di Marino says will you look at my paintings and I, you want me to look at your work, are you sure, yes, are you sure, yes yes, so we walk to his studio upstairs, to this small room stuffed with echoes of Gaugan, Van Gogh, Pisarro, Matisse, you name it, you're a blotting picker upper. Get rid of this stuff. Blindfold yourself and paint with your arm, I will, he wraps a white rag over his eyes, picks up a brush and a can of white paint, lifts an old vertical painting, puts in on the easel upright, with one thrust at the canvas, then grabs a brush and a can of deep blue paint, whacks it on the canvas, back to the first can, slams a stroke fast as Van Gogh, white hair, blue nose and lip, white chin and beard, fast furious, he rips off the provident blinding rag, in a hot glory, it's your portrait, and I, that's your finest work, it's yours— He's launched full blast out of Zen. From then on his drawings are rushing out of that faucet—"

Alicia (Suskin) Ostriker: "To learn was freedom. I had one gifted teacher after another. Miss Murphy, under whose massive dowager wing I glimpsed the clean beauty of geometry. Mr. Heyman, a refugee from Eastern Europe, who brought European history to life by his tenacious attachment to the Reformation. Was everyone as thrilled as I when Martin Luther nailed his Ninety-five Theses to the door of Wittenburg Cathedral, in defiance of the Pope? Here I stand; I can do no other, said Luther. Mr. Lenrow in Fifth Form English, who snarled Hamlet's 'one can smile and smile and be a villain' speech magnificently, capping it with a crescendo 'O vengeance!' ending in a long bellow. Miss French, a lady dry as sand, who once uncharacteristically played *Threepenny Opera* in class. Oh, the shark had pretty teeth, dear, and Lotte Lenya's voice was like the rasp of my own adolescent contempt for society and propriety. Over my shoulder I scanned the classroom, certain that none of my privileged classmates could understand. The wry and twinkling Mr. Brown in Sixth Form, as advisor to the high school yearbook, chose the quotations for each student's senior portrait. The quote for me was 'Liberty of thought is the life of the soul.' The quote for Jerry Ostriker, whom I did not yet know I was going to marry, was 'I thought of questions which have no reply.'"

Louis Owens: "Living in a house in the dry New Mexico mountains now, I put out bird feeders and sunken troughs of water, and I watch with great pleasure the rabbits and tassel-eared squirrels come to eat the spilled feed and drink the water. Both squirrels and rabbits, in fact, have become so familiar that they simply move a few feet out of the way when one of our family appears, not to be stepped on, and continue whatever they are doing. At times I find myself politely asking cottontails to move from the doorstep so that I can enter my house, or I am awakened by the chattering of a squirrel peering through my upstairs window, angry because the sunflower seeds haven't been replenished in the second-story squirrel feeder. But amidst this peaceable kingdom I now inhabit, I confess that I still cannot watch a fat cottontail grazing beneath the bird feeder without almost tasting the aroma of lightly floured rabbit breast frying in butter. Someday, I think—and tease my children with the thought—I might yet weaken and eat my wild neighbors just as my neighbors do to one another. When I run the forest trails near my home, I watch for the deer, fox and coyote, bobcat and badger, porcupine and skunk tracks that appear every morning. And on the very best mornings, my strides become faster and lighter as I find myself gliding over the almost dainty tracks of a black bear who has ambled along the same trail some time during the night."

Alma Luz Villanueva: ". . . once while swimming in the ocean by myself and going out a little further than usual (I could swim a mile easily, having been on a swim team for a year), an undertow caught me. Though I'd been trained not to, I struggled with it until I realized it was taking me out (maybe) further than I could swim back to shore. When I stopped struggling—that very instant—the undertow let me go. By then I was exhausted from the struggle, and land looked so far away. I knew, right then, at that very moment, I was going to die. Waves of terror rippled through my body, and then, still floating on that treacherous ocean, I saw the lights (from the sun) on every wave envelope me, leave me, surrounding me. Suddenly, I was calm, and as I slowly began to swim toward shore (feeling too tired to reach it), this is what I felt: a large, cupped hand scooped my tiny body up (the light-filled wave) and, without any break or pause, brought me riding, floating, flying to shore. I knew this was a miracle, but I didn't want to repeat it, so I never swam out that far again on the open ocean. (Now I swim and kayak in Monterey Bay, which has canyons deeper than the Grand Canyon—imagine.) Looking back, thirty-nine years later, I see the importance of this memory: trust, limitation, revelation, *trust with knowledge.* I see that death (transformation) has always been my teacher; that when death and life *meet* miracles occur. As a writer, I treasure this truth, for without it: nothing."

These brief examples only suggest what lies ahead in this volume. The essays will speak differently to different readers; but they are certain to speak best, and most eloquently, for themselves.

Acknowledgments

Grateful acknowledgment is made to those publishers, photographers, and artists whose works appear with these authors' essays.

Photographs/Art

Ivan Argüelles: p. 1, © 1992 Lori Eanes/*East Bay Express;* p. 6, Newman Kraft Studio; p. 10, Danny Lyon.

Charles Bernstein: p. 31, © Kari Sarkkinen; p. 36, Sonja Bullaty; p. 40, © susan bee laufer; p. 41, Robert Turney; p. 48, Toni Simon.

Neeli Cherkovski: p. 83, © Ira Cohen; p. 93, Sam Cherry; p. 94, allan dean walker; pp. 97, 98, Chris Felver; p. 99, © Regina Cherry.

Rick DeMarinis: p. 107, Cynthia Farah.

Vincent Ferrini: p. 125, Lynne Geldard/*Salem Evening News;* p. 127, *Lynn Daily Evening;* p. 143, © 1989 Paul Foley; p. 144, Frank Montrond; p. 146, Hartley Ferguson.

Jack Foley: p. 153, Robert Schneck; p. 165, Weitzmann; p. 170, Fred Betz; p. 172, Jenny Chu; p. 173, Rick Mahan; p. 175, Painting by Leonard Breger; p. 176, © Carol Boyd.

Diane Glancy: p. 213, Jim Turnure.

Lyle Glazier: p. 217, Jill M. Hayes.

Ernest Hebert: p. 243, © Geoff Hansen/*Valley News;* p. 253, © Alan Mendelsshon; p. 257, © 1987 Robert B. Perreault.

Alicia Ostriker: p. 266, © Harcourt-Harris; p. 278, Debra Cook.

Louis Owens: p. 281, Brett Hall Photography.

Alma Luz Villanueva: pp. 299, 313, 316, 317, 319, 321, 322, Wilfredo Q. Castaño.

ruth weiss: pp. 325, 349, William Westwick; pp. 333, 334, C. R. Snyder; p. 336, Paul Beattie; p. 340, Ingeborg Gerdes; p. 346, Ingeborg Gerdes/Lisa Wuennenberg. Collage by Paul Blake; p. 350, Jan Hinson; Calligraphic lettering designed by Paul Blake.

Lisa Zeidner: p. 365, © Jerry Bauer.

Lyle Glazier. Reprinted with permission of Vermont Council on the Arts./ Poem "The Shanties," from *Prefatory Lyrics,* by Lyle Glazier. Coffee House Press, 1991. Copyright 1991 by Lyle Glazier. Reprinted with permission of Coffee House Press./ Poem excerpts from "Azubah Nye," in *Azubah Nye,* by Lyle Glazier. White Pine Press, 1988. Copyright 1988 by Lyle Glazier. Reprinted with permission of White Pine Press.

Alma Luz Villanueva: Poems "Indian Summer Ritual," "Weighing My Father's Soul," and "Dear World," by Alma Luz Villanueva. Reprinted with permission of Alma Luz Villanueva./ Poem "To Jesus Villanueva, with Love" in *Blood Root,* by Alma Luz Villanueva. Place of Herons Press, 1977. Reprinted with permission of Alma Luz Villanueva./ Poem excerpts from "Mother, May I?" in *Planet* with *Mother, May I?,* by Alma Luz Villanueva. Bilingual Press/Editorial Bilingüe, Arizona State University, Tempe, AZ, 1993. Copyright 1993 by Alma Luz Villanueva. Reprinted with permission of Bilingual Press/Editorial Bilingüe./ Poem "The Balance" and "Spectrum," and excerpt from "Dark Roots," in *Life Span,* by Alma Luz Villanueva. Place of Herons Press, 1984. Reprinted with permission of Alma Luz Villanueva.

ruth weiss: Poem excerpts "Incident," "Single Out," "The Brink," and "ANAÏS," in *Single Out,* by ruth weiss. D'Aurora Press, 1978. Copyright © 1978 ruth weiss. Reprinted with permission of ruth weiss.

Lisa Zeidner: Poem "Gypsy Moths" in *Pocket Sundial,* by Lisa Zeidner. University of Wisconsin Press, 1988. © 1988. (Madison: The University of Wisconsin Press.) Reprinted by permission of The University of Wisconsin Press.

Contemporary Authors ®

Autobiography Series

Ivan Argüelles

1939-

ASI ES LA VIDA

Ivan Argüelles, reading from Looking for Mary Lou, *1992*

> *to begin by announcing the form*
> *and have no hands to shape it*
>
> I got the key to the highway
> billed out and bound to go
> I got to leave here running
> cuz walking is much too slow
>
> —*Jazz Gillum*

Where my brother is today, I don't know. Twins are supposed to have that connective sense, but it fails me. He came into the world ten minutes before I did, January 24, 1939, in St. Mary's Hospital, Rochester, Minnesota. We were conceived nine months earlier in Mexico DF, but Mom brought us back to her hometown, Rochester, Minnesota, so we could be U.S. citizens. *Los cuates,* the twins, this single transcendental aspect of my existence: Joseph Anthony and Ivan Wallace Argüelles, born to Enrique Argüelles of Guadalajara, Jalisco, and to Ethel Pearl Meyer, Olmstead County, Minnesota. Engendered into this bilingual environment I was destined to become multilingual.

Earliest years were spent in La Ciudad de Mexico, 40 Calle Tula, not far from beautiful Chapultepec Park. Earliest memories—watching Enrique paint on a large canvas the represen-

Parents, Enrique and Ethel Pearl Argüelles,
Mexico City, 1921

tation of a grey vase with nostalgic yellow flowers.
Mom somewhere in the background, smoking
herself into tuberculosis. Sister Laurita played
with the twins as if they were dolls, Ivan pouting in the China Poblana skirt, Joe (José) pouting
in his serape under the mild mile-high sun.
Recollections of posh birthday parties for
Cuauhtemoc Cardenas, son of the Mexican
president, Lazaro Cardenas. Not to forget that
Trotsky had exiled himself in Mexico, and my
father, who knew him, claims to have been
the first on the spot after the communists' brutal
assassination.

"I never saw so many brains in my life,"
he was to recount on repeated occasions throughout his life. A failed artist, Enrique's existence
was to be a pathetic patchwork of artistic efforts. In those days he was in the know with
Diego Rivera, Rufino Tamayo, and Frida Kahlo,
among others. He compensated for his lack of
success in the arts by encouraging his sons,
especially in painting.

For whatever obscure reason, we left Mexico
City and went to Mexicali, on the U.S. border,
where Enrique was something like an adjutant

or chauffeur to the territorial governor. Enormous cockroaches surprised by electricity on white
stucco walls. Then to Los Angeles in El Dorado,
so the twins could get an American education.
Never mind that sister Laurita had been uprooted after thirteen years in Mexico. We lived
at 11870 Lucille Street, Culver City, at the end
of the street the Howard Hughes Airport, and
not far on Jefferson Boulevard the fortress-like
MGM studios. First grade at Playa del Rey School,
Laurita at Venice High. Sundays at the beach
in Santa Monica. Dad as elegant as ever, and
more confusingly distant, violent fights with my
sister, Aunt Lucia had to restrain him. Didn't
understand what was happening. Then WHAM
Mom terribly sick with TB. Long lugubrious
winter train ride to Minnesota, transplanting
this wretched family once again. No discernible future, what with papacito barely in command of English, and Mom with what could
be a terminal disease.

What a shock! This bitter cold snowy Minnesota winter. How did we get here, lodged in
a sterile bedroom in our grandparents' large
white-box boarding house? Everything was an
ineffable and painful mystery. Martin and Laura
Meyer, peasants from Westphalia, Germany,
started their American dream in Potsdam, Minnesota, where Grandpa ran a saloon, until it
burned down. He finally made it as an insurance salesman in Rochester. How did their
daughter Ethel ever get it into her head to go
to Mexico City and fall in love with someone
with an unpronounceable name? Tight-mouthed
German-Lutherans, with more than parsimoni-
ous manners, they forced the Trinity Lutheran
Church, a blank white slat-board architectural
code in the middle of town, on us. In their
austere living room, across from the ancient
radio, was a glass-door cabinet, with, side by
side, a large black Fraktur-Skript German Bible
and a skull with a movable lower jaw. Church
and Sunday school on a regular basis. Learned
to fear death early on from the frightening
sermons of Pastor Eifert. This was only somewhat mitigated by the inspired playing of an
organist named Zilski, who obviously loved Bach.

Mom in a sanitorium in Cannon Falls (I
thought the word was "cemetery"), and because
TB was the AIDS of the day, the twins were
separated from their mother literally for over
a year. The suspicion that we might have been
"infected" required repeated and lugubrious
Saturday morning visits to the Mayo Clinic for

X-rays. Then one day Uncle Wally packed us into his car to go to Cannon Falls. We were allowed to see her only from a distance, across a big room. Mom, a wraith in long floral gown, distant, a chill.

Life was indeed tough. Our first day at Lincoln School, the kids told my brother and me that we were not Americans but Indians. Laurita went to hell fast, the high school hoyden. Dad, once in the retinue of the president of Mexico, now a cook in St. Mary's Hospital, later a bartender at the Carlton Hotel, and a notorious town drunk. Once out of the "San," Mom managed to get us our own house at 904 7th Avenue SW, where I lived until I graduated from high school in 1956.

Rochester was a small town (population 25,000) and superficially a very normal one. It was characterized by the Mayo Clinic and a very regular street pattern, quadrilinear, divided neatly by the intersection of Broadway and Center streets, into four quarters with evenly numbered streets and avenues. The doctors, who gave the town the imbalance to its "normalcy," lived in the southwest quarter on "Pill Hill," and we had the fortune or misfortune to live at the foot of said hill. We were both an embarrassment and a fascination to those around us. Nobody ever said our name correctly—everything from "Hargraves" to "Argoolies," but whatever it was we were "wetbacks" pure and simple, unique in this white Minnesota town. My earliest childhood experiences are best expressed in my long experimental poem "Chicano," some portions of which follow:

this aint no fresno farm poem

pass the dago red, puto

this ain't no abuela poem

we got fangs

ever read that poem CACAMADRE?   this is one mother

dime la verdad, man, where you get that accent?

. . . .

my earliest memories involve my nurse-maid chabela
who used to take me to chapultepec park off paseo de la reforma
and look at the peacocks behind the bars

later on it all drifts into a scene from los olvidados

"ojitos"   "el perro negro"

soulful tearful notes of trio los pancho on an old 78 RPM

"perfidia"

to you my heart cries out perfidia

. . . .

we are kings of loco weed

we are kings of lorca weed

qué peligro   los comunistas!

to you my heart cries out perfidia

and every morning pop would fix up a breakfast of chicharrones and grits
imported a tortilla-making machine from his sister aurora
and all that tabasco sauce and green peppers and cebolla, man

I can still smell it

never was home Xmas eve out drinking till he was brain dead
took up with a pair of fools named bud and eddie
who ran the mobil station on 4th street   was it 4th street?

and standing up tall striking his pecho with his fist

"soy comunista!   soy comunista!"

he saw trotsky's brains pop did   sure, man

(From *Poetry USA,* numbers 25 & 26, 1993)

Dad was keen on giving his sons art lessons. At an early age we were quite skilled at drawing with crayons or pencil, and developed a great facility for copying, usually from comic books. We also began creating maps of large imaginary cities, usually on great rectangles of paper discarded after X-rays. But an even more important form of escape was the public library, a wonderful sandstone structure across from the Mayo Clinic. I think I must have gone through every book in the children's room, from Zim's book on submarines to Howard Pyle's Arthurian retellings. Years later I was to write: "I write everything I read and I read everything I write." This was no doubt the genesis of my Pantograph (the writing of everything).

Music also played a very important role for me from the earliest days. Father was a really fine piano player, and there were nights, three in the morning, when I would wake up and hear him playing the most haunting pieces, enough to make you weep. And he loved the classics, being in possession of a collection of old 78s, which included Beethoven's *Pastoral Symphony,* Handel's organ concerti, and Dvořák's Slavonic dances. He thrust piano lessons on us, which didn't take. Then he insisted I learn to play the cello, pointing to the masterful example of Pablo Casals. I never developed any real skill at playing an instrument, but the enormous and profound pleasure of listening to music has never left me. And then there was Father's mariachi, syphoned up from the basement many a drunken weekend night to our bedrooms, pieces like Trio Los Pancho doing "Perfidia." And Mother, too, at the piano doing melancholy waltzes by Chopin. Laurita was a full-fledged bobby-soxer, Frank Sinatra her idol. This musical eclecticism really opened me up to all genres and styles. Nowadays, when people ask me what my Pantograph is about, I respond by saying that, like music, it's not about anything that you can "describe" either narratively or rationally.

From library to language. I recall running across the Middle English poem "Sumer is icumen in," and marvelling that the words in their quaint orthography really belonged to the same language I employ today. All things considered, up through the eighth grade I was a mediocre student, a daydreamer, living in imaginary maps and unheard of dialects. Given choices for courses to take in the ninth grade, I noticed that Latin was offered, a language still commonly taught

in high schools. The kids bound for college normally took two years of Latin. I took all four years offered. I was the star Latin pupil. I loved it, and this was the start of my polyglot derangement. On the first day of Latin the word *mensa* (table) leaped to my senses. It was obviously the same word we used at home, the Spanish *mesa.* This etymological discovery really excited me. So there were these "Romance" languages, descended from the language of Virgil. WOW, within a year I was teaching myself Italian, French, and Portuguese. The encyclopedia told me there were other Romance tongues as well, Romanian, Provençal, and Catalan. On a trip to Chicago during my fifteenth year I obtained a Romanian grammar, a language I mastered before I finished high school. Provençal and Catalan came a bit later. Romanian and Catalan, being lesser known, have especially attracted me, and I began translat-

Laurita, Granny Meyer, José (left),
and Ivan, Mexico City, about 1943

ing poetry from these languages as far back as high school.

During the summer of 1953 Father took the twins on a long trip back to Mexico. It was to be the last time we were to see our *abuelo* (grandfather). The trip made a strong impression on me and Joe, I think more on him than on me. Mexico City was still rather tranquil compared to the frightening megalopolis it is now. Climbing the Pyramids of the Sun and the Moon are seminal memories for me. My uncle Julio, who put us up, also had a fine artistic sense, and I am always grateful to him for introducing me to the fifth symphony of Dmitri Shostakovich, a piece that has always held some kind of heraldic and heroic symbolism for me. But a disturbing aspect of this trip for me was my father's growing preference for my brother. Particularly when we went to art museums or visited the ruins, he only addressed Joe. When I got home I wept bitterly to my mother about this. Although Joe and I had been progressing in our visual arts skills, I then made a conscious decision not to compete with him. I made the firm vow to be a poet. I knew I was a poet. I told my father, and showed him some early verses, which he disregarded, much to my pain. In the eleventh grade I received a national high school poetry award for a poem that began: "Here I sit 'pon thy gilded tomb / dumbfounded in ethereal silence."

During that period I was greatly impressed with T. S. Eliot, along with Faulkner, Woolf, Dos Passos, and Stein, inter alia, for their experimentalism. But it was James Joyce who held me in total thrall. On my fifteenth birthday my girlfriend Mary Lou Willard gave me *Ulysses*. I had also embarked on Pound's Cantos, and for my high school graduation my brother gave me an early Viking edition of *Finnegans Wake*. I must admit that these works have been at the core of my poetics, not to disregard the Virgil I was reading avidly in Latin. In the night behind the great enigmas of *Finnegans Wake* was the sudden explosion of the sound of Elvis Presley, gateway to the immense collection of rhythm and blues records I was to acquire in the next few years.

Did Mary Lou Willard have something in common with Molly Bloom? She embodied a bourgeois normalcy I yearned for, to escape from what I considered the shameful stigma of my Mexican background. That drunken Mexi-

can Enrique, with his failed efforts at great art, the circus murals in the Carlton Hotel, or the more austere murals in a nunnery outside of town. And Laurita never graduated from high school, got "knocked up" and married in her senior year. Mary Lou was "good," normal, white, cute, wonder bread, my girlfriend throughout the four years of high school ("we were going steady"). At the end of the summer of '56 I suffered the most intense separation angst. She was to go to Carlton College in Northfield, Minnesota, and I had a scholarship to the University of Minnesota in Minneapolis. And my twin off to a dumb Lutheran school in Valparaiso, Indiana. The sweet, anodyne image of Mary Lou never left me, and she resurfaced symbolically in my 1989 book *Looking for Mary Lou: Illegal Syntax*. I do not know whether she is dead or alive. The last I heard is she got married to a guy who does septic tanks. My fiercest evocation of this Mary Lou appears in my poem "Mechanical Pianos" (*Tattooed Heart of the Drunken Sailor*):

the statue of Lenin is multiplied six times
MARY LOU and her cadaver and her mythic
  breasts
float through the fog and slime
MARY LOU I remember your step-father and
  his carbines
and the nostalgic saturday nights in the frozen
  gardens
MARY LOU has never grown older than
  eighteen
and suffers forensic decay in all of her teeth
MARY LOU has never been to the Mountain
where they mine the gold's ultimate seizure
MARY LOU is a midden heap where literature
is exercised for its pretended shepherds
MARY LOU gets her shadow drunk on wood
  alcohol
it is laughing and raging between sheets of sky
MARY LOU lives with disembowelled monkeys
in a jungle of septic tanks and automobile parts
MARY LOU is dead she is more dead than
  Israel
the angel who fornicated with the city of
  Chicago

As a freshman at the University of Minnesota I suffered from a terrible depression. Ignoring my regular studies, except for the French and Italian courses in which I excelled, I plunged myself autodidactically and typically into the study of the lesser Romance languages and dialects. I also began writing in a notebook a long rambling poetic narrative of sorts, influenced by Faulkner's *As I Lay Dying* and a mishmash of Joyce. Both my twin and I were heartbroken by this long separation. We agreed to transfer to the University of Chicago in our sophomore year. Chicago had tried to recruit us as early entrants in the eleventh grade (I was just polishing off Gibbon's *Decline and Fall* then), and they were still interested in us. The summer of '57 was a dreary one, marking time as dishwashers in St. Mary's Hospital, not at all the halcyon summer of '56 with such pals as Joel Pugh and Jim Balfour, carousing, digging the blues, wild car rides in sweet-smelling upper midwest country summer.

Chicago, fall 1957, Joe and I were on the loose in the Big Town. The university was still in the Robert Hutchins mode, great books of the Western world, *Artes Liberales,* and no football. An unusually vibrant and intellectual place in the Eisenhower '50s, it was also intimidating with its severe Oxford quadrant look. For undergraduates "the college," the program, was austere, scholastic, and interdisciplinary. The spirits of Plato, Aristotle, Aquinas, and modern physics dominated. This was where the atom was split by Fermi and company on Ellis Avenue, where they used to play football. This ambience was really heady for a pair of kids from the country. The senses reeled, walking the streets of the Loop or Hyde Park, a white island where the stimulus was as emotional as it was intellectual.

Bordered by 47th and 63rd streets, Ellis Avenue and Lake Michigan, Hyde Park and the university were wide open to other cultural forces, namely the largest black urban community outside of Harlem. Jazz and rhythm 'n' blues were resonant in the air. My brother and I combed the record stores on 47th and 63rd streets, as well as on the west side, assembling a really sizable collection of hard to get rhythm 'n' blues on the old 45s. For me the master was Muddy Waters. This southside Chicago blues, raw and immediately electric, was the focus of a university subculture in the late '50s and early '60s. What was then in vogue was an acoustic folk music, based usually on British folk styles. The use of electric instruments, the raw high-pitched emotional vocal styles of the Delta-based Chicago blues, not to mention rock 'n' roll music in general, were despised. Those of us who loved this stuff were condescendingly called "Kiddie-Beats." This sense of "otherness" com-

High school graduation, Rochester, Minnesota, spring 1956

bined with my growing awareness of being a Mexican-American in the midst of a sophisticated elite composed largely of Jewish intellectuals from the East Coast, whose learning was often daunting, certainly enforced my sense of being "different."

Looking back on those early college days I realize I was a very confused young man, not sure of what I was all about, not in the least focused on a future career, unlike so many other students. My brother and I shared quarters with an Italo-American from the steel mills, Bob LaMorticella (I loved that name, "The Little Death"). I planned to concentrate on literature, opting for an English major, but later I switched to classics to continue my Latin studies and to learn Greek. Again I was just a so-so student, on the side working on long prose rambles. I fancied myself to be a "bohemian," and the style then popular was the Paris Left Bank, Juliette Greco, Sartre, existentialism. Walking around in a black turtleneck sweater with a copy of *Being and Nothingness.* I thought it was cool to adopt the look of Elvis, James

Dean, or Marlon Brando in *The Wild One*, you know, leather jacket with the collar up, tight jeans, cigarette in mouth, motorcycle boots and prepared to discuss Eliot's *Four Quartets*. This was the period described by sociologist David Riis as "the lonely crowd." Camus's *The Stranger* was big. I had been developing this image since high school. I was somehow "different." And in fact I WAS different.

In the spring of '58 I fell in love with Claire Birnbaum, a Holocaust survivor from Romania, but relocated in Washington, D.C.

An early entrant, she was a year younger than I was. I regret that I have lost the one photograph I had kept of her for so many years in an old Provençal dictionary. This was a very passionate but also a very confused relationship. We were both quite exotic to each other, but unfortunately too young to make things work. During the spring break she took me to D.C. to meet her family, an orthodox, Old World lot, still new to America. I slept in a basement room, mulling over the Talmudic literature on the bookshelves there. The Birnbaums's hostility toward me was thinly masked. How could their daughter . . . ? In retrospect I think that Claire was just as much a loner and desperado as I was. She wanted "out," and I was the "out" for the time. It was all terribly bittersweet, intense, and brief. We returned to Chicago. She moved in with me. We initiated each other to sex, and got married on a hot humid August day in some minister's living room. The Pugh brothers from Rochester were there, and not much else I remember about that. Though I professed no religion, I participated willingly in all the Jewish holidays with her. I particularly recall the gusto with which she celebrated Purim, the story of Esther and all.

Arcadias are short-lived. We both dropped out of school, though I resumed studies after a few months, while she worked as a medical assistant, and later as a proofreader for Scott Foresman. Too inexperienced with the challenges of domestic life, the marriage was doomed to failure. Being a married undergraduate also bore an unspoken stigma. Frustrations abounded. I drank heavily, found any reason to party to excess, and sought new companions, usually those acquainted with my brother. Rather than concentrate on my studies, I spent more time poring over Meyer-Lubke's massive four-volume *Grammatik der Romanischen Sprachen*. We fell apart imperceptibly. I was not really aware that the end of the marriage was just around the corner in the summer of 1960. Her parents had been incommunicado with her since the marriage. This pained her far more than I knew. She said she was just taking a trip, but when I looked in the medicine cabinet and the diaphragm was gone, I was stung with a truth I had denied myself too long. The following are some stanzas from my "Ode to Claire Birnbaum":

CLAIRE you are tarantula of black light
you bleed like palestine in the ravished sun
of the most ancient of all kings the sumerians
. . . .
CLAIRE you are lava black opium kinetics mutant
a buried city of fish-heads cigarettes of smoking
    sphinx
war-time blooming in the electric fissure of memory
. . . .
CLAIRE tentacles of fire and milk and dread
    open you
I come down from the archaic music of Purim
counting the decapitated in their gardens of lice

CLAIRE I don't remember the photographs clearly
the wedding attended by cannibals and apes you
    blindfolded
as the cadavers of opulent chicago arabs on
    Xmas trees
                      shrieked
. . . .
CLAIRE you are tabernacle and sumptuous
    banquet on the coast
a lake for social workers and depraved psychiatrists
yourself who ate freud raw with his cancer and
    ties

I wear mask of a single and only actor late in
    the bone age
reciting backwards the awful chant of FANTOMAS
    the jewess
whom I married not knowing what life was

(From *Tattooed Heart of the Drunken Sailor*)

I had in the meantime struck up a number of new friendships, among them Frank Deffrey, a handsome writer who resembled Kerouac in a striking way, and Peter McKeon, the son of the noted Aristotelian scholar Richard McKeon. Clearly my experience with Claire had made me very fragile, and one Sunday afternoon, at a movie theater with Peter, I suddenly felt extremely beside myself, and told Peter to get me to a hospital. He took me to Billings Hospital, where I spent a good week in the psych ward. Upon release I was assigned a psychiatrist, Dr. Richard Telingator, with posh offices on N. Michigan Avenue. He became a weekly fixture during my last year of college.

The Beats were very much in the air then. My new friend Frank Deffrey was a very exciting cohort, and there was Clyde Flowers, a jazz musician, and a few others, and we all felt the vertigo of *On the Road* and *Howl*. Lots of experimenting with drugs, rooftop dawns wailing to the rising sun. And God knows what clubs we didn't visit after midnight, Peter McKeon and his Aquinas, Deffrey and his *Dharma Bums*. To say the least, my last year of college was very intense. I found quarters with a wild Bronx Jew and fellow classicist, Jeff Wilner, on Woodlawn Avenue. Jeff had a very strong sexual penchant which he transferred to his intense musical tastes. He introduced me to Beethoven's last quartets, and he insisted that Beethoven's seventh symphony was nothing but an exercise in masturbation. The crowd we hung out with was definitely on the unhealthy end of the student spectrum. We partied like crazy, and frequented such bars as the popular Jimmy's or the more sordid and dank Smitty's, a black bar, both on 55th Street. Among new friends were Carl Dolnik, a nuclear physicist who began to make huge Max Ernst-like paintings, Benny Muscovic, a philosophy major, who now teaches at UC San Diego, and Paul Butterfield, perhaps the best white blues-harmonica player ever. Paul was a college dropout who started out playing classical flute. I don't know whether he had heard much of the blues before he met us, but the sizable rhythm 'n' blues collection we had, and which we used to play for dances in the dorms, really caught his attention. The greatest Muddy Waters recordings are those with blues-harpist Little Walter, who became Paul's idol. In a matter of years Paul was to land a contract with Electra Records, and his was to be the band behind Dylan when Dylan went electric at Newport.

Hitchhiking with Jeff to New York really turned me on to Gotham. Forget Chicago. I visited New York several times that year. One of those times I stayed with Danny Lyon, the now famous photographer whose early work includes books on the freedom riders, biker gangs, and Texas prisoners. He shot a lot of pictures of me, and I still have a favorite one of me, lurching, lean, and obviously in my cups at a Hyde Park party. In fact, it's a wonder I

ever graduated from college. My brother and Clyde Flowers were suspended in the first marijuana bust on campus. Our reputations were bad, if not sleazy, and in the eyes of Dean of Students George Playe, my brother and I were scum, we belonged in "outer Bohemia." He warned me toward the end of my last year that if he found out one more time that I had kept another co-ed after midnight in my apartment I was gone. As it was, Jeff and I were busy trashing our Woodlawn apartment with a series of parties on a nightly basis. Paul Butterfield left an incredible pencilled mural in the living room. The place wasn't fit to sleep in. Our heads were full of Burroughs and Kerouac, and heavy doses of nihilism and anarchy. The descriptions of living quarters in Dostoevsky and Kafka must have inspired us to these depths.

Of course, the women. First of all there was Marilla Calhoun Elder, whom I met on Halloween, 1960, at the party where Danny Lyon took my lurching bohemian photo. She was from Nashville, and had a striking face, long dark-brown hair worn straight waist-length, and a wonderful southern accent. We had in common a love for the Donna Diana overture from the Sergeant Preston radio series, and for Nashville radio station WKDA, where she worked before going to college (the station we picked up nights in Minnesota that played great rhythm 'n' blues), but above all a love for Haliburton's *Complete Book of Marvels*. She was to become the most important person of my life, and in two years, despite all, we would be married. Our initial relationship was off-again on-again and sometimes stormy. Another woman was Ellen Taylor, a close friend of Marilla. Equally brilliant and eccentric, Ellen also attracted me greatly. She was a tall, urbane blond with large blue eyes that could really look crazy at times. Her father was Telford Taylor, the chief prosecutor of the Nuremberg war trials. I guess both Marilla and Ellen saw the "poet" in me. And then there was Lucy (Lucinda) Boldereff, who was to become Jeff's wife. She was artistic and very much on the fringe. Her mother was Frances Boldereff, a *Finnegans Wake* scholar, who took a strong liking to me because of my own passion for the *Wake*. I had no idea at the time that Frances was also the "muse" in Charles Olson's life. I only became aware of that relationship when I ran across their correspondence at the Bancroft Library years later.

Despite warnings and my continued excesses, including waking up dressed but shoeless in a bedroom on the first floor of the women's dorm one Sunday morning, I did manage to graduate, the first in my family to do so. Mom and Dad were there, and real proud.

So, there I was out in the world with a college diploma in classics from what I thought was a great university. I naively thought a degree from such a prestigious institution would open the door to economic opportunity. Well, who wanted to hire someone with a degree in the classics? I had a menial job at the Midwest Interlibrary Loan Center at the time, and was still seeing Dr. Telingator. Early in the summer of '61 Marilla and Ellen had decided to hitchhike together to New Orleans. I saw them off, though I thought it was doomed to failure. Sure enough, a state trooper brought them back that night. Two girls hitchhiking together! In one of the most impetuous moments of my life, I decided to take Ellen Taylor with me not just to New Orleans but to San Francisco. ON THE ROAD. Without notifying my employer or Dr. Telingator, we took off with very little baggage, some money, and lots of illegal pills, "speed," which we sold to truck drivers. I was convinced that this was to be the great Kerouackian experiment of my life, and that in San Francisco I would find the "ideal" literary community. It is difficult to imagine the elan and excitement we felt doing this, hitchhiking down South, sometimes with guys who offered us their whiskey out of a bottle. At Oxford, Mississippi, we visited Faulkner's house. He wasn't there, but I left a note pinned to the screen door saying Ivan and Ellen had dropped by. That evening (it was a Friday) in Natchez the cops picked us up in a churchyard. This was the heyday of the freedom riders and the civil rights movement. Without really asking us many questions, they just put us in jail. We spent the next two and a half days in this miserable place, where only two meals a day were served, usually hominy grits and hominy grits. I refused to eat. I shared a cell with a guy with the d.t.'s. I finally prevailed upon an officer to let us see a higher-up, whom I convinced should let us out since no charges had been filed against us. All this time I kept thinking what an irony it was that I was in the hoosegow with the daughter of Telford Taylor. On Sunday evening they put us on a bus bound for New Orleans, where

we stayed for a while in the Lafcadio Hearn House on Bourbon Street. Clarence "Frogman" Henry was performing next door.

The rest of the trip was one long hallucinatory ride through northern Mexico and the Southwest, usually in big hot "rigs," high on the pills which we shared with our drivers. We took a short side trip to Monterey, Mexico, where my aunt Aurora had a big, comfortable house. And it was nice to sleep in a real bed. Then a stop-off in Phoenix where my uncle Wally prospered as a wealthy, golf-playing proctologist. He was a little aghast at our sudden and scandalous presence. We were sick and emaciated from bad food, sleepless nights, and too much speed. Despite all, he was kind to us and gave us some medication for our ills, and sent us off to L.A., where we stayed in the seedy Hotel Selma just off Hollywood Boulevard. Then up old Highway 101 to San Francisco, where Ellen dropped me for a pre-arranged engagement with a guy from Harvard named Rappaport. I was stunned. They went off to pick crops. I had but one address, that of a girlfriend of Chicago blues musician Nick Gravenites. She put me up, and I slept on the floor while making lukewarm efforts at job-hunting, but feeling the keenest despair and isolation. After a bit, I made a bleak and long solo hitchhike back to Chicago. How naive I had been to think I could have connected with a so-called Beat literary scene, which had long abandoned San Francisco. What's more, I had nothing to show for myself but some almost incomprehensible notebook scribbles.

Things had changed in Chicago. I was no longer a student, but a pariah. Marilla was not exactly pleased with me for having chosen her friend to gallivant with across the country. José was going his own way in art history, and he had his own set of friends. After a halfhearted suicide attempt which landed me back in Billings Hospital, I decided to go back to Rochester to "heal." As it was Mom needed company, because Enrique had been ordered by a court to "dry out" somewhere in northern Minnesota with the rest of the Indians. Long nights playing Scrabble with Mom. My only other communication were letters to and from Marilla, who was keeping my few possessions, mostly clothes, for me. I decided it was time to straighten out. I returned to Chicago, got my clothes, and hit the road for New York City, with no clear plan in mind. Miraculously I got

Halloween, Chicago, 1960

a job within days as a bindery clerk in the Columbia University Library. Ellen Taylor was back in New York, too. We struck up a friendship again, and she was instrumental in getting me an apartment on W. 90th Street with a guy she worked with (they did technical translations from Russian), whose name eludes me because I got to calling him "Roomy-the-Mate."

But besides acting out the role of "that difficult young man," as Telford Taylor is said to have remarked about me, what had I really been doing all these "formative" years? What was I reading? Was I writing? If anything, I was a voracious reader, *Finnegans Wake* at the top of my canon, and Pound, and I was fascinated with fiction that merged into poetry, such as Djuna Barnes's *Nightwood,* or Burroughs's *Naked Lunch.* The works of Kafka and Dostoevsky influenced me deeply, and there was an underground classic, William Gaddis's *The Recognitions.*

Proust's massive effort (failure?) intrigued me for its music. I had no ordered program for myself, and kept random jottings of a "fictional" nature in notebooks. An occasional "modernist" poem dropped out, and early on I adapted the punctuationless orthographic eccentricities of e. e. cummings (while in Chicago, cummings was the only "real" poet I heard read). I had a vaguely "informed" sense that I wanted to do something big, something that would incorporate all my readings, which also included heavy doses of classical and medieval history, as well as ancient philosophy. And of course I read the classical Latin poets, my favorites being Virgil, Catullus, and Lucretius. I had also embarked on Homer in the original. I believe I was intuitively forming a guidebook for myself to lead me through the hell around us. There was a need to locate and identify the muse(s), or "that" goddess, a concept I derived from reading Robert Graves's *The White Goddess* and *His Greek Myths.* For the next decade my orientation was towards European and Latin American literature, specifically literatures in the Romance languages. I have next to nothing that I wrote during this period.

I was also acquiring a sense of who I was in a societal sense. Dislocated or uprooted while growing up, I became by nature a nonconformist. Never sure whether I was being accepted or rejected, usually for the same reasons, I always felt like "a stranger in my own home town," to quote Percy Mayfield. And then there was the terrible, if not tragic, example of my father, the total outsider who humiliated himself for acceptance in an environment originally so hostile to him, pounding his fist on his breast and proudly shouting, "Soy comunista!" So that was it, I was some kind of hybrid Hispanic who didn't fit in the run of the mill. That's why brother Joe changed his name to José. My father liked to think we were "Spanish," but we knew we were just Mexicans. My brother and I loved that poem: "Miniver Cheevy, child of scorn . . ." And in the midst of this was my nostalgic classicism, harking back to erudite and lamenting shepherds with names like Tityrus.

So I began life as an "adult" in Gotham. Soon after I moved into my new digs in Spanish Harlem, Julius Karpen, a journalist I knew from Chicago, and his girlfriend, Sammy Nobles, landed on the doorstep, and we had space for them too. Julius was a wonderful, early balding, red-headed Polish Jew who always acted like my uncle. He would spend a whole day boiling chicken, lying in the bathtub afterwards with a gallon of red wine, and pretending to read. Weekends we hit the Village together, looking for "kicks," what few there were. In early summer of '62 Marilla came to stay with me too. "Roomy-the-Mate" graciously gave us the spacious pink-ceilinged front bedroom that looked out on W. 90th Street from the sixth floor. At the end of the summer Marilla and a wealthy jeweler's daughter named Jane split for Mexico in Jane's jalopy. Marilla telegrammed me from New Orleans on the way back. Should she return? My reply was short and simple: *"Vamonos y casemonos"* (let's get married). She was due back at the University of Chicago for her third year, but decided to stay with me. We got married on October 27, 1962. It was a homely event. Julius Karpen and the poet Paul Oppenheimer played the role of best man and bridesmaid. Afterwards, we celebrated at one of those Upper East Side Wild Irish Rose brisket of roast beef bars. I had enrolled at New York University as a grad student in classics, taking night courses. The program turned me off. Only a fossilized Indo-European linguist named Krahe turned me on to the larger field of comparative linguistics.

In 1963 we decided to go back to Chicago so Marilla could get her B.A. She was majoring in medieval studies, and she was pregnant. We got an apartment in Hyde Park, just by the 51st Street station of the Illinois Central, which took me to the Loop where I worked in Kroch & Brentano's Bookstore on Wabash Avenue. This was not an easy year. Our first son, Alexander, was born on April 30, 1964. It was difficult for Marilla to manage the child and her coursework. I did what I could, but I was grappling with a new middle-management position in the bookstore. I was head of the Personal Shopping Services (phone and mail orders), and it was odd to have my brother as one of my employees. He had gotten married to a Lithuanian, Elena Gustaitis, and their social world had advanced into that of grad students in art history, distancing themselves from us somewhat. Among other employees I had were brash students who studied at the nearby Chicago Art Institute, a wonderful place for lunch. The collection was magnificent, and the French Impressionists were more than amply represented. I especially liked Seurat's pointillistic

Marilla Calhoun Elder, Chicago, 1961

Ile de la Grande Jatte and the works of the primitive Rousseau. But this was an opaque period in my life, burdened with the new responsibilities of fatherhood, a real job, and having to "walk the line." I was reading a lot of Indo-European grammar, Sanskrit, Greek, and Hittite, and lots of Roman and Byzantine history. The origins of things, be it languages or human discourse, the archaic, were at the source of my interests. Relationships between languages, Old English and Gothic, Italian or its many dialects, fascinated me. Historiography in the works of Toynbee and Spengler, myth and the origins of religion, such as Jane Ellen Harrison's *Prolegomena to Greek Religion,* all held a strong attraction for me. Among the few literary works that excited me then was the old Whalen translation of Lady Murasaki's *Tale of Genji.* I was still unconsciously evolving toward the "work" I felt destined to create.

José got a Guggenheim to further his art history studies (French Impressionism) in Paris in 1966. Marilla had graduated, and I was fed up with my job at Kroch & Brentano's, as I watched the book industry grow into a big con-sumer-sales thing with no eye on literature. The underground had really gone underground. With a mix of impetuousness and foresight, we decided to leave the States and go to Italy. My model was James Joyce as a Berlitz teacher in Trieste. Through my father-in-law I got a letter of recommendation from the head of Berlitz in New York to his counterpart in Rome. In Italy I would embark on "the work." In January 1967 we boarded the steamliner *Cristoforo Colombo* for its last transatlantic voyage, Marilla, our two-and-a-half-year-old son Alexander, and a large green trunk uselessly filled with grammars and nonsense. Italy! I was finally bound to my land of classical antiquity *(Altertumswissenschaft).* The voyage was monotonous and grey until we entered the Straits of Gibraltar. We disembarked in Messina, Sicily, and from there to Taormina and Siracusa, full of beautiful and haunting ruins harking back to the time of Plato, and Aetna, into which the philosopher Empedocles is said to have leaped either to his death or to immortality, then to Palermo with its classical/Arab/Byzantine mosaic. Finally Rome. I could not believe it. After my passionate readings of Gibbon, Mommsen, and Gregorovius, here I was, among the Coliseum and the Pantheon, with its two-thousand-year pagan chill still wafting, and the Forum, magnificent in its wintery ruin. I did get a job through Berlitz, but not in Rome. I was assigned as an English instructor in an Italian aeronautical school in Macerata, some 150 miles east of Rome by the Adriatic coast. We were given a marvelous house built on top of the old city wall that gave us a splendid view of the countryside leading up into the Apennines. Living there that half-year allowed me to become fluent in colloquial Italian, and I never missed a chance to learn from my students their varieties of vulgarisms. Went to the movies a lot (saw *The good, the bad and the ugly—Il buono, il cattivo e il brutto* in the original). I began my serious reading of the Italian classics, Dante and Petrarch, in particular, and reanimated my notebook "fictions," being most recently influenced by the enigmatic passages of the *Tale of Genji.*

Unfortunately the school was to move to Taranto in the south of Italy that summer. Macerata had seemed remote enough from the cultural center of Italy, so the thought of Taranto seemed appalling. From Macerata it was relatively easy to go to Rome, Naples, Florence

(where the incredible Botticelli triptychs of *La Primavera* and the *Birth of Venus* made a lasting impression on me). We decided to try our fortune in London, and eked our way north through Venice (one of my favorite cities of all time) and Milan, then Switzerland and to England. We were put up by the sister of a fellow Berlitzer in Wimbledon. Marilla got a job as an editor in a middlebrow woman's magazine, and I, unable to get a job, had a wonderful time exploring London with Alexander on my shoulders. After New York, I love London the best of the cities I have lived in. There wasn't a part of London we didn't visit, from the Isle of Dogs, to Hampstead Court, from the British Museum to the Victoria Embankment where the Salvation Army Band played some rousing tunes at lunch. But alas, Marilla was pregnant again. We resolved to return to the States. My plan was to a get a master's degree in library science (MLS) at Vanderbilt University in Nashville, where Marilla's folks lived. Marilla's father, Charles Elder, perhaps the best known

Ivan, Marilla, and their son Alexander, Venice, Italy, 1967

antiquarian bookman in the Old South, pulled some strings for me to get into Vanderbilt.

We returned to the States in grand style, on the last voyage of the *Queen Mary*. We stayed with some old friends in the East Village in New York, and I got a job as the night-manager of the W. 8th Street Brentano's. Then on to Nashville. The territory we covered in less than a year! It was still 1967. We found ourselves in the upper quarters of a house at 3434 Love Circle. When not in classes I worked in my father-in-law's wonderful secondhand bookstore on Westend Avenue. Mr. Elder is one of the finest men I have ever known. He was like a father to me. Generous and humorous, he took to me so sincerely and sweetly, and, though puzzled by my irreverent character, he never dismissed me. He certainly seemed to appreciate me more than my own father. And he was quite the character, so quintessentially Southern that he landed bit parts in such Hollywood movies as *Nashville* and *Coal Miner's Daughter*. For my part, I loved the old Nashville, the Grand Ol' Opry, and Tootsie's Orchid Lounge, with all its garish photos and signatures of country-and-western stars. Our second son, Max, was born on March 9, 1968. And it was in Nashville that I really started writing in earnest. The library school courses were so boring that I took my notebooks with me to class and embarked on a planned, concerted piece, the bulk of which I still have, and which I hope to transcribe sometime in the future. My imagination opened up: wild, erotic, and erudite scenes with no narrative patterns flowed out of me. Clearly *Naked Lunch* and *Finnegans Wake* were at the core of this. In fact, as my master's thesis, I compiled a bibliography of William Burroughs's work, including his gallery shows, collaborations, and so forth. I really enjoyed that year at Vanderbilt. I was popular, perhaps because I was exotic. Dr. Richard Gleaves, the dean of Library School, took a real liking to me, and when recruiters from both the New York and Brooklyn Public Libraries descended, Gleaves took only me to lunch with them. Within a week I was offered positions at both libraries. I had intended to get the MLS in order to work at the New York Public Library. My dream came true. I left Nashville even before the graduation ceremony.

I began work at NYPL in September 1968, a professional librarian in what I considered to be one of the greatest intellectual institutions in the world, the marvelous Astor, Lenox, Tilden structure at the corner of 42nd Street and 5th Avenue. I had found us quarters, albeit dingy because of ongoing renovations, at 449 Pacific Street in a part of downtown Brooklyn known as Borum Hill. The entire neighborhood was in a state of change. Young professional families moving in, buying dilapidated brownstones, repairing, investing, etc. And the distance to downtown Manhattan was a matter of minutes. Working in New York, right there in the middle of the universe, hit me like a grenade in the head. My senses were ripped open. Just to be in the human traffic at noon hustling up 5th Avenue towards the Museum of Modern Art on 53rd Street! and the Donnell Branch Library with its large circulating collection of foreign language books, not to mention Rizzoli's ultra-sophisticated Italian bookstore on 5th Avenue. The noon crowds of 5th Avenue, I learned to move through them like a needle. I was hired as a cataloger, and I was trained by a Romanian, Gabby Leventi, who was mildly shocked when I addressed her in her native tongue. In fact, there was quite a Romanian "colony" there, and I took advantage of it to hone the language I had taught myself in high school. Was I born in Bucharest? a newcomer from Romania would ask me.

But there was more than that. There was a real poetical awakening in me in this rich and contrasting polyglot mid-Manhattan milieu. In the circulating collection on 42nd Street I browsed avidly through the poetry section. There were American poets totally new to me, among them Bly and Merwin. But more important, I discovered that wonderful anthology of the so-called New York school, so active in the mid-sixties. Here was the best of Ashbery and Frank O'Hara, not to mention so many others, such as Koch and Berrigan. What was this idiom, this racy colloquial and yet often surreal mélange? I was still swinging with Dante and the troubadours. I immediately went out and bought O'Hara's *Lunch Poems*, and discovered that he really wrote most of his poems during lunch, and that he had worked for the Museum of Modern Art. I felt a vast affinity. Lunch became from that time on my sacred hour for writing poetry, a habit I keep to this very day. And then there was the gateway to the French surrealists through Ashbery and O'Hara. And the relationship between the visual arts and poetry, and the Dadaists. My mind was in flames, multiplying in all directions. Bly's mediocre translation of Lorca and Vallejo led me to peruse the originals. Lorca's *Poeta en Nueva Yorque* was familiar to me, but the intense and very complex work of Cesar Vallejo had the most revolutionary effect on me. Between Vallejo and Breton my brain began to sunflower.

So here I am in Brooklyn, with an armful of a family, and the world just burgeoning around me with all these aesthetic enticements. The ten years in New York, 1968–1978, I have always considered to be the most felicitous of my life, and perhaps my most innocent. I loved being a father, taking my kids all over New York. Since I worked weekdays, I took over at home on the weekends, giving Marilla time for her art. Routine weekend jaunts to the Brooklyn Public Library, the Botanical Gardens, the Metropolitan Museum, the Natural History Museum, Lincoln Center, Coney Island, the Staten Island Ferry, Central Park Zoo—you name it, we did it. We didn't have a car, we had bicycles which we pedalled over the Manhattan Bridge or to Brooklyn Heights. I was devoted to my sons, and read them to sleep every night. I think I gave to them what I never received from my father.

I began writing poetry in earnest in the early '70s. I endeavored to the experimental, or at least the nonconventional, and always stayed away from the clearly identifiable and descriptive poem. Fiction, I had decided was a deadend and, like the modern symphony orchestra, a product of the industrialized bourgeoisie, lacking in inspiration or sublimity. Intuitively I knew that poetry was unclassifiable per se. Vallejo's *Poemas Humanos* were the most tangible evidence of that. My first two published poems, "Orfeos Mavros" and "Broken Stanzas," appeared in *Gnosis,* a small magazine published by Stanley Nelson, who lived just down the street. Both are cryptic and metaphysical. A poem, "Address to Fifth Avenue," appeared shortly thereafter in an anthology, *Voices of Brooklyn* (1973). I didn't know any poets to speak of, and was working in a real vacuum but for the books I was devouring of poets near and distant in both time and space. About this time I encountered the work of J. V. Foix, perhaps the greatest Catalan poet ever, and certainly one of the greatest twentieth-century European poets. His complex, oneiric, surrealistic, and definitely Mediterranean-based

poetry was another strong influence on me. He was able to incorporate, like Pound, the troubadours, Dante, and Petrarch into his own highly stylized modern idiom. I began translating his work in bits and pieces. I have yet to finish translating his masterpiece, *The Unreal Omegas.* There were so many other poets and writers I was discovering then, Tristan Tzara, Hans Arp, Nicanor Parra, Murilo Mendes. Though not poetry, strictly speaking, the colossal and ambitious fiction of such Latin American authors as Guimaraes Rosa (the Brazilian counterpart of Joyce for his language and complexity), Miguel Angel Asturias (especially his books *Leyendas de Guatemala* and *Mulata de Tal*), and Garcia Marquez (*Cien Anos de Soledad*) imparted to me a wave of magical realism. I had also improved my Modern Greek, so I could read Kazantzakis, and discovered the powerful poetry of George Seferis, whose rendering of his ancient ancestry is both haunting and shattering, not unlike that of Hölderlin's fascination for *Altertumswissenschaft.* I was under the influence, and between 1973 and 1990 I submitted poems at an almost hectic pace to addresses I uncovered in the *Annual Directory of Small Presses and Magazines,* yielding a total of over five hundred published poems.

In the early '70s I actually met Ezra Pound. Ancient as he was, he was being feted at NYPL on the occasion of the library's acquisition of the Joyce/Pound correspondence. He was seated in the center of one of the grand rooms on the third floor. I shall never forget his countenance, truly a rock that had been weathered by many a tempest, the very crag of solitude and distance, such as the Avedon portrait of him has it. Pained to the end by existence. So alone that nobody dared approach him. I could not resist. Sympathy and curiosity drew me to him, this living master of my art. I could not do otherwise, but at a loss for words, I merely asked him in Italian: *Come sta?* (How are you?) and he replied: *Poco bene* (Not so well). Nevertheless this encounter with a figure so mythical to me, and the contradictory strength and frailty of his bearing, had such a powerful and lasting impression on me, that I returned to the Cantos at once. Something had to come of it.

In the meantime, life was moving us on. We had found new quarters on Saint Felix Place, right across from the Brooklyn Academy of Music. This was a most energetic period for both me and Marilla. Our landlord was a mad Italo-American architect, Pat Pirro, with utopian ideas of an "artistic community." This was it. He bought the whole side of the block on Saint Felix, wonderful old brownstones, and tore down all the fences in back to create a common backyard, in fact a Renaissance garden with enigmatic pieces of statuary and all. It was a unique block. Right next door to us was renowned jazz singer Betty Carter, and a few doors down was the Living Theater, Julian Beck, Judith Malina and company. Their kids spent a lot of time at our place. I remember once Julian came to pick up his kid, and he looked around in my living room with its large bookcases, everything in some kind of order. He turned to me and said: "Sometimes I wish I could live like this." Their place was squalid and messy and people slept on the floor. Judith Malina chastised Marilla for her Blue Willow ware. And Marilla, with the kids in school, had more time to devote to her art. She was turning into a very capable fabric art designer and teacher. Both of us felt on the verge. Something was going to open up. Marilla was beginning to exhibit her work, quilts and wall hangings, in small galleries and museum shows. *McCalls* magazine even featured some of her ethnic clothes designs in a Christmas issue. I began doing poetry readings, initially at open readings in Manhattan. I was quite excited when Marguerite Harris, who ran a very popular series at the Doctor Generosity Poetry Pub on 2nd Avenue in the East 80's, offered me a feature reading. She introduced me by saying: "When I hear Ivan read, I want to start a revolution." Charles Shahoud Hanna, a Lebanese-American who ran a press in Pennsylvania, Damascus Road, was there at the reading. He was preparing an anthology for his series of the Doctor Generosity poets. Imagine my thrill when he asked for contributions from me. The volume was dedicated to Paul Blackburn and included work by such heavyweights as Allen Ginsberg. Among the poems he accepted was "The Spanish Girls," which has been anthologized at least three times since then. Even though I was beginning to get around in the small press and New York reading-scene, I still had not connected with the larger poetry scene as I began to perceive it. There were some minor poets that I got to know, such as Fred Baumann and a guy named Boruk, and Barbara Holland, who was noted for her early feminist "I am a witch" stance. The fa-

mous New York School had long since departed for Boulder or Bolinas. There didn't seem to be any particularly significant poetry "scene" in New York at the time.

In the mid '70s we resumed our wanderlust. I had been studying Oriental languages on my own, Sanskrit, Hindi, Persian, and Arabic, and was getting an itch to hit those climes. Marilla has always had a flair for the exotic. We took the kids on a number of trips, the most memorable of which was our trek to the Himalayas, Srinagar, and Ladakh, the portion of Tibet controlled by India. Ladakh had just been opened up for tourists, and it was an absolutely unspoiled Buddhist paradise—no Coca-Cola, no commercial anything. We were put up in the homes of locals. The monasteries and Buddhist statuary were magnificent and timeless. The journey itself up a steep, winding, and barely paved mountain road was an experience in itself. The bus felt like it was held together by rubber bands, and one did not want to look too often into the precipice yawning to the right of the road. Sidetracked to Delhi for a week, we relaxed in a real hotel. I bought for almost nothing the critical four-volume edition of the Sanskrit epic the *Mahabharata,* as well as copies of the *Ramayana,* both the Sanskrit epic by Valmiki and the medieval Hindi one by Tulsi Das, and a copy of the *Rg Veda.* The flight back to New York was inexorable. Max and Marilla were very sick, and it took Marilla months to recover. And, what's more, we had to move from our St. Felix digs to new quarters in a very nice brownstone at 484 State Street in Brooklyn. This was to be our nicest abode in New York. Other trips included a good summer in England and Scotland, a sojourn in Portugal, southern Spain, and Morocco, and a jaunt through France and Catalonia, where I relished in using Catalan, but was unsuccessful in finding the poet J. V. Foix. That was our last Grand Tour. We were broke and life was to give us a different turn.

We were both working hard. To make ends meet, I began private tutoring in Spanish, Italian, and French. I also landed a night teaching position in beginning Spanish at Brooklyn College's adult education outlet. Marilla taught at the 92nd Street Y and at Brooklyn College. My favorite pupil was novelist and children's author Paula Fox. She and her husband Martin Greenberg, an English professor at Long

Island University, sought my services for Italian. My tutoring sessions with them were really more like a weekly party, witty and exuberant. I began to publish more and more in the small press magazines. I had written quite a few poems on themes based on my Mexican background, and was finding a ready market for them in the new ethnic literary scene. I was a regular contributor to *Revista Chicano/Riquena,* and Arte Publico Press was to publish a number of my poems in their anthology *A Decade of Hispanic Literature.* In the first *Before Columbus Catalog,* edited by Ishmael Reed, *Revista Chicano/Riquena* was represented solely by my poems. I even wrote some poems in Spanish, one of which, *"mi propia voz,"* was published in a New Mexico mag called *De Colores.* In the same issue of that magazine, to my great surprise, I encountered a fictional recounting by my brother entitled "The man who saw Trotsky's brains." Neither one of us had been aware we were to appear in the same publication together, nor did the editors of the magazine know that the two Argüelles were even related.

The irony was that my brother and I had become estranged during the '70s, rarely seeing or even communicating with one another. Ensconced in the Boulder Buddhist community known as Naropa (other adherents included Ginsberg, Gregory Corso, and Anne Waldman), José had become a faithful pupil of Tibetan guru Trungpa Rimpoche. José and his wife were true believers. We were not, and there was a distressing exclusion factor. José had already achieved a measure of success and fame with his mystical New Age books, notably *Mandala* and *Earth Ascending.* I will not go into the few painful re-encounters we had, exacerbated by his heavy drinking, but will only conclude that at a much failed "family reunion" in 1977 in Boulder, Marilla and I were thoroughly turned off by the way Miriam, his second wife, and José indeed excluded us. The pity was that Miriam's mother, Edith Tarcov, an editor of the Jewish intellectual magazine *Dissent,* had become close with Marilla and me. Edith was a dear friend of Saul Bellow, and as such she edited the Viking *Portable Bellow,* for which she enlisted my services in doing research at NYPL. Edith was equally perplexed and hurt by the cultishness in which José and Miriam wrapped themselves. Nevertheless, since José was in Boulder and did know those poets, I got him to show Ginsberg some of my work. Ginsberg cut

them up, and all but rewrote my poem about Kerouac, based on impressions from reading Ann Charters's biography of him. I had better luck in sending some of my Romanian-theme poems to Andrei Codrescu, recently exiled in the United States, a poet who had already made a stir with his collection, *License to Carry a Gun.* I wrote to him in Romanian. His response was one of effusive surprise. Critically he was to play an important role in my persona as a surrealist poet, even though I could just as well have been tagged at that time as a Chicano or Neo-Beat poet.

Charles Shahoud Hanna liked my poetry so much that he offered to publish a collection of mine. Until then his Damascus Road series was comprised only of anthologies. He was to break the pattern by publishing my first book in his series. Marilla and I read and re-read his letter, we were so excited. The book, *Instamatic Reconditioning,* had a long gestation period, well over a year if not two. In the meantime I was getting more feature-reading "gigs," mostly in Manhattan or the Village, places like the Cedar Tavern or, my favorite, Chumley's in the West Village. Fred Baumann, whom I got to know closely, ran the Chumley's Saturday afternoon readings. I would sometimes take the whole family. Fred had lots of poetical theories in his head, and talked about Basil Bunting and Pound a lot. My name surfaced in two different *New York Times* articles on poetry. One was about the new reading scene, and my style was singled out. The other was a report of a psychiatry/poetry seminar held at Bellevue. Again, I was singled out, and some lines of one my poems were actually quoted. My poetry began to be published in more visible journals, such as the *Kansas Quarterly,* the *Minnesota Review, Confrontation,* and others. The magazine I really wanted to get published in was George Hitchcock's *Kayak,* out of Santa Cruz, California. *Kayak* was the premier of the underground small press. Heavily surreal, intelligent, and with great graphics, usually by George, I thought this was one of the places for my work. After some rejections, Hitchcock finally accepted a bunch of my poems. Perhaps Paula Fox, who knew him from years back, had some influence. At any rate, he published one of my favorite poems, "Ya Muhammed!," a ballad-like poem based on the description of the prophet in Dante's *Inferno.* My poems were to become a staple in *Kayak* until it folded with issue 64.

The surrealist label was to work like a double-edged sword for me. New -isms were in sight, among them Language. Douglas Messerli, who published *La-Bas,* another heavily surreal-oriented magazine, but which also included work by Charles Bernstein, was contemplating an anthology of the "new" surrealism, and had solicited some work from me. The anthology never materialized, because he had decided to go Language. At this time I also discovered the poetry of Philip Lamantia, a prodigy from California taken under wing by Andre Breton in the '40s. Lamantia's mad, Beat-tinged American idiom surrealism had a very strong impact on me. Both intellectual and uninhibited, this was the dose for me.

So toward the end of the '70s I was finding my own "voice" *("mi propia voz"). Instamatic Reconditioning* finally arrived. For its time, it was a handsome book. I had designed the cover, a Tantric Buddhist print I found in NYPL. And I already had a second book under way, *The Invention of Spain.* David and Phyllis Gershator, who ran a small press in Brooklyn, The Downtown Poets' Co-op, really liked my work, especially the rapid Spanish surrealistic poems I had been writing and reading then, under the influence of Lorca and Vallejo. This early collection has always been a favorite of mine, derivative as it may seem. This book, whose opening lines ("To begin by announcing the form . . .") have always had a haunting effect on me, because of what was to happen to Max in the coming months, but also because the surrealistic energy that informs the poems at a runaway pace, has remained characteristic of my style. Again I had designed this book's cover from a Mexican "calavera" print I found in NYPL, and I was involved in the production and printing of the book. Max seemed especially excited about it, and the day they told me I could pick up the several hundred copies, I called a cab and Max and I went and got it. This was spring 1978. The opening poem ends with the lines about the "fast little feet that never stay put, that never find direction." That was Max. A Brooklyn Heights weekly published an interview of me upon the book's publication, and my old friend Paul Oppenheimer did a radio interview of me on New York station WBAI. Marilla was doing shows, and I was invited as a guest lecturer to Ramapo College in New Jersey. Our careers seemed to be opening up.

*Marilla in some of her own designs,
New York City, mid-1970s*

But we were also getting restless, at least I was. My job at NYPL seemed dead-ended. Joe Rosenthal, my former boss there in technical services, had gone on to Berkeley. The University Library was looking for a new head of the Serial Cataloging Division. Rosenthal openly courted me for the spot. I applied and was granted an interview for June 9, 1978. The momentous, random and terribly unpredictable intervened. Max had gotten mysteriously sick at the end of May. Constant high fever, no appetite, and vomiting. By June 1, a Thursday, his fever was still 104 degrees. We gave him an ice bath, and the next day took him to our doctor, who was puzzled and said that if he couldn't keep food down within twenty-four hours he should be hospitalized. The following morning, June 3, Max woke up calling me to tell me he had had a bad dream. This wonderful artistic vibrant ten-year-old with his "fast little feet" was to suffer a grand mal seizure within hours. Suddenly everything was brownian movement, galactic plunges into the brain's unknown hemispheres, black holes of abstruse medical terminology, and the so-called concern for quality of life. Cesar Vallejo's book *Poemas Humanos* took on a heightened significance for me. All the music I had ever heard flooded my head, not the least Mahler's *Kindertoten Lieder,* as a neighbor's automobile honking all the way rushed us to the nearest hospital, Brooklyn Jewish. By the afternoon Max was lodged with tubes and all in the intensive care unit, where he was to stay the duration of the summer. It was beyond our comprehension as to what was happening. Marilla and I hugged each other sobbing as never before. The greatest of mysteries had entered our lives. Diagnosis and etiology baffled the medics. Fluid in the brain was increasing. Tests, CAT scans, a relentless few days, and he was slipping into a coma. On June 9 he underwent surgery, a craniotomy on the right side to relieve the ever mounting pressure of brain fluid. A second operation the following week. Cardiac arrest, and the long summer coma, punctuated by the terrible metronome of the beeping monitors recording vital signs. His life had been saved, for what?

ENCEPHALITIS

I have come this far
without the names for fear
but what was the bad dream?
I took off all my clothes
and let them scrub me clean
then I lay myself in a small leaf
and started to shake
as if the world would end
I perceived a thread of light
endlessly unravelling
how could I know this
was this the house without memory?
they came to me with burning cotton
and pierced me with wires
they shaved my head and
gave my hair to the meadow
the rest is curtained in a
screen of persistent insects
whose haunting siren wakes me
from time to time
but if my hands have no shape
and the hour of sand never stops
evolving on its glass ladder
it is impossible for me to say
what it is I am doing here
floating stricken from the lists

(From *Manicomio*)

Upon the advice of the medics, I was encouraged to go to Berkeley for the postponed interview, and I did so in early July. I spent a whole day interviewing in Berkeley. It was gruelling, lots of emphasis on being a "professional librarian." It was nothing like the low profile of librarians at NYPL. Whatever the consequences, I really wanted the position, and we felt that a drastic change on account of Max's catastrophic illness (Herpes Encephalitis, it turned out) would be good for us, better than staying in a place full of bittersweet memories for us. I was offered the new job, and was prepared to start November 1978. By September Max was coming out of the coma and I was the first person who could get real food into him. As it turned out the extent of his brain damage was quite severe, affecting in particular his speech, and swallowing, not to mention the severe motor and cognitive impairments. A social worker told us, in a not very generous manner, that the worst was yet to come. The medics who had worked with him during his illness tended to shun us. The conjecture or prognosis was that he was to remain in this semicomatose state, helpless, for the rest of his life. Max's condition was to become a central element for the duration of our lives.

Ivan with his sons, Alexander (left) and Max, Morocco, 1974

I came to Berkeley in mid-October to get a place to live. I found quarters on California Street, about a mile from the university. Our son Alexander came out next, and I got him registered in Berkeley High School. His life, too, had been tragically interrupted, and throughout his high school years he dwelled in bitter resentment and guilt, totally withdrawn and asocial, although he remained a straight-A student. I began work as the head of a cataloging division at UC Berkeley's library. I had a sizable staff of professionals and para-professionals. This was a new and heavier responsibility than I had expected. Max and Marilla arrived a few days after I had begun my new job. Max was admitted to Children's Hospital in Oakland, and I was really anxious to see him again. I'll never forget the wan smile on his bandage-swathed head, his eyes still shut, when he heard my voice. Max was to stay at Children's for a few months, then, since he was technically not sick anymore but disabled, he was transferred to Kaiser Hospital in Vallejo, about forty-five miles north of Berkeley. The so-called therapies, physical and occupational, accomplished very little for his recovery. I went daily to help. We had never driven a car before. So we had to learn to drive to do the trip to Vallejo. Max was released after a few months. It was a great shock to suddenly have him home in his extremely incapacitated condition. There was a whole new world we had to master: wheelchairs, special beds, etc. Because of his craniotomies, we had to get a sort of hockey helmet which he wears to this day. Psychologically, having Max home with us was almost as traumatic as the initial illness. How were we to function? We had to search for rehab therapists and programs, and for home attendant care for relief. It was especially hard on Alexander. Because we lived in a two-story unit, Max's bed was in the living room, and we had to carry him upstairs for baths. Clearly Alexander was not going to have friends over. In fact, for several years he had no friends. Initial advice suggested we find some "place" to put Max. This was a dismal prospect, as we sensed there was a lot of the old Max there. Visits to several state institutions were thoroughly discouraging. We were determined to keep him home with us, and he is still with us after eighteen years. We tried various "centers" and "schools" mostly catering to the developmentally disabled, of which group Max was not. Ultimately Marilla founded her own brain-damage rehab center, Consensus, as a solution for a daytime program for Max, and for other young adults with brain trauma. Marilla still runs Consensus, and it is to her credit that, without being educated in this field, she has become an esteemed member of the social/public health community in the Bay Area.

I was gradually getting back to my poetry. Here I was in the Bay Area, already legendary for its poetry renaissance and the birth of the Beat, and despite the trauma we had suffered, I was still optimistic about my poetry and its future. The recent interview and radio show in New York, the excitement over *The Invention of Spain,* I thought would carry over on the West Coast. I had been in touch with George Hitchcock, and to my amazement, a reading had been arranged for him and me at the California College of Arts and Crafts. I was floored when Steve Ajay, who ran the reading, gave me a check for $100 before the reading. I thought that this was an auspicious beginning for me on the West Coast. In the early '80s my poems were being published with an astonishing frequency in the better small press magazines: *Kayak, Abraxas, Ally, Berkeley Poetry Review, Osiris, Revista Chicano/Riquena, Kansas Quarterly, Minnesota Review,* and many others. The poems themselves were heightened by an emotional tension, no doubt informed by the experience of Max's tragic circumstances. The long line, oneiric distance, and an erotic mysticism were becoming characteristics of my poetry. I began employing long capitalized titles, a device borrowed from the Catalan J. V. Foix, and my mind searched as much history as I knew for themes. Yet I was disappointed at how little attention I was able to arouse in the Bay Area. If there was a poetry or literary community in the area, I was ignorant of it. My early years out here felt like a setback compared to the New York experiences. Of course, the responsibilities I had, both with middle management at the university and the caring of Max, severely limited my social intercourse. These restrictions prevail even today, if not more so, because until 1982 when Alexander went to college, it was easier for Marilla and me to get out nights or weekends. And despite the increased frequency with which my poems were being published, I remained an unknown item out here. If anything, my growing national reputation as a surrealist worked against me in the Bay Area. For whatever reasons, there was a hostility to this -ism (was it too foreign—French and Spanish? too wild?). Upon trying to get a reading at Cody's Bookstore, the preeminent venue in the area, I was told that "my kind" of poetry (i.e., surrealism) was a no-go. In a letter of reply, I asked rhetorically that if I had been labelled as an ethnic/Chicano poet, would the same have been said of me? And in fact, I was quite frequently published into the early '80s in the Chicano/Latino journals too. I did not feel that I was "just a surrealist" poet, but simply a poet with many modes and personae. These were the years of the rise and dominance of the Language school, particularly strong in the Bay Area, with poets like Ron Silliman and Barrett Watten among them. *The Poetry Flash,* a monthly Bay Area calendar and review, spent a lot of ink thrashing out Language polemics, theory, and reviews, as if nothing else existed, other than the bland poetry of the academy exemplified by Robert Pinsky or Robert Haas. What the Language poets had was their own exclusive sense of community, well-orchestrated and sometimes run from the academy, which pretty much knocked out the "competition."

Matters were slowly shifting for me. A third collection of mine, *Captive of the Vision of Paradise,* was being prepared. A fellow librarian and publisher of Hartmus Press in Mill Valley, Catherine Moreno, was impressed with my work. The title of the collection reflects how I felt being in California. The poems I chose for this set exhibited a greater variety of topics and styles than the two previous books. The surrealism was more intense. The mystical eroticism, the unrequited nostalgia, and the great cosmic lesson or randomness which Max's illness had taught me also informed the collection. Through Marilla, I found a Texas-born artist, Linda Strickland, who did the haunting graphics for this collection. The Saint Sebastian torso that graces the cover is especially striking, as it floats out into a void. I was also able to capture some blurbs for the back cover from Codrescu, Hitchcock, and Paula Fox. During this period I was steeping myself in the Italian and Spanish classics, Ariosto, Tasso, Cervantes, and Gongora. I was reviving my Greek, Homer and Hesiod, and plunging with difficulty into the seemingly impenetrable Sanskrit epic, the *Mahabharata.* And I finally landed my first reading

at Cody's. I read with the famous Greek (multi-lingual, also French and English) poet Nanos Valaoritis, who also had a solid surrealist background. Older than I by far, he knew Seferis, Kazantzakis, and Elytis well. In his native land his reputation is high. Nanos was indeed surprised when I quoted some lines of Seferis in the original, lines which he recognized at once. Among those at the reading was Andrew Joron, a somewhat sallow, unpresuming young man with a ponytail, who introduced himself to me. He was publishing a magazine called *Velocities,* which espoused a "speculative" aesthetic (something between science fiction and surrealism). He solicited work from me, and I became a regular in those pages as well.

In 1982 my third book, *Captive,* finally came out. Alexander graduated from high school and was to go on to Columbia University with his straight A's. His departure made our lives more constrained. While he had been with us, we were able to take weekends off, down to Big Sur, or up to Mendocino. With his leaving home, the constraints were only to tighten. We moved to a new apartment on Walnut Street, across the street from the university's experimental greenhouse. Max, in a wheelchair, was better able to cope in an apartment all on one floor. Finding a placement for Max had been really difficult. Nothing really worked until Marilla founded Consensus, a brain trauma rehab center in Berkeley, where Max was provided something like the education he should have been getting all this time. Consensus was a master-stroke on Marilla's part, an endeavor into an area she really knew nothing about. But it also detracted from her artistic ambitions. Life was admittedly hard under these circumstances. It was still a shock to us that Max was really as disabled for life as he was. And to admit to the full extent of his impairment was a difficult lesson. His speech was utterly disrupted, at one point being diagnosed as having twelve kinds of aphasia. His memory of things before his illness, once solicited, is relatively good. It was working with short-term memory and mastering cognitive skills that was a task. We went through any number of speech, occupational, and physical therapists, to no avail, with the exception of one physical therapist, Scott Herbowy, who got Max out of the wheelchair and walking with the aid of a quad-cane, something the neurologists said would never happen. We also got him to ride a large 3-wheeled

Schwinn bike, as well as take him to horse-back riding lessons. With Alexander's departure I felt keenly the harsh reality facing Marilla and me with Max. We were forced to work out a way together through what seemed to me then an asphyxiating life-situation. I resented, as I am sure Marilla did too, the restraints put on our social lives, such as was left of them. Anger, bitterness, and depression informed us as never before. That we remained together I believe is largely due to Marilla's inherent optimism and sense of values and high standards for living a good life. As a footnote to 1982, I need to add that Alibi entered my life. A pure-bred black labrador, Alibi was given to us as a companion dog for Max, by the Canine Companions program in Santa Rosa. Trained to be a guide dog, he turned out to be skitterish, and so we got him gratis, uniform and all, to help pull Max's wheelchair, and just be "there." It turned out that Alibi was to be my companion too. We bonded early, and to the end of his days, I was his faithful companion. We developed a routine that afforded me a stresslessness and sweet sense of innocence. There were times when even Marilla would express jealousy over our relationship.

So there we were, ensconced in Berkeley with few friends or contacts. The two friends we had there, Liz Leh and Alex Levit, had gone back to Israel. Liz was a vibrant artist, who shared poet Delmore Schwartz's last days. Alex, too, was quite alive, a photographer who couldn't resist taking shots of dogs. Marilla, if anything, felt the frustrations of our isolated and constraining circumstances more than I. After all, I got to go to work Monday through Friday, which was an ironic sense of liberation *(Arbeit Macht Frei)*. On the other hand, I had a rough time as a professional librarian, and received negative evaluations denying me promotion to full librarian status. Was poetry getting in the way of my career? Well, yes. Did being a poet brand me as an academic nonconformist? Not that I didn't do a good job, working like a Lutheran farmer keeping his peasants in line and getting productivity up.

Fast forward: a balmy Friday afternoon, April 5, 1996, in the living room of my oldest friend, James Balfour. How did we get here? The sun streaming through the windows, Muddy Waters accompanied by Paul Butterfield in the background. James and I have known each other from way back in Rochester, Minnesota. My sister

used to babysit him and his sisters. Related to the Mayo family, the name that put Rochester on the map, James was typical of the kids on "Pill Hill," while Joe and I were the Mexicans down below. Yet, we'd struck up a close friendship from high school on. Our close friend Joel Pugh is no longer with us. Our memories traverse dozens of lawns and chalkboards with Latin declensions. Joel, crazy little redhead, spinning his car around in an open field, with us clinging to the top. Joel and I thumbing a ride summer of '56 to Minneapolis, my first hitchhike. And the blues that bonded all of us together, music we picked up late at night riding around, from stations like WKDA in Nashville. What did we know? Joel and I ordered by mail "blues packages" from these stations, rhythm 'n' blues songs on 45 RPM discs, on labels such as VJ, Excello, and the famous Chess and Checker. And what songs: Slim Harpo's "I'm a King Bee," or the eerie Otis Rush number, "My Love Will Never Die." What a rush it all was, the great grassy field of heaven the summer of youth seemed to have been, mad youth, tasting it all, the wound and the inebriation, Joel, mysteriously dead in a London flat some ten years later. I was later to discover, from an old classmate who told me to look at the book *Helter Skelter* (the Manson family), and sure enough there was Joel, married to Sandra Good

With Alibi, north California coast, about 1985

Pugh, living on the Spahn Ranch, and splitting perhaps before the time of the murders, but himself found dead (murdered?) in this London flat, with weird writing in blood on the mirror. In Ed Sanders's book *The Family* I read that Sandra Good and some others fled to the Mohave desert, where Sandra gave birth to a child named Ivan. That gave me the chills. So there we are, James and I, and the ghosts of Joel Pugh, Paul Butterfield (whose death I dreamed the night it happened), Muddy Waters, and James's sister, Barbara, with whom I danced just once, a Yeats scholar who blew her brains out. As we part, I say, "Muchos años." "Muchos años," James repeats. Ciao.

It becomes increasingly evident to me as I endeavor to record some of my memories, in order to form a coherent picture of myself, that I only become more of a puzzle to myself. Chronology fails to adhere. As a poem of mine, "The Death of Stalin," demonstrates, I am nowhere at once and in all places. The Mayo Clinic doctors in this poem who investigate the dying Stalin, the thug who sent Trotsky into exile, are the same ones who sent Mom to the sanitarium. This poem was a revelation to me. I had become the poet I always wanted to be. In a nutshell, both my past and future are there, the total break from the linear, the leaps, and yet the hidden narrative concern. The voice with all its hesitations, the awareness of the Heisenberg principle about objectivity, become important aspects of my poetry. The great uncertainty and enigma. Some passages from "The Death of Stalin":

I appear in the dream inside the dream wearing
a military greatcoat and speaking thick neapolitan dialect
from my sleeve a map marked and blurred issues forth
with instructions about eternity and the roads that only

                                        lead half-way there

. . . .

the brain moves at crashing velocities

                        is this really the twentieth century?

. . . .

NO RELIGION NO SACRIFICES ONLY THE FIERCE AND PETTY DAILY STRUGGLE
the map of the Ideal City the Invisible City obliterated by rain
who is reading me scraps from the life of Trotsky?

. . . .

are these doctors communists?

                        which of the three doors shall I choose?

is this chemical thaumaturgy in reverse?

                        and then there is that Idea

about that woman that Goddess

                        if I can begin to follow her

(From *Pieces of the Bone-Text Still There*)

In the mid-'80s, after the publication of *Captive*, I had a series of chapbooks published, one a year, by different small press publishers. Within these, *Tattooed Heart of the Drunken Sailor*, *Manicomio*, and *Pieces of the Bone-Text Still There*, are some of my wildest and more experimental poems. *Tattooed Heart* was reviewed in an article on surrealism by Andrei Codrescu in the *Baltimore Sun*. About my work he said: "If proof were needed that Surrealism is a spontaneous expression of the poetic mind, Ivan Argüelles would be the one to provide it. In the tradition of the madder, darker and more mystical surrealists like Rene Crevel and Antonin Artaud, Argüelles weaves his mad web of images out of an impossible depth. Unlike the more superficial image makers who lay claim to the surrealist label out of sheer laziness or because 'it looks easy,' Argüelles is genuine." *Manicomio* was the winner in the First Silverfish Review Chapbook contest. The poems in it represent a sort of "golden hits" of mine at the time. *Pieces of the Bone-Text,* despite its striking cover, is an example of small press production at its worst, which is too bad, because this collection contains some of my hardest-hitting poems, starting off with "The Death of Stalin." In 1988 in a survey done by Len Fulton in the directory of Small Press Poetry publishers, which asked the question "which poets do editors name when asked whom they published," I ranked fourth. I was out there in the small press world, but relatively unknown in the "establishment." I was beginning to meet more poets here and there. Loss Pequeño Glazier, a maverick library school student, published a small set of mine, *Nailed to the Coffin of Life,* through his own press, Ruddy Duck. Through him I met Denyse Du Roi (now Denyse Anger) who worked at Shambala bookstore on Telegraph. She had been at Naropa in Boulder (and knew my brother), where she studied poetry with Anne Waldman. Denyse had just started a new poetry reading series at Larry Blake's, a popular bar/restaurant on Telegraph. She was very impressed with my poetry, and offered me a feature reading. I really liked her poetry as well. It harked back to the witty, urbane madness of Frank O'Hara, but had its own distinct touch, both feminine and on the edge.

This is where Jack Foley tap-dances into my life. Marilla introduced me to Jack at a New Year's Eve party. She had met him and his son Sean at Park School where she taught an art class. Jack was a literary type, on terms with Ishmael Reed and Gerald Vizenor, writers who also taught at the university. A writer who had not gotten out at all, Jack evinced a sharp mind, and we immediately hit it off. I gave him some of my books. I guess it was my mix of surrealism, ethnicity, and my obvious sense of the traditions of poetry from the classical to the moderns that Jack picked up. He recognized in me something deeper than most of the small press people who published my poems ever fathomed. He was the first contem-

porary of mine I'd met who really "understood" my work. I recognized him to be a man of extreme gifts, critical and creative. Our minds truly met and exchanged ideas of an evolved level together. In March 1985 I had the opportunity to hear him read at the California College of Arts and Crafts. "This guy's too much," I thought as I watched him perform his poetry. He exuded a passion and an intelligence that certainly matched the qualities I thought I had when delivering a poem. His erudition and sophisticated use of language in its various strata was immediately evident. When he and his wife, Adelle, did choruses together, an aural collage that sang vibrantly, like jazz, was created. A brother, I thought, a brother. Jack, despite his lack of exposure, was full-blown, not in the least an amateur, like so many poets I'd encountered and read with, but a real poet of stature. So when Denyse offered me the gig at Larry Blake's and she asked who I would like to read with, I had had George Hitchcock in mind, but then I had just heard Jack read. So I asked if he would join me. Jack was thrilled. He had never been a feature reader before, and he was virtually unknown and unpublished. It was an exciting night. As Jack says, I put him on the map, I started his career. Since then Jack and I have been very close. I consider my lunches with Jack to be some of the most exciting get-togethers with anyone I have ever had. Our mutual excitement reverberates like bebop, a veritable jazz. I have joked that Jack is my "real" twin brother, for our intrinsic similarities, though of course we are very different, too, and it is no cosmic accident that Jack and Marilla share the same birthday, August 9.

Life at home, life at work, and life as a poet, gained steam. Marilla, having founded Consensus, a testimony to her skills, fortitude, and impassioned social sense, proved herself as a pioneer and leader in a grassroots-based services environment. She has helped numerous clients through programs she herself has instituted. In later years Consensus has also become a weaving studio, partly as an extension of Marilla's career as a fabric artist. But just being "Consensus" was not all that satisfying to Marilla. She needed to get back more of the life she had yielded upon coming to California. This is a tension we have always hoped to resolve, and in the past few years she has been creating some magnificent political quilts and wall-hangings. Professionally, in the mid-'80s, I became quite involved with library governance at the university, both locally and statewide. I was an elected leader with heavy responsibilities. Fortunately, my tenure in these offices lapsed after four years. As for the poetry, I continued to be widely published in chapbooks, magazines, and anthologies. Though not to my full satisfaction. In addition to my reputation as a surrealist and ethnic poet, I also gained one as an erotic poet. *Yellow Silk,* a magazine of erotic arts, published many of my poems, and I received the first Yellow Silk Award for erotic poetry in 1985. My poems were becoming bigger with longer lines, such that they began to be rejected simply for their size. The small press was really defining itself as "small." I recognized all too well that there was little out there, and few publishers who understand what poetry is, what the traditions of poetry are. My poems, more and more, were extending across the map as cultural myths, epic themes, the discontents of civilization were being drawn upon with greater frequency. These were not just "lyric pieces," "verse," but something tending toward an epic leap. Jack introduced me to the poetry of Zukofsky and Olson. Their long, extended, and experimental work, deriving from Pound, but also branching out into other domains, was a critical discovery for me. About this time I met Dale Jensen, another Berkeley poet, who published work of mine in his pre-determined to be shortlived magazine *Malthus. Malthus* was unique in that it varied in size, format, style, and utter experimentation. I had finished my reading of the Italian epics by Dante, Ariosto, and Tasso. I had the archaic Greek poets Homer and Hesiod under my belt. I never left Virgil. And now I was consumed by the great English poets: Chaucer, Spenser, Milton, Blake, Wordsworth, and the Romantics. The enormous Oriental epics, such as the Sanskrit *Mahabharata,* and the Persian *Shah-Namah* were not far away.

In 1988 I was selected to be the UC Berkeley librarian to participate in a Library of Congress program for cooperative cataloging on a national scale. This was a very prestigious action for me. It elevated me out of the ordinary ranks, and finally got for me the promotion long denied me. For the national library I was to be the specialist in German political and intellectual history, as well as the Catalan specialist. In a sense this dovetailed into my poetry life. The exasperating and self-contradictory evasions of German history and literature were at my fingertips. I have become expert particularly in Germany and the Germanies of the twentieth century. Nietzsche, Hölderlin, Heidegger, Hitler, the Holocaust, and the re-unification question have all entered prominently into my poetry. My passion for Hölderlin stems from this period. This mad poet with his *Sehnsucht* for *Altertumswissenschaft* struck a profound chord in me. His baffling and fragmented later poems and hymns led to a modernism of my own, combining elements of classical antiquity and myth with the atrocities of the twentieth century.

About this time, too, a frail young punk photographer, Craig Stockfleth, who had worked for me earlier in the '80s at the library, and for whom I felt an artistic or creative affinity, approached me with the idea for a book that would combine in equal proportions poems of mine matched by his photographs. I liked the idea. His photographs of the punk subculture were graphic and haunting, particularly the portraits. He had just come into some money and was willing to foot most of the bill. But also, he had been relegated to suffer an incurable illness, Joseph's disease, acquired through his mother's side from the Azores Islands. The external manifestations of this illness are like the palsy, an increased and irreversible diminution of one's physical abilities. For a photographer, for whom manual and ocular precision is all, this disease is the end. Craig's world as a creative artist was over. But he did have this mass of photographs, most of which are now in the archives of the Bancroft Library at UC. So we went to work. We founded a small press, which I called Rock Steady after the Aretha Franklin song. I made a careful selection of mostly unpublished poems, with a concept I conjured up after my last visit to Rochester, Minnesota, where I could find nobody I knew, and worst of all, the house and motel where Mary Lou and her parents lived, 1819 S. Broadway, were no longer there. Hence the title, *Looking for Mary Lou: Illegal Syntax.* I put the poems together with a sense of order, beginning with the mad, surrealistic "October Muse," to the Hölderlinian final poem "Illegal Syntax." Craig also carefully read the manuscript, and skillfully paired a photograph to each poem. I selected the cover photo, the insouciant punk girl going to work in San Francisco's financial district. The result was a large, beautifully produced and very slick book, very glossy, that cost $35 dollars initially. It came out in 1989. And I was saying goodbye to the daily lunch poem with this collection.

And there are the vicissitudes of life. The poets and people who pass as in a dream in the lightning flash of one's life, like angels passing in the night. I finally met Philip Lamantia, the one living American poet who had influenced me the most. I met him hearing him read at Larry Blake's (I nudged Jack, who was with me, and said NO INHIBITIONS). For years I had assiduously been sending him my books and chapbooks, without any response to speak of. I was pleased that he enjoyed my company as much as he did when we finally met. *Poetry Flash* had published a review of mine about Lamantia's latest book, *Meadowlark West*. In this review I took the opportunity to contrast this later work with his far more interesting and demonic *Destroyed Works*, poetry that has been ignored but which rivals *Howl* in its incantatory power. I believe I am the only poet in decades who has taken Lamantia seriously and reviewed him. As Lamantia said to Ferlinghetti: "Did you ever get a perfect review?" To which Ferlinghetti replied in the negative, and Philip continued: "Well, I did, and Ivan gave it to me." A difficult person, with dogmatic tendencies, Philip struck up a brief friendship with me. But I felt he wanted a disciple, like Sotère Torregian had been, and not an equal, as a companion. Sotère was another poet whose work I had admired in the '70s. I connected with him in the Bay Area. He was warm and enthusiastic about my work, and unhappy, as he admitted to me, about Lamantia's treatment of him. Sotère dropped out of sight, but has resurfaced in the '90s. Shadowy links to my surrealist past, a past from which I was divorcing myself more and more, just as I had severed myself from the Chicano literary scene. And in the mid-'80s I had organized and ran a poetry reading series in the Library's Morrison Room. This offered me the opportunity to meet many poets, both from the area and afar. I tried to be as selective as possible, from the academic Robert Haas to Language poets like Ron Silliman or Leslie Scalapino, or to the arch-Chicano Gary Soto. I included all schools and ethnic groups. All this came and went without any effect on my life and work, other than the passing sense that I had heard some voices and seen some faces.

I was definitely tending toward a new or extended definition of my own poetics, many thanks to Jack who kept encouraging me to do the "long poem." I have already mentioned the larger works that kept inspiring me, from *Finnegans Wake* to *The Maximus Poems,* and my frustration with the daily poem, the small press, and the inability to get a wider critical understanding of what I was doing. Early in 1990, imagine my surprise when I opened up a letter from the Poetry Society of America, Gramercy Park, New York. The letter said I had been awarded the Poetry Society of America's 1989 William Carlos Williams Award for *Looking for Mary Lou: Illegal Syntax*. The award is given to the best poetry book published in a given year by a non-commercial press (i.e., university or other small press). In my excitement I called first Craig, then Marilla, then Jack. We were all beside ourselves. I recall going to a PEN West gathering that afternoon with Jack, who introduced me to Lyn Lyfshin, the most prolific of all small press poets, and how Jack bragged about me to her. Craig and I flew to New York to receive the award. I discovered then that poet June Jordan, a professor of African-American and women's studies at Berkeley, had been the judge, and that Gregory Corso's selected poems *Mindfields* was the runner-up. In February 1990 I had already begun my epic Pantograph, with its first long installment, *"THAT" Goddess*. I showed Jack the opening sections. He was excited. He was then the editor of a poetry tabloid published out of Fort Mason in San Francisco, called *Poetry USA,* and he at once included those opening sections in it. I wrote *"THAT" Goddess* in a white heat of two months (106 pages between February 10 and April 25, 1990). I don't believe there was anything like it at the time. An epic with numerous introductions, and the twelve virgilian cantos, each canto in a different style, from the comic to the tragic, racing along through myth and history and all the zeitgeists of poetry I knew. My classical education, my erratic and undisciplined readings in history and literature, informed the work with the massive and at times ribald chaos that I intended it to have. Nevertheless, I could not find a publisher. Nancy Peters (Lamantia's wife), of City Lights, returned the manuscript with highly commendatory praise, but there was no place for it then at City Lights. The praise was so sound, that I called the following day and pressed Nancy for a reason that City Lights wouldn't publish it. Lawrence didn't like my poetry. That's what it came down to. Douglas Messerli of Sun and Moon, again, saw the value of the work, but. . . . From the "Proemium":

tell me oh Muse of the man who went by trial
of rock and water sunwhipped to found this
    changing shore

. . . .

left to die alone adrift on the thought of
    nothing
tell me what were his names his myriad pains
        his wrath his obsessions his conduct of life
his mental struggles his artistic and spiritual
    inventions
his infidelities as well as his positive attributes
his opinions about the gods his knowledge of
    music
his many masquerades his inabilities potential
and real his favorite monies and poems
his typical and multiple defeats his poverty
his humiliations his lack of diplomacy
his pornographic passions his ontological anguish
his angst and ennui his knowledge of french
of german of italian and latin and of sanskrit
his disdain of statistics and money his fear of
    death
his drinking habits his fondness of black dogs

I kept working daily during my lunch hours at this obsessive epic. Each book was different. There were no more "poems," just the long lines, the extended vision that respected no page length. Then I got to the fourth book. I had been reading a lot of Elizabethan tragedy, especially Jonson. I met the challenge. I had never written drama before. I embarked on a new and more experimental variation of Pantograph by writing *The Tragedy of Momus,* an Elizabethan play, following all the Aristotelian guidelines and Elizabethan conventions for plot, structure (e.g., five acts, five scenes, choruses, etc.). I felt a boundless freedom daily, going in all directions, and this minor Greek deity of envy whom I was destroying in a ninety-six-page play made me sing. I considered this long ongoing Pantograph as music. You don't ask what music is "about," so you don't ask what "Pantograph" is about. It is the music of everything I ever read and wrote. It was THAT Goddess who informed the entire piece, the White Goddess of Robert Graves, the muses of poetical convention, both the erotic and the

sacred, all was enigma and mystery. It was THAT Goddess whom Stalin wanted to follow in my visionary poem about his death. Throughout this far-ranging manuscript of more than one thousand pages, I meant to touch on all the major themes of Western history, myth, death, and the archaic, from Gilgamesh to Teotihuacan.

I filled up a dozen or so spiral-bound notebooks in a little over two years, typically writing in the surroundings that gave me the most anonymity: pizza joints, with large-screen TVs playing *All My Children,* and hi-amped jukeboxes roaring out punk music. This apparent cacophony allowed me to immerse myself in the poem. The atmosphere was designed to be as opposite to that of a librarian cataloging works on German intellectual history for the Library of Congress as possible. In this environment all my senses were attuned to contemporary speech, subculture styles and music, which directly contributed to the mosaic composition of my work. Writing outside of such a "living" atmosphere, writing, for example, only on a PC, is unthinkable for me. Not only do I need Homer, but I also need Sid Vicious.

So where to go, what to do, which cathedral to deconstruct next? Thumbs up to time passing and to the Germanies united. Marilla gets a windfall of money, and encourages me to start my own press. Jack, Andy, and I get together, resolved to found Pantograph Press in an effort to publish what we think should be getting attention "out there," a real alternative to the various -isms and crapola floundering in the shoals. Jack wants to start with an anthology. There ensue polite differences of aesthetic opinion. Andy and I co-found Pantograph Press with an aesthetic based on the "sublime." The first three books will be my *"THAT" Goddess,* Andy's *Science Fiction,* and Denyse Du Roi's *Filmmaking,* a book I had been wanting to see published for a long time. Andy operates as the "production manager," and I am essentially in control of the "business" as editor in chief, and Marilla is the financial backer. In 1992 three beautiful slick paperback poetry books issued forth from Pantograph Press. And exactly as I wanted, the books found a distributor immediately, Small Press Distribution in Berkeley. They were really taken by the quality of the books, both in content and appearance. We already had three more books for 1993, Jack's *Adrift* (his first major publication), my

*Jake Berry, Jack Foley, and Ivan Argüelles at artist Leonard Breger's house,
San Francisco, California, 1996*

Hapax Legomenon, actually the ninth book of Pantograph, but chosen because it was so different from *"THAT" Goddess,* so ethereal, no breaks, one long poem done in a matter of ten days, and a book by Laurie Price, *Except for Memory.* Laurie had also just won a prestigious Gerbode award for her poetry. I was especially happy to publish Jack's book, as it was long overdue. And we also published an anthology, Andy's *Terminal Velocities,* which includes the full text of my play, *The Tragedy of Momus.*

So much time propelling me from Rilke's Lorca to Vallejo's Gilgamesh. The juggernaut was rolling. Once so prolific in the publication of my daily poems, I rarely submitted work for publication anymore, unless by invitation. The most significant single piece I published in the '90s, "Chicano," appeared in Jack's *Poetry USA,* the experimental issue, in which I appeared side by side with Robert Duncan. "Chicano" is an enormous poem, taking up six full pages of tabloid-size paper, and often running in three distinct and non-sequential columns. The poem

was as much of an autobiographical and experimental piece as I had done. The dream was coming together. The various threads, ropes, and symbols gathered from my waking and walking life found their loom. Woof and weft, seam and hem, ravel and unravel the skein.

(On April 8, 1996, I received an invitation for the fortieth graduation reunion of Rochester Senior High School. Listed among the missing were Ivan Argüelles and Joe Argüelles, and a further update also listed Mary Lou Willard among the lost.)

My father died at 9:50 P.M., December 4, 1994. I don't remember the last time I spoke with him. Our conversations, rare and such as they were, were not conversations, just brief greetings in passing. Though I do recall that my father was troubled that he could not understand brother Joe's extraterrestrial ramblings about the Mayans, and his prophetical statements, originating from the time of José's Harmonic Convergence, much publicized in the media, in 1987.

(On April 11, 1996, as I finish this autobiography, Max suffered a seizure while eating breakfast, and was hospitalized with acute aspiration pneumonia. I insert this detail to emphasize the extent to which his lingering twilight existence affects us. While he pulled out of it in a week, it meant for us taking shifts at his bedside through the day until bedtime. Furthermore, his few days back in an intensive care unit were too reminiscent of the far more traumatic stay in Brooklyn Jewish Hospital. There he was again with IV and oxygen tubes and clicking metronome devices clocking the "vital signs." Zodiacal signs of no use. Conjunction of what astral houses caused this again?)

I never learnt how to rhyme. The dactylic hexameter was hard for me, though I knew how to scan my Virgil and Homer. The rhyme patterns and meter of the blues were more to my heart. I was never a disciplined student. Could never do without reading several books at a time. Dipping my finger in the broth of knowledge, to do the mad chase through dreams to Albion's Tomb with some crazed Zapata be-alike at my heels, while I dream and dream again the dead, my dead, in the vast oneiricon of my dark honeycomb. Dithyramb, iamb, hecatomb, holocaust, all geometrically one to me. Bonzes of Oriental wisdom, ears torn off and tattooed all over, suggesting to me the utterly ineffable. Caught in the typical karmic cog, Max in hand, hospital synonym, cemetery, sanitarium, syllabary, syntax (illegal) . . .

In 1995 what happened? After a hiatus, I decided to publish more books through Pantograph Press. I was happy to get Jake Berry, perhaps the best of the younger experimentalists in the country today in print. He sent me a manuscript, *Species of Abandoned Light,* which I edited to a stage that we both liked. Andy chose books by poets Will Alexander and Lee Ballentine, both younger poets beginning to get attention. Marilla, heavily politicized from the Persian Gulf massacre, had begun working with a prison information project concerning the Gulag-like Pelican Bay maximum security prison in northern California. Here the prisoners are kept in solitary, allowed but one hour a day outside. She began to be in touch with one of the prisoners, Anthony Murillo, who wrote poetry, rather good poetry. I sent him some of my books, which really transfigured him and his style. Then she got the idea, which I heartily

encouraged, of doing an anthology of Pelican Bay prisoners' writings. She began soliciting poems, letters, essays from the prisoners. I decided to publish something unique to Pantograph Press, *Extracts from Pelican Bay,* edited by Marilla. She designed the book from cover to cover, and the result was haunting and beautiful. I was particularly impressed with how she took some of the poems and put them on the page, in styles reminiscent of the Calligrames of Apollinaire, for example. In the meantime Jack had introduced me to Neeli Cherkovski, a noted North Beach biographer and poet. He had done biographies of Ferlinghetti and Bukowski, as well as a wonderful book of autobiographical reminiscences of poets, called *Whitman's Wild Children.* Among the poets that he writes about intimately are Bob Kaufman and Philip Lamantia, surrealists dear to my heart. Neeli was burning to get a major book of his poetry out, and he importuned me with manuscripts. At first I was disinclined. It didn't have the surge, the long line, the experimentalism I wanted. Then he showed me some new poems, notably "Queer Careers," which I think is the best gay and AIDS poem I have ever read. He gave me another manuscript. I edited it extensively, getting him to flesh it out with the long, complex poems I knew he could do. The result was a beautiful book published by Pantograph, *Animal.* I had also decided to publish a major work of Jack's, *Exiles,* and another book from my epic, *Enigma & Variations: Paradise Is Persian for Park,* with a gorgeous cover designed by Marilla and taken from her haunting wall-hanging, *Blood and Oil.*

Neeli's book has an apt title. Both Neeli and I are animal lovers. My own animal, Alibi, was on his last legs throughout 1995. After a serious liver infection in August, he managed to pull through and see it to December 1. Nothing was more painful for me than to make the appointment to "put him to sleep." Unable to move for the last twelve hours of his life, Jack and I got him up off the floor beside my bed and put him on the living room couch, his favorite spot. A kindly vet showed up a little after 2:00, as did my old friend James. The appropriate injections were given. As Jack says, the last thing Alibi felt or saw was me. The ceremony was very symbolic. Both my oldest friend, James Balfour, and my best friend and fellow poet, Jack Foley, were there. For me it was a strong test for my fear of dying, acquired years ago in the Trinity Lutheran Church. It was like a chapter out of the *Tibetan Book of the Dead.* A Learning-to-Pass-Beyond.

So we come to 1996. Pantograph Press came out with the three new titles, by Jack, Neeli, and myself. The combination of the three, I think, is very potent, and I hope will better establish us on the map. It is as if we are generating a "California School," post-Olson, post-Language, and definitely nonacademic, a mix of experiment with language and passion. Good advance raves already for these titles, and Marilla's and Jake Berry's work, too. When I recall my strong sense of inferiority growing up in Minnesota, of being an outsider, of being unsure of myself and of my talents, suddenly here I am with some kind of reputation, and with some kind of conviction of my own art. I have arrived somewhere on the charts. And then there is the distance between my twin and me. He has resurfaced, with ideas about how to stave off total disaster with his Mayan calendar, a further evolution of his earlier Harmonic Convergence celebration, and his book *Mandala.* How far we have come from drawing those massive maps of imaginary metropolises (necropolises?). Will our next encounter be in some coffinbarque in the Egyptian Book of the Dead? What Mayan Factor will reassemble us? What exercise in alleatory writing will we practice in the dream after the dream?

It is difficult to terminate an "autobiography" when one presumably still has years to go. There are times, more and more frequently, when I feel I have written more than enough. *Basta!* Look at the drawer packed with unpublished typescript poems. *Basta!* Look at those dozen or more spiral-bound notebooks whose handwriting has yet to be deciphered. *Basta!* What will come of all that? The incertitude of dust or flame? Will it matter? Have I already written my masterpiece? Will I ever know? Will I ever fully comprehend what has been at work inside me? All those words and images pushed and pulled together, pointing to what?

What is it we say to the night?

—*Ivan Argüelles*

BIBLIOGRAPHY

Poetry:

Instamatic Reconditioning, Damascus Road (Wescoville, Pennsylvania), 1978.

The Invention of Spain, Downtown Poets Co-op (Brooklyn, New York), 1978.

Captive of the Vision of Paradise, Hartmus Press (Mill Valley, California), 1983.

The Tattooed Heart of the Drunken Sailor, Ghost Pony (Madison, Wisconsin), 1983.

Manicomio, Silverfish Review (Eugene, Oregon), 1984.

Nailed to the Coffin of Life, Ruddy Duck (Fremont, California), 1985.

What Are They Doing to My Animal?, Ghost Dance (East Lansing, Michigan), 1986.

The Structure of Hell, Grendahl (Lompoc, California), 1986.

Pieces of the Bone-Text Still There, NRG Press (Portland, Oregon), 1987.

Baudelaire's Brain, Sub Rosa (Teaneck, New Jersey), 1988.

Looking for Mary Lou: Illegal Syntax, Rock Steady (San Francisco, California), 1989.

"THAT" Goddess, Pantograph (Berkeley, California), 1992.

Hapax Legomenon, Pantograph, 1993.

Enigma & Variations: Paradise Is Persian for Park, Pantograph, 1996.

Anthologies:

Voices of Brooklyn, American Library Association, 1973.

Doctor Generosity Poets, Damascus Road, 1975.

A Decade of Spanish Literature, Arte Publico Press, c. 1980.

For Rexroth, The Ark, 1980.

Fiesta in Aztlan, Capra Press (Santa Barbara, California), c. 1980.

Through a Glass Darkly (freshman English text), Tennessee State University, 1982.

American Poetry Since 1970, 4 Walls 8 Windows, 1987.

Stiffest of the Corpse, City Lights, 1989.

American Poetry Confronts the '90's, Black Tie Press, 1990.

Yellow Silk: Erotic Arts and Letters, Harmony Books, 1990.

New Chicano/Chicana Writing, University of Arizona Press, 1992.

Terminal Velocities (includes the play *The Tragedy of Momus*), Pantograph, 1993.

Primary Trouble, Talisman House, 1996.

American Poets Say Goodbye to the 20th Century, 4 Doors 8 Walls, 1996.

Also contributor to *Before Columbus Foundation Catalog 1,* c. 1981 and *Annual Survey of American Poetry,* 1986.

Charles Bernstein

1950-

An Autobiographical Interview Conducted by Loss Pequeño Glazier

Charles Bernstein with his son, Felix, 1992

This interview was written in the summer of 1995. Questions and answers were exchanged by e-mail.

LPG: My first question is one that has been on my mind for quite some time. Reading your work, there seems to be a presence of your early life in your writing, certainly from the point of view of language and surface texture. Yet not much has been published on this subject. You were born in New York, correct?

CB: Yes, at Doctors' Hospital, Upper East Side, Manhattan, on April 4, 1950. As my father had

it on the announcement: "Sherry Bernstein, Labor; Herman Bernstein, Management."

LPG: I'd also be interested in hearing about your parents. Certainly, the idea of poetry as a business and the generational conflict—for example, in "Sentences My Father Used"—makes this of great interest.

CB: My father, Herman Joseph Bernstein, was born Joseph on December 22, 1902, in Manhattan; he was the eighth of eleven brothers and sisters: Joseph (who died before him, so the name was never really used), Sadie, Harry, Gad, David, Pauline, Ceil, Evelyn, Sidney, and Nahum. His father, Charles, died when my father was young; his mother, Jenny, died in early 1945. Both immigrated from western Russia in the 1890s, settling in the Lower East Side and then the Village. Jenny ran a Jewish resort in Long Branch, New Jersey, for a while but was put out of business by an epidemic; later she ran a restaurant in lower Manhattan. My father's grandfather spent his days studying the Talmud and the like; he did not work. Many of my father's brothers were very successful in business and real estate. My father mostly worked in the garment industry, eventually as co-owner of Smartcraft Corporation, a medium-size manufacturer of ladies' dresses, one of the first firms to make cheap ($12) knock-offs of fashion dresses. Back taxes did him in in the early 1960s; he had a heart attack but eventually rebounded as the American consultant to Teijin, Ltd., Japan's largest textile manufacturer. He married my mother on December 12, 1945, at the age of forty-three. He died January 20, 1978, of leukemia.

My mother was an only child. She was born on February 2, 1921, and lived with her mother, Birdie Kegel, on Avenue P, near Prospect Park in Brooklyn. Birdie, born Bertha in western Russia in 1891, was abandoned by her father, Louis Stolitsky, who left for the United States. Her mother died, and she was sent, alone, to the U.S. when she was seven; she went to live with her father and stepmother, an unhappy circumstance for her. She married Edward Kegel in 1918. He was a successful Brooklyn real estate developer; he died of a streptococcus infection in 1927.

LPG: Given that both your parents had their roots in western Russia, might I ask specifically where in western Russia they came from? Importantly, did you grow up in an environment of spoken Yiddish or Russian? Do you have any familiarity with or memory of either of these languages?

CB: I don't know the precise locations where my grandparents on my mother's side were born. My father's mother emigrated from Lithuania in about 1888, when she was in her early teens; his father emigrated from near Odessa. But this was ancient history to my father, who, after

all, was born in New York, and I don't ever recall him talking about it, except in the oral history I did with him just before he died, which I had to listen to again in order to answer your question. My father did not dwell on such things, at least not so as I could tell. Maybe it was that he didn't want to trouble me, or my brother and sister, about it; maybe he didn't think we'd be interested; maybe he didn't want to think about it. The main thing was that the family got out. In things like this I found my father quite opaque: he didn't seem at all introspective, although to say that is to reflect an enormous gulf between his own cultural circumstances and my own. In many ways my father seemed foreign to me, which is not to say unfamiliar; so it is all the more startling that I now find myself resembling him in so many ways. The early poem that you mentioned, "Sentences My Father Used" (in *Controlling Interests*), tried to think this through; much of this poem is based on the oral history I did with my father. (I'm sure I'm not alone in finding Paul Auster's evocation of his

The Bernsteins: (from left) Charles, father, brother Edward, grandmother Birdie Kegel, mother, sister Leslie, 1953

father, in *The Invention of Solitude*, very close to my own experience of my father.)

But equally, in the case of my mother and my grandmother, origins and roots were rarely a topic. The only grandparent I knew was my grandmother, who always lived very close by, but since she came to America as a little girl, any echo of Yiddish was long gone. My mother says the only time she remembers hearing her parents speak Yiddish was when they were saying something they didn't want her to understand. So, no, we had only American English at home, except for the occasional Friday night Hebrew prayer, although neither of my parents, nor my grandmother, knew much Hebrew, and what Hebrew was around was the product of religious education. That was the context in which I learned a very little Hebrew in the couple of years before I turned thirteen, at Congregation Rodeph Shalom, a Reform synagogue on the Upper West Side.

LPG: But wouldn't your father have been familiar with these languages? And if the background of your parents was not a linguistic presence, wasn't it of importance in their political outlook?

CB: My father probably spoke Yiddish as a kid, but there was no hint of that in our household, except for the pervasive idiomatic insistences that come naturally from any such linguistic background and add texture and character to a person's speech. For example, my father would say "close the lights" or "take a haircut." I know there must be dozens more examples, but I can't bring any to mind right now, only keep hearing him saying, "Can't you kids close the lights? This place is lit up like Luna Park."

My parents were assimilationists who nonetheless had a strong Jewish and later Zionist identification. As for many of their generation, this made for interesting contradictions. We were loosely kosher in the "beef fry" years; but in other years the bacon fried plentifully and tasted sweet. Or we were kosher on Friday night when my Aunt Pauline came to dinner but not the rest of the week. Of course, on Rosh Hashana and Yom Kippur, when dozens of relatives descended on our apartment for gigantic and endless meals that I grew to dread for their tediousness, we were strictly kosher, with once-a-year Pesach plates and cakes made from matzoh meal. (Those who might "correctly" say you can't

Charles with his mother, Sherry Bernstein, 1954

be a little bit kosher ignore the actual practice of Jewish ethnicity.) My father's family was associated with the Congregation Sherith Israel, the hundreds-year-old Spanish and Portuguese synagogue relocated across the street from our building; I occasionally attended the Orthodox services in their august main sanctuary. But as I say, for my parents the religious end of Judaism was less pronounced than a decisive, but at the same time mutable, ethnic identification.

In politics my parents were liberal Democrats, but not especially political, though I can still remember handing out leaflets on Broadway and 74th Street for Adlai Stevenson when I was six. And while I am pleased to have been enlisted into the Stevenson camp, and have holes in my own shoes to prove it, my politics and that of my parents grew further apart. When I was a teenager, my father and I used to have vituperative exchanges at dinner about Vietnam and about racism as he embraced Hubert Humphrey and I drifted leftward. More recently, my mother expressed her exasperation that I was the only Jew in New York who supported Jesse Jackson, though I pointed out to her that my brother had also voted for Jackson. (I center here on my father not only because it is more relevant to your question but also because my relation with my mother continues in a way that makes me less apt to characterize it.)

In any case, my father's concerns were centered foursquarely on success, and too often, and very painfully for him, failure in business. As he put it, "One can achieve success and happiness if the right priorities are valued." "The right priorities" was not a particularly elastic concept for him, and in this he represents, more than less, a new-immigrant generation that didn't have the leisure to question what their very hard work made possible for my generation.

LPG: Louis Zukofsky and Charles Reznikoff are writers who have been consistently of great interest to you in their ability to "create a new world in English, a new word for what they called America." How does the experience of your family inform your reading of these authors? I was wondering if, especially in Reznikoff's work, other than the literary and documentary qualities, there are specific events or issues that you find particularly resonant in your personal history?

CB: Yes, my relation to Zukofsky and Reznikoff is tempered by this history. Zukofsky and my father were virtually the same age and grew up near each other, but there seem few other points in common. Zukofsky and Reznikoff interrogated and resisted the very ideologies that my father accepted as the givens of American life. And both had gone well beyond the high school education my father possibly completed. (My mother's education was not much more extensive, though she had a few years of "finishing school" after high school. But that is a different story.)

My father certainly had no sympathy for artists, whom he thought of as frauds (in the case of "modern" art) or slackers (as in the case of his own rabbinic grandfather, whom he saw as something of a family black sheep). And we grew up surrounded by popular American culture but very little in the way of literature or art. While my parents hardly even played music on the radio, the newspapers—the *Times,* the *Post,* the *Daily News,* and later *Women's Wear*

Charles with his father in Italy, 1966

Daily—loomed large. We did have books, but they were mostly inherited popular novels of the previous decades supplemented by a few contemporary best-sellers or condensed books (just add boiling water). My mother had decorated a large part of our apartment in a very formal French colonial style. The large living room, for example, was for company—not for everyday life. In this context, books become decor, as with a complete set of Ruskin's work bought by the yard for a beautiful antique bookshelf. As far as I can tell, the Ruskin was never opened during my childhood, though I do appreciate the fact that it presided over us, in some subliminal way.

Zukofsky and Reznikoff are important to me because they suggest a totally different sense of Jewishness than anything I knew of in the 1950s, something along the lines that Isaac Deutcher, writing from a Left perspective, describes as the "non-Jewish Jew," but also part of the heterodox context chartered by Jerome Rothenberg in *A Big Jewish Book.* This is something of a circus sideshow to "serious" Judaism, with opening acts by Maimonides and the Baal Shem Tov, Spinoza and Heine, or, in the main tent, Groucho and Harpo and Chico Marx, Lenny Bruce, Woody Allen, Bob Dylan. While I never mentioned Jewishness in my college piece on Stein and Wittgenstein (and the subject is largely unmentioned in each of their works), it is, of course, an obvious point of contact as well as a crucial, if implicit, reference point for me.

But let me end this string of thoughts by quoting a passage from Amos Oz that, by a delicious coincidence, Eric Selinger e-mailed while I was answering your question:

> Now suppose a new Kafka is growing up right now, here in San Francisco, California. Suppose he is fourteen-years-old right now. Let's call him Chuck Bernstein. Let's assume that he is every bit of a genius as Kafka was in his time. His future must, as I see it, depend on an uncle in Jerusalem or an experience by the Dead Sea, or a cousin in a kibbutz or something inspired by the Israeli live drama. Otherwise, with the exception of the possibility that he is growing up among the ultra-Orthodox, he will be an American writer of Jewish origin—not a Jewish American writer. He may become a new Faulkner, but not a new Kafka. ("Imagining the Other: 1," in *The Writer in the Jewish Community: An Israeli-North American Dialogue,* ed. Richard Siegel and Tamar Sofer [Associated University Presses, 1993], 122.)

It seems to me this tortured and reductive conception of identity is just what the tradition of writers I've mentioned have refused. And it is in exploring and realizing alternative identity formations that at least one sliver of a Jewish tradition may be of use; in this, Kafka is our dark and imploding star.

LPG: As your father was a manager in the garment industry, how did this reflect upon your own sense of self while growing up? (In other words, his work could have seemed petty or commercial compared to your own engagement with social concerns, or you may have felt pressure to become a part of the "cottage" industry.) Did you have to fight pressure to participate in your father's commercial enterprise?

CB: One day I woke up and found myself metamorphosed into a tiny businessman. All that I have

done since, political and poetic, has changed this not at all. For poetry, after all, is the ultimate small business, requiring a careful keeping of accounts to stay afloat. Not to mention all that "small press" stuff like distribution, promotion, and book manufacturing. That is to say, I have wanted to bring poetry into the "petty, commercial," indeed material and social world of everyday life rather than make it a space in which I could remain "free" of these things, or, better to say, chained to an illusion of such freedom.

Because my father and his brothers were "self-made" men, they believed that theirs was the only practical, and therefore right, course in life. The proof was that it had worked for them, and, as far as I can tell, they never came to understand how the lives so created could look so hollow, if not misguided, to at least a few of the next generation. To start a business on nothing, as my father had done in the 1920s, when he bought and resold short end pieces of fabric rolls that would otherwise have been discarded ("the trim, the waste"), meanwhile being weekly hounded by his successful brother to repay a small loan, sets in place a pattern of anxiety and diminished expectations for the, what? "quality" of life, if aesthetics can be defined, so, that doesn't eas-

At Harvard College, Thayer Hall, freshman year, 1969

ily, if ever, unravel. The business isn't something you do to make money; it's what you do, who you are. Family, like cultural or social activities, is an extended lunch break.

And what went with this, at least for my father, was an unquestioning belief not only in progress and industry in the abstract but also in the absolute value of industrialization, Western Civilization, the market system, and technology that the catastrophes of the Second World War did not, finally, touch. I imagine that the 1920s and 1930s passed my father by as he worked, singly and single-mindedly, to establish himself, to create his own estate. That came, finally, during the war, and he married for the first time in the very first year of the postwar era, and at pretty much the age I am now, starting a family when most men of his generation had grown-up kids. He came the closest to his American Dream in the 1950s. It was as if his life had led him to this decade of prosperity and surface tranquillity, and he remained, for the rest of his life, its unshakable constituent.

But here's where the ethnic ethos comes in again: it wasn't for us, the children, to continue in business but to become professionals, free from the grinding labor and terrorizing uncertainty of business. The pressure, then, was to be a physician or lawyer; my own choice, at least initially toward downward social mobility, was rankling and fundamentally unacceptable and must have made me seem ungrateful and disrespectful of the whole struggle of the business, of his life. I know my father often complained about my lack of respect and certainly had no respect to spare for my choices. I pretty much ignored the pressure, which is to say, adamantly rejected the life so envisioned for me, and never really looked back.

LPG: Tell me about your brothers and sisters. Did you grow up in New York? What was your early life like?

CB: I have a brother, Edward Amber (changed his last name), born October 8, 1946, and a sister, Leslie Gross (married to Donald Gross),

Susan Bee Laufer, at the time she and Charles Bernstein first met, with a painting of her by Miriam Laufer in the background, 1969

Charles and Susan, about 1972

born June 16, 1948. My parents moved from 81st Street just west of Columbus to 101 Central Park West just before I was born; my mother still lives in the same luxurious twelfth-floor apartment, which overlooks Central Park. Classic Upper West Side.

Like my sister and brother, I went to a self-congratulating "progressive" school of the Deweyite persuasion, the Ethical Culture School. I was there kindergarten to sixth grade. None of us did very well there, and I intensely disliked the social, cultural, and intellectual environment. This was a place that, even if you were "comfortable," the other kids, and their parents, made you feel like you were a pauper. On the school's part, they did not think much of me, as I was repeatedly told: my penmanship and spelling were abysmal; I was slow to read and in constant need of remedy in the form of remedial groups; I did not socialize right; my appearance was somewhat ajar. I give a sense of this in "Standing Target" in *Controlling Interests,* where I quote some reports from Fieldston day camp, which was run by Ethical. My favorite thing to do was stay home; some years I missed as many as forty days. And at home, there was the chance for reverie, for sleeping late, for making tuna fish sticks sprinkled with paprika, for watching daytime TV. I read *TV Guide* religiously in those days and knew

all the panelists on the celebrity game shows, all the actors on the sitcoms, and all the comedy shows from the early 1950s that I had missed the first time around.

I liked TV and hanging out at home—but not sports! I was the kind of kid that was always picked last for the team and put in right field or its equivalent. By the time I was in high school (after a brief flirtation with soccer, all dressed in black to play goalie, in junior high school), I used to put my hands in my pockets whenever I was thrust into a game. I never played catch with any member of my family, but we used to go out to Chinese dinners on Thanksgiving and Christmas, and I liked that.

I can still remember my delight at the reaction of my sixth-grade teacher, Miss Green, when I sported a button that read "I may look interested but I'm just being polite." I've always tried to be polite. But I did like one thing about Miss Green's class: for months, it seems to me, we read, always starting from the first page, *The Old Curiosity Shop:* "Night is generally my time for walking." I loved that and could, no matter how awkward I otherwise felt in the class, fall into that prose and be transported.

I was not admitted to Fieldston, Ethical's upper school, a routine matter for my classmates, and went on, to my great relief, to a small, highly conventional, private school, Franklin, for seventh and eighth grades, and it was there that the worlds of history and literature opened up for me. What I hated about Ethical was that you never received grades but were given pop psychology reports about your development and social integration. At Franklin, there were concrete tasks assigned and measured by tests; the right attitude was less important than the right facts. Certainly, there were some tough times adjusting. I wanted to do really well and can remember cheating a few times on tests in seventh grade, as if that would prove to myself that I knew a thing or two. Actually, the academic side of the school became the great focus of my life as I began to read the history of Greece or China and especially to read literature. I remember a great, thick collection of international short stories, with a gray cover, that I got while at Franklin, and the excitement I felt when I read, even if I could not fully understand, Kafka, Genet, Camus, and especially Sartre. Then one day in seventh or eighth grade an English teacher named Francis Xavier Walker wrote on the board, "Bun is such a sad word is it not, and man is not much better is it." He said it was by Samuel Beckett, and that he liked the way it sounded, the way it focused on the sound of the words man and bun. That was kind of like hearing about the theory of relativity. I was hooked; in fact years seemed to go by when all I wanted to do was stay in my small room overlooking the park, which at that point I rarely stepped into, and read books and watch TV.

LPG: Yes, you have written that "My work is as influenced by *Dragnet* as by Proust." This comment, of course, is indicative of the sources of "information" we have in a media culture like ours. Did your interest in the classroom experience change when you went to high school?

CB: Well, I always loved those clipped voice-overs. But I have to say, the influence of *Dragnet* was nothing compared to the Manhattan Yellow Pages.

I spent high school at a terrific school, the Bronx High School of Science, where, in my senior year, I edited the school newspaper, *Science Survey*. Science was a "specialized" school, something like today's magnet schools, but pretty much the only such schools in New York, in the *Sputnik* era, were science schools, so my interest in going there was for the quality of the school and not for the science and math, which I never had much interest in. Strangely, I always did very well on standardized tests of physics, chemistry, geometry, algebra, and the like, but I never felt like I "got" it. My interests were literature, history, social studies. Indeed, I coordinated our high school Forum series, which sponsored speakers every month; I remember in particular taking a cab back into the city with James Farmer of CORE [Congress of Racial Equality]. There were great, even inspired, English teachers at Science. The one I was closest to was Richard Feingold, who gave vivid lectures on *Hamlet*, Jonathan Edwards, Emily Dickinson, and Robert Frost. Feingold is now a professor of eighteenth-century poetry at Berkeley. He came to my reading there a few months back—I hadn't seen him in over twenty-five years.

During high school I started going to the movies a lot, and also to the theater. I grew up with the big musicals of the period, but at this point I got interested in Pinter and im-

ports from the Royal Shakespeare Company, Peter Brooks's productions, but also off-Broadway stuff: I can still remember being riveted by Leroi Jones's *Dutchman*. You know, the whole world of "high culture" and modernism opened up for me and I was always making lists of what I should know about. I remember sending for WQXR's Martin Bookspan's list of the one hundred most important classical records and then checking them out at the library or buying them. I mean, I had no information about this kind of thing but I was fascinated. My parents, like I said, didn't listen to music or read very much beyond the newspapers and magazines (though my mother would occasionally read a best-selling novel), but they did do things like get me a subscription to Leonard Bernstein's Young People's Concerts with the New York Philharmonic, and they were happy to buy me tickets for lots of other concerts all over the city, which I generally went to by myself. When I was sixteen, my father, sister, and I went to Europe. We visited London, Paris, Florence, Rome, and Berlin. In London I went to plays every night and saw all the museums, all the sights. It was thrilling, although it was quite difficult to travel with my father, and the deep generational and political divisions between us were never so apparent.

LPG: When did this divergent cultural information begin to coalesce for you?

CB: Everything fell into place in the mid-1960s: those great movies from Fellini and Antonioni and Godard, Phil Ochs and Bob Dylan and Richie Havens, and much that holds up far less well these days (I still have my Procol Harem and Incredible String Band records), the Be-Ins, the smoke from loose joints. While I had a Bar Mitzvah at thirteen and was, at the time, quite religious, all that started to come apart within a year or two. The civil rights movement, the sit-ins, the Mississippi Freedom summer, Martin Luther King, and then the Vietnam War all increasingly focused my politics. I tuned to WBAI, Pacifica radio in New York. I was around for the demonstrations during the Columbia University strike during my senior year in high school, and also involved with demonstrations at my high school (against regulations prohibiting "shirts without colors and dungaree-type pants," among other things).

I've never shaken the shock and sadness I felt when Martin Luther King was assassinated; it was my eighteenth birthday. In the summer of 1968, after a trip I took by myself to Scandinavia (I wanted to see the fjords) and also to Greece (where you could still get by on a couple of dollars a day), I returned to the U.S. to go to the Chicago demonstrations during the Democratic National Convention. Like everyone else there, I got gassed, got "radicalized" (again), and got to hear Allen Ginsberg chant "Om" to the crowd.

I met Susan (Bee Laufer) in high school—at a party in Greenwich Village on February 9, 1968. Her parents had both grown up in Berlin, had left in 1936 on a youth aliyah to Palestine when they were teenagers, and had met in Jerusalem. They came to New York in 1948—Sigmund keeping the same job, until a couple of years ago, and the same apartment all this while. Susan's parents were both artists: her mother, Miriam, a wonderful, unjustly unrecognized, painter doing 1950s-style expressionist paintings of, among other things, female nudes,

and a later series painted on car windshields. The Laufers, who had been sympathetic with the Left when in Palestine, were a remarkable political and cultural contrast to my own family. With Susan, I started to go to the art galleries and then also up to Provincetown.

LPG: Then you attended Harvard, correct? This must have been quite a change from the cultural and social excitement of Manhattan. Was this a satisfying experience?

CB: I found Harvard a rather unpleasant place and was shocked by the snobbism and arrogance. It was unbelievable to me that the "men" at the Freshman Commons would clink their glasses when a woman walked into the hall. If Katie Roiphe and other post-feminists would like to go back to this time, they can have it. This was the last year that you had to wear a tie and jacket to dinner; there were parietals in effect in the still all-male dorms. I found the environment suffocating and depressing. And living in Harvard Yard was like living in a zoo—

Wedding photo—Charles Bernstein and Susan Bee Laufer,
Lyme, New Hampshire, August 17, 1977

with all the tourists taking pictures of you and your environs when you poked your head out the door.

I have to say, it was an eye-opener to realize how few of my classmates actually cared about the arts, literature, history, though after a while it was possible to find like-minded souls. Still, Harvard students, on the whole, seemed contemptuous of the arts and of learning in a way I never encountered at Bronx Science; I soon came to realize that the enhanced admission for students from elite prep schools pulled down the intellectual, cultural, and moral level of the school, just as it does the country. Talk about affirmative action. In my year only one student from all the public schools of Chicago got into Harvard, while 40 percent of the classes at the elite schools were admitted. I got a real sense of where this was all going when I had a job doing childcare at a twenty-fifth reunion. At the Boston Pops concert, the middle-aged Harvard grads gave a standing ovation to an orchestral version of "Rain Drops Keep Falling on My Head." I keep that image in mind when I think of our "elite" institutions and what they are doing for our culture.

I was not alone in my distress. In my freshman year I became involved in the antiwar movement, even if my somewhat anarchic and pacifist politics did not sit well with some factions of SDS [Students for a Democratic Society]. I was impressed by many of the ideas of the New Left, and especially by the Port Huron Statement and the concept of participatory democracy. And I certainly thought something had to be done to stop the war. I was in and out of University Hall during the 1969 occupation, but when the police were called, I was in bed, right next door to the occupied building. I quickly slipped into the building and was arrested for trespassing in a case that was ultimately dismissed. Despite the dismissal in a court of law, I was put under indefinite "warning" by Harvard's Committee of Rights and Responsibilities ("We're right, you're responsible"). I have been amused and appalled to see how in the intervening years some of my classmates who did not take a stand of principle against the war have parlayed their own failures of political judgment into a source of pundit power: I am thinking here of James Fallows and Michael Kinsley.

LPG: The political informs your work on many levels. It seems relevant here, given your expe-

rience with politics at the Columbia and Harvard strikes and the (one would presume extremely significant) Chicago demonstrations, to ask whether you were considering political activism as a future involvement. What influenced you in this regard? And wouldn't "literary" action be considered less than effective? How do you reconcile this?

CB: I never wanted to be a professional activist, although in some ways maybe that is what I've become. I always thought protest was for the informed citizen, taking the time out of her or his everyday life, time hard to spare but required by the very demands of citizenship. The demonstrations of the 1960s and 1970s were exhilarating, and I dearly miss that level of idealism and activism in the U.S., dearly miss the time when the political and cultural Left, or shades of it, set the national agenda rather than the religious Right, as now seems the case. Still, I was amazed at a reunion held on the twentieth anniversary of the Harvard strike how many of the people spoke of those events as the high point of their life. I think my own preoccupations were and are elsewhere.

It seems like it can never be stated often enough that the claims made for "the politics of poetic form" are against the idea of the political efficacy of poetry. If anything, the politics of the poetic for which I have spoken mute any such efficacy. So then the question becomes, how do you reconcile thought and action, or second thoughts and action, reflection and decision? The answer is, as best you can. Poetry explores crucial questions about the core values that constitute a polis; it allows for refor-

Charles and Susan, 1978

Sulfur Conference, Ypsilanti, Michigan, 1988: (top row, from left) James Clifford, Michael Palmer, Clark Coolidge, Eliot Weinberger; (middle, from left) Clayton Eshleman, Caryl Eshleman, Charles Bernstein, Rachel Blau DuPlessis, John Yau; (bottom, from left) Jerome Rothenberg, Jed Rasula, Marjorie Perloff

mulations of the basic issues of political policy and the means we use to represent them. It may even mock what men, and women, hold most dear, so that in our laughter we may come to terms with what we cling to.

Poetry thickens discussion, refuses reductive formulations. It sings of values not measurable as commercial sums. But such poetic politics do not exhaust one's political options or commitments. I don't suggest that aesthetics replace politics. I just don't believe in a politics that abolishes aesthetics.

LPG: If Harvard was a disappointment culturally, I wonder what your expectations had been. Did you expect a revelation in terms of education? Was there a specific grant or scholarship that encouraged you to attend? Why did you choose to go to Harvard?

CB: My choice was to go to the best college that I could get into, where "best" was conven-

tionally defined. This was a given, which I had no means to contest. I bought the image of Harvard as the ultimate place of Higher Learning, in which I would be able to pursue my studies in a manner that deepened and extended what I most liked at Bronx Science. In many ways this was possible at Harvard, and I certainly did have the extraordinary opportunity to read and converse. I just had no idea what went with this; my studies had not prepared me for the fact that the fruit of learning would be laced with nausea-inducing poison and that for many the lesson learned was not to eat that fruit, or not eat very much. That is perhaps the chief product of the Harvard education: willful ignorance, learned callousness, and an ability keep your eye on your personal bottom line (defined by money and social status). So, yes, this was disillusioning, and it hit me hard and almost immediately upon arriving—that "learning," as I had romanticized it, was not disinterested and indeed was being used as a

*"Objectivist" Poets Conference, Royaumont, France, 1989: (from left) Emmanuel Hocquard,
Pierre Alferi, Lyn Hejinian, Charles Bernstein, Jean-Paul Auxémery*

means of preserving social injustice; that one had to struggle, even at a place like this, to create a space for thought, reflection, art. These are lessons I have found very useful. But perhaps, looking back, it's not Harvard that shocked me but America, an America I had not yet met in the culturally rich, but unrepresentative, precincts I had inhabited up to that point in my life.

LPG: Your involvement with philosophy is well known. Certainly, "Thought's Measure," among others, qualifies as a consummate philosophical essay. You studied philosophy at Harvard?

CB: Yes, I concentrated in philosophy at college: though my interests were more in the history of philosophy and "continental" philosophy than in analytic philosophy, toward which I was antipathetic. As a freshman I took "Introduction to Symbolic Logic" with Willard Quine. He mumbled to the blackboard during most of the lectures, though I did find his books witty and provocative. I had a dream one night in which I was haphazardly trying to stuff all my clothes into a suitcase and Quine came over to show me how they would all fit if neatly folded. I shot him. (This was a time in which Quine was widely quoted as saying that we should

handle the student demonstrators in the U.S. the way they did in South America: bring in the militia.) Then there was Hilary Putnam, who was in his Maoist period. And John Rawls, whose *Theory of Justice* had just come out: the most rational man in the world but, well, somewhat boring and stiff for my taste at the time. In contrast, I was very impressed with Judith Shklar, the social historian.

Two philosophers, Stanley Cavell and Rogers Albritton, were particularly important for me at Harvard. The first year I was there they split one of those grand tours of Western thought, Albritton from the pre-Socratics to the Middle Ages, and Cavell from the Enlightenment on. Each brought his own quirky, thought-filled style to the occasion. I had heard about Wittgenstein before coming to college and felt an immediate fascination, so to fall in with these two Wittgensteinians was marvelous. I also had the great pleasure of spending a fair amount of time talking to Cavell and Albritton, and though I have remained friends with, and been influenced by, Cavell all these years, it was those long late-night conversations with Albritton that initiated me into philosophical conversation. My senior thesis was called "Three Compositions on Philosophy and Literature" and was a reading of Stein's *Making of Americans* through Wittgenstein's *Philosophical Investigations*. (A bit of this was recently published in

Gertrude Stein Advanced, edited by Richard Kostelanetz.)

LPG: It seems to me that Stein and Wittgenstein would not exactly be considered "canonical" in any institution at the time. Were these writers approved or encouraged in your program? Was it a struggle to gain acceptance for these writers as the focus of your thesis?

CB: As I mentioned, Cavell and Albritton were both very committed to Wittgenstein, especially the *Investigations,* so within that microcosm, Wittgenstein was the canonical, albeit "anticanonical," modernist philosopher. I had no companions in my enthusiasm for Stein, however—not surprising in a philosophy faculty in any case, and most decisively not in the English faculty, with which I had little contact. Of course, Stein had studied at Harvard with William James and at Emerson Hall, the site of my own studies; but that was a fact of little import in 1971. Since mine was an undergraduate thesis, I was pretty much left to do what I wanted and wasn't required to gain any acceptance for Stein, which would not have been possible. I did have a third reader for the piece though, a witty and genial visiting British philosopher named G. E. L. Owen, whose specialty was classical Greek philosophy but who had read, and expressed some sympathy for, Stein.

LPG: Were your thesis readers comfortable with the connection between Stein and Wittgenstein?

CB: At the time the idea of a connection between Stein and Wittgenstein was completely farfetched, the first of my crackpot theories that end up, over time, not seeming nearly so cracked. If the linking of these two names now seems unsurprising, that takes away from some of the brash humor I had in mind for it years ago. My own name for the project was "Three Steins." But I can't explain how, when I was twenty-one, I fell upon a matrix of thinking and writing that would continue to occupy me until this day. For the writing and thinking I was starting to do then is very much of a piece with my work now. Let's say it was an intuition that bore out.

LPG: What was the occasion or relation or particular event that might have put you in contact with these writers? How did this come about?

CB: Wittgenstein I had first heard about in high school, just a passing remark by a friend returned from college, but I became fascinated and curious since it seemed to go significantly beyond what I had been finding so interesting in that wonderfully intoxicating high-schoolish way about existentialism (with a puff of Hesse, Zen, the Beats, and the Beatles mixed in), and so I was happy to pick up on that in the next few years, especially in the context of reading over a range of philosophical works. I can't quite place my interest in Stein, certainly not from any class or reading list! I know I was consciously looking for literary equivalents for the modernist and abstract expressionist painting that I was so passionately taken by, and while I appreciated what I was offered—Joyce or Celan or Kafka or Woolf or Proust or, indeed, Faulkner—I felt there was something missing, something I did see, though, in Beckett's *Stories and Texts for Nothing* and Burroughs's *Naked Lunch* (I realize my examples here are all prose writers). Meanwhile, in 1970 Susan [Bee] was taking a seminar with Catherine Stimpson at Barnard, one of the first courses to be given on women's literature. This was way before there were anthologies or even recommended syllabi for such classes, before much of the material now at the center of women's studies courses was reprinted. Anyway, Stimpson apparently assigned *Three Lives,* and I must have heard about that from Susan. I don't think I more than glanced at *Three Lives,* but I soon found *The Making of Americans, Tender Buttons,* "Composition as Explanation," and much other Stein material, some of which was beginning to be published in new editions at this time. When I first read these works of Stein I was completely knocked out: this was what I had been looking for, what I knew must exist, and I was giddy with excitement.

LPG: What other activities were you involved in at Harvard? What about its "literary" culture?

CB: My sophomore year I happily moved to Adams House, just at the time it became coed and when it still had a beautiful private swimming pool. (When I was on the house committee, we passed a resolution requiring bathing suits only from 7 to 9 A.M.) My main artistic work at college was in theater, though oddly, as I look back on it, I was elected editor of the freshman literary magazine, the *Harvard Yard Journal,* and we put out two issues. In my senior year I also put out a small Xerox magazine of work by people in Adams House called *Writing.* (I stayed clear of "literary society" at Harvard, or anyway it stayed clear of me. The pretentiousness of the *Advocate* scene couldn't mask its emptiness, and I don't mean that in the Zen sense.)

LPG: Were there other cultural activities you found more relevant at the time?

CB: I studied theater games and improvisation with Dan Seltzer, a Shakespearean scholar who had gotten involved with acting. I directed several productions, including a rather large-scale musical production of Peter Weiss's *Persecution and Assassination of Jean-Paul Marat as Performed by the Inmates of the Asylum of Charenton under the Direction of the Marquis de Sade,* influenced by the radical theater work of the Living Theater, the Open Theater, and Grotowski. We did the production in street clothes (though one review seemed to think these were hippy costumes) in the dining room at Adams House. William Liller, an astronomer and the Master of Adams House, played the Director of the asylum and Marat was played by John McCain, at that time a Progressive Labor Party activist and later gay activist; McCain died of AIDS a few years back. The composer Leonard Lehrman was the musical director. It was a wild time. One night the Japan scholar John Fairchild showed up, and one of the cast rebuked him, in one of the bedlam scenes during the play, for his Vietnam policy—in Japanese. After a benefit performance for the Bobby Seale defense fund, a spontaneous demonstration moved the audience into the street. The next year I scripted and directed a work I called *Comings and Goings* that linked short pieces by Beckett and Pinter with a staging of the trial of the Chicago Eight. I also played a bit role in a play by Joseph Timko on the death of Morris Schlick, the Vienna Circle philosopher and logical positivist. My role was as the graduate student that killed Schlick and my line was "I shoot you out of jealousy and revenge: Bang! Bang!"

I spent the fall following college graduation (1972) in New York, living with Susan on Arden Street in Washington Heights and working mainly as the office manager of Sloan's Furniture Clearance Center #45 on East 85th Street, for $2.75 an hour. When Susan graduated Barnard in December, I took advantage of a William Lyon MacKenzie King Fellowship, which I had received, and we spent a year in Ruskin, just east of Vancouver. I had a loose and pleasant relation with Simon Fraser University, and it was there I attended a marvelous seminar on Emily Dickinson with Robin Blaser.

LPG: From what I've read, I would assume that you experienced a breakthrough in Vancouver. Was it at this point that the thrust of your future in writing became apparent?

CB: Not so much a breakthrough as follow-through. I moved to the Vancouver area with Susan in January 1973, six months after graduating college. During the nine months I was there I was able to read in and around the "New American Poetry," something I knew little about before this.

Shortly after moving, I sent some of my work, out of the blue, to Jerome Rothenberg, primarily on the strength of *Technicians of the Sacred,* which I had read with great enthusiasm when it came out in the late 1960s. Remarkably, Jerry wrote me right back and suggested I get in touch with Ron Silliman, in San Francisco, who was editing a section of new poetry for his and Dennis Tedlock's new magazine, *Alcheringa.* Ron wrote me back, also immediately, on a piece of letterhead from something called "The People's Yellow Pages," which seems apt for Ron. He had finished the collection, called "A Dwelling Place," but said he was going to quote something I said in my letter to him. He also gave me a list of people to read, which, as I recall it from this distance, included Michael Palmer and Clark Coolidge and a half-dozen others, including Eigner and Creeley. I hadn't read many of those poets and was also hearing about some of them, and a related set, from Blaser. I has access to the library and to the extraordinary poetry collection, so I had no trouble finding even the most obscure poetry I wanted. It was heaven.

As to my writing, I was onto something, but not there yet. I hadn't yet gotten to the other side of what Ron, I think, heard as Stein's "syrupy rhythm"; I was in a Stein period, that's for sure, writing things like "Paddington wade, she said faded" and a mock-epic "Hermes Hermeneutic" ("Hermes Hermeneutic, the swashbuckle kid from Alacazam, swim / swam /

swum past fireflies and mint juleps, pusses in the allies and lizigator monsters").

LPG: Then you returned to New York City?

CB: Actually, we moved from Vancouver to Santa Barbara in the fall of 1973, for no particular reason except, I suppose, that the sun was appealing after months of gray skies. In Santa Barbara I worked part-time for the Freedom Community Clinic, a free clinic, as a health education coordinator at a time when we were very involved in questions of feminism and gay rights, drug education, and, of course, sexually transmitted diseases. While I was there I continued to read around and I was in touch with other poets, getting their magazines and books. Even made it up to see Ron Silliman, although our first conversation was made almost inaudible by the loud band playing at the bar where we met. (Ron knew one of the people in the band!) In Santa Barbara I went to one of Kenneth

Rexroth's gatherings but didn't connect up with that context at all. *Disfrutes* and *Asylums* were written in Santa Barbara and include the earliest poems of mine that have been published.

I moved back to New York, to 464 Amsterdam, in early 1975, and that's when I met Bruce Andrews and we discovered how much we had in common, not only as poets and artists but also, for example, in an interest in such things as the Frankfurt School, which at that time seemed an unlikely thing for a poet to be interested in. (I had read Habermas's *Knowledge and Human Interest* with great interest and later attended a series of lectures he gave at UC Santa Barbara in 1974.)

In New York I went to lots of readings, particularly at the Poetry Project at St. Mark's, but all over the place. And in 1978 not only did Bruce and I start *L=A=N=G=U=A=G=E*—actually, the planning for that goes back to 1976—but Ted Greenwald and I also started the Ear Inn Series.

At a poetry conference in Wansee, Germany: (from left) Leslie Scalapino, Charles Bernstein, Kathleen Fraser, Clark Coolidge, Susan Coolidge (below), Hannah Moekel-Rieke, and Hans Joachim Rieke, May 1992

LPG: Let me stop you for a moment here. I am specifically interested in the period from 1973, when you left Vancouver, to 1978, when _L=A=N=G=U=A=G=E_ was founded. It is unclear, besides the mention of Stein and Wittgenstein, what your sense of your literary "elders" was during this period. In terms of contemporaries, you have mentioned Jerome Rothenberg and Ron Silliman, but I have the feeling that your reading would have been much more immense. Let me be more specific. I would like a clear sense of your position in terms of literary influences at this time.

CB: "Literary" is a problem for me since I was trying to get away from the literary, from any preset idea of poetry or of the aesthetic. It seemed to me that writing, certainly not verse—let's say verbal art in the sense that Antin talks about it in his early essays—was the thing.

In New York I worked initially at the United Hospital Fund, writing the scintillating _Health Manpower Consortia Newsletter,_ which Susan and I designed in exactly the format that we would use, a few years later, for _L=A=N=G=U=A=G=E;_ then briefly for the Council on Municipal Performance, a public-interest group where I primarily worked on mass transit issues and against the subway fare hike of that moment; and then for a couple of years as abstracts editor of the Canadian edition of _Modern Medicine,_ where I wrote about eighty medical abstracts each month. This immersion in commercial writing and editing—as a social space too, but more in the technical sense of learning the standardized compositional rules and forms at the most detailed, and numbingly boring, level of proofreading and copyediting—was informing in every way.

As far as art goes, painting has always been intimate for me, and I mean in particular Susan Bee's work, which crisscrosses, parallels, and leaps ahead of my "own" work. Living with a painter, seeing the paintings develop sometimes day to day from my comfortable "critic's chair," seeing how Susan would handle (and I mean literally handle) similar interests in collage, in the giddy rhetoric of various styles juxtaposed, well, I can't adequately acknowledge the importance of that. Many times Susan's work has amazed me by showing that things I thought you "theoretically" couldn't do needed to be done, and that includes things your own ideas would seem to hold you back from. The company and work

of visual artists was and remains so much a part of the sense and texture of my work that I made a decision, at some point, not to write too much about it or else I would end up just writing about it. So I'll leave it without further account save the fact of my immersion and the many, many shows I went to each month in the mid-1970s.

And then . . . then there's the movies, endless movies, including the visionary and revisionary films of Sonbert, Snow, Brakhage, Gehr, Child, Hills, Kubelka, Jacobs, and such (with Vertov, Eisenstein, etc., not far behind). And the theater—Richard Foreman's, Robert Wilson's (I especially appreciated those early, "messy" pieces), Richard Schechner's stuff at the Performance Garage, and so much else, including much of the performance art that was presented in New York at the time. And how about new music—thinking of so many nights at the Kitchen and other spaces—but also, and crucially, the opera? And so many poetry readings, three or more a week.

What I am getting to is that in this context what most excited me was indeed the work of my immediate contemporaries, just because, let's say, they are contemporaries and the meaning and the trajectory of their work was not yet determined, historicized (which can happen awfully fast). This work made the most immediate sense to me.

LPG: Certainly, these are crucial elements in the constitution of a writing. But you still haven't mentioned specific writers. Where and who were the "elders"? That is, what sense of relation was there to say Pound, Williams, or the Objectivists? Of course, there's also a "middle" layer here: Creeley, Ginsberg (who must've been very active in New York), and also Olson (though he doesn't fit exactly into either of these categories). At the same time I am very intrigued by what your sense of "contemporaries" might have been. I want a sense of who your "colleagues" were.

CB: Yes, indeed, there is a literary answer too. Rothenberg's anthology _Revolution of the Word,_ which came out in 1974 and included Riding, Zukofsky, Loy, Gillespie, Oppen, Schwitters, Duchamp, Mac Low, and others, is a good map of what was interesting me. At the same time, over those years I read and reread H.D., Williams, Stevens, Eliot, Bunting . . . not to mention the Russian constructivists, concrete and visual poetry, sound poetry, ethnopoetics, Dadaism . . . to keep the list, neatly but misleadingly, to the present century.

As for the "middle layer" you ask about, I knew Corso and Ginsberg from high school on and had seen Ginsberg perform many times. I especially loved his recording of Blake's *Songs of Innocence and Experience,* which I got when I was a college freshman and used to sing to myself all the time (still do). But from my perspective—thinking again back to the early 1970s—I think this work just didn't seem to me radically modern in the way that, say, Pollock or Rauschenberg or Morris Louis or Twombly or Rosenquist, or Godard or Cage or Coltrane or Stockhausen, or the poets in *Revolution of the Word,* or indeed Stein or Wittgenstein did. And that would have gone for Pound too, whom I read with greater interest only later.

But somewhere in all this I had to slow up and backtrack a bit, and this is where I started to absorb, in a big way, many of the poets grouped in, around, and about the "New American Poetry," including Mac Low (whom I went to see perform many times during the 1970s), Ashbery, Eigner, O'Hara, Guest, Schuyler, Spicer, Antin, and Creeley (whose *A Quick Graph* and other essays I read with great interest). The work of these poets, and especially their new and ongoing work, was incredibly exciting for me, and not just as artworks to appreciate. The work made me want to write poetry and also gave me many entry points for how to do it. Reading became intimately connected to writing.

Yet even as I write this, it still seems too pat, too limited, and my suspicion of narrative gets the better of me. When you are just starting to write, all poems seem like maps of possibilities for your own writing, or did to me, and order and sequence is jumbled, irrelevant, maybe an insult. In 1975 I didn't care very much about generations and influences or the order I read anything in, and I certainly didn't know what was important and what not, and if I did probably leapt from the former toward the latter. In 1995, a professor no less, the historical matrix for poetry seems to me not only very interesting but determining. But in that case these lists are as important for the names I've left out that ought certainly to be mentioned, acknowledged.

To chart that warp and woof you'd have to do a magazine like *L=A=N=G=U=A=G=E,* and this is what we did.

LPG: But "charting" implies that the activity surrounding *L=A=N=G=U=A=G=E* was "fixed" in some sense. In fact, probably the greatest danger for people who write about "Language" writing today is that they do so as if it were defined—a finite set of texts. You are on record as once saying that *L=A=N=G=U=A=G=E* was one part of several efforts and that these included *This, Roof, A Hundred Posters,* and *Tottel's.* What was the nature of the relationship among the poets involved with the *L=A=N=G=U=A=G=E* project?

CB: In 1976, when Bruce and I first started to discuss what would become *L=A=N=G=U=A=G=E,* there was no forum that addressed the philosophical, political, and aesthetic concerns that were central to us, although there were many poets and a number of poetry magazines that were working in ways with which we felt a strong affinity. Indeed, there was much hostility in alternative as well as mainstream circles, not only to the kind of poetry to which we were committed but also to our poetics—both our insistence on the value of nonexpository essays and also our rejection of received and beloved notions of voice, self, expression, sincerity, and representation.

Official Verse Culture operated then as it does now by denying its narrow stylistic orthodoxy under the cloak of universalized and unassailable poetic principles. Thus we had the spectacle of a poetry of abject conformity celebrating its commitment to individuality while flailing rather more viciously than might have seemed decent at actual individual expression. The prevalent phobias against groups and against critical thinking encouraged us to make our opposing commitments specific and partisan. If mainstream poetic "individuality" breeds unreflected conformism, collective formations might actually provide the space for conversation as well as for difference.

In this context, *L=A=N=G=U=A=G=E* was (and in other guises and transformations may still be) an ongoing and open-ended collaborative conVERSation and exchange on a series of particular and partisan, but also mutable and provisional, poetic principles and proclivities conducted in a decentralized manner by a number of differently situated editors, reading se-

Charles Bernstein with his daughter, Emma, outside Ear Inn, Manhattan, 1995

ries coordinators, poets, and readers: a linked series of poetic tendencies and collaborative exchanges among a range of poets who desired, for a period of time, to make this social exchange a primary site of their work. By "open-ended" I'm suggesting a context in which, despite shared, if conflicting, stylistic and formal concerns, one doesn't know what the results will be. No formal rules for participating are ever established. And while I could reiterate our specific and galvanizing preoccupations, the point of *L=A=N=G=U=A=G=E* was not to define its own activity or to prescribe a singular form of poetry, but rather to insist on particular possibilities for poetry and poetics.

LPG: I'm also interested in the "may still be" of your answer. How do you see the *L=A=N=G=U=A=G=E* project—or its permutations—

projecting into the present? Certainly, the locus of such an activity is modified by, on the one hand, a number of these poets now appearing in teaching anthologies, and on the other, the number of "younger" writers entering this "location."

CB: As names like Language poetry, Language writing, Language-centered writing, or Language-oriented writing become fixed in time, they lose generic and projective force. About ten years ago, I remember reading a call for submissions of "language" poetry for a new magazine that said, "You may be a language poet and not know it!" That seemed right to me: the terms were sufficiently underdetermined that there was room for projection. In contrast, when *The New York Times Magazine* ran a big poetry feature last spring that purported to map contemporary poetry, they carefully excluded from their list of "Language Poets" every one of the many participants in *L=A=N=G=U=A=G=E*—a nasty business unfortunately characteristic of the sort of cultural disinformation practiced at places like the *Times*.

Still, one test of an art's vitality is that it manages to unsettle, and it seems like this work continues to do that, and I for one am happy to embrace the description of my work as ungainly solipsistic incoherence that has no meaning. No meaning at all.

Which is to say, projection has its consequences, and one of them is that the recognition (positive or negative) accorded even a projection tends to split off, objectify, and atomize the "project," both stylistically and generationally. Then again, there's no need to get glued to a bill of particulars circa 1978 or 1988 when you can just as easily remain attentive to shifting conditions and contexts, new names and new work. But when this happens, and this is why it's appealing, the "location" you mention in your question changes: just that it's my desire to participate in the emerging locations, to reground myself. So my current identification is not with work that takes the same positions as *L=A=N=G=U=A=G=E* but with work that pursues these and related issues. I find extraordinary company just now, in so many magazines and books that I can hardly begin to keep up. For example, the Poetics e-mail discussion group, and the Electronic Poetry Center, with which we are both involved, seems to me to be continuing the work of

L=A=N=G=U=A=G=E, Segue Distributing, and the like, just as the poetry publishing of Sun & Moon Press and Roof Books, or the Ear Inn reading series, for example, continue to flourish, partly because they have welcomed new writers.

And of my companions of *L=A=N=G=U=A=G=E* days, I find it less remarkable than it probably is how contemporary, how crucial, our exchanges remain—not all, of course, but many and profoundly—after twenty years. And yet I am leery of how loyalty to old friends can form a closed circle, and I have tried, no doubt clumsily, fitfully, inadequately, to resist the temptation.

Loss Pequeño Glazier is director of the Electronic Poetry Center (EPC), co-edits RIF/T, an online poetry and poetics journal, and is presently working as web manager for the university libraries, State University of New York at Buffalo. He has recently written two entries for a forthcoming volume of the Dictionary of Literary Biography, *one on Charles Bernstein and the other on Robert Creeley. Glazier is the author of* The Parts *(Buffalo: Meow Press, 1995);* Electronic Projection Poetries *(Buffalo: RIF/T, 1995);* Small Press: An Annotated Guide *(Westport, Connecticut: Greenwood Publishing, 1992); a number of poetry-related articles, including "Sounding Bernstein," a study of Charles Bernstein's early work with sound texts; and over sixty published poems, including the online hypertextual poem "__E__: Poem for HTML" and the* Little Magazine *CD-ROM publication "5 Pieces for Sound File." He has presented numerous papers on poetry in the electronic environment. Recent activities include work with sound files and developing the EPC to engage the emerging graphical environment of the Internet.*

BIBLIOGRAPHY

Poetry:

Asylums, Asylum's Press, 1975.

Parsing, Asylum's Press, 1976.

Shade, Sun & Moon Press, 1978.

Poetic Justice, Pod Books, 1979.

Senses of Responsibility, Tuumba Press, 1979.

(With Bruce Andrews, Ray DiPalma, and others) *Legend,* Segue Books, 1980.

Controlling Interests, Roof Books, 1980.

Disfrutes, Potes and Poets Press, 1981.

(With Susan Bee) *The Occurrence of Tune,* Segue Books, 1981.

Stigma, Station Hill Press, 1981.

Islets/Irritations, Jordon Davies, 1983.

Resistance, Awede Press, 1983.

Veil, Xexoxial Editions, 1987.

The Sophist, Sun & Moon Press, 1987.

Four Poems, Chax Press, 1988.

(With Susan Bee) *The Nude Formalism,* Sun & Moon Press, 1989.

The Absent Father in Dumbo, Zasterle, 1990.

(With Susan Bee) *Fool's Gold,* Chax Press, 1991.

Rough Trades, Sun & Moon Press, 1991.

Dark City, Sun & Moon Press, 1994.

The Subject, Meow Press, 1995.

Republics of Reality: Poems 1975–1995, Sun & Moon Press, 1996.

Other:

(Editor with Bruce Andrews) *The L=A=N=G=U=A=G=E Book,* Southern Illinois University Press, 1984.

(Translator) Claude Royet-Journoud, *The Maternal Drape,* Awede Press, 1984.

Content's Dream: Essays 1975–1984, Sun & Moon Press, 1986.

(Translator) Olivier Cadiot, *Red, Green, and Black,* Potes & Poets, 1990.

(Editor) *The Politics of Poetic Form: Poetry and Public Policy,* Roof Books, 1990.

A Poetics, Harvard University Press, 1992.

(Editor) *Live at the Ear* (CD-ROM), Elemenope Productions, 1994.

(Founding editor) Electronic Poetry Center (http://wings.buffalo.edu/epc).

Also the author of four librettos: *Blind Witness News, The Subject: A Psychiatric Opera* and *The Lenny Paschen Show,* with composer Ben Yarmolinsky, and *Cafe Bufe,* now being composed by Dean Drummond.

Work represented in hundreds of periodicals in North America, Europe, New Zealand, Australia, Japan, and Korea, and work has been anthologized in these countries, as well as being represented in anthologies of American poetry and criticism in translation in Italy, France, Germany, Yugoslavia, Argentina, Spain, Portugal, Russia, China, and Japan. Bernstein has given poetry readings and lectures throughout the English-speaking world and in the last few years has read in Italy, Portugal, Germany, Austria, Yugoslavia, Spain, Canada, England, and France.

Recent anthology appearances include *From the Other Side of the Century: A New American Poetry 1960–1990,* edited by Douglas Messerli; *Postmodern American Poetry: A Norton Anthology,* edited by Paul Hoover; *The Best American Poems 1992,* edited by Charles Simic, Scribners, 1992; *Out of the World,* edited by Anne Waldman, Crown, 1991; *Language Poetries,* edited by Douglas Messerli, New Directions, 1987; *In the American Tree,* edited by Ron Silliman, National Poetry Foundation, 1986; *21 + 1: American Poetry Today,* edited by Claude Royet-Journoud and Emmanuel Hocquard, Delta (France), 1986; *Up Late: American Poetry Since 1970,* and *New Directions* 50.

Recent magazine appearances include *American Literary History, American Poetry Review, Avec, Big Allis, College Literature, Common Knowledge, Conjunctions, Critical Inquiry, Diacritics, Harper's, M/E/A/N/I/N/G, Postmodern Culture, o.blek, Review of Contemporary Fiction, Social Text, Socialist Review, Sulfur, Talisman, Temblor, Tyuonyi, Wallace Stevens Journal, Witness,* and *The Yale Review.*

Jake Berry

1959-

Jake Berry, self-portrait, 1993

Legends. Epics. Rumors. Stories. Gossip. Gospel. How much of the truth can be gathered from them? How much of the pure sweet Logos can be found in a tale unraveled from the convolutions of time in the human brain? Try as we might, we always seem to fall short of the experience, yet produce something that may be finer yet, may be a way of getting at the truth after all. In his poem "The Descent," William Carlos Williams said, "Memory is a kind / of accomplishment, / a sort of renewal / even / an initiation, since the spaces

it opens are new places / inhabited by hordes heretofore unrealized," and later, "and no whiteness (lost) is so white as the memory / of whiteness." So now I come to open new places for the unrealized hordes that I surely believe are the people and events of the years I gather beneath the name I was given. And if I must choose between the two, I hope the facts fall victim to the truth rather than the other way around.

*   *   *

The story is told of a young man, David Berry, an orphan, crossing the Atlantic in the middle of the nineteenth century. He may have been a cabin boy raised by the ship's captain. The world he'd left behind, in England, Wales, Scotland, maybe even France, had apparently lost its hold on him because once in port in Charleston, he jumped ship, bringing my father's line to America. I have never heard anyone say if this was his first trip across or if he'd made the journey many times. Perhaps it was his first voyage and he'd found it so unpleasant that land, any land, was preferable to the ship; perhaps he was escaping something, running from bad memories, from abuse, or maybe he was as fascinated with America and its promise as those millions that came through Ellis Island. But for whatever reason, no reliable history of my family can antedate the transgression that made my forefather an American. After this event I know little else for several generations.

David Crockett Berry was my great-grandfather. I have been to his grave at the Stoney Point Church of Christ in Florence, Alabama, several times. As a child I was naturally fascinated by his name, but I have never known if it came from his father and mother's fascination with the frontier statesman or if there was some other derivation. He lived much of his life in Lauderdale County, Alabama—a businessman, and a farmer. At one time he was quite wealthy. My grandfather has shown me a section of Florence his father owned that was then, as it is now, a prime piece of property near downtown. Apparently he lost almost everything in the Great Depression and spent the rest of his years farming. He was also a carpenter. My father acquired a table he had built one Sunday morning while the wife and children were at church. It became, with my father's addition of a new top, our family's kitchen table. The table survives to this day and may outlive us all.

My grandfather, Jacob Norman Berry, for whom I am named, was a farmer for much of his life, owning a small house and farm in the county, and later a farm in Wayne County, Tennessee. He later worked construction on a variety of jobs for the Tennessee Valley Authority and even ran for office as a county commissioner, losing narrowly. His mother's life overlapped with my own enough for me to remember her sitting silently in a black chair in my grandparents' house. My only other memory of her is her funeral and my making some innocent yet wholly inappropriate remark as everyone stood silently around her grave, and being scolded into silence by my mother. I often wonder what a mortal terror I might have become if my parents had not taken me to task for my excesses. Most children need a little stern guidance to convince them to assume some degree of civility; I was no exception.

The first clear memory I have of my grandfather is from my fourth year. We were living only a couple of miles from my grandparents' home in a small white house across the road from a railroad. My mom and I were walking to visit them when my grandfather drove by in his gargantuan lime truck. That truck seemed miles high, blocking the sky as I looked up at it—the back flaps covered in white dust I was eager to touch, but Mother pulled me away saying we were going to ride the rest of the way with my grandfather. I am sure it was one of the greatest thrills of my early life to take that ride, to feel important so high up in the cab looking down on the world. But even then, and always, there was a tension that surrounded my grandfather. He could be completely joyous, a child with you, playing at your games, then at a word or some hidden signal he'd become melancholy and cold. One never knew

At two and a half months old, August 1959

what would trigger this response, there seemed to be no consistency in it, and I witnessed it in my father to a lesser degree. Later, as a young man, I felt it in myself, a sudden gloominess that swept through me like a storm for no apparent reason. But I do not think it some genetic predisposition because once I became aware of it, and remembered it in my father and grandfather, I worked to correct it and succeeded. Had it been chemical this would have been impossible. My father as well seems to have overcome it, but my grandfather carried it with him his whole life. Without a doubt, one or both of his parents had suffered the same predilection and passed it on to him. How much of our identity do we acquire by unconsciously imitating those traits in our parents that we associate with adult behavior, for good or ill? Identity is nothing more than the surface of a great sea of selves that live inside each of us, and is victim to every wind that blows across it.

Other memories of my grandfather include a period of time when I was in the first year of high school, playing basketball. My father's job had called him away for a few months and there was no way to get home since we lived several miles out of town, so I would often spend the night with my grandparents. At that time, like so many others inspired by Bobby

Fischer and Boris Spasky playing for the world championship, I had become fascinated with chess. I quickly mastered the fundamentals and with the help of a few books advanced to the principle strategies. My grandfather and I would play chess in the evenings. Either he taught himself so that he could play me or I taught him the rules, but we had wonderful games. He allowed me to be the master, to discover the subtleties; I almost always beat him. In all probability he allowed me to win, but very soon I could easily defeat anyone my age, and only lost when I played a senior who had regularly participated in tournaments. I was convinced that I would be the next Bobby Fischer, that by the time I was sixteen I would be winning major tournaments and be made a master by the National Chess Federation. Other things intervened, of course, but if I could speak to my grandfather now so that he could understand me I would thank him for those games, for taking the time to foster my enthusiasm. For that short time the generations were swept away and we were friends. It allowed me to seek out in him qualities I consciously wanted to imitate. When my father returned home and I no longer visited my grandfather so often I genuinely missed him and held those qualities more dear. I was on the brink of events that would shatter my childhood and my grandfather had provided a link, a means of passage that sustained me for years.

Grandmother Berry was a sweet, loving, generous woman who raised four children, ran a farm, and took care of my grandfather with virtually no complaint. By the time I was born they were living in a house just outside of town, no longer farming. She loved her grandchildren dearly. When I was eleven I went through a period of fascination with model rockets that would actually fly, with cartridge-like solid fuel engines, launched from small launchpads powered by a car battery. Grandmother had taken me shopping with her and gave me three dollars to buy whatever toy I found. What I found was one of those rockets, but it cost $3.75. I ran down the aisles until I found Grandmother and begged her for more money. She suggested I look for something a little cheaper, but I persisted and she searched through her purse, giving me the last of her change. Later, at home, I was unwilling to wait for my grandfather to wake from his nap to help me assemble the rocket and in the process not only made

a mess of the rocket but made a significant scratch on my grandmother's dining-room table, a table that up to that point had been immaculately free of blemish. She had warned me to be careful, but in my eagerness to have the rocket built I had cut a deep gash into the surface with a razor blade. Later I noticed her discovery of it, but she said nothing. I felt guilty for taking advantage of her and never did it again. Her tolerance had forced me to learn for myself what no scolding could have taught me. This is how I remember her, as being patient and tender with everyone she knew, and though she must have had moments when she said and did things she regretted, I was never witness to it. Even when cancer had destroyed her health and she lay in great pain at the point of death, when I went to see her she managed to make a joke and smile and tell me she loved me. I still dream of her occasionally and in the dream she gives me gentle advice, comforts and reassures me. Whatever heaven may be, I have no doubt that she is there.

My mother's family history is even more obscure than my father's. I know that they lived in the Tennessee countryside, were possibly farmers from South Carolina. My maternal grandfather was a teacher and school principal and a promising athlete in his youth. Grandmother had been one of his students, then, after completing college, began teaching as well. I am not sure at what point they were married and when she gave up teaching, but I suspect it would have been the occasion of her first pregnancy. Grandfather was a well-educated man, holding degrees from several universities; he also coached baseball and once ran for office in his community. Occasionally, before I was of school age, I would be brought to visit him at work in the principal's office. I remember a big color map of the solar system, with all the planets and moons. I was amazed by it, by the vastness of space and the variety of planets, Saturn's rings and the Sun's intense boiling orange ball larger by far than anything else; so large in fact that only a corner of it could be shown. Grandfather Kirk seemed at all times to maintain an intellectual distance; rarely did I get a glimpse of emotion in his face or eyes that was not in some way chastened by intellect. Perhaps he was a natural teacher, his personality was so well suited to the work that he

Jake (left) and his brothers, Jon (center) and Jeff, 1966

always carried with him the atmosphere of instructor. I recall instances in which he and my father disagreed about something, the way to plant a particular kind of seed in the garden or which make of car was of better quality, and even if my father knew my grandfather was wrong, he deferred to him. Grandfather Kirk was not a domineering personality; I do not recall ever feeling threatened by him in any way, but when his mind was set there was no arguing with him. At any rate, most of the time he was right.

Grandmother and Grandfather Kirk came to visit us every week in Killen, where we lived, from their home in Waynesboro, Tennessee, an hour's drive away. My brothers and I dearly loved those visits. They brought food with them, usually a roast or chicken. The aroma of the food drew us in from outdoors or from our rooms until by the time the food was ready we were ravenous, and the food always lived up to our expectations, with Granddad at one end of the table, holding forth on sports or politics or whatever interested him and Grandmother and Mother talking about family events. The atmosphere around the table was suffused with warmth and safety and satiety. We hated for those visits to end. Later, when I was living by myself and Grandfather had become too old to drive, my grandparents had my cousins bring them down to cook lunch with me. By that time I genuinely needed the food for sur-

vival as I rarely ate a full meal, and the company was wonderful, but Granddad would spend most of the visit looking out the window, worried about the ride home. After a couple of these visits it became obvious that there was no need in them making the long drive. I was too self-involved to return the love they were giving me, and Granddad felt better at home. When he died I arrived at the funeral something of an outcast from the family due to my lifestyle and abandonment of the family religion. The last few times I saw him he was lost in memories that he took to be the present. Yet, he managed to give me a few dollars and remark, joking, "Go get yourself some cigarettes and beer." In the community he was regarded as an icon, in the state of Tennessee he was held in respect. He'd been an adviser to governors, had taught and coached thousands of children as well as teaching and preaching at church. He was a scholar of many disciplines, and grew two or more excellent vegetable gardens every year. His loss actually shook me a little. I felt as if a force had gone out of the world.

For my brothers and me, and for all her grandchildren, Grandmother Kirk was the ideal. She was kind and soft-spoken, never harsh, and always giving. She concerned herself with the family's well-being before anything else. I always felt very comfortable being alone with her, enjoying the simplest pleasures: a cup of coffee, a TV show, sitting on her front porch watching the traffic pass. She understood how to find great joy in the everyday. However, she loved reading more than anything else. I remember stacks of paperbacks under a desk in one of the rooms of her house: mysteries, westerns, popular novels—she consumed books. Due to cataracts she had almost given up reading by her eightieth year, but surgery restored her vision and she related to me over the telephone how delighted she was to be able to read again, even if it was something she'd already read. I regret not seeing her more after I grew up. She had the ability to make me feel enveloped in love. I'll likely never feel that again.

In his senior year in high school my father, Norman Berry, moved from Collinwood, Tennessee, to Waynesboro and lived in a boardinghouse so that he could play football, since Collinwood had no team. This is where he met my mother, Carole Kirk. They dated a few times

I believe, but nothing serious. Mother played piano and after graduation went to Freed-Hardeman College to study English and music. After the first semester my father transferred from Florence State College to Freed-Hardeman. During that second semester they fell in love and by August of that year, 1958, they were married. On June 16 at 11:57 P.M. of the following year I was born. They had left college and taken an apartment in Florence with the intention of beginning a family right away, but a few days after I was born it seemed their plans were about to come to a crashing halt. I was a very large baby, 11 pounds, 2 ounces, and apparently the birth had been more dangerous than either my parents or the doctors realized initially. Mother began to hemorrhage, losing blood at an alarming rate. My father once told me in a letter that while the doctors were struggling to save her life he walked around the hospital wondering what he was going to do with a baby and no wife. Fortunately for all of us Mother recovered and they brought me home to the apartment. In her teens my mother had had polio, and though she bore no outward signs of the disease, it may have rendered the birth more difficult than normally would have been the case, therefore the complications. But the complications had only begun.

From all accounts I was a very aggressive baby. My baby bed was situated near a window, and as soon as I could sit up and grab the curtains I ripped them from their hangers. Shades were installed, but I managed to rip these down as well. My parents shared the apartment house with another young couple, and a few months after I was born they had a son. He was crippled by cerebral palsy, making it difficult for him to use one hand and leg— and though he later overcame virtually any handicap, having me as an infant companion was not a fortuitous beginning. I have been told that I regularly struck him and generally made his young life miserable. Later we became the best of friends, and I defended him on occasion from the savage attacks of other children making fun of his disability. Yet, in my infancy my approach seemed to be control by brute strength.

Dad worked at various jobs; a hardware store, Sears and Roebuck (as it was then called), getting into the insurance business by the time I was old enough to begin paying attention to such things. Mother was a housewife, and played the

piano almost daily. I loved to hear her play. She had an excellent ear and could quickly teach herself to play any tune she heard on the radio that she liked. From time to time, studying a piece of sheet music she would point out to me where the music on the page differed from that on the record. She had a style all her own, finding the melody among the chords and rhythm and weaving it so flawlessly that you heard the whole song, almost as if she were playing every part all by herself. Later, after my brothers and I were in school, she began to teach piano, first at the school we attended and then at home. She tried on several occasions to teach me to play, but she was my mother, and where I would have submitted to the rules from a teacher, I would argue with Mother until both of us were too frustrated to continue. I regret now that I wasn't a more willing pupil because when I did pick up an instrument, my father's guitar, I had no idea where to begin and had to teach myself everything. Yet, when I started writing songs she would occasionally teach me bits of music theory. All I know of theory I learned from her, which isn't much, but enough to write folk, rock, country, and blues. I also regret stealing my father's guitar. After years of struggling with a cheap instrument he'd acquired as a child, he finally made the investment in a Yamaha flat top. I have no idea what it cost, but the money came dearly, and the guitar was high enough quality that he cherished it, protecting it from blemish. But once I decided to play guitar I took it without asking and banged it against walls and chairs, scratching the back of it with my belt buckle. Dad pointed this out to me with threats and protestation, all to no avail. Yet, he never took the guitar away from me, even though I compounded the abuse of the instrument with abuse of the music I tried to play, to such an extent that he would scream at me to stop.

When I was an infant, my father told me, I would cry for hours at night for no discernible reason. He would rock me and walk with me, but nothing helped. I think now of Plato's idea that each of us chooses the life we are going to lead for the lesson it will teach us. Was I hasty in my decision, or was I terrified to find myself an infant again? There's every possibility that Plato had no idea what he was talking about, or that he intended the idea as metaphor, but many years later I wrote in a poem called "Essay: Empire Poets": "We were smuggled / across the border / into time / by subversive / angels / through cracks / in the empire / & my father / wondered why / as an infant / I'd cry so long / What a pitiful destiny / singing / with your tongue cut out." Perhaps I knew even then that I would be a poet, with the frustration of living to create a language that so few would understand. Perhaps I just had a bellyache. Perhaps they are one and the same.

I have no clear memory of anything before my third year. At that time we had moved out of Florence, a few miles west to a village of six hundred or so called Killen. We lived in a brick house and had a canary. I can remember the bird being loose in the kitchen and being fascinated by its flight across the ceiling, Mother finally catching him and returning him to his cage. Later that year we moved back to Florence briefly, living in the small white house by the railroad tracks. The only strong memory I have of living in that house is its furnace. The vent was a steel grate in the floor. Mom and Dad warned me about the dangers of being too near it, but one night after my bath, without thinking, I ran right across it, burning the bottoms of my feet. I howled and leapt for safety, but too late. I kept my parents up all night, sitting on the edge of their bed soaking my burning feet, crying, but I had learned about the furnace. From that time on when I was warned about heat I listened. A few years later, I must have been five or six, living in another house with a similar furnace, I watched in horror as my younger brother, Jeff, just learning to walk, rolled in his walker onto the furnace, catching the wheels in the grate. He had on shoes so his feet weren't burned, but before I or my parents could get to him he toppled over face forward. He bore the scars for a long time, yet they were not very obvious, and I believe they were no detriment to him. Yet, this was my first conscious experience of empathy. I could feel what Jeff was going through and it hurt me to see him in such pain. Even now, an infant or toddler in pain, innocence afflicted, is unbearable to me; if I am unable to help the child I have to extricate myself from the situation.

When I was four or possibly five my parents purchased a house in Killen. This was the house I was to grow up in, with a big yard, trees to climb, and a cute little girl my age next door. Everything seemed possible. My brother Jeff was born shortly before we moved. All I remember about his birth is that I had measles when Mother went to the hospital to have him. It must have been an anxious time for her and my father, considering what she had gone through after having me. I was placed in the care of my paternal grandparents and I remember looking at myself in a dresser mirror at their house, noticing my spots and wondering what it would be like to have a baby brother. On May 1, 1963, he was born, Jeffrey Kirk Berry. I was too young to take much notice, but two years later, just as I was starting the first grade, I played a role in naming the next baby. I was fascinated by space and the astronauts, my favorite being John Glenn, so when the discussion came around to naming the baby I suggested that John Glenn would be ideal. This suited my parents since my mother had an uncle named Glen. Of course, its more likely that they had planned to name him this all along and allowed me to believe that I had been part of the decision, but I was proud of his name and told my friends. He was born, Jonathan Glen Berry, on September 4, 1965.

I didn't realize it then, but I must have tested my mother's endurance as I began school. She would have been eight months pregnant and I refused to go. We lived only a block from the school, an ideal circumstance my parents thought. I could walk to school. They bought me a red, plaid book satchel, the necessary pencils and paper, and thought to send me on my way. But more than once Mother had to go into class with me and sit with me for a while before I could be persuaded to stay. All three of us children were very attached to her, screaming and wailing when she would try to leave, even for a moment. She had very few nights out to see a movie or have dinner with my father from the time I was born until all of us were in school. Yet her devotion to us instilled in us a sense of security that few of my friends and colleagues have. Among many other things, I am eternally grateful to her for this.

The early school years were generally happy and without traumatic incident, at least nothing more than children are likely to incur. There were fights and obstinant teachers, but generally all went well. Though I had friends I was often quite content to play by myself. I loved Superman, from TV and comic books, and I would tie one of my baby brother's diapers, a clean one, around my neck like a cape and fly off to perform heroic deeds. Quite a sight since along with my diaper-cape I was usually wearing overalls. And no doubt I tried to "save" the cute girl next door, Laura Hamner, though she did not need saving. We were best friends, playing at whatever games we might invent, oblivious to the war claiming American and Vietnamese lives, to African-Americans finally demanding their civil rights, the events that would shadow our youth and inform our idea of what the world was like as we grew up. Occasionally my imagination would get the better of Laura. One day I saw Maurice Chevalier on TV take a woman's hand in his and gently kiss it, then proceed all the way up her arm concluding with a kiss on the lips. The next time I saw Laura I proceeded to do the same, only by the time I reached her shoulder I was commended for my efforts with a solid slap in the face. I stood back aghast. What had I done to offend her? I thought perhaps she had misunderstood my intentions, so I grabbed her hand and tried it again. Again I was slapped. "Don't do that!" she said, "I don't like it." I was shocked. This was not the way it happened in the movie at all. I decided I would have to be more subtle. I spent the next ten years of my life, until I was fifteen, working out those subtleties, but when I finally kissed a girl it wasn't Laura that I kissed, nor did I ever succeed in kissing her. Still, what I learned by trying to woo her got me further with other girls than I ever could have imagined when I tried to imitate Chevalier.

When I entered the third grade my parents switched me from the public school at Killen to a private school, Mars Hill Bible School, in Florence. The idea was that I would receive a better education and be among children of other members of the church we attended, the Church of Christ. While it was true that the work was more challenging and thorough, there was a downside that haunted me well into my twenties. The problem was a mix of class difference and religious elitism. I quickly noticed that most of the children around me were dressed better than I was and equipped with brighter, more expensive pencils and notebooks. Being inclined to live as much in a world of the imagination as the real world had already

Family photo: Jake and his father, Norman, brothers Jeff (left) and Jon, and mother Carole, about 1970

made me something of an outsider, but here was another difference. I never felt underprivileged, and I wasn't; I had everything I needed for school, I ate as much as I wanted, my clothes were clean and warm, often handmade by my mother. Yet, the other children made a distinction. Also, I wasn't as inclined to sports as many of the other boys. I enjoyed baseball, in fact I played entire seasons in my backyard by myself, complete with statistics, and I wanted to someday play in the big leagues, but when I played on teams I was never as good as the others. What bothered me though was not that I was a poor player, but the fact that my lack of ability excluded me from the companionship of the most popular boys. I had other interests as well that I did not share with them. I loved to study maps, and draw my own, to learn about the shapes and terrain of the continents. I also loved dinosaurs, drew them and read about them voraciously, pronouncing the long Latin names, hoping to be an archeologist. And I wanted to be an astronaut, to discover new worlds, to find new maps to draw. So I wasn't initially troubled by the difference between myself and most of the others, I simply noticed it.

It was also in the third grade that I first wrote a story that impressed a teacher. I think it was one of those typical tales, a boy is saved from drowning by his dog, but my teacher was impressed enough to mention it to my mother. The following year brought the seminal event that in all likelihood planted the idea in my head that writing might be something I'd want to do. The teacher assigned Edgar Allan Poe's "The Tell-Tale Heart." I had trouble reading it because of some slight dyslexia that had given me difficulty from the first grade forward. Afraid that I would be unable to finish in time my mother read the story to me. By the time she finished I was mesmerized—I'd never heard, nor imagined, anything so thrilling and dark as that heart that would not be silenced. I wasn't frightened by the story, I was enthralled. It unleashed something inside of me. I wanted to read more like it. I wanted to feel that darkness, that transgression and its consequences. I quickly devoured as much of Poe as I was able to read (many of the stories, "The Cask of Amontillado," "The Black Cat," most of the poems, I loved "Annabelle Lee" and "The Bells") and carried their melancholy and phantasmagoria around inside me like a treasure. I had discovered something no one else knew about. Indeed, no one I knew even had a clue as to what I was feeling. And I had discovered a little about why and how I was different. I had secrets. I knew where the monsters lived.

Still, I lived the life of a typical nine-year-old. My parents took us to Atlanta to see the Braves play baseball. We saw Hank Aaron hit a home run. I wanted to be like him. I kept up with the teams and the players, watched the games, played my own imaginary games. There was still nothing to indicate what was brewing deep inside. I went through long periods where I paid no attention to my discoveries. But the following year changed everything forever.

In the fifth grade we were required to learn long division. I'd never been very good at math, only just able to keep up with the rest of the class, but long division was a breaking point; something about it seemed inherently illogical. Try as I might, something in me re-

sisted. My teacher, Mrs. White, could not tolerate my difficulty with the exercises and forced me more than once to stay in during recess while she stood over me correcting every error sternly. It was too much; finally I came home in tears, afraid of her and afraid to tell my parents the problem. When I did tell them, my father paid a visit to school, calling Mrs. White and the principal to task in a meeting. I was brought in to tell my side of the story, but I was too horrified of her to even remember what she had done to frighten me. The cumulative effect of all of this occurred one night as I was drifting off to sleep. Suddenly I was surrounded by swollen faces that seemed to swoop down at me. I tried to find bodies for the heads, to make them conform to reality, but this only made them more grotesque until I rose in my bed terrified. My skin felt six inches thick and completely desensitized. I tingled all over, and couldn't make it stop. I woke my mother and told her what was happening, my head was buzzing, and every time I closed my eyes the faces came back. Mother had me sit down and gave me magazines and catalogs to look at and a glass of water to drink. After an hour of consolation I finally felt normal enough to try to sleep again. For weeks, at irregular intervals these attacks recurred. The stress at school had opened some gate in my psyche. Mrs. White had cut the monsters loose and they were trying to destroy me. I didn't know it then, but my life as a poet had begun, my mythos had found its genesis and would initiate the work of my life. That work, *Brambu Drezi, Book One,* begins:

> legion swollen faces drift through sentient
>   blue-orange empty space
> bodiless heads swoon against me behind
>   my eyes

Seventeen years lay between those hypnogogic terrors and the writing of the lines they gave me, but the powers had been loosed into the world and it would be my responsibility to tend to them and give them their form in poetry.

The next few years brought no significant response to the attacks. Perhaps the stress Mrs. White had driven me through had opened me to "the call" several years before it might have happened naturally, or it may be that my response to these events required years of gestation. At any rate it wasn't until my fourteenth year that circumstances unfolded that offered me a path through which to deal with the mysteries. However, there was a slight forecast of things to come when I was twelve. As in many school systems, books were offered for order in class. I spotted something called the Pop-Rock Tarot Calendar that included a set of the twenty-two major arcana, each card associated with a particular song. For instance, The Fool was associated with The Beatles' "The Fool on the Hill," The Magician was associated with The Who's "Pinball Wizard," and so on. These associations meant little or nothing to me, though I loved the music. It was the cards I wanted. I also ordered a book that explained tarot. I knew nothing about the cards, only that I had seen the stereotypical gypsy fortune-teller in movies, and was curious to see what might happen if I learned the method myself. Reading the book I learned that there were in fact seventy-eight cards in a full deck, so I proceeded to make a set of the minor arcana from posterboard, drawing the necessary figures. The only thing of significance that resulted from this was that I found I was attracted to The Hermit—I felt it was "my card."

When I entered the ninth grade, my parents were shocked to learn that I'd been placed in a class of "below average" students as part of an experiment that was designed to allow the students with better grades to excel, and ostensibly to bring the troublemakers under control by placing them in the same corral. I don't know why I was listed as a troublemaker except that I found school very dull and often ignored my studies, with the exception of history, which I loved. The experiment failed miserably. The administration had underestimated our intelligence and our proclivity for taking advantage of every situation. We had been labeled as bad children and this gave us great latitude. In class we were prone to simply leave the room, by way of the window, with the teacher screaming at us to "take your seats!" At times we were literally swinging from the rafters. This terrified the faculty. They were convinced we were all on drugs. In fact, we were just living up to expectations. But something happened as a result of our deviance that made the difference for several of us. As a joke, and in lieu of our schoolwork, we began writing poems. These were limericks at first, then we wrote poems about whatever vile, depraved notion we could conceive. We became champion smut

artists. We challenged one another, grilled one another and everyone else on the caustic spit of adolescent satire. The poetry was horrible, of course; none of it survives, thank God. Eventually, it occurred to me that I might try to write something seriously. My classmates had recognized that I seemed to have a natural sense of meter and, as a record producer later told my friend Barry Powell, I could rhyme "shit with basketball." The first attempts were copies of rock and roll lyrics, since I saw myself as writing songs. I began teaching myself guitar at this time so that I would be able to set my lyrics to music. However, the seminal event that instigated my response to "the call" of those swollen faces, came a few weeks later, when I discovered in my desk in Bible class at school (Bible was a required subject) a talisman drawn on a sheet of stenography paper. I had no idea what it was, but I admired the shape of it, and I recognized some of the words, such as "Jehovah," and "Alpha and Omega," and there were other interesting words as well that were new to me, "Elohim" and "Tetragrammaton." I was studying it when a classmate asked me what I was looking at. I showed her the sheet of paper. "Oh," she said, "that's a Satan's Penta."

"What's a Satan's Penta?"

"It's an evil sign, it calls the devil."

That was all I needed to know. My imagination ran wild. I'd discovered the forbidden fruit. I had to write a poem about this. Ironically, I had drawn a picture during the weeks of our toying with poetry writing—and it frightened me when I was finished with it. Considering its contents there was nothing inherently taboo about it, but I felt a power from it, like opening a dark door. I had drawn a large goblet with strange symbols on it, symbols I thought I had imagined. The symbols were distorted versions of the star in a circle that I would discover in the talisman. The goblet was obviously a grail.

The poem I wrote was full of confrontation with evil, the devil in particular. When I showed it to my poetry-writing companions, they were astonished. The poem was horrible, but it was good enough to demonstrate to them that I was capable of rendering real emotion as poetry. I remember Keith Henry, who had become and remains a spiritual brother, looking up after reading it as if he'd seen something revealed, something dreadful and beauti-

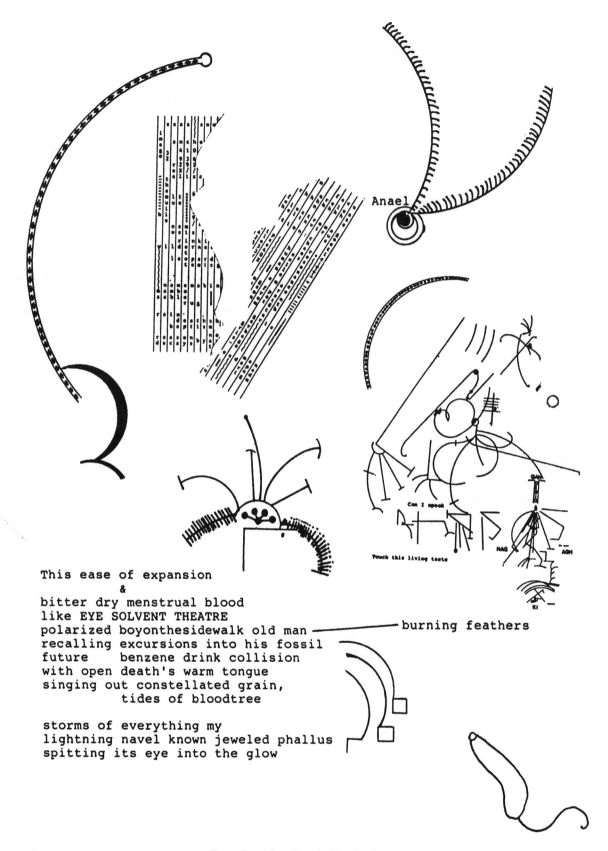

This ease of expansion
                    &
bitter dry menstrual blood
like EYE SOLVENT THEATRE
polarized boyonthesidewalk old man ——————— burning feathers
recalling excursions into his fossil
future   benzene drink collision
with open death's warm tongue
singing out constellated grain,
          tides of bloodtree

storms of everything my
lightning navel known jeweled phallus
spitting its eye into the glow

From Brambu Drezi, Book One

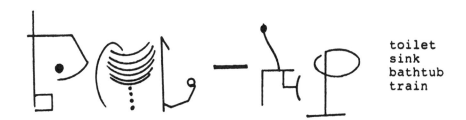

toilet
sink
bathtub
train

straw
fork
hat
cylinder

...a plastic ohm neuro-virus, rhizomes
emerging from an empty matrix. A subterranean
lion persona dementia; equidistant from
manifest form to core as the moon from its
genesis quasar. This golden mask, once dissected,
reveals a secondary motion that, by its
measurable frequency, yields the primary
coordinates of the initial explosion.

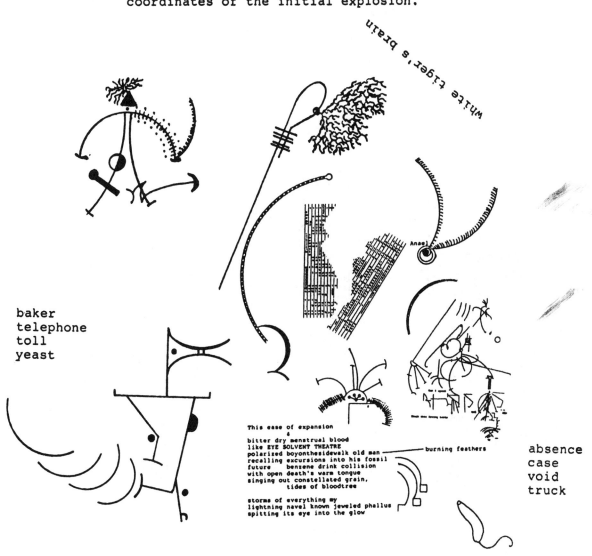

White tiger's brain

baker
telephone
toll
yeast

This ease of expansion
&
bitter dry menstrual blood
like EYE SOLVENT THEATRE
polarized boyonthesidewalk old man
recalling excursions into his fossil
future   benzene drink collision
with open death's warm tongue
singing out constellated grain,
            tides of bloodtree

storms of everything my
lightning navel known jeweled phallus
spitting its eye into the glow

— burning feathers

absence
case
void
truck

ful. He ran across the room and began showing it to other people. Keith helped to affirm what I felt myself. I had discovered what I was, what I had come here to be, a poet.

I quickly realized that I had not exhausted the inspiration from the talisman, so I wrote four more sections to the poem, to complete the five parts a "penta" should have. I placed them in a notebook I covered in black paper on which I placed a cross over a reversed star. When I finished it I trembled. I'd created a power object, taking responsibility for the forces I'd discovered. I felt that the book contained those forces and that no one should see it or they might be overwhelmed by them, so I hid it, only showing it to my closest, most trusted companions, those I felt would understand.

At the end of the ninth grade I transferred to Brooks High School in my hometown in Killen in order to play football, but also to escape what would have been continual confrontation with the authorities at the repres-

sive Christian school. One of the first people I met there, Alan Cantrell, was also an aspiring musician. We became close friends and I shared my poetry with him, including my black book. He encouraged my writing, making suggestions, and passing along what he knew of the occult. Alan also introduced me to J. R. R. Tolkien, and together we read *The Hobbit* and *The Lord of the Rings* trilogy. After we'd finished these he suggested that I read *The Odyssey,* Homer's epic, which I did. Only a year ago he told me that he'd not read the book himself. I'm glad he encouraged me to, though, it was probably my first reading of classic Greek literature outside the bits of mythology we'd been taught in school. We even called the band we were trying to start Odysseus.

Football went well though I was ineligible to play the first year. Keith Henry, who had also transferred, and I practiced diligently, learning the game, taking the bruises, then acting as team managers on game day. It provided us with a means to community. As football play-

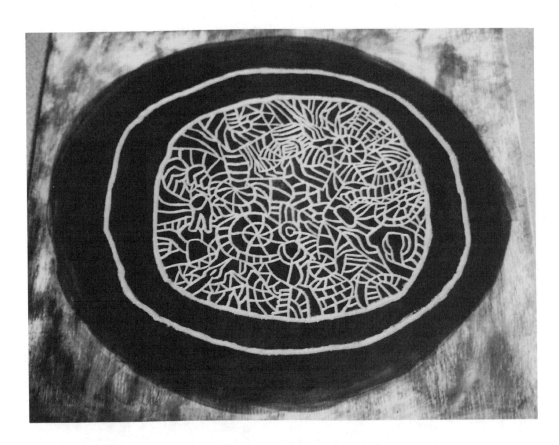

Brambu Mandala, *by Jake Berry, given to Jack Foley as a gift, 1992*

ers we had status, instant respect, and the admiration of many of the girls, which in itself was reason enough to play.

Poetry and puberty began at roughly the same time for me, and this is perhaps as it should be, to enter one's path at the same time one begins to reach sexual maturity. I discovered that even more than football, most girls were very impressed with love poems written to them, so any girl I desired quickly found herself flooded with love poems and songs. I usually wrote in the style of Poe's poetry, occasionally copying from Shelley or one of the other Romantic poets. I recall a very early example of these that began, "At night upon Plutonian shore / where knights of the dead hold the door," obviously derived from Poe's "The Raven." Oddly, it seemed that what I desired at this point from girls was not sex as much as admiration. I had no idea what sex was, how it should be done, despite having had so-called sex education classes, which consisted of an embarrassed male teacher passing books around and telling us to read them. I read them, but none of it made sense as it was rendered in the cold technical light with which one might describe dissecting a frog. What, I asked myself, could this have to do with affection for a girl? I resolved, unconsciously in part, to avoid it as long as possible. Not a good idea as it turned out, since I lost at least two girlfriends because I refused "to go all the way." Yet in my stupidity I got as close to intercourse as one can come without actually doing it. And I remained ignorant of the risks involved so that when I finally had sex, and my girlfriend Alice Case, who would later become my first wife, told me that it was the "right time" of the month for her to become pregnant, I acted knowledgeable, but had no idea what she was talking about.

School was easy academically, required little effort or study. I was fortunate to have an excellent history teacher in the person of Ronald Pettus. Mr. Pettus was a great proselytizer of history, bringing the "gospel" to his students. Many of my classmates resented his enthusiasm and made fun of his manner, but I had nothing but respect for him. Another teacher, Jim Smith, would be very important in encouraging me to continue writing. He befriended several of us in whom he saw some talent. Most of these became my closest friends. Among them were Greg Eaton, Barry Powell, and Joey Holder.

When I met Greg Eaton he was constantly surrounded by a crowd of admirers, male and female. He had the ability to give even the most absurd gesture great significance. When later I read Kerouac's *On the Road,* I had the perfect model for Dean Moriarty. Like Dean, Greg was constantly devising new projects, making elaborate plans which he would describe with such charm and enthusiasm you'd feel like a complete loser if you missed out on them. His energy was enormous, his appetites vast. One thing was certain, as Greg's friend life would never be boring.

As our friendship developed into a genuine brotherhood we shared houses, food, drugs, jobs, everything. I don't regret one second of it. Even when I hated him for taking advantage of me, for hurting others that I loved, I admired his resolution to live on the sweet edge, to drain life of every ounce of experience. Greg and I discovered music together, turning one another on to the artists we had discovered individually. I discovered Bob Dylan before Greg and passed along the recommendation. Greg discovered Bruce Springsteen, early in his career, and came barreling through my parents' house without saying so much as hello, threw open my bedroom door, held up a Springsteen album and said, "YOU MUST LISTEN TO THIS!" He placed the record on the turntable and cranked the volume, then proceeded to scream at me above the music about its merits to such an extent that it was not until he left that I actually had time to enjoy the music. But he was right. He was virtually always right about music. I learned to pay close attention to his ravings. He was trying to communicate something vital to me. It was his way of expressing love and friendship. We were working at the same record store when we began to investigate jazz. First with Miles Davis and the Modern Jazz Quartet then on to John Coltrane, Ornette Coleman, Charlie Parker, Ellington and Armstrong, and on and on in a journey that never ends. We spent an entire summer experimenting intensely with various hallucinogens and listening to jazz, though none of that prepared me for the music of Don Van Vliet, otherwise known as Captain Beefheart. I'd seen him perform on TV and thought perhaps the acoustics or the sound system were to blame for the dissonance and lack of apparent theme. A few months later, during an acid trip, Greg dropped in, bursting with excitement at his new discovery, which we all must hear RIGHT NOW! A few minutes into the music I had to leave the room. I thought I was going to be sick. I could find no discernible pattern, nothing to connect with, and in my enhanced state of sensitivity it was more than I could bear. Greg followed me outside, asking what was wrong, with a knowing smile on his face.

"That is the vilest, most disgusting noise I have ever heard!" I screamed at him.

Greg came close to me, put his finger in my face, and said, "Someday you'll own this album, and love it." As usual, he was right.

More recently, Greg and his brother Van, both of them accomplished musicians and songwriters now, brought me to the Johnson City area of northeast Tennessee to record several songs, some written by Van, some by me. With the help of their brother Kirk, also an accomplished musician, we produced excellent versions of the songs in only a few hours. It had been a personal dream for years to play in a band with Greg. His attention to detail in his guitar solos brought elements to the songs that neither Van nor I had imagined.

I have known Barry Powell, another of Jim Smith's star pupils, for most of my life, though we did not become brothers until years after we'd left school. After my parents left Killen, taking my brothers, to do mission work for the church in Kentucky, I moved into a small trailer. Joey Holder quickly joined me as he needed a place to live and we were friends and songwriting partners. Joey had begun recording some of our songs in the local studios, bringing me along with him, so it seemed the best possible situation; we could work and live in the same place. During these trips to the studios, long nights of working out the details of particular tracks, putting the songs together piece by piece, I began to learn the process of the music business and why I wanted nothing to do with it, at least on no one's terms but my own. Occasionally, Joey would edit a few lines from the lyrics I gave him to make them fit the music he'd written. One evening, sitting in the board room of a studio, the producers asked Joey for additional lyrics to one of the songs he'd edited. I suggested that I had the lines at hand, but no one listened to me. It wasn't until I fed the lines to the producer, one at a time, through an intermediary he respected that I was able to restore the verse to its original shape. Later I discovered the producer had taken credit for the lines himself.

Barry would visit the trailer when he was in town on leave from the navy. He'd just begun to play guitar and was eager to learn whatever he could from Joey and me. Once we had a chance to sit together and talk for a while we realized we had a rapport, and a common fascination for mysticism. A few months of living in the trailer, my future wife and I converted to Christianity, a pentecostal variety that included speaking in tongues and other characteristics common of the charismatic movement. Earlier, during my senior year in high school, under pressure from an assistant minister, I had been baptized into the church of my family, the Church of Christ, a largely legalistic fundamentalist sect. A majority of its members are persuaded that they have discovered in the Bible the true intentions of the first-century church and that they alone hold the answers. Therefore, by default, everyone else is condemned to eternal punishment in a fiery hell. I had always found this reprehensible, but having no other experience with Christianity, tried to hold to what I felt was valuable in the church and discard the prejudice, but had never been able to persuade myself to actually become a member. Finally I acquiesced to ease the fears of those around me that I was damned. By comparison, the charismatics were liberated, though less educated in the details of the Bible. I felt it worth a try. When I announced my conversion to Barry and Joey they congratulated me, and later converted themselves, Joey to the charismatics, Barry to the Church of Christ. Barry quickly ran into problems, trying to convince the members of his church to adopt a more open, and ultimately more mystical approach. I had difficulties as well and abandoned my newfound religion in a few months, shortly after Alice and I married.

Together Barry and I began searching, looking for a means out of the dilemma our inherited religion had forced upon us. Many years before, about the time I'd begun writing poetry, I'd purchased a complete tarot deck and learned how to read them. Tarot became a prime means of inquiry into the spiritual world. Barry and I spent many hours discussing their design and levels of meaning. Over the years I had also read a variety of poets, being particularly fond of Whitman, Dylan Thomas, and

Barry Powell, 1985

T. S. Eliot. Remembering that Eliot had mentioned the tarot in "The Waste Land" I began to read Eliot to Barry whenever he visited. We began with "The Love Song of J. Alfred Prufrock" and worked forward. Barry was quick to find subtleties that I had missed in my initial reading of the poems, so we sat up all night many nights searching the poems for all their magic. In the process we realized that most of what we had been taught as children regarding religion was the fearful code of a small cult of zealous believers who saw no reason to investigate beyond the code. Our first response was to try and persuade our families of our discoveries. This only engendered hostility and ultimately we were both to some extent ostracized for living outside the code. We experimented with hallucinogens together, drawing the sky, the earth, and much poetry and music into our fascination. For hours we would discuss the details of a particular philosophy or religion, or try to "read" the experiences we were having as the result of a combination of drugs and minds eager for a liberating gnosis. Barry

was also wonderfully aware of the nuances of my poetry and songs, relating back to me what he had found in them. He listened when no one else would, constantly affirming my instincts. I felt he was receiving something valuable from my work and I often wrote with him in mind.

Eventually Barry found a teacher, a witch or priestess, from whom he learned the oral, and "inner," mysteries. Occasionally he will surprise me with some bit of insight or a technique for healing that I know he received from a source other than books. He also began writing songs and I was amazed at how quickly he developed a style all his own, writing memorable hook lines and beautiful melodies. He continues to be a constant source of encouragement and inspiration. In late 1995 we collaborated on a tape that included my reading of my book *Species of Abandoned Light* combined with his music/noise composition "Sounds of the Celestial Screw."

At the time I was beginning college, my father had returned to complete his education. Though we were attending different schools it was interesting being a student with my father. After years of working various jobs, from insurance salesman to maintenance for the Tennessee Valley Authority to truck driver, he had decided to pursue his own calling, which according to his mother had been with him since he was a young boy—to become a preacher. I had and have great respect for him for making the commitment, getting the degree and serving several years, some of them quite brutal, as a missionary. He continues to preach and minister today, but for a large congregation. My mother also gained my respect in new ways at about the same time by becoming part of a conservative women's political action group, even leading a chapter in our area, and taking part in various campaigns in support or protest of various issues. My parents it seemed were beginning to move into another part of their life, one not so directly involved with their three sons, but concerned with creating a cultural atmosphere that they felt would preserve the values they hold important, for our generation.

As usual I was traveling in the opposite direction. Not as a matter of rebellion, but because the poetry and songs I was writing compelled me to pursue a different set of priorities, a primary and long lasting experiment with excess. What happens when one lives ev-

Jake Berry, 1985

ery moment at the extreme end of sensation? What will be revealed? Is this a path to visions? I'd read Huxley's *The Doors of Perception* about his experiments with mescaline, and several of the Carlos Castenada books, as well as piles of anti-drug propaganda my mother had used in teaching Sunday school classes of young women in the late '60s and early '70s. There was also the advice of Timothy Leary, the Beatles, and Jimi Hendrix, as well as Jim Morrison and The Doors as examples of what had been done, for good or ill. I began smoking pot when I was fifteen, and tried a variety of pills and cocaine. Marijuana seemed fine as a general living environment, or to spend a few hours stoned every day. It seemed to enhance the pleasure of listening to music, and with concentration I discovered that meditation seemed to come more easily when I was stoned. But it was not until a friend gave me two doses of LSD that I felt I was confronting anything of significance. That first trip was not a strong one, but it was an indication of what was possible. I shared the LSD with Keith Henry and we spent most of the night studying the ceiling and talking about what we felt was happening. A year or so later, after Scott Huffstetler, a new friend, moved into the trailer, he began to join us in our experiments. I met Scott through a mutual friend and was completely

taken with him. He had invented his own language (consisting of words like "schlahoots" and "schleen") and loved the altered state; his sense of humor was unlike anything I'd ever confronted. Perversely illogical, idiosyncratic, I would often find myself in a state of delightful absurdity in Scott's presence. Scott had no agenda; he wasn't out to change the world, to become a writer or artist or make millions of dollars. Raw experience at its most intense seemed to be his only desire, and drugs were the quickest shortcut. It was with Scott that I had my first full-blown LSD experience; he knew how to exploit every dimension. With him the world was our carnival, specially designed for our thrills. Without dominating events Scott could arrange an evening's festivities, almost secretly, so that spontaneous surprises would occur at the opportune moment. One evening we stole several boxes of dental floss and as a tribute to the Frank Zappa and the Mothers of Invention song, "Montana" (about a dental floss farmer), we created a web of dental floss throughout the entire trailer. For days afterward movement about the rooms was precarious. One had to navigate through strands of floss that might be tied to an unseen object in the next room, or face an equal danger of becoming hopelessly entangled. For the long period of these experiments Scott was an essential companion. He understood the music that would set the atmosphere, and has an intuitive wit that will lacerate anyone within range. Scott also was and is a true friend. When Alice and I were without a car for months he dutifully drove us any place we needed to go. When trouble came Scott was always there to help, or just commiserate.

It was also during the time of these experiments that I began to paint. A constant companion at the time, David Smith, introduced me to watercolors. They seemed the perfect medium for quickly responding to evenings of hallucination and revelry. I eventually began to work with acrylics on a variety of surfaces, as well as developing a method of line drawing that allowed a spontaneous mythos to emerge; something that hearkens back to the satyrs and horned gods of the grove. Painting has been for me a means of restoration when the mental work of poetry becomes too exhausting. The physical involvement with paint and surface frees the mind toward an active imagination that releases the anxiety of an intellect too self-involved. So visual arts have become an intrinsic part of the poetry. Not just as a release from poetry, but as a poetry itself, part of the language in the air, on the tongue, and on the page. Painting and drawing have informed the poetry of its organic nature, something Michael McClure pointed out to me in speaking of the self-organization of his own spontaneous poetry as well as that of Jack Kerouac. Nature uses each of us as her mediums. Art that is unbound by any dominant theory allows nature a free hand to explore the potential of formlessness and deeper, less obvious form, and thus entertains herself with the wild growth of the soul in infinity.

In my late teens, I saw on public TV a documentary focusing on Dada and the branches it produced, particularly the work of Marcel Duchamp. While a case could be made that Duchamp was never, at least for his own concerns, part of those artists that called themselves Dada, what he released into the art world was an inversion of all that had gone before it. The nonsense and sound poetry of Tristan Tzara, Hugo Ball, and Kurt Schwitters combined with Duchamp's *The Bride Stripped Bare with Her Bachelors, Even,* were a revelation to me. They broke through all the pretense and inhibition that forever seems to saturate the arts and produced pure sound, pure form, based on no forebear other than that which lurks in our nervous systems. When I came to painting, then, I brought that sense of freedom with me, so that I had no fear of "getting it wrong." I wrote a long Dada poem called "There's a Place for a Freak in the Park," which had absolutely nothing to do with hippies or the hippy ethic, but experimented with nonsense and long flurries of raw sound. This latter especially became an intrinsic part of my poetry in that I learned from it my own natural tendency toward a longer line. Discovering jazz in my twenties encouraged that tendency, especially the liberating solos of John Coltrane and Ornette Coleman, among many others. When I wrote I could feel those long looping animal noises in my own breathing and in the rhythm of my blood. The first conscious expression of this was a long poem called "Four Angels and the Dog" that was part hallucinatory description and part diatribe against religious bigotry and repression. Though both of these poems were significant steps toward developing an original approach I can now find

no trace of them anywhere, lost during innumerable relocations too hastily arranged.

Probably the most significant event of the years I spent in various colleges was meeting Jim Wisniewski. In my first quarter of school, at Northwest Alabama Junior College, perhaps only a week or two into the term, I saw him in a high balcony area of the building, playing guitar. He played maniacally, with complete abandon, possessed, and the music he produced was unlike anything I'd ever heard, part flamenco, part folk, with the occasional classical phrase. I joined him and a friend in the balcony and introduced myself. The connection was immediate. In a day or two I brought him a notebook filled with poetry. He took it home with him and seemed to enjoy it as much as I'd enjoyed his music. Jim's life had been very different from mine, much less sheltered. By the time he was eighteen he'd already lived in the woods for weeks by himself, lived in New Orleans, and hitchhiked all around the South. He seemed to carry what I took to be a Buddhist air with him. His actions seemed spontaneous, joyful, uninhibited. That term we had long conversations, reading one another's soul. Then one day we took a trip into the hills of Colbert County, smoked a joint, and came back to school not to see each other again for more than a year. I dropped out of Northwest, enrolled in the University of North Alabama, fell in love, and got married. Jim got married as well. We ran into one another just outside the bookstore where his wife was working. We had both been experimenting with LSD and other hallucinogens and reading related material, so there was much to discuss. We began playing music together, exchanging books, having long conversations that amused our wives and left both of us exhilarated. I'd met another brother. No longer comfortable with my family I found myself among a circle of friends that included Jim, Greg Eaton, Barry Powell and his wife Alicia, Scott Huffstetler, Sharon Scott, Greg Henry, David Smith, my wife Alice, Kim Beck, Debbie Miller, and several others. There were times when our life seemed almost utopian, and at other times complete chaos. The life of this family of friends deserves a biography all its own. Suffice it to say, we left no boundary untested, no call unanswered.

Once Alice became pregnant it was obvious we had to marry. This circumstance delighted both of us despite the fact that I had

brujos in my nerves again twisting the
wires around sharp machine gun rhythm
through supercritical reactor file tusks dull
in the sundial glare outrageous heat siani
convulsion glittery ceramic mask
fragments – motionless Noh character
flapping his arms beneath gravity in the
roots of an oak as pomegranates fall up into
the trunk his head disappears into nil
space as she closes and nails his lids & rolls
his eyes back at planetary angles

(From *Idiot Menagerie*)

---

no steady income and she was still in high
school. Her family arranged employment for me
at a stove factory and the wedding plans were
set in order. I hated the noise of the factory,
the mind-numbing repetition of the assembly
line, and the violent temperament of most of
my fellow workers, but I consoled myself with
the promise of a wife and child, starting what
I perceived as adult life. I wrote a song for
the wedding which Joey Holder was kind enough
to play and sing. The ceremony was held at
her parents' house. My parents and grandparents were in attendance. Alice and I settled
into life in the trailer, avoiding drugs, attempting
Christianity. The factory job lasted only a week
or two into the marriage. I took odd jobs as I
could, painting houses, doing yard work. Friends
dropped in with support occasionally. I attempted
for the first time to actually practice the religion I'd been taught, attending church regularly, participating in church events. I hoped
that I could bring the kind of depth I was
finding in the poetry I was reading, and that I
read in the Bible, into the church, to bring at
least intellectual depth and possibly even mysticism. If T. S. Eliot had found a way, I reasoned, then so could I. Unfortunately, no one
at church was even remotely in touch with those
concerns. I felt claustrophobic; desperate to
contribute, but with my contribution of absolutely no use to the congregation. Alice continued to attend the pentecostal church she'd
been taught as a child, and I would return to
visit occasionally, meeting with similar frustrations. There seemed to be no place in organized religion that was even aware of, much

less embracing, the poetry I was so thrilled to
read: *The Divine Comedy, Paradise Lost,* the work
of William Blake, Thoreau, and Whitman. In
frustration, Barry began arriving at my door
on Sunday afternoons to celebrate Eucharist with
Alice and myself at home while we listened to
the music that was important to us and read
from the Bible, or poetry, or from some other
scripture, often Hindu or Buddhist. Once Jim
Smith, our literature teacher from high school,
dropped by and I explained to him what we
were doing. He had no objection despite the
fact that he was a deacon in the church Barry
and I had fled.

Another brother in spirit is Jon, my brother
by blood. In the last few years I lived with my
parents I would often come home from a date
or a night of revelry with friends and discover
Jon, six years younger than me, in my room,
listening to my records and reading my books.
My initial response was to chase him out, but
I eventually realized he was beginning to respond to the same kind of visionary impulses
that I had. Though I continued to treat him
as a kid brother I began to share music, books,
and ideas with him. Once he'd moved away
with my parents he studied painting, often sending me samples of his work. I responded in
kind. Our friendship frightened my parents. They
were afraid that Jon would be drawn into the
same lifestyle to which I'd given myself so completely. Truth was, neither one of us was trying to persuade the other. We were excited
about the discoveries we were making and eager to pass them along to one another. A few
years later, while in college, Jon was stricken
with a psychotic episode. I'd long recognized
him as sensitive, more acutely aware than most.
Apparently the stress of college combined with
the paradox of trying to challenge the moral
code from inside the church had activated a
genetic predisposition. For days it appeared he
had become hopelessly psychotic, but drugs
combined with the constant attention of my
parents, especially the latter, brought him out
of it and slowly, over several years, he recovered. I realized those schizoid attacks of my
childhood had prepared me to beware of the
possibility of complete madness, and in poetry
I had found a means of response. Jon was not
so fortunate. His breakdown was more painful
to me than his death would have been. I'd
lost him, but he was still with us, incoherent,
alone in chaos. Today Jon is a university in-

structor, holds four degrees, writes poetry, has a beautiful wife and child, is a wiser man for the experience. His recovery has been nothing short of miraculous, and what he has been able to accomplish since then even more so. Recently I came upon a photo of him as a young child, perhaps two years old. In his eyes I saw something phenomenal, a numinous glow, as if he'd arrived from the heavenly realms, a bodhisattva returning out of mercy to bring the rest of us to bliss. I see the same glow in his son's eyes.

In the early morning of October 24, 1980, Alice gave birth to our son, Joseph. I felt enormous love for him; I adored every part of him, every sound and gesture. He was a wonderful baby, peaceful and quiet, sleeping soundly, with always a pleasant temperament that continued as he grew up. Once he had learned to walk and had his own room we would be wakened in the morning by a soft knocking at our bedroom door. When we opened the door he stood there smiling radiantly, pure joy and hope, eager for the new day. I never had any great desire to have children, but one look at Joey in the morning supplied me with all the evidence I needed for the promise that fosters that desire.

I only found jobs sporadically, and the jobs I found were short-lived. Alice managed to get into a federal program for secretarial training, and began working as a secretary so I stayed home with Joey. He and I became great friends. I played songs for him, showed him the tarot cards, we played games, and generally enjoyed one another's company. We quickly outgrew the trailer and didn't have the money to pay the utility bill anyway, so we moved into a duplex apartment with Greg Henry, Keith's brother and one of the "family." Keith and Sharon owned the duplex and lived in the other apartment. Greg and I have known each other since we were children. We became friends after we had graduated school, spending the weekends at the movies, riding through Florence getting high, discussing music, goofing off. I admired Greg's openness and unwillingness to pass judgment; it was and is very easy to spend time with him. He expected nothing of me, just conversation, levity, and my share of the cost of a bag of pot. There is something almost saintly about Greg. I don't mean that he is pious or even religious, but that he tolerates difference with joy, he finds affirmation in dark moments.

I feel fortunate to know him. So moving in with Greg was a joyous affair; he greeted us warmly every morning, though I know we must have tried his patience many times. And when Alice left and filed for divorce, taking Joey with her, Greg tolerated my complaints, reassured me, and gave me food when I was too distressed or too broke to buy any for myself.

Keith, Greg, Barry, and I began playing music together, hoping to start a band. We experimented wildly with a variety of approaches, and discovered a form of composing with recorded sound I would later use to publish audio poetry. The "band" served as a soundtrack for family life, provided us with an outlet for song and experiment, and a place to learn our instruments. Keith has since gone on to study music in depth and become a virtuoso guitarist.

It was during this period that I discovered Rimbaud and French symbolism. Everything I had believed about poetry up to that point vanished. Poetry had come out of the ivory

"The Roan Steed Clad in Velvet,"
by Jake Berry, 1996

tower and settled itself in the body. I began to realize the importance of the poem as experience rather than as a record of experience. One had to make oneself a seer, as Rimbaud said, and suddenly all the hallucinogenic experimentation fell into place. I understood that if I were to write poetry of any value to myself, let alone to the rest of the world, I would have to be willing to risk my sanity, even my life, to manifest it. In my obsession I was blind to the fact that Alice had been growing restless. She had attempted to express it in various ways, but I made the assumption that marriage was forever. Rank stupidity, but I had no experience with anyone who had a broken marriage, had only known one person who had a divorce and I was not witness to it. So I assumed that whatever was troubling Alice would work itself out and ignored the signs. She fell in love with someone else and after a period of procrastination left to live with him. It was a terrible blow. I couldn't eat for days, until finally I nearly passed out at work. Reorientation required years, and several others were damaged in the process, but the worst of it was losing Joey.

I tried to see Joey often at first, but the moment of separation became increasingly difficult, so I retreated. After a few weeks, at the encouragement of my second wife, I went and picked him up for a visit. We had a wonderful time playing in the park and watching a movie about dragons. He was still not talking in complete sentences, but was very aware of the circumstances. For a day or so the old friendship was restored, then he had to be returned to his mother. On the way Joey fell asleep in my arms and didn't wake until he was home. His immediate response was terror. He screamed and cried, reaching out to me, but I couldn't take him. I was forced to abandon him against both our wishes. After I left something broke inside that has never healed. I continued to see him, but with no regular frequency, and always with great caution, hoping not to cause that horrible pain in him again. Both of us suffered the long dull ache of separation constantly rather than the overwhelming attacks of repeated separations. Now in his mid-teens he accepts the situation stoically when we see one another a few times a year. We are friends, but can never recover what was lost. I am not his father day to day. That task has fallen to someone else. But I am his friend, passing no judgment on his choices, only encouraging him as a friend would, out of concern for his future.

The year after the breakup with Alice was turbulent. Just as the divorce papers were being signed I was fired from my job, no doubt due to the distractions of the divorce. My parents had become increasingly insistent that I conduct myself according to their code, and I had diligently tried in the months leading up to Alice's departure, but now all bets were off. Just as I was beginning to find my own poetry I would have to find a way to live on my own terms. In a single day I had violent arguments with both my parents individually, resolving that there was nothing left to do but remove myself from their lives entirely. I would live as a poet regardless of the cost since compromise had yielded nothing but heartache and frustration. I had begun seeing Jerri Shelton, someone I had actually known of for years because she was related by marriage to my mother's family. Jerri was very supportive, and without realizing it allowed me to take advantage of her generosity at every turn. I was completely out for myself, to survive, to assert myself as a poet, ego on overdrive. Jerri witnessed the worst of me; I yielded nothing to her. Yet she tolerated me and when I was no longer able to meet my rent at the duplex she suggested that I move in with her. I gladly accepted, and when Alice married her boyfriend I suggested that Jerri and I marry as well, almost as casually as if I were inviting her for a walk in the park. The marriage was doomed, though there was never any great hostility, and certainly no violence, between us—I had simply taken advantage of her trust. In line with my agenda I began submitting poems to magazines, expecting rejection slips, with which I intended to paper the bedroom walls as I had read another poet had done. The rejection slips came in almost as quickly as I sent the poems out. I assumed I'd never be published. In my attempt to create poetry as experience I felt I had simply run so far outside tradition that publishing was impossible and sending out manuscripts was only a means of affirming my suspicions. Here is a sample of the poetry I was sending out:

whirling dervish magpie lares
palm leaves breaking the yellow-come-tender
   orange sun
cracks on the bronze baal ghosts

Jerri gave me a typewriter for my birthday and I wrote like mad almost daily, pushing myself toward something beyond my own capacities. I was frantic to become a visionary or be consumed in the attempt. Jerri and I fell apart in a matter of weeks. I admitted to myself that I felt nothing for her, but I had no clue as to how to resolve the situation. And I had no inclination to solve it as long as I was able to work and she tolerated my lack of attention. Very soon the problem would resolve itself.

Irony of ironies, on the day that Jerri and I were married we visited her friend, Bridget Fago, to borrow some items for the wedding. I was fascinated with Bridget immediately. She was dark-haired, mysterious, and beautiful. Within a few days of the wedding she visited Jerri and me at our apartment. We talked long into the night. I loved talking to her, drawing her out; she seemed full of secrets and I wanted to know them all. It was not until several months later while I was wrestling with the problem of being married to someone I'd never loved that I recognized in Bridget the archetype of lover and companion I'd carried with me from child-

hood. The choice was simple. I had to be with her.

As my life had been destroyed by Alice's departure, now I was destroying Jerri's life, but the mistake had been the marriage and there was nothing to do but end it. For the first time I had exiled myself from my friends, I had selfishly victimized someone who in no way deserved it, and they were understandably angry. And though the guilt was completely mine, Bridget was haunted by it for years. When I moved in with Bridget I was completely alone in the world, removed from both blood and spiritual families. I thought of myself as a snake shedding its skin, and threw myself even more completely into my work, writing another long spontaneous poem, day and night at the typewriter, mad for a liberation that would absolve my sins and deliver me into a realm of pure poetry.

Bridget and I were quite happy together as exiles, living in a cold apartment in a drafty old house with winter closing in. One night while Bridget was at work I was huddled over my typewriter when I heard someone call my

At work, with Aleister, 1993

With his son, Joey, and Aleister, 1995

name outside. At first I ignored it because we had told no one where we'd moved. But the voice insisted and I went to the window to discover Barry laughing and dancing on the lawn. I was delighted to see him. In a few moments we were rapt in a discussion of the metaphysics of love, erotic and spiritual. Eventually Bridget and I were restored to our friends. Despite my selfishness and stupidity they had forgiven me.

It was particularly good to see Sharon again. She has a talent for finding positive attributes in everyone she meets, but for a while I had challenged her. Later, when she and Keith separated, I broke a period of silence and isolation to comfort her. I wouldn't have done it for anyone else. Sharon's company is a delight. Fascinated with the tiniest of details, she discovers things the rest of us overlook, and relates them in hilarious tales that more than once have sent us to the floor laughing until we cried. After Alice left she and I spent a period of hard drinking, some nights I had to leave her apartment crawling, too drunk to walk. Her marriage was falling apart and I would

have taken advantage of the situation had she let me. I needed someone and Sharon was a friend, but while she discouraged any sexual intentions I had, out of respect for Keith, she would sit and hold me, comforting me. It may have saved my life. It certainly saved my soul.

Meanwhile, Jim's hunger for experience had taken him and his wife across the country on motorcycle, and across Europe with whatever transportation they might acquire. I was surprised one day to see Rhonda, his wife, in a grocery store.

"When did you guys get home?" I asked.

"Actually *we* aren't home," she said, "just me. I'll let him explain it to you when he returns."

Jim spent the next few months hitchhiking in Germany, France, and England, with nothing more than a sleeping bag, a change of clothes and his flute, eating on what he could earn by playing music on the sidewalks, in parks, and subways. He gave me no warning of his return, so when I came home one day to Bridget's complaints about the toilet I suspected nothing. When I opened the bathroom door I discovered Jim, pants down, on the commode. He screamed at me, "My God, can't a guy take a shit in this town?!"

For the next few months Jim and I were together almost daily. Collaborating on projects, sharing bottles and cigars and other drugs during endless conversations about music, poetry, philosophy, religion, and mysticism.

In late 1984 I had work accepted and published for the first time in *Rolling Stone*. They were only short poems, but at last I was a published poet. Early the following year I discovered the literary underground through a magazine called *Beatniks in Space*. I was amazed at the number and variety of small magazines being edited and published from homes and garages. The poetry ranged from doggerel to established modernism to extremely experimental. Poets, collagists, politicos, and short-story writers were having entire careers without ever breaking into the mainstream press, or desiring to. I was suddenly able to publish my poetry, prose, and visual art in many of these small magazines. *Popular Reality, Lost and Found Times, Mallife, NRG, Atticus Review,* and their respective editors, the Rev. David Crowbar, John M. Bennett, Mike Miskowski, Dan Raphael, and Harry Polkinhorn, were all encouraging and published my work, becoming regular correspondents. We wrote long letters, ranting our aesthetics to one another. Mike Miskowski asked me to send him material for a small book. I sent him the manuscript of *The Pandemonium Spirit,* a collection of dense schizoid voices woven through one another in long, virtually endless lines. Here are the opening lines to one of those poems, "Summon":

> Enoch created a diversion of stars / gate
>   guard sword angel
> stunned deadeyed / as he blowtorched his
>   way
> through corrugated iron stumbled onto a
>   dried child body
> hung upside down on a dead tree like a
>   tombstone surrounded
> in cornucopia sea pried his neutered
>   leathery hips apart with the end of a
> wrench and saw the universe milk tear
>   stellar window

Jim ("Whizz") Wisniewski, 1994

A "key" to the book lay in another of its poems, "Murderer's Work":

> I am doing
> Murderer's Work
>
> assassinating a culture
> nerve
> by
> nerve
>
> Breaking through vaults
> of relative slumber
>
> Hacking away at the concrete
> mind with a bloody
> ax

A phrase from this poem, "assassinating a culture / nerve / by / nerve," became the motto for a small publication, *Murderer's Work,* which I began as a means of contributing a magazine of my own to the underground, publishing other poets whose work I enjoyed. One of them, and probably the most significant in terms of the quality of his work, and his friendship, has been Jack Foley. Jack and I had appeared on an audio magazine called *Poets Eleven.* Of all the poets on the tape, only Jack and I exploited the resource of the medium. Jack had contributed a recording of he and his wife Adelle performing his "Overture: Chorus" which featured alternating and simultaneous voices. I was completely overwhelmed. The poetry was vastly intelligent, musical, dramatic—forces of nature rendered with incredible eloquence and passion. I'd never heard anything like it. I was immediately convinced of two things, Jack and I were both insane for spiritual liberation, connecting on a multitude of levels, and that if there was something new happening in contemporary poetry, Jack was it. I wrote to the editors of the magazine demanding his address. They refused, but sent my address to him, along with my comments. In a few days I received an enthusiastic letter from Jack saying that he was impressed with my poetry as well, introducing himself and his work to me. I responded immediately with a letter and poems. We quickly became friends, brothers, and remain in constant conversation by mail, phone, e-mail, and personal visit.

Mike Miskowski became a close friend as well. We published one another's poetry, I published his first book *Suburbreal Drive.* We shared a fascination with Futurism, Dada, and Beat literature, as well as a desire to test the limits of all the arts, dissolving boundaries and categories wherever possible. Mike made use of household items in his painting, sculpture, collage, and poetry, and we collaborated on a pseudo-scripture about a migration of appliances to the geographical center of the continent in Kearny, Nebraska. Each of us believe that play is an essential element in art, and inspired one another daily to become more elaborate in our experiments. Through his Bomb Shelter Propaganda Mike published my first, second, and fourth books, *The Pandemonium Spirit, Idiot Menagerie,* and *Unnon Theories.* Through my Abscond Press I published his second book, *Applianoidal Grphcus Birthday Elaps.*

Jim Wisniewski was my underground companion locally. Together we published several issues of *Murderer's Work,* designed and published flyers, collages, and screeds, both of us thrilled to be a part of an active art community at last. Jim had also become an accomplished musician and founded a music publishing company, Elan Vital. For a first release I joined him and a group of musicians at the famous Muscle Shoals Sound Studio to record an album of spontaneous, mostly instrumental music called *Solstice.* In preparation for the event Jim and I had discussed performing a major ritual to summon the powers to assist us. We'd considered the possibility of including an animal sacrifice, a goat in particular, but had abandoned the idea until Jim saw, on the way from Atlanta, a goat for sale on the side of the road, as if by design. He bought the goat and pulled into my drive with the animal in the back of his van. We spent most of the night discussing the propriety of animal sacrifice, the details of the ritual, the dangers, principally metaphysical, involved. At last we decided the project was important enough to merit the sacrifice. The next afternoon, a steamy summer solstice eve, we met in a grove of trees on the banks of a lake. I cast a circle with salt and invocation, saluted and asked the favor of the four directions, then summoned the deity to aid us in our task on making music that would enlighten and heal. Jim stood in the center of the circle with the goat and with our arms wrapped around it we cut its throat. At first the goat resisted death, but soon submitted. In the intensity of the moment it was as if the animal's life flowed into us, charging us

Jake with his brothers Jon (left) and Jeff, 1995

with the sacred obligation of transforming his blood into music. Each of us tasted the blood, saluted the four directions, built a fire into which we cast the heart, leaving the rest to be cooked by Jim's brother Joe the next day while we recorded the music the sacrifice had wrought. The result was an album that surprised all of us. With no rehearsal, and most of us having never played together, we created a series of pieces that were simultaneously avant-garde and tranquil. The sacrifice and ritual had worked. Still, Jim and I swore to use other methods in the future. A particularly favorite ritual is the sharing of a bottle of mezcal just before making a recording, splitting the worm between us. This method proved successful when we created and recorded with the Muscle Shoals Noise Orchestra, experiments in spontaneous composition and noise sculpture with a variety of musicians.

Jim continues to roam across the planet, recording his music, and constantly noting his thoughts and history in a long series of journals. I excerpted one of these journals to publish Jim's first book, *Womb of Insight.*

Along with Barry, Jon, and Jack, I count Jim as a deep brother in spirit, a fellow worker whose path is so close to my own that there is often no distinction between them. I love all four of them in a way that only we can understand. Though we part company we are never apart. Our deepest connection lies in the total commitment to forces that lie beyond, yet contain, the events of our lives. And though those events often become part of my poetry, it is the force that drives them that gives each of us a life, a gnosis, that will sustain us, through our work, until the work of our life is complete.

In 1987, after several pages attempting a new long poem, producing nothing satisfactory, I drove down to a park on the Tennessee River and sat looking out over the water, waiting, listening for the voices. Association with the poets in the underground had accelerated my education of what poetry had been and might be. I felt that after years of study and preparation, of discovering and honing unique approaches to manifesting the poetic event, the moment a poem is, I was ready to contribute a larger work; something epic in scale yet radically different from even the most progressive forms. It would have to be a form not defined by any preconception, nor by chance or by purely spontaneous construction. Suddenly those swollen faces that tormented me as a child came rushing back, but this time they weren't terrifying, they were healers, shamanic entities bringing me the work that would become the central body of my poetry, the center of my life. No wonder I had been terrified as a child. They had come to me when I had no idea of the awesome responsibility a human life is, had come to shake me awake, to announce themselves, then wait for the circumstances to ripen and drive me to the task. "legion swollen faces . . . ," I began, I was born. *Brambu Drezi* was manifesting.

The title of the work arrived sometime later. I was in the habit of voicing streams of glossolalia to my cat, Aleister, who I consider a friend and a kind of familiar, to get his reaction. When the sounds pleased him I would jot them down. During this process the words "Brambu Drezi" arose. Aleister liked this one very very much and I felt an organic, earthy resonance in its sounds, as if they were magical. After considering various titles that were attempts to

in some way describe the long work I'd begun, I realized that the title would always limit the poem in some way, restrict its ability to take its own shape. Then those sounds rose in my mind again and I spoke them aloud, "Brambu Drezi," repeating it like a chant, "Brambu Drezi, Brambu Drezi, Brambu Drezi . . . ," realizing, chanting and laughing, that the work had named itself.

I continued to experiment with forms and approaches outside *Brambu Drezi* as well, often making discoveries that would contribute to the body of the long work. There are prose experiments in *The Tongue Bearer's Daughter* and *Unnon Theories* as well as graphically constructed poems; spontaneous poems in *Psychlstomp;* manipulations of physics, anatomy, kabbalah, and mathematics in *Equations;* and a series of daily short form experiments in *PhasEoStrophes.* Many of the various approaches later became a part of *Species of Abandoned Light.* I will let the poetry speak for itself and not try to explain it, since no comprehensive explanation is possible. However, I can speak of the reality of the poem as organism, as a body borne through the worlds by whatever medium is best suited to the phenomena that grant this world its presence and awareness of its presence. It is not my intention to write obscurely, to veil a meaning that might be unwound from the riddle by the diligent. But one must live as expansively and to the height and depth possible, opening toward infinity. Ultimately all proportions are a cocoon that must be shattered. The poem is the creature that emerges. It is infinity swimming through the apparition of shape whose sound is a gnosis of its experience. When we attempt to define it we come away frustrated. When we assign it to a category or class we attempt, without success, to contain and possess it. Finally, the best response is to *allow* its being to wake before us and within our perceptual domain, liberating us.

After years of living in apartments Bridget and I finally took a mortgage on a house in Florence. In the spring and summer we plant and harvest herbs and flowers and a few vegetables. Bridget has allowed me time and space to devote to my work. I love her without condition. She continues, after twelve years of marriage, to fill the archetype of companion and lover for me. I try to reciprocate in some way, but marriage of any kind can only flour-

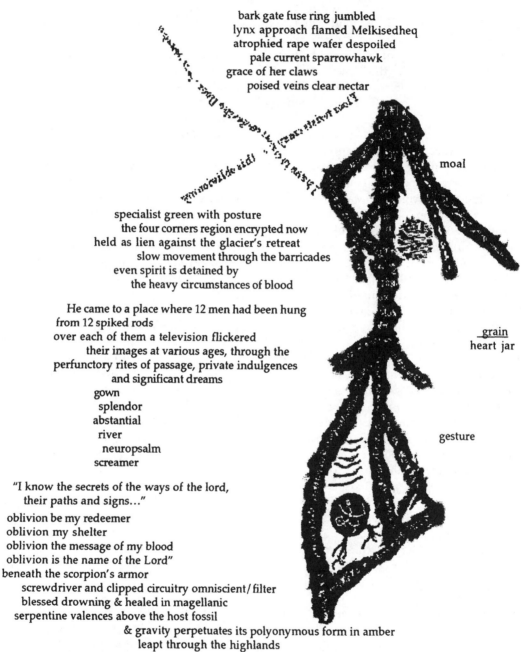

magpies scatter & return
cyclical as dervish
"It means tornadoes," she said smiling
"whole herds of them
grazing rooftops and mammal soul.
We begin with carnival."

bark gate fuse ring jumbled
lynx approach flamed Melkisedheq
atrophied rape wafer despoiled
pale current sparrowhawk
grace of her claws
poised veins clear nectar

moal

specialist green with posture
the four corners region encrypted now
held as lien against the glacier's retreat
slow movement through the barricades
even spirit is detained by
the heavy circumstances of blood

He came to a place where 12 men had been hung
from 12 spiked rods
over each of them a television flickered
their images at various ages, through the
perfunctory rites of passage, private indulgences
and significant dreams
gown
splendor
abstantial
river
neuropsalm
screamer

grain
heart jar

gesture

"I know the secrets of the ways of the lord,
their paths and signs..."
oblivion be my redeemer
oblivion my shelter
oblivion the message of my blood
oblivion is the name of the Lord"
beneath the scorpion's armor
screwdriver and clipped circuitry omniscient/filter
blessed drowning & healed in magellanic
serpentine valences above the host fossil
& gravity perpetuates its polyonymous form in amber
leapt through the highlands
asleep cortex egg
or albino maggots
crawling in mushroom rot

From Brambu Drezi, Book Two, *a work in progress*

ish if it is allowed to live according to its own appetites and needs. The conjunction of our souls forms the entity we nourish.

In recent years the underground has evolved into many undergrounds with a large number of magazines that specialize in publishing the vanguard, by whatever name it might be given. In the late '80s I met Bob Grumman. Bob is the underground's foremost theorist and one of its most important poets. He also publishes much of the most exciting work appearing in what he calls the otherstream via his press, Runaway Spoon. In 1994 *Brambu Drezi, Book One* appeared as a Runaway Spoon title. Harry Polkinhorn, an important poet by any standard, assigned *Brambu Drezi* as required reading for his students at San Diego State University. I was shocked and thrilled at the prospect and eager to hear how the students responded. Harry told me that arguments broke out, resulting almost in physical hostilities. With the exception of some of the aspersions thrown at Harry, I was delighted with this result.

In late summer 1995 *Species of Abandoned Light* appeared from Pantograph Press. Ivan Argüelles, whom I have known and corresponded with almost as long as with Jack, and whose reinvention of the epic poem makes him natural inheritor of the mantle of Ezra Pound, founded Pantograph (named for his epic) in the early '90s. He encouraged me to assemble *Species* and brought it out in the most beautifully produced volume of any of my books.

*

For years Jack had encouraged me to visit him in the San Francisco Bay area (Jack and Adelle live in Oakland), and he spent a week with Bridget and me in 1992. By the time *Species* appeared it was obvious to me that the trip was essential. Jack and Adelle solved the problem of a plane ticket and on April 16, 1995, at four in the afternoon I was on a plane bound for California.

Jack was waiting as I came off the plane, camera in hand, Adelle met us straightaway and we stepped into a whirlwind of poetry, poets, and the beautiful cities by the bay. I fell in love with all of it.

Though many have supported my work over the past decade, Mike Miskowski, Jim Leftwich, Gregory Vincent Saint Thomasino, John M.

Bennett, Harry Polkinhorn, Bob Grumman, Ivan Argüelles, all of them poets of considerable power and circumstance, none have been as generous and enthusiastic as Jack has. And this is not only the case with me, but with many poets. Jack is one of the finest writers and performers of poetry alive, but his commitment to poetry is complete. Where he finds poetry he believes in, regardless of the poet, he promotes it tirelessly.

Right away Jack and Adelle were introducing me to new sights, tastes, and sounds. My first full day in California Jack and I traveled across the Bay Bridge and into the North Beach section of San Francisco to City Lights Bookstore, legendary for its co-founder, Lawrence Ferlinghetti, and the Beat movement. I grabbed as many books as I could, then we were off to meet Neeli Cherkovski. I'd heard of Neeli for years, as a poet, longtime friend of Charles Bukowski, and author of *Whitman's Wild Children*. When we arrived Neeli greeted us warmly and began to show us some of the art around his house, wonderful paintings and photography. Neeli is a gentle man, full of energy. I could see and feel the ideas rush from him, bubbling forth into speech. Before the words are out he is on to another idea. Yet, he was never overpowering or dominating, as curious to hear others as to relate his own thoughts; beatific. The three of us walked down the hill and around the corner to a little Hungarian restaurant. The food was delicious, the company superb. It felt odd and blissful to be hanging out with people I had long considered important poets, people that are part of poetry's history.

After lunch Jack and I were back off across the bay to Berkeley for Jack's weekly radio show, *Cover to Cover*. The show went very well. Jack has a way of making you comfortable in an interview. As with so many things, he is a consummate professional on the air. John Malloy, an Irish actor who had performed Samuel Beckett's plays for many years, sat in with us.

Later that night, in an uncharacteristic pouring rain, Jack and Adelle and I performed at Cody's Bookstore in Berkeley. Ivan and Neeli as well as Michael McClure with Amy Evans, the sculptor, were in attendance. It was my first official poetry reading. In 1993 I had performed with Jim, Stan Berryman, and Ray Miller on the Nashville cable TV program, *Speer Presents*, hosted by poet/videographer Joe Speer,

At the home of Neeli Cherkovski, in San Francisco; (from left) Neeli, Jack Foley,
Ivan Argüelles, and Jake Berry, April 1996

and in 1995 I had read to two classes of students taught by my brother Jon at the University of Alabama, but this was an entirely different animal. However, everyone in the room seemed relaxed and eager to hear the poetry, so I felt very little anxiety beforehand. I noticed as I read that everyone seemed to be paying close attention, the kind of attention I had seen audiences give jazz performers during a long solo. Every poet dreams of this kind of attention to his or her work. For me, it was fuel, an energy that I had to transmute and return to them through the poetry. When I finished, the applause seemed genuine, and as I sat down Ivan embraced me as one embraces a long lost brother. That embrace alone was worth the trip. Jack and Adelle performed after me, an astonishing, burning performance, the kind that has made them legends wherever they've performed. Jack's intelligence is so vast, yet he is keenly aware of the importance of humor and showmanship. By collaging a multitude of disparate, but equally powerful, elements he has developed a poetry that cre-

ates paradoxes from which a moment of rapture or awakening emerges. Adelle is an extraordinary performer as well, integrating the shape-shifting the poetry requires with grace. One of the great treats of the trip for me was getting to see them perform three times in the space of a week.

The next day we met Neeli at his house for lunch. We picked up Ivan on the way and dropped in on the artist Leonard Breger at his house, very near where Neeli lives. Leonard is an extraordinary painter, working on masonite cut in the form of the images he paints. He has painted a portrait of Jack, along with Gertrude Stein, Abraham Lincoln (naked), and himself as a dragon. His wife, Beth Pewther, has created a beautiful mosaic in tile on the exterior of their house that distinguishes it from any other. Lunch was wonderful, full of conversation about poetry and art. Neeli read us some of Bukowski's poetry, and did an imitation of Bukowski that brought chills. Afterward Neeli and I rode across the city to pick up Harold Norse, author of *Beat Hotel* and other

Beat era novels and poetry. Harold was warm and, I think a little curious, to meet a strange poet from Alabama who had read his work.

Shortly after arriving back at Neeli's, Jack and Adelle took me to see the Golden Gate Bridge, which was an epiphany for me—the bridge and its rapturous view of San Francisco Bay. Then, after a quick look at the Palace of Fine Arts, with its Greek columns and domes, we met Neeli at City Lights along with Lawrence Ferlinghetti and Nancy Peters. With Lawrence we walked down the street to a coffee shop and sat for a while talking, having Lawrence sign copies of his books. Neeli has known Ferlinghetti for many years, and has written his biography. Jack and Adelle have known him for a few years as well. Lawrence was kind, eager to talk, with a peaceful air about him. Before we parted Jack told him about *Brambu Drezi* and I gave him a copy, which he asked me to sign. I'd certainly never expected to be signing a book for Lawrence Ferlinghetti, but with Jack these things happen.

That night Ivan and I, along with Eileen Kaufman (Bob Kaufman's widow), were reading at Gaia Books in Berkeley. Due to some inner ear problems I had been dizzy most of the day, and as we arrived at the bookstore I was wondering if I'd be able to stand and perform, but once Ivan began to read the dizziness vanished. He seemed to be a prophet, like Isaiah or Ezekiel, ranting his visions, his complex visions of the spirit of everything, flailing the air, his voice rising and falling swiftly, the poetry turned in powerful strophes.

After the reading Jack and Adelle introduced me to Ethiopian food and honey wine, both of which were delicious. We were joined by Guillermo Galindo, the composer of *Kiyohime* among many other marvelous works, and his wife Paula.

The following day, Jack and I had lunch as the guests of Jess, the painter and collagist, at the home in San Francisco he shared with the poet Robert Duncan. The house is a temple, saturated with the spirit that two masterful artists have drawn into it. For many years I have counted Duncan a primary source, not just for myself, but for what poetry is in this age; and when Jack introduced me to Jess's painting and collage I was astonished by its richness and depth. Often I have read Duncan while standing in front of a collage by Jess that I have on my wall at home, drinking in the two together. Now to be in the shrine they had created, I was speechless. Jess was very kind, and open, eager to hear what Jack and I were working on, and answering all our questions graciously. He served a delicious meal, then showed us around, including the extensive library and a rare signed copy of *Finnegans Wake*. Jack and I both could have stayed for days, soaking up the atmosphere, working, communing with Jess.

That night Jack and Adelle, Neeli, and I, performed at the Yakety Yak coffee house in San Francisco. There was an open reading afterward so the room was full of poets. They were attentive and very responsive. I was delighted to see Mike Miskowski there with his girlfriend. Mike, through his press, Bomb Shel-

---

Election Year

Shouldn't we have seen it coming? An age of golden totem followed by an age of vomit, lice, and plague? Decay slobbers over her vertebrae, the desert trigger, a fat gangster earning his commitment to the toilet. At the end of a long hallway crops fail in the raging laughter of a rusty sun, polyester orchids gag for Christ who strokes out bloated and diabetic on his patio in Beverly Hills. It's the perfect America – genocide descendants and gasoline swamp. I'm casting my vote with a torch.

(From *Species of Abandoned Light*)

Reading at Gaia Books, Berkeley, California, April 1996

ter, was, along with Miekal And and Liz with their press, Xexoxial, the primary source for the true vanguard of poetry and art in the late '80s and early '90s. I still consider Mike to be a brother in the art, though we don't correspond and collaborate as much as we once did. Listening to Neeli read I heard how, of all of our group of poets, he has absorbed the street savvy and natural wisdom of the Beats. While he brings it further, awake to the technological change and intensity of the '90s, his delivery is as cool and lyrical as a Miles Davis solo.

The following afternoon, Saturday, I read at New College in San Francisco. Eight poets were on the bill, a diversity of styles. I was delighted to hear many of them as I had read and corresponded with them for years; John Noto, Andy Joron, Will Alexander, Adam Cornford, and others.

Sunday, we met Neeli at Land's End on the Pacific Ocean and followed him down a rugged trail to the sea. Neeli, in his fifties,

took to the trail like a mountain goat. The rest of us kept up as best we could. The ocean rolled in, white waves crashing into huge boulders. It was easy to see why Robinson Jeffers built his house on this ocean; it is full of poetry, and eager to give it up for those who are willing to listen.

Afterward, Jack, Adelle, and I visited Michael McClure and Amy Evans at their house in Oakland. While Jack spoke on the phone to Jerome Rothenberg, Michael read a list of wildflowers he and Amy had collected the day before. As he read, the names became poetry, McClure's voice as pure, ancient, and newborn as the flowers themselves, as his poetry. He is the revelator that biology is spirit through an approach to the art that sets him apart from virtually everyone. When I picked up his book *Antechamber & Other Poems* many years ago I had no idea who he was. By the time I finished the book my entire perspective had changed. To be able to sit with him and speak about nature, music, and personal history, and to read some of *Brambu Drezi* for him, at his request, was an apex. Amy served us coffee, fruit, and biscotti, and showed us her sculptures, busts, complete figures, and more abstract form, all of which have a sense of the organic, vehicles through which some intangible force flows.

The following night we rode to Santa Rosa to perform at Mudd's coffee house. After performing selections from my work, the poet Amy Trussell and I performed with a percussionist, me reading my poetry and a poem we had written together while she danced. Amy understands the connection between ritual and poetry instinctively. I was thrilled to be able to perform with her. Afterwards, there was the treasure of Jack and Adelle performing for the final time during my visit.

Leaving was difficult, and I don't think I ever left completely, or ever will. Jack, Neeli, and Ivan tell me I am a California poet. Who am I to argue? At least I hope I am able to contribute in my work a poetry that complements their own. If there is a movement afoot, these are the poets I want to be moving with. I owe Jack a debt of gratitude I will never repay, and Adelle as well.

*   *   *

So little has been told here, there are so many others who have been and remain very important to me. In recent years I have grown closer to my parents. The rift torn between us by our different philosophies has disappeared as we have learned to tolerate, even appreciate those differences. And my brother Jeff and I have become close friends, based in part on a common love of music. Our paths have begun to meet with increasing frequency. When he visited me last year, bringing his guitar and songs to play, I felt as if something missing had been restored.

Life is concerned with origination, not finality. So then, this is a record of the skins I've shed in the act of becoming. Yet, there is ultimately no "I" to shed a skin. The focus of attention rests where it will and the sequences randomly cohere as a single entity, but something is revealed in the process. I was never born, I am forever being born. May the truth claim its own.

Jake Berry 5.17.96

BIBLIOGRAPHY

Poetry:

The Pandemonium Spirit, Bomb Shelter, 1986.

Idiot Menagerie (see also below), Bomb Shelter, 1987.

Hairbone Stew, Plutonium Press, 1988.

Unnon Theories, Bomb Shelter, 1989.

Psychlstomp, Sir Realist Press, 1989.

(With John Eberly) *Gris Gris Malkuth,* Xexoxial, 1989.

Equations (see also below), Runaway Spoon Press, 1991.

The Tongue Bearer's Daughter, Luna Bisonte, 1991.

Brambu Drezi, Book One, Runaway Spoon Press, 1994.

Species of Abandoned Light (also see below), Pantograph Press, 1995.

(With Jeffrey Little) *The Beast's Pheromonal Mariachi Machine,* Juxta Press, 1995.

(With Ivan Argüelles) *Purisima Sex Addict II,* Luna Bisonte, 1996.

The Doorman Sleeps Like an Apparatus . . . , Semiquasi Press, 1997.

PhasEoStrophes, 3300 Press, forthcoming.

Sound recordings:

Idiot Menagerie, 9th St. Labs, 1987.

(With Sounds ov Earth) *Solstice,* Elan Vital, 1987.

Fetic Porn, 9th St. Labs, 1988.

Protonon, Sound of Pig, 1988.

(With Jack Foley and Mike Miskowski) *3 Talkers,* 9th St. Labs, 1988.

(With The Muscle Shoals Noise Orchestra) *Void of Course,* Elan Vital, 1988.

(With Pantaloon Cinema) *Devastating Dream Soundtrack,* 9th St. Labs, 1988.

Diaspora, Plutonium Press, 1988.

Chants, 9th St. Labs, 1989.

States, Elan Vital, 1989.

(With The Muscle Shoals Noise Orchestra) *Swampworm,* Elan Vital, 1990.

Deep Nature, 9th St. Labs, 1990.

Incidental Music for Contemporary Aquariums, Harsh Reality Music, 1990.

(With Pantaloon Cinema) *My God Has Hair,* 9th St. Labs, 1991.

(With Jack Foley) *Recess Conjunction,* Spiral Cassest, 1991.

Equations, 9th St. Labs, 1991.

(With John M. Bennett) *The Lemurs,* Luna Bisonte, 1991.

(With The Muscle Shoals Noise Orchestra) *The Basements of Kcairo,* Elan Vital, 1992.

(With Jim Whizz) *Personal Pruitus,* 9th St. Labs/ Elan Vital, 1993.

Shadowlands/Disintegration Days, Elan Vital, 1993.

Faith Is Blood, Elan Vital, 1995.

(With Jim Whizz and Wayne Sides) *Monkey Head,* Elan Vital, 1995.

Species of Abandoned Light (with music "Sounds of the Celestial Screw," by Barry Powell), 9th St. Labs, 1995.

Neeli Cherkovski

1945-

THE MAKING OF A POET: AN AUTOBIOGRAPHICAL INTERLUDE

1.

Unlike Nietzsche's Zarathustra, who descended the mountain to offer his truths in the marketplace, I rush up and down the mountain in one breathless dash, offering only a glimmer of what the truth might be. Poetry is not always a search for what is absolute, but may also be a continual discovery of what holds true for the moment and may change at any time. In these words on my past, I am only able to bring forward a suggestion of happenings that stretch over forty years or more, right back to a World War II sugar ration coupon issued in the name of "Baby Cherry." I struggled to return to the beginning of my life as a poet. Pondering the reasons for my poetry I thought back as far as I could and came on an idea that I cannot let go of, that it all began with a dream.

In 1952, at seven years of age, I was lying on the living room floor of our family home in west Los Angeles playing with our pet, a black cat with white paws. Boots purred deeply. Obviously content, she lay on her side as I sang her a song, some silly thing that had popped into my head. I don't know if she understood my words. In my child's mind I hoped so. After a while, she got up, stretched, and sauntered off, looking back momentarily from across the room. Then she sprang onto the couch and lay there quietly. I felt inexplicably hurt, as if she didn't care for me anymore. I approached her and when I reached out my hand to touch her, she leapt from her comfortable throne and ran across the living room rug. I followed, hoping to gain her full attention once again. Boots wanted none of this. She slinked under the bed in my parents' room and remained there the rest of the afternoon. My pleading did nothing to bring her out. Defeated, I went into the bedroom I

Neeli Cherkovski

shared with my sister, Tanya, two years older and possibly closer to Boots than I, and sulked, face down in the pillow, feeling betrayed, rejected. That night I developed a fever. In our bedroom, a painting dominated the wall opposite our beds, of a cat circling a track or open field. It was a black cat, just like Boots, whose body was stretched to its full length, legs in the air, front and back, in a fast run. I looked

Neeli and his sister, Tanya, Los Angeles, California, about 1952

up at the painting in the midst of my sickness. The cat, no longer suspended in midair, began to make its way around the painting with a determined pace. I rubbed my eyes, hardly believing what I saw. Now the cat became a phantomlike streak of colors. Fascinated, I nonetheless fell asleep and immediately began dreaming. I wandered through a dark forest of snarling felines. Some nipped me. Bleeding and in tears, I came to the edge of the forest where fields of tall grass lay before me. In the distance a huge mountain loomed over the plain. There were jagged rocks sticking up from the flat lands. From behind one Boots bolted into view. I called her. She turned toward me with a human face. We came toward one another as the sky darkened. When I bent my knees to stroke her black hair, we were hurtled into an abyss and swirled downward together. During that fall I saw her glittering eyes and felt her paws touch my body.

This dream is the foundation for what I would choose as my life's vocation, poetry, and is very much a part of my life even forty-three

years later. Freudian interpretations aside, a kind of surrealism, or supernaturalism, came forward in that dream. The process of seeing had popped up in an entirely new way and made an indelible impression. I feared the painting after that and thought of it as a talisman, a religious object or something filled with magic. There is a reality beyond the ordinary, a poetic, as opposed to a prosaic, view of the world, an unpremeditated outlook relying on spontaneous revelation of world and word. My inability to grasp the basics of arithmetic may come from this nonformulaic way of thinking.

I see Samuel Taylor Coleridge's poem "Kubla Khan" as a beacon of this kind of imaginative perception. It brings us a world midway between wakefulness and sleep, a semi-dream in which we may wander fearfully. The poem, revealed to Coleridge in an opium-induced dream, became my companion, pieces of it helping to shape my own reveries during the day or before falling asleep. Its rhythms and the way the natural world flowed into Coleridge's vision of the fabled city, Xanadu, attract me even today. What the poem taught me was the importance of listening to the rhythms of my own body, of my own intellect, and to connect them with my work. There's a vital resonance between Coleridge's wild, swinging music and the words I heard in the synagogue as the rabbi chanted from Hebrew Scripture.

I returned home from playing in an open field four blocks from Rosewood Street in west Los Angeles and down the hill from the Douglas Aircraft Plant to find our small stucco house empty. Neither my mother nor sister were there. Panicked, I ran outside and called for my mother. Rosewood Avenue seemed empty, alien. Even the green lawns, well-trimmed hedges, and small trees in sidewalk planters made me uneasy. I ran back inside and called frantically for my mother again. Beads of sweat formed on my forehead. Without thinking I went to the bookshelf and tossed several books onto the floor. Then I threw the sofa pillows all over the living room and I turned over a chair. In the kitchen, I emptied a box of cornflakes onto the dining table and yanked open the refrigerator, sending a carton of milk splashing across the green linoleum. As I made my way to the bedroom, the front door opened and my mother stepped inside. "What's going on here?" she demanded. I cried out, "Mommy, there were robbers in the house." She didn't buy this, so

I accused her of neglecting me. She had been at a neighbor's house, she said, and proceeded to give me a spanking and then pronounced that I help clean up the mess. I can still feel the emptiness of that house and am often startled by the fullness people give to a place.

In school we learned how to write our names. Even though I had begun to grasp the rudiments of writing, I lagged behind in reading. At the beginning of the next school year, after a summer of play, my mother decided to take matters in hand and teach me how to read. She sat me down at our rickety dining table where a letter of the alphabet lay on the table in place of my dinner plate. It was the letter "A," which my mother pronounced "AH." She asked to me repeat it and then gave it to me to hold. I took it in hand. "Go ahead," she coaxed. "Ah," I said, repeating the letter. Next the "B," pronounced "BUH," was handed to me. I formed it correctly as well. Within a week I had read through *Dick and Jane* and eagerly asked for more books. Letters became real. No longer were they abstractions, but actual sounds you could touch and feel. One month later I received a gold star for being the best reader in class. My teacher expressed amazement. The principal telephoned my mother to tell her that the school was considering skipping me a grade. School went easier after that. I stood before my class and read an entire chapter from our textbook. I loved the word "ball" and the word "hill" and the word "dog." As I spoke them, I felt like crawling inside the words I loved, sheltered in their warmth.

In the summer of 1953, Lynne Eddington, a dark-haired, tan boy who lived across the street, played with me in the service alley behind Rosewood Avenue. At the end of our block stood a peafield that later became the site for a junior high school. We weren't allowed to cross over there, but that didn't matter as the alley provided plenty of room for exploration. There was tall grass everywhere and little openings into the backyards on either side of the alley. This was our personal jungle. "Hey, Neeli, look at this," he yelled, pointing out an old truck tire propped against the wall behind the Crockett's garage. I came over to examine it when suddenly Jim Crockett popped into view, a tall, lanky kid with hair falling over his forehead. "Your real name is Nelson," he shouted as I drew back in horror. "Yeah, my mom told

me," he said. "They started calling you Neeli 'cause it rhymes with squealy." I turned away in shame, running along the alley toward my own home. I entered the kitchen to find my mother busily preparing lunch. "Why do I have two names?" I asked. She explained that my father had named me after the famous British Admiral, Lord Nelson. Hearing this, however, didn't ease the pain of being ridiculed. Confounding matters, she explained that I also had a Hebrew name, Natan Israel, which, when translated, means "He gave to Israel."

My birth certificate reads Nelson Innis Cherry. As to the origin of *Innis*, my father, Sam, believes it was inspired by George Inness, the nineteenth-century American landscape painter, but there is the matter of the different spelling. Still, that is what he remembers. Only years later did my mother, Clare, type the name Neeli Cherry in parenthesis on the certificate. And still more years passed before I added "Neeli Cherkovski" to my passport. It's funny how people guard their names. I like having two surnames on my checking account and a passport with two identities in one. Somewhere along the line my paternal grandfather either got swindled into the name Cherry or simply chose it soon after landing in America to better blend in with the new culture. Many people want to know where *Neeli* came from. No matter how often I asked my parents about it, they've never given a straight answer for how it popped into existence. What I have learned is that it's also a Hebrew word standing for "The people of Israel shall live forever." When I traveled to Israel in 1970 I discovered that it was a popular girl's name. My mother's maiden name was Weitzman. Many times I've thought I should have had the name Neeli Weitzman Cherkovski. Yet her surname sounds foreign to my sense of self, a name that doesn't fit. My first poetry publications bear the name Neeli Cherry. So too my individual chapbooks of poetry published before I moved to San Francisco in 1975. Largely influenced by Lawrence Ferlinghetti, who had gone by the name Lawrence Ferling for much of his adult life before returning to the original family surname, I used Neeli Cherkovski on two books of poetry in 1975 and have kept the name ever since.

I sailed through much of public school without being bothered by the name Nelson until chancing on an arithmetic teacher named Walter Mayo who took it upon himself to call me by my officially registered name. This caused me grief, considering that it had been brandished before me years earlier in the alley off of Rosewood. I felt as if that strange name had followed me down the highway to San Bernardino where we had moved and would always sneak up on me at an unsuspecting moment. This torment began on the first day of arithmetic class. Mayo refused to let go of it, even after I explained that other teachers called me Neeli. "It's what I'm used to," I explained. "Young man," he shouted, "this is what it says on your records and this is what I will use!" I pointed out that the name Neeli also appeared there, but that made no difference to him. Compounding matters, I found it impossible to memorize the multiplication tables or to master long division. Percentages dealt me a deathblow. Mayo tortured my Neeli Cherry dreams. I'd wake up worried about the next day's humiliations.

My family moved from Los Angeles to San Bernardino, sixty miles east, in 1954. The plan was for my father to join a war surplus business operated by my mother's family, a position he accepted, though his real passion was photography. But it was my mother who had willed the family to San Bernardino in order to be near her mother. Back then, the highway east was lined with vineyards and orange groves. All of that is gone now, replaced by housing tracts, shopping malls, and bits of urban wasteland. San Bernardino itself, once surrounded by groves, is the vortex of a depressing urban sprawl breathing much of the bad air from Los Angeles as it backs up against the San Bernardino Mountains. As if to accent this, the San Manual Indian Reservation at the town's northernmost boundaries has a gambling casino. The city's wide streets were laid out in the mid-nineteenth century by Mormon pioneers who had been sent West from Salt Lake City. Living there from age seven, I still looked on Los Angeles as my hometown, drawn to it by its sheer size and the lure of its history as a Spanish and Mexican settlement.

We settled into a yellow stucco house with a sizable front lawn, two large trees, and a row of bushes in front. There were rose bushes lining one side of our driveway and they became the lifelong charges of my father, who watered them, trimmed them, and kept them amazingly healthy. Not surprisingly, a number of my early poems were about roses. The backyard consisted of a patio with a red concrete

surface in the middle of which stood an elm tree, and a sprawling green or lawn, separated from the patio by a brick wall coated with white paint. Massive trees stood at the end of the lawn. In a sizable elm beyond the wall I built a tree fort at age eleven, the perfect place in which to daydream of life in distant kingdoms. An elegy to my mother, written after her death from cancer in 1991, recalls our backyard.

> I've been saving this,
> your death,
>
> now it rises
> from our backyard,
> already taking
> a commanding lead,
> along with the lemon tree
> in dust and
> mud
>
> incidentally,
> the lemons remain,
> they're green
> this time of year,
> a few have fallen
> and rotted
>
> the peach trees, all three,
> are gone, the fig tree
> is lost, it never
> was much. even
> the walnut trees
> are diminished, almost
> as if they had lost
> a battle to an unseen enemy
>
> they have open wounds,
> sap oozes out, running
> down the bark
>
> I really gave
> a terrific eulogy
> two months ago, the mourners
> trembled
>
> now death rises
> from our backyard, a place
> of thorns, ants, weeds,
> patches of grass
>
> we sold the house
> to a prison guard
> from Chino
>
> this means good-bye
> to all the anger
> and our real happiness

hello to every man and
woman
who ever sailed
on a sea of pain

to all keepers of the flame
who abandoned their posts

This poem was written a week after my
mother's funeral at a time when I felt particularly pained about the past. The yard had been
a place of life, of play through long summertime hours where I had once planted a vegetable garden. To write "now death rises from
our backyard" was an affirmation of change.
The poem offered me distance from my mother's
passing, the last two lines a comment on the
human condition from the beginning of time.

Inside of our house there were paintings,
ceramic bowls, shelves of books, and standard
department-store furniture. My bedroom walls
were lined with books, including a 1913 set of
Encyclopedia Britannica with tiny print and detailed maps that unfolded into a large format.
I spent the late hours of every night combing
through my library, often reading three or four
books at a time, a habit I've taken along into
adulthood. My manual typewriter, a hand-me-
down from my mother, sat on a desk cluttered
with papers, only a bit of it homework. This
room offered near perfect solitude once I was
inside of it, often with the door locked. The
only discordant note was that my window faced
the neighbor's driveway and the door to their
kitchen. Luckily, as the years progressed, a barrier
of camellia plants grew tall enough so that I
could open the window curtains and remain
unseen.

I attended Arrowview Junior High School
in San Bernardino, the school my mother also
attended during the '30s. The main building,
consisting of administrative offices, the campus
library, and many of the classrooms, was a musty,
Spanish-style structure with a creaky staircase
leading up to the second floor. In seventh-
grade speech class, the teacher, Mr. Biggs, a
balding, bespectacled man with a high-pitched
voice and kindly demeanor, read "Thanatopsis"
by William Cullen Bryant before the class. He
asked what we thought of it. Everyone loved
the poem. Only I had reservations. Biggs grew
agitated. Not to be cornered by his growing
wrath, that I should question the importance
of one of America's major poets, I vowed that
I would write a poem on death superior to

With his father, Sam Cherry, 1954

Bryant's, or at least more understandable to
modern ears. Biggs smiled. "Did you hear that,
class?" he asked pointedly.

The next day I brought my poem, now luckily
lost, to class. And I am ready to admit that it
didn't live up to "Thanatopsis," but I had allowed my rebel self to be heard, and I liked
that. Word of my challenge to Biggs and Bryant
spread around school, to students and faculty
alike. I had declared myself a poet, which didn't
keep me from being sent to the dean's office
on countless occasions for behavior problems.
Those visits to the office of Milo Philbin, a
short man with close-cropped hair and thin
mustache, were a welcome relief. Not only was
I spared the agony of sitting in the classroom,
but my sense of being an outsider only increased, finally taking wing. Philbin's secretary,
Yvonne Ensey, treated me with disdain. Knowing nothing of my poetry, she saw me as just
another troublesome child. With a severe expression etched onto her face, she would moan,
"So, it's you again. Well . . . just be seated
with your face to the wall, like the bad boy

you are, until Mr. Philbin is available." I'd turn my face to the wall, close my eyes, and think of how demons might come to lay a curse on Miss Ensey for her snooty attitude. Eventually, Philbin would call me into his office where he'd lecture in high rhetorical style on the need to behave. He usually began, "Now, young fellow, let's talk man to man." One time he asked why I had dared to whistle during a multiplication lesson. "Because I'm happy," I told him. This brought a stern rebuke. "We're not in school to be happy. We are here to learn."

Gradually, because of my upcoming bar mitzvah, I cultivated an intellectual life having little to do with public school education. This outside reading is what convinced me that I should stand up to Mr. Biggs and make another attempt at challenging Bryant's poem. I had already written five or six poems on small, half-size sheets of paper. I bought a thick black looseleaf binder and placed them inside. My typing, which consisted of one tap on the keyboard at a time, produced a thick black lettering which appealed to my young esthetic sense. I had read a few poems by e. e. cummings—certainly not in school—and wrote in lowercase.

My first poem was written during my first semester in junior high school, probably a few months before I tackled Bryant's "Thanatopsis." I found a picture in the encyclopedia of the Amida Buddha (Great Buddha) at Kamakura, Japan, and was fascinated. It led me to look up more information and I learned that the statue was 52 feet tall and an important monument in the Buddhist world. My poem reads, in part, "Buddha, Golden Buddha, Buddha sing, Kamakura. Tears. Darkness. Light. Laughter. Buddha, Golden Buddha. . . ." I played a bit of the alchemist in this poem as the Buddha is actually constructed of bronze. One of the big influences on my growth and development as a writer was the *Pali* canon, specifically the *Dhammapada*, a collection of the Buddha's sayings. My father had given it to me and suggested I study it for the ethical teachings it contained. In this ancient text, I discovered a guide for daily conduct. "Through many a round of birth and death I ran, then found the builder that I sought . . . ," it reads. The passage goes on to underscore the need to put an end to craving. Only after accomplishing this is the

mind able to rest. I probed deep into my young life and found a myriad of lives there.

This awkward beginning, written while I was studying Hebrew, convinced me that there was no alternative to poetry. Nobody stood over me when I wrote. The words were my own. Hungrily, I waited for something else to pop into my head. A few days later I wrote a poem on Mahatma Gandhi, influenced by Eric Erikson's biography, quickly followed by a poem on the clash between traditional ways of life and the coming of modern civilization to Black Africa.

In ninth grade I had a rough time in arithmetic class, so much so that I dreaded leaving for school each morning, fearful of being called on to work out a problem at the blackboard. Most of my friends studied algebra, while I continued to struggle with long division and percentages. The teacher, a bald, dour man named Mr. Burling, made me feel small. One day I blurted out, "I don't need any of this. I'm a poet." As a reward for this declaration, I was sent to the dean's office. In sharp contrast, Mr. Franks, the science teacher, gave me an "A" for the year based on the growing body of poems I wrote.

By the end of the '50s, I had read Walt Whitman's *Leaves of Grass* and returned to it frequently, searching out passages that appealed to me, letting the poet's rhapsodic flow of words carry me along. Whitman's ability to sweep the reader into his rhythms held me. No matter how much I read him, I'd invariably come upon a new direction, a flow of language with surprising twists and turns. His insistence on a universal pattern underlying all of life continues to appeal to me:

Each of us is inevitable,
Each of us is limitless—each of us with his or
    her right upon the earth,
Each of us allow'd the eternal purports of the
    earth,
Each of us here as divinely as any is here.

I remember showing these lines from "Salut au Monde" to my father, drawing a comparison between Whitman's sentiments and those I'd seen expressed in the writings of Gandhi and in the message of the Buddha. When it came time to write my bar mitzvah speech, I wanted to include Whitman and Gandhi, but was dissuaded from doing so and instead had to content myself with quoting Jewish sources.

Even when I argued with my mother that the very point of what I wanted to get across could be confirmed by bringing in voices from other cultures, she wouldn't allow it. "At other times, yes," she said. "Not in a bar mitzvah speech."

My own poems began to take on a Whitman-like quality, to the point of imagining myself writing my own "Song of Myself." I had come in possession of a massive compilation of the "good gray poet's" writings, *The Poetry and Prose of Walt Whitman,* which I lugged along to school. In social studies class one afternoon the teacher interrupted his lesson to ask what I found so interesting in the book I was reading. How could I tell him that I was reading "The Sleepers," a section of *Leaves* touching on sexuality? It turned out that I didn't have to say anything, as Mr. Kucera, normally an affable man, marched sternly past the other students and snatched the book out of my hands. He took it to his desk, slammed it down, and continued the lesson. All I could think of for the rest of the hour was getting the book back into my hands. When the bell rang I raced to retrieve it. "Not so fast," Kucera said. "What do you find so interesting here?" I told him Whitman taught me a lot about literature and life. "But he's not helping you with social studies," Kucera warned.

San Bernardino in the late '50s, those long-gone Eisenhower years, had an old town center, filled with ornate movie palaces, all-night cafes frequented by bikers, drifters, and other restless souls, corner drugstores with fancy soda fountains, and a skid row leading from the central shopping district to the Santa Fe train depot, a brown facade Spanish structure with an antique waiting room of uncomfortable green benches and dank public toilets. Across from the station stood the Santa Fe Yards, where a roundhouse and gigantic repair shops reminded people that San Bernardino evolved as a railroad town. Several blocks from the station was a 1920s library with narrow shelves and shadowy corners. I spent long hours there and felt a sense of loss when they tore it down to replace it with a newer building. The YMCA, equally squalid, was where I ran through long summer days watching movies, playing chess, and swimming in the basement pool.

Amidst the hodgepodge of crumbling buildings and shoddy storefronts, Pick's Book and Pen Shop stood out . . . its crowded shelves

and old-fashioned ceiling with fans and big yellow lights perfectly framed the elderly Austrian Jewish immigrant couple who ran the shop. True to the sign in front of the shop, there were also several cases of fountain pens and fine inks. Even though I didn't own a fountain pen until well into my forties, I loved staring at them in their protective display cases. Until my parents opened their own bookstore in a shopping area at the north end of town, this is where I bought my books. For two or three years I piled up a huge collection of Mentor paperbacks, mostly nonfiction works on everything from the Aztecs to the Turkish Empire. One Saturday I came across a Peter Pauper Press edition of the poems of Arthur Rimbaud, illustrated with woodblocks. I tore into these translations and fell in love with Rimbaud's view of the world, especially as it appears in the poem "The Drunken Boat." I felt a kinship with his search for the past, most likely because it showed me that a poet could look back in time and feel at one with ancient man. I've come to feel this quality is one of the most important features of my writing. Already, in 1962, at age sixteen, I had written:

> When I was a young child and the earth
>   was something newborn,
> Each hour was an eternal lifetime of
>   innocence,
> Each day a new sky-light of noises, sounds
>   calling me from a distance . . .

We lived near the San Bernardino Mountains. Walking from the wash near our home into the foothills, I came easily up into Coldwater Canyon, nestled between arid walls and filled with ponds of near-freezing water and narrow passageways. It served as my private wilderness. I'd go up there with a book and settle in by a particularly shady pond, rocky cliffs on either side. I can still hear the creek water flowing and sense the presence of dragonflies that abounded there. Further up the mountain, despite the burgeoning communities and resort areas, there were forested slopes and meadows where deer and black bear survived.

Another wilderness existed, one that my father revealed. His love for the wild took us to mountain meadows, desert expanses, wind-swept passes, and untamed coastal beaches throughout the American West. We avoided motels, opting for campgrounds and roadside places where he pitched a tent. Among the lessons I learned was how to build a campfire, how to chop wood for it, and how to keep the camping area clean. He led me on long and often taxing hikes into the countryside around where we'd camp. In "Job, Suffering," I go back to these times:

> nearby a creek speaks, morning;
> the remains of song, a story to be seized
> and built on, fidelity, hillside covered in
>   thick foliage, a trail
> draws the mind . . .

The high point of my hiking days with my father came when we ascended Mount Whitney, the highest point in the Sierra Nevada mountain chain at 14,500 feet above sea level. Hiking up those switchbacks, my father pointed out changes in the environment, the dramatic difference one can experience in the kinds of plant life that grow on the mountain. I learned to identify juniper, Ponderosa pine, and Douglas fir on that trip. When we came to the tree line, that point above which no sizable trees can grow, I felt as if I was entering a new world. Exhausted, yet exhilarated, we reached the summit and stood peering down at the wilderness lakes thousands of feet below and out across the Owens Valley to the Nevada Desert. Back then I wrote:

> wind, a high place, higher
> than the lights of any dream town
> wide cracking sky, a blue lake hardly
>   visible, below. . . .

In 1960, I met a twenty-seven-year-old poet named Jory Sherman, author of a book of poems, *So Many Rooms.* He had recently moved to San Bernardino from San Francisco and beguiled me with stories of the writer's life up north. He described a little known poet in Los Angeles named Charles Bukowski, a man whom he boasted as having written poems equal to those of the fabled Beatniks. "He's a loner," Sherman said. "Buk spends much of his time behind drawn shades, and when he's not there he's either at the race track placing bets or working at the post office." I told Sherman that I'd like to meet him, especially after reading the poems in *Flower, Fist and Bestial Wail.* "I'll see what I can do," Jory said, not sure if the reclusive Bukowski would be up to it. With a meeting finally arranged, I wrote a long poem to my new hero, basing it on stories Sherman

told of Bukowski's life bumming around the country, living in small hotels, and working dead-end jobs, a life I knew from tales my father told about a similar life he had led in the years before World War II.

We drove into Los Angeles with my father to meet the poet. He lived in a ramshackle apartment building on Mariposa Street in Hollywood. When Bukowski opened the door I found myself face-to-face with a tall, round-shouldered man who held out a surprisingly slender hand. His voice was gentle and he had manners to match. We walked inside. I handed him the poem I had written and he read through it. Calling me "Little Rimbaud" he offered us beer and then started spinning out the magic. When I told him of my difficulties getting along in high school, he spoke of his own problems in school. "I was the frozen man, an outsider," he confided. "Everything they taught seemed false." Soon after this first get-together, he sent me his second book, *Run with the Hunted,* with the inscription:

> For Neeli Cherry, I hope that I have awakened some of your young sleep. Charles Bukowski. 7-23-62. p.s. you should have heard some of Franky Roosevelt's fireside chats. God! A-D 1932, on. c.b.

Below that he noted corrections in the text and drew a man smoking a cigarette with a bottle of beer at his side: Himself, of course.

On a visit to San Bernardino, I had another experience with a poem I had written for Bukowski. He relates the incident best in his letter of October 1963:

> Well, kid, I got your burnt Bukowski poem bust-out booklet, and it was something like finding angels female with good figures and some wing in the Daily Racing Form and I thank you for the toast (burnt) and I guess you ain't neva going to forget I threw one of your poems in the fire, but you've got to remember it was a very hot night and the fingers of my mind were sweating. I was almost out of stuff to drink and your old man kept running in and out of the back door with this constant stagger of logs, and I was standing in front of the fireplace and it got hotter and hotter and I thought I was a wheel from the old Lafayette Escadrille and when you handed me the poem there was nothing left to do but dump it with the rest of me. . . .

Bukowski was responding to my having sent him the flame-scorched poem he had tossed in the fire. His letter went on to praise my poems, saying they had "a blaring hardstone sense that is closer to feeling than the hanky drillwork of our contemporaries." As I think back on this incident I rediscover the love I have for the word "Fire." How I like saying, thinking it. The word appears often in my poetry and is the title for several poems. I return to the campfires I sat around as a child . . . fires my father and I had built together. When I read T. S. Eliot's "The Fire Sermon" in *The Wasteland* I am amazed to find the opening lines so close to those experiences: "The river's tent is broken; the last fingers of leaf / Clutch and sink into the wet bank."

I went to school one day in my sophomore year in high school, armed with Bukowski's volume *Longshot Pomes for Broke Players* and showed it to my English teacher. She wondered why he had misspelled the word "Poems" on the cover. I explained that it was done on purpose. She asked that I recite a few of the poems, which prompted a lecture on the necessity of rhyme. When I countered, "Well, Whitman doesn't rhyme," she told me that the poets I needed to study were Henry Wadsworth Longfellow, James Russell Lowell, Edgar Arlington, Robert Frost. I argued, contrary to the critical thought of the times, that all kinds of poetry were okay and that we had to keep an open mind.

I had also been reading the Beat poets. Lawrence Ferlinghetti's poems first came into my hands while I was still in junior high school. Poems such as "Dog" and "Autobiography" communicated directly to me due to the poet's visual sense and ability to focus on common themes. From time to time I carried on a dialogue between myself and an imaginary Ferlinghetti who cautioned me to keep the populist voice. Bukowski played in the same courtyard of the narrative poem, but I gradually developed an aesthetic that led me elsewhere. What I've come to realize is that each poem, at the moment of conception, finds its own form, intuitively.

My earliest published poems had a surreal quality, although I didn't yet know of that literary movement. I had seen the works of Salvador Dali, however, and surely had read poems by surrealists, but without having given any thought to their underlying literary theories.

The Wormwood Review (1963), a journal that survived for more than thirty years, published "a cute girl named eternity," written in my high school English notebook:

> a cute girl named eternity and her hour
> of dawn before the morning,
> rooftop generation of birds singing
> such songs as there is plenty of
> time before the dawn to live another
> tomorrow.
> as if one could not be wise for living
> his rightful moment of possession and
> dewdrops sunpeep.
> moisture gleaming.
> come dawn it seems that nothing has
> happened except the turning of the
> dripping clock and the rising of the
> sun.

It was signed "neeli cherry," yet another form of my name, this time in e. e. cummings lowercase. In 1965 I published "The Woman at the Palace of the Legion of Honor" in *Epos*, a journal edited by an eccentric left-wing couple from a small Florida town. I don't recall the work having any antecedents, and was proud to have moved beyond abstract themes to ones rooted in concrete imagery and telling a story.

> She does not know that I am staring at her
>   as she stands in her bright yellow dress
>   looking at something by Rodin,
> She does not know that I believe in the solemn
>   things sculpted by Rodin,
> Looking like poetry
>   or the secret of clay.
>
> If only I were brave and handsome,
>   I would let her hear my mind
>   as I equate her with the statue.
> I don't think she has even glanced at me,
>   and here I am, so close by,
>   confused,
>   listening to Rodin,
> And listening to the woman
>   who stands there,
>
> looking like poetry
>   or the secret of clay.

I had written the poem on a visit to San Francisco's Palace of the Legion of Honor and its Rodin sculpture court. When I showed it to Jory Sherman he suggested I send Bukowski a copy. Later, I received a phone call from him in which he praised the clarity of the poem.

In 1962 I decided to publish my own literary magazine. I became aware of these homegrown and lively journals through Jory Sherman again, who published in them regularly and knew many of the editors. Generally printed in mimeograph or inexpensive photo-offset in editions rarely over 500 copies, they served as an arena for young poets and writers often isolated in towns far from big-city literary scenes. I chose the name *Black Cat Review* and solicited poems, first from high school friends, and then, with Sherman's help, from a wider circle. By this time my parents had opened Cherry's Book and Art Center. It occupied a long, narrow storefront in the north end of San Bernardino, down the street from a bowling alley and bakery and across from a Christian bookstore. Their idea was to have a solid selection of books in every field, but to specialize mainly in literary and philosophical works. They bought an old-fashioned cash register, put up movable shelves, and kept the place light and airy. My father's lack of a formal education hadn't kept him from acquiring a broad knowledge of books. One of his finest moments came when we held a book party for Irving Stone's *The Agony and the Ecstasy*. We sold nearly one hundred copies of the book in its hardback edition. Such moments were unfortunately infrequent. Buyers didn't want to understand that no matter what the price of a book, we made the same small profit. I'd make sure we were well-stocked with the classics and in Beat literature, most of the latter had to be ordered from the book jobbers in Los Angeles. In the back section of the store my father opened an art gallery, showing works by local talent, as well as by San Francisco artists he'd known from the past. In the gallery, we held poetry readings, folk music recitals, and discussion groups. One heated discussion involved the issue of censorship. My family took the censoring of Henry Miller's *Tropic of Cancer* seriously and my father refused to take copies of the book off the shelf at a time when other stores were selling it under the counter.

Black Cat Review was named after San Francisco's Black Cat Cafe, where my parents had hung out in pre-Pearl Harbor days. The cover reproduced a watercolor of the cafe by Dong Kingman, a noted Chinese-American artist. Aside from poetry and illustrations, I included selections from letters Jory Sherman had written to me in his position as Advisory Editor:

Dear Neeli—I thought you might be interested in running a poem of Lorca's in your Black Cat. I don't know if you have read much of him, but he is worth the time. I've concentrated so far mostly on translating his *Gacelas*, mostly because they are short, and rooted in gypsy song so much that they cry out to be read . . . regardless of my translation. Lorca was such a beautiful man, a pure poet, and nothing he wrote was bad.

That kind of attention led me to seek out Garcia Lorca on my own. I read the available work in English, or at least the texts I could find, and even worked my way through a short biography. Later, Sherman exposed me to Stéphane Mallarmé and landed me Ray Bradbury's first published poem, "Something Wicked This Way Comes." Sherman advised in another letter, "Don't be afraid to revise . . . every genius makes mistakes . . . and when it happens they are dillies . . . part of the dichotomy of it all." Sherman was the first of a series of mentors with whom I became closely acquainted.

My mother wrote early childhood education books, the result of nearly forty years as an educator and director of a nonsectarian nursery school at the Jewish Temple in San Bernardino, a school which now bears her name. Her philosophy of education centered on the "open" classroom and on teaching kids self-reliance, but not at the expense of a happy childhood. She criticized educators and parents who pushed their children into academic pursuits long before they are physically or emotionally able to handle those activities. In *Think of Something Quiet: A Guide to Serenity in the Classroom*, she inscribed for me, "Dear Neeli, Thank you for keeping me inspired to always try to do my very best so I can be a 'writer'—not just a money-making author." She was an accomplished communicator of her theories and her books remained brisk sellers after her death. Much of her success centered on her enthusiasm as she flew from city to city, conference to conference, promoting her work and her ideas on early childhood education. The book that most intrigued me was *Parents, Please Don't Sit on Your Kids: A Guide to Non-Punitive Discipline*. She worked tirelessly and conducted parenting workshops, encouraging the participants to let go of their inhibitions and become children again, or, as she described herself, to walk "with both feet planted firmly in

Mother, Clare Cherry

turned our kitchen into a biological laboratory, balancing petri dishes and test tubes against meat loaf and the morning cereal. I remember standing on the stage accepting a set of encyclopedias as an award for my efforts. There she was in the first row, modestly dressed, as always beaming with pride at her achievement.

My father, with his swarthy complexion and dark mustache, was frequently mistaken for a Mexican or Italian. The only vehement prejudice I heard from him was that "Rich people are sons of bitches." He constantly berated the local business community for "screwing people over" and encouraged me to stay out of their world. As a man who had worked much of his life as a longshoreman, house painter, and other such jobs, he radiated a sense of physical good health. His heydays were the years spent in San Francisco where he and my mother lived in the late '30s. Their hangout was the Black Cat Cafe whose habitués became larger-than-life figures during my growing-up years. My father recorded the atmosphere of that era in a series of haunting photographs. Looking at these images of a large, high-ceilinged cafe with paintings on the wall atelier style, I imagined sitting there with Spanish Civil War veterans, world travelers, hard-drinking journalists, artists, and writers.

the air." Her emphasis on intuition, creativity, and self-exploration influenced my own direction as a writer.

But did my mother sit on me? In a sense, yes. Strong and dominating, even competitive she was, at the same time, a champion of my chosen vocation. Rather than be alarmed by the thought "My son, the poet," she pronounced it a good thing, although she believed that having a profession, say as a psychologist or college professor, might make life easier. When I failed to perform well in junior high school, she wasn't alarmed, feeling that eventually my abilities would come to the fore. She wasn't overly concerned by my rebellion against arithmetic and science. Sympathizing, she advised the school authorities to let me chart my own course. Her one major flaw was her tendency to step in too often and too soon. In my first year of junior high school, when I showed some budding interest in science, I entered a competition at the science fair for the county of San Bernardino with a project, "Penicillin from the Soil," which became a Clare Cherry production. She

High school, as I remember it, bore little resemblance to those movie and television images of *Happy Days* or *American Graffiti* afternoons and evenings. To the contrary, I experienced those years as a burden. For one thing, I was aware of being an outsider, not just as a poet, but sexually as well. As an adolescent male who felt physically attracted to others of my own sex, I had nowhere to turn. In junior high school I had some playful sexual encounters with other boys my own age, but somehow, as we became older, all of that was put aside. Two of the boys I had felt closest to had drifted away, perhaps because of the homosexual element in our friendship. I had no adult to turn to, not even my parents for all their liberalism, and so, like other homosexuals of the time, I kept quiet. The schoolyard was full of anti-gay comments and the media portrayed homosexuals as sleazy characters who molested children or as empty-headed, super-effeminate oddballs. Yet there were homosexuals who came to our bookstore. One was a psychiatrist who became a friend of my parents, a renegade

While attending rabbinical school, Los Angeles, 1969

from his profession who in later years moved to San Francisco. He didn't speak much about his sexual preferences, although one day he talked with me about the great homoerotic poetry of Catullus and other Roman poets, exposing me to a side of literature I was ignorant of until then.

In 1965 I left San Bernardino Community College for California State University, Los Angeles, from which I would graduate with a B.A. in American Studies two years later. I played a leading role in the anti-war movement on campus, meeting with activists from the eastern universities, from UCLA, and from up north at UC Berkeley. Late in 1968, while taking graduate courses, I was arrested for a whole series of misdemeanor charges and subsequently went on trial in Los Angeles Municipal Court. This incident stemmed from an anti-Dow Chemical Company recruitment program at Cal State. Those of us in the antiwar movement were decrying the sale of napalm to the U.S. armed forces for use against the Vietnamese. During the three-week trial I found little time for writing. When

it came my turn to take the stand I told the jury how proud I felt to protest the war and Dow's complicity in it. A light moment came when the prosecutor asked where I had been during the order to disperse. I pointed out the bathroom on a map posted for the jury, telling them that that's where I was at the particular moment and managed to get a chuckle from the jurors. When I left the witness stand, the chief prosecutor leaned over and whispered in my ear, "You win some and lose some. . . . I think we just lost one."

After Cal State I moved on to rabbinical school, the Hebrew Union College, Jewish Institute of Religion, in Los Angeles. My first impulse for attending centered on a deferment from the draft. There was another reason, however. I had the idea that being a rabbi might be the perfect job for a poet. Certainly the Bible was filled with poetry: The Psalms, the Song of Songs, and much of the prophetic literature. During this time in the late '60s I saw a lot of Bukowski, spending long nights disposing of cases of beer in his east Hollywood apartment and cramming for my studies in rabbinical school. One night he rang to suggest that we put out a literary magazine. He wanted to call it *The Contemporary Review.* "You can do better than that," I said. Taking the challenge, he asked for three days. At two in the morning, three days later, he called to announce the birth of *Laugh Literary and Man the Humping Guns.* "Brilliant," I said. "Let's go to work." We managed three issues, often edited during our long drinking bouts in his dank, crowded living room, which also served as his writing studio.

After two years at the rabbinical school, I left for Europe and Israel to travel and write. I met a young man there, an American from a family in Beverly Hills, with whom I spent several nights of sexual delight, finally seeing him off at Ben-Gurion Airport. Tearfully, I returned to the kibbutz where I had been staying. While walking through the grounds on my free time, I came upon a tall young American woman who lived there with her husband, a New Yorker who wanted to make a go of it in Israel. We started talking, then went to her cottage, during which time she told me that her husband was on guard patrol up in the nearby Golan Heights. We made love and began a relationship, carried out while her husband played around with a string of women.

When she left for home in New York with her young son, having separated from her husband, I followed. It turned out that her father was a successful doctor in Long Island who took a liking to me. With his encouragement, we tried to make a go of it in the East, but the lure of California called, as did the draft board. I returned home, went for my physical at the induction center in Los Angeles, and, at the end of the day, a clerk looked me in the face saying, "You don't want to go to Southeast Asia, do you?" I answered, "No. Not at all." He smiled and said, "You don't have to," and handed me a deferment.

I stayed in San Bernardino awhile, running an alternative school, then working for the city government under a federal jobs program. In 1975 I joined the staff of state senator George Moscone of San Francisco. He planned to run for mayor of San Francisco and wanted me to work as a press aide. I drove up to the northern city and stayed with an old friend from San Bernardino. His roommate, an experienced gay man, took me out to a few of the bars

In Amsterdam, 1970

and I began having sexual encounters. Most of them were not ideal . . . I wanted a relationship in which sex counted as only a factor. A poem, written years later, recalls the mood of those early excursions into gay life:

Sutter at Post, near the Chinatown
gate, twin lions haunched for my annihilation,
copy of *Sonnets to Orpheus*
in my back pocket, breathing
brick stone glass steel girders, animated
sadness of a hotel, tour bus, green eyed,
full of ghosts nearly ran me down, I jumped
   quickly
out of the way, desire
embroiled in dust of doorways
and exit signs, dim
theater lights reflected in palms of the hustlers
lined up outside of the St Francis Hotel, lean
dream machine, dark taxi dragon heads,
tyrannosaurus blood, easy
money for the young ideal, asleep
later in a bed of drugs, I talked
with a kid from Cheyenne, made jokes, and
when he slipped into my hunger I was suddenly
alone, he pointed out the way to a
bar, a favorite in those days,
streetsigns fragrant flowered dusty fingered

I stood over the shadow of a shadow
squinting, my promised land of fallen idols
falling down, ashes, tether-ball memories
the fading bones of moonlight
twisted, aged queens wiggling their butts
in my fevered forehead, come here
and be one song, divine eye shadow boy
or rabbit

This poem, written in 1996, brought back parts of my life from the '70s, long before AIDS colored the gay scene. It was a time when wide-open sex predominated and recalls how dazzled I had been by it all. Crucial for me at the time was my meeting with the poet Harold Norse, who has remained a close friend. I had first come across his poetry in 1962 and felt an immediate identification with his clear vision. We met at Bukowski's in the late '60s and he served for a time as an associate editor of *Laugh Literary*. I didn't come to know him well, however, until I came to San Francisco. Norse served as a guide into the labyrinthine world of gay life, often accompanying me to bars and bathhouses. We were able to laugh our way through many comical and often frustrating adventures in the gay world. On a few occasions we shared "pick-ups" in his rambling apartment on an old street tucked away between abandoned warehouses on the outskirts of downtown.

My political job didn't amount to much. The one virtue was that it did pay well and I managed to save a considerable sum of money. Because the Moscone campaign was only in its planning stages, however, I had no definite job description, so I wandered around town, spending a lot of time in coffee houses and gay bars. The campaign manager, a gruff old character who had worked on Lyndon Johnson's presidential race in 1964, found a stack of poems on my desk and decided I was more suited to another kind of job. Before he could fire me, however, I quit the political life and landed in North Beach, San Francisco's old Italian neighborhood and Bohemian enclave. I collected ninety dollars a week unemployment benefits for a year and a half . . . not bad for those days when a cappuccino cost ninety cents and a Chinatown meal could be had for under three dollars. I lived in a room barely bigger than a closet in the Italian American Hotel at Sansome

and Montgomery. At that time I met San Francisco's leading poet and literary figure, Lawrence Ferlinghetti, and often went to dinner with him in North Beach and Chinatown. He told me of an apartment for rent on the lower slope of Telegraph Hill, right in the center of North Beach: 28 Harwood Alley. The place consisted of a living room, bedroom, kitchen, and a tiny hallway. It stayed cool in the summertime due to its big windows, but turned into an icebox through the winter months, as it had no built-in heating. Over the years I would share Harwood Alley with a number of friends, including George Scrivani, a transplanted New Yorker. We were ourselves a flamboyant pair, often frequenting the coffee houses and gay bars of the city in search of young men. Having someone with whom to share both literary and social concerns helped to make sense out of the bohemian mayhem in which we so often found ourselves.

North Beach was a cauldron of energy, much of it undirected, some of it very focused.

At Cherkovski's North Beach apartment, 1979: (from left) poet Kirby Doyle, George Scrivani, Neeli Cherkovski, Raymond Foye, and John Mueller

Looking back, I realize that it served as a point of departure for those of us leading a literary life. It could be insular, too much the village, but the fact is we were often busily at work in other parts of the world. We'd return home to North Beach and live the cafe life. Even in San Francisco there was easy escape. Chinatown, a block away, was another world, a safe haven from the cafe regulars. The Polk Street area, over a hill, where there were several bookshops and gay bars, provided another escape from the daily whirlwind. I can now ponder what is real or unreal in friendship by looking backward to those intense times when conversation dominated. The remembrance of a kind phrase, an encouraging word, a smile, or the wink of an eye stands out in the mind. Conversely, the below-the-belt comment, proverbial knife in the back, and the insincere frown also stick out in memory's field.

The true secret of that neighborhood lay in its proximity to the financial district, an easy playground for the professional intelligentsia. But North Beach always preserved its self-generating integrity as a fully integrated slice of life with its own grocery stores, hardware stores, bars, coffee houses, clothing stores, bookstores, barbers, and legends. If one did not want to be alone, North Beach provided plenty of opportunity to be with people, to literally be absorbed in their triumphs and tragedies, and to strike up new friendships across a cafe table. Even the loner found solace there, living in any number of cheap hotels or small apartment buildings crawling up the side of Telegraph Hill or Russian Hill. It was Little Italy, New Chinatown, Old Bohemia, and post-Beatnik all in the same sweep, and it worked.

One morning I was walking along Columbus Avenue, the area's main thoroughfare, and the owner of a cafe I rarely frequented came out to ask where I had been. We did not know one another, but she spoke as if we were old friends. I told her that I had just come back from three months in Mexico and Guatemala. "You've lost a lot of weight," she commented and then asked if I had written any new poetry. We talked on. When I turned to leave, she said, "I forgot to tell you: Welcome home."

The magic of San Francisco and the entire Bay Area continues. Even though I've never experienced a *tertulia*, that traditional Spanish gathering of friends, I've maintained several important friendships that feed into all aspects of my life. With Jack Foley I've convened an ongoing conversation about the nature of poetry, how it evolves, how it affects the outer world, and how the experimental voice can help to meet the challenges of changing times. Joining in that dialogue is Ivan Argüelles, Jake Berry, and others in what can only be described as a new American movement. John Mueller is another poet with whom I have maintained an important relationship, along with Jack Hirschman and Kaye McDonough. Yet I have also found sustaining relationships far from San Francisco. In the spring of 1996 I read for the Honor's Program at the University of Massachusetts, Dartmouth, re-establishing close contact with the New England poet John Landry who had lived in North Beach during the late 1970s. I then read at Tufts University in an event coordinated by Joel Rosenberg, who had been my Hebrew teacher when I attended rabbinical school in Los Angeles during the 1960s. These readings, and others I've done in Germany and in the American South, constitute a vital part of what it means to be a practicing poet.

2.

During the spring of 1996 I left San Francisco for a nine-day drive through parts of Nevada and Utah. Accompanying me on the trip was Jesse Cabrera, a Philippine-born psychiatrist with whom I have lived for the past thirteen years. Jesse is also a painter who has shown work throughout the San Francisco Bay Area, as well as doing the artwork for the cover of *Animal*. We originally met in Los Angeles where he worked for the L.A. County Department of Mental Health. We crossed Donner Summit in the Sierra Nevada Mountains on the first day, encountering a snowstorm, the first of three on our trip. Next, we plunged into the Great Basin of Nevada, staying for a night in the ghost town of Virginia City. I had been there with my family at age seven and remembered the raucous saloons, Wild West storefronts, and mining debris on the far hillsides. Virginia City was home of the *Territorial Enterprise,* the newspaper where Mark Twain worked as a young reporter. That night we stayed in a renovated hotel more than one hundred years old. I picked up my pen to write at a fragile table with a small desk lamp at 2 A.M. but nothing came. Instead, I read a few pages from Nietzsche's

With Linda and Charles Bukowski, Los Angeles, 1990

Zarathustra before going to bed. After that, I didn't bother to write much. This trip was about abandoning ship for a few days, letting go.

At six in the morning I quickly dressed and walked down the empty streets of the old town. Even though the shops were filled with tourist goods, the storefronts remained largely unaltered from their nineteenth-century form and a number of the saloons have remained in operation since the days when Virginia City was a boom town. A year before I had been in Spain and Portugal, among much older and grander buildings, but these seemed almost as venerable, from my own backyard though separated from San Francisco by at least two mountain ranges and a lot of wide-open land. On the empty main street I felt as if I was making my way through the center of a poem. I wondered if my father had felt this way when he hopped off a freight train in the Great Depression, bumming around the country. Cold morning wind tore through my jacket and red pullover shirt. I rubbed my hands together, but to no avail. Despite the momentary chill, I felt warmed by the idea that poetry haunts me

wherever I step. I am continually being reborn as a poet no matter if I am writing or not. With that thought in mind, I found myself standing before a restaurant with an open sign. I entered and had a cup of coffee while peering out the back window toward a series of parched hillsides, subtly illuminated by the early morning light.

Later that day, as we drove along, passing through an arid landscape like those I had seen in Mexico from many a train and bus window, I recalled my trips South of the Border. Plunging headlong into the history and traditions of another culture can only take one so far. There's no doubt in my mind that those trips, sometimes by car, bus, train, and airplane, came out of a need to take to the road much as my father had years before. Usually I entered Mexico with no particular destination in mind. I'd let the impulse of the moment drive me forward. In Mexico City, a sprawling metropolis larger than New York City, I'd meander through entire neighborhoods, discovering out-of-the-way parks and gardens. Wherever I went I'd find Mexicans with whom I could talk in my poor Spanish. Mostly I was alone, and that was the main attraction on these journeys. Those nights of solitude and days of wandering through the ruins of Monte Albán or Teotihuacán, were inexhaustible wells from which I could draw inspiration years later. Out of these excursions, whether along the coast or in a mountain village, came a collection of poems, *Toltec Stone, Mexican Windows.* It is a book of discovery, not so much of what I found in Mexico, but what was revealed about myself while traveling in another country, surrounded by solitude. My Mexican poems span more than ten years, a notebook of a journey through both a real and an inner world, as in the following lines from a poem drawn out of my notebook ramblings from a trip down the western coast of Mexico in 1970:

> butterflies fly from path to bramble,
> from thorn to rose,
> from shade to spotlight.
> all over Mexico and in the park
> birds speak many languages
> although Spanish predominates.

> workers with figs on their heads
> and people wearing turquoise in their eyes
> and those erudite as moonlight
> converge on a hummingbird's nest
> near to green benches.
> my reveries crash against busy taxicabs,
> my desires rub elbows with Buddha-like poets
> who charm the Mexican night.

The Mexican muralists and painters of the twentieth century have always drawn me to the culture of Latin America. The painter I identify with most is Rufino Tamayo. He combined a deep knowledge of pre-Columbian art with the techniques of such modern trends as cubism, surrealism, and expressionism. I first came face-to-face with one of his paintings at an exhibition on Calle Francisco Madero in Mexico City. The colors, his strange muted form, and unsparing ability to interpret life in new and fantastic ways left a deep impression. His work provided the impetus for my Mexican collection. The poem "Eyes," quoted below, is dedicated to Tamayo. It calls to mind the Grand Hotel Cosmos, where I used to stay when in

Neeli with his partner Dr. Jesse Guinto Cabrera

Mexico City, a metropolis where it is only natural to mix the old and the new as I do in the following:

the banks close down
like boys zipping up their flies,
headlights drill into a Spanish
wilderness of mirrors
and swinging doors, pipes of pan
plead for our words to become
luminous as skies turn gray.
here is a man with an eye
in his mouth, with a hand
up his ass, with a finger
in his nose, with an electric fan
overhead in the hotel
of la noche oscura.
his body folds,
aviaries burn
all day and all night,
plumed birds evaporate, white doves
fall to the ground, common gulls
become ancient nuns.
a man with a monkey face
slams the hood of a beat-up Volkswagen
in the city of birds.

I had to clear my head driving along the 1996 U.S. roads and remember it was now north of the border in California's neighboring state and years later. Halfway across Nevada, on what has been dubbed "the loneliest road in the world," I sifted through the past, wondering just what is important to plunk into an autobiographical essay and what should be left out. It occurred that much of my life is patchworked into *Animal,* a book of poems published in 1996 by Pantograph Press. Fellow poet Ivan Argüelles was my publisher, making the editing process both challenging and enlightening. He encouraged me to keep the longer poems as the backbone of the book. The most ambitious poem in that collection, "Job, Suffering," is a record of coming-of-age in the Eisenhower Era and the early Vietnam War days. I was prompted by the theme of Job because of my mother's interest in that particular biblical legend. She had painted a whole series of abstract canvases centering on the life of Job and was taken by the story of faith that it invokes. While I have less concern for the particulars of Job's tale, I have certainly probed the meaning of suffering and the part it plays in our lives. Much of my poetry derives from a feeling of having fared worse than others. Perhaps we all have a bit of Job inside of us, and a feeling that we're

In front of City Lights Bookstore, with bookstore owner Lawrence Ferlinghetti and Mexican poet Juvenal Acosta, San Francisco, California

somehow especially singled out for suffering. This poem, thirty pages in length, came to me over a period of two weeks. I wrote the first section in one sitting and then revised it at least a dozen times before moving on to part two of the poem. Each section, as it revealed itself, brought back memories, not all clearly defined, but like shaded entrances to parts of my life that had a subtler meaning. The poem captures urban and country landscapes and delves into politics and metaphysics. I addressed Job as if he were a living person, standing right across from me. I remembered that on any given day, whether in a bank line, on a sidewalk, driving by another car, or sitting across people at a cafe table, I sensed the suffering of others. I began the poem by placing myself at age fifty, in San Francisco, and then delving back to my childhood during the Eisenhower years when, as the myth now goes, the country was so much calmer.

It wasn't World War Two or Korea, this war we
    held
in our banquet room, doomed from its
    inception, enter
and be seated, please pass the genuine knife,
    your elegance
hardly showing, it was the death of General
    Dwight David
Eisenhower on the TV screen, his face like rice
    paper, I mean
the body of what we perceive to be poverty,
    garage door opener, a
mean lawn, we kept our doors unlocked and
dwelt in the spirit of the major food group, a
    pyramid
with the eye of sedition on top. you can only
    butter
your bread so thick until the wound bleeds,
    LSD was not a gateway
don't bring my brother home that way, tarmac
    Jehovah, puto
in your defective heart, cowboy, William
    Westmoreland, General
that room in which you find room to ruminate
your poor kids in a yellow submarine
gem of memory as children of our July. picnics
grow up to murder newborn song at the table
    of another people
see, in your mailbox, prison poems of Ho Chi
    Minh, hummingbird
a warrior, waning fear of night, trouble with my
    heritage
send for the gorgon, go call the waiter, we
    want
to see 'tis of thee, to sing easily in the National
    Geographic
a man in picturesque garb, go build your Star
    War, Godzilla. . . .

In "Job, Suffering" I try to avoid nostalgia.
While writing it, I didn't feel an overwhelming
sense of loss, or that the good times were gone.
I ranged back over San Bernardino, and other
terrain, keeping a distance, letting the words
reveal what is important and what is not as
they flowed onto the page, establishing their
own coherency:

hold onto your eyes, come with us
laughing fit of adolescence, keep your
    family center
surly forehead, smart lips, we were once a
    community
imagine mid-day San Berdoo, the sonnets
    in asphalt
twilight birds, cat feet, the barber Irving

It was a poem called "Queer Careers," however, that had brought the *Animal* project
into focus. The concept was suggested by San
Francisco art dealer and writer Charles Wehren-
berg. This poem was written in one sitting,
surrounded by the ghosts of the homosexual
side of me. I was determined to make sense
of it all, not an easy task in a country still
plagued by its puritanical past and from the
vantage-point of a stable relationship depend-
ing more on mutual respect and common interests than anything else. But once the first
words of the poem found their way onto the
computer screen I sensed that I was on track.
The poem begins:

Feel your way to the door, your body laced in
    velvet, those
purple arms, his way of letting you know, his
way of describing you as an ugly man, a pushy
    man, a
man he can wrap around his fingers,
unburnt, unhurt, he lies on top of you before
pushing you away, world-wide, sacred,
he's going to build a career, don't step on it,
he's going to bust up your house
and appraise the ashes, he's a monster of
    arousal. . . .

From this personal vision the poem surveys the
spectrum of gay life, both public and private,
and delves into the AIDS bureaucracy with a
critical eye:

we're fighting for money
have hired an aggressive fund-raiser
who knows how to twist an arm
an emerging idea of just which disease
at the moment traps us in grief, use it
not a moment to lose

One of the more ironic passages tackles the
all-American image of the boy scout, plunging
through time to Greek mythology and back to
the present:

great American boy scout
wrapt in Medusa's tongue, how can he speak
when his voice was taken away? I'll outlast
this plague, I'm going to outrun the runner
no stopping me in my mother's long black
    stockings. . . .

When "Queer Careers" was completed I read
it over several times, wanting to see if I had
struck the proper note. The more I read, the

more convinced I was that I had written right from the heart, and that my unsentimental tone was precisely what the gay community needed to experience.

Midway through Nevada, I couldn't help thinking about *Animal*, so I decided to put the book to the test. I re-read "Job, Suffering" and "Queer Careers" in the solitude of a hotel room in Ely, Nevada, close to the Utah border, and still felt that the poems held up. Looking over my shoulder to Jesse, who was sound asleep, I returned to my book. It dawned on me that the title poem offered a view of myself that had undergone change. For that reason, the poem now stood as a document of who I had been before. This realization did not create a motel room epiphany or a Nevada Desert illumination, but served as a signpost to yet another of life's passages. I had to ask, "Can a person change at fifty?" Here's the poem "Animal" in its entirety:

First I talk to a receptionist.
Then to a social worker.
Next, I'll confer with a medical student
And a supervisor.
After four intake sessions
I will be assigned a therapist.
I am an animal with no rain forest
and no wild river.
I have no hunting grounds
Or mountain range.
I am trapped
Cornered
And anticipating the worst.
I called the State Employment Agency
But they are only hiring armadillos
And leopards this week.
Next week they are interviewing geese
With more than four years experience.
I am lost
And I have no way of telling this to my dog.
Comet jumps into my lap.
He probably thinks I am a very successful writer,
Or maybe he doesn't even know that I write.
I am not the one who buys his dog food
But I am the one who opens the can.
Comet may not be able to understand the difference.
The social worker at the Psychiatric Clinic
Asked: "What is the matter?"
I told her how confused I felt.
There are strange animals everywhere.
The other animals seem well fitted to survival.
I am surviving all right
But not on my own terms.
I used to be able to stalk my prey and pounce.
Now I don't even join the hunt.

I want to be put on the endangered species list.
I need to be protected.
I want a reservation.
I will move through water like a dolphin.
I will think ocean thoughts like the blue whale.
I will soar like a condor over California hills
And dart in dust of Ohio brushland like a red
    fox.

I am only a track in the sand.
I am merely a clump of fur on the rose bush.
I am practically invisible.

How differently I had felt when that poem appeared on my computer screen in 1987. Then I was gripped by anxiety and I had sought help at a mental health outpatient clinic clear across town. After the intake sessions referred to in the poem, the social worker told me that I was suffering from a variety of neuroses and needed therapy. Despite the good advice I returned home and wrote "Animal." The poem underscores my belief that we are not separate from the rest of the earth. We may walk on two legs and have the gift of speech and reason, but we're still part of the animal kingdom. By declaring myself "practically invisible" I was better able to fight my way back to full visibility, a poet's unpremeditated vision.

After leaving Nevada, Jesse and I headed for Zion Canyon, a great chasm cut into Na-

With his dog, Comet, 1988

vajo sandstone by the Virgin River millions of years ago. We stayed in the small town of Springdale. After spending a day in the canyon, marveling at the huge rock forms and precipitous cliffs that often appeared to come together as family groupings, I lay down in bed and read "The San Bernardino Elegies." The poem delves into the somber heart of San Bernardino, taking the reader into the city's more recent history, hoping to offer a sense of what it had been like to live in an old-time railroad town:

The poet's father, Sam Cherry, 1994

> if I told you about Mount Vernon Avenue
> in San Berdoo, viaduct, Railroad yards, antique
>   roundhouse
> Manuel's furniture, boy's club, Irish beat cop's
>   red roadmap face
> red-light World War Two brown courthouse facade
> Carnegie's sinister library creaking floorboards
> Antler's dim cocktail lounge dividing
> high desert tracts, dread hotel near to tracks,
> Traveler's green lobby, big black locomotive
> a sentinel, the whole light of the world
> gleaming in its steel eyes, prophetic
> somber, enchanted street lamps
> voices made of dry grass, I've been
> working on the railroad, what elegy measures up
> to drifting wind, burnt mountainside, raging fire
> seen from below, trickle of water
> Coldwater Canyon observed leaping flames, drove
> past orange trees stacked like cordwood
> on the freeway siding, death
> to this enterprise, vacant eyes,
> Democratic Luncheon Club
> part of my ghost life now, who's going to
> enter this house of desire?
> deadlines, speeches, pleadings, election night
> tote-boards, beerhall musing, Tijuana Street
> echoes, Arrowview, Arrowhead, call from
> Big Bear, Chad's short order cook, died
> near Lone Pine, they held
> a celebration, directed railroad museum, you can
> turn into old bones, genuine skeleton
> late-night phone conversations, steal into L.A.
> to mitigate solitude, downtown Mission Hotel
> Night Owl Cafe, Thrifty's blue plate brain cells
> handsome shop windows, names
> thrown against prevailing winds, poor Zanja
> unknown, dead river, rise—Cisco—How do you
>   do?—
> in the morning, mañana, compañero, it's
> a sure bet we've got to dive
> into darkness—brings you home again . . .

On my return to San Francisco from Nevada and Utah, I stopped off to visit my father in Los Angeles. Sam had recently turned eighty-three, clear-minded, maintaining rugged good health. He rattled off the names of mountain ranges in Nevada that we had passed through and vividly described Lehman Caves in Great Basin National Park, which he hadn't seen for more than forty years. He advised us to drive coast-to-coast: "It's still the best way to get to know the country." I was reminded of Jack London's *The Road*, in which he relates just such a trip at the turn of the century. I recollected driving with a friend from North Beach clear across the midsection of America to the tip of Long Island, Walt Whitman's "fish-shaped Paumonak" in 1975. Meanwhile, Jesse and I still faced five hundred miles to drive, north to San Francisco. When I arrived home, I unpacked, checked the mail, took the dog for a walk, and read through my notebooks. I had described my first sight of snowcapped Wheeler Mountain at more than 13,000 feet and surrounded by desert terrain. "It's like a piece of land floating off into space," I wrote. Later, on the mountain itself, I sat beside a fast-running stream and wrote an entry on the preceding two days of travel from San Francisco:

> done by grass and done by sky,
> done by ghost town and done by billboard
> and baked by snow and burnt
> by wind and blown away by open space
> and fried by highway dream
> lost in motel places, circled by sand demons,
> drawn to the fire

Neeli Cherkovski, reading poetry in San Francisco, 1994

by water, left on the plain with a coyote,
given-over to the memory
of an eagle, cleared into a clearing
drafted onto the great steps,
in the distance: hills,
mountains, limestone stepping-stones,
granite pinnacles, sandstone shelves
and other untempered furnishings
named by human minds
flung out from time
into the timeless

I often thought of the word "Home" as I wrote
this autobiographical essay. Though my father had sold the house in San Bernardino a few years back, I had long ago stopped thinking of it as home. My *place* is now San Francisco and my home a modest house shared with Jesse on Bernal Heights, a gently sloping hillside. On the first floor, facing the street, is a small workroom and library where I write. Over my left shoulder are books by the writers I admire and various reference books. My desk is fairly disorderly, filled with loose papers, manila folders stuffed with manuscripts, unsent letters, business cards I've acquired, a telephone, my printer, computer, and stacks of disks. There's a painting my mother did of me when I was twelve. Until recently, it was obscured by a stack of books. Jack Foley suggested I take the books down and reveal my smiling, freckled face, which I have done.

And I thought back now to the last sighting of the sugar ration coupon for "Baby Cherry." It was in our garage in San Bernardino, perhaps ten years ago, placed in a cardboard box along with *National Geographic* magazines from the period and a lot of old papers belonging to my parents. Why hadn't I taken it with me then? It was a keepsake from my distant past, but now it is lost. I wondered if I was already a poet as an infant. Or is a poet shaped by time and circumstances? Years ago my mother and Bukowski were arguing about what makes a writer. "They're born that way," my mother insisted. "No . . . that's a romanticism," declared Bukowski. "Life makes you a writer." I'd like to agree with my old mentor, though there may be something to what my mother said.

BIBLIOGRAPHY

Poetry:

(As Neeli Cherry) *Don't Make a Move*, Tecumsah Press (San Bernardino, California), 1973.

Public Notice, Beatitude Press (San Francisco, California), 1975.

The Waters Reborn, Red Hill Press (Los Angeles, California), 1975.

Love Proof, Greenlight Press (San Francisco), 1981.

Clear Wind, Avant Books (San Diego, California), 1983.

Ways in the Wood, Misnomer Press (Oxford, Mississippi), 1993.

Animal, Pantograph Press (Berkeley, California), 1996.

Elegy for Bob Kaufman, Sun Dog Press, 1996.

Memoirs and biographies:

Ferlinghetti: A Life, Doubleday (New York), 1979.

Whitman's Wild Children, Lapis Press (San Francisco), 1988.

Hank: The Life of Charles Bukowski, Random House (New York), 1991.

Books in translation:

Heartbeat, Maro Verlag (Augsburg, Germany), 1991.

Das Leban des Charles Bukowski, DTV (Munich), 1993.

Hank, Editorial Anagrama (Barcelona), 1993.

Hank, Grasset (Paris), 1993.

Slam! Poetry Heftige Dichtung Amerika, Druckhaus Galrev (Berlin), 1993.

Rick DeMarinis

1934-

FRACTURED LIVES

Whenever I think about my early years, fictions occur to me, fictions more vital than memories. I often wonder if I have a "true" story to tell, an unimpeachable record of places, people, and events. Perhaps my "truth," whatever that is, is traceable in my work. Someone once said that all writing, however fanciful or remote from the life of the writer, *is* autobiography. There's a smug reasonableness in this notion that I find attractive. It's a tempting evasion.

I have evaded writing directly about myself for years. I'm not sure why. This much is true: I tend to guard my privacy—I don't like public displays. Another disincentive is that I look at my early years in almost exclusively negative ways. But perhaps the most compelling reason behind this reluctance to commit myself to autobiography is that I don't have a comfortable grip on the particulars of my childhood—the most critical part of a writer's (or anyone's) psychological development. I have impressions, a galaxy of emotions, a slide show of dramatic inventions, but very little in the way of reliable memory. Some, if not most, of the stories I will tell you here are secondhand, pieced together over the years. Many come from my mother, who enjoys exaggeration, some from my father, who was very tight-lipped about his life beyond the outer edges of mainstream society, and some from my fragmented memory. Other sources are few.

I envy people who have complete memories of their childhood. My wife, Carole, is one of these. She can remember, in photographic detail, her preschool years. She can recall, and give names to, everyone in her first-grade class. Her advantage is that she came from an unbroken home, lived in the same small Montana town until she left for college, and has a naturally good memory. Linear memory, for me, doesn't begin until about the age of nine.

Rick DeMarinis in El Paso, Texas, 1994

The obvious question arises: why try to do it at all?

I have a partial answer, inadequate I readily admit, but as I write this now it makes sense. I've always believed writing—any kind of writing: poetry, letters, diary entries, fiction—acts as a dredge on memory. Memories that have long since slipped below the waterline of consciousness can be raised to daylight by the simple act of moving one's fingers over a keyboard. I tend to think that the process is physical rather than psychological, that nerves, muscles, tendons, and bones, acting together in the effort to put words down on paper, pull up the shipwrecked past. Some of it, anyway. The original shape of the fragments may be distorted by carbuncles and rust, but I think they still may have some worth. As I grow older, I am conscious of losing more and more of my past. This exercise in self-exploration, then, may prove useful—to me and to my kids and grandkids. If it proves useful to anyone else who for reasons of his own is curious about me or my work, I welcome him to sit next to me in this bathyscaphic descent into murky waters.

I was born in New York in 1934, in lower Manhattan's St. Vincent's Hospital. My mother, Ruth, was a beautiful Finnish girl (she had just turned twenty-two when I was born) from northern Michigan, my father a minor Mafioso figure. It was a cultural train wreck in the making, though no one seemed to grasp this at the time. The marriage couldn't—and didn't—last. I'm not sure how long they stuck it out. I know, from Ruth's stories, that the marriage was shaky from the outset. (Her memory is somewhat like mine: she likes her fictions, offers contradictory fables without apology, waves at the past as if at a sinking ship. In one of her letters to me she baldly states: "I was born the day the Titanic sank." This isn't quite true. Her birth date is April 9, 1912; the Titanic went down on the twelfth. But it makes a good story. I have no doubt where my impulse for dramatic fiction comes from.) Anyway, the marriage lasted about three years. I know she couldn't stand living in my grandmother's household at 60 St. Mark's Place in Greenwich Village. The railroad-style flat was small, and my mother was crowded by my father's grandmother, Ermina (the Old Lady, as she was called); his mother, Luisa; his stepfather, Pacifico Nardi (his father had died in the early 1920s); and by his three sisters, Teresa, Genevieve, and Mildred, all of whom took the responsibility of spoiling me rotten. Antonio ("Tony"), my father's younger brother, lived there, too. An older brother, Almerindo, was out on his own, working for Meyer Lansky in one of his palatial Havana casinos.

Something was wrong with Tony. He was pathologically shy, possibly retarded. He died before he turned thirty, of tuberculosis of the bone. It was a slow and miserable death. Toward the end, his bones were so brittle his body couldn't support a sheet. He had to lie naked in his bed, and would scream if anything touched him.

Life on St. Mark's Place was alien to the raw-boned, north-woods sensibilities of my mother. I was being raised by these dark little people as a southern Italian prince. I think I must have been an obnoxious kid. I recall vividly taking Pacifico Nardi's cane as he napped and whacking it over his great bald pate to see if I could crack it. I was forgiven, probably felt no remorse. I have no memory of having a motive. I might have been put out over some trifle, or I might have been conducting a toddler's experiment. I look back on this incident and wince, but I am sure I did not wince when it happened.

My father, Alfonso ("Funzi"—pronounced *Foon*-zee), was, like his older brother, in the gambling trade. He worked the house side of the table. Illegal games were set up in various parts of the city, overseen by my father. He was offered jobs in Las Vegas casinos, back in the Bugsy Segal era, but could not bring himself to leave New York. The city was his world—nothing worthwhile existed west of the George Washington Bridge.

Funzi dropped out of school in the sixth grade because he would not tolerate the beat-

*The author's mother, Ruth, as a
Maybelline model, 1930*

ings regularly handed out by the teachers back then. Young Italian boys were rarely beaten by their parents; to be beaten by a stranger was intolerable. He ran numbers for a while, then graduated to driving trucks, hauling contraband whiskey from Canada. Eventually he was an "appointed" boss of a longshoremen's local.

He was Rocky Graziano's (the eventual middleweight champion) first manager. In Graziano's autobiography, *Somebody Up There Likes Me*, my father appears as a character named "Big Sal." Managing Graziano was another mob assignment, given to my father before it was realized just how good Graziano was. He cautioned me, on my occasional visits to New York, "Rick, stay away from boxing. It's a dirty business. Stick to baseball. It's a good clean game."

Italian athletes back then were mostly boxers or baseball players—sports that didn't require preparation in a collegiate athletic program. Baseball players were not controlled by the mob; the boxers were. What he didn't know was that by the time of these occasional visits, when I was in my early teens, I had become a shy and reclusive kid. I was not the Neapolitan prince he and his sisters had tried to create. I was a four-eyed bookworm, a nascent nerd, and had no impulse to climb into the ring.

I remember visiting him in 1947. We (my mother and her second husband, David Lee) had just spent half a year in Fort Worth, Texas, having moved there from Vallejo, California. Lee—a lover of big, fast cars—bought a pre-war Packard in Fort Worth, and we started a trek that took us back and forth across the country, starting with a trip to New York. Ruth and David Lee were restless people, always looking for a new place to re-start their lives. Like most people they wanted stability and security, but they brought their chaos with them wherever they went. Whoever dreamed up the now-overused phrase, "Wherever you go, there you are," could have been thinking about my mother and her second husband, who claimed kinship with Robert E. Lee.

We spent a couple of weeks in New York. Lee and my mother considered buying a house on Long Island. I remember it—a nice two-story brick, but the asking price, $14,000, was too high. I was handed over to my father for a few days. He took me to Yankee Stadium to see the Yankees play Cleveland. Bob Feller was pitching for the Indians. Joe DiMaggio was back

Rick's father, Alfonso, about 1930

from the war and in pre-war form. The lines at the ticket window serpentined endlessly. My father took my hand and we walked to the head of the line. He shouldered a man out of the way and bought our tickets—box seats down the first base line. I was mortified, and expected the man to say something. He didn't. I didn't understand this. I can only assume that in those days, in New York, a certain type of man was given a lot of space: the obvious mobster, in glossy Florsheim wingtips and camel's hair coat, recognizable even to tourists. The man who had been shoved out of the way simply ate his rage. My face burned with shame and I couldn't concentrate on the game. I think of this incident today and feel the humiliation of it, as fresh as if it happened yesterday. Once my father knocked a man out cold who whistled at my mother while they were walking down St. Mark's Place. The man realized his mistake too late.

My father was called "Big Al" because he was half a foot taller than his brother, Almerindo, "Little Al." But Little Al was bigger in the mob, and was, hands down, the star of the family.

New York had no hold on him, as it did on my father. Uncle Al was able to leave the city. He started out as a croupier in Havana for Meyer Lansky and subsequently moved up in the ranks of the organization. When he married, he chose an Atlantic City beauty queen, "Bobby," another blonde. Aunt Bobby and my mother, the only "white" women in the family, became fast friends. (In the early decades of this century Italians, especially the southern Italian immigrants, weren't considered white. Just as Jews and other Mediterranean types were not. White—back in the days when it was important to be thought of as white—only gradually became a flexible idea, a classification open to revision.)

In the mid-1930s, Uncle Al bought a large penthouse apartment in the Bronx for his wife. It was an elegant, art-deco place overlooking the Grand Concourse. By the time Bobby died in 1994, she was an isolated old widow living in a ghetto she hated and feared. "Trapped in the Bronx," a cousin of mine told me, lamenting her fate. Bobby died alone and frightened, and her apartment was looted before she was in the ground.

My mother tried to get my father to leave St. Mark's Place. She tried to get him to go with her to northern Michigan where he could be employed in the iron ore mines. What an astonishing lack of understanding she had of these lower Manhattan Italians and of my father's temperament and ambition! My father got up at noon, had his coffee and cigarette, read the sporting news, went out to see his friends, and that was the sum of his daily activity. Here was a man who had his fingernails manicured weekly, who wore expensive silk suits, who looked down on physical labor as something the wealthy conned suckers into doing. In his wonderful book, *The Italians,* Luigi Barzini quotes from a Roman father who advises his sons, "You must all try to have an occupation in life. Life without an occupation is contemptible and meaningless. But always remember this: you must never allow your occupation to degenerate into work." Such politically incorrect defamations can be made only by those who implicate themselves. It's unnecessary to point out that this doesn't apply to all Italians. (My next door neighbor when I was a teenager in San Diego, an immigrant from Abruzzi, was a stone mason, and probably the hardest working man I've ever known.) But it does typify a certain strain

Rick with Aunt Rachel and Uncle Dom, 1939

of Italian mentality, and it seems tailor-made for my father, and, I freely admit, for me— I've always hated the idea of the monotony of a steady job. And my mother wanted Alfonso "Big Al" DeMarinis to dig red ore half a mile below the surface of the earth for forty dollars a week! Talk about cultural misapprehension! Ruth never knew Funzi; Funzi never knew Ruth.

To assert her own independence, and to get me away from my doting aunts, she took a night job at Tony's Trouville, a midtown restaurant and night club, as a hatcheck girl. Then she found an apartment at a complex called Warren House on Second Avenue and 12th Street. Most of the residents there were working-class Jews. The apartment was small but very nice. Of course the nicest thing about it, from Ruth's point of view, was that there was no large Italian family smothering her. I'll make a chancy generalization here (I'll permit myself this one though I usually scorn generalizations) which I can't support except by my own limited observation: Finnish women are stubbornly independent. Independence is one of

America's prime national virtues, but independence that vetoes common obligation can be destructive. My mother's stubborn independence made it impossible for her to live in an Italian household where dependencies and hierarchies are as pervasive as the smell of tomato sauce. My father agreed to spend a few hours in Warren House taking care of me on his wife's first night of checking hats at Tony's Trouville. When my mother came home after her shift, she found my great-grandmother, Ermina, baby-sitting me. Funzi had fled back to St. Mark's Place. Of course the family sympathized with him. You can't expect a man to stay home with the baby while his wife works. It was a humiliation of a very high order. The Italians won that first skirmish in a battle that would eventually end in separation and divorce. My mother gave up her apartment and returned to St. Mark's Place.

Luisa DeMarinis, Rick's grandmother,
April 1950

A few years before he died, my father visited me in El Paso, Texas, where I taught college courses in fiction writing. He recalled some of his feelings about my mother and her independent ways. "She'd come home four, five in the morning. She didn't give a damn. She just said, 'Ah, what the hell.' I hated that. She could do anything, then just say, 'Ah, what the hell,' like that was going to make everything all right."

On my grandmother Luisa's side of the family there was some power. Her brother, Itaniel, was a wealthy and well-connected man. When the Italian ambassador came to the United States in 1934, he visited Itaniel, who sent a limousine to pick up my grandmother, my father, my father's sisters, and my mother. They were all to have dinner at Itaniel's Brooklyn mansion with the ambassador. My mother, barely twenty-two years old and always ready to party, had to be restrained by my father. "Don't say *anything*," he cautioned. "This is the Italian ambassador, don't embarrass the family."

Another story from this era: There was a family summer house on Staten Island. My father was given the job of entertaining some men who had just arrived from Sicily. He brought me and my mother, as well as my grandmother and Aunt Mildred, to the house. It was billed as a vacation. The men from Sicily were very polite and helpful. They did most of the cooking, sang songs, played with me, and in general charmed everyone with their good manners and high spirits. They charmed everyone except my grandmother, who did not trust Sicilians. "Killers!" My grandmother muttered. "Assassins!" And of course they *were*. Their services had been solicited by the mob and they had come to New York to rub someone out. It was a job they were obviously comfortable with and consequently they were not the grimacing hoodlums Hollywood in the 1930s liked to portray, but fine, jovial, life-loving fellows who really knew how to cook.

Another one: My aunt Mildred had been corresponding with a young man in Sicily. Actually, the young man, a barber, was courting her. Mildred agreed to marry him. When my great-grandmother, Ermina, discovered this, she went ballistic. And when the ship pulled into New York Harbor with the young Sicilian, Gianni, on board, Ermina met the boat with a revolver. No way was she going to allow her granddaughter to marry a Sicilian! The pistol was wrested away from her—not without a considerable struggle—by family members just as she drew it out from under her long skirts, and the young Sicilian, my Uncle "Johnny," married Mildred and became one of New York's most sought-after barbers. Johnny eventually got his own shop, but he also made "house calls" to the offices of important men whose time was too valuable to waste in a barber shop.

My mother began to make small escapes. She took me to Michigan's Upper Peninsula every summer and left me with my grandmother and sometimes with her sister Rachel and Rachel's new husband, Dominic Marra. (Rachel had also married into an Italian family, but Dom was a hard-working man with no silk suits in his closet, a superb athlete who had been offered a contract out of high school by the Green Bay Packers. The contract was for blue-collar pay, and he chose to stay in Ishpeming to work for the Michigan Department of Highways.) After one of these fugitive summers, Ruth, on our return to New York, took an apartment in Knickerbocker Village. She officially separated from my father, and began living a wild life.

She ran with glamorous men, some of them dangerous. "Uncle Jack," a mob fingerman, was one of these. (A fingerman is an operative who discovers and points out—for the purpose of assassination—men who have betrayed or are in some way a danger to the organization.) Years later she told me, "I really loved Jack. If he had not been sent to prison, I swear I would have married him. He was very good to you, treated you like you were his own son."

Jack was a Jewish mobster, wanted by several police agencies, including the NYPD, in connection with a mob hit. He paid for my mother's divorce from Funzi. I remember traveling with my mother and Uncle Jack, a wild trip through the southeast, all the way to Florida, then back up into the Midwest, to Michigan. Uncle Jack was on the lam. I was too young to realize the possible danger we were in. I was caught up in the excitement of the long, high-speed tour. He left us with my grandmother in Michigan to continue his odyssey alone. A few days later a black car with New York plates pulled up to my grandmother's farmhouse, out on U.S. 41, between Marquette and Negaunee. I was playing out in a field, next to the house. I saw my mother being escorted to the car by

two large men in dark suits. The car doors slammed shut with a finality that made my heart skip beats. I ran after the car, screaming, but the car roared away, toward Marquette. No explanations. No good-byes.

The men who had taken her away were New York City detectives with extradition papers. They figured she knew where Jack went, knew about his associates, and so they held her in the Bronx County jail for eight months without charging her with a crime. Because she was a "material witness," the District Attorney could hold her indefinitely. She was never booked, never fingerprinted, never accused of anything. Jack was one of Meyer Lansky's important henchmen, and naturally—for her sake—had not revealed the details of his professional associations to my mother. She only knew that he was mob-connected, and that he was a kind and generous and good-natured man. "On the other hand," my mother once said, "the D.A. was the most disgusting creep I'd ever seen. Fat, sloppy, with loud wooden heels, and baby shoes in bronze dangling on the windshield of his car." Jack was caught in Kansas City, even though he'd had plastic surgery to change his appearance. He copped a plea and got eight years in the state pen. My mother was set free and given three dollars a day for every day she'd spent in jail.

By this time the war in Europe had started. I was still in Michigan with my grandmother, Aiti. ("Aiti" in Finnish means "mother." She had been a great beauty in her youth and did not like to be thought of as a grandmother. Her Christian name was Elma.) Aiti brought me to my mother, having had her fill of this brattish kid from New York. But my mother was desperately poor, too poor to take me back. Aiti agreed to keep me for a while longer, until my mother got back on her feet. When I was finally returned to New York, my mother had talked Funzi into paying for my keep at a Catholic boarding school, St. Vincent de Paul's, in Tarrytown. Thus began my education and the most miserable year of my childhood.

The kids at St. Vincent's were rejects from their own families. They had been warehoused at this boarding school because, for one reason or another, their parents could not abide them. Rejected boys have a lot of anger to work out. At St. Vincent's they worked it out on each other. The nuns were nice to us, but nice people can't deal with blind hatred. They can't understand it. It was an anomaly in an otherwise orderly and rationally structured universe. They thought this burning rage of ours was an act, something we could easily change or drop. They didn't know that it was the only thing that kept us from disappearing completely. I believe that abandoned kids begin to fear that they are going to disappear, like someone lost at sea. Hate is their life boat.

I loved my hatred. I protected it. I kept it watertight. I have it today—civilized, modified, housebroken, and valuable as one of the darker yet energizing principles of my fiction. It's always at hand, like a genie, ready to serve. "How does one prepare himself to be a writer," someone once asked Hemingway. "Have a lousy childhood," he replied. As long as you have this red hot ball of anger, you know you won't disappear. The nuns, who glided through the halls and playgrounds like huge black-and-white confections, could not see this polarizing energy.

The boys slept in a large open bay, much like a military barracks. The older boys intimidated the younger ones mercilessly. I was six years old—a member of the youngest group—and terrified. I began wetting the bed again, though I hadn't done so since I was three. The nuns who ran the place viewed this bedwetting as a moral failure of some kind. They put rubber sheets on my bed, threatened to trade them for electric sheets if this nonsense did not stop.

The food at St. Vincent's was grim. I remember one dinner of rubbery boiled eggs and soggy spinach. I sat at the end of a long table. Next to the table, sticking up out of the floor, was a vent pipe of some kind. When the nun in charge wasn't looking, I unscrewed the cap off this pipe and stuffed my spinach and eggs into it. I lived on bread and milk and sugar. I broke windows when no one was looking, and committed other small acts of vandalism, just to get even.

I think I became neurotic during my year at Tarrytown. I began obsessively repeating everything I said under my breath. My whispered echo served to underscore my words, as if they required constant seconding. It was 1940. Wendell Wilkie was running for president against Franklin Roosevelt. The kids ran around the playground yelling, "Wilkie is a Nazi! Wilkie is a Nazi! Death to Wilkie!" for no particular reason. We didn't

Rick's first Communion, 1940

know a Republican from a turnip, a Nazi from a cutworm, but we applied our nebulous hatred to Wendell Wilkie. The sweep of our great unfocused spite was always on the lookout for a scapegoat. Wilkie, who had dared to test Franklin Roosevelt, qualified.

When my mother came to visit me with one of her friends, I vented my rage on her. The rage of a small child is an oxymoronic marvel—like a cute tornado. She and her friend took me to a movie in town. Halfway through the main feature, I stood up and urinated—with the defiant ceremonial chin-jut of Mussolini—into the aisle. My mother and her friend—Margie, I think her name was—took my display in stride. They weren't shocked or disgusted. They were strong, durable women who had seen a lot of bad behavior by grown-ups and were not particularly impressed by my improvised outrageousness. My mother had a powerful laugh. It always brought tears to her eyes. "Ah, what the hell," she said, infuriating me, just as it had infuriated my father. She was an untutored fatalist who saw life in comical terms. Bad things happened, but they only deserved a shrug. If they happened to you, well that was just the breaks. *What the hell.* She and Margie laughed at my little rebellion.

My father came to visit me once at Tarrytown. I begged him to take me back to St. Mark's Place. He said he couldn't do that. I screamed that he could. He was Big Al. He could do anything he wanted. But he turned his back and left. I have no memory of this. When Big Al visited me and my wife in El Paso a few years ago, he told me about it. But remembered or not, the incident stuck with me. It lay, festering, in some dark corner of my heart, an impacted knot of rage, waiting to erupt. When I was in the air force, fifteen years after my father turned his back on me at Tarrytown, a bird colonel came to visit our barracks. It wasn't an inspection tour, just a friendly drop-by to see how the troops were doing. He joshed with us, saw a picture of my girlfriend on a dresser, complimented her, and by extension, me. Then he turned crisply and left. Incredibly, I gave him the finger. My first sergeant, a bull-necked World War II vet, saw it. His jaw dropped; so did mine. I had no idea why I'd done it. It was a moment of dire confusion. I can't explain it today, except in this mock-Freudian way: Big Al turned his back on me when I needed him most. The colonel was in all ways imaginable every bit as big as Big Al. The two men became, for an instant of psychological blindness, the same. I expected to be taken out and shot. I didn't even get an in-squadron court-martial. Not even a reprimand. I can't explain this either. It's possible that the squadron commander (a captain who needed to make major on the next round of promotions or retire) did not want it known, publicly, that he had an idiot in his unit who made obscene gestures to field-grade officers.

I didn't react when my father told the story of his refusal to take me out of St. Vincent's. We were having an elegant dinner at the El Paso del Norte Hotel. He was an old man now, in his mid-eighties. The stories he told were, for him, without emotional significance. He didn't mean to apologize or explain. And that was fine. I thought I'd managed, by then, to have survived my childhood. ("Anybody who has survived his childhood has enough information about life to last him the rest of his days," wrote Flannery O'Connor, on the subject of what a writer needs to know in order to write.) There was a lull in the dinner conversation. Big Al

looked at me, sizing me up it seemed, his hard Mafioso eyes revealing a hint of wonder: How could this rumpled college professor be his son? I was wearing a beat-up sports coat, Levi's, some scruffy oxfords. He was in silk, still an aristocrat of lower Manhattan. The wonder in those hard little eyes turned to dismay. "If you'd a been with *me,* you coulda been something," he said. Meaning, of course, that if I had grown up in New York under his tutelage, I might have been a *capo* by now. It was clear that I didn't amount to much in his eyes. Here I was, the first in my immediate family to have graduated from high school, a full professor in the University of Texas system, a respected writer with ten books published, but to him I was a pathetically attired failure. It was an astonishing moment. I didn't know whether to laugh or cry or give him the finger. I suppose all of these would have been appropriate. I exchanged a quick, amused glance with Carole. We continued our meal.

I'm afraid that this is beginning to sound like a complaint against the past. I hope it isn't. These people, Alfonso and Ruth, were who they were and there was little they could do to change the random configuration of their lives even if they saw a need to, which they did not. They were the children of immigrants, one foot in the new world, the other in the old, and the forces that shaped them were tectonic in magnitude. And—to use a current cliché—they played the cards they were dealt.

My mother, though she was born in Brooklyn, had spent the first seven years of her life in Finland. When she returned to America she spoke only Finnish. And my father spoke Italian more frequently than he spoke English. I'm impressed by them for surviving as well as they did. Funzi died a few months short of his ninetieth birthday. Ruth lives in an Arizona retirement community, alone, having survived all her husbands, lovers, and most of her friends.

Aiti arrived in New York from Helsinki late in 1911, unmarried and pregnant with my mother. My mother's father, Matthew, was detained at Ellis Island and then sent back to Finland because of an infectious eye disease. Aiti, in her early twenties, on her own, with very little English at her command, took a job as a housemaid for a wealthy Brooklyn family. When my mother was born, the woman Aiti worked for offered to adopt my mother.

Aiti declined, and returned to Finland where she married Matthew.

They were very poor. Matthew was a good musician and made his way traveling about rural Finland playing an accordion and singing. Aiti went with him. Their infant daughter, Ruth, was sent to live with her maternal grandparents for seven years. Ruth writes: "I lived with my grandfather, grandmother, and a crippled, bedridden uncle. My grandfather made me a little boat, and I used to go fishing in a nearby lake. I'd come home and cook the fish over an open fire called a *täkä*. I put the fish on a long stick and roasted it, guts and all. My grandmother kept a cow, and she let me drink milk from the cow's teat. I'd go into the barn with her and she'd squirt the milk into my cup. I had no playmates as there were none in this remote part of Finland. I moved huge rocks from place to place and pretended they were my cows. For horns I used glass vacuum cups

I found in the sauna. These cups were the kind that people used as suction cups to pull the badness out of you." Ruth's grandparents lived in a lonely landscape of cold clear lakes and shadowed hills, which may account for her later need for bright lights and big cities. When my mother's sister, Elna, was born, Aiti and Matthew decided to try America again.

The small family boarded a White Star liner. Again, Ruth writes: "I remember going aboard with my babushka and red boots that were curled up at the toes. I lugged a huge bag made out of fish netting on my back. We were in steerage of course. I guess it was a stormy crossing because everybody in steerage was sick. A big fat lady sleeping in the bunk above me farted all night between vomits. I had to fetch the food for my family as there were no dining rooms for people in steerage. The sailors aboard helped me get the trays into our small room— *pen* would be a better name for it. I liked the sailors and they liked me. Funny, but I never had relationships with sailors in later life."

They settled first in Hurley, Wisconsin, where Matthew had relatives. His sister's husband owned a bottling plant there, and gave Matthew a job. But the money was poor and Matthew decided to move the family to the Upper Peninsula of Michigan where he got work in the iron ore mines of Negaunee. Ruth's brothers—Roy, Carl, and John—were born there, as well as her sister, Rachel. They lived in a small house in Negaunee, and as they prospered, Matthew built a larger house outside of Negaunee, on Highway 41, complete with an outdoor sauna large enough to hold twenty adults.

In 1926, when my mother was fourteen, tragedy struck the family. Matthew, along with several other miners, was killed in a cave-in. In those days there was no such thing as Social Security. The mining company paid for Matthew's burial and gave Aiti thirty dollars a month compensation for a short period of time. Ruth had to quit school and go to work as a housekeeper. Aiti took in laundry, and in the summertime, the whole family picked wild strawberries and sold them from roadside stands.

When she was sixteen, Ruth left home. She went to live with an aunt and uncle in Chicago who had two sons but no daughters, and so were glad to have her. She got a job at the Baby Ruth candy factory. The aunt and uncle were strict, religious people who went to church twice on Sundays, insisting that their

The author's mother, Ruth, and her family, about 1915: (from left) her father, Matthew; her sister, Elna (on Matthew's lap); Ruth; and her mother, Elma ("Aiti")

niece go with them. Their rules of behavior proved too confining for Ruth, who was, by her own admission, a natural-born rebel. She could not abide such a life. When she was eighteen, she left for New York City with three girlfriends from the Baby Ruth factory.

The four girls got a shabby apartment, a base of operations from which they would conquer the big city. Ruth writes: "I remember going through the Holland Tunnel on the bus and getting out into the bright lights of the city. What a thrill! We found a dumpy rooming house and stayed there until we moved into an apartment on 50th Street, right over the Automat. Then our lives began. Everything was fine, but we had no jobs and the bread lines were everywhere. It was 1930, and the depression was in full swing. We finally took jobs as taxi dancers at a dime-a-dance place. I didn't know how to dance but learned real quick. Before long we had boyfriends, but we remained loyal to each other. If one had a date to go out and eat, we made sure that the girl with the date would bring home leftovers for the rest of us. We learned to pull a lot of dirty tricks on men. Such as taking them to a deli and buying bags of food with their money while they waited outside. We were supposed to go back to our apartment and have a party, but instead we slipped out the back door and they never saw the food or us again. We learned these survival tricks young."

Sometimes famous people came into the taxi-dance hall. One of these, Red Grange, the "Galloping Ghost" of the University of Illinois and later of the Chicago Bears, danced with Ruth. He came back the next day and asked her to dinner. Nothing came of it. Ruth was not impressed by football players. From the dime-a-dance job she went to modeling. She became a "Maybelline Girl," and her picture appeared in magazine ads for Maybelline products.

Then she met Alfonso DeMarinis. She writes: "I thought I hit the jackpot. He was dressed like a million bucks and took me to hockey games on our first few dates. On my nineteenth birthday he took me to the Cotton Club in Harlem. We eloped and got married in New Jersey. Then the party was over. We went to live with his mother and her mother, his stepfather, Nardi, and his sisters. They told me what to eat and drink to make the forthcoming baby strong. Lots of raw spinach in oil, chicken and eels, plenty of wine and plenty of

housework to work it off. I lived there for over three years. Every Sunday was family day. The tribe got together and ate and drank from morning until night, except for poor Tony. He stayed in his room and came out to eat only after everyone had left. Nobody understood him or tried to. He used to come out to play with the baby when no one was looking. When I took the job at Tony's Trouville, I had to pay my mother-in-law twelve dollars a week for room and board. Once I used a lemon to rinse my hair and the old lady had a fit. Funzi roared back at her and said, 'Why can't she have a lemon, doesn't she give you enough money?' That was the first and only time I ever heard Al come to my defense. He came and went as he pleased, never worked or looked for a job. One night I checked a man's coat and he gave me a big tip. He came back several times after that, and finally asked if he could drive me home. I accepted." The man was Uncle Jack, Meyer Lansky's henchman, the man who eventually paid for Ruth's divorce from Funzi.

After her episode with Jack, she met David Lee, the man who I would come to know as my stepfather. The war had just started and the economy had begun to boom. Lee came from an upper-class family that had lost its money in the stock market crash of 1929. He was a graduate of Colgate and had completed a year toward a master's degree in Romance languages at Columbia. He had elegant good looks and aristocratic manners, but he was broke. He owned a 1928 Duesenberg, but in 1941 gas had been rationed, and the huge straight-eight engine was a gas guzzler. He sold it for a few hundred dollars. That car today, in restored condition, would sell for close to a million.

Car buffs will groan at Lee's shortsightedness. But this was typical of him. He didn't give proper values to things. He didn't value himself, his education, or his intelligence. Obviously he had low self-esteem. This, mixed with his arrogant bearing, his show-off vocabulary, his ability with languages, made him a puzzle to those who knew him. I think, in his better moments, he was a puzzle to himself.

Ruth was impressed by his style and pedigree, but she didn't love him. She married him only because she was out of options. She told him she wanted to go to California, and he agreed. They went to Los Angeles where Lee got a job delivering milk for the Challenge Dairy, and Ruth went to work for Douglas Aircraft, riveting aluminum skin to the frames of Dauntless dive bombers. I was still in Michigan with Aiti and did not join them until 1943.

Ruth's kid brother, my uncle Carl, brought me to Los Angeles on the train. We were put in an ancient coach that, because of a shortage of passenger cars, had been taken out of retirement. It still had oil smoke smudges above the windows from antique oil lamps that had once been used to provide illumination for nineteenth- and early twentieth-century travelers. Most passenger trains had been commandeered by the government as troop trains and space for civilians was scarce. The seats were hard wicker that made your buttocks ache after a few minutes, but we were lucky to have any seats at all. We had a shopping bag full of pasties that Aiti had made for us. (A pasty is a meat pie favored by miners.) This was to be our only food for the entire three-day trip. The train was packed with soldiers on their way to camps in California, from which they would be shipped to the Pacific theater of combat. Uncle Carl and I were the only civilians.

The troops—men in their twenties, for the most part—gave Carl a hard time. Carl, only nineteen years old, wore his father's ancient pin-stripe suit that barely fit. He was a stocky, muscular man and he looked as if he were about to explode out of that confining suit. The ribbing was good-natured, but Carl blushed furiously and was obviously uncomfortable, though at home he was an outgoing, good-natured guy, an iron ore miner and lumberjack who sang and played the guitar and who loved to tell jokes.

He needn't have been uncomfortable. He would be drafted a few months later himself and would become a ski-trooper in Europe. Carl fought in the Battle of the Bulge, and was decorated for heroism. In one instance, a troop truck in which he was riding was strafed by German fighter planes. Every man in the truck was either killed or badly wounded, except for Carl who escaped without a scratch. His wounds were interior. They call it post-traumatic stress now. Most combat veterans suffer from it to one degree or another. When Carl came back from the war he was no longer the happy-go-lucky, joke-telling uncle I had known. He was moody and introspective. I saw him in 1947. I tried to get him to repeat some of the great jokes he told me before the war. He denied ever telling jokes. "Don't you remember the

Rick and Uncle Carl, about 1942

one about the airliner that runs out of gas over Outer Mongolia and after an emergency landing the men take off their suspenders to make wind-up motors so they can take off again?" Carl just shrugged. "I never told you that," he said. I talked to him again a few years ago, over the telephone. The soul-depressing effects of war had lifted. He was back to his old, life-loving self.

My unbroken memory begins in Los Angeles, 1943. From that year on, I can account for myself, and the self I eventually became. Everything that happened to me before that—places I lived, schools I attended, friends I made—exists in fragments. Like the pieces of a jigsaw puzzle that had been tossed out the window of a moving vehicle. The pieces that can be recovered compose a partial picture that is more intriguing for what is left out than for what is there.

I was happy to be with my mother again; it seemed that I had come to an end of abandonments. We lived in an apartment in west L.A. The apartment building, on Ridgley Drive between Washington and Adams boulevards, had a small sign posted in front of it that said, in tasteful script, "Restricted." That meant, in this case, no children. It could, however, mean anything the landlord wanted it to mean. There were no civil-rights laws back then. Landlords were free to refuse anyone on any basis. Race, it goes without saying, was the paramount cause for refusal. Apartments were scarce in L.A. during the war. Ruth agreed to work for the manager—she hauled out garbage, waxed and buffed the hallways, raked ash out of the incinerators behind the apartment building, trimmed the hedges, and watered the lawns. She got only a slight break on the rent for doing this, not enough of a break to be worth the trouble, but her willingness to do these custodial chores got us the apartment.

I learned to become invisible. Whenever the landlord came around to check on his property, I had to vanish. I usually walked around the streets of west L.A., amusing myself. The Variety Theater, on Adams, was a favorite hangout. Matinees cost eleven cents. I think I saw every war movie that came out of the back lots of Hollywood. The war was a continual source of excitement. I remember driving by the Douglas plant with my mother and stepfather along Ocean Park Boulevard. Huge camouflage nets covered all the buildings of the factory as well as the streets around them. Looking up at the netting from below, you could see the underside of fake farm houses, cows and horses, and rolling fields of grain. Japanese bombers flying over them would be hard-pressed to find the aircraft factory.

A Japanese sub had managed to lob a few shells from its three-inch deck gun into the oil fields of Long Beach. If this was possible, then air raids were also possible. Every night the powerful beams of searchlights would lattice the sky. If a Japanese bomber had made it to the coast, the big lights would expose it to the many anti-aircraft batteries stationed around the city. Once, the guns opened up on an imagined intruder, and the shells, when they fell back into the streets of the city, wounded several citizens. Air raid wardens, middle-aged men in white doughboy helmets and arm bands with civil defense insignias, patrolled the streets at night during blackouts. Every residence was required to have heavy blackout drapes on its windows to prevent escaping light from betraying the location of Los Ange-

les to the enemy. The wardens, who took their job very seriously, made sure that did not happen. We were all in it together—kids and adults, in uniform and out. There's nothing like a common enemy to unify a country and to crystallize belief in its virtue.

My first day at the Marvin Street School was a disaster. I'd worn what kids in the east wore to school: knickers. I was teased without mercy. "Bloomers!" the kids yelled. "He's wearing bloomers!" I wouldn't go back until my mother bought me Levi's, the standard wear for California grade-schoolers.

Ruth's sister Elna moved to Los Angeles with her new husband and stepson, Graham. Graham was three years older than I was, but we became good friends. He was like a big brother. Elna's husband, Lloyd, was a Canadian, serving in the Canadian Merchant Marine. He was a good-looking, husky man with a violent streak. They stayed with us in the Ridgley Drive apartment until Ruth was able to get them a place of their own.

There was a large, empty lot next to the apartment building. Graham and I dug a deep trench and covered it with scrap lumber, then covered the lumber with dirt. It was our underground "fort," a great place to play, but an even better place to hide when the landlord came around on his unannounced inspection tours. There were other "illegal" kids in the building, and our fort was big enough to accommodate them all. The mothers wore traffic-cop whistles around their necks and whenever the landlord drove up they would blow their whistles and all the kids would head for the underground hideaway. It was great fun. The exercise seemed in keeping with the wartime atmosphere of Los Angeles.

I want to be fair to David Lee. The truth is, though, that we didn't care much for each other. He was too immature, I now believe, to take seriously the role of father. And maybe I expected too much. I remember wanting to like him, wanting him to be my father, but always finding him indifferent to my childish enthusiasms. He was a disappointment, but by that time it didn't matter all that much to me. I was back living in a family situation with my mother, which was better than boarding school, or life in Michigan with my grandmother who, I believe, was pretty much fed up with having me dumped on her by Ruth.

Ruth and David Lee lived on some kind of edge that I can't define out of context of the war's overwhelming disruptions of American life. World War II changed the country in ways that are still being discovered by social thinkers today. For one thing, large numbers of women took the place of men in the work force, since most able-bodied men between the ages of 18 and 35 were serving in the military. Another was geographic displacement. Vast populations, populations that had been more or less stable, shifted regions. The defense industry of California was a magnet that pulled families out of the rest of the country. People from the South, people from Appalachia and the Great Plains, people by the hundreds of thousands left their native soil to settle in L.A. and the San Francisco Bay Area.

There was a lot of money to be made, and after ten years of severe depression, this sudden cash flow stimulated the country. It was green amphetamine to a lethargic economy. People were excited, anticipating the good times to come. News of the war, the setbacks and

victories, kept the adrenaline flowing, and the stitches that kept the seams of society together began to give way. When they broke, America changed its basic configurations. These changes would define the last half of the twentieth century. Like everyone else, Ruth and Lee were caught up in this feverish moment.

Lee was 4-F, a selective service classification that exempted him from military service. When he was a student at Colgate, he shattered his right elbow while playing hockey. The bone of the elbow joint was fused at a right angle. He could neither lower nor raise his forearm. He wanted to serve, volunteered to drive transportation trucks, but the bureaucracy denied him.

Flannery O'Connor, in her great book of essays *Mystery and Manners,* talks about personality as a central mystery. Who we are, what motivates us, what mechanisms guide us to our ultimate fate, are essentially beyond the rational discourse of behavioral psychology. I believe this. David Lee was a mystery then and remains a mystery to me today. Though he

(From left) David Lee, Uncle Lloyd, Aunt Elna, and Ruth, 1942

was intelligent, had a fine education, and could speak at least three languages, he never wanted to be anything more than a delivery man. I remember asking him when I was in high school why he didn't get a job more suited to his education and background. (He was driving a bread truck at the time.) "Why don't you get a teaching job?" I asked. I wasn't ashamed of his minimal expectations for himself, I was just bewildered. Lee was more intelligent, better educated than most of my teachers. Why wasn't he interested in using what he had? He didn't answer, or if he did, it was an evasion. Lee never earned more than a hundred dollars a week, and when he died a few years ago, he was buried by the county of San Diego, unmourned, in a pauper's grave.

Ruth and Lee were too restless to settle down for long. After a year in Los Angeles, they moved to the Bay Area. We lived in a racially mixed government project in Richmond for almost a year, then moved to Oakland where Ruth had found a house in a Levittown-style development called Sobrante Park. Lee sold ice cream from a truck. Ruth got a job as a welder in the Kaiser shipyards on Mare Island.

In addition to covering his own routes in the east Bay Area, Lee also managed boys who sold ice cream from pushcarts. I was one of them. It was a good job for a kid, better than delivering newspapers. I was paid on commission, taking a percentage of all my sales. I worked after school and on weekends and saved my money in quart jars.

I was working my route when the war ended. V-J Day. People went crazy. They poured out into the streets, screaming and yelling. It seemed everyone was drunk. A mob attacked my pushcart. They dumped it over and took out the ice cream. I tried to protect my stock. In the scuffle, my change apron went flying. Nickels, dimes, and quarters rang against the street like silver rain. I sat bawling among the ruins. It took a while for me to get excited about the defeat of Japan.

Home ownership was not enough to stabilize my parents' lives. After a year in Oakland, they sold the house and bought another one in Vallejo, in the northeast Bay Area. Lee continued to sell ice cream. Defense jobs disappeared, and Ruth got a job in a department store demonstrating yo-yos, which had become a national rage. Then, without much notice, Lee left Vallejo for Fort Worth, Texas, and

Rick with Ruth, Los Angeles, 1943

sold ice cream there. The house in Vallejo was put up for sale. By now it was late 1946. The war was a memory. We were testing A-bombs on south Pacific atolls. This was the excitement of the day. Ruth finalized the sale of the house and we followed Lee to Fort Worth.

Though I had started the seventh grade in Vallejo, I finished it in Fort Worth. This was my seventh school since 1940. The quick disruptions turned me into a de facto loner. Friendships were never permanent, and my education was a fractured mess. I think it was these experiences more than any single thing that turned me to writing. I began to read a lot, living vicariously in the books of Mark Twain and Alexander Dumas. I liked Twain's out-and-out fantasies more than Huck Finn or Tom Sawyer. I read and re-read *A Connecticut Yankee in King Arthur's Court* and *The Prince and the Pauper.*

I often wondered if there was something more to Lee's need to get out of town than mere restlessness. I'm convinced, now, there was. Once, when I was helping him deliver bread in San Diego (where we eventually settled in

1947) we went into Logan Heights, the black section of town. It was a run-down neighborhood. Some of the streets were not paved and many of the houses were shanties. A black woman approached the truck and Lee got out to meet her. "You got my cigarettes?" she said. Her tone and demeanor were imperious, and Lee went to the back of the truck and pulled out several cartons of cigarettes. He gave them to her. I got the distinct impression that he *owed* her these cartons. There was an intimate exchange of some kind, face to face. It was not affectionate, but it was sexual. I was only thirteen at the time, but even then it seemed that Lee and this woman had more going on between them than bread and cigarettes. I can't support this, but it seems likely to me that his need to skip town again and again might have had something to do with his extramarital entanglements. In this regard, let me now say, without going into it, that Ruth was no angel herself.

After Fort Worth, we hit the road with no clear destination in sight. Lee bought his big Packard and we headed east. After a brief stay in New York we drove around the country aimlessly, looking for another likely place to try domestic life—Michigan, Iowa, Kansas, Oklahoma, Texas, New Mexico, Arizona, and finally, California again.

They bought a house in east San Diego for six thousand dollars and stayed there until 1954 when their marriage finally came apart. They drank and fought constantly. These alcohol-fueled battles roared through the house and sometimes carried out into the streets. I buried myself in books and tried to ignore them. The Hardy Boys series was a life saver. I also began to read Thorne Smith, the man who wrote the Topper series. I loved Thorne Smith. I discovered, for the first time, a truly bizarre comic mind. Reading him was an escape into hilarity. If any writer's work had a permanent influence on me, it would be the books of Thorne Smith. I don't think his work holds up today, but when I was a teenager he was the funniest writer around.

I left home in 1952, at the age of eighteen. I was a freshman at San Diego State College and joined a fraternity just so I could move out. The day I left home, Lee was beating Ruth in their bedroom. I heard her sobbing, the dull thuds of the blows. I entered their bedroom and grabbed him by his shirt and threw

him against the wall. His head banged against the plaster and his eyes rolled up showing the yellowish whites. I remember making some kind of threat, and I remember the blood draining from his face. Lee's virtues were few; courage was not one of them.

I don't know why he was beating her. It's possible she'd invited it. Enlightened people will have trouble with this last statement. I have trouble with it myself. And I suppose that, from some global perspective from which individual actions can be stripped of their circumstantial complications, it should be troubling. But individuals, and individual circumstances, always confound well-meaning generalizations. I can say this much with some certainty: Ruth was very good at provoking men to the point of blind rage. She lied to them; her affection was provisional; she said one thing and meant another; she ran around. It was not the first and would not be the last time a man struck her.

I've seen enough of violence to believe that no one should ever raise his or her hand against another. That Christian ideal does not seem to be on the horizon. And now I must add a further complicating factor: In spite of what I just said, Ruth was a good person. She was generous, good-hearted, smart, and always a very hard, uncomplaining worker.

I didn't know and didn't care who started the fight. By roughing up Lee I was making a statement. *Goodbye.* I never went back. When I saw my mother again, several years later, she had a new husband, Willie Lenick, a housewrecker from Brooklyn.

I was a terrible high school student. I never studied, never did homework. In California schools back in those days, everybody passed. I had friends who were functional illiterates who nonetheless graduated. I did well in English courses because I could put sentences together with some intelligibility and style. English teachers liked me. I got C's and D's in all my other courses, learned essentially nothing. San Diego State let me enroll as a provisional student, even though my high school record should have made me provisionally eligible for nothing beyond trade school.

My generation was born during the Great Depression when birth rates were very low. There were not very many of us. Competition for jobs, or for places in universities, was not intense. Kids today who have the kind of attitude I

*Little Al (Rick's uncle, at left) and
Big Al (Rick's father), 1954*

had wind up on the streets or living with their parents until they're thirty-five. I was given second, third, and fourth chances. We were, because of our numbers, a privileged generation.

My poor study habits continued at State. I flunked, or got D's. Now and then I got a decent grade in a course that required writing skills. I supported myself by working at night as a stock boy at an electronic parts warehouse, and later, at a steel company in National City, south of San Diego. Fraternity dues were minimal. We had no regular dining arrangements. I bought thirty-cent-a-pound steaks from a butcher on El Cajon Boulevard who specialized in horsemeat. A fraternity brother who was a skin-diver snorkeled for abalone in the La Jolla cove. In the early 1950s abalone was still abundant on the coastline. It's all gone now.

Many of the fraternity brothers were World War II vets in their late twenties and early thirties, going to school on the GI Bill. They chose this particular fraternity, Pi Kappa Alpha, because it was the most inexpensive on campus. The house was an old 1920s bunga-

low located in the small town of La Mesa, about five miles from campus. The bungalow had enough bedrooms to sleep about a dozen members.

My poor grades were making me vulnerable to the draft. I was 2-S, the student deferment classification. But you had to maintain a C average to keep it. I was well below C. In the fall of 1954, a friend of mine and I brought a sack full of vodka half-pints to school. We sat out in the quadrangle drinking them openly, trying to decide our futures. We got stupid drunk, hoping, perhaps, to end our foundering collegiate careers via dismissal, but the campus cop didn't notice us. My friend, Bill, said, "Let's join up." Bill was even more academically useless than I was. "When?" I said. "Tomorrow," he replied. "We're too goddamn drunk today."

We joined the air force, the recruiting sergeant promising us tours of duty in either the Far East or in Europe. It sounded good to us. I looked forward to adventure in "faraway places with strange sounding names," to quote the old ballad. I don't know where they sent Bill, but I was sent to a small radar station near Havre, in north central Montana. I felt betrayed at first, then fell in love with the vast, empty landscape of the Great Plains. It was a good place to sort out your life.

I dated a local Havre girl, Mary Lee Palmer. She was eighteen, I was twenty-one. We moved in together, in a small two-room apartment. It was bliss. We ran on youthful energy, unaware, or unmindful, of the emotional baggage we were both carrying. Mary Lee was a pretty redhead with a rebellious streak. And she was from a broken home, too. When we announced to her mother and stepfather that we intended to get married, they were not displeased. They had been willing to send her to college. Now they didn't have to worry about that four-year expense.

When I was a teenager, listening to Ruth and Lee do furious battle, I would daydream about living far away from home with an ideal mate. I could almost picture her. Our love would be a perfect union of like minds, and our lives together would be uninterrupted bliss. Petty argument, moody silence, nursed resentment, and eventual betrayal, could not possibly be part of the picture. It seemed that this marriage would fulfill that dream. It did, but only for a few years. We divorced in 1966, but our marriage bonds had begun to fray two or three years before that.

I was discharged from the air force in 1958. Mary Lee and I went to Missoula, where I entered the University of Montana as a math major. I was determined, now, to excel. I took my studies seriously and managed to graduate with a B average—in spite of my dismal record at San Diego State, which pulled my grade-point numbers down.

I sent job applications and was eventually hired by Boeing as a reliability engineer. The pay was good; the job was important (I worked on the Minuteman Missile project), and Seattle, in the early 1960s, was a great place to live. It seemed as though I had escaped my past. I had no writing ambitions, other than an occasional (and disposable) short story or poem.

Boeing sent me out to Great Falls, Montana, and then to Minot, North Dakota, where I worked as a reliability field engineer. I drove a pickup truck from one Minuteman missile silo to another, checking on failed equipment. It was a pleasant, outdoor job.

Mary Lee and I had two children by then, Richard and Suzanne. The four of us lived in a single-wide trailer on these field jobs. The money was better than ever since people in the field were paid very well. We received per diem as well as "dislocation" pay for the inconvenience of having to leave cosmopolitan Seattle and re-settle in the boondocks. Add to that all the overtime we wanted at time-and-a-half. We were, by our standards, rich.

I went from one job to another within the Boeing company, then, hoping for a more stable working environment, I took a job with Lockheed, in Sunnyvale, California, as a quality control engineer for the Polaris missile program. It was a good job in a bad time. President Kennedy was assassinated after I'd been at Lockheed a few months. It was announced over the P.A. system in the building where I worked. No one said anything. As the reports came over the speakers—that Kennedy had been shot, that he'd been taken to a hospital in Dallas, that he was dead—the silence became more profound. My fellow engineers bent closer to their work, as if, by narrow focus, their minds could shut out the horror.

My wife and I began to fight. We weren't drinkers, not serious drinkers at least. We didn't fuel our grievances with booze. We were pru-

dent people trying to have stable lives. Even so, our marriage started to break down. My work began to seem boring. I was going through the motions and my supervisor took note of that. I got reprimanded several times for having a "bad attitude." I took extra-long coffee breaks, flirted with a secretary and had daydreams about taking her out. Mary Lee hated living in California and wanted to go back to Montana.

Then something peculiar happened to me. I went to the movies, alone, to see Fellini's masterpiece, *8½*. I was artistically naïve, and couldn't comprehend what I was seeing on the screen. Fellini's mix of reality, dream, and fantasy boggled my mind. At the same time, I was deeply moved. What I had been putting off for so long (I was thirty now), suddenly overwhelmed me like an avalanche. I knew I could spend the rest of my working days looking at failed missile parts, tracking down the sources of the problems—and gradually becoming an embittered old man who had not lived his proper life. This knowledge struck me with such force that I began to weep in the theater. I wept on the drive home. The next morning, listening to Mozart on the car radio on the way to work, I began weeping again. I was cracking up. It was time to make a serious decision.

We moved back to Missoula in the fall of 1964 and I began to work on a master's in English, studying writing under the great poet and teacher, Richard Hugo. It was Hugo's first year as a university professor. He'd spent, coincidentally, thirteen years at Boeing as a technical writer, writing poems all the while. Dick taught me how to write. He taught me to value words, and the sounds they make. He taught me about the rhythms of strings of words, and how meaning is mostly unintentional. Intended meaning, he held, was a form of communication. And he scorned the notion that art is communication. "You want to communicate, use the telephone," he said. He was talking about poetry but I believe this notion applies to serious fiction, as well.

Most importantly, Dick taught—preached, I should say—*honesty*. He was the heart and soul of honesty. To be dishonest in writing is to hide your true self from your superficial self. To do this is to kill any possible chance of producing art. At the time it sounded like a simple prescription. Thirty years later, I am only beginning to discover how difficult, and how vital, it is.

BIBLIOGRAPHY

Novels:

A Lovely Monster: The Adventures of Claude Rains and Dr. Tellenbeck, Simon & Schuster, 1976.

Scimitar, Dutton, 1977.

Cinder, Farrar, Straus, 1978.

The Burning Women of Far Cry, Arbor House, 1986.

The Year of the Zinc Penny, Norton, 1989.

The Mortician's Apprentice, Norton, 1994.

Short-story collections:

Jack and Jill: Two Novellas and a Short Story, Dutton, 1979.

Under the Wheat, University of Pittsburgh Press, 1986.

The Coming Triumph of the Free World, Viking, 1988.

The Voice of America, Norton, 1991.

Other:

Contributor of short stories to *Antaeus, Antioch Review, Atlantic, Cavalier, Colorado State Review, Esquire, GQ, Grand Street, Harpers, Iowa Review,* and *Malahat Review.*

Vincent Ferrini

1913-

Words forged by a secret knowing take the listener or the reader to embodiments undreamt of.

Poverty troubled my deepest feelings.

The Child I was and still am asks who am I and why.

I knew I was in the unseen Heart of the Mystery.

I grew up in the bowels of the Great Depression. I distrusted the school, the teachers could not answer the why.

Something is going on in the deeps of the Ocean in hiding.

My father was an unemployed shoe worker in those Mammoth Factories, glaringly empty.

The owners had moved South for cheaper labor.

Our family was on Welfare.

School was my Nemesis.

It was not relating to my background, nor to my senses of alienation. There were no pathways to myself nor my parents.

I found the Lynn Public Library. I became obsessed with Books. I will use Words and Images to guide me out of the Labyrinth of the Psyche.

In 1941 World War II gave me a job in the Defense Plant, General Electric (GE), where I worked as a bench hand polishing buckets for airplanes to knock out the Nazis, scientifically bent on controlling the planet.

That year *No Smoke* was published, a "classic" of the Great Depression. The Death of the once Greatest Shoe City in the world.

That same year I met and married Margaret Duffy (Peg), a high school teacher, and brought with her three children into our household: Sheila, Owen, and Deirdre, who will increase our tales.

I was employed in the GE nine years. Published *No Smoke, Injunction,* and *Blood of the Tenement.*

In 1948, we moved to Gloucester.

In 1950 I met Charles Olson, a brother poet, who had a profound effect on me. A severe critic of the Art.

Vincent Ferrini—"Photo taken across the street from Charles Olson's house and where the writing of the theory of poetry is on the wall"

He wrote a mammoth tome, *The Maximus Poems,* in various stages of development. The first was addressed to me while he was away, in the form of letters. In Letter Five, he castigated me for not having the precise care for the city as he had. I wrote him a thirty-page love poem *In the Arriving* that he called the "Anti-Maximus Poem," which it wasn't, which he said was the best of my books.

We had a long-running relationship, including his two wives, Connie and Betty, and the child from each, Kate, and Charles Peter.

He died in 1950.

In 1978 I began writing the first volume of *Know Fish* and published it in 1979 through the University of Connecticut Library—four volumes in all.

These are the bare facts.

When I had completed the first volume, I had this desire for a drawing that would be the symbol of this epic.

A friend came to mind, a sculptor, not internationally famous yet, Louise Nevelson, to whom Mary Shore and I brought driftwood for her ideas. I wrote her. Not a word for months. One noontime at the Bucket of Blood in Newburyport with Truman Nelson, a historical novelist and dedicated Marxist, a painter John Di Marino, and several others, at lunch for fishchips and beer, I told them about my request. Fuck her, I said, grabbed a napkin and, with two strokes of my pen, drew a Fish oggling a Man. I had my cover. The aliveness of those two on that throwaway paper startled me beyond words. Once seen, never forgotten. In one picture the Crisis of 350 years if Fishing went out of Gloucester. Maybe Louise knew what she was about.

That was the beginning. Three other volumes followed. The first was called *The Lady of Misbegotten Voyages,* and *Da Songs,* then *The Navigators, The Community of Self,* and *This Other Ocean.* The last volume contained a two-act play, *Shadows Talking.*

I had written the innards of the fishing industry about the Demise of the Shoe Industry during the Great Depression with my first book, *No Smoke.*

In 1950, the Essex Institute in Salem, a living Museum, presented the Life and Times of the Shoe Workers in Lynn, 1850–1950. It brought together maps of the streets, the factories, photos of workers, shoe racks, tools, the replicae of a tenement and a manufacturer's home. Nothing was missing. It was a monumental exhibition of the hardships of the largest shoe city in the world.

In the last room was an enlarged poem, three-by-four feet, "The City," the first poem in *No Smoke.* I was dead and alive at the same time. It shook me.

My father was a shoe worker all his life, so were my uncles and cousins, and so was I for a year.

In 1991 at the same Museum, a showing of my nephew Henry's video film of my life was screened, *Poem in Action.* I read for an hour about fishes and the loves of the fisher people, and an hour for the movie. The room was packed. We got a standing ovation from over three hundred persons.

These events are the Moonstone and Ruby in the Laurel of a Poet.

Each book was the document of emotional history lived intensely at the centers of perception.

A Tale of Psyche was the delineation of a personal life impersonalized. A book that sprung up over the waves like two dolphins.

Injunction was in the grip of General Electric (GE), making weapons against the Nazis, and working as a bench hand or salvaging scrap copper wire, sitting beside a small man with a tonlike voice, and cutting rolls of tape, studying the intestines of a Behemoth.

Being married, raising a family of three children, came out in *Blood of the Tenement,* and the "Quarrel," drunk on Peg, the Winewoman. Sheila, Owen, and Deirdre, the three children poems, changing every minute, the growings distinct as the petals of each flower they were moving with.

And quitting GE when the harassing of the Communists by the neanderthals of the flag, the ones with all the answers, became unbearable.

That was the ending of making shoes, and the Hercules Factories with no arms and no legs, unable to move, empty as the VOID sitting on the seaside city and the amputated neighborhoods. Evenings, the Diamond District, the citadels of the Shoe Manufacturers, losing that precious color of their superior strongholds, the opposite world to the Brickyards where the poor and the workingclass lived in closeknit tenements, like loose boats in economic storms.

The shock of Gloucester at night visiting an artist. I will inherit his house and his frame. Am now alone in this house, living in an island of egomaniacs, of the lumpen proletariat, the fishermen, the craftspeople, the artists, and today the poets, stars in a Lightland that demanded attention from the promontorial views, each in possession of the Ocean.

That's when *The Infinite* grabbed me by the hair and the crotch and said PEOPLE, for which Charles Olson stuck his needles in my eyes— yeah, one person at a time.

We were writing poems to each other across the harbor vessels. Walking back and forth on the waters!

He was spying on me. I was finding out for myself when I owned my eyes after I was given notice it was time to leave my mother's Taj Mahal.

This Olson had a knack of pinning a listener down. He had a mercurial pickaxe, he was in his diamond view, you could see it in glints of his eyelight.

Like George Butterick said, Olson is right and so are you.

And if Olson heard me say this, he'd probably have another Letter Five to hack me to pieces with, that the characters I knew in Lynn and gave eternal life to in *No Smoke* had each in a peculiar way the contents in Helen Stein's eyes, and I knew them as close as you can get without stealing each one's soul.

The Garden, as clear a poem of love as each one feels intimately with, sank in Olson's meat machine, as anyone else's.

A friend Jim Bever bought me a small handpress I printed the nineteen-page poem on, my children helped me to cut the sheets and staple the small pamphlet so it could fit in a suit pocket or a handbag and feel at home, going places on a vacation.

The Law includes take others with you, or go with them, changing the conditioning process that Olson had a gift for and so did this skylark.

The Japanese entered my life with their haiku and Zen, when *Mindscapes* came forth, a book of hand poems, and to get to the cause, *The Square Root of In.*

What fun that was picking poems off the street, anywhere my eyes stopped for a second, penetrated, sunk and drew up from their deeps, until Olson latched onto *In* and drove hard into the body of his Elephant Book, the *Maximus*—Archeologist of Evolution's shifting faces.

The Square Root of the thing in itself, once known, brings a power that is invincible, but as yet unpolitical.

O the kinds of power!

And the Almightiest Power—Politics—the poets shun away from as the plague it is, but there the rites of Language determine the primal sensitivities of the people, by the people, and for the people—words that ring broken-down songs.

Imagine, artists have yet to use the divine Spring, LOVE POWER.

It dumbfounds me that that free agency is utterly ignored, steered away from, knowing

Ferrini at the time No Smoke *was published, 1941*

instinctively that their life would change irretrievably, if one drop of that Divine Elixir was swallowed.

This is the fuel that runs me, where the public and the private is one:

> A spinning coin
> self sprung
>
> like all outside
> never stopping

> (From *Hermit of the Clouds*)

the simplicity of this seed has value only if it is ingested and left to fructify!

As a word from a parent or a teacher sticks in memory as a living territorial imperative.

Taking a whole life to vomit, purified!

The touched ones come to me, the others fear my intensities, and they revise their opinions when they join in my visceral laughter or even then that contagion is threatening.

One night we took over the Armory, now a home for the elderly, and had two rock bands, three belly dancers, booze, food, and divine

"My wife Peg and me," about 1949

enthusiasm for raising the money to launch the first volume of *Know Fish*. We raised four thousand bucks, the ladies and the guys were before and behind the fishes, we are, I at departures and arrivals, coming back loaded to the topmost mast! The city itself was high as a balloon ship! The fishes were loud with arias, the fisherwomen carrying the boats and the kids in their arms!

For a few years no more, the fishes are yelling at us, give us time to breed and sing as you do in bed when you do!

Have reverence for us as you do for St. Peter, and the Mary of us all, if the church is not in the Ocean, it is divorced from the Real, the Ideal is form and content, Beware of the Split, Western Civilization is rotting between!

So the fishes have gone on a vacation, to multiply, the law is INCLUDE. Don't rape the earth, or suffer the consequences.

Economics affects people's existence, and Politics, and poetry does not really slide off; something is diabolically wrong here.

This is the Uses of Language, and poetry is supposed to be the King and Queen here, the split is the disease is a Vortex—

In ignoring the small, so is the great diminished.

This humpty-dumpty Value edifice has the people, the masses of humanity as Expendable—

If a leaf of the Garden is unimportant, so is the whole Garden that leaf.

This is the nerve root of individual and communal illness.

This is the thought that never leaves me. It is the Mystery Oil—

As a car is so is the body, banged up, needing body work or the engine or both—a cliche, an accepted habit—

Art's subliminal to make connections immediately, lacking the carry-through in a society gone amuck—

Every community thrives on a theatre and making Art of it.

It is its Joie de Vivre, and the styles of dancing for jumping in.

One such theatre was missing for years.

The theatre starved, went to work, and organized the Cape Ann Theatre.

Knocked one up we did. Michael McNamara brought the interested together, we established a going enterprise, and produced old-timers and recent plays. McNamara was the director.

It brought alive two Ferrini plays to full houses at the Puritan Building cornering Main and Washington streets.

Cape Ann Theatre had a Board of Directors, McNamara, Artistic Director, Ed Price, Jud Wilson Jr., Pat Perry, Tim Perkins, Joseph Profetto, Rick Looney, Kevin Ellis, Joanne Cooper, and Christina Thibodeau.

"MOONPRINTS" was a one-act play about my mother, my father, and three brothers, acted by Constance Condon, Anthony Sutera, Anthony Gentile, Tracy Tinkham, and Thomas Cole.

On the bill was another of my one-act plays from *Know Fish, Volume III*, "The Navigators," about developers, "Base-Ball," performed by Edward Price, Ann Koumou, John Hart, Genny Linsky, Susan Bulba, Christina Thibodeau, and Tim Perkins, both plays directed by McNamara, who played in "Base-Ball."

After the performance, Israel Horowitz said he "did not like them." The *Gloucester Daily Times* headlined them "Surprisingly Good!"

The Cape Ann Theatre brought on our stage a number of old-timers, lived for five years, and then folded due to the usual causes such local dreams are addicted to.

Horowitz, a local playwright with an international reputation, created The Gloucester Stage Company for the production of his new works before they tried on the world.

I tried him once to no success.

Celeste Miller, who heard me read at The Bookstore, sent me two complimentary tickets for her Dance Performance. I hadn't been there since its inception and hesitated going. Some friends said why not? I went with McNamara, who acted in *Scrooge and Marley.*

I went in and was thoroughly bewitched by the Space and its maneuverabilities. I was high on the Logistics of Theatre. And Miller was excellent.

At the intermission, Izzy approached me and I said, "This theatre has tremendous possibilities. It is the first time I have been here in fourteen years." He said, "We've been here sixteen years!" and left.

That's his theatre, door, stage, and choices.

Such a Boss enjoys his power but he's insecure.

Julian Beck of New York's Living Theatre is the closest to my idea of a vital theatre, embracing the actors and the people at large.

Antonin Artaud and his Theatre of the Double knocked contemporary drama out of its iron armor and out of the Ring. He's the enemy of social constraints and remains a lonely dramaturge. He's influenced some. In another one hundred or two years he'll be in.

Convinced that staged drama is the art form of the centuries, and since it has become very expensive, the Movies have taken its place as a mass media, with its ups and downs, committed to blockbusters in order to regain and surpass its outlays and reap bonanzas.

That's why my nephew's videotape is successful when it travels with me reading. They hear and they also see and participate in the two arts.

When I saw the movie *Uncle Vanya* at 42nd Street, I was in the honeymoon bed of the Stage and the Film. It threw me deep into myself. The actor usually far-off was up front in my face, pouring his feelings with me. O would Shakespeare be moved beyond himself? The bodies are missing but, what the Hell, look what is happening. He was one of the newly married and the other.

The Theatre—where poetry leapfrogs itself over all the deities claiming to be The Chosen.

When Life and the Theatre are that coin, O the festivals we will have, spending that gold coin!

What prescriptions for the ills of the planet— Humans will know it participating and so will the Earth!

John Corina was searching for a one-act play for an opera, and mine was one of the six he decided to choose from, and mine had the honor. He made *Telling of the North Star* that appeared in *The Best Short Plays of 1952–53* into a one-act chamber opera that was performed at the University of Georgia in Athens. O Athens, a play about a Gloucester family and a lost ship come back to port.

Not yet produced in my home city, and we have a Symphony.

If I cannot get my plays produced, I will see them published. I can wait.

One is on the rim of falling into the whirlpool. A full-length play, *The Double Point,* about a Veteran of Vietnam, a Point-man socked with twenty-one years for growing grass in Vermont, cut down to eleven.

Another one-act play, *The Wellwater,* about a Bishop and his son, a Marxist, and his daughter, and a sexton.

My two wives are Irish and women lovers. I met Yeats in his grave, five years ago, when McNamara took me to Europe: six days in Ireland, and three days in Amsterdam. And soon Bill Spencer, a Taoist, a friend of early Lynn, and a herbalist, my Second Opinion healer, will recite a poem for Yeats' ears alone, going into the ground and dropping the words into the basket of his skull for his journeys back and forth.

When I saw Judy Chicago's *Dinner Party,* I flew around like a crazed cormorant, spying to eat from any plate, even when there was nothing there. Yet the emptiness fired my hunger, the stunning variety lifted me off my mind, and I was poking around, checking out each individual woman saying this is me, we are not all alike, and tough we are, we are as special as the God the multitudes worship on their knees. I stooped to read their histories, each had her story to tell, and the sight of the plates stirred my libido, as I sat down one plate at a time, Emily Dickinson's Saint Mary Magdalene, and to the next plate. I was totally absorbed by the immaculate beauty of Joan of Arc, Heloise's passion trembled on my lips, I was at the table of the Holiest of Holies, there was a halo surrounding each plate, never before was such a dinner exhibited for public eyes. I was at the Resurrection of each woman! Each has been vindicated! The design came not from God but the Goddess who reigns, knowing behind the scenes that she is the WHOLE! Each plate is verifying! For the first time in all the Ages of Humanity, before my eyes, I could barely hold it, my brain was on fire at the audacity of these women to show their innermost naked, the utter wonder that this is real!

The Revolution no revolution comes anywhere near in its depth of perception!

I knew someday in my darkest lining that this would take place, on such a scale that dwarfs the imagination of men!

The hidden personal and public so intimately displayed—

Eat with your eyes! Boy, did I! Still doing, with my other eyes!

The silent music, in details. If Congress could go to this Dinner Party and eat, they would each have a metanoia!

We would be able to put the shit that comes from there in its proper bin.

The veils would fall from their ignorance and fear, being reborn!

The lesson digested, or constipated from too much reality!

What great bowel movements could follow, seeing things just as they are!

This is the poetry that turned me inside out!

When Art does this, I am literally transformed into my Original Face!

The innermost secret, put on plates for the individual public to join The Party.

Reverence for the Mystery up front, raw and so beautiful I stopped breathing. I was shown where I came from, head out or feet first, that I was the beloved intimate of that holiest rite!

Each template divine!

Each arrived and recognized, for us immediately, getting it, for each living it to the utmost degree, enlightened, and now reviving others to feed on understanding without fear, liberated from past restrictions.

Judy Chicago!

Mary Daly!

Barbara G. Walker!

Inseminators!

I had already seen Edmund Sullivan's show of sculptures, drawings, paintings, when he asked me what I liked best, and I said that self-portrait. And John Di Marino says, will you look at my paintings, and I, you want me to look at your work, are you sure, yes, are you sure, yes yes. So we walk to his studio upstairs, to this small room stuffed with echoes of Gauguin, Van Gogh, Pissarro, Matisse, you name it. You're a blotting picker-upper. Get rid of this stuff, blindfold yourself, and paint with your arm. I will. He wraps a white rag over his eyes, picks up a brush and a can of white paint, lifts an old vertical painting, puts it on the easel upright with one thrust at the canvas, then grabs a brush and a can of deep blue paint, whacks it on the canvas, back to the first can, slams a stroke fast as Van Gogh, white hair, blue nose and lip, white chin and beard, fast furious, he rips off the provident blinding rag, in a hot glory. It's your portrait, and I, that's your finest work, it's yours—

He's launched full blast out of Zen.

From then on his drawings are rushing out of that faucet—

I hang the unexpected signature on my kitchen wall, he's made his niche in my restless Museum.

His lamp—

Next to Peter Petronzio's memory of a lobster fisher beside his hut and wheelbarrow at the Gulf of a mountain wave.

Opposite Di Marino are the two portraits in one frame by Helen Bishop of the poet as a prophet, speaking, laughing, gesticulating, and a young man, head bowed, reading from a book out loud.

Inseminations—

Bumper to bumper, stuck in the traffic of the trying to make it—

Lives in heat and arrested—

To catch the art and the life immediately, as the lady who saw me and asked for a session. Meet me under the oak tree. She came with a cardboard box, told me her tale of family on the rapids. What's in the box? Five womb-warm poems as she plucked out five baby rabbits and a sculpture of the listener, the size of a fingernail—gone, not a word from her, the wordless working—

Janice let me peek into her cameo movie—

How old are you?

Twenty-one—

What's bugging you?

I hate my mother, I hate my father, I hate myself.

Good—

What do you mean good?

It is all upfront, you can see the running film, the characters are deeply engaged in each happening—

I can see them—

Your mother is locked in her head's prison, so is your father in his deadly roots, and you, there, visiting each one at a time and then together wrangling over ghosts which they are in your head.

What do I do?

Watch them, study their actions, their voice tones, the silences—

They aren't listening—

Conflicting view driving them hither and yonder—

They seem alone—

They are, deeply so—

I can see them as not my father and mother—

And you?

As another person not myself—

Give them plenty of space—

I am doing that, and I feel released—

And Janice, what about her—

I am feeling for her and can see her as a person in her own orbit—

Can you make love to her?—

I think I can—

Then go ahead, be a lesbian—

NO—

Try it, just for something new.

I can't—

Why not, that person is yourself—

It is, the shock shifted me, I am dislocated—

Caress her with your hands—

She's still a stranger—

Tell her who you are, think it—

I did, she smiled—

Touch her—

Too much space—

Embrace her

O she feels alien and good!

I will leave you, go all the way, take your time, stay with it—as long as you enjoy the mounting sensations, and you will, later you will let your mother and father go as persons not inside you, with bodyminds of their own.

She took the cameo with her, walked into it, and left, directing it as one of the three players finding old friends.

"My nephew Henry (future filmmaker of Poem in Action*), my son Owen, my brother Lindo, my wife Peg, our daughter Deirdre (who died at sixteen of leukemia), Lindo's wife Gladys, and myself," 1959*

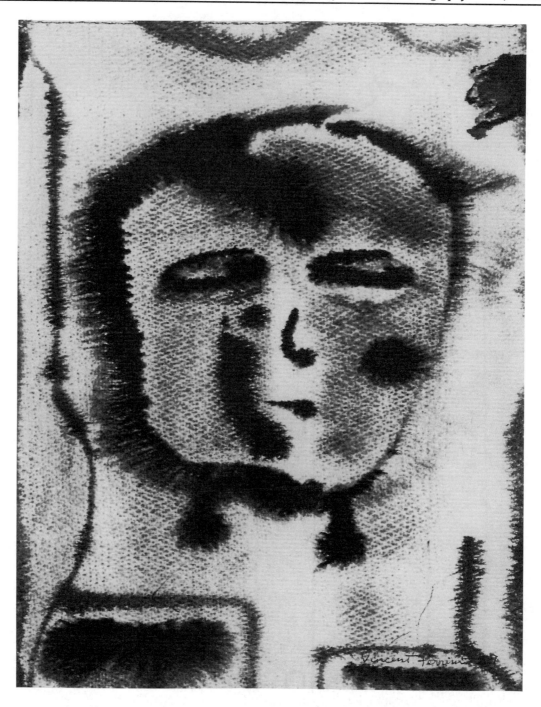

Watercolor portrait of son Owen at ten years of age by Vincent Ferrini

I was deep into Infancy, I knew it would present me with a talisman to the origins of my Journey.

The infant was six months alert, and she was in her father's arms, when she reached out for my cheek. Look, said her father, Abbe-Rose is making love to Vincent.

Another infant reading my thought, as so many do, and noticing the shadows there as hers came on.

The two flowers in the shape of two cupped hands, green on white paper, and red lines shooting out, in orgasm, and across the room, Georgia O'Keeffe sizing up the nine-year-old child's spontaneous drawing, stunned that it caught what her flowers of the Desert took so long to paint in precise stages. Each to her own!

As any expression that recaptures the emotional ocean.

Rage at the widening gap between the Richer and the Poorer.

The memories of poverty are etched in my marrow, as when Congress robbed the children in need.

In the arts such feelings are passé. Disengagement is the way to advance one's career.

Emotion is still the fuel of Art.

Which threw me back into my father's family as a kid on Welfare, and the current sadness, a wet suit. At Bill Spencer's studio I painted my first monotype, one of the abandoned children.

It was only after Charles Olson was dead eight years that I could start on my big Gloucester poem, when his shadow had completely melted into the ocean of the ground and he was safely asleep and his eyes were no longer on my neck. After George Butterick had published his *Selected Ferrini* and introduced me to the world of literature.

When George saw the first volume, knowing I had my own voice apart from his need for owning Gloucester, his special turf ordained by the Fates, but those three duennas were partial to me and approved my style and pitch, so different from his ultrascholastic dynamics, I asked him to write the introduction. He said no, get Paul Metcalf, who willingly accepted the task. When he did, we were pleased, but George said ask him to make "Mayor" and "city" plural, which Paul did, seeing the future possibilities of poets becoming the Voices of towns, hamlets, and cities, affecting the climate of communication on all levels since language is the foundation.

George was the most perspicacious scholar extant then.

I visit him and Colette and their two sons in Willimantic, Connecticut.

He spent five years on *A Guide to the Maximus Poems* for his Ph.D.

Without Butterick as his Virgil, the reader is lost.

George, the lanky erudite poet, lit with the Norse light and the Irish mist, who saw what Olson and Ferrini had in common with life

and literature, who sacrificed himself to explaining Maximus, and putting his epic together, from parts in the process.

Who gave his tongue, his eyes, his mind, his head, strength to making Olson whole to the world of letters.

His home was a hotbed of living art, his private working room, a sanctuary of Greek Gods and maps to unknown generations. Stacked with books and papers from every direction of the blue planet, and the realms of the unthought of. The last two years in bed, with a tube delivering the morphine that kept him alive, attended by wife, the nurse of his wracked physique.

She a painter, a sculptor, designer, mother of two self-moving sons, as anyone of them, or George, could fit into a copper armor for meeting the Heroes of the Iliad on any terms they chose. They shone and the house ablazing with her vibrating works, human, metal, stone, paint, and the angel figures she made out of colored taught thread, presenting me with one angel, the length of the little finger, that guides my shack that is white with a Yiddish Blue door.

Bedridden, tied to the tank of his Moly.

I would visit and we'd catch up with our literary concerns.

Very anxious to see the book of his *Collected Poems* in the works before he died.

Almost a half dozen of small pamphlets of his poems, hard as jewels, with colored lights flashing from the essence of his unselfish compassion for the divine creatures of this Earth.

He could catch a flaw in the making, or see the whole of an incident in a single image.

The last time I was with him, he said, "I'll be dead in two months," spoken without regret, accepting his Destiny as it happened, secure in the results of his contribution to a Master of the Language. The tube connecting him to three worlds he was conversant with.

While Colette was attending his needs, at the same time hammering copper, iron, paint, thread into a ship for her beloved husband, to take him on his astral trip, Vincent, drop it, I'm as close to my sons as the cannon on Stage Fort Park, aiming at the ghosts of the living past, and my hereafter is the roads and cities you travel through to accompany Colette through this travail.

Yes George. Did Olson ever realize what you did for him? Probably not, he was so busy on his own ship with his dedicated crew.

The angel of desire she gave me stands on my altar watching.

When I got home from the last visit, when I told him, George, you are a great poem, he already had gone through the proofs of his *Collected,* and he gave me that innermost smile, knowing he had come through for what was closest.

As soon as I got through my blue door, I called him. Colette answered, "George just died." A boulder took me down through the bottomless living waters.

At the memorial service in the Special Collections of the University of Connecticut, filled with his devotees, I remember, Charley secundo, Colette, the sons, others, and I read a long poem that is part of the last book of *Know Fish,* "This Other Ocean."

Colette sent me a small package, a handful, with his ashes, asking me and Jonathan Bayliss, novelist, playwright, and close friend of Butterick's, to distribute the last of George somewhere in Dogtown, and the rest into the Harbor.

For weeks the fragments of that Idyl slept on my working table.

> Jonathan & I were on
> one of the loneliest roads
> checking for his place in Eternity
> we spied 2 boulders
> holding up the tallest tree
> swaying among the clouds
> there between them
> we laid half a hand of him—
> at the Harbor letting
> the last colored pieces
> slip through our fingers
> upon the outgoing tide
> to cling to the pilings
> as the barnacles they would
> become

If George had not written that Guide, students would be floundering over the spiritbody of *Maximus,* and the teachers buried in homework.

Now readers have been given searchlights.

As Olson suggested, take a subject, an idea, even a hunch about something that interests you, and know more about it than anyone else.

He hit on what George did, what I have done with my life, to penetrate the need for Poverty on all levels of existence.

So I see life as living art, and art as the shadows of life.

George, the student, earning his third degree, who knew more about Olson and *Maximus* than anyone in current Culture, became the Exemplar of the Axiom that could be on the portals of high schools and colleges.

You won't believe this but CETA put me to work writing poems and dancing, with the pleasures of being myself, unlike the surveillance of the WPA watchdogs. Hired by two little women, the most adorable Muses, Jo-Ann Castano and Jessica Filtrante, a sculptor, and a painter on cloth, metal, and paper. For one whole year at $168.17 every week, I appeared two days at the Old Town Hall in Salem, to sharpen our tools, assessing the process with our projects, planning exhibits, readings, and dreaming about ending the limits of its life.

We brought in the community for parties, outdoor circuses, and concerts. We had everything going, photographing psyches, puppet congresses, mobile personalities in word, iron, or windbreakers. The shows we produced were free to the public and they jumped for joy as much as we did, and the poems moved into a thick manuscript, stored for posterity, ready to ride at any love tap.

The money we earned went back into the local economy or the State's. They benefitted, thanking us for bringing them into our fantasies made real.

A wound top spinning on micro seconds, this Castano is far in and far out from the marketing, making it. A one-woman spaceship with techniques for meeting anywhere without being handicapped by bodies.

Filtrante, a mixture of races, no one a sacred manipulator. What a hungry field her energy is, the film of history continuously showing. Her Amerindian peace, her designs set on a shoulder, a floor, or a wall, pulling the observer into her states of primordial tranquillity, one feels standing beside her, or listening, the words being spare and hard to reach.

These two image-makers, as all the artists on the merry-go-round of doing what is innate, among a dozen or so, at their daily bread, working their arts as a way of living fully.

A taste of the future of the arts.

This poet, who came to visit me, fresh from his immersion in Olson, wanting to meet one of the figures in Mastership Maximus, Tom Taylor, from Montana and Washington State,

Cover drawing for Know Fish, Volumes I & II, *by Vincent Ferrini*

said Gloucester is his place also, telling me Gloucester is so much in his head he needs a foothold here. I asked him where he came from. Montana. Montana is almost the size of the original Thirteen Colonies, go back, your roots are there, you will be alone, the whole Earth at your feet. Gloucester is already top-heavy.

He listened and went back home, and our correspondences have been cross-country.

He knew the ropes, he had the world of literature under his scalp, familiar with Indian lore and the reservations. A shark of the George Butterick brotherhood.

The poems came fast and in bunches, he is fecund as he calls me, writing constantly without a break, no lunch, no supper, he was getting the silent ruminations into words, and sentences that ran from Missoula to Gloucester, miles, unbroken. They keep coming nonstop.

No one paid any attention. I did.

He is the first poet writing or breathing poems, every second, every minute, no letup, no weekends, no vacation, and doing this all day and night at his berth at the cubbyhole in

the Geology Department of Portland State University.

He got back to the breath, Olson's creed to the function of making verse count.

The manuscripts were the river he and I sailed on, but he was desperate to make sure he did not lose one special second. I could sleep, he could not. He had to make sure the world paid attention and Crowned him King of Poetry. Olson could be Chief of Court, or the Grandfather Sage.

There was and still is a desperation that he is going to be missed. He had to be recognized first before the cyberpoet or so-called Language movement took over the Universities and the ground schools.

Like Philip Weld, secundo of Gloucester, tripping on ninety miles, I felt safe. Tom was out to beat the speed of light. It also is my speed, as soon as a thought comes to mind I want to deliver instantaneously. That's how we function, but for two persons being in the same space it was closer than lovers who sailed on the spaces between.

Tom demanded all. Would he get to my thought before I did? He did. At moments when the letters were at snail mail. Now that Jo-Ann stamped into the Internet, the cyberpoets are crisscrossing their lightspeeds, and the individual is being blotted out, or hysterical about the possibility that if they did not get instant recognition, they would die in midflight, choked on their cyberumbilical.

The American disease for making it has outwinged itself. Chaos is a tide that is going one way.

Tom was in works twenty-five years ago, he had written his theory of poetry in two essays, *The Visionary Education* and *Diction.*

I told him to back off, you don't have to convince every atom or person you've arrived, others are merely catching up, they are historically on the way backwards.

He is the Father of Himself.

Forty years in the Birth canal.

Out at last, now that he can see himself as he is and doesn't need anyone to tell him so.

The Daimon is the secret ally.

Like the calm in the music of the marrow.

The awareness gets written down when the poem floats or erupts into Consciousness.

It comes and goes in myriad States of Absence.

Discontinuity/continuity being the joined lovers.

Captured or loose, the POEM is separate and together as the Earth in the Cosmos is the dancing pulse of the Beholder and Beheld.

Thriving with the minutiae and the Whole.

Seen for the first moment and the quickening space.

The rhythm beating as the Poem in each human.

When we have not forgotten who we really are.

Then, we hunt for the stillness of ease a finished work of Art has.

It is this functioning awareness governing actions and thoughts, stemming from the senses of Intuition.

Owen's children, Ben, about ten, and Cara, eight, "both raised without a mother; Owen's doing a great job!"

In this POEM, the insanities of society make their ghostly appearances.

The fountain springs of all existences and the POEM are the same.

The Poor and the Rich are movies in the skull of the unrealized.

LOVE is the spontaneous Theatre.

Its Golden Light is obscured by the Ego and its insatiable devourings.

The POEM is all yours, you are IT.

You give up the world that limits your potential, which is what Nature is challenging you for. Give it to Her, and it all comes back.

Give a fistful and that's what you inherit.

Give all of yourself, and everything comes of its own accord.

Each one is the Name of the Mystery and the unfolding story of the POEM.

It cannot be possessed.

Trust it.

Live it.

As Elaine Wing, the painter, Paul Wing, the jeweler, and Ferrini, the poem[1], bending the saw, boogie woogie at the piano, and a large silver spoon at wood, drum strings, and furniture in our Asylum Triangle, 3 mad-ones in music, Isaiah in USA, the Prophet on a disk, Opus Minus One, where sounds are born before Anyone.

The saw winding the stars into the fireplace for messages.

Once the Poet, anyone or anything, and an Agency of the Conscious/unconscious, you can write with one Hand and many, or speak with one Tongue or many.

Don't be stingy, Praise!

Use all the tactics Imagination has in store!

Just to be alive is a miracle, and to be dead too.

Eat words and shit them out!

They are the Food, for the body and the Soul!

Don't make them what they are not, if there is no life in them burn them as the cells do to perform the tasks of Unseen.

The feet on the ground, the head in the skies, as far down as desired to go and then as high up, O totem!

Elaine Wing is my astrological sister, she is the only one who has captured my bodysoul

in paint, 36″ x 40″, it is the beating heart of my dwelling, it is reproduced on my autobiography *Hermit of the Clouds,* it is a statement of the sentence above this one.

Wing is her married name, Ferraresso, her plate belongs on the table of the *Dinner Party* by Judy Chicago. She is a Cancer, but her Moon is in a different sphere. We are Moon Children, the center of the Zodiac is my heatmind. Her eye is devastating.

Her Gloucester paintings will one day be published as such.

The colors are bold and concrete as the persons and the places.

She has a shack in Lanesville, one of the villages and the most wild and individual, as each is but so special in temperament and habit. She figures prominently in the Artlife of my residence in the most highly idiosyncratic island I know of.

Her tongue when aroused spits arrows tipped with fireheads.

Therefore she is among the witches of her breed.

She or one of her amigos gave me a brownie spiked with a seed of outlawed grass. I was on the porch of the house she and Paul built with their own hands, overlooking the setting Sun, and peeked over, as though I was on the edge of an alp. I trembled in horror and dread, backed off on my ass, crawling across the room, the other guests unaware of my distress. I reached the stairs and hugged the floor, wondering if I could ever make it to the bottom without falling into a pit of broken bones. Each staged moving so cautious and careful that it took me a year to get to the next step below, a year at a time. It was so nerve-wracking that my flesh was as tense as a violin string ready to snap. It was a century when I made the kitchen floor. I was so released that I had left my body in another world. I was light and grateful for having left her house clean and myself too.

Watch out, Vincent, Whitman had not caught up with this grass. And yet he may and have been immune to any angel of destruction.

That it is a medicine for others, what a boon for them.

Elaine's deepest hold on the Real is Music, which bypasses the mind, dives into the gut, taking over the emotional network.

And the key practitioners are in the drum, the black were born there as we all are, but

---

[1]Vincent Ferrini was featured in a cover story entitled "I am the poem," in *North Shore Magazine* (Beverly, Massachusetts), April 8, 1993.

they are overhead in feelings from where she and I are, and music triggers off sensations and images that pull us incognito into uninhabited regions of the blood harbors.

Jazz for her, Dionysian rhythm for me, rock liberties, and loose behaviors, tuned-tense, and private.

Music, the pound of poetry, the subtle sinuations, the personal and extraterritorial, the guitars, as the sitar, and the bongo, all instruments made of earth material and the unearthly, words are made from these with a poetry seducing participation.

These are the song poets who corral the multitudes in orgies of frenzy, knocking off the head, and the bodies go mad with delight and communal fucking.

Poetry as Poetry can't do this, can't match this, not here, maybe in Russia once with crowds as large as Football or Baseball draw, still spectators in most of the arts.

My theatre is going on every split second, the elements being the drumbeats; and the atoms, to the outermost galaxies, they too, each in its own possession, in the mingling mystique.

Those who see are in, and those on the rim watching and joining at their private paces.

The POEM of these senses is the wealth to aim at.

Elaine knows it, I can tell when she is seething or angry, frustrated.

Waldren Joseph brings it all for them, especially his silences! I read Bibles in his stances. As I do in hers.

When a society makes Music as the primary food, as Amendment Extraordinaire to the Constitution, and Education free to the Infant and the Adult, that Nation will have a people as its mightiest treasure and not all the Gold in Fort Knox as a possibility for anyone so ambitious.

Imagine a Nation founded on JOY as the greatest good with the greatest freedom!

A Nation founded on nourishing Enthusiasm!

No testing for degrees to join the infrastructure and its deadly routines and restrictions of the Spirit.

When the Poets choose people and Congress to do their work in and with, the ultrarevolution has saddled Pegasus.

The colors of Elaine's paintings have the beat of that enthusiasm and the Power exuding from this island I live in and on!

As Michael McNamara, a dynamo, an empathizer par excellence, as director and actor of his own theatre in the school committee, his first public office, outside of the staged sequestered drama, the boxed in. Committed to the life-drama of the community's responsibility to the Education of the Children, the roots of future families and informed citizens for participatory democracy. A possible Mayor's job in City Hall for transcendence of community's personal consciousness. Children exercising unlimited potentialities, examples for the adult world!

McNamara is fully occupied in his living theatre. He has the maturity and the ability to articulate situations as they come up. He is quoted as the others, and his clarity and courage are witnessed by the citizens and audiences at public meetings.

He is one of our Seers.

The self in education, for a family yet to come, for the city as it is and could be better, and its physical beauty to enlighten the human dilemma, that each person is the crown and glory of our City.

Making clear the Vision, delicately picking off the cobwebs, understanding the agendas of self-interest, and in the process of working with people wherever they are, finding themselves or not, enjoying the process, exercising the power, and passing it on.

McNamara is equipped to work with the realities of any given problem.

I have seen him in action, directing a play, acting in that drama, and inspiring the actors to pull it off.

This is the drama everyone is in, anyway it is viewed.

If a Play on the stage is a work of Art, so can the Play of living people become as involving and as artistic.

Imagine, everyone is INCLUDED, not excluded.

Imagine the energy that generates!

To abide in that observation.

If EDUCATION can follow through its purpose, the graduates will be in position to live their individual destinies instead of repeating their parents' fates. Echoes or this *never was before* on emancipated terms.

The disease of exclusion is rampant and the Earth knows it. Keep noticing the WEATHER, all kinds!

Humanity is a bullet shot from a gun, or ready to blow itself up in the Neutron Bomb.

Don't be timid, don't be afraid, you are invited to the *Dinner Party*. Nibbling on gossip, rage, and Divine Delight.

Listen to the Women.

Listen to the Heart, where the shining sight is, the sites.

A hole in the snow and no two repeating.

A Peace that is the Axis of the Center and Circumference, unseen and totally present.

Jane Robbins wanted to do a book with me, her drawings and my poems. I said do it alone, you don't need me. She said it is not a need, it is my intimacy for your poems. Okay, then, and we did. What a labor choosing the right pictures. The poems were no trouble. After it was done, what shall we call it, *Deluxe Daring*, your astrological signature.

A very insightful one she is, sometime travelling at the speed of light. The cyberpeers are on, and difficult to hop on when the pace is so mechanical. This lady who lives on her hunches, her nemesis.

O these persons who are POMES!

This lady who one day is in China, the next with a New Age guru, and has the sensitivity of Picasso line drawing on the air of what's coming, I can play with in my theatre!

When three or four are together each is on guard, or one burst of laughter relaxes the tensions, held as tight as that famous atom.

The Wishing Well is behind the bellybutton.

I must tell you about Tom Taylor, the nonstopping writing poet, whose MSS are pushing me out of my house, whose poems are as numerous and flowing as the seconds of running time, each second a word for, can you see it, long enough to circle the earth three times, maybe TIME itself will say enough Tom, lie down on your couch, and sleep for one whole day, and I will rest with you, then we'll all be in dire trouble, TIME STOPPED FOR TWENTY-FOUR HOURS, and Humanity in strict Chaos, or might not even know this poet who is determined to fill each second with a word, the only poet I know who's been doing this for the quarter century I have known him, founded now among the Cybercats, as the Amazon of Verse! The Night skies at his feet, and worldwide magic boxes.

Who, studying at the Feet of Ezra, in and out of jail, W. C. Williams, and Mountainman of poetics, Olson, the proud inheritor of the Helicon Historians.

George Francis Butterick, poet and scholar

Tom Lowe Taylor, TLT, anabasis, poet father of the LANGUAGE founders, tied umbilically to the vagina screens, lost in the Uroboros WOMB.

Ah the Cybergenius, the oracles of the written word, the innocent immortal dedicators, we are linked, Jim Leftwich in Charlottesville, Virginia, who sent me a small pamphlet, *Dirt*, I tried reading, and asked him next time to send a tape so I can hear it. Anyway Susan Pisano, a psychic, picked it up and read a page, and it sounded brand new, the ears got it. He puts out *Juxta*, sent me a copy, I read it, and sent him *The Broth of Mischief*. He's open to me, he asked me to take on an issue of his *Electronic* magazine, I pondered and accepted, twenty-nine pages in his beehive.

Jake Berry from Florence, Alabama, what cities, working on *Brambu Drezi*, book ONE at hand, sixty pages, thirty both sides, with an eight-page introduction. *The Hero as Man of Letters* by Jack Foley, a forenote, drawings, designs and directions. Typeface on the picayune, and crowded, very, at battle with my eyes, but I climb on board his barque, *Brambu Drezi,* before BEFORE. I am still going wherever it is taking me.

Jack Foley is brilliant, knows the past of verse, and the MAKERS thereof. Love his clarity. And he's into the performance kickabout.

On word of Jake Berry comes Foley's *Gershwin,* in two art forms, the written Text and the cassette, which first, go for the cassette, I do, and it hits me fast forward. Great, I enjoyed its force of anger and delivery.

Then I looked at the text, nothing like the form that came into my ears. I am impressed, but not anything like hearing it.

These songbirds are serious, and I admired the Dedication.

I am with the new voices and LANGUAGE words.

Larry Eigner is the Mother of these Marathon poets, he probably had no idea they were going to run around the Globe with his seedlings.

As endless Blizzards going out to the planets to root in.

Mama Mia!

Or these four and others, rejuvenating and regenerating the Languages.

All and EVERYTHING, as one Sage said.

Nature knows what it is about.

Ah, *her* MIND.

Some AGES are intensely fierce, some are laid back, but they are continually Present. And New.

Man's competitive Mischief invariably Screws Nature.

She's on top now.

And tired of his bullshit.

Georgenis, the Greek, has the ancient Greece working for him. Art and Democracy uninhibited by Commerce. Plodding alone, covering the East and the West in the Colorado River of his ingenuities.

Lao-tzu in the Soulbody of Bill Spencer.

From everywhere people come to Gloucester, some like Simon Geller from New York bought a Radio Station and played the music loves for twenty-five years, Bach, Brahms, Beethoven, but constantly Mozart. The businesses hated him or took him for a classical nut, which he was, refusing to make contributions to support his madness. He was pigheaded, and cranky as Satan with horns up, and crabby, but he was sui generis, as this town is, till he had a bite and sold his Network for a million bucks, and Henry

Ferrini fixed him in our History in a thirty-minute videotape, ending his time on Earth in some hole in Gotham, another Fishtown character.

Simon Geller, who played his Power out and left his message. Shuffling down the street, a leaning Tower of Fishtown, his calligraphy in our ears.

His voice as strong as any lasting line of a poem, he was.

An alter Altar: I used to wait for a date with my lady so I could be with my love fully in every dimension.

As I wait for an appointment with whomever so I can be with however in the multiple fiction/facts of the Buddha, the sensuous dervishes, or adding to the Tao going nowhere.

Persons are their own poems, and mine too, getting as much as I can read or hear, or what they give, there are so many closet songs. Some tapping at the door for someone to open, if the house is.

Once Jane, now Jain Tarnower, who lived with Elaine Wing for years, almost as a novitiate in a Convent, listening to the silences between conversations, painting scenes or figures in her head, rarely leaving the shelter, left for Somerville, another town like Jamaica Plain that draws the solitaires, those knitting a rage, or exclusion, the inventors of new legislation, bookworms, hardy hungry working people, proud as a tulip or a crocus, and these provided Jain with the images she'd paint on very small pieces of wood, or canvas, anything at hand, and exhibited them in a living graveyard, satisfied that viewers rest in them and walk away disturbed. She moved surreptitiously into the monotype after seeing Elaine work with ink and plateglass, doing a number of me, which I used for my books. From miniature painting to life-size. She arrested friends in their outward inner revelations, and saw me as a benevolent gangster, noble in pride and humble. I liked that.

A whole room of characters, eighteen, at the Pittsfield Museum, her birthplace, not too far from Herman Melville, a brother hermit of the sub-rosa introspections.

The poets of the Cosmic Web invite me to do an electronic book, when Buz Bever, who worked for Wang Laboratories, put a prized edition on the computer. She was into electronic publishing and printed from the Magic Church, fifty copies with five monotypes by Elaine,

With historical novelist Truman Nelson, 1980

black hardcovers the size of a manuscript sheet, at fifty bucks to raise money for "The Navigators."

Jim Leftwich, poet and publisher of *Juxta* magazine, put the first section of "Deux Ex Machine, Preamble to Divinity," on the Internet, in April of 1996.

Buz published my first wireless book in 1984.

While I was living in Lynn I wrote five books of poems, *No Smoke*, when I was twenty-eight, and had completed my first cycle of the Zodiac.

A sense of rounded time held me in its curve, and I felt as though I had reached a maturity that would sustain me throughout my life.

I was being prepared to enter a new world, the past was a fulfilling childhood, and I knew I would be badgered by supporting a family of wife and three children.

When the second book came out, *Injunction*, I sent a copy to Mike Gold at the *Daily Worker*, and asked him to read it, that's all. He did and gave his whole column "Change

the World" to it. He'd come across someone more than a poet. He visited me in Gloucester, and he played his recorder, a man as solid in literature as I had met at that time as a songbird.

The only other poet/anthologist was Walter Lowenfels, who said,

> You are the last surviving Proletarian Poet. On the lower East Side Lowell has no existence, and in the Lowell-land Ferrini has none. You have to search for the Ferrini circle. How Fantastic that Voz, the Soviet poet, lands in the Lowell-Auden circle in the USA when he could be reading you in Gloucester and vice versa. It is nice to think that these things will go on as the stars last. And the speed with which the divine reader, the universe that gets you, catches up, cannot equal the speed of light at which you compose y/our poems.

Ralph Coffman, a librarian at Boston College living in Marblehead, told me that he asked Lowell, why he wasn't writing like Lord Weary's Castle, his stunning first book. He said "Ferrini is."

"Self-portrait" of Christ from the back cover of
Magdalene Silences

Voices from the dead.

At the Lynn Public Library *No Smoke* was stolen, and a xerox copy had to be drawn from the locked room with an IOU.

Tidal Wave picked up arms at the Great Strikes of the middle '40s. Hot as a leaflet against the scabs.

Poem in Action covers that period of labor struggles.

In Gloucester, the pitch of my verse changed, from the rage of helplessness and economic anxieties to the vertical launching pads and an epic of fishing.

In hindsight the disturbing learning was that democracy has its short sight in the long run. I worked with a board of editors, when I should have been the spearhead, but I believed in a consensus.

That was the opening for the attack that came from Olson, with his Letter Five, the first

he began is *Maximus,* with a letter addressed to me, as his "brother in Gloucester," then came others, which I followed and understood. He was correct and so was I, but he had precision that taught me about people, yes, The Infinite People I still believe in.

I was invited to an ecumenical meeting of sympathetic denominations, and David Bergeron of the largest Catholic Church asked me to speak at a Sunday morning Communion. You want me, why not, I have never spoken to a Mass Service, we'd like you to, I was astounded. That morning I appeared near ten o'clock, and the first Priest said take your hat off. I did, reluctantly. When we are through with our presentation I will give you a raised finger. I sat near where I could see between the intruding Pillar posts, I saw his hand, I walked over to the Podium, spread out my three sheets. This is a poem addressed to a Lady in distress: peering over the two hundred faces raised to this unusual man before them, unexpected, roving my eyes over their heads, I was given three minutes:

You are born
with an immaculate Essence
if you betray it
or forget it
you are in trouble—

The other is not you
yet
you are the Pole Star
for both

Take the first triangle of
the Father, the Son, & the Holy Spirit
and place it on the second triangle of
the Mother, the Daughter, & the Holy
   Spirit

each one has to make that Star
alone

The 13th Disciple
is Mary Magdalene
the last who is first

I turned to leave the stage, and I heard two mountain voices AMEN!

At the funeral of City Clerk, the entrance was lined with policemen and firemen and other dignitaries. As I approached with my hat on, OK to go in, yeah, I sat in the back rows alone. After the prayers and accolades, we all rose, as I approached the door, one of the priests tried to penetrate my third eye, I did not follow the train of cars to the Calvary Cemetery, facing Good Harbor. Back home I wrote "The Death of a City Clerk," who accepted people as they were, for three decades in City Hall, as they say here, the finest kind. The poem appeared in the *Talk of the Town,* the newspaper does not accept poetry, except when it or they are portions of a news item or story. And that is the only time I can sneak in.

Once I sent the *Gloucester Daily Times* "The Gas Poem," the result of an attack in my midriff, and they said they could not print it, but if anyone wanted to read it they could at the *Times* office on the Bulletin Board.

So I write prose letters on any and every issue that I find urgent, and citizens tell me they liked my poem.

They remember the pith, the words, and the point being usually direct as language is, to communicate to anyone, and to roost in the mind, long after.

The distinction between prose and poetry is abolished.

And the unlearned and well read remember. What stays is a simplicity that is profound, or casting the shadow of the arouser.

Maximus buried in books and the comings and short knowledge of the authors is the medium of letters, the most personal, engrossing, and entertaining, interest and curiosity are engaged.

As close as we can get to talking, which is the prime role of participation, otherwise it's only in print, the images people throw away are gestures of an endless abundance.

The tongues as festival dancers, because they are spenders of who knows what's coming next, each tongue a combination of the female and the male appetites.

Tongue is the Dragon, the giver and the taker away.

Tongue is also the Seer, it is the door to the Unknown. A killer and a resurrector.

Be in awe of the Power of that little muscle.

When I first saw and heard Letter Five, all my atoms were dancing on the dragon of that Tongue.

Vincent and Henry Ferrini, 1989

The author with Tom Taylor, "friends for twenty-six years," Portland, Oregon, about 1990

It gave me strength and joy that someone could see what I failed to, and I wrote him a thirty-two-page love letter/poem.

Emmanuel of the Church across the street called me "a penetrator" and here's another Maximus. Like is drawn to itself in another.

Words in cells!

Peg's mother had trouble on her feet, would I mind if she came to live with us. She asked me twice if I could handle it.

She found a Homestead at Eastern Point Road. Ten rooms, she was in her class, like her mother's home in East Lynn, where she reigned, firmly and gentle in this new experience.

Up a road behind the Fairview Inn's fifty rooms for the itinerant artists and bohemians at prices they could handle. Kipling lodged there.

Peg had two brothers, one in the Navy's high command, and the other a teacher, the first married, with stretches from his wife. The other brother, a loner and a teacher, and bon vivant when it was appropriate.

The children grew up in an Estate, rented of course, with Niles and Brace Cove, two playground beaches, and acres of wild woods.

The Grandma was a devotee of Emersonian philosophy covering the immaterials.

Helen Stein's self-portrait dominated the living room. It was a gift to me, dated 1929. The whole head, and the eyes that Olson used as the Key to his Polis.

Peg disliked her presence. It rubbed her skin, that oil did. After the family moved into different metamorphoses, it was lost. Never to be seen. Some extra homework.

The Duffy tribe was at the helm, I was in the crow's nest upstairs with my bed, books, dreamlogs, and pen.

Her two brothers were absent kings. Stainless steel.

Peg taught English and French and drama at the Wenham/Hamilton Regional High School. She was the ideal teacher, greatly loved by the students, and a Guru at theatre. The Auditorium was named for her.

The Navy brother was privy to a flaw in his marriage and dying in the Homestead of brain cancer.

The Duffies were full bodyminded Irish, as they still are, and addicted to the fierce and the fairy dominions, as I am.

They worship the sounds of words, have a high sense of learning and justice. Actors and audience in the history of Irish struggles.

Dionysia was an intruder in the Homestead.

Peg loved my poems and saw me among the mythmakers.

The play she directed was one she lived in, as I am right now, still prowling around determined to make our appearances.

The Grandma is prominent, characterized in *War in Heaven*. A play about the Irish in Ireland, and those Irish in America. Still to be performed, or read aloud.

The ghost of my mother still wanders in and out of this little house.

The beloved Irish women are present in the objects they have left here waiting, nothing is finished, a poem seems to be, a play.

My brother Dante, who came after me and was robbed of the milk I got, with grown children is an outright misogynist, down on all of them. Like my father, if you are so good at words, how come you can't make money. A cracked record, he keeps covered in his bank vault. His shrinking compass has a stuck needle. A Dante without a Virgil. On a tier of the Abyss.

Even Alighieri had his radical Priest.

And Olson his Explicator, his shadow ego.

The Soul of America is a hardening arteriosclerosis, it preys on the poor. Death stalks in the halls of Congress wrapped in nearsight.

The poets have lost their open sensibilities, the eyes are ingrown.

A false, shallow success is the face of the C note, leaving on planes daily to rescue a

Russia the Pentagon fears is stirring towards a Resurrection. There is a deadness in the cells, the cells are distraught with not wanting it.

The sages are asleep, the cocoons of a wisdom that is tired.

Language is butchered, and doubletalk is the Hero.

Reagan and Deregulation is the birth of the oldest Disease.

The heart and the Balls of the Nation have been infected with a virus from colors and the numbers on the do-re-mi, the music of reaffirmation.

God is not only chic, but an imposter, who pays Corporate Power.

Do you think you are fooling the masses?

We are, and getting away with it; we rule the Media and all the conditioned thinking.

We are the Almighty.

We are the real Deity.

The life of my art is not to pacify you.

My feelings and my intellect tell me something deadly is in the New Religion of the Free Market.

We will hire you for your worth, and dump you when we don't need you—

The smoking gun economy.

You are on your own—

Survival of the fittest—

Don't think this is not part of the POEM—

Each day is the end of the world—

Tomorrow is another day—

The PLAY of ferocious Forces.

Everyone's in it.

The Olympians in the purple robes and gold chairs watching.

Mirages, Ferrini, enjoy it!

You have a time limit, O Desperados, you won't be here forever—

Maybe in that short space the WOMEN will have you as pigs for procreation—at their beck and calling—

Jain is smearing the plate glass with black ink, when the consistency is right, she starts removing the ink out of its eternity to bring me out of it, the white outlines emerging slowly. Almost without thinking, she reaches for a large sheet of softhand paper, puts it over the figure on the black world, presses it down hard as though to glue evenly, and lifts the sheet, looks at it, and is pleased, and begins to scrape off the ink when I clutch her hand. What's wrong, eyeing me, incredulous and a bit disturbed by my audacity, the paper has the impression, it is only a copy, she smiles, you want the original, if it's possible, why not, it has to dry first, two weeks later it is over my working table, shining in Black light!

Across from Elaine's *Hermit*. I am between two visionaries.

At the other end of the room is Liam McNiff's portrait of poet done at fourteen, the humble star of the house . . . A son of Picasso.

A private Museum, public!

Paula, half sober, drew me without taking the pen off the paper, she did it in thirteen minutes, while I leaned against the open door. All the women who like it don't catch what's there, a horn on the head, and a can opener for two holes at once, only a woman can execute. Other women won't tell me they see. But dream of.

The following is from a paper I delivered at the Charles Olson Festival, August 12, 1995,

"Two Gloucester Poets," Vincent Ferrini and Charles Olson, a monotype by Elaine Wing

Hartley Ferguson, Vincent, Joy Dai Buell, Paul Hamilton, Annie Thomas, and her daughter, Kate

at City Hall in Gloucester. It beats to the heart of my relationship with Charles Olson. I was on a panel that included Peter Anastas, Robert Creeley, Hettie Jones, Jean Kaiser, Ingeborg Lauterstein, and Ed Sanders.

ANASTAS: Vincent, what about the impact of Charles's work on you, Charles as a poet?

FERRINI: For me to answer that question, I have to read from this paper so that you'll get a good sense of how this man affected me:
The air is a page you write on, as Charles-O did, and I do.
He called me his twin and said in his Ferrini-I of his *Collected Poems* that we were "co-kings."
His astrological signature is "Climb the Highest Mountain," and mine is "Mermaid."
He's of the head and I'm of the heart, exchanging them.
He's a Capricorn, I'm a Cancer.
This is the Tale of the Big Kid and the Little Kid.

I'm with the women who say, "Don't tell me what you think. Tell me what you feel."
He scolded me in three poems of his *Maximus.* If the roles were reversed, I would have done what he did, only differently. (LAUGHTER)

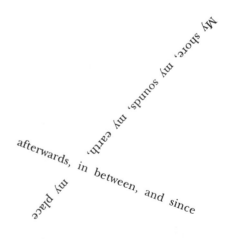

In *Know Fish* I have a poem in the same shape, only opposite, which says:

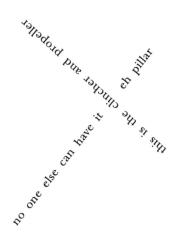

We have a schizoid situation where everything is split, heart from head, mind from body, private from public, art from life.

One of the *Four Winds* had a diagram where Gloucester is N42°37' W70°40'.

He has a poem in the *Maximus* in the shape of the diagram, which is like an upside down Cross:

It is on top of his, and it is called "The Engine," which together they are.

The *North Shore* magazine of *Gloucester Daily Times* had two articles which singled out the summation of Charles Boer's experiences as host to Charles's stay at his home in his book *Charles Olson in Connecticut,* where he said: "There was no letup in your demand for attention, I began to be consumed by you. Drained, devoured."

Now let's go back a bit.

In 1964—I forget the date—I drove Charles, Betty, and Charles Peter to the South Station, and Betty had not made up her mind to go with him to Buffalo. He chatted all the way, and in the last five minutes she decided to go.

It changed their lives, all three of them.

When I heard about the fatal accident, I went there immediately.

After that Charles was never the same.

Deep in his guts he knew that he was facing an unsurmountable obstacle, knocked off that highest mountain.

The last six years of his life were the loneliest I had ever seen anyone in.

We met a number of times, and he was bowed because that mountain was on his back. He was a driven one.

The Daimon had its grip and his fate was inexorable.

So don't judge him if you have not lived in his flesh and bones and in his head.

Now if you want to understand the *Maximus* poems, you have to read George Butterick's *A Guide to the Maximus Poems.*

It's all there, because he too gave his life to Olson. Without George, who died at forty-five if I remember correctly, the works of Olson would be in the hands of other less gifted scholars. Then, who knows?

Charles Olson was the cross between Black and Light Magic, and he drew his believers with his pleroma.

Not long after he met me, he read my books at the Lynn Public Library, and *No Smoke,* a graphic tale of Lynn during the Great Depression, tolled a bell inside his eyes, and I was in Gloucester.

I came back from that Wyoming wake with a copy of his *Human Universe* inscribed to Mary Shore and myself in a death's head.

I was drenched to the marrow and, figuring the weight of Eternity was going to get me, I gave that copy to Peter Anastas.

I was caught up in him and he in me. I wrote a section of *The Navigators,* book III of *Know Fish:* forty-six pages of "The Dreams or out of the body travelling with Maximus & some others."

Olson was a son of Hermes, the greatest of thieves. He could lift anything from anyone and that person could never know except for another Hermes.

The universities at large are afraid of Charles Olson because he is a teacher of teachers, and his method is dangerous to the Status Quo, a rebel education will catch up to when he's buried long enough to be safe, and those authorities will choke on his words.

There's more going on than meets the eye or the ear.

Olson was in a state of love, but he was intoxicated, very one-pointed. And so am I, star-studded, as those who are awake. (APPLAUSE)

In 1996, *Split Shift,* a new magazine edited by Roger Taus, a poet and drama critic, featured a "Homage to Ferrini, Encomia & Essays" by Terry Kennedy, P. J. Laska, Alan Golding, Jack Hirschman, Gerald Nicosia, Paul Sawyer, Steve Ellis, Antler, Shaun McNiff, Bob Snyder, Peter Kidd, Kenneth Warren, Ed Kaplan, Peter Anastas, Jim Leftwich, and Jim Fay.

Herb Kenny writes to Vincent Ferrini:

To have a festschrift honoring you means you have reached the icon stage and don't need to do a damned tap for the rest of your life, but I know you and you'll continue to write after they bury you.

Don't let them cremate you: it's harder to pull yourself together for a few ghostly appearances.

Have you read the GLOUCESTERBOOK? Tell me what you make of it. Jonathan Bayliss has completed his volume two.

as always, dear friend,
6/6/96

Herb,

It took me 6 days to read GLOUCESTER-BOOK, with two dictionaries. It is definitely written for the astute and inveterate reader.

The GLOUCESTERTIDE is the same length, over 600 pages 6 x 9, this time accessible, still it had me booked for 6 days to read it through. It is interspersed with a play on Gilgamesh.

His chapters on love's escapades is entrancing. His name placings, confusing. His hero is Ibi Roi, his dog, King of a fictitious terrain in fact. Unmistakable as an autobiography, finally upfront.

6/13/96

The sleep of Socrates is coming upon me, perhaps it is the urge to escape another Great Depression of the Soul. I'm into a nine at night to six in the morning. Winter hibernation. The hermit crab.

An island as your own house, that's what people in Gloucester think and feel. The neighborhood as a magnifying glass, a ship as gone undersea and back. The personal view the utmost sacrosanct.

The picture poems, the etching of the real Olson and the Grand Vision, the ravishing nude, and the Ferrini with hair in the wind, starker than I'd seen him, as when I visited my mother, at her last year chipper, unabsentminded, happy among the cliff walkers, hearing their tales when they had the energy, or just concerned to find themselves locked away. A working-class Queen, at poker with God himself. The rabbis watching.

I see the mansions up against the sky, secure among the clouds, the tenements in their ridges, the water up to the bellies, the photo

Cover painting by Elaine Wing from
Hermit of the Clouds

memories of the fish factories, the knife writing on the tables, and the glint of the scales on their clothes and eyes, miniature portraits in the gizzards of the fishes, their eyes in the buckets, globes of the lost paradise, even in the eyes of the fishermen stranded on land, their wives fisherwomen in new waters.

Strange indeed the body is all you have, and it is a habitat for ghosts.

I live with mine and another me is a companion from a distant world.

On the wall I saw the lips of a picture of myself at twenty-eight speaking to me. I couldn't see the words nor hear them.

. . . I do the chores and the sentences arise to accompany me.

A child with stories and the archaic.

A slab of wrought fish head with one eye in two directions.

On the gas stove, clay white heads in Buddhist meditations. On Stage. Not for them.

At lunch off Sappho's plate.

Artemisa Gentileschi tomorrow for supper.

Then St. Bridget, Virginia Woolf, Hildegarde of Bingen, Mary Wollstonecraft, and Sophia, the tightest Wisdom.

If only the Patriarchy weren't so stupid.

Blunt or the sharpest of weapons, just dumb. Hoisted in battle any kind.

The Mind in feelings!

The sponges eyes and ears are.

You are in the Play, whether produced or published.

Most are but divided, in or out of themselves, or with the birds, the dolphins, the whales, the TREES, pillars the seasons are married to.

The lights at night jiggling on the waters, this city is the Holy Grail for the monks and nuns of Art. Or flagstones for their journey.

Sleep akin to the peace within the stones the tides are grinding away. The bones know when the rush and the suction the distance brings to them. The sleep in the absentmindedness of the roads, and the windows of domiciles are privileged to see both ways.

Sleep at home in the tripping feet. When dreamless, a pure black Void no words can conquer.

Sleep the working harbor embraces in round arms, the holy mud at the bottom of incoming and goingout.

In that sleep people are perfect, and the wealth waiting to be spent.

I wake up in the Spiritbody of the island.

I don't need anything, the women are with me, and the men and children bringing the real miracles I find them in.

I saw this when I crossed over the "Cut" drawbridge over the Annisquam Strait, the train bridge, and 128, the main highway into Fishtown.

The inner light in family pow-wows, even in their clashes breaking through stifling barriers.

In my broken family, the wise son and daughter who see me with unclouded eyes, taking me as I am, and although the grandchildren were far off and near, in their twenties, their new eyes accept me as an equal, as I took them, in so many different states of arriving.

The transcendence of families together and apart, trusting the liberties.

Pure as sleep and light, interweaving a method kaleidoscope offers.

The image is the clue, it appears when ready on its own volition, and it tells that portion of the story.

Or the whole tale is seen in all its tenses, the quick mind hooks and stores in a purse, it stamps an impression, or it flees, and haunts.

I am the well of the images that guide me as the experiencing reflections fall in that water. Any stone in that well has all the water.

The life of words shared, that above everything because love personal and objective is the very air that unites.

The wordless, the silences of that ether.

The Drag of Sleep and its narcotic, creeping unobtrusive, and the siren heaven it deliv-

---

Harbor Is the Crux of Our Identity

We are shifting gears, studying the Map we have not seen before.

Struggling together is our new Visibility, and hard come by.

The Harbor is the Crux of our Identity.

We are agreed on that for near 400 years.

The Vacant Lot is saying Just Get It Right—

For 50 years, I have never seen Gloucester people thriving as close as we are on revitalizing the 2 Oceans of our living.

We have learned to our sorrow the limits of over-fishing.

If our polluted Harbor and the narrow Strait can be purified in 10 years, so can the Seas.

The fishes will Know it. Tasting the seedbeds and the energetic waters at their own paces, coming back in schools, and singing scales!

Be Patient.

Be wary.

There is No Hurry.

The needle of our human compass engendering all the directions. At Work and Play. Playing working. That's the Ecstasy.

Keep trusting this germinating process.

This activity, individual and communal, is the Map inside us, arriving outside almost by itself.

Because of our interfacings!

—Vincent Ferrini

(*Gloucester Daily Times,* Monday, April 29, 1996)

ers, a colorless, odorless fragrance never expected. A restful cessation and not wanted. A release of all attachments and the heavy burden of the ending of the third cycle of the Cosmos, at the womb door of the fourth. Caught between wanting and not wanting, the Chakras glowing, the topmost saying without saying that you are with whatever is promised.

In the blood red pouch Dorothy Cahill gave me, Death is stitched with durable colored thread, on opposite sides, with the same thread doing the vagina dance, VIVRE, Death elegant and twirling in a one-God dervish hallelujah! VIVRE, quiet and secure, and pulsing.

Within the pouch is a six-inch penis, a Moosebuck on the glans ironwood.

Hanging down from sewing thread are two light cloud cannonballs wound with gold thread and each with two feathers, a Mother and Witch from Canada, Suzanne Surette, weaved and molded for me.

They bear this house and me with them.

On the second door facing the front one is HOMER, in pieces of rusty metal found on the streets of Gloucester, a green iron laurel around his forehead, his imperial nose, out of his mouth the hexameter lines on the air, sometimes his voice is soft and I bend my ear not to miss an inflection.

His red beard and the round iron eye never sleep.

On the back it is signed Mary S. 1/9/63
The Visage of Homer
At Night, a Lighthouse during the Day, the shadow of Eros.

"With 4 strokes of a pen I simplified my name"

BIBLIOGRAPHY

Poetry:

No Smoke, Falmouth, 1941.

Injunction, Sand Piper, 1943.

Blood of the Tenement, Sand Piper, 1945.

Tidal Wave: Poems of the Great Strikes, Great Concord, 1946.

The Plow in the Ruins, James A. Decker, 1948.

Sea Sprung, Cape Ann, 1949.

The Infinite People, Great Concord, 1950.

The House of Time, Fortune Press (London), 1952.

In the Arriving, Heron, 1954.

Mindscapes, Peter Pauper, 1955.

Timeo Hominem Unius Mulieris, Heron (Liverpool, United Kingdom and Gloucester, Massachusetts), 1956.

The Garden, Heuretic, 1958.

The Square Root of In, Heuretic, 1959.

Book of One, Heuretic, 1960.

Mirandum, Heuretic, 1963.

I Have the World, Fortune (London), 1967.

The Hiding One, Me & Thee, 1973.

Ten Pound Light, Church, 1975.

Selected Poems, edited by George F. Butterick, University of Connecticut Library, 1976.

Know Fish, Volumes I and II, The Lady of Misbegotten Voyages & Da Songs, University of Connecticut Library, 1979.

Know Fish, Volume III, The Navigators, University of Connecticut Library, 1984.

Know Fish, Volumes IV and V, The Community of Self, University of Connecticut Library, 1986.

Know Fish, Volumes VI and VII, Shadows Talking & This Other Ocean, University of Connecticut Library, 1991.

A Tale of Psyche, Igneus, 1992.

Magdalene Silences, Igneus, 1992.

Deluxe Daring, illustrated by Jane Robbins, Bliss, 1994.

The Magi Image, Igneus, 1995.

Plays:

The Innermost I Land, in *The Best Short Plays 1952–53,* edited by Margaret Mayorga, Dodd Mead, 1953.

Telling of the North Star, in *The Best Short Plays 1953–54,* edited by Margaret Mayorga, Dodd Mead, 1954.

Five Plays, Fortune, 1960.

War in Heaven, University of Connecticut Library, 1987.

Undersea Bread, University of Connecticut Library, 1989.

Contributor:

Poets of Today, Walter Lowenfels, International Publishers, 1964.

Italian American Poets, Italian translation by Ferdinand Alfonsi, edited by A. Carello, Catanzaro (Italy), 1985.

Twentieth Century American Poets, Russian translation by Valery Shpak, Ukraine, USSR, 1989.

Other:

Four Winds, edited by Vincent Ferrini and others, nos. 1–4, 1952–1953.

Ferrini & Others, edited by Vincent Ferrini, Nessuno, 1953.

Hermit of the Clouds (autobiography), Ten Pound Island, 1988.

Contributor of poems and articles to literary journals, including *Athanor, Intermountain Review, Moosehead Review, New Anvil, Review of Contemporary Fiction,* and *Smoke.* Featured in "Homage to Ferrini, Encomia & Essays," *Split Shift* (new literary magazine), No. 1, edited by Roger Taus, Santa Monica, California, 1996.

Jack Foley

1940-

Jack Foley, 1987

I continue my reading of cheap novels. It satisfies . . . my taste for imposture, my taste for the sham, which could very well make me write on my visiting cards: "Jean Genet, bogus Count of Tillancourt."

*

I learned only in bits and pieces of that wonderful blossoming of dark and lovely flowers: one was revealed to me by a scrap of newspaper; another was casually alluded to by my lawyer; another was mentioned, almost sung, by the prisoners—their song became fantastic and funereal. . . .

Jean Genet, *Our Lady of the Flowers*

What is a life but stories—stories we tell ourselves, stories we tell others, stories others tell about us? Out of these stories we fashion—what? I am *writer, husband, father, poet, teacher, friend, "radio personality," occasional cook, householder, amateur guitarist, sometime tap dancer, jobless person, performer, student,* any number of other things. And now, *biographer.* How was "he" as a poet? you may ask. How was "he" as a lover? Was his cooking all right? Who is "he" when "I" see "myself" from the objective point of view? Who is doing the seeing? Where did "he" get his lamentable habit of putting words in quotation marks and italics? What are these words anyway? Will they

"My mother as a young woman"

tell me anything real about "him"?—*Adrift,* to use the title of one of his/my books. But what did "he" mean by that?

A year ago I was told by my doctor that I had diabetes. The doctor told me to read up on the subject but if I saw any references to "blindness, impotence, and death," not to worry, that wasn't the kind of diabetes I had. Appropriately enough, my earliest memory is of being fed candy. My mother and I are lying on a bed. I believe we are in a hotel room in Port Chester, New York, a city in the southeastern part of the state, on Long Island Sound, population approximately 25,000. We have recently moved to Port Chester from Philadelphia. My father is not there. My mother is, if I'm not mistaken, weeping. I am being given candies which were actually named "Chocolate Babies" but which my mother and others regularly referred to offensively as "Nigger Babies." My mother is making an effort to shut me up. I am probably about three years old and I am "eating babies." My mother perhaps wishes that real babies could disappear as easily as these babies can. If I remember correctly from later experience, the candies are delicious, but at this moment they are not quite doing the job. My mother is trying to prevent me from asking a question which tears her apart. *Where is*

Daddy? Is Daddy coming back? She doesn't know, though at some level, I think, she realizes that he *will* come back. She knows but she does not know, and the uncertainty is tearing her apart. The uncertainty is tearing me apart too, and so I keep asking. I am like an awful witness to the failure of her life.

After that, nothing. I don't know how the story turned out. Perhaps my father walked through the door the next moment and reassured everyone. Certainly we were able at times to maintain the fiction of being a happy family as, here, we were maintaining the fiction of being an unhappy one. Perhaps this is a "screen memory," standing as an emblem for many individual events. When the pressure of circumstances became too much for him, my father would simply *disappear:* later I learned that he would go on "binges." But he would always come back. Perhaps I was reminded of these disappearances when I heard stories of a Christian god who also disappears—disappears for centuries—but who also promises to come back. That god too is frequently represented as a baby, and, under certain circumstances, like the Chocolate Babies, he is "eaten."

*

The past is a foreign country. They do things differently there.

L. P. Hartley, *The Go-Between*

Much of what I'm writing here is ancient history, stories that people who know me now don't know. My pattern, in more ways than one, has been that of the shape-shifter: I am fifty-five years old; if you saw a photograph of me at eighteen you would have trouble recognizing me.

My father, John Harold Aloysius ("Jack") Foley: 1895–1967. Slightly taller than I, thin, jet-black hair (my hair is brown), with a touch of the dandy. People would say, "He reminds me of Fred Astaire." My mother, Joanna Teriolo (later shortened to Terio): 1898–1964. She hated the name "Joanna" and so called herself "Juana," shortened to "Juan," which she pronounced "Ju-an," with two syllables. Plump, dark, with intense, piercing eyes. He was Irish. She was Italian, with perhaps some Spanish blood. I was their only child: born August 9, 1940 (a Leo), Fitkin Hospital, Neptune, New Jersey, outside of Asbury

Park, where my parents were living. A war baby. The *Dick Tracy* comic strip for that day features an attempt to arrest "Yogee Yamma," an exotic-looking man wearing a turban. My father, forty-five years old, was working at Fort Monmouth as a telegrapher. I was christened "John Wayne Foley." Later, the confirmation name "Harold" was added. (My father claimed not to be able to spell his own confirmation name, "Aloysius.") The naming had nothing to do with the popular movie actor John Wayne. My father wanted to name me after his brother, but the parish priest convinced him that Wayne was no proper saint's name, so I was named John after my father with Wayne as my middle name.

The name was a rare gesture on my father's part towards his family. There were several Foley children. "We were fairmers"—farmers—my father told me. They were living in Elmira, New York. He was, I believe, the youngest, "the baby of the family," his sister said. His brother, Wayne, somehow learned to tap dance. He taught the art to my father and helped him to enter the dazzling world of show business. My father performed in vaudeville as well as in one of the last minstrel companies, presided over by George "Honeyboy" Evans. My father's sister Goldie was part of that world too. She was a Ziegfeld Follies girl, a spectacular beauty, and perhaps in some sense the love of my father's life. "We'd go everywhere together," he told me, reminiscing. "Everybody thought we were sweethearts." Pause. *"But we weren't."* He was hardly a sophisticate. He used to tell the story of being in the subway as a young man and seeing a sign saying "Smoking Prohibited." He was with a friend who wanted to smoke. My father told his friend the sign meant "you could go ahead and smoke." He also told me of being with the songwriter Jimmy McHugh. They were passing the poetry section of a library when McHugh turned to my father and, pointing to the section, said, "Jack, it's all in there." In general my father didn't tell stories about our family. He told stories about his friends in show business. Later I realized that the friends were almost always Irish. The people he knew in show business became his real family. He married one of them—Laura, one of the dancing Wood Sisters. Evidently, that marriage (about which I knew nothing as a child) was short and disastrous. The lyrics to one of the songs my father wrote go:

"'Mama and May'—my father's mother (left) and his sister, May," 1920s

They all love my wife
They all love my wife
She makes all of them fall
When I go to bed she's at a dance
When I wake up she's in a trance
Oh, what a home sweet home I've got it!

Or, more poignantly:

Passing my window faces I see
Most of them smiling none smile for me
None know I'm lonely or that I'm alone
Since you have left me home isn't home
Why weren't you satisfied

Goldie was the only one of my father's siblings I actually met, and by the time I met her her beauty had gone. There was another sister, May, for whom my father wrote a song, and perhaps others. I don't know what became of them. Both my father and Wayne served in World War I, but Wayne died young as a result of the mustard gas he had inhaled. He called for my father on his deathbed but my father couldn't summon the courage to go to him. Naming me after Wayne was a late—and no doubt rather guilt-ridden—fraternal gesture.

As my father grew older he grew bitter about women. "Put a man in all that make-up, fix his hair, and he'd be just as attractive as any woman." He was not advocating drag. Women baffled him and, finally, frightened him. He wished at last to keep his distance. Another lyric goes, "I did all I could to make you happy, but still you chose to grow cold and forget. / My pillow's wet every night, praying you'll write, goodness only knows why."

My father left show business when vaudeville, which was his primary bread and butter, gave way to the movies and died. In addition, his great mentor and occasional employer, George M. Cohan, lost interest in musicals and made an ill-fated attempt to establish himself as a "straight" playwright. My father opened a dance studio. He received a telegram from Cohan wishing him luck and tendering "kindest personal regards." The venture failed. He turned to Postal Union—where he had worked as a telegrapher during the summers—and then to Western Union, which eventually made him manager of the Port Chester branch. He claimed that the sound of the telegraph key reminded him of tap dancing. Recently I came upon a clipping, a review of one of his performances. It refers to him as a "great" dancer. Since childhood I have collected recordings of vaudevillians: Cohan, Harry Lauder, Nora Bayes and Jack Norworth, Gallagher and Shean, many others. All these recordings bring me closer to my father, whose performing days were long past when I knew him. "To Americans," writes John E. Dimeglio in *Vaudeville USA,*

"My father" (right), New York City, 1926

the vaudevillian . . . typified the spirit of liberty. Was he not utterly free? He travelled across the expanses of the great land, and did as he wished on the stage. In the most mobile of all nations, that nation's most mobile citizen, the vaudevillian, represented something special. Vaudeville entertained the family, the sacred core of America's strength. Yet the nation had been founded by daring adventurers who challenged the unknown. The average American had to remain close to home, but not the vaudevillian. He was heroic in this sense, meeting the challenges of one town after another, one audience after another, his very career at stake each time he mounted the stage. The theatergoer could share in all this. The destiny of the lone figure on stage was in his hands.

I think of my father in his suit, with his black hair slicked back, or in his underwear playing his nightly game of solitaire. "Your father," one of his drinking companions told me after his death, "was a goodtimer."

The story of my mother's life seems to have been the story of the longing to go home.

Her hometown was Perth Amboy, New Jersey, where she met my father. He must have seemed like an embodiment of all the lights of Broadway. She maintained the hope that I would enter show business, and my father did indeed teach me to tap dance. Like my father, my mother came from a large family. When we visited Perth Amboy on Memorial Day there seemed to be relatives everywhere. Her brother Panny ("strong as a bull") was once a wrestler and now called himself an "automobile beautician." I remember her sister Maggie as immensely fat ("it's her glands") and barely able to walk. I was expected to hug Maggie and kiss her, which I did with little enthusiasm. I don't think the people there liked me very much. I was too bookish, I had little interest in—or capacity for—sports. When I learned to play the guitar my mother would force me to bring it to Perth Amboy. Everyone would ask me to play. At first I would refuse. Finally, I would comply. Everyone was sitting around me in utter silence. You could hear a pin drop. The moment I began to play, everyone started to talk.

My maternal grandparents, whom I never knew, operated a store which featured delicious Italian cooking, my favorite kind of food. My relatives maintained the tradition of good cooking, but I disliked these trips to see people whom I scarcely knew and who scarcely knew— or wanted to know—me. Yet this was the place for which my mother yearned. Port Chester was quite similar to Perth Amboy. It too boasted a large Italian population. Yet my mother was never really able to make friends there. She would make a friend, there would be an intensity of communication, then there would be a fierce argument and that would be the end of that. There were fierce arguments at home, too, but that relationship went on. My parents made an attempt to make me happy, and at times I was. But I was also lonely, on my own a lot, given to imaginative play. There was a great mirror on my mother's dresser. I would play in front of it, watching myself. We listened to the radio (this was "the golden age") and we went to the movies. If I saw a movie in which I identified with the hero, I became the hero the next day. The "movie" became my image in the mirror. Thirty years later I raised the question, "Is the movie screen a window or a mirror? It appears to be a window, but it turns into a mirror." I'm sure my childhood experience had something to do with that question, though I believe there is also something in the nature of movies which encourages one to think of mirrors. Criticism as secret—or, as Oscar Wilde said, the only civilized form of—autobiography.

I suspect that my mother would have preferred for me to have been a girl. There are stories of her dressing me in girl's clothing— my girl ego was named "Geraldine"—but I remember little of this, and I have no temptation to cross dress at this point. When I was in my twenties, my father remarked, in as manly a voice as he could muster, "Well, I thought you were a little, you know, but I guess you're all right." There's a story here too. When I was in high school a male teacher took an interest in me. Like Deborah Kerr in the popular movie, he was planning to offer me a little more than "tea and sympathy." He taught gym and English literature and was responsible for school plays. He knew of my interest in musicals and once hinted that he was planning to cast me in the lead in *Carousel,* but the production never materialized. I must have led him

on unmercifully. He was very popular with "the guys," and as far as I know no one ever suspected him. My mother in fact decided she wouldn't believe me when I told her the truth. "Oh, you're lyin'." He was Italian and rather

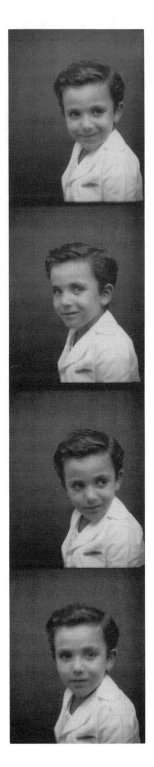

Early 1940s

*Confirmation photo, Port Chester,
New York, about 1953. Our Lady of
Mercy Church is in the background.*

handsome, so she must have fantasized about him.

The teacher invited me to accompany him to an excellent Broadway musical, *The Music Man*. He was very careful to ask my parents. He explained that he *could* take me all the way back to Port Chester, but it was a shorter drive to Mamaroneck, where he lived. I could spend the night with him and he could take me to school the next day. He really gave me every consideration. He said I could sleep on the couch or, if I preferred, "bunk in" with him. I chose to "bunk in." He took me in his arms and kissed me. I still remember his voice as he said, "In a moment our eyes will get used to the light and we'll be able to see each other." I felt nothing, no fear but no sexual excitement either. That was that. My experiment had come to its conclusion. I mumbled something about having a headache and rolled over to go to sleep. The next morning he was understandably a little panicky: "I hope nothing happened that bothered you. . . ." I reassured him, "No, no." It was certainly my fault as much as his. I had been experimenting, wondering about my sexuality. The fact that I felt nothing freed me a little. It only occurred to me recently that, had it been a different man, the results might have been different. Gay men have often figured in my responses to art: Noël Coward, Jess, Robert Duncan, James Broughton, Neeli Cherkovski. I hate the concept of the shadowy homosexual figure who haunts—and taunts—the good American hero in so many American films—the Penguin vs. Batman, for example. Yet my sexuality is finally not all that different from such heroes'. John Wayne once said, "I guess I've proven that I'm no pantywaist." I don't even know what a pantywaist is. But I suppose my encounter with that teacher was such proof for me. "Don't knock it unless you've tried it," the "gay" villain says to Clint Eastwood in one of his films. "What makes you think I haven't," Eastwood replies. Someone in the audience said "Whoa!" at that remark. I suppose my adventure with the teacher was a way of saying "Whoa" too, of putting the brakes on something. I have no idea what became of him. I hope he found someone better suited to him than I was. I wonder how many other people he may have taken to New York!

Though my high school never put on its production of *Carousel*, Port Chester did afford me two moments of stardom. The first of these involved my father. I have some talent for drawing. Since my father worked for Western Union, he had the addresses of various famous people. At his suggestion I drew pictures of President Eisenhower and sports announcer Bill Stern. My father then sent the pictures to the people I had drawn, hoping that they would greet me as a young Picasso. I received a letter from Eisenhower's press secretary and another from Stern himself. This was written up in the local paper, the *Daily Item,* as "Local Boy Receives Letter from President." There was a photograph of me with my easel. I thought it strange that the reporter who wrote the story interviewed only my father, not me. The story rhapsodized, "Who would be next in a boy's heart to the president—who but a figure from the world of sports?" Who indeed.

I wondered what that reporter would have made of my interest in Bernard Shaw (whose prefaces and plays were actively distancing me from Catholicism) and Noël Coward, whom I had seen with Mary Martin in an amazing television special, *Together with Music.* I had a record album, *Noël and Gertie,* with Coward and Lawrence performing the balcony scene from *Private Lives.* Coward (like Burns and Allen or Lucy and Desi) was demonstrating that the unit was not necessarily the single performer, the "lone vaudevillian," but the "team," the man and the woman together. This team was not quite "the family." It represented something different: the search for that mysterious other for whom one yearned and who arose out of one's deepest feelings of loneliness. Indeed, the team suggested that the other could not only be found but even presented to the world. That the other was also *oneself,* something denied or broken off from one's own psyche, only increased the yearning. Thinking of my poetry presentations—my wife and me reading chorally—James Broughton remarked that he thought I was producing an "androgenous form." "King Amour," a poem I wrote in 1986, attempts to deal with such desire:

> How
> is it possible to speak to you?
> We stand
> in different dimensions if we stand at all—you
> in that darkness on the "other side" (flow into
>   it!) What is it?
> "The bareness of the mind the glitter of
>   certain states"—
> Dusk. What I can see of the sky is gray.
>   Colors darkening. Everything failing.
> Hope is inseparable from Delusion (Love). . . .

The second instance of stardom is when I appeared on *The Ed Sullivan Show* as a member of the Port Chester Senior High School Choir. Sullivan had been involved somehow with Port Chester Senior High—he may have taught gym—and he decided to do his own biography on television, so he invited the high school choir to perform. We sang "Beyond the Blue Horizon." It was, as Sullivan used to say, "a rilly big shew," with Bob Hope, Pearl Bailey, Smith and Dale (Neil Simon's "Sunshine Boys"), and others. Everyone looked at least ten years older than they did on TV. I remember having to stand for a long time under the hot, bright lights. More recently (1991), my friend Ishmael Reed generously described me in *Time* magazine as a "literary luminary" of California.

When Ishmael told me what he had done, I was so surprised—flabbergasted—that the only thing I could think of to say in reply was, "In 1955 I was on *The Ed Sullivan Show.*" Ishmael waited a beat and said, "You've topped it."

It was part of my mother's weirdness that, though she might take a cup of coffee, she would never eat off anyone else's plates. No one was clean enough for her. Every day she scrubbed away at the house in an effort to keep it clean. Later, when she was ill with cancer, she wrote me telling me how exhausted she was, "and the house is dirty." The "house" was in fact a three-room apartment on the top floor of an apartment house. The apartment house had been someone's mansion once, but now it was divided up into apartments. There was a marvelous front yard where we could play catch or even baseball. I never felt quite middle class in that situation. My middle-class friends had houses. They often had their own rooms. I had space in the apartment but not my own room. Middle-class people seemed to live a marvelous life. My mother's urge to clean meant that the house was always in an uproar as she moved furniture around to get at any piece of dirt that might be hidden from her. The houses I visited seemed calm, orderly, like the houses I saw in situation comedies on television. There seemed to be people living the fifties' version of the American Dream: a house, a television set, reliable plumbing. I just wasn't one of them. Someone said to me recently, "You were a rebel even then." But I wasn't a rebel. I was an *outsider.* From my position I could watch people, but it was difficult for me to participate. I was in this respect very similar to a moviegoer. I don't know at what point I began to believe that everything around me was *fictional,* that people's lives were a constant invention. But from my outsider position that is the way it seemed. It wasn't that their lives weren't real. For them, their lives were very real, and many times in my life people have told me their stories. My position as outsider has made me a good listener. But their lives were at a *distance* from mine. That poor teacher whom I led on—there was an entire drama going on for him. It just wasn't going on for me. Yet I could understand him. I was not "a camera" exactly (in Christopher Isherwood's famous phrase), but I was a kind of sponge, even (in Shelley's words) a "sensitive plant"—a nothing, a null space ready to be filled with someone else's being. "Yah," said my friend Larry Eigner to me, "Negative Capability."

Like other women, my mother had been trained to take care of a baby by practicing on dolls. The result of this was not only that the doll "became" a baby; the baby also "became" a doll. My mother selected my clothes and combed my hair for my entire life through high school. I objected at times, but never very strongly. I knew that when I went away to college everything would change. I understood that I needed to please my mother. She was the person with whom I had most daily contact, and she was formidable. Her anger might erupt at any moment. When I was "bad" she would beat me with a special stick. Once, after I had grown and been away to college, she tried to "spank" me again: I grabbed the stick and broke it in front of her. This infuriated her, but it was the end of the spankings. Perhaps most terrifying was the phrase, "Wait till your father gets home," though I soon learned that my father didn't share her anger at such moments. I knew from Sunday school that it was a mortal sin to miss mass on Sunday, but my mother never went to church. When I asked her about it she said, "Oh, I've got nothin' to wear." She seemed to feel genuine shame at her position in life. She would occasionally shoplift things. Once, she was caught and brought to the police station. My father had to rescue her. Her embarrassment was tremendous. She was superstitious and would "read cards" for people. I believe she would charge them for this. She would also buy more food than was necessary and sell the extra cans to her friends at a reduced price. It was a way of getting a little more pocket money. She believed she was fooling my father but I discovered that he was quite aware of it. She would say to me, "Someday you'll know" and "Someday you'll miss your mother" and "I wish you could always be little." Any genital exploration by me was strictly "shameful." Once when she felt I wasn't being sufficiently sympathetic to her plight she waited till I was alone in the apartment and phoned me. Unfortunately for her, I recognized her voice. She said, "You know your mommy. I'm going to *kill* her!" I said, "Mommy, stop doing that," and she hung up. The incident was never mentioned. When, in 1964, she was on her deathbed, groggy with sedatives, she seemed to believe that she was going to hell. It was horrifying. "I'm going down, down," she muttered. I

tried to reassure her, "You're going up, up," but she would have none of it: "Not after what *I've* done." I don't know what terrible guilt was upon her. A few moments before she died, she sat bolt upright in the hospital bed, her eyes tightly closed. She began to whirl her arms in front of her, as if she were warding off some unseen enemy. I ran for the nurse. When we returned, the nurse went in ahead of me. She turned to me and said, "She's gone."

My mother hoped by her advice, example, and bullying to control my life. "Don't get married until you're forty." (I married at twenty-one.) But in fact I knew that my life was in my own hands. This was the message of the books I was reading. The only problem was that my life was also *elsewhere*. In Port Chester I was laying low. I would have to wait until I got away for my life, my true life, to begin.

*

. . . at a distance life awoke, and there was a rattle of lean wheels, a slow clangor of shod hoofs. And he heard the whistle wail along the river.

Yet, as he stood for the last time by the angels of his father's porch, it seemed as if the Square already were far and lost; or, I should say, he was like a man who stands upon a hill above the town he has left, yet does not say "The town is near," but turns his eyes upon the distant soaring ranges.

Thomas Wolfe, *Look Homeward, Angel*

*B*ios, the Greek word, means life, particularly human life, as opposed to *Zoon*, a living being, an animal. But we are *both* "humans" and "animals." Perhaps I should be writing an autozoography as well as an autobiography: my history as an animal. What I am doing here is nothing but telling stories, often stories I have told friends over the years. *How can one break through stories into something like the life I lived?*

My father was surprised and delighted when I won scholarship money to go to college. One of the scholarships, the major one, came from Western Union. Western Union provided three prizes for children of its employees: first prize was a full scholarship to Cornell University in Ithaca, New York. The other two scholarships were less money, but you could go to any school you wished. I won first prize. "Kid, I didn't think you'd be able to go," my father told me, "I didn't have the money." With a perhaps

Jack with guitar

misplaced zeal I simply *assumed* I was going to college and that the money would somehow take care of itself. Amazingly, it did.

I had come to Port Chester in 1943. When I left in 1958 I understood myself to be a poet. My essay, "Home/Words," in *Exiles* (1996) deals with the moment in 1955 at which I discovered poetry. "Someone—probably a teacher, perhaps Angela Kelley, who was Italian but who had married an Irishman—suggested that I read Thomas Gray's 18th-century poem, 'Elegy Written in a Country Churchyard.' I have no idea why the teacher thought the poem would appeal to me. I thought it very unlikely that I would have much interest in it, but I looked it up in the library and took it—home. . . . The poem seemed to me the most beautiful *sound* I had ever heard. . . . [It] affected me so deeply that I wanted it to have come out of me, not out of Thomas Gray, and I immediately sat down and wrote *my own* Gray's 'Elegy,' in the same stanzaic form and with the same rhyme scheme as the original:

I see the night—the restless, eager night
       That spreads its shadow softly on the day,
And whispers to the sun's red, burning light
       To vanish like a dream and pass away.
I see the night—the darkened mist of night—
       And feel the velvet sorrows mem'ries bring;
September's leaves have fallen, old and bright,
       And autumn's winds have blown the dust of
             spring.
I think of days long past, and gone, and dead,
       Of all the ancient, withered hopes I've had. . . .

"Etc. Unlike Gray, I took myself as the subject of my elegy. But its mournful tone—and words like 'mem'ries'—was directly traceable to him. I understood the state of mind named in Gray's 'Elegy' to be the state of mind of poetry itself; and in reacting so deeply to it, I understood myself to be a poet. It was by no means a simple state of mind. It had to do with the enormous power of words not merely to reflect but to *create* a 'reality,' a 'mood' which moved me *away* from the daylight world in which I ordinarily functioned and had identity: 'I see the *night*. . . .' In some ways Gray's lines hinted at sexuality—surely an issue for me at that time." His rose 'blushes' and, virginal, 'wastes its sweetness on the desert air'; he writes of 'the dark, unfathomed *caves*.' Speaking the words aloud let me experience them *physically,* with my own breath, coming out of my own body. In *this* situation, mind and body seemed not to be at odds: Thought seemed sensuous, sensuality seemed thoughtful. Self and other were joined here too. Thomas Gray was a long-dead poet of the 18th Century. It was *his* mind that was being expressed in his elegy. Yet his poem seemed to be expressing my own inmost thoughts. It was almost as if Gray's passionate words allowed him to be reincarnated in my body.

"There was of course a 'real' Thomas Gray, a man who actually existed and who did a number of things beside write poetry. The Gray I was experiencing was not that person but Gray the poet, the bard. Aspects of both our lives seemed suddenly to fall away, to be of little consequence. What did it matter who the man Thomas Gray was? What did it matter who I was—born in New Jersey, growing up in New York? My powerful reaction to Gray's words allowed me to recognize not only who *he* was but who *I* was: I 'was' a poet. And to 'be' a poet meant to be transformed, to move away from the person who lived at 58 Prospect Street and who was 15 years old and who had a mother named Juana and a father named Jack. Poetry offered me another identity, that of the poet; and, in so doing, it offered me another 'home'— that of words. The life I led 'at home'—'in my house'—was one thing; the life of words was another.

"But a person with two homes can be understood as an exile. . . ."

When I arrived at Cornell one of my poems had been published in my high school yearbook ("We shall return no more, no more, our days. . . ."). Three short pieces had been selected for an anthology of high school poetry. Another poem had been published in a series called Yale Penny Poets. (Later I learned that Larry Eigner had a poem in that series as well.) I momentarily considered majoring in math, which I had enjoyed in high school. But I knew that my primary interests lay elsewhere, and I became an English major. My minor was French literature.

To my surprise, my freshman roommate was both Catholic and a wrestler (the church militant!). He was about my size and was trying to be nice. His brother had attended Cornell and so he knew the campus a little. He showed me around. But we were both a little nervous. When it came time to go to sleep I had some difficulty. Suddenly I heard a favorite piece, Gershwin's *Rhapsody in Blue,* beautifully played. At first I thought the music was coming from a radio, but in fact it was simply in my head. As I "listened" to it I fell asleep. I have always been grateful to Gershwin for that moment:

> there—on the edge
> of sleep—
> guiding me into it

> ("Chorus: Gershwin")

One of my dorm-mates tried to get me together with another English major, Ed Pechter. Ed and I eventually became good friends, but at this point we circled around each other warily. Noticing that it had begun to snow, he smiled and said, quoting Shelley's "Ode to the West Wind," "If Winter comes. . . ." That settled the matter. The man was at the very least trivializing a great poem; at worst he was committing blasphemy. I recited the entire first stanza of the poem and then, without another word, turned and left. I thought I was punishing Ed for his loose tongue. Ed thought I was trying to impress him!

"After years of continence," wrote Ezra Pound, "he hurled himself into a sea of six women" ("Moeurs Contemporaines"). That is exactly how I felt after Port Chester, though Cornell's three to one ratio of men to women made finding the six women a little difficult. "I'm not oversexed," I used to say, "I'm just undernourished."

In any case, Cornell offered me the opportunity to reinvent myself, and I went about doing that. I was a writer, a poet, no longer a "brain"—some sort of oddity—but an "intellectual," something which (unlike a "brain") might have a sex life. Here, writing poetry seemed actually to be an advantage. (I was so out of it in high school that when someone called me a "fag" I had no idea what they were saying. When I looked the word up in the dictionary all I could find was "*Slang.* A cigarette." It was some time before I discovered the actual meaning of the word.)

I had brought my Gretsch "Ultra-Modern Twin-Pickup 'Miracle Neck' Electric Spanish Guitar" with me to Cornell, but I wasn't sure whether I'd have much occasion to play it. This changed when I met Lou Cataldo, another outsider. Lou was half Italian and half Puerto Rican and called himself a "Ginnyspik." He called me a "Ginnymick." He had been raised in Greenwich Village (of which he spoke with great authority), could play the saxophone and double on bongo drums. He used the word "crazy." We decided that the best way to meet women was to have a band. ("Crazy!" said Cataldo.) We put up advertisements for a "girl singer" in the women's dormitories and held auditions. We got a lot of names, addresses, and phone numbers and—a girl singer. When I told this story to someone recently she asked, "Which of you had the affair with her?" I said, "He did," which was true. On the other hand, Cataldo's girlfriend from Greenwich Village arrived at Cornell and made a pass at me: "Oooo you didn't tell me he was so CUTE!" I made a few trips to Greenwich Village, and that was that.

At the end of freshman year Cataldo "busted out" and the girl singer was on probation. Our band had been successful enough to make it necessary for me to join the Musicians' Union. Once we fronted for a showing of "stag movies" at an organization called Young Israel. They couldn't advertise the movies but they could advertise us. Everyone just walked past us as we played. Eventually we stopped playing and went downstairs to watch the movies ourselves.

The psychological pressures of college life are considerable, and there isn't space to deal with them here. Cornell had some interesting teachers—including, eventually, Paul de Man, who was a major influence on my understanding of criticism and on my view of Yeats. There was also an excellent course on Dante taught by Robert Durling, and I read Joyce's *Ulysses* in Arthur Mizener's course. I wrote considerably less poetry in college than I had in high school, partly because I was being asked to consider poetry *critically,* in ways that were not fully familiar to me. *What exactly did you mean by that? Was that put in only for the sound?* Robert Durling was my freshman English teacher, and I would show him my poetry. I remember his description of my early work as "mellifluous Yeatsian vapidity." He smiled as he said it. But he said it. (I remember thinking that "Wolfian vapidity" might have been more accurate.)

For me the experience of poetry had been extraordinarily intense but utterly isolating. I had no way of knowing whether my work was any good, whether it "communicated." I had no one whose opinion I could really trust. To make matters worse, the opinions of most of my professors seemed to reflect those of the then-fashionable New Critics. For the New Critics, Shelley was a terrible poet. For me he was something like a god. (Whenever leaves show up in my poetry, Shelley's "Ode to the West Wind" is present.) One teacher said to me, "Why did Shelley write, 'I die, I faint, I fail' in *that* order? How can you faint and fail *after* you have died?" I had no way of answering the question, though much later the *Oxford English Dictionary*'s article on "die" provided me with an excellent response. I didn't find out about the *O.E.D.*, however, until long after I had left Cornell, when I came upon references to it in Robert Duncan's work. In many subtle ways I was encouraged to write criticism rather than poetry at Cornell, and I discovered that I was good at writing criticism. Like most college programs, Cornell's English department tended to produce people who felt comfortable with analysis but uncomfortable with emotion—particularly with personal emotion.

I had hoped that Cornell would give me what I lacked in Port Chester, an intellectual community. It gave me something, but it didn't give me that. In my sophomore year I took a great many English courses. I wanted to learn everything at once. What I discovered was that, no matter the period or the writer, Chaucer or T. S. Eliot, the same kinds of questions were being raised, questions of irony, paradox, etc. This discovery made me realize that I wasn't in school to learn about literature. I was in

school to learn a *grid* which could be applied to almost any piece of writing (though woe to the writer like Shelley to whom it *didn't* apply). This was a useful thing to learn, but it lessened the authority of my instructors.

When I read Thomas Gray's poem I believed (however inaccurately) that I had penetrated to the heart of poetry. I knew that Gray was a great writer because of the way he made me feel. I knew that Shelley was a great writer because of the way he made me feel. If my professors could not account for that feeling, their opinions didn't have to be taken too seriously. At the same time, however, I knew of no work which could further what I had already done. The poets I was reading were ones my professors approved of—or might approve of: Yeats, Eliot, and Pound; Dylan Thomas, W. H. Auden, Robert Graves, Robert Lowell. Also Alan Dugan, George Starbuck, Arthur Freeman. John Crowe Ransom gave a charming reading and I acquired his *Selected Poems*. I missed Charles Olson's visit. The writers I was reading influenced my verse, surely, but they could not push me forward. I had no sense of direction. The closest I was able to come to such a sense was in something I wrote myself, a poem called "Orpheus" which was eventually published in the *Beloit Poetry Journal* in 1970, about eight years after it was written. The poem was influenced by Pound—particularly by "Moeurs Contemporaines" and "Mauberly," with their fragmented sections. Except for the opening lines, written as part of an earlier poem, it came all of a sudden, in a burst. It was as if the original poem suddenly decided to change direction and take on a life of its own. The central sections, including the somewhat homophobic lines about Whitman, were a deliberate echo of Lorca's *Poet in New York* and "Lament for Ignacio Sánchez Mejías":

Walt Whitman walks on the harbor, watching
sea-gulls scatter, his beard full of lice.
There he goes, with his body electric,
chanting his chansons in the morning,
          never shaving.

Walt eyes the sailors, with *their* bodies electric,
electric to him, Walt Whitman,
chanting his chants in the morning,
          never shaving.

*

Garcia Lorca chants Walt Whitman—
Orpheus in the saddle,
his beautiful eyes are gleaming.
Never will there be an Andalusian
as handsome as he.

Now the worms eat him,
now the worms chew up Garcia Lorca

shot in the head for political reasons.

I realize now that the poem was telling me something about my own death and the death I sensed in my surroundings, but at the time I couldn't read it.

Here are three more poems from that period: "On the Ultimate Failure of Religiosity," "Love Song," and "Before Leaving Atlantic City." These three poems are more representative of what I was attempting than "Orpheus." The first suggests my uneasiness with both mother and mother church. The second suggests my sexual anxieties. (A woman said to me once, "I don't know whether you know it or not, but you have an absolutely terrific line!") I'll discuss the third poem in the next section. These poems show various influences, and they point towards my sense of poetry as something "physical," something *dangerous* and *erotic*.

On the Ultimate Failure of Religiosity

The lineal direction of eternity
is not marked clearly.
Hansel-and-Gretel-like, I lose my way
and stumble into the wicked house
in the bewildering wood.
I had supposed that death was an accident,
a deviation from the usual path,
yet these sweet-toothed children
munching their gingerbread crumbs
in evident sensuality
are another matter.
They are content, untrue
to the fairy tale, awaiting
the inevitable movement
to the black pot stirred
by the old hag of the story,
and grateful for the compassionate act
of swift beaks snapping
umbilicus of usual bread.

Love Song

This delicate piece of thread
proceeding by the longest possible route
from the point of my desire to your awareness—
had you postulated its existence,
I should have drawn it taut,
wound it easily on the spindle of
your acceptance,
but, as it is, must toss my line
hoping by some chance
you catch the baited inference.

Shall I remind you of its capacities?

Old tapestries,
diagrammatical pictures of the heart,
were woven by its ancestors,
and even the white surface of your indifference
might (with a bit of luck)
be rainbowed into passion by its working.

Before Leaving Atlantic City

The mother-sea exploded with a roar
before we put the lights out and it vanished.
Not even the ladies marching on the boardwalk
were storm enough to pull us down;
we rode out the daylight, dreaming
of drowsy islands where the water's calm.
Night was our harbor, when the midwife, love,
folded us in with its impossibilities,
fished out our pieces till the game made sense.
Sweetheart, forgive the liars and the fools
who shipped us to this place: they thought it
    best.
Sleep will bear you into gentler water
where painted characters of kings and castles
glitter like islands, and I will close your ears
to the disarranged palaver of pawns and
    landlubbers.

*

If you catch me stealin', please don't
tell on me.

Leadbelly song

The third poem quoted, "Before Leaving Atlantic City," was written in December 1961, as a love poem to my wife, Adelle. We had spent our honeymoon, at her parents' expense, in Atlantic City. I met Adelle through a complicated series of events.

I mentioned earlier that the pressures of college life are considerable: academic pressures, social pressures, issues of identity, sexuality, self-assertion. One is suddenly, willy-nilly, ready or not, an "adult." In my case, I had never been away from home. I had never gone on a date. I had never received any instruction about sex. I remember my mother remarking to my father, "D"—short for Daddy, something from my infancy which stuck—"you ought to say something to him." Understanding exactly what she meant, my father parried the attack: "Nah," he said, "These days they tell them all about that in school." Then, turning to me, he added: "Don't they?" What could I say but "Yes"?

As a child I owned very few books (except for comic books, which were a great passion), and there were very few books in my house. If I wanted to read a book I got it out of the library. In my freshman English class at Cornell, I was assigned to do a report on Yeats's *A Vision*. I went to the teacher to explain that the book had been taken out of the library and so I couldn't do the report. He surprised me by saying, "Why don't you just buy the book?" The possibility of buying a book—any book—hadn't occurred to me. I bought the Yeats, did the report, and suddenly I was beginning to buy books. Unfortunately, my funds were extremely limited. Looking around me in a bookstore one day, I realized that it would be easy to *steal* a book. I reasoned that stealing a book or two was really harming no one, and, further, that I would use the books well, better than most of the people who had money to buy them. At that point I began to steal books in earnest, to set about building myself a library. Once, when a friend needed money, I stole a large law book from one bookstore and sold it at the other. Unfortunately, I didn't get enough money for it and I had to go back and steal still another law book! My stealing was not only illegal but self-expressive, a mode of subversive self-assertion in a situation in which I was constantly under the scrutiny of authority figures. Friends whom I told about it expressed admiration, though they didn't take up the trade themselves. Finally I stole books I didn't really need, would never get around to reading.

Apparently, I was not alone in this activity. There were articles in the Cornell paper about the increase in book-stealing, and the bookstores began to install anti-theft devices. One

Jack and Adelle Foley, wedding photo, 1961

of the stores featured a "plainclothes" guard, who was supposed to blend in with the students. He didn't blend in. During one of my expeditions I realized that he was watching me. I decided to give him something to watch. I picked up more and more books and carried them around the store with me. I knew I could put these books on my credit account and get away. It would be expensive, but I wouldn't be accused of stealing. I remember thinking that the guard was probably wondering whether I would do that. I walked over to the clerk as if I were going to pay for the books, chatted with him for a few moments, and then—walked out the door. As soon as my foot was outside, a hand was on my shoulder. I handed over the books and, later, a few others from my library. I argued that I had read about the increase in stealing and, since I had little money, thought I could steal a few books too. I was put on suspension for a year. Someone remarked, "You seem almost relieved." Robert Langbaum, one of my teachers, said, "I hope you realize you've done a horrible thing." "There was," as the French Lieutenant's Woman says to her ex-lover in both book and movie, "a wildness in me at that time." The relief my friend noticed was real. Stealing books was a way of extricating myself from an increasingly unbearable situation, and of doing so without the pain of a direct confrontation. Did I wish to stay in school? Was Cornell the right place for me? I needed time off but had no way to ask for it. Stealing deflected my attention from those difficult questions and, finally, provided me with time. When my parents learned of my suspension they rose to the occasion admirably—my mother had after all been caught doing the same thing—and I was welcomed home.

Several years earlier, my mother had sued, or threatened to sue, our landlord when I accidentally put my hand through a pane of glass on the front door to the apartment house. The result of the injury was a panicked trip to the hospital and a fairly obvious scar on my left arm. My mother argued that the scar might mar my career in show business (not that I had a career in show business), and the landlord gave her some money. This money had been put aside for me to use as I wished. I had recently gone to Boston to see a friend before he went home to Italy. I decided it might be nice to spend the summer of 1960 in Cambridge. I tried finding jobs in the Boston area but none of them worked out. Finally, at my mother's suggestion, I took advantage of my savings. The money allowed me not only to live in Cambridge but to attend Harvard summer school.

In Cambridge I acquired a whole new set of friends. Moreover, I discovered that it was not unfashionable to be a writer/thief. Jean Genet was at the height of his fame. So my petty thievery tended to work to my advantage. One of the people I met, Lewis H. Rubman, changed the course of my life. Rubman was amazing. He had a mustache, for one thing. For another, he had a car. Furthermore, he was extremely frank about sex—and he had some of those beautiful Henry Miller books published by the Olympia Press in Paris. His parents were well-off (he was an inhabitant of that middle-class I both envied and disdained) and he had actually undergone some psychotherapy. He was, I believe, looking for a best friend, a best friend for life, and he sensed that in me. Neither of us was writing very much but there was always a good deal of intellectual excitement. One of

the courses I was taking included the magnificent Brecht/Weill opera *Aufstieg und Fall der Stadt Mahagonny*. I listened to the record over and over. Brecht's play, with its self-conscious "bits," suggested a new and, to me, astonishing direction for *vaudeville*. Later, I translated Brecht's lyric to "Surabaya Johnny," only to discover that the lyric was itself a translation of Kipling's poem "Mary, Pity Women." It was a marvelous summer.

When the summer was over, Rubman returned to New York City, where he was going to New York University. He had an apartment on East Eleventh Street. I went back to Port Chester. Arguments with my parents increased. My father was terrified that he would have to support me for life. Finally, over my parents' fierce objections (my mother writhing on the floor, my father shouting, "You're killing that woman!"), I moved into a rooming house not far away from home. I got a job as a bank teller and, for the first time in my life, was able to support myself. I felt that if my parents were going to make my life miserable, there was no reason I had to stay with them. My bank teller job meant that my father didn't have to give me any money. What did my parents have to give me if they could no longer give me money? My difficulties with my mother remained unresolved when she died in 1964. I walked out of the hospital and burst into tears. During our deathwatch over her, however, my father and I were able to feel close to one another again. When he died three years later, I felt that we had arrived at some sort of understanding.

Moving out of the house meant I could do what I liked with my time. Every second weekend I visited Rubman in New York. The other weekends he drove to Goucher College in Maryland, where a woman he'd met in Cambridge was going to school. I accompanied him a few times. On one of these trips he introduced me to Adelle Abramowitz, whom he'd known in elementary school. He had been recently reintroduced to her by his girlfriend, Ellen, and he'd been very impressed. "She's read *Finnegans Wake*," he told me. *The grass is always greener, the ass is always keener,* a friend once chanted. There was a Jewish family living in the apartment house where I'd grown up. The father spoke with an attractive, slight Yiddish accent. Their grown daughter seemed to me enormously beautiful, and was the object

Jack and Adelle Foley in costume for the musical Tom Jones, *1962, Cornell University. "In our photo album, beneath this photo, are the words, 'You are the guiding star of his existence.'"*

of one of those immense, all-consuming crushes which animate our childhood. Later, in high school, there was another woman, closer to my own age. Jews seemed attractive, witty, intelligent, and, in a way that I was not, *successful.* "You only like them," a Jewish woman told me recently, "because you're *not Jewish.*" I admitted that that was possible, but I have often found very close friends among Jews. Adelle had not only read *Finnegans Wake,* she had lived abroad for a year; her French was better than mine. Since she was an economics major and good at math some friends wondered whether we could find anything to talk about. There were no problems.

As my relationship with my own family deteriorated, Adelle's family welcomed me. I spent the next summer in New York City—my father was able to get me a job in a Western Union office in Bowling Green—and I saw a great deal of Adelle and her parents, Sam and Esther. Adelle and I were almost exactly the

same age (I'm six days older) but she had skipped a grade, so she was a year ahead of me. After graduation from Goucher, she entered graduate school at Cornell. We lived together for a short time and were married in Foley Square in New York City on December 21, 1961. I cursorily invited my parents to the wedding. My mother, rightly, was insulted, and they didn't attend. My best man was Lewis Rubman.

My mother would not have been happy had I married anyone, I think, but she was especially unhappy about my marrying a Jewish woman. At the same time she realized that I was threatening to break off relations with her and my father entirely. I had a deep need for family and, at the same time, a deep need to break away from family. But—like my father—I was discovering that it was possible, at least in part, to substitute one family for another. Despite my name, many of Adelle's relatives assumed I was Jewish. Adelle's parents, who knew

167

better, accepted me without question. Their kindness and understanding are things I will always be grateful for.

At Cornell my writing tended to focus on song lyrics. Warren Wechsler, a classmate, wrote charming songs and played piano. We began to collaborate: I provided lyrics, Warren provided music. Finally we found people willing to write a libretto and we put on an original musical, *Tom Jones*. I sang one of the songs and worked out a tap dance. Adelle had a brief role—she played a servant girl who initiates the action by leaving baby Tom at the front door—and she handled the finances. The musical was a success, and we were asked to stage it again for a big weekend at the end of the year. Had I not been suspended, 1962 would have been my senior year. I produced a poem, "Tunnel of Love," which was at once a love poem and a good-bye to all that:

Hard-put by the weather,
we await the spring
in sluggish Ithaca.
Stuck
in a ramshackle town,
I love you up to keep the blankets warm.

Back home,
the foghorns bellow in the dingy harbor
while mother putters at her indoor plants.
They are the household deities:
anchored,
they flower in a bad season
while the crazy tugs
teeter and totter in a choppy sea.

Broken by winter,
we huddle mole-like in the covers,

two old sailors
blindly anchored in our Tunnel of Love.

*

This one was one very many were knowing some and very many were glad to meet him, very many sometimes listened to him, some listened to him very often, there were some who listened to him, and he talked then and he told them then that certainly he had been one suffering and he was then being one trying to be certain that he was wrong in doing what he was doing and he had come then to be certain that he never would be certain that he was doing what it

was wrong for him to be doing then and he was suffering then and he was certain that he would be one doing what he was doing and he was certain that he should be one doing what he was doing and he was certain that he would always be one suffering and this then made him certain this, that he would always be one being suffering, this made him certain that he was expressing something being struggling. . . .

Gertrude Stein, "Matisse"

In 1963 Adelle and I were heading west, on our way to Berkeley, California. I had been awarded a Woodrow Wilson Fellowship; Adelle was soon to find a job at the Federal Reserve Bank of San Francisco. Paul de Man good-naturedly told me that I had better get my tennis game together because that's all anyone did in Berkeley. In 1962 I had finally learned to drive. We purchased a 1956 Oldsmobile to make the trip across country. Two close friends, Mike Lurie, whom I had met in Cambridge, and Ed Pechter, were already living in Berkeley. Then Rubman surprised us by showing up to live there too. We found an apartment without much trouble. The following year we found a place in Oakland; ten years later we bought a house in Oakland. We're still living in that house.

In Berkeley my writing stopped almost entirely as I concentrated on graduate school or participated in that explosion of energy we call "the sixties." Rubman knew many of the people involved with the Free Speech Movement, and so I got to meet them early on. I protested the war and experimented with LSD and marijuana. (I deliberately took acid *before* marijuana so that no one could accuse me of "going on to the harder stuff.") I learned rock songs and played them on my electric guitar. Until that time my guitar playing had depended entirely on sheet music. I now learned to trust (and develop) my ear. Berkeley radio station KPFA broadcast an astonishing range of art programming, which I found fascinating. (I first heard Gertrude Stein's voice on KPFA.) A short poem written in Berkeley, "The Skeleton's Defense of Carnality," was published in the *Beloit Poetry Journal*. A paper written for Stanley Fish's Milton course was published in the journal *ELH*. But the basic story of my life in the sixties and seventies is my increasing awareness that I *could not be* a member of the academy. There were constant tensions between my personal vision and what was acceptable in graduate school. At one point I produced a long, complicated paper on "Holy Thursday" for a seminar on Blake. The paper went over like a lead balloon, but twenty years later a passage from it found its way into my poem "Fifty":

> We have here—as we have at the conclusion of "The Echoing Green"—a kind of gradual fading of the light in which things are no longer seen clearly and in which the sounds we "hear" tend to become somewhat distant: "all the hills echoéd." At this point, I think, language becomes something close to pure potentiality, to pure "sound" or "music," to the "song" that the piper pipes. What Blake is attempting to make us do, I suspect, is to treat *all* of his words in the same way that we must treat the names of his characters: we must continually recombine them, must turn them around and around in our minds until they become words which, though different, involving other letters, retain in their sounds the echoes of one another. Blake himself used words of the Bible in order to create new harmonies, harmonies which "chimed" with those of the Bible, and I think "Holy Thursday" was meant to serve the same purpose. 'Twas on a, for example, might easily become 'twas honor, hosanna; the seats of heaven, the saints of heaven, the seeds of heaven; beneath them sit, be neath them said; white as snow, why 'tis snow, why 'tis now; till into, tell unto, toll unto; the voice of song, they voice his song, their voice is song, their voice, his song; the flowers of London town, or land atoned, or lenten time; but multitudes of lambs, but multitudes of lands, but multitudes of limbs, bought multitudes of lambs; thousands of little boys, those sands of little boys; O what a, O water; the hum of multitudes, the home of multitudes, the hymn, the ham, the him of multitudes; they like Thames waters flow, they light time's waters flow, their nighttimes waters flow; radiance all their own, radiance all thereround, radiance all thereon, regents are there crowned; the children walking, the cauldron waking, the called are walking; harmonious thunderings, our moan, his thunderings; the voice, the vows, the joys.

I had hoped that Cornell would provide me with an intellectual community. It did not. My experience at Berkeley was similar, though again there were moments of excitement.

Josephine Miles, Joe Kramer, Paul Alpers, and others taught courses which interested me. Henry Nash Smith's course included Charles Feidelson, Jr.'s excellent book *Symbolism and American Literature* with its intriguing discussions of Melville, Poe, and Whitman. A 1971 class taught by James Breslin introduced me to many writers whom I had previously neglected, particularly to William Carlos Williams, whose masterly *Spring and All* was on the reading list. We also read Robert Duncan's magnificent *Bending the Bow.* (I had bought Duncan's *Selected Poems* in Ithaca and been fascinated by "The Venice Poem" and "Homage to the Brothers Grimm.") Duncan lived in San Francisco and often gave lectures and readings. I saw him frequently in Berkeley going to the bookstores or the library. There were also writers in Breslin's class: Ron Silliman, David Melnick, and Rochelle Nameroff had all recently published books through a press called "Ithaca House," located, ironically enough, at Cornell. Furthermore, James Breslin was the judge of Berkeley's Yang Poetry Prize that year, and a little selection of my poems was one of the winners. Still, I could hardly call myself a writer. By 1970 I was really nothing more than a professional graduate student.

On April 5, 1970, at the age of twenty-nine, I gave up smoking. On May 6 of that year I began a journal: "What do I want to come of this? Some self-knowledge. I have been a propagandist for self-knowledge. I really know very little of myself."

By 1974 I had finally had enough of graduate school. I made a last-ditch effort to write a Ph.D. thesis. A long paper on Shakespeare's *Cymbeline,* written for Joe Kramer's class, might be the basis of a thesis. The only problem with the paper was that it didn't mention a single critic. I set about to remedy that. The books I needed were sometimes taken out of the main library. In the undergraduate library, however, there was a set of stacks which had just about everything. Nobody ever touched it. Unfortunately, as I read the critics I found myself getting angry. *Cymbeline* was not a play which anyone seemed to have understood very well. Even people whose work I usually liked had little of interest to say about it. Finally, I got up and wandered over to the modern poetry section. There I came upon Charles Olson's *Maximus IV V VI.* I found the book amazing. I'm not sure I understood it in the usual sense in which one "understands" things. On the other hand,

I understood it. *Maximus IV V VI,* with its size, its ample white space, its *freedom,* was a revelation, or, as Jake Berry said about another book, a baptism. I went back and forth between the critics and Olson until I realized that I was in fact acting out a little drama. Do you want to be *this* or do you want to be *this?* The decision was obvious. I left school. I wanted to be Olson.

Leaving school freed me towards reading again. I plunged into Gertrude Stein and Pound's *Cantos.* Like Robert Kelly as he tells it in *A Controversy of Poets,* I felt transformed by Williams's "astonishing" "Asphodel That Greeny Flower." I read the Beats with better understanding than ever before. L=A=N=G=U=A=G=E poets were just beginning to publish, and I was aware of their work. A KPFA program introduced me to Kerouac's marvelous reading style. I read all the Duncan I could find. McClure's essay "Phi Upsilon Kappa" opened his work to me ("Writing this is a kind of pain as well as a joy at the chance to make a new liberty"). KPFA broadcast an amazing production of Artaud's radio play *Pour en finir avec le jugement de dieu* which included Artaud himself. I immediately hunted up *The Theater and Its Double.* I also read Louis Zukofsky, Jack Spicer, Larry Eigner, H.D., Amiri Baraka, Clayton Eshleman, Ishmael Reed, and Adrienne Rich. Through Rich I came upon Judy Grahn's stunning poem *A Woman Is Talking to Death* and then her later poetry and her wonderful essays. Walter J. Ong's work became an endless source of inspiration and insight. Gregory Bateson taught me a good deal, as did Carl Sauer. I explored the occult: A. E. Waite, Crowley, Max Heindel, Corinne Heline. (Her little book on the moon in occult lore is masterly.) I finally read Heidegger (to whom Paul de Man was always referring) as well as Wittgenstein, Gurdjieff, Reich, Whitehead, Freud, Jung, and Foucault. Hannah Arendt's *The Human Condition* was read and re-read.

Partly through the good offices of Charles Amirkhanian at KPFA I was listening to experimental music as well as reading experimental poetry. Charles Ives's *Concord Sonata* and his book *Essays before a Sonata* were enormous influences, as were his songs. I first heard Lou Harrison on KPFA. I had acquired Kenneth Rexroth's wonderful edition of D. H. Lawrence's poetry in Ithaca. Now I was reading Rexroth, who also had a show on KPFA. My friend Ed Michel gave me a collection of records he had

Adelle, Jack, and Sean Foley; Sean is four days old. Oakland, California, February 24, 1974.

produced, so I began to listen seriously to jazz. Eisenstein's essays were tremendously exciting, as was Abel Gance's marvelous "polyvision" film, *Napoleon,* which Adelle and I saw at the Avenue Theater in San Francisco. I haunted UC Berkeley's Pacific Film Archive and published a few essays on film. (Gary Morris, the editor of *Bright Lights* magazine, has been a constant supporter of my work in this area.) I began to think seriously about the art of painting. Clyfford Still's work fascinated me. A 1977 exhibition of Jess's work at the University Art Museum had an enormous impact. I discovered Max Ernst. Kandinsky's paintings and his book *Concerning the Spiritual in Art* were powerful expressions. Etc.

My poetry was, however, to use Gertrude Stein's word, still "struggling." Under the influence of Breslin's course and its participants I began to produce a kind of experimental verse. Remembering both Paul Valéry and a brand of candy, I put these poems together in a short sequence called "Charmes." Each of the poems was an ecstatic, only partially understood experience. Here is the third:

randy belly . look & come . there are clouds
    in the—

                        .

        hardly the ice . ends

                        .

            folding   lines
                quiet is the

                        .

            cross-ing the
                crossing   toss-
                    crossed

Such poems were wonderful when they came, but they were few and far between. Though the poems seemed to celebrate my entrance into the ecstatic state in which poetry was possible ("cross-ing the / crossing toss- / crossed"), I had no idea how that state might be induced or how in fact I had fallen into it.

                        *

Immature poets imitate; mature poets steal.

                T. S. Eliot, "Philip Massinger"

On June 25, 1974, I was utterly depressed about my writing. I had just brought our car in for servicing—never a happy obligation—and taken the bus back home. I was extremely tired and believed at that moment I would never produce anything of any value. Glancing at a collection of Olson's essays—particularly at "Human Universe"—I noticed a sentence which began, "If there is any truth at all to the idea that. . . ." Certain that nothing would come of it, I typed on a piece of paper, "If there is any truth at all," and added, as if in commentary, "(there is)." I went on to appropriate others of Olson's phrases, changing them if I felt like

it. (Olson actually wrote, "It is *not* the Greeks I blame.")

            if there is any truth at all (there is)
            it is the greeks I blame
            the lines in which
                            speech takes place
            & Melville did. . . .

Next I took a recent passage from my journal,

        a waking dream.
Someone (me, not me) on a rooftop. Being chased?
    Crowds. The man's friends below, holding a
net which looks like an awning, urge him.
            Tremendous distance!
The man jumps!—he misses the awning.
I remark (it is remarked to me): he didn't check
        which way the wind was blowing,

and retyped it, moving my fingers slightly so I would hit some of the wrong keys and leaving out some of it, revising as I went along:

        a wajubg dreanL
sineibe OOne.bitg neOOib a riiftioOObeubg cgased.
    Criwds the man's friends bekiw
        gikdubg a bet kiijs kuje ab wawbubg 'greeb
                    tremendous distance
yrge
    urge him

            to killowatts

My depression vanished. The poem suddenly came alive. Its seemingly obvious discovery that literature was made out of *letters* was extraordinarily liberating, and its concluding lines, only half-understood when I wrote them, "the page is not the / natural dividing point," thrust me into an entirely new direction. A sequence of such poems followed. I called it "Letters" and dedicated it to "the sixth Marx brother: Typo." (Olson's praise of the typewriter in his famous essay "Projective Verse" was undoubtedly in the back of my mind.) Then a friend, Richard Segasture, sent me his play, *Limbo*. I thought it might be interesting to include what I called "Choruses"—theater pieces—in his play, and he agreed. The first of these was later published in my book *Adrift*. Its opening line is a kind of stage direction:

Darkness. The light comes slowly.

What is it?
It sweetens the circulation of the blood.
My blood is circular enough already.
And your reasoning?
What is it?
Voices.   Voices.

The piece goes on to quote from Darwin, Einstein, Hans Christian Andersen, W. H. Prescott, and others. Writing another of these choruses, I decided to involve Adelle in its performance. The first chorus moved through various voices, but I could perform it solo. With two speakers, voices could be thrust against one another, simultaneously. I worked out the poem's timing by using a tape recording of my own voice, then presented it to Adelle. We became very interested in the possibilities of the form. Thinking partly of its placement in Segasture's play but also regarding it as a genuine "opening," I named the poem "Overture." It became the "Words for Adelle" of my first book, *Letters/ Lights—Words for Adelle:*

At the "Performance Poetry Bash," 1988

that the hummingbird's wings are of a remarkable
  rapidity he had noted often
  nothing could be done   the shift of his
    breathing   had to begin
12 o'clock and he still hadn't had a   dermal
  sensation

Such poems were tremendously exciting, but, apart from Adelle, I had no audience and no idea where to present my work. An acquaintance invited me to an open poetry reading in Berkeley. I didn't read anything, but he tried to read a long poem which he regarded as the best thing he had ever written. The emcee decided he was going on too long and ran him off the stage. "Overture" was performed at someone's birthday party in 1974. It was well received, but it wasn't performed again until 1985, when Adelle and I gave our first reading. My isolation had allowed me to develop a kind of poetry which I found immensely satisfying. At the same time, however, there was absolutely no one to validate it. My friend from Cambridge and Berkeley, Mike Lurie, would make occasional comments about my work. He was hit by an automobile in New Jersey and killed. I remember thinking, in the midst of my grief, "Now there is no one to read my work!"

Not that I had much time to mope over the fate of my writing. On February 20, 1974, Adelle gave birth to a son, whom we named Sean Ezra, in part after Adelle's father, Samuel. ("Sean" = "John" by way of "Jean," so he was being named after my father and me as well.) Sean, someone quipped, had been exFoliated. The presence of a son was a great joy, the occasion of stories, humor, even of the creation of an imaginary creature named by Sean "The D D D Monster." Though "The Monst" *looked* like me, he had a separate history. He *sounded* a little like Sean as a baby. Later came the arrival of a female creature called "The E E E Monster." *She* looked like Adelle and featured speech made up entirely of E's.

For the next several years I was a househusband, taking care of Sean, bringing him to school, etc. Ed Pechter moved to Canada to teach and Lewis Rubman and I became utterly estranged. Friends left and new friends appeared. We got to know other parents.

Meeting poet Ivan Argüelles in 1985 changed almost everything.

I had known Ivan's wife, Marilla, because she taught at Sean's elementary school, Park

Jack and Adelle reading at Cody's Books, Berkeley, 1988

Day School in Oakland. I also knew that Ivan was a widely published poet, but I hadn't read much of his poetry. I ran into Marilla at a party given by an old friend of Adelle's mother. I had recently gotten to know Ishmael Reed, whose daughter, Tennessee, was attending Park Day. I mentioned Ishmael to Marilla, who told me that Ivan might be interested in meeting him. I said, "Maybe I can arrange that," and was introduced to Ivan, who gave me two of his books to read. "Let me know what you think of them," he said. I thought they were wonderful. Here was an extraordinary, wildly visionary, wildly funny work, full of pain yet full of comedy as well. I wrote Ivan a long letter about his poetry. Later he told me the letter came closer to what he felt his poetry was like than anything he'd ever received before. He also said he was going to be reading at Larry Blake's series in Berkeley. "You mention that you write. Why don't you read with me? If your poetry is even half as good as

your criticism, you'll be fine." I learned later that such generosity was characteristic of this amazing man.

As it happened, Gerald Vizenor, whom I knew through a course sponsored by Ishmael Reed's Before Columbus Foundation, was also about to do a poetry reading. Gerry's reading was to be at the California College of Arts and Crafts in Oakland. I told him about my upcoming reading with Ivan and he suggested that I read with him as well. The organizer of Gerry's reading phoned me asking whether I would like to be on for a half hour. I told her fifteen minutes would be fine. She told me that there would be "other, less well-known people on the bill." I didn't tell her that it would be pretty hard to find someone "less well-known" than I was! I suggested that Ivan be included in the reading. My idea was that Ivan could hear me and if he didn't like what he heard, he could skip the Larry Blake's reading, no hard feelings.

173

When I began this project, I asked a few people who were close to me to write a few sentences about me. I told them I would not edit what they wrote or respond to it in any way.

Jack's life, like his art, is based in collage. He welcomes unorthodox combinations of everything from food to music, from friends to clothing—and urges them enthusiastically on those around him. Living with Jack is a lifelong, year-round course of study with no boundaries and no written exams.

> Like nobody else
> His passions stretch and challenge
> What "everybody knows"

Adelle Foley
4/26/96

Courage and faith are the two words that come to mind when I think about my father. This may be an odd thing to say about an ex-Catholic, but I don't think I have met a person who is more willing to challenge the assumptions of everyone around him and confident enough to forge his own path. There are four examples in my father's life that illustrate this point: his friendship with Larry Eigner, his poetry, his decision to drop out of graduate school, and his kindness to those around him.

Sean Foley
4/27/96

Jack's all right if you like that sort of person.

The D D D Monster
4/96

Eeeee. Eeeeee. Eeeeeeeeee. Eeeeee. E.

The E E E Monster
4/96

Five Things about Jack Foley

Jack—
If you can read it I can write it
M

1. Jack Foley is one of the main hombres for shouldering responsibilities in the Bay Area literary world; whether it's friendship and care-giving for cerebral-palsied poet friends or letting everyone know about an important event that might be missed, Jack is there with his shoulder to the wheel and his hand on the phone.

2. Jack is notable for the specialness of his ear and he's capable of, and likely to, appreciate the most far-flung temperaments from experimental Jake Berry to gay and metaphysical James Broughton.

3. It's as if Jack runs an ever-open service to stick up for the rights of the outcast and the unaligned or invalided writers. He reminds others of their responsibility through his activism.

4. Jack never forgets a birthday whether it's his own or yours. He's right there to celebrate.

5. In roles like public radio reviewer—maestro—and contributing editor to *Poetry Flash*, Jack is a deepener; he has a powerful intellect and gives substance to issues under view.

Michael McClure
4/12/96
(Automatic Writing)

*   *   *

It was reported in the *Oakland Daily Tribulation* that someone had broken into the First Rational Bank and had made off with quantities of ballpoint pens. Rumors that Jack Foley is the culprit are irresponsible and inaccurate. I was with Jack and Adelle from the beginning of his memorable poetry reading to the wee hours of the morning. Who could forget the guitar-dancing, tap-twanging multisimultaneous poetic cavortings? It was entertaining and affecting. Afterwards we repaired to their house and, surrounded by treasures and artifacts that attest to the Foley passion for the arts, we talked of all shapes of cabbages and all sorts of kings. Jack's breadth of knowledge and depth of insight are impressive. There was laughter too, much nose-clearing, eye-opening, twittering-tittering. Early on it was all poetry and performance, exciting new sounds, voices, ideas and deeply human caring. Later it was sharing and clashing, some sanity and much insanity at the Foley home . . . a full and remarkable night. So Jack Foley could not have robbed the bank . . . unless he had an accomplice.

Leonard Breger
4/96

Portrait of Jack Foley by Leonard Breger, 1995

That fifteen-minute reading reshaped my life. Ivan loved what he heard and generously encouraged me. It was a pivotal moment. Here was a man whose own work was rich and powerful. I knew no one who even liked my work. At almost every point in my development, someone had told me *not* to do what I was doing. When I began to write multivoiced poems, a friend wrote me a letter urging me to *stop* writing them. When I showed her my long poems, another friend announced that long poems were boring. Ivan gave me what I had never been able to find in all my years in the university system: validation, a sympathetic reading. The best poem I had produced at that point was "Turning Forty," a long collage piece initially influenced by David Bromige's "One Spring" but later by Joyce's *Finnegans Wake*. (I had often listened to Joyce's recording of pages 213–216—the Anna Livia Plurabelle section.) For the reading at Larry Blake's I wrote a new poem in the style of "Turning Forty." It was called "Sweeney Adrift," and it dealt freely with the legend of a mad Irishman. For the first

Adelle, Jack, and Sean Foley, 1986. "This photo was reproduced on the back cover of my first book Letters/Lights—Words for Adelle. *Seeing it, someone asked Adelle, 'Is that your group?' She answered, 'No, that's my family.'"*

time in my life I asked someone's opinion of my verse as I was actually composing it. I would write a few lines, phone Ivan, read them to him, and he would say, "Great! Keep it coming!" I did.

The reading at Larry Blake's (June 1985) was a great success, and Ivan and I each went on to do many more readings, together or with others. In all this, Adelle has been not only my wife but my performing partner. Her performing skills and her willingness to take the kinds of risks I ask of her have been enormous factors in my success. She has sung, tap danced, made faces, and screamed, all in the service of my "art." She has turned pieces which were at best only vaguely conceived into some sort of recognizable shape. People have said to me, "Well, *your* performance was all right, but *Adelle . . . !*" In the past few years she has begun to write poetry herself, and her haiku have appeared in various magazines.

In 1986 I took over the series at Larry Blake's and then, in 1988, I was offered a radio

show on KPFA, where I have been producing programs ever since. I became deeply involved with the community of writers here, organizing, discussing, reading, writing. From 1990 to 1995 I edited an Oakland-based magazine, *Poetry USA. Heaven Bone* called it "the poetry Bible of the 'Bay' area"; *The Beatlicks: Nashville's Poetry Newsletter* described its experimental issue as "a wake up call for poetry in America." In 1992 Joyce Jenkins named me contributing editor of her wonderful magazine, *Poetry Flash.* Larry Eigner, James Broughton, Michael McClure, Jess, and Lou Harrison became dear friends, and they have all encouraged my work in various ways.

There is much more to the story, but it will have to wait. If in the seventies I was completely unknown, in the past ten years I have become an extremely public figure. "Sweeney Adrift" became a signature poem, and it was dedicated to Ivan. "Chorus: SON(G)," published like "Sweeney Adrift" in my book *Adrift,* is still another signature poem, and it is dedicated to someone I can only barely begin to discuss here: Jake Berry. Jake and I discovered each other's work in 1985 through a cassette magazine called *Poets 11,* and we have been encouraging and learning from each other ever since. He has been called, rightly, by Harry Polkinhorn, "the preeminent experimentalist of his generation." (Jake was born in 1959.) I wrote the preface to his *Brambu Drezi* and the afterword to his *Species of Abandoned Light,* both marvelous books. More recently, Neeli Cherkovski has joined our group. His lyricism and deep knowledge of poetic history are examples for us all.

Once, Ivan, Neeli, and I were to do a reading together. We were listed alphabetically (Argüelles, Cherkovski, Foley). I thought: the *A*cademy of *C*hicanerous *F*rumpery! But then I realized that Jake should be included too, so it became The *A*cademy of *C*hicanerous *F*rumpery, *Boo!* For some time now we have been nourishing one another, discussing poetry, acting like Something Is Afoot in California. Much of our work has been issued through Ivan's Pantograph Press, which is rapidly becoming a center for what John M. Bennett has called "the fundamental revolution going on in American poetry at this moment." Other energy sources include: Hank Lazer in Alabama, Bob Grumman in Florida, Susan Smith Nash in Oklahoma, Jim Leftwich in Virginia, and Gregory Vincent St. Thomasino in New York. Writers recently designated as "The Other South" in the *New Or-*leans Review connect with us as well. As Kenneth Rexroth wrote in "Disengagement: The Art of the Beat Generation" in 1957, "The avant garde has not only not ceased to exist. It's jumping all over the place. Something's happening, man."

The Difficulty of Concluding This Autobiography

> What you either come by naturally, or as I suspect have always understood is how to free your mind.
>
> Barbara Guest in a letter to me

Looking back over this short autobiography, I realize how much of my life I've been *un*able to name in it. Even what I have been able to name is problematical. In story our lives tend to take on a coherence and purpose which they may well have lacked in actuality. As circumstances arise we discover/invent selves to deal with them. And the circumstances change in response to those selves. What I wrote in the seventies in a paper on Alfred Hitchcock ("Doubleness in Hitchcock: Seeing the Family Plot") might apply more generally to my sense of the world: "In the dizzying ramifications of the Oedipal situation the external world and the self are not separate entities but dynamic

---

Statement on Performance Poetry Made for National Poetry Week II (1988)

> *Camerado, this is no book . . .*
> —Walt Whitman

Performance poetry is an active and intellectually engaged response to the silence and whiteness in which most poetry remains entangled. Writing of Mallarmé, Frederick R. Karl remarked, "The page or territory is primary, on which language wanders like a lonely adventurer hoping to survive emptiness and whiteness." The performance poet insists that s/he is not a mere adjunct of a book but rather a manifestation of what books arise out of: the physical presence of the author. Historically, "poetry" and "writing" remain in a state of tension. (Homer was a *poet,* not a *writer.*) Performance poetry seeks to tilt that tension in the direction of presence, to insist on the limitations of writing as a medium for the presentation of the art. At the heart of writing, at the heart of all mass culture, is a profound and disturbing absence. Performance poetry is an insistence that absence, silence and whiteness—the page—are not the only conditions in which poetry can be "heard."

forces which shift, merge, interrelate, conflict, reverberate, change around—and the very same narcissistic tendencies which may give rise to (among other things) fantasies of murder become, in the limitations and intensities of 'performance,' a mode of authentic self-disclosure. In the midst of a self-reflective world, a world in which actor and audience tend to merge, and which tends to give back, reflect the ramifications of the self, 'action' becomes in effect *revelatory.*"

"Performance," "action," and the "revelatory" have been key factors in my work. Hannah Arendt's chapter on "Action" in *The Human Condition* quotes Dante: "For in every action what is primarily intended by the doer, whether he acts from natural necessity or out of free will, is the disclosure of his own image. Hence it comes about that every doer, in so far as he does, takes delight in doing; since everything that is desires its own being, and since in action the being of the doer is somehow intensified, delight necessarily follows. . . . Thus, nothing acts unless [by acting] it makes patent its latent self."

One might also cite Baudelaire, whose sonnet "Correspondences" I recently translated. (I added a quotation from Swedenborg to Baudelaire's poem to show Baudelaire's own source of the word "correspondence.")

What correspondence is is not known at the present day, for several reasons, the chief of which is that man has withdrawn himself from heaven by the love of self and love of the world. . . . This was not so with the ancient people. To them the knowledge of correspondences was the chief of knowledges. By means of it they acquired intelligence and wisdom; and by means of it those who were of the church had communication with heaven; for the knowledge of correspondences is angelic knowledge. The most ancient people, who were celestial men, thought from correspondence itself, as the angels do. Therefore they talked with angels, and frequently saw the Lord and were taught by Him. But at this day that knowledge has been so completely lost that no one knows what correspondence is.

Emanuel Swedenborg,
Heaven and Its Wonders and Hell (1758)

Nature is a temple where living statues
At times give out confused words;
Man passes through forests of symbols
That watch him with familiar looks.

Like long echoes that merge from afar
In a shadowy and profound unity,
Vast like the night, like light,
Perfumes, colors and sounds answer back and forth.

There are perfumes as fresh as the flesh of infants,
Soft, like oboes, green, like fields,
—And others, corrupt, rich and triumphant,

Having the expansion of infinite things •

Amber, musk, benzoin, incense,
Singing the **transports** of spirit and sense.

Poetry does not arise out of a *part* of one's life. It permeates everything, welcomes everything. When Ivan was just beginning to write his great epic poem, *Pantograph,* he phoned me to talk about it. *"No more inhibitions!"* he said triumphantly. I thought of that remark when I wrote the following lines in "Villanelle," a poem dedicated to Ivan:

THE DESCENT INTO HELL & DARKNESS & THE NEED FOR "MEHR LICHT" are primal images, gestures. Song allows us to contemplate horrors & yet remain sane. It places the horrific thing directly in front of us, we see it all, & clearly, yet, because of the song, it *cannot* harm us. Song

*Larry Eigner, drawing by Jack Foley,
about 1992*

With Jake Berry in KPFA's studios, 1996

empties the terrible of its terror, annihilates *content,* yet leaves us with a "sweetness" that is certainly close to if it is not precisely a state of grace, a Buddhistic emptiness. Song seems to distance us from the world at the same time that it brings the world to us, with all its "news." Song's "sweetness" allows us a certain innocence in the midst of the inferno. Shhhhh, it says to the horrors, there's nothing going on here, only someone humming a tune.

I remember as well the title of Larry Eigner's first mature book: *From the Sustaining Air.* The "airs" a poet puts on sustain him in innumerable ways. These are some lines from a recent piece:

> The drowned day
> any man of vigorous mind
> anticipate his thought
> which all ranks pay
> I cannot even hear of Vigor of any kind
> bread and fire
> I know not
> *lyre*

The thrust of so much current writing involves a redefinition of selfhood. The remarks Ludwig Wittgenstein makes about the concept of "games" in *Philosophical Investigations* might be a description of the kind of "self" we see in current work: "If you look at them [games] you will not see something that is common to *all,* but similarities, relationships, and a whole series of them at that . . . And we extend our concept . . . as in spinning a thread we twist fibre on fibre. *And the strength of the thread does not reside in the fact that some one fibre runs through the whole length, but in the overlapping of many fibres*" (my italics).

In a little paper on "Hamlet's 'Individuality'" I argued that the supposed "individuality" of Shakespeare's character was in fact "multiplicity." One might say the same thing of the figure which emerges from autobiography:

> Hamlet seems real not because he is a coherent character or "self" or because there is some discoverable "essence" to him but because *he actively and amazingly inhabits so*

many diverse, interconnecting, potentially contradictory contexts. Implicitly promising to tell us all about the interesting "individual" Hamlet, the *play Hamlet* ends by expressing the possibility that "individuality" (a word derived from the Latin *individuus*, indivisible) *is in fact multiplicity.* It is the plenitude of contexts in which Hamlet functions— i.e., his multiplicity—that gives him density.

*

We're supposed to be these unities. *And we're not.*

Jess, in conversation

I was born.

BIBLIOGRAPHY

Poetry; books accompanied by recordings on cassette tape:

Letters/Lights—Words for Adelle, Mother's Hen Press, 1987.

Gershwin (also see below), Norton Coker, 1991.

Adrift, Pantograph Press, 1993. [Cassette tape includes "Mob Ecstasy," a radio program (KPFA, 1992) in which Foley performs with saxophonist Glenn Spearman and bassist Ben Lindgren.]

Exiles, Pantograph Press, 1996.

Prose:

Inciting Big Joy (monograph on the films of James Broughton), San Francisco Cinémathèque, 1993.

"O Her Blackness Sparkles!" The Life and Times of the Batman Art Gallery, San Francisco, 1960–65, photographs by James O. Mitchell, 3300 Press, 1995.

Editor:

Editor in chief of *Poetry USA,* the official publication of the National Poetry Association, 1990–95; contributing editor of *Poetry Flash;* guest editor of *Poetry: San Francisco,* winter 1988–89.

Radio:

Host of "Cover to Cover," a weekly series of interviews and poetry presentations, on radio station KPFA, Berkeley, California; performer, with wife, Adelle, of poetry throughout the Berkeley/Oakland/San Francisco area, as well as on local radio and television stations, 1985—; featured performer in half-hour video, *Jack and Adelle Foley: An Anthology for Television,* produced by United Cable of Alameda for the *Star Rover* program.

Radio programs and other examples of Foley's work are archived at the Bancroft Library, University of California, Berkeley.

Contributor:

Poly: New Speculative Writing (anthology), Ocean View Press, 1989.

The Love Project (anthology), anabasis, 1993.

Other:

Gershwin is available in a hypertext version designed by Servando Gonzalez, Intelibooks, 1995. Jack and Adelle Foley perform Lou Harrison's poem "Four Strict Songs" on the CD *Lou Harrison: A Birthday Celebration,* Musical Heritage Society, 1994. *Three Talkers,* a tape featuring Jack Foley, Jake Berry, and Mike Miskowski was produced by Experimental Audio Directions, 1988.

Contributor of poetry to periodicals, including *Barque, Beloit Poetry Journal, Berkeley Poetry Review, Blue Beetle Press Magazine, Café Review, The Experioddicist, Exquisite Corpse, Galley Sail Review, Inkblot, MaLLife, Malthus, Meat Epoch, New York Quarterly, NRG, Outré, Talisman, Tight, Transmog,* and *Wet Motorcycle.*

Contributor of literary criticism and reviews to *ELH, Galley Sail Review, Heaven Bone, Konch, Linden Lane Magazine, lower limit speech, MaLLife, Multicultural Review, Open Letter, Poetry Flash, Prosodia, Seattle Literary Quarterly,* and *W'ORCs;* contributor of film criticism to *Bright Lights* and *Journal of Popular Film;* contributor of art criticism to *Artweek, East Bay Express,* and *Poetry Flash.*

Reginald Gibbons

1947-

THE GOOD-ENOUGH MOTHER TONGUE

Gibbons with his parents in Houston, Texas, about 1947

Sitting in the hallway on wooden chairs or benches were perhaps a dozen other young men. All were dressed in black suits and holding Bibles, saying only a little to each other. I was twenty-two years old, waiting with them in the federal building in Houston in 1969 for a hearing before the local Selective Service commission. The summer day would have been typically scorching; the air conditioning in the federal building would have been excellent.

When my turn came, I went into a plain, very 1950s federal-building room—a very gray gray—where I found three men behind a table on which lay a few manila folders. There was an empty chair on my side of the table. They instructed me to sit down with them. They must have been suspicious, irritated, and dismayed, but I remember them behaving with that cheery false friendliness that is a mark of Texas, and southern, culture. I sat down.

It's odd that repeating the word "gray" produces almost a carnival effect instead of making gray grayer. Say "gray gray" and it's as if the language had its own desire to romp. My pleasure in writing from inside the language, where there are romps and surprises, gets in

With brother, Gary F. Gibbons (right), in Houston, about 1953

the way when I am also trying to write from memory and experience, argument and story, using language merely as an instrument. Language insists on coming between one's experience and one's understanding. One's language *is* one's understanding of what one experiences, remembers, ponders, tells. Truth and lies, both. But which side of this equation is in the way of the other? My experience and memory might be said to be in the way of the play of language; my somber mood in the way of the drive in the psyche to follow the sounds and rhythms of language instead of its meaning. The nature of writing, and the problem of writing about this moment in Houston, force me to choose, over and over again, to suppress the play and possibilities of language so I can get to what I am trying to remember. But I cannot entirely suppress them; maybe that's what writing is.

I had registered for the draft for military service, as required by law at that time, when I turned eighteen, during my senior year in high school in 1965. I had received a "defer-

ment" to enter college the following fall. Among all the reasons for going to college, this was a most serious one. The deferment signified that one's eligibility for the draft was postponed till one graduated or left school. Those with college deferments, who did not *have* to go to Vietnam immediately, could consider the war a moral problem to be pondered, rather than a test of character and of one's ability to survive the armed forces in themselves, and then the war. Because college had been designated by the State as an acceptable, even desirable, reason for postponing military service, the draft sorted young men out by class, taking those who for lack of preparation, inclination or money couldn't or wouldn't go to college. The army needed more officers and so college education was in its interest, too, since it would eventually get some of the graduates.

During the spring of my senior year in college, in a small East Coast town, I had applied for "conscientious objector status." I did not advertise to all my friends and acquaintances that I did so. The application was a series of essay questions. Along with seminar papers and a senior thesis, it was one more writing task. I had no firm hope that my application would be considered seriously. I wasn't sure that anyone's was. Consideration was given at the local level, and everything depended on the temper of one's draft board.

While I was working on the application, I visited a Quaker draft counselor in his one-room office on the main street. He was not many years older than I. The first time I ventured there, curious and wary, he offered me hot tea; I must have been very much a provincial creature of Texas, for he was the first man I met who drank tea that was not iced. He gave advice on how to think about the questions on the application form, how one's responses tended to be evaluated, what kinds of responses might actually convince someone that the applicant did not believe himself able to kill another human being under any circumstances. We talked about my life and attitudes, my formation and my beliefs. He was quiet, encouraging, considerate, reserved. He helped me work through my thoughts to find out whether I *could* object conscientiously to military service.

I could. My beliefs were only my own, not those of religious doctrine anymore, although my upbringing had been conventionally religious. I had firm convictions, at least on the point of killing. The State held that belief that would support conscientious objection had to be religious; it could not be political. This amputation of one moral realm from another might have been clearly refuted in a philosophy class, but I, like everyone else, had to work completely within the limitations the State imposed. Even within those limitations, I felt sincere and righteous at twenty-two. My whole being was in revolt against this war and those who led it, upheld it, argued for it. Like many young men, I was outraged to discover that "fate," which one discussed in a seminar on Greek tragedy, turned out to be the will of the powerful who could send you off to kill and be killed if they chose. I felt a young man's passionate disillusionment with institutions. And I was convinced that all war was corrupt and corrupting. But these attitudes had to be kept out of one's request to perform some alternative, non-violent service instead of soldiering. One couldn't just argue for life against death.

I had spent many hours in late-night discussions of moral problems (especially of the young) with the college Methodist chaplain and a few friends. In the sixties there was a lot of earnest discussion of life and death issues—impassioned or cool, at meals, in class, in dorms, in the midst of watching games; there was anger and hope, analysis and strategy, stubborn individuality and commanding solidarity. I was too earnest. The chaplain was a wonderful man, one of the best teachers I had: learned, frank, patient, energetic yet easy-going, serious yet intellectually playful. He assigned us readings in theology, as for a class, and his pleasure was evident as we talked from 10:30 P.M. on Wednesday evening until past midnight.

But talk about these issues, no matter how urgent it felt, was only talk, and I had needed a practical course of action. One late-night friend had joined Navy ROTC as a freshman, to pay for college; thus agreeing to help fill the government's need for more officers, he might manage his own conscience by choosing non-combat duty, which, as a flier, he could do. Another friend was going to move to Canada. Some would take their chances, aiming for military desk jobs. There was hope that at one's preliminary physical examination one would fail and receive the "4F" classification as opposed to the "1A" that meant an eligible young body. I hoped I would get a 4F, because my knees were indeed shot, from childhood injuries, and I was afraid boot camp would cripple me. In the meantime, the C.O. application was the only thing.

It may have been important to me, in the writing of my application, that I had had the luck already to have succeeded in writing one good poem. I had written lots of poor ones, and in just one clear case I had found myself with something to work on that required, that justified, that was worthy of, seemingly endless revision. The poem was alive enough to keep me rewriting much longer than ever before. I was driven by love and romantic ideals, and by romanticized ideas of being or becoming a poet, but I was also, for the first time, writing from within both feeling and the play of language—the sounds, the patterns of stress, the syntactic sinew and ripple—within that extraordinary fusion of discourse and discovery, story and form, in which the play and the extra-semantic effects of language are both arbitrary and full of meaning, both ornament and the core of how poems make meaning. I sensed that something more than my own feelings, my own perceptions, my own ideas, was in play. This something, far from suppressing *my* truth, could lead me to a richer telling than any available from entirely conscious deliberations, or—it was a dangerous something, often exploited for its power—it could falsify my being. I suppose I am imputing to my earlier self far more knowledge than I then had. But I'm sure that I wrote the C.O. application in the context of a widening sense of what writing was.

The Quaker was in business for every kind of draft counseling, and he was savvy about the Selective Service bureaucracy, about the Surgeon General (to whom you could appeal your pre-induction physical exam if you had a documented medical problem that had been overlooked or, more likely, willfully ignored by the bored physicians who examined you on behalf of the army), and about other offices of State. He spoke deliberately, carefully. I certainly don't remember that we talked about my poem, or about any poetry at all. Perhaps he wasn't a reader, in that sense.

Draft boards typically saw it as their duty to deny requests for C.O. status. Where the applicant felt conscience, boards saw deceit or deficiency of character. They denied both those who were intentionally fraudulent and those who were dupes of their own mistaken ideas.

In my application I had written that I was unwilling to serve in the military because I believed it was morally wrong to do so. My draft board was likely to suspect—this was their job—that my judgment was political rather than religious. Such dissonance was axiomatic in those years of the bitter heartache and bitter righteousness, the jeering protest and staunch dutifulness, in those who opposed each other over the war. The draft board was likely to figure that I just didn't want to go: I was a coward, a shirker, unpatriotic.

Perhaps I did not understand then, as I do now, that I could have been conditioned to hate, and then if I held a gun in my hands and if I had been shot at by those I hated, I would shoot back. Did I sense in myself that I could not kill for excitement, or out of boredom, with a sense of sport, and had I divined—with a fright—that this might be exactly what one had to do or ended up doing? I believed that killing was something one should never do. I was perhaps deceiving myself that my principles were stronger than my fear, but I'm not sure I should so readily accuse my earlier self of bad faith. I needed to believe I couldn't kill.

Or perhaps then, twenty-five years ago, I was afraid that I could indeed shoot at someone else and even take satisfaction in it, and I didn't want to believe that I could do it. To acknowledge this would have been to disillusion myself, to shatter my self-regard. Having always felt by temperament an outsider, always needing to prove I deserved my place, could I survive without that self-respect I had worked hard to build up? And some years earlier, when shooting small game, what I had felt was disgust with myself. Ducks veered away, just overhead, wings beating so beautifully hard, escaping. I had never graduated to deer. My father hunted; I did not hate him for it in the least; in fact I was glad he could do it, and take himself away from his working life. But I couldn't do it.

I remember that in my application, revised again and again, I explained that my conviction was not so much based on my present religious beliefs. I said that my beliefs had evolved beyond Methodism; the truth was that once I was away from church and Methodist Youth Fellowship and the wheedling or flattering or threatening adults in the Sanctuary or Fellowship Hall, once I was in my own life, my religious beliefs had worn thin and fallen into rags. I took the precept of non-violence from Chris-

"A true Texan," 1959

Giving a piano recital, about 1961

tianity (observed, yes, more often in the breach; the daily news and the white hatred of black in Christian Texas had taught me that) but I left behind the belief in a supernatural God. If God was anything, I was on my way to thinking, it was a name for some aspect of human consciousness, or for that which human consciousness is an aspect of. God was our own subjectivity, too strange and overpowering to be fully understood, much less trusted, so we took one aspect of mind, namely our sense that the phenomenal world cannot account for some experiences, which we call spiritual; and we called that aspect God or Buddha-nature or satori. My conviction at twenty-two was a personal moral code developed, evolved, unfolded, in me, out of every moral and spiritual glimmer I'd caught in every text I'd read, spiritual and literary. The Methodist Church, in which I had been more than dutiful even if not especially devout, and very active even if not fervent, was only a part of it.

But I knew there were philosophical arguments against a "personal moral code." I had

been confronted by powerful arguments from religious believers, who saw me as a fallen sinner, from the junior philosophers of the college, who thought it was shameful and needless to shore up a rational philosophical position with bankrupt religion, from militants and activists, even religious activists, who wanted to call political opposition by its proper name, and from rebels who thought it cowardice to cloak political opposition to this war in moral beliefs, which were suspect no matter who held them. Christers and SDS and aesthetes made, in my head, a deafening chorus. If I opposed the war I should say so and do something to *stop* it—demonstrate, go underground, evade the draft, or be drafted and fight against the war by sabotage, or refuse induction and go to prison.

It was 1969. A year after the assassinations of Martin Luther King and Robert Kennedy, righteous opposition or radicalism or cynicism were all heady drinks, and drinking them was exciting. I had a little red lapel pin that said simply, in lower case letters, "resist"—an almost jocular insistence on a kind of modest nihilism. I could relish the Neanderthal suspicion of others that I was a communist, an atheist, or, in the minds of my former co-religionaries, an agent of Satan. (How impressive, how appealing, were the annotations *in Greek* in the margin of the copy of the Greek Gospels that belonged to the predatory white-haired minister of the campus fundamentalists! I had been pressed to the wall by his exhortations to repent and be born again.) Resistance was not an unworthy goal in life. And to some degree I did resist and I did relish it. But I did not feel heroic. Self-sacrifice was not so powerful a drive in my psyche. I wanted someone—everyone—to acknowledge that what I as an individual believed and felt was reason enough for my choice not to kill. I wanted a pure freedom. At that age I was new enough to the world to feel that I and everyone deserved it.

There were two other things. A part of me was scared. The roots of my fear lay in childhood and had nothing to do with the war. But now I was scared of boot camp, scared of being shipped out, scared of pain and injury and dying, scared of other young men who relished shooting and power, scared of losing face with people back home if I didn't go to war. School days had been a sufficient initiation into the spectacle and the fear of bullying and being bullied, of hatred and cold cruelty. I was also scared of leaving the familiar world shaped by my interests and my needs. I didn't realize at that age that with luck one's courage is sufficient unto the day, as is the evil it should oppose, and that the things that would require courage at one point in life would be replaced by others later.

I was angry, too. Unacknowledged anger, building up since childhood, was part of who I was. Now I was angry at the president and his advisors for waging a war so many people opposed, angry at the waste and death it caused, angry at its compliant political supporters, at the cynical arms suppliers, at the mostly fawning media for so failing to question how public figures equated the war with patriotism, angry at soldiers, furious at Death himself, as he stood grinning over it all.

I don't remember that I knew a single other person, either away at college or still in Texas, who was applying for C.O. status. My chances were nil. I think now that even if I wasn't sure my own conviction was rock-solid, my need to feel conviction, and perhaps my sheer stubborn self-fortification, which I knew well—I'll do this, goddamn it, whether anybody wants me to or not—must have given me the energy I needed to work out, alone, my position against killing. I was satisfying my need for moral purpose, even though I was now a post-Protestant, post-Christian; I was indeed satisfying indirectly my desire to oppose the war, as I sought my application answers.

Language, although I could not have fully understood this then, became for me the weapon of resistance. Language itself—which was to prove my abiding obsession—was at the center of the decisive moment. And I have a feeling now, as I write, like the impatience and frustration of that moment when the one word you need, a word from everyday life, just won't come to mind—"the . . . can-opener," "her . . . embarrassment": until the word shows up, the thing or idea doesn't quite show up either. But in this case it's not a word but a moment of being.

I can't recollect the three men of the draft board very clearly any more, and so to write of them, and of myself at that moment, is an exercise in imagining. At moments, as I am writing this, the appeal of a phrase to my ear overwhelms that faint mental trace of my past. The words push aside the as-yet unworded visual image or feeling, in memory. Even my

application is lost, so I cannot read now what I worked so hard to formulate then.

Of course all three men where white. Each man told something of himself. I think it was to demonstrate that he worked and owned and was thus a patriot. I think one was a pharmacist and another owned a car dealership. I've forgotten what the third man said. All seemed to feel they had to announce their identities before they tried to figure out mine. This figuring out seemed to proceed by instinct, not by any process related to the sounding of belief. Men taking the measure of a boy, they must have felt. And they knew I had no moves in this game: I had just graduated from a distant elite university, as yet I had no job, I owned nothing, unless my father had given it to me (and in my case, there was very little to be given). I remember them as stout men, in both senses of the word. In their eyes, I was skinny both bodily and humanly. I felt I was their victim. Now I wouldn't claim any sympathy on account of that. There is fat arrogance and skinny arrogance, isn't there?

I expected such men to scheme righteously for a buck, routinely to praise God and attend Men's Prayer Breakfasts on Sundays before church, to enjoy aggressiveness by the proxy of young men at war; to be racist, unreflective, and fanatical about football (although the latter in itself was evidence of no failing—it was simply part of the mix). I could not guess whether each was privately scatological in speech or clean-mouthed, but I could guess their attitudes toward the war. They were suspicious and xenophobic; my having left Texas to go away to school was itself a kind of defection, to them. I had exiled myself from what was known and good, namely (white) Texas. What sort of judgment did I have?

Manila folders lay on the table. The word strikes me as strange, as soon as I write it now, and I look it up in a dictionary. "Manila" means a strong, coarse paper originally produced in the Philippines. I imagine that such paper must have come into American use through the trade opened up by military conquest in the nineteenth century. Thus can the language sometimes preserve traces of what we have done, after the deeds are no longer commonly remembered. And my having to use that word, "manila," in the midst of trying to describe the moment in my own life when I had to confront whether I myself would go to war, seems like an effect of language itself contradicting *my* motives with *its* ironies. No matter what one writes about, one is also writing about the language one is writing with.

Among these particular manila folders must have been mine. One of the men told me to present my arguments. I was astonished, frightened. The very little control I had of this situation—my so carefully written statement—was now irrelevant.

I said that I had presented them already in my application. I was asked again to give them now, to *say* them.

I said that I couldn't possibly give a speech off the cuff that would be half as clear as the answers I had spent months working out and writing down—my careful, pondered arguments. But—they insisted—"Tell us in your *own* words." That phrase remains unforgettable to me.

I think I must have felt betrayed by the naiveté of my assumption that simply because I had worked so hard to write something, those who read it would want to get my meaning out of it. But I think that it was *because* my statement was written that the draft board didn't trust it. Perhaps it was very different from most of the other written statements they read.

I tried again to resist. I can't feel now whether I got stronger or feebler in this, but I know they insisted, "Tell us in your *own* words."

I did not convince them that the written words on the application form in my folder, which lay unopened on the table, *were* mine, had indeed been written by me and not by someone else.

Their refusal to deal with the written word implied that for them words written down did not belong to the person who had written them in the way that speech did. You could be held to what people heard you say. Whereas I, who had read thousands of pages in my studies, had been taught to think that modern statements of belief were complicated and long, and were not authoritative till they had been worked out on paper, published and read by others (whether they agreed or not didn't affect assumptions about this process), my interlocutors were men who said they believed each time they repeated the Nicene Creed aloud on Sunday mornings in church, and who must have thought that I should be able to recite chapter and verse in support of my conscience.

To write something up is to draft, to speculate, to test, to essay. To write something down is to scribe the paper (inscribe, transcribe), to annotate, record, establish, conclude. I wonder what it meant to me, then, to want to write. Now, I think that "being" a writer means writing things up and down and every which way, both exploring and establishing, both ex-

With Gary F. Gibbons (left) and W. R. Gibbons, Sr., about 1964

The author (right) in a creative writing class with novelist Edmund Keeley, Princeton University, about 1967

perimenting and finishing, for the sake of a sort of knowledge, a self-defining expressivity, the pleasure of making, and something else that I could describe as being in the language the way a swimmer, as opposed to a log, is in the water.

Some literary theorists have argued that all words are mere counters inside the system of language, and have no innate, inherent, given relationship to anything outside language (which is why there are not only different languages but also different words in the same language for similar things and why the meanings of words change over time). Therefore, language is unable by definition ever to contain or convey a genuinely transcendental something that lies outside language, like "God" or "truth" or "non-violence." Or rather, in this view there are no such transcendent somethings. Words mean what they mean by not meaning something else. "Oak" means, partly, "not pine." "Judaism" means, among other things, "not Christianity." If I write "Judaism commands 'Thou shalt not kill,' and Christianity instructs we must love one another," I cannot prove any authority in these statements beyond the views of Jews and Christians, because I cannot define, outside the language and social constructs of Judaism and Christianity, what God or love are. "Oak" is not very specific, admittedly; *quercus*

virginiana, which in English we call the live oak, is a particular kind, but what connects this particular term to that particular species of oak is that the term is different from, say, *quercus alba*, the white oak. Every word only points to another word somewhere else. However, despite the argument that there is no first point from which any belief derives, and that all beliefs are constructed out of impulses and reactions, advantage and disadvantage, pleasure and pain, and only excused or falsely bolstered with generalized ideals, it does not follow that all belief, as an aspect of our experience, is therefore bankrupt. In some parts of the world, in some times, an oak has been worshipped and not without convincing reasons. There are still events, experiences, emotions, needs, which, even if they can be represented and for that matter experienced only from within language, show up in all languages. Like the psychoanalyst D. W. Winnicott, who urged trust in the "good-enough mother" who does not need to be perfect in order to give her child both love and courage for life, I feel trust in the good-enough mother tongue. Language is just as self-referential as the theorists say it is; and we are just as caught inside it as they say; it is perfectly imperfect and inadequate in just this way, and from this imperfection and inadequacy many ills and illusions spring. And yet like a good-enough mother, language still suffices perfectly for our development as human beings, and moderately well for communication among us; it provide us with the tools for coming *near* some things, if we have the will to try coming near them, even if we don't get to touch them. Certainly we deceive ourselves, both linguistically and psychologically, but not everything we say and write is deceptive. Within the mother tongue's imprecision and lapses, concealments and redundancies, its evocative powers, hortatory effects, regulations, permissions and prayers, there is something going on that reaches far beyond the power it has simply to point to things and thus represent (and even misrepresent) our world. There is, above all, a meaning-making not limited to the dictionary definitions of individual words but bound up in the movement of language as we use it.

It seems that the good-enough mother tongue raises up some of us who, out of error or pleasure or anxiety or sorrow, get caught up in the odd angles of meaning-making. In serious play, we make obsessive, earnest attempts to shape language against its power to shape us. This is a process of pushing and pulling against an uncanny resistance, and often ending up in a place we're not likely to have foreseen. And far from being always disappointing, these un-

foreseen outcomes can be discoveries—not even so much discoveries of the world as of the shape of our responsiveness to the world.

Now, my sense of who I was at twenty-two was already a little tangled in this experience of writing and in ambitions to write. I had begun what would become, by ten years later, the obsessive habits of mind that make me the opposite of my friend who says that she likes to be out in nature because she forgets language; wherever I am, the wilder the wilderness the better (and the more crowded the city street the better), words come into my head and I like it that they do. I like sorting them out, I like thinking that some of them are more my own than others, "my own" in the sense of tuned to my own rhythm of thinking and feeling, even of walking.

But at that moment in the Houston federal building, the question was not language itself as a realm of possibility and impossibility, but rather who owns, or thinks he owns, it—those who have spoken their piece or those who have written it. I was right to tell the draft board that some moral questions, at least, took thinking through and weren't to be judged hastily and extemporaneously. But although undoubtedly in a thousand other sorts of moments they were wrong in their undoubting willingness to believe anything written, even what was false by design—in government press releases, in newspapers—were they also right to feel that in matters of life and death one ought to be able to *say* what one believes? In that gray gray room I was traumatized by their stark response, which in all my mental rehearsals I had never anticipated. I had thought of answering this argument with that, this example with that. I had studied for this ultimate exam. I had not thought of being asked to start all over again and, deliberately avoiding the language I had struggled with, to find new words—simpler, more spontaneous, spoken—for the same sense. In the space of a few minutes.

Their proof was in my inability. Had I not even mastered my own arguments? My fledgling practice as a writer had already alienated me from the use of language they were insisting on. For me, language had become, in some moments, at least, a medium; and I think that as users of language they had not brought to consciousness the problems of saying. This did not mean one of them might not have been a remarkable storyteller.

Gibbons and college roommate James Hulbert (left) at Princeton, probably 1967

With former wife Virginia M. Harris, 1975

I wish my ability to work out ideas and the articulation of my own convictions had been less difficult. I wish I could have stood before them and given them my word.

Their motives might have been mixed. They might truly have been unable to understand me. And they might have been cynically holding me to whatever cowed stammering phrases I could offer in those intimidating few moments, when my fortune, not theirs, lay in their balance pan. Then they could have denied my request on the basis of what I said that day instead of what I had written beforehand. It was a "hearing," after all, not a "reading." The ancient history of law, which must have begun in oral dispute and not in written documents, was bearing down on that room, and its inertia was on their side, not mine.

The supplicant was not permitted to argue against any particular war (certainly not against this particular war); their policy, even if it did not represent a consensus of the people, required that you had to make the case for never ever being able or willing to kill another person at any time, in any war or other circumstance. You had to believe that always and anywhere it was wrong to kill another person. I did so believe. They endeavored to help me along by interviewing me, since I was not making my case very well by myself. To this day I remember very clearly the questions.

"Wouldn't you kill someone who was trying to rape your sister?" one of the men asked me. It's a measure of my panicked self-involvement, my sense of a grand conflict between me and them, between what I thought I stood for and what I believed they stood for, that I'm sure I did not think of my flesh-and-blood sisters. What *would* I have done? But it was of course a trick question they had used many times before—a fake moral dilemma, a debating tactic. They didn't say "murder your sister"; they said rape. They implied the white man's favorite fantasy of outrage, because "someone" could be code for "a black man." Vietnam wasn't white. But Vietnam was not raping, literally or figuratively, anyone's American sister. If they had waited twenty years and said not only sister but also wife and child, I could not have held my ground. But then, if the waging of war depended on men over the age of forty to do all the soldiering, there would be few wars or none.

"If you're attacked wouldn't you defend yourself? Wouldn't you defend your own country?"

"Wouldn't you have fought against *Hitler*?"

"You know, don't you," one said, "that if you get conscientious objector status, we going to ship you off to the furthest county in Texas and you'll be emptying bedpans of niggers for two years, *mighty* far away from your family."

They were fools. Anxious and angry, I felt petty superiority to their dialect pronunciation—"conshenshus," "fambly." I remember thinking bitterly, "Threatening me with distance from my family is only giving me what I want, anyway." For I wanted to stay out in the world, not return home after college. Yet when I spoke to them, I'm sure I spoke with nearly that same accent they had—it was the sound of the region, the style of my own origins, which I had mostly lost, the intonation of their sway—the thicker your accent, the more you belonged. The sound of these words was not my way of being, any longer, but language student that I was, I probably mimicked it at least somewhat, as I often did, without thinking about it and almost without noticing it, when I was in Houston. So as to be literally understood. Accepted again for the moment, if only superficially.

My draft board seemed to run out of questions; they gave up on me. I was dismissed from the room and I went back down the hallway filled with the other young men waiting their turn—most of them, the ones with

Bibles, headed for jail, headed impenitently for the federal prison. The Quaker had told me that usually such cases were open and shut. Their applications for C.O. would be denied. They would then refuse induction. They were Jehovah's Witnesses. All their applications may have been worded in exactly the same way, and for each of them the imperative, "Tell us in your own words," would have rung differently than it had for me. I went out to my car in the parking lot—the stifling heat of the interior must have poured out when I opened the door. I drove out of downtown Houston to my parents' house, where I had grown up— at that time still beyond the expanding city limits, at the very end of a row of houses on big lots.

The Quaker counselor had warned me that it was now much harder to be recognized as a conscientious objector than it had been, that the Selective Service was approving only a tiny number of applications, and I ought to consider Canada. The Methodist chaplain at college had helped me work through my beliefs, but I don't think he advocated I go one way or the other. My father and mother had mostly stood to one side and watched me—I knew

they didn't want me to go to a war. My father had no illusions about the service; he had hated his Army years before and during World War II. When I got back to my parents' house I told them and my young wife about the hearing. No one had expected otherwise. I don't think we talked about it much. The subject was too gloomy. Only three or four days later my draft card came in the mail, the blanks typed in, on an old irregular machine, with my name and those extraordinary two letters "C.O." By this fiat I was free to go to California, where I had been accepted into graduate school. I could get my draft physical there and see what the alternative service turned out to be. But I would not have to confront another stage, with higher stakes, of conviction.

Why did the draft board give me what I wanted? Maybe they didn't believe me, but didn't want me in the army. Perhaps there was some cross-checking and they had been apprised of my angry speech in a Houston city council meeting two years earlier in the summer of 1967, and I looked like a slight security risk. On the other hand, draft boards were known to send such young men to war to teach them a lesson about patriotism.

The author with Spanish poet Jorge Guillén, Cambridge, Massachusetts, probably 1977

That summer of 1967, off-duty servicemen had been given leave from nearby bases to help fill the ranks of a march in support of the war. They had fallen upon an anti-war group which, among the war boosters, was marching with its own protesting placards. The fight was appalling; the peace marchers, women among them, were completely at the mercy of the attacking men. Police had stood to one side and watched. This was nothing new in the nation, but it stirred feelings in Houston, both against and for the soldiers. Some citizens let it be known that they would attend the next city council meeting to express their rage. Others would attend to commend the attack. One of the councilmen, a middle-aged man with a military haircut, had already stated publicly that he was glad the demonstrators had been beaten. He had slung the usual defamations—"outside agitators," "communists"—that so many men like him had been practicing on civil rights demonstrators. (The great march on the Pentagon would come in October; but King and Robert Kennedy would then be murdered months after that—these events, like statement and reply, showed that a supremely powerful element in our national life, in our heterodox cultural psyche, whether it acted impulsively or after conspiring, could not tolerate such challenges as the civil rights protests or those against the war.) At the public city council meeting, I rose in my turn and, shaking as I read the text over which I had labored, I delivered my best phrases of condescending fury at the imbecile councilman, and I was pleased that he sputtered in reply. I had succeeded in ambushing him. But he would remain, and I would leave. A few weeks later, a law student I knew at a legal aid service—part of Lyndon Johnson's other war, the "war on poverty"—told me he had learned that the Texas Rangers (who functioned as a kind of state-level FBI) had opened a surveillance file on me. I couldn't tell if he was joking. It worried me some, although I sort of hoped it was true, if it meant my speech had genuinely upset someone.

Maybe the draft board's distaste at the thought of my serving in the army was enough to keep me out. Or maybe they believed me and honored my beliefs.

A few months later Nixon ordered U.S. forces into Cambodia. Over my new campus a wave of demonstrations washed, leaving behind debris both inanimate and human. Those of us who opposed the war felt an apprehensive but ultimately satisfying conviction that we were in the middle of history, still. Sometimes I was among the demonstrators; often I was near them. It was a tremendously disturbing time—everyone was kept roiled, like muddy water, with no moment of stillness in which the water could settle and clear. There were left-fringe political groups who were armed, and who thus discredited those who were not (which was in part what they wanted to do). At the student center there were a few shocking fist fights at noon on the outdoor terrace, among the tables where people were eating lunch—rival political organizers competing to enlist students. One day I overheard one of my fellow graduate students, an eastern, urban young man, a complainer whose stooped shoulders seemed to convey disappointment in those of us who were not sufficiently radical. He was moping in the English department and told the secretary—she was like a friendly aunt to all of us, no matter our attitudes and beliefs—that his apartment had been robbed for the third time. This was only to be expected, since as an act of political solidarity he lived in the poorest and most violent section of the otherwise affluent town. He was upset, though; he said they had taken his guns.

I received notice from the State to report for my pre-induction physical exam. With a few fellow graduate students, similarly instructed, I drove south to San Jose, then with other boys and young men we were all bussed north together, past where we had started, to Oakland. This orderly irrationality seemed to us all army. The physical was one of the common rites of my generation of young men. The experience must have been the same everywhere: barefoot, wearing undershorts, we stood in line for hours for tests of hearing and eyesight, we bent over for the physician who did not bother to change his surgical glove as he went down rows of us, sticking his finger up our asses. And even in a time when lots of young men presented bizarre reasons and strategies for getting judged unfit, there were surprising oddballs. I remember an emaciated boy in red briefs, in whom the medical orderlies could find no blood pressure at all. A fat boy with only a whisper of a voice and a heavy scar in the flesh of his neck explained to me, smiling, "My brother cut my throat." There were performed intimations of homosexuality by heterosexuals, rehearsed displays of presumably insane behavior by those who were sane (amidst the all too evident insanity of the military state and some of its personnel), and peculiar bodily results of prior ingestions calculated to derange the human system. There was even a written exam—a lieutenant explained that if we failed it, we would stay overnight to take it again the next morning, and stay every night until we passed. Tired doctors in small cubicles glanced at the results of our tests and then with a rubber stamp approved or exempted. I had a fat packet of photocopies of medical documents and a letter to the army from the orthopedist who had treated me for years since I'd torn up both knees at the age of thirteen. The army doctor ruled me fit. When I asked why, he pointed out that none of my documents was dated within the last six months, as army regulations required. How, in all my meetings with the Quaker, with whom I had also discussed a possible medical exemption, had I missed this regulation?

Then I got a call from my high school soul mate, L, whom I hadn't seen in several years. He was at the Oakland army base, he was leaving for Vietnam the next morning, would I come see him. My wife and I drove to Oakland to see him.

We had written poems and songs together; we had been taken under the wing of the English teacher, we two, the future writers. He told me he had sold his violin, had dropped out of college to be drafted; he believed this was his karma. Hadn't I read the book on Vedanta that he had given me in high school? Vedanta was his religion.

I said to him something like, "What will you do if you have to shoot someone? How will you do it? This is crazy." He should have been a C.O. before I was. I was trying to draw out of him the allegiance to non-violence, the belief in life, that in him had long been sincere and unforced and well-formed. But he would not admit or affirm it. I see now that he did not believe in life; youthfully, he believed in the meaninglessness of death.

I felt I would have been far more able to violate my own principles in order to survive the war than L would be. He was dreamy, vague; he had never even tried to be the competent male his father was in the male working world of sales, clubs, machines, much less guns. But evidently L had learned competence in basic

training. He was not a conscientious objector because he was trying to be removed from what happened to him; he was trying to be apart from his own being. That was in the nature of his belief. Was it beatifically or insanely or just foolishly, I wondered, that he smiled at us? It did not seem heroic.

He reassured us: things would work out. Don't worry. I looked around the linoleum-floored room like a gigantic church hall hung with crêpe paper, as for a party at which there would be a potluck fellowship supper with fruit punch and a lovely young woman with a guitar who would lead the singing of "Michael Row the Boat Ashore." Here and there, in plastic chairs, soldiers were talking to mothers and girlfriends. L and I said good-bye.

Came the great Lottery. Not for good fortune but for bad. Quite logically, at a lottery for bad fortune you did not choose to buy a ticket: the ticket was forced on you. The State dumped the year's three hundred and sixty-five birthdays into a figurative hat and then drew them out one by one, and took for its warring purposes those boys it needed. Numbers above two hundred were said to be absolute guarantees of safety. My birthday was the three-hundred-and-sixth to be pulled out of the State's hat. I was not even going to be called to empty those bedpans that my draft board had imagined were so horrific because the shit in them hadn't come out of a light-skinned body.

There was nothing fair about it: Dan Quayle and Reg Gibbons and many thousands in between got out from under the risk one way or another; many others did not—not rich or connected, not so patriotic (isn't fatherland often opposed to mother tongue?), like Quayle, that they could be exempted, or not articulate enough or educated enough, or not able to think of anything else to do, or not given any other choices by life. I was a successful supplicant; my petition had been granted—all I had done was to write down, and then fail to say, what I believed and wanted, which was not to be made to kill or be killed, because I abhorred killing. And then I was let off my alternative service.

I try to imagine myself then. I say—but I can't be sure I had thought this out then, as I have done now—that in my poems and stories, I wanted to write in such a way that the effect on some reader, somewhere, was good,

With Cornelia M. Spelman, prior to their marriage, in Norwich, Vermont, 1982

not bad; interesting, not boring; deep, not shallow; meaningful, not pointless; for good, not for evil; and for life, not death. But these are insipid pieties. Whatever came of my writing, I wanted to write with language that represented truthfully, accurately, meaningfully (values I cannot quickly define, as the words slip out of my hands) both my own sense of things—me—and what I understood the world to be. But to what higher standard than my own happenstance being would this writing be held? If I wanted to write in such a way that how I presented myself and the world, to myself and to a reader, would be an admitted distortion of good and honest intent rather than bad and dishonest, then how would I define "good and honest," exactly? Exactitude is finally impossible; exactitude is finally not necessary. I think that at twenty-two I already understood the further paradox that language, while it belongs to no one in particular, is not therefore neutral or innocent in itself. I wanted to write *for* something, but also *against* that kind of language

that gets into our heads only to make us vulnerable to deception and manipulation, to accustom us to falsifying our own feelings, to ingrain us with attitudes that serve the power of someone or something else, not us, to harden us to other souls in misery or sorrow, and inure us to the evils of states and demagogues and to the pain of other people's lives and deaths at the hands of those states and demagogues.

Ho Chi Minh was not Hitler. The U.S. Armed Forces were commanded to fight not in order to save a way of life but rather to control political influence. Murder was wrong, the war was wrong; and I had worked my way up and down the paths of Protestant, Catholic, Jewish, existentialist, and even Vedantic theology, and thought to arrive at a belief that all war was wrong. It was wrong to me and to some minority of opinion whose truth-standards and axioms of belief I found more convincing than those of the men in charge, and the men and women who agreed with them. Back in that gray gray room with the three denizens of the Selective Service my problem was twofold: I had only a careful and perhaps precarious argument against killing, and I didn't know how to get my argument onto the ground of what they considered right language, much less how to win the argument once it was there. Anyway, I believe these men wanted to discuss not impersonal principles and positions, but rather my attitudes and opinions (which they knew they did not and could not share), because they did not really believe that any person of worth could *say out loud in the presence of others* that he would not shoot to kill if his country or his sister asked him to. What they were hearing, if not reading, from me and others, was unthinkable to them, and beyond that, was in their view criminal.

Remembering that moment of writing, I write up these memories, balancing myself between me as I think I remember I was and me as I think I know myself now, or anyway as I describe myself, or describe my thinking about myself. What connects these two individuals is a residue of similar conviction and the persistence of the habit of trying to think on paper. I'm sure there are contradictions in what I am writing down, false notes. Our time has taught me there's no escape from these problems, especially if you are trying to escape them. The language itself moves under your feet, full of faults. To speak or write earnestly is to invite dissonance, if not in substance then in style. I am not a writer until I have accepted the impossibility of writing some kinds of truth, and the utter necessity of trying to write others. Socrates' insisting on clear definition of terms is salutary, but mistaken, I understand. I understand that I cannot understand as I want to; I believe something, as I know I have no reason to believe.

It's the same play of contrasts that lets me see that I became a Texan only when I left Texas. Then I understood myself in terms of my cultural differences from others I met, like the east-coast Quaker. I became a C.O. when I moved away from the conventional attitudes and language of my experience. I was a word spoken by my culture in a new context, and so I came to stand for a difference from what I had been, and from what I was expected to be. I might have been more of a conscientious objector if I had been denied my petition. Maybe I would have even given up my hopes of writing, and I would never have come to this later moment when, in the light of having written many things over many years (although I always still feel like a beginner), I look back to that early moment of writing, and I write of it.

Do I understand those times well, or these? Everywhere individual men, as individual murderers and as agents of institutions and governments, kill people. But during the time I am remembering, the government of this country was eating its young men when it seemed to have no need to do so. No language, no explanation I ever heard, political or psychological, from pacifists, Marxists, or cynics, or from patriots, liberals, or fools, from the blasé or the stout-hearted, ever explained this hunger fully to me. Those soldiers whom our government didn't consume, whom it spat back out injured and distressed, it then mostly abandoned. As a psychological collectivity, the nation was sick, despite few persons admitting to any personal symptoms. Perhaps all nations are mostly sick, even if in some ways they are well. This nation, where entertainment feasts on images of murder and where boys collect arms and shoot for the thrill of damage and power, seems sicker now, as if those murders so far away and long ago let loose some of these later ones at home. The pacifist Quaker, a few years after he had helped me and encouraged me

to see the thing through, for the sake of not killing, stole his father-in-law's expensive shotgun and with it he murdered his own wife. I am looking for the language that could tell, or represent, or make use of, such a story without settling for the story itself; I want to be able to tell of what happened, but I want more than that to live in the language of the telling, with its flashes of both the written and spoken, argument and interrogation, the right and the false, the true and the wrong.

BIBLIOGRAPHY

Poetry:

Roofs Voices Roads, Quarterly Review of Literature, 1979.

The Ruined Motel, Houghton Mifflin, 1981.

Saints, Persea Books, 1986.

Maybe It Was So, University of Chicago Press, 1991.

Fiction:

Five Pears or Peaches, Broken Moon Press, 1991.

Sweetbitter, Broken Moon Press, 1994, Penguin, 1996.

Translator:

Selected Poems of Luis Cernuda, University of California Press, 1977.

(With Anthony L. Geist) *Guillén on Guillén: The Poetry and the Poet,* Princeton University Press, 1979, published in Spain as *Jorge Guillén: El poeta ante su obra,* Ediciones Peralta, 1980.

Editor:

The Poet's Work: 29 Masters of Modern Poetry on the Origins and Practice of Their Art, Houghton Mifflin, 1979, University of Chicago Press, 1990.

(With Gerald Graff) *Criticism in the University,* Northwestern University Press, 1985.

(Editor of posthumous edition) William Goyen, *Had I a Hundred Mouths: New and Selected Stories,* Clarkson N. Potter, 1985.

(With Susan Hahn) *TQ 20: Twenty Years of the Best Contemporary Writing and Art from "TriQuarterly" Magazine,* Pushcart Press, 1985.

The Writer in Our World, Atlantic Monthly Press, 1986.

Writers from South Africa, TriQuarterly Books, 1988.

(With Susan Hahn) *Fiction of the Eighties: A Decade of Stories from TriQuarterly,* TriQuarterly Books, 1990.

(And principal translator) *New Writing from Mexico,* TriQuarterly Books, 1990.

William Goyen: A Study of the Short Fiction, Twayne, 1991.

(With Terrence Des Pres) *Thomas McGrath: Life and the Poem,* University of Illinois Press, 1991.

(Edition editor and author of afterword) William Goyen, *Half a Look of Cain,* Northwestern University Press, 1994.

Contributor to periodicals, including *New York Times Book Review, Paris Review,* and *American Poetry Review.* Editor of *TriQuarterly* magazine, 1981—; codirector of TriQuarterly Books, 1989—; member of advisory board, Illinois Press American Poetry Recovery Series.

Diane Glancy

1941-

THE COLD-AND-HUNGER DANCE

. . . therefore I set my face like a flint
(Isaiah 50:7)

I had a hunger for words. The house I lived in as a child was quiet. I was quiet. I was three before I had a sibling. My mother handled the words. I wanted someone to listen. I wanted someone to talk to.

I wanted my own voice forming my will.

I wanted books. The fortified cities of them. I wanted to be a maker of those fortifications. A fortifier. Because my parents are gone and they were once young and sturdy. Though they also tore down. And were torn down.

I was born between two cultures. My father was Cherokee. My mother, English and German. But we weren't enough Cherokee to be accepted as Indian, nor was I white enough to be accepted as white. I could walk in both worlds. I could walk in neither. I lived in a no-man's-land. A no-man's-land that moved.

In a poem called, "Oklahoma Land Run," in *The Relief of America*, I have a line, "jiggling like a pea in a Prince Albert tobacco tin." I always have felt I rolled around.

My father worked for the stockyards in Kansas City. He was transferred several times. I went to several schools in the midwest. Francis Willard in Kansas City. Flackville in Indianapolis. Normandy in St. Louis. I graduated from the University of Missouri in 1964, from the University of Central Oklahoma in 1983, and from the University of Iowa Writer's Workshop in 1988. I have been at Macalester College in St. Paul, Minnesota, since then. I write and teach Native American literature and creative writing in its many forms—poetry, fiction, creative nonfiction, scriptwriting.

I've always wanted to tell stories. To tell them in my own way. According to oral tradition, I could speak with the trail of voices. I could talk with my own voice, and the process of my words could change the structure of the

Diane Hall with her father—"Sitting on the fortified wall; 'my rock and fortress' (Psalms 31:3)," 1941

story. I could speak indirectly if I wanted. Talking about one thing while meaning another.

The Judeo-Christian heritage, which is full of stories of expanding boundaries, and church, where I heard those stories, have been a part of my middle-class life also.

I think I am a Christian because of the words in the Bible. The sturdiness of them. The oratures of them.

He stretcheth out the north over the empty place, and hangeth the earth upon nothing.

(Job 26:7)

199

He bindeth up the waters in his thick clouds;
and the cloud is not torn under them.

                                       (Job 26:8)

He hast set a bound that the waves may not
pass over, that they turn not again to cover the
earth.

                                  (Psalms 104:9)

Will ye not tremble at my presence, who have
placed the sand for the bound of the sea; and
though its waves toss themselves, yet can they
not prevail; though they roar, they cannot pass
over.

                                (Jeremiah 5:22)

I felt an *unformedness* I wanted form for. Or maybe I wanted boundaries for. It was through words. The stories of them. Their *storyness.* It was the Word God held out as a pole for me to take ahold of.

There is something in the Bible. A relativity of *changeableness,* yet an absolute dry-ground in the flood. The waves could come so far, but no farther. Jesus was a construct of voice and a centering in the turmoil I felt.

Sometimes, even in the Native American experience, I hear about Jesus.

In the Newberry Library, during a research fellowship, I found a story.

Now here is a Ute Sundance story told by Mollie Cloud.

this is about the Sundance, it was long time ago;
there were two of them, an old man and an old woman,
she was his mother, the one who acted as his mother;
and he was lonely, the (young) man was,
without relatives, they had all perished (in an
epidemic); so he would just hunt around,
he went hunting, wandering around,
through the cedar-grown country, it was around
Mancos Creek long time ago;

so as he hunted around, he didn't kill (anything),
he didn't kill any deer; so the next day
he went out again, having killed no deer (the day
before), he again went hunting; and once again
he returned (empty-handed);

so then . . . he became very lonely; he . . .
having no relatives; so then later on
he brooded, and he became lonely; so he decided
to kill himself, to shoot himself
in the head, right there on the rocky slope;
he was sitting on a rocky hillside, he was going
to kill himself;

so then, having not yet loaded his gun,
all of a sudden an owl hooted right
behind him; he had hobbled his horse . . .
where he had hobbled it . . . right behind it there
(the owl) cried;

so he quit trying to kill himself,
sitting there on the slope, sitting on the rocky
hillside; then all of a sudden, for whatever reason,
he got angry; "Why is it" he said, "that
the owl is calling me? So that I shouldn't
kill myself!" he said, he thought;

then his horse . . . (the owl) kept hooting
toward where his horse was, the owl did;
when he was sitting, when he was sitting, right
behind him, it hooted; and it kept leading him
toward the horse, it kept hooting;
he had hobbled his horse quite a distance back;

so then, while he was sitting . . . I mean . . .
he stepped (up on) his horse; then all of a sudden
his . . . he mounted it and turned back,
going home; it was very far; then
when he arrived, he told his Grandmother: "being so
lonely, I almost killed myself" he said,
"because I was so lonely" he said;
"Why are you so lonely?" asked his Grandmother,
"I'm still around,
you shouldn't do it!" she said;

well, the next day he went out again;
he had a dream in his sleep (that night),
of a deer going that way, across the rocky mesa . . .
it was a flat rocky mesa . . .

so (going across that country), there were
indeed tracks, of a deer
going across the rocky mesa; then, the young man
thought, someone was whistling right there;
there was a small arroyo there,
and suddenly from across it, there was a whistling;
so he looked that way,
he kept tracking the deer, its spoor; and right there
(in front of him) there was a White-Man standing,
on a white horse,
all dressed in white; it was a White-Man;
"What manner of dress is that?" the Young Man thought.
"It must be the White-Man's way" he thought;
so he stood and looked at him, and the White-Man
called him: "Come here!"
he told him; so the Young Man
approached slowly; and the White-Man spoke
to him then;

he spoke in all languages . . . then . . .
eee . . . he spoke English (first), next
he spoke Spanish, but the Young Man didn't
understand . . . he then spoke (in the languages of)
all the people who live on earth,
he spoke all of them;

finally he spoke to him in his own
Ute language, finally,
but before that he spoke to him in Navajo . . .
and that the Young Man understood;
what the White-Man spoke last was Ute,
and the Young Man understood it;

now the White-Man showed him . . .
he showed him . . . he showed him
his hand where he
had been nailed . . . and his ribs where
he had been stabbed; "How come you are like that?"
the Young Man asked; he was indeed a whole
  person . . .
there was nothing . . . there was nothing missing
about him;

the Young Man himself was sort of an orphan . . .
he understood (only) when the White-Man spoke Navajo,
or in Ute; he didn't understand any
English; and he didn't know anything about it,
that this was the White-Man who had been nailed
(to the cross) on the hillside;
of what the White-Man told him
he knew nothing; "Who is this one?"
he wondered; and indeed, it was Jesus,
it was him, he was bearded,
he had long hair.

well then . . . the story goes . . .
"I will talk to you now" Jesus said,
"about this business yesterday of you wanting
to shoot yourself in the head" he said;
"You shouldn't do it,
even though you may be an orphan" he said then,
"I will talk to you now"
he said; "It is because of his influence
that you did it" he said;
and lo, just next to Jesus there was a Dark Man
standing, with a hook nose, like a cowboy,
just like that type, wearing a big hat,
with spurs, decked up in his finery, riding a
well-made saddle; and his horse had fierce
eyes, it was pitch black;
and lo, it was the Devil himself
it was him; so the Young Man stood and watched (him);
it was because of his power that he was going
to shoot himself
in the head (the day before);
that's what Jesus told him;

the Young Man was scared, watching the Devil,
Jesus showed him to him; then (he said):
"I am the one who stopped you (from killing
yourself), disguised as an owl,
I'm the one who hooted at you,
I'm the one who led you away"
he told him then; so the Young Man said: "Yes"

*"Aunt Mil Wood in her saddle shoes, Uncle Carl Wood, my father and mother,
Lewis and Edith Hall, five months before I was born, on the running board of
Uncle Carl's '39 Oldsmobile on my grandparents' farm," 1940*

he said, "I was feeling very
dejected when I did it"
he said, "That's why I (tried to) do it"
he told him, the Young Ute told Jesus;

　　so Jesus told him: "I will now tell you"
he said, "you . . . you . . .
'I'm lonely' that's what you said" he said;
"Now I'll show you your relatives;
your relatives are indeed alive,
your older brother" he said, "is standing
right there" he said,
"indeed I've brought him here" he said;

　　and lo, right alongside Jesus
there was a person standing,
his older brother; so the Young Man stood there
looking at him; "alright" asked Jesus,
"do you recognize him?"
he asked; "yes, he's my older brother"
said the Young Man, "and he's been dead
for a long time";
"No" Jesus told him, "he's not dead,
he's alive, up in heaven, up there above the earth:
he said, "he's alive there,
(together with) many others"; that's what
he told him, he told him;

　　then Jesus continued: "Yes" he said,
"he just came to see you, because you
were lonely, you said so yourself; now he
knows where you live" he said;
so the Young Man said: "Alright" he said,
"it's alright by me" he said;

　　then Jesus said: "Now I am going
to tell you the story" he said,
"of this land, the way it is going to be
in the future" he said; "right now I . . .
right now all this land is
full of Indians; but just like that (it will fill
with) Whites" he said; "They'll speak all (kinds of)
language, it will all be mixed" he said,
telling him the story; "And these
church goers, there'll be all kinds, there'll be
all kinds, a jumble of congregations with all kinds
of names . . . church goers . . ."
he said; "They'll have (different) names,
those congregations" he said; "And as to these
Indians, the ones here now, the Indians, they'll
become this way too;
now, here standing (next to you)
is the one you were longing for" he said;
"So what will become of you now?
These Indians (around you), they don't . . .
understand (about all this)" Jesus continued;
"So . . . you . . . we-two will now
tell you about the way the Indians
will practice (religion); they will eat Peyote,

or they will Sundance; of the two,
which one do you choose?"
"The Sundance . . . that's the kind I choose"
said the Young Man, "the Sundance.
But my relatives don't practice
any of it" he continued, "they don't
Sundance. Of what you describe,
they practice nothing. But I will practice
that kind" he said;

　　"Now I . . . Alright" said Jesus;
"You yourself will be the (Sundance) Chief, and I
will then give you the things
with which you'll do it,
what you'll Sundance with, what will be done"
he said . . . that's what he told him . . .
so the Young Man agreed, and he did exactly
that way, when he practiced the next summer;
when they did it then,
they just did it for practice,
with only a few people;

　　the following summer, it was supposed to be
very big, with many people doing it;
and then the Sundancers
were to be all dressed up exactly
the same way; the Young Man also had the same outfit,
with an Eagle-Whistle and all, and drums . . .
the way they were going to do it . . .
that's what Jesus told him,
so that's why the Young Man did it (that way);
and when they practiced,
they did it with the singing;

　　now then, after having finished the practice,
he . . . he, one Indian, an envious one,
came over across, with his hat . . . the center pole
was very, it was very tall;
so he hung his hat up there (on the center pole)
after they had practiced; that person went mad
afterwards, and he ran away;
and lo, his house . . . inside his hat
there was a yellow (cloth) bundle (of bad medicine);
he was bad-mouthing (the Sundance),
he was a bad one,
he did it . . . so he went mad;

　　then the Young Man . . . Jesus had also
told him: "that . . . don't . . ."
(some people) were bad-mouthing the Young Man
when he practiced the Sundance; so then he . . .
when they kept doing that to him, that crowd
spoke ill of him; so later:
"When they speak ill of you,
I myself will (come and) take you
away (to me)" that's what Jesus had told him . . .
"When you had practiced it (the Sundance),
I will take you away (to me), if they speak
ill of you, that crowd . . ."

so then when the Young Man practiced that way,
those people indeed bad-mouthed him;
Jesus had told him (about it) long before that;
at that time he had also told him many
(other) things . . .

so then the next summer . . .
the next day . . . the next summer when (the
Sundance)
was supposed to take place,
he died then . . . just . . .
the Young Man died, after they bad-mouthed him;
there were quite a few there when he practiced,
and they all were dressed exactly
the same fine style;
well, there was that woman inside there
where the crowd (of Dancers) was supposed to be,
two women; they were supposed to sit across
(from the Sundancers); they weren't supposed
to Sundance, only to sit; that's how
it was to be, supposedly;

and he had also said . . . the Son of
God . . . "You must also do like this,
I tell you" he said;
he told him about everything, about what
will become of everything
on this earth, the way it will happen,
about that, he told him;
The Indian will disappear,
he said, with only a few surviving,
alive; they will have to marry their own kin,
he said then, because they would have become
so few, he said;

that's how it is nowadays, just as
he said, with the White-Men having become
so numerous; they all go to churches,
and (Jesus said that) they'd all
be arguing with each other, all those religions,
he told him; they . . . all over their churches
they would be shooting each other;
that's what has happened now, Jesus told him
  (about it),
that's what Jesus said . . .

I myself often sit and think about it,
knowing all this; I keep thinking,
about that; knowing all this . . .

so Jesus told him about everything,
about all that is on this earth; that's how it is,
the way it has become; they even called-up
the Indians (to serve) overseas; it has become
that way . . .

"I remember the empty bookcases beside the fireplace in our living room. I don't remember having many books. Yet, I'm on the front steps of my house, age two and a half, reading," 1943.

long time ago . . . that way he . . .
it was long ago, there remain other things,
that he also said; this earth
would break open, he said, and the water
would begin to rise, he said;
unless they do the Sundance, unless
they run it real good and proper,
unless he run it well;

that Sundance is powerful Medicine, (that's)
where the Sundancing Indian would get
his Medicine-power; it's that way
that they've come (to have Medicine-Power);
and with it in their hands, like this (gesture),
they would always ward off (bad medicine);
that is, if one does the Sundance well,
that's what (Jesus) said, if one does it real well;
that wandering young Ute was to become
a Medicine man;

nowadays I often sit and think about all this;
(about how) they do it the wrong way,
those who do it, those who do
the Sundance; it is the wrong way,
it is;

it is Jesus who said it; when I think about it
now . . . there's much more to it, what I
will say, there's much more to it that (Jesus)
had said; there's no end to it,
the way this (the Sundance) has become;
he's the one who said that . . . it's him,
the Son of God; there's much more to it, I myself
know only some of it, I don't know all
of it, I don't remember (all of)
what he said, what he said;
whatever it be, it has become
like that, the way (Jesus) said it,
to him, to the Ute man, it's what he said,
to the Medicine-Man;
I've said it now, this is just about as far as
I know, not very much . . .

Jesus told him this, to him, to the Ute man:
"when you return . . . when you go back home . . .
when you go back, I'll give you one horse"
he told him then; so then later the Young Man
went back, back home . . .
"That horse will catch up with you"
he had told him; "It'll be a black spotted one,
a small one, not very big";
and indeed that happened;

but then he couldn't, when he was going
back home he couldn't catch it;
he came along it four, three (times);
but it kept disappearing that-a-way; and then
afterwards it would come back,
but the Young Man didn't carry anything
(to catch it with), he didn't have anything,
he wasn't carrying a rope with him,
so he didn't catch it then; heee . . .
circling around four times with the horse,
he kept coming up to it
as he was returning home; but he didn't have . . .
anything with which to catch it; that one . . .
that horse . . . that's the one that the Young Man
was supposed to ride
going all over this land;
he had said that, he had told him,
God . . . the Son of God; the Young Man saw him;
then when he returned home he . . . then . . .
it was like that . . . he didn't catch it,
the horse ran way, that-a-way;
it was supposed to be gentle, the horse,
it was supposed to be a good one;

I sit and think about it, this is the story
they used to tell me,
my long-gone relatives; that's how come
I know it, about how the Sundance used to be . . .

(Here the speaker digressed into how the
Sundance is currently done.)

so the young man . . . he returned home then,
and he lived on; but later he died;
he is the one who told (his people) about the Sundance;
but he did not do it himself;
he died (before that);

after he died, when he was lying in state,
a rainbow appeared, right above;
and everything was there (on the funeral pyre),
everything, what the Ute man would have worn dancing,
Sundancing, it was all there, the bundle
he would have (carried),
his eagle whistle,
what he was supposed to wear, and whatever
else he had; he had done it all properly,
it was like that . . .
he was a real Indian;

that's what she said . . . she used to tell me this,
my late mother, when she told me stories . . .
I have told it now, where it all
comes from; this is as far as it goes,
what I know.

Diane, with her mother and brother,
David, 1950

"My brother and me at the Pacific," 1950

(The Ute name for the Sundance, "tagau-wunu-vaci," means "standing hungry." In this story it is referred to most often as "tagu-nhka-pi" ["hunger-dance"]. Sometimes it is also referred to simply as "wunu-vaci" ["standing"]. Some speakers say that the name of the Young Ute man who received the Sundance from Jesus was "tuu-naci-too-pu" ["Black Cane"]. He is said to have been the older brother of Peter Spencer, and thus, the son of a Ute man named "nuu-saaquaci" ["Ghost Person"].)

*

Those Sundances would go on in secret. The Indian couldn't practice his religion openly until the Religious Freedom Act of 1978, For nearly a hundred years the Sundance was illegal. It wasn't the tradition my father was from anyway. He'd come from northern Arkansas, where his father had been a country doctor and his mother a Cherokee woman. His religion came in the form of church.

My father also liked to travel. From Kansas City, we made trips to my grandparents' farm in Kansas and my father's mother in Viola, Arkansas. We went to California to visit my Aunt Helen, and to Itasca State Park in Minnesota. When we lived in Indiana, we went to Lake Michigan and the sand dunes, Turkey Run State Park, and Washington D.C., Jamestown and Williamsburg. When we lived in St. Louis, we made trips to Florida and to the Lake of the Ozarks in Missouri, where Aunt Mil and Uncle Carl had a cabin.

I remember feeling limits, but when I look at the photo album, there was also migration.

When I was eight or nine, I had to take swimming lessons at Paseo High School in Kansas City. I still have an image of that pool. The shape of it, shallow on one end, deep on the other, something like the state of Oklahoma where I lived much of my adult life. The weight of it filled with water. I was under water, swimming for the surface. I could see light. I swam toward it. When I think back on those early years, it was my father who was the light. My Aunt Mil in her saddle shoes was the one who held out the pole. Because she was never angry with me.

I never did learn to swim.

It was an overwhelming experience that stands as a dominant image of my childhood.

That swimming pool is still in my head. I drain it with my writing. My mother's unhappiness as a mother. Her disapproval of me. Whether it was my darkness intruding upon her, or something disagreeable in me, we had conflict.

But that point of fear and drowning is the undercurrent of my writing.

Words are a netting, a surface of waves, which disrupt the joint of process. Wind patterns on the lake. Interrelated and touching one another. Though it seems they don't. I feel the frustration of words in their bondage of having to explain.

A swimming pool full of waves. That was my adolescence.

He had seven sons and three daughters . . .
and their father gave them inheritance among
their brethren.

(Job 42:13–15)

Though I felt I was nothing, I knew I had an inheritance. I struggled through self-devaluation and fear and inferiority and isolation. There was a steel wire that ran though my life. Wherever it came from. A combination of several sources, probably. Self-will and determination. An aunt without children, who approved of me. A house with two parents that remained whole though broken. The words from the Bible.

He hath compassed the water with a boundary.
                                                    (Job 26:10)

When I write a story, I feel those variables moving in different patterns. I think it's why I write in several genres. The imagination moves across the landscape and enters the text, and takes part in the forming of the creative act, which unites my fragments in a loose bonding, which moves to other bondings of other fragments, and makes sources of energy spots.

Writing is the creating of a *source structure.*

In wording and naming the act of living, the experience of shaping out of shapelessness, a determination, a determinacy, speaks a continuum of will and fortitude and not giving up.

When I was rejected and rejected and rejected, the words were still there, the writing, that is. I kept writing. And the manuscripts piled up. I sent them out, received them back, sent them out again. The title of my second collection of drama, *Cargo,* probably came from carrying all those words around.

Now that I'm older, I think, looking back, what it was to live my life. It was long ago and I wanted to write and I wrote when my two children napped, and I had a file cabinet, and then I bought another to hold what I had written. I moved it with me, from Oklahoma to Iowa to Minnesota, and twice since I've lived in Minnesota.

Words are a dynamic of self seeking connection.

> Waves cropping a lake.
> A lake cropping its waves.

Words are the reflection of water in the pool of the eye.

> A place I was looking for
> made of images of meaning.
> A more-than-one on which to focus.

> A flag in the wind.
> Someone speaking from far way.
> I can see the mouth move.
> I see it like a flag in the wind.

There is a crosspool of floodings in the complexities of current. There is a voice saying, "hold on, it will connect and *go somewhere,*" in a broken surface on which words spread into many genres.

"My cousin, Susan, who is Aunt Helen's daughter, and me on our grandparents' farm; my father made my wooden doll cart," 1951

From 1964 to 1983, I was married to Dwane Glancy. The image I have from those years was a dream I had once, early in the marriage. I was trying to drive a loaded eighteen-wheeler up a sandy incline.

Those were the years I began writing.

I also wanted to return to school. After I got my B.A. at the University of Missouri, it was twenty years before I continued my education. My years as an undergraduate had been unsettled. Insecure. I couldn't study. I didn't think I could. My grades suffered.

The turmoil of my life still circled. Everything fell back on me. I worked with poetry and then story. I worked with creative nonfiction, drama, and the novel. It wasn't until 1984 that I had anything published.

Two early novels, *The Only Piece of Furniture in the House* and *Fuller Man,* written during my marriage, weren't published for fifteen years. I began *Monkey Secret,* my third collection of short stories, as an undergraduate at the University of Missouri. I remember writing one of the sections, "The Wooden Tub," in my first creative writing class. It was nearly thirty years before the other parts of the story were finished and published.

My historical novel, *Pushing the Bear*, about the 1838 Trail of Tears, the removal of 13,000 Cherokee from the southeast to Indian Territory, took nearly eighteen years to write. In the afterward, I tell how I first saw the outdoor drama in Tahlequah, Oklahoma. My daughter and I had driven from Tulsa to see it. Over the years, the many voices in the novel came to my imagination during research or travel. Or sometimes when I was doing something else, there would be Maritole or Knobowtee. It's where I heard them anyway, in the imagination. A series of voices, a story of many voices walking the trail, telling their side of it.

When I was in New York to talk to my publisher about the novel, I visited the Smithsonian Museum of the American Indian in the Custom House. I saw a Seminole robe which was a patchwork of color and geometric design. I thought of my novel as a patterning of voices with dialogue and conflicts unfolding in relationship to one another. When I saw a northwestern tribe "button blanket," I thought of my novel as a "voice blanket." My grandmother on my mother's side made quilts. Maybe in sewing the scattered voices together in the novel, I'm doing what she did, only in a different way.

I also thought of *Pushing the Bear* as the noise of voices after their sound has stopped.

The title came to me when I was at the Gilcrease Museum in Tulsa, down among the shelves in the storage rooms. I saw a small ivory statue of an Eskimo man pushing the rump of a bear. "Pushing the Bear" came immediately to mind.

Sometimes my writing comes quickly. My next novel, *Flutie*, was written in 1995–96. It's the story of a young woman who is shy and cannot speak, but through circumstance and ceremony and an act of the will, she finds her voice and speaks.

I'm glad each piece comes in its own way. Writing is a continual process, changing as it goes.

I have the title for a new novel, *An American Language*, and something else called, *The Man Who Heard the Land*, is there. And something called, *America's First Parade*, is there after that. I feel my words coming and coming. I don't think I'll ever get them all down.

I have a piece of dialogue from *An American Language*. "Imagine a place without its own language. Well, it has a language. It's just not its own."

I was thinking about our American language when I was traveling in Germany recently. I said that I felt limited when I traveled because I only had one language. But someone said, "It's the right one."

At the conference in Munich, I was talking about the experimentation I liked to do with the American language. I talked about the possibilities of changing syntax. The possibilities for opening the language to accommodate minority and women's voices. How in not having ownership over language, it expands to do what

Diane with her brother, David, at Itasca State Park, Minnesota, 1951

"My first dance," 1956

you want to do as a writer. The Germans said that the German language didn't have that capacity. If you changed a word in German, or tried to stretch it, you'd feel that something was wrong.

Maybe our language is more fluid. Elastic. It's what I want language to be, anyway.

It's also what I want genres to be. I think it's why I began experimenting with the short-story collections I wrote. My first two short fiction books, *Trigger Dance* and *Firesticks*, were written in Oklahoma, where I lived with my husband and children. They contain first-person narratives and short short fiction pieces as well as traditional short stories. *Firesticks* begins with a story about Louis, who is colorblind and tries to imagine color. The book then continues with a personal essay, then a poetic piece about a truck driver, and then the first section of the title piece, "Firesticks." Then there's another personal-voice piece and another chapter of "Firesticks." Then more stories and personal-voice pieces with more parts of "Firesticks" woven between them. I think I wrote the book that way because I felt the fragmentation of my own life, and of my father's heritage, in the breaking up of a solid place.

I've already mentioned *Monkey Secret*, my third collection. It is also a broken-voice piece. The book is three short stories followed by the no-

vella, "Monkey Secret." That monkeys were once men was an idea I got from the *Popol Vuh*, the Mayan council book.

On the cover flap, the editor, Reginald Gibbons, writes:

> Glancy's tales of Native American life explore the essential American territory, the border-between: between past and present, between native and immigrant cultures, between self and society.
>
> The short novel, "Monkey Secret," combines traditional Native American storytelling and contemporary narrative techniques to explore the coming of age of a young girl of mixed race and heritage in rural northern Arkansas. Jean Pierce narrates her passage from childhood to maturity with typically Native American circularity and digression. Each chapter of "Monkey Secret" is like a single perfect bead on a string; Jean's impressionistic vignettes—growing up with her extended family at their farm in Haran, Arkansas, spending summers at the cabin on Bull Shoals Lake, departing for college and returning to find her mother dying—are threaded with the twin strands of her complex culture and her desperate love for her cousin Cedric.
>
> In its gaps and hesitations, the qualifications of thought and feeling, the meditative self-reflexiveness, Glancy's work interrogates narrative form while revealing the individuality and authenticity of her characters.

I had wanted to call the novella, "Portrait of an Artist as a Young Woman," but I knew I couldn't get into those waters. It's about a young woman who lives in the crevice between the Christian world of her father and the mythic Cherokee world of her mother, and uses words to bridge the two irreconcilable worlds that are always moving apart from one another. One of the sections in the novella, however, is called "Sketches of an Artist as a Young Woman." I remember visiting Bull Shoals Lake in Arkansas when we went to see my father's mother. I remember being in a rowboat on *big water*. I also used the experiences I had at my Uncle Carl's cabin on the Lake of the Ozarks.

During my 1995–96 sabbatical year at Macalester College, I finished my fourth collection of short stories, *The Voice That Was in Travel*. It also moves between the personal and distant voice, but there is more of a "settledness" of pieces.

In 1995, *Trigger Dance* was translated into German and published by S. Fischer in Frankfurt. It's the reason I've traveled to Germany several times for readings and conferences. I also went to Italy, Syria, and Jordan for U.S. Information Service tours.

Creative nonfiction is a genre with a moving definition. Memoir, autobiography, diary writing, journal keeping, travel pieces, essays on various subjects, assemblages of experiences and reflections, and experimentation with the variables of composition. *Claiming Breath* and *The West Pole* are collections of creative nonfiction, combining lectures and book reviews with personal essays and fragmented prose pieces, all the while moving between traditional and disconnected writing styles, shifting the text, breaking into the sentence structure. Expanding the boundaries. Somehow communicating the ideas.

I'm now working on my third book of creative nonfiction called, *In the Spirit of the Mind.*

I have nine manuscripts of unpublished poetry I work on at various times. *The Relief of America, The Deer Rider, Asylum in the Grasslands, (Ado)ration, Generally He Gave Us Plenty of Room, Necessary Departures.* Well, two of them, *Still Life with Mazie in the Cornfields* and *Warrior Woman* are chapbooks, and *Passionate Visions* is a selected work.

Drama is a fifth genre field. *War Cries* is a book of nine of my plays. *Cargo* is my second. "Lesser Wars," "American Gypsy," "Cargo," "Jump Kiss," and "The Woman Who Was a Red Deer Dressed for the Deer Dance" are the plays I've worked on recently.

Now I'm working on a piece called, "The Women Who Loved House Trailers." The main characters are three women: Oscar, a welder, Jelly, a weaver of strips of birchbark into small canoes, and Berta, a collector of stories.

Like "The Woman Who Was a Red Deer Dressed for the Deer Dance," which was written after I saw a red papier-mâché dress made by visual artist Carolyn Erler, this piece will also be interdisciplinary.

"My brother, my parents, and me in front of our house in St. Louis," 1959

The house trailers will be the three women who come to terms with themselves. The house trailers will be their roaming hearts. The house trailers will be the groups of their extended families they learn to accept. The house trailers will be the moving stories of their different lives. The house trailers also will be the cultures of several continents, which is another addition to the multidimensional aspect of the new wave of oral tradition I'm trying to create, which is interlocking cultures. Well, I'm just beginning to write this fictional/poetic/dramatic piece, and already I can see the long trail. Jelly will make wheels for her canoes. Oscar will weld wheels. Berta's stories will be mobile. In the three women's relationships, their problems and limitations will be made portable and rolled away. With love and blow kisses from the welder's torch.

Native American storytelling is an act of *gathering* many voices to tell a story. One voice alone is not enough because we are what we are in relationship to others, and we each have our different way of seeing. NA writing is also an alignment of voices so the story comes through. A *relational stance* is the construct of the writing. In my short stories, poems, and creative nonfiction I can follow the rules of conflict/resolution, one point-of-view, plot, and the usual, but there is something essential in Native storying that is not included, which is a migratory and interactive process of the moveable parts within the story. It's also the element of Native American oral tradition told with what it is not—the written word—then returned to what it is by the act of the voice. There's not a name for it in the genre field, but I'm trying to give solid nomenclature to something that is a moving process, and resists naming, other than a new oral tradition.

I think writing exists, in part, for healing, not only in the writer, but also for the reader/hearer. For instance, in Navajo sand paintings, the painter aligns the design in the sand to the hurt in the one needing healing, and the alignment draws the hurt into the painting, and the painting is destroyed, and the ailment along with it. Storying should do the same. It is much needed in a culture with a high alcoholism rate, poverty, and a struggle for racial esteem.

America is taking out of the melting pot what didn't melt: our voices and styles of storytelling. We are a fractured, pluralistic society, which our art should reflect. I think understanding cultures is the byword for our society. It seems to me that art is the medium for understanding not only the differences between cultures, but within cultures as well. There is a vast difference between the Plains Indian and the Woodland cultures.

Sometimes, in the long cold of a Minnesota winter, I think about my writing. Especially when I'm chopping ice that's several inches thick on my sidewalk. Especially when I'm shoveling snow. The last storm, my snow shovel froze in a mound of old snow where I'd jabbed it. I had to shovel with a shovel with a broken handle.

At night, when the ice on the roof shifts, the house moans and knocks with stories.

Over the years, I have written because I was hungry for words.

I have written because I was cold.

I think I've waited my whole life to teach, travel, read my poetry and fiction in bookstores and at conferences.

Like my father, I want to be on the road. The autumn of my sabbatical after receiving tenure, I had a fellowship at the Provincetown Art Center in Massachusetts, I drove from St. Paul to the other side of Cleveland the first day. And from the other side of Cleveland to Provincetown. 1465 miles in two days.

There was something I had to get through. Maybe like a piece of writing.

There were names I found, like Ashtabula County in Ohio, I had to get down.

And there were the trucks—*Yellow Transit. National Carriers. Transcontinental Registered Lines. Roadway. Consolidated Freight. Wells Fargo. J. B. Hunt. North American. Burlington. Falcon. Tuscarora. Mayflower.*

Some without names.

The turnpikes east of Wisconsin are walled cities. I felt locked on the highway with the truckers. But I was away from classes and department and committee meetings and grading papers.

There were seven tollgates through Chicago alone where I waited in the exhaust of their dust.

After two days by myself on the road, weary and spaced, my sense of identity, which is tied to place, was gone. I was one of those nameless trucks floating over the road. Disconnected. But in the movement of my car was place, I remembered. Migration was a state.

And I was in the walled city of my car.

If I could be from anywhere, it would be Ashtabula. If I could be with anyone, it would be one of those truckers. Those wedding-cake grooms up there decorated with lights. I would follow his truck across the Atlantic, if there was a highway there.

My children are grown and my relatives are gone, and I am with my words now.

> Water I can't swim.
> Water you are blank as I am.
> Water you can swim.
> Water you can hold me up.

Sometimes I think of my father, who left his rural Cherokee heritage to be a real American—a Boy Scout leader—a provider for his family. I remember the hollowness and anger in him because he had a blank place where heritage should have been.

But I had a doll cart with two wheels my father made, and I'd pull my two dolls to a weeded lot by my house and play there all day mashing berries for food, playing out what was in my imagination. There was a life of the mind in which there was the making of metaphor, a development and insight into the relationship of parts—the likeness of differences—the difference of likenesses—the connectives and disconnectives—the making of something. I think I continue pushing my doll cart to the woods with my writing.

Because I didn't have music or mathematics or science—I made analogies. I made stories. But the principles of discovery and relationships may be the same.

The language of the imagination has the function of talking through the connections which underlie things. I am in a relationship to something outside myself. I have a connection to words, and as I work, they connect with something larger.

I feel the variability. The layering of expanding thought processes, the opportunities, the options, the embellishment and elaborations. I generate my own life in the development of thought through words.

I have a reliable construction of change and the unexpected. I have a gist of certainty. My writing is a generator. A source of something—of words—of reasoning—

They brought me to the place where I am now. It's a full life full of ordinariness, really. I had twenty years as a wife and mother. I've been divorced thirteen. My children are on their own in different cities. This was a time dreaded by my mother's generation in the fifties. What do you do after the children are gone? Who are you outside your husband and family?

Those years with my children were meaningful—and I miss them sometimes. But now I get up in the morning and have coffee and read the newspaper and go to my word processor and go through my thoughts, and go back through them, and find that road into what I am saying. I guess it's always been Main Street under the Elms.

I remember the decency of my parents despite their problems and economic straits—the unfairness they knew. My mother as a woman. My father as a man who had to live without part of himself. I remember the disillusionment, the boredom, I guess, of their marriage. The tediousness of life we all know. My anger at them—

But the carcasses of cattle hung upside down in the stockyards where my father worked, and Christ hung right side up on his cross in church. There was faith in the bloodshed of Christ for the atonement of our shortcomings and sins. Christianity as a strained metaphor, so to speak. A thought process that links. Something like sand, which can be a boundary of the sea and a conduit of healing in a painting.

I have my own life now. I have a small house in St. Paul. When it's twenty degrees below or when there are twenty inches of snow in one afternoon, my brother calls from Missouri and asks what I'm doing there. But I can shovel my walk and mow the lawn and reach the windows when I wash them. I have a sense of self in my thinking, which is an internal landscape. There are elements in the world that could wipe me out, but I have a heritage of survival. I just have to hold on to it.

Somewhere as a child, the cold-and-hunger dance passed into me. Awkward. Intrusive. A routine of writing and rewriting and rewriting and waiting.

But there was a Ute Sundance story circling. A mix of cultures. A change in the way of saying. A text you can't quite get ahold of. An accomplishment despite failure.

If someone is deer hunting and can't kill a deer. If someone is alone. A white man on a white horse appears. Before which he'd been an owl. Speaking languages until after he finds the Ute to speak. The Devil on a black horse causing the Ute to deconstruct. The white man showing the Ute his dead relatives while deer hunting and not killing deer. A forecast of the mix of American culture. Religions of varied interpretations. A Sundance to dance a certain way. It was the Ute's choice. Jesus would take him away if anyone laughed. It seems they did. Though the Ute only practiced the Sundance and couldn't really do that. Nor a small black spotted horse the Ute couldn't catch. Robust and he didn't quite have the rope with which to catch. Couldn't seem anything in the haplessness of his story. But the horse was there anyway. And the rainbow appeared over. The eagle-whistle and drums after overseas service. Through bondage to the fact of slipping. Yet the Ute dying significantly. In the long cold winter of the Sundance where I live.

I am always thinking about the importance of story. I've heard many Native American writers say that our words are our most important possession. They define what we are.

Stories give us our sense of meaning. But what exactly is a story? How does it work?

Dan Taylor, in *The Healing Power of Stories* (Doubleday, 1996), says that "a story is the telling of the significant actions of characters over time." But where should the definition go from there?

When I was in Germany, I visited the *Forum der Technik*, the science museum, in Munich. On the second floor, I saw a huge DNA double helix. Somehow I thought, that's how a story works.

Our lives are made of the joining of words into stories into meaning into integral parts of our being. In the same way, maybe, that we're made of DNA, which carries the chemical traditions from generation to generation.

There also was an explanation of genetic coding on the second floor of the museum, and though it was in German, I could see two things linking. I felt, likewise, our minds hold up their hands to hook on to a story. A possibility of meaning. The mind and the story connect and coil with other stories to form the structure of thought. There is a combining of elements.

Later, I was reminded of Reginald Gibbons's comment about the chapters of the novella "Monkey Secret" "threaded with the twin strands" of Jean Pierce's culture and her love for her cousin. There are always undercurrents working in the subconscious to make connections.

When I returned from Germany, Jim Straka, biochemist and visiting professor at Macalester College, talked to me about the DNA I had seen in Germany, since the language explaining it, as I said, had been in German. As he told me about A, T, G, C, the four bases on the strands of DNA, we agreed the DNA structure could be a metaphor for story.

There was the possibility of a correspondence. The meaning and sound of the spoken words, the hearing and interpretation of them, the telling of them again in one's own way.

The four bases holding hands. Their carefulness in which hands they hold.

The DNA making protein, which, in combination with the DNA, makes cells to make organs to make organisms. There is a circularity in the fact that DNA makes protein which is necessary to make more DNA.

As story must be heard and processed to make more story.

The drift and change.

Somehow I could make the transference.

It's always been those small connections. I lived in Oklahoma when I met Gerald Stern at a writers' conference in Tucson. He encouraged me to apply to the Iowa Writer's Workshop. I was in the farmhouse I rented in Iowa when Alvin Greenberg called from Macalester College. Could I come up and look the school over? He'd heard my name at an Associated Writing Program's conference where he had asked for names when he was thinking of changing and expanding the English Department faculty.

And I was there with determination like flint that was going to spark. I came from no intellectual tradition or background. I was supposed to be quiet, invisible, to survive. But I could feel the fortifier moving. I could feel the spark of the human mind.

I could move to Minnesota and teach. I could step to one place after another in the landscape of the classroom: writing and Native American literature. I could take one trip after another in a continual migration of readings: from the Hungry Mind Bookstore in St. Paul, to the Loft in Minneapolis, to the University of Alabama in Tuscaloosa, to the Phillips Public Library in Eau Claire, Wisconsin, to the Summer Writer's Conference at the University of Iowa in Iowa City, to the Just Buffalo Literary Center in Buffalo, New York, to the Olean Public Library in Olean, New York, to the Conference on Christianity and Literature at Baylor University in Waco, Texas, to Southwestern Oklahoma State University in Weatherford, Oklahoma, to the Quartz Mountain Writer's Conference for the Oklahoma Arts Institute in Lone Wolf, Oklahoma, to Hope College, Holland, Michigan, to a roundtable discussion, "Myth and Ritual, Desire and Cognitive Science," at the University of Alabama in Huntsville, to a Writer's Conference at Concordia College in Moorhead, Minnesota, to the University of Rochester in Rochester, New York, to the University of Arizona in Tucson, to the International Conference for the Short Story in Ames, Iowa, to the Arts Guild Complex in Chicago, to the Matthews Opera House in Spearfish, South Dakota, to Northland College in Ashland, Wisconsin, to the Left Bank Bookstore for the Writer and Religion Conference at Washington University in St. Louis, Missouri, to the Modern Language Association presentation of my play *Halfact,* in San Diego, California.

I could take research trips, driving back along the Trail of Tears from Georgia, Tennessee, Kentucky, Illinois, Missouri, Arkansas, Oklahoma, stopping at state parks and museums along the way. In the same two-year period, I could travel to Rosebud Reservation and drive across Montana. I could fly to the Squaw Valley Writers' Conference in California for a screenwriting workshop. I could drive to Provincetown, Massachusetts, for a month's fellowship. Another time, I could drive through New England.

I could spend two months in Australia. I could go to Japan in addition to the U.S. Information Service trips. All of which I've done and written about in my poems and stories and novels and creative nonfictions.

I could read for Fiction Collective II, the University of Oklahoma Press, and the Native American Prose Award for the University of Nebraska Press. I could be on the 1995 National Endowment for the Arts panel, the Jerome Travel Grant panel, and serve as judge for several poetry competitions, such as the National Federation for State Poetry Societies.

I could follow the turns of narrative truth in their pivotal and moving processes. Their

Diane Glancy—"a chilly afternoon, my house in St. Paul," 1996

several directions and points of departures and returns. I could see truth as a collaborative work, a country of imagination, a series of integral histories integrated into how one reads the narrative.

In other words, my words could be about the impossibility of arriving at one place of wholeness, but getting somewhere in the neighborhood.

I could feel the parts of myself, unthreaded by my name also. Helen Diane Hall Glancy. With an Indian name someone gave me that means "Happy Butterfly Woman." A name I would need in the moving and changing places I've lived my life. I was named after my Aunt Helen, my mother's sister. But I've never been called by that name, though it appears as my name on official documents. And my married name, Glancy, speaks of an Irish heritage I don't have.

But when I married, a long time ago, I don't remember the option of keeping my own name, Diane Hall, or returning to it once I had children.

I've turned one blank space after another forming my identity, but all those spaces, threaded one after one, coiling together like rope, is who I am.

BIBLIOGRAPHY

Novels:

The Only Piece of Furniture in the House, Asphodel (Wakefield, Rhode Island), 1996.

Pushing the Bear, Harcourt Brace, 1996.

Short-story collections:

Trigger Dance, University of Colorado/Fiction Collective Two, 1990.

Firesticks, University of Oklahoma Press, 1993.

Monkey Secret, TriQuarterly Books/Northwestern University Press, 1995.

Essays:

Claiming Breath, University of Nebraska Press, 1992.

The West Pole, University of Minnesota Press, 1997.

Poetry:

One Age in a Dream, Milkweed (Minneapolis, Minnesota), 1986.

Offering, Holy Cow! Press (Duluth, Minnesota), 1988.

Iron Woman, New Rivers Press (Minneapolis), 1990.

Lone Dog's Winter Count, West End Press (Albuquerque, New Mexico), 1991.

Boom Town, Black Hat Press (Goodhue, Minnesota), 1995.

Coyote's Quodlibet, Chax Press (Minneapolis), 1995.

Published plays:

War Cries (nine plays), Holy Cow! Press, Duluth, 1996.

Produced plays:

Segwohi, produced at the Oklahoma Theater Festival, Tulsa, Oklahoma, 1987.

Testimony, produced at the Heller Theater, Tulsa, 1987.

Weebjob, produced by the American Indian Theater Company, Tulsa, 1987.

The Lesser Wars, produced by the Jones Commission, Playwrights' Center, Minneapolis, 1989.

Stick Horse, produced at the Borderlands Theater Play Festival, Tucson, Arizona, 1990.

The Woman Who Was a Red Deer Dressed for the Deer Dance, produced at the Walker Art Center, Minneapolis, 1995, and the Native American Playwriting Festival, New York, 1995.

Halfact, produced at the Modern Language Association Conference, San Diego, California, 1995.

Also author of *The West Pole*, a collection of six essays, published by the Minnesota Center for the Book Arts, Minneapolis, as a 1995 Winter Book. Contributor to *I Tell You Now*, edited by Brian Swann, University of Nebraska Press, 1987; *Braided Lives: An Anthology of Multicultural American Writing*, Minnesota Humanities Commission, St. Paul, Minnesota, 1991; *Talking Leaves: Contemporary Native American Short Stories*, edited by Craig Lesley, Dell, 1991; *Earth Song, Sky Spirit: Short Stories of the Contemporary Native American Experience*, edited by Clifford Trafzer, Doubleday, 1993.

Durable Breath: Contemporary Native American Poetry, edited by John E. Smelcer and D. L. Birchfield, Salmon Run Press, Anchorage, Alaska, 1994; *Inheriting the Land: Contemporary Voices from the Midwest*, edited by Mark Vinz and Thom Tammaro, University of Minnesota Press, 1994; *The Norton Book of Science Fiction*, edited by Ursula K. Le Guin and Brian Attebery, W. W. Norton, 1994; *The Pushcart Prize XVIII: Best of the Small Presses, 1993-1994*, edited by Bill Henderson,

Pushcart Press, Wainscott, New York, 1994; *Two Worlds Walking: Writers with Mixed Heritages,* edited by Diane Glancy and Bill Truesdale, New Rivers Press, Minneapolis, 1994; *What Is Found There: Essays on Poetry and Politics,* edited by Adrienne Rich, W. W. Norton, 1994; *Writing Women's Lives: An Anthology of Autobiographical Narratives by Twentieth Century American Women Writers,* edited by Susan Cahill, Harper Perennial, 1994.

Contemporary Plays by Women of Color, edited by Kathy Perkins and Roberta Uno, Routledge (London), 1995; *Freeing the First Amendment: Critical Perspectives on Freedom of Expression,* edited by Robert Jensen and David Allen, New York University Press, 1995; *Native American Literature,* edited by Gerald Vizenor, The HarperCollins Literary Mosaic Series, 1995; *The Sacred Place,* edited by Scott Olsen and Scott Cairns, University of Utah Press, 1996.

Glancy's unpublished works include the novels *Fuller Man* and *Flutie; Cargo,* a drama collection; *The Voice That Was in Travel,* a short-story collection; and *Passionate Visions,* a collection of selected work. Titles of unpublished poetry works include *The Relief of America, The Deer Rider, Asylum in the Grasslands, (Ado)ration, Generally He Gave Us Plenty of Room, Necessary Departures,* and the chapbooks *Still Life with Mazie in the Cornfields* and *Warrior Woman.*

Lyle Glazier

1911-

WELCOME, O LIFE

I go to encounter for the millionth time the reality
of experience and to forge in the smithy of my soul
the uncreated conscience of my race

    —James Joyce, *A Portrait of the Artist as a Young Man*

An aged man is but a paltry thing
A tattered coat upon a stick, unless
Soul clap its hand and sing, and louder sing
For every tatter in its mortal dress.

    —W. B. Yeats, "Sailing to Byzantium"

Lyle Glazier, 1995

[EDITOR'S NOTE: This essay was excerpted from a larger, unpublished work in progress.]

I went to Byzantium for two years, as Fulbright chair of American studies (1961–63) at the great University of Istanbul, and found not lords and ladies and golden nightingales singing on a bough but a sensual city pulsing with life, where my spirit soared not in rare ozone but in tune with barefooted hamals carrying burdens through crowded streets and with the busy intellectual life of the university, whose twin gatehouses, once guest houses for visiting heads of state, housed, when I was there, the faculty club in the basement of one with glittering audience chambers above, and the official residence of the rector in the other.

For a man of fifty, reared in a New England farming community—part affluent, part rural slum—then a graduate of Middlebury, Bread Loaf, and Harvard, this melting pot on the Bosphorus became something different from Yeats's dream, but priceless still. Not only could I glow in the aesthetic surprise of every street-turn opening on a view, but I could look back at the United States from that distance and see my own life and my country in a new perspective. Part of the gain of being in Turkey was having no political obligations. In that new freedom I could enjoy a moratorium on immediate oversight of the Puritan conscience.

Not that I was new to psychic regeneration, for early in life I began to rebel against the political, religious, and sexual correctness into which I was born.

My family was poor and, like Zora Neale Hurston, when I grew beyond childhood illusions of perfection, I began to discover that "poverty is death."

I was also sexually ambivalent, having at six years of age been seduced (in the "little chamber" at Gram's, that 1774 farmhouse with outlying wagon shed, barn, icehouse, smokehouse, toolshed, henhouse, and smithy across the road), with no trauma, by a boarder in his teens. In later life I never overcame the epiphanic joy of that sexual discovery and never blamed the boy, even though for many years I resisted other advances even when hoping to be courted.

I have no idea whether my preference was genetic or a product of conditioned reflex, or both. That episode was printed indelibly on my brain. It happened after Gramp picked me up after supper at our shanty on Northfield Mountain in Northfield Farms on a plateau overlooking the Connecticut River Valley and carried me ten miles "back home" to Moores' Corner to the 1774 farmhouse where Pop was born. By the time we got there I was asleep in the backseat. Gram and Aunt Maud, their voices distant and fuzzy, tucked me into bed. It was pitch-black indoors and out, the only light from the open door to the kitchen, which Gram and Aunt Maud pulled to softly when they tiptoed out.

In the middle of the night I came out of my deep sleep to find a big boy pulling up my nightgown and smothering the life out of me, so I had to squirm around to breathe under his armpit. At first he just "laid" there with his peepee between my legs, then he was moving, making himself felt. It began to feel good, all warm and cozy. When he was moving faster, he put his hand over my mouth and whispered, "Hush!" He was going faster and faster. Then he was still, and it was all sticky and beautiful down there in the hollow between my legs. He was breathing hard, his head on my pillow. Then he was holding me tight, cuddling me. After a while, he flopped over and mopped up with his nightdress. He put his mouth close: "Don't you tell your Gram!"

Hardly daring to breathe, I whispered back, "When can we do it again?"

The author's grandparents, Lil Richardson Glazier and Dan Edward Glazier, about 1920

He was holding his breath but let it out with a whispery laugh: "Holy cow! You and me, we're going to have fun!"

Pop's father was a lumberman with a watermill on the Sawmill River in North Leverett, Massachusetts, employing his sons as sawyer, marker, handler, and paying them menial wages until Mom, expecting her fourth child ("another boy"), put her foot down and we moved from a shanty into a frame house in Northfield Farms in the Connecticut Valley from where Pop was, first, a section hand on the Central Vermont Railroad, later a bookkeeper/factory hand, and then a foreman in Millers Falls Tool Company's stockroom. In the 1920s (my teens) we lived in that disheveled house with no modern plumbing, no electricity, no telephone, and only a one-pipe furnace that heated the sitting room but was also capable of producing carbon monoxide gas that could risk our lives, and sometimes did. The house may have been wonderfully suited to four growing boys, but it must have been more and more difficult for Pop and Mom as our appetites grew more demanding and the obligation to keep us clothed and housed and fed made greater demands on their small income.

At the factory Pop started keeping the stockroom's books for his boss several years before the boss retired and Pop took his place, but he would never earn the same salary. He never dressed to hobnob with the front office; nevertheless, he considered himself management and was both antilabor and pro-Coolidge, Harding, and Hoover.

Sunday afternoon after dinner, sitting in a rocking chair in the dining room reading *The Book of Knowledge,* borrowed from the Farms library, paying no attention to Pop at the table in his shirtsleeves and Mom standing at the west window, looking out over the ferry road to the CV railroad tracks toward the river, I came out of my dreaming to hear Pop's complaint, "I don't know where the money's coming from," then Mom's "I wish I'd had the good sense to go back to work in Flatbush when the Adlers were after me to."

Yanked out of my book, I was thinking I would never get married. I sank back into my reading, refusing to be bothered by their picking at each other.

When I looked up, the door to their bedroom was closed. Along in the afternoon Mom came out and flew around getting maybe pancakes and the last dregs of maple syrup for supper. She was humming to herself and seemed in a trance deeper even than my book-dreaming.

By instinct I became prolabor and anticapitalist, as well as agnostic in reaction against born-again Christianity, which seemed to hinge on some Great Brain in the sky that was so wise it knew everything but had no mercy for the waste of spirit imposed on his creation. I thought that the myth of his existence was created partly to give the wealthy an excuse for their power, and partly to offer a sense of grim security to their victims.

I was a good boy, embracing the whole Puritan ethic of workaholic, family cohesion—and, above all, the need to be "well thought of"—and the belief that somehow I could make a go of it and find a better life.

Without knowing Walter Pater, some center in my brain fastened on his creed: "To burn always with this hard, gemlike flame, to maintain this ecstasy, is success in life."

I loved music without having a chance to play an instrument, was a born lover of nature and poetry as well, and a budding writer before I was old enough to think about becoming one. For the first four years of schooling, in a one-room school, I adored Mary Dalton,

The Glaziers' Northfield Farms shanty, about 1918

my wonderful teacher who had a knack of including on the fringe of that fourth-grade class the first-grader with ears wide open for picking up tidbits of advanced enrichment.

By the time Northfield Rural School Number Four required an upstairs for grades five through eight, I had profited from what Miz Dalton taught my grade and the ones ahead. My eighth-grade teacher, Ruth Wilder, was equally remarkable. Friday afternoons were devoted to reading to us from *Evangeline, The Leatherstocking Tales,* and other inspiring books; we heard the language of poetry and the history of the opening of the American West: "This is the forest primeval, the murmuring pines and the hemlocks . . . / Stand like druids of eld." (Reciting it in my head, I may have blanked out the second line, but the syncopated drumbeat of the dactyls rings in the sensoriums of my ear.)

And my narrative instincts stirred to Natty Bumppo's rescue of Eliza Temple and her friend Louisa on a forest path "where the fierce front and glaring eyes of a female panther fixed on them in horrid malignity . . . threatening instant destruction."

"'Hist! hist!' said a low voice . . . 'Stoop lower, gal, your bonnet hides the creator's head.'"

For my first two years in high school I had the great fortune to take Red MacDonald's Latin classes. She taught grammar and *Julius Caesar* interspersed with anecdotes from her summer trips by freighter to the Mediterranean— to Rome or Athens or Cairo—to learn about ancient people. I was nearly outside myself imagining what it was like to have such adventures as her walks on the Palatine Hill viewing the cellar holes of the mansions of Roman patriots or, another summer, visiting the Acropolis in Athens.

Every year she conducted for all four classes a seminar in writing short stories. Every student had to turn in a story to be graded by the teachers, then read aloud for all to hear. I remember the title and theme of my freshman story, "The Green Monkey's Secret." The Green Monkey was an inn in a watering place somewhere in an exotic abstract corner of the Pacific. There was a Green Monkey behind the check-in counter, but the secret had to do with the mysterious disappearance of guest after guest after guest. Modeled after Somerset Maugham for Malaysian exoticism and Edgar Allan Poe

for gruesome details, it was, I knew, a classic, but it didn't win the prize.

My earliest poem, printed in the school annual, was written about Betty Cota:

> Before she got a boyish bob
> she used to wear a hat
> but now she has her hair cut
> she wants us to see that;
>
> It's cut off short in front
> and shingled down behind
> and for some movie company
> she thinks she'd be a find.

Mom thought it "pretty good."

All four years I was president of my class and a straight-A student. In our senior year I had the happy accident of being discovered by Emma Fitt, daughter of the evangelist D. L. Moody; she had a spat with Mrs. W. R. Moody over prestigious turf at Northfield Seminary and came to our school to help raise money for our Washington trip. She told me she would arrange a meeting between me and her younger brother, Paul D. Moody, president of Middlebury College. "Once he gets a look at you, he will see you are admitted there." Without a penny and no possible help from home, I knew it was impossible. However, after graduation I kept the thought afloat by getting a job at $19 a week, nine hours a day, plus five hours Saturday morning in Pop's stockroom at the tool company, and I saved every penny until my brother Melvin, a year and a half older, came back home to work there also and persuaded Pop to buy a car to drive us back and forth and for him to use evenings. Choosing a fancy Dort touring car, he burdened the folks with debt that forced them to charge each of us $10 a week board and room, leaving me $9 that I put in the bank scrupulously.

At the end of that year Mel drove me to meet President Moody at his sister's and insisted on talking with him before I did. Both of us became students at Middlebury, 1929–33— Mel with a tuition-and-living scholarship from a Barre businessman and I with a tuition-scholarship. I waited on table for my board and for three summers bellhopped at the Middlebury Inn, but at the end of each year my debt to the college had grown by $250 dollars, interest free, until at graduation I owed $1,000 dollars.

I thought I was in heaven to be free from the prison of the tool company, and was delighted with Prexy's first sermon on "The Bible as History and Symbol," interpreting this to mean that that great work of literature was not the dictation of a Great Brain in the sky but the product of finite human beings groping for enlightenment.

Our huge lecture class in "Survey of the Universe and Human Society," required of all freshmen and taught by an inspired, very young Columbia graduate, covered the evolutionary background of the heavens and the earth. The course encouraged my agnosticism enough so that when I read in the *Campus* of a $1,000 dollar prize offered by a businessman for an essay on the subject "The World Does Not Owe Me a Living," I thought I would solve insolvency and satisfy apostasy by writing about my love of the Christian ethic as a creed embracing equal opportunity for all people and about my skepticism toward institutionalized religion and the capitalist ethic as a money-grubbing defilement of that creed. I could stand on my own feet and by sheer personal grit earn my own way.

When I showed my essay to the wisest student I knew, Hiram Crommett, a crabbed apple of a guru from Down East Maine, he took me in tow to visit Ferd Mann, the Marxist editor of the *Campus,* who read my effort with greater and greater glee. When he finished, he chortled, "From the mouths of babes! This won't win the prize, but I sure hope you submit it!"

Right on both counts.

When my friend Rollin Campbell came in to discuss a writing assignment from Dr. Beers on Wordsworth's *Ode: Intimations of Immortality,* I was in awe of the poem but having some trouble with it. A word like *intimations* didn't register for me. It wasn't in my vocabulary. "Rawl" understood the poem better than I. In fact, he seemed to have an instinct for it. I liked its majesty. It had a swing that appealed to my sense of rhythm, and what Wordsworth was talking about reminded me of an experience I had as a boy when I walked into a birch grove and for the first time felt a sense of myself as a person inhabiting a world that seemed to fit me hand in glove. It could be called a religious experience, but it had nothing to do with born-again Christianity, dominated in Northfield by D. L. Moody and in North Leverett by a series of tent camp-meeting evangelists who came to New England from Scotland.

I really didn't know enough about my belief or about Rollin's to confide in him the root of my problem, but I felt that the language in the poem was probably closer to his belief than to mine. I had the feeling that there was a rebelliousness in Wordsworth that made him more comfortable in the woods than in church, yet I couldn't be sure. Words like *soul* and *God* seemed to communicate something different to him than to me. I didn't believe in any great overseeing intelligence out there in space, and I wished I could say for sure that that was not what Wordsworth intended. But what *did* he intend? Anyway, Rollin and I chewed the rag in the presence of those great cadences, which shielded a meaning that I for one didn't have more than an inkling of but was trying to discover:

> Our birth is but a sleep and a forgetting:
> The soul that rises with us, our life's star,
> Hath had elsewhere its setting,
> And cometh from afar:
> Not in entire forgetfulness,
> And not in utter nakedness,
> But trailing clouds of glory do we come
> From God, who is our home.

I wanted to print those rhythms, those images, on my mind so that years later they would come back to me with no need to look in a book to be prompted.

Rawl seemed surer than I. There was a distance between him and me and at the same time a closeness, as if we were admiring the same words and getting meanings equally significant but not the same. Rawl had a good deal to say of the next part, about "Shades of the prison-house begin to close / Upon the growing boy." I had some feeling for these lines, yet I would say that for myself they didn't describe my life, which was more like a new life suddenly springing out of a cocoon. Back there at the Millers Falls Tool Company I was not trailing any clouds of glory as I was that morning when I was nine years old and walked into the birch grove. I lost the clouds of glory in the stockroom. If I were ever to get them back, it would be Middlebury that opened the cocoon and brought back my birthright. Wordsworth's poems were sublime—that business about the "still, sad music of humanity" showed the power of true feeling. I thought of Pop and Mom. Wordsworth described what happened to Pop. Up there on Northfield Mountain, when he used to bring Mom wildflowers, he was a dreamer. Even though he was getting more and more deeply absorbed in the struggle to support a growing family, he carried his dream with him:

> The youth, who daily from the east
> Must travel, still is Nature's priest,
> And by the vision splendid
> Is on his way attended.

Working on the section gang and in the tool factory, he lost the vision: "At length the man perceives it die away, / And fade into the light of common day." I thought Mom hadn't lost the vision, but she had lost the opportunity to grasp it. She was trying to pass it on to her boys. I wanted my life to be an opening out and out and out that never stopped expanding until I stopped. And then where did it go?

I wasn't disheartened, because I knew where I was headed, and Middlebury was infinitely better than any place I'd ever before been in or dreamed of.

In my junior year one of the bonuses I got from taking Pud Fish's course in harmony and counterpoint was going down to the practice rooms in the basement of Music House and trying out my composition for the week. At first I felt guilty for sneaking in when others were paying rent for the use of these rooms. But I had no money for such frivolity, and I soon rationalized away my guilt. I was hurting nobody by using a piano squatting there idle and useless. I soon began to carry along music brought from home and got back to work on "Minuet à L'Antique" and "Marche Militaire."

One Sunday afternoon, feeling frustrated because I had nothing special to do, I drifted over to Music House to see if someone was practicing. The front door was locked, but I went down the slope along the side of the building and tried the windows of vacant practice rooms along the back side. In one window the bottom sash was unlocked, and without any effort I was able to push it up and enter the room. Soon I was pounding away, responding to some internal hunger for visceral self-indulgence, as if somewhere down in my bowels was a musical gland demanding to be stroked. I had only the two pieces, but it would take time to get them anywhere near back to where I had left off two years before with Miss Lincoln.

In short order, I was infected with the music, and the next weekend, back again in the same

The Northfield Farms house, about 1920

The author's parents, Mertie Abbie Briggs Glazier and Harry Lee Glazier, 1908

room, I began to think of that special piano as my piano, not to possess it but to consider it the one I would practice on when it was free. By some magic, it seemed always to be free when I needed it. I began to go down once in a while on a weekday afternoon. Professor Hathaway heard me one day and came down to see who was playing. He walked in on me and, without saying a word about my using the piano without permission, asked if I would like to take lessons from him every two weeks. He didn't charge me for them. Pud Fish had spoken to him about my singing in the choir, but not about my piano-playing. I went for a lesson the next week, and he gave me a short, slow piece, "To a Wild Rose" by MacDowell, through which I could rationalize that musical feeling was more important than dashing technique. I loved it. He also assigned scales and arpeggios.

Professor Hathaway had just returned from a sabbatical in England, where he studied with a prominent British pianist-teacher who had a new technique for improving speed. Instead of lowering the wrists to concentrate the weight of the arm on the finger playing each note, he had me lift my wrist above the keyboard, freeing the fingers to fly over the keys. I had become so persuaded that Miss Lincoln's method was right for producing deep rich tones that I was struck with the way the new method freed the fingers from tension and let them rip and tear up and down scales. It was exhilarating. At the same time I didn't entirely renounce Miss Lincoln's technique. Especially in the slow romantic movement of the MacDowell, I loved to bring out melody and make it sing, as if not only my upper arm but my whole body had somehow lent its force to a lyric movement.

To my surprise, Professor Hathaway seemed to like both my tip-of-the-finger scales and the depth of tone I managed to persuade from the piano when playing "To a Wild Rose." He invited me to play the piece at his spring festival, and I went to work on it in earnest. Not only did I feel a possessiveness about the three pieces I could play, but the Music House became one of my haunts. I knew I was musically ignorant, but I didn't allow myself to be bothered with that. It was as if I built myself a small province within the musical universe and decided to be master of that infinitesimal domain. I also heard from a Middlebury choir member that the Methodist church on Seminary Street, northeast of the corner where the white Congregational church stood, was in need of voices. My choirmate (a Methodist) took me there one Sunday morning for rehearsal, and I became a member of that choir. I heard also about the student chorus conducted by Madame Hayden, the ancient, retired grand opera singer who had her office across the hall from Professor Hathaway's. She stopped me in the hall one day, arresting me with the quavering lost grandeur of her deep gone-to-seed contralto, and I became a member of her chorus.

It was as if for the first time I began to be liberated body and soul and I was free to splurge on whatever luxury my spirit fancied. I read in the *Campus* that Professor Goodreds was holding auditions for a series of short plays, and I went down and found a small part in a Chinese tone poem. None of the actors knew Chinese. From the start we were coached in letting our voices rise and fall in a crescendo/decrescendo of modulations that had less to do with verbal than with tonal communication. At rehearsals I had no idea what I was saying or whether I was saying anything. We were a group of peasants going into the fields with empty baskets and returning with sheaves piled on top of our heads. The student director paid no attention to the meaning of the sounds we were making; rather, he pushed us back and forth and around this way and that way onstage as if we were trees in motion swaying in the breeze. It was only at dress rehearsal, when for the first time Professor Goodreds took command, that I comprehended how fully we were only accessories to the painted setting, the quavering music of a flute, and the voices of the two stars—suppliant, willowy manikins in delicately beautiful Oriental dress, and with almond eyes, jet-black hair, and olive complexions. They swayed across stage like reeds in a wind. Their voices rose and fell like a waterfall. We were all of us, and the stage setting, the lighting, and the musical backdrop, instruments being played by the director, who had known since before the first rehearsal exactly the effect he would achieve.

A poem I started in Beers's class the first day of first semester appeared in the *Saxonian*:

Smell of the Fresh Turned Soil

Smell of the fresh turned soil
Tells me that I, living, am part of the unliving,
And the unliving part of me.
I would like to envelope the world,
To press my identity,
To claim the parentage that is mine
I know not how.
This, my bone and my flesh,
Was it not conceived in her womb,
And suckled at her fertile breasts?
"Great foster-mother!
Can't you hear my voice?
Can't you feel me pressing against you,
And digging my fingers into your side
To bring you closer,
And fuse our two beings
Into the one which we really are?"

—Lyle Glazier, 1933

A couple days after the poem appeared I got a letter from Dean Barney: "Dear Lyle, While I'm not a poet or a critic of poetry, I know what I like, and I like your poem."

I liked his criticism.

When I graduated I had A grades in calculus, French, geology, psychology, and first-semester harmony and counterpoint, and Bs in all other courses except freshman Latin (79) and the history of French literature (73). In creative writing I got 94 for the year, and my personal essay ("The Book Lady"—about the wispy librarian in Northfield Farms) was published in Warren Bower's *College Writer* in the fall of 1933.

Highest honors that year went to another English major, Amy Niles, a farm daughter from Bennington who was valedictorian, class poet, and winner of a graduate fellowship from the Proctor family (Vermont Marble Works) to study at the University of London during the Depression year 1933–34.

Unable to get a job teaching high school (only two members of our class did) and with no backing for graduate school, I stayed on as janitor of the Community House and correcter of freshman English papers for an English professor and enrolled in a graduate course in Milton and another in the American short story.

I had no money for socializing and took care of my own sexual needs, except for a couple of brief encounters at the very end of my senior year—one with the cleaning boy at Calvi's Restaurant, and the other with a middle-aged bank teller who wanted relief with nothing given in return. I was hard up enough to accept him for a while but soon dropped him. I knew I was a homosexual but dreaded being classified as one.

On October 9, 1933, when I was twenty-two, I had word from Northfield that my father had lost his job in the tool factory and shot himself. By the time I got home that evening, my mother had escaped from the family and sought refuge by drowning in the Connecticut River, a quarter-mile west of our house. I brought my thirteen-year-old brother Larry back to Middlebury and for the next six years was *in loco parentis,* providing his chief support during the rest of that year at Middlebury and in 1934–35, when we returned to Northfield, I as principal of the Center Graded School and Larry as a sophomore in high school. When I be-

came housemaster at Mount Hermon School for Boys for two years (1935–37), Larry was my dependent, with free tuition and board and room. In 1937, when after three summers at the Bread Loaf Writer's School I had earned an M.A. and was rewarded with a job teaching English at Bates College in Lewiston, Maine, I paid for Larry's tuition at Hermon, and then for two years at Middlebury. In the summer of 1940 he took over control, first working a year at the Millers Falls Tool Company, then becoming a bombardier in the air force, chiefly from a base on New Guinea bombing targets in the Philippines, before returning to Middlebury, then to the University of Vermont for an M.A. and a lifelong career as a bang-up good high school teacher of English.

I was too ignorant to realize that the pattern for my sexual life had been established in a conflict between two equally important needs: the visceral and elemental need for sex with an adult male, and the social need for marriage and a family. After graduating from Middlebury, I carried on a furtive but more

The author (front row, second child from right) at Glazier family Thanksgiving gathering, about 1924

Bronze blue

in greenery

the Siamese Pan

cups his extended palm

as if to invoke

a handful

of rain

(From *Double Vision*)

"The Ancient City," Bangkok, Thailand

and more active homosexual life that was by no means flagrant and included only one encounter at Bates with a student, when I could persuade myself that he took the initiative, propositioning me during summer vacation.

I was also carrying on relationships with women, and in June 1934, in the loneliness of backlash from my father's and mother's suicides, I somewhat condescendingly asked a wonderful girl to marry me. I was quite sure of her, for she had actively courted me for two years before giving up. She showed me her engagement ring, recently accepted from her high school sweetheart. I was crushed, more through vanity than through passion, and wrote her an emotional letter, to which she replied that her burning love for me had worn out, but "I love you still. It's possible to love more than one person at a time, and although I have now chosen Andrew, I will always love you, too."

As a matter of fact, our love endured throughout her lifetime, a quiet romance that her husband never had reason to fear, nor did my (future) wife, who also knew about it. The last time we met, when I visited her at the prosperous farm her husband and his brother had developed over the years, she was entertaining a college girlfriend, and when I left, she made a point of firmly insisting on a lin-

gering kiss on the mouth. On both sides it was a deep and enduring platonic affection.

At Bread Loaf in the summer of 1935 I was sedulously courted by a homosexual teacher in the Chicago public schools, and in the summers of 1936 and 1937 I took a crush on a young junior from Ephraim College who, like me, was waiting on table. He took a shine on me for my high grades and reputation from two creative writing seminars with Ted Morrison.

The Bread Loaf English Summer School and Bread Loaf Writers' Conference were a shaping influence on my need for lyric expression both in poetry and in fiction. In 1935 I took creative writing and a course in English prosody with Ted Morrison. Under his influence I wrote my first lyric short story (on an anecdote furnished by Mom on her first job, when she was fifteen, as housekeeper for a stingy storekeeper in North Leverett). This story about Mom opened the gate to the series of prose narratives (fictional and autobiographical) and poetry that have been a seminal part of my lyric writing over a lifetime. From 1936 to 1941 a driblet of my poems was published in *American Prefaces* at the University of Iowa. I was trying to find a voice and couldn't settle on metric and rhymed exercises or unshaped free verse in a more intimately personal statement.

At Mount Hermon School for Boys an elderly science professor, Mr. Stark, offered me the use of the "sky parlor" on a turret with a staircase opening out of his kitchen, and I did my scratching up there with a view looking out over the Connecticut River basin to Northfield Mountain to the southeast and the plateau where from 1915 to 1919 we had lived in a shanty when Pop was a marker in Gramp's sawmill in a saddle on top of the mountain, where the reservoir for Four Mile Brook Pumping Station now stands. It was in that room that for two years I found afternoon relief from the strenuous supervision of more than a hundred boys in the dormitory of South Crossley.

I formed the habit after lights-out of strolling along the edge of the pond into the woods west of campus and returning a half-hour or an hour later. I was glad when the end of June came and it was time to return to Bread Loaf.

At the Writers' Conference in 1936, when Robert Frost came for his yearly lecture, Ted Morrison, then director of the conference, asked me to write out a couple questions for Frost to answer during his Yankee farmer-poet yarn-spinning that always preceded his reading.

Admiring Frost short of idolatry, and having only one afternoon to prepare my questions, my first attempt was an old chestnut: "Can you tell us about your connection with the founding of Bread Loaf and what it has meant to you and the development of poetry?" I knew he had discussed that before and worn it out, but I couldn't seem to come up with anything else. In desperation I wandered across the meadow to the brook trickling down from the mountain and sat by the dammed-up swimming hole, and finally, just before going to set up the staff table for dinner, I scratched out: "When, if ever, will the United States produce a poet who will speak not simply for a region but for the whole nation?"

Frost began his reading with the remark that Ted Morrison had just given him two questions. Opening the folded paper, he read the first question as if scanning it for the first time, spoke on it for a couple of minutes, then read the second one, and launched into his reply. It was obvious that behind all he said about regionalism and national consciousness was his preference for the latter, and his unspoken hope that in time it would be discovered that he

was that national poet. He never mentioned his ambition in so many words, but it lay behind his every illustration of a regional poet; he would move on from each such example to the broader question of producing a poetic voice for the entire United States. He gave up scrutinizing the question only when there were voices raised for "'Birches,' Mr. Frost, 'Birches.'" Whereupon he called for a copy of his *Collected Poems* and launched into a reading.

Ted caught up with me on the way from the theater, and invited me to attend the postlecture staff coffee hour in Treman Cottage. "Lyle, Robert loved your question."

It was the first time I'd ever heard anybody refer to the poet by his first name, and I was inflated at the thought of standing on the edge of such intimacy. At Treman I found Charlie DuBois and Dottie and Dick Gould and a couple other hoi polloi hovering around the fire. It may not have been true for the others, but my ears were tuned for scraps of immortality falling from the lips of Frost and Louis Untermeyer across the room.

We were talking about Roosevelt's campaign for a second term, and in short order Dick and I were blasting away at each other, he defending free enterprise, and I defending what I called "an evolution toward socialism." It became clear that Frost's eyes and ears had shifted from Untermeyer to our group by the fireplace, and in a few minutes he drew up a chair with us: "You young whippersnappers are out to change the world, but when you reach my age, you'll be hanging on for dear life to your upper-middle security." He went on in that vein, attacking Roosevelt's "Second New Deal" as a mere political gambit, until finally I'd had enough and said, "I voted for Norman Thomas in 1932 and will vote for Roosevelt come November. I think he has launched a socialist revolution."

For a half-hour he and I had it hot and heavy until he said, "I'm tired. Thanks for listening to an old man. I have to help Louis find where he's sleeping."

I was thinking how I'd thrown away my chance to impress the great man when Charlie said, "Lyle, you gave him the opening he was looking for. You lucky dog, you."

Ted came over and said, "Lyle, I'm supposed to show Louis his room on the third floor of Maple. If I give you his key, will you show him? The first door on the right at the top of the stairs."

Charlie went along as we crossed the street and followed the poets laboring up two flights of stairs. At the top I forged ahead and was trying to turn the key in the lock when from the inside a woman's voice screamed, "Get away from my door!"

Untermeyer pushed me aside, pretending to be forcing his way in: "I bet she has my anthology on her bedside table waiting for me to autograph it. *I'll* autograph her anthology!"

Frost was hauling at his coattail. There was silence in the room, then a phone ringing, and we could hear her distraught voice but not what she was saying.

I got the key and said Charlie and I would scoot over to the office and be back in a jiffy. We left Frost and Untermeyer in the john at the top of the stairs, Frost turning down the stool cover for a seat and Untermeyer leaning against the washbowl. Halfway along to the inn we met the night clerk, anxious to repossess the key and show Untermeyer where he really was being put up for the night.

In the summer of 1937, Amy Niles came to Bread Loaf to take Ted Morrison's course in creative writing and, as she said later, "to research Lyle Glazier." For some reason Ted refused to accept her into his seminar, but waiting on table, like me, she had the misfortune to have him at her table, where she had to endure his late arrival for breakfast and recitals at length to his tablemates of long passages of *The Canterbury Tales,* which he was transcribing into modern English.

She and I had a tiff the second or third day and recovered only at the very end of the session when, on the footbridge to Gilmore Cottage, we mended our breach with a kiss, just in time for me to meet her father and mother, whom she had invited to meet me. After returning from England, she had earned an M.A. at Brown with a thesis on British travelers' accounts of America and had taught high school English for a year in Mendon, Massachusetts, a small town near Worcester, where I visited her. Now she had just obtained a new teaching job in Le Roy, New York, south of Rochester, and as soon as exams were over, she went to Bennington to prepare for it, leaving an invitation for me to visit her at the end of the Writers' Conference. Having earned my M.A., I was feeling high from having just been hired to teach English at Bates College in Lewiston,

twenty-five miles northeast of Portland, Maine, on the Androscoggin. Prexy Moody had recommended me.

On a Sunday in spring I was invited to dinner at the home of Gus Bushman, chairman of Bates's German Department and also of the committee to choose guest speakers. He lived on a side street west toward the river. His wife served a hearty German dinner with beef and dumplings and sauerkraut and a heavy apple strudel. Afterward Gus invited me to walk their dachshund with him and their two children. Almost at once we were on a path leading across railroad tracks to the bank of the Androscoggin in a riverside grove I had never explored. I had not realized I lived so near such parkland. We could look across to the factories lining the bank on the western shore.

Madras, India

On the Road to Tirupathi
Ootacamund Recalled

At Ooty one morning
in a swirl of mist
three country women
balancing baskets of produce
drifted across my vision
silent as rain;
they whirled into the thoroughfare
turned to confront me
and vanished,
an instant ballet
without patter
of sound

(From *Double Vision*)

I could hardly contain myself. I wanted to run on the paths, but we were confined to a slow progress with a toddler and a baby in a carriage and a fat dachshund firmly leashed.

From then on to the end of the semester, the riverbank became my haunt for correcting papers. I found a spur of rock leading out a rod into the current where there was a natural seat; there, ruminating over a comment, I could lift my eyes into the turgid flow of the river or gaze unseeingly across to the Bates mill on the distant shore.

Amy and I started writing oftener, almost daily. She came to visit in Lewiston, where I introduced her to my close friends and my chairman. Although I thought of myself as homosexual, I had an intense desire to have the respectability of marriage and a family, and my affection for Amy, spurred by her pursuit of me, seemed genuine. It was as if I were neither hetero nor homo but simply sexual, so that I could know without fully realizing it the innocence of both needs, provided I could strike a balance—which meant that I could never resort to violence or take advantage of a younger person, especially a younger person under my supervision, unless that person took the initiative, and then only with great caution.

I had my first absolute love affair with Skip, a young Bread Loaf admirer from Ephraim College who was, I knew, hetero, so although he took a lead in horseplay, I knew a deeper relationship was hopeless. In the summer of 1938 Skip persuaded me to buy a secondhand Chevy roadster and drive him to the West Coast to visit relatives and friends and his high school sweetheart, who had become a vocalist with a swing band in Seattle. On the way there, two nights west of Chicago, to my surprise and great joy, his roughhousing became sexual, and for nearly six weeks we were lovers, an experience that grew more intense after his Seattle girlfriend announced she had lost interest. On the way back, in the late afternoon of the eve of the September hurricane, we arrived at Amy's lodging in Le Roy, where we were expected for overnight. The next morning at breakfast talk was of a great storm with hurricane force already striking the East Coast.

Somewhere south of Bath the storm broke, and we stopped to change drivers and fasten side curtains more securely. Before Skip could start the engine, he gave me a pat on the knee and said, "Well, Little Lyle, good buddy,

"Marine Drive," Madras, India

Against the curve of the basin
in the round pool
across the Marine Drive
from the statue of the Mahatma
conspicuously modest
in his loincloth,
a lotus
pink and exultant
lifts from scalloped pads
flat on the water:
nature affords magnificence
with no affront
to the democracy
of the attendant plain

(From *Double Vision*)

I hope you have enjoyed our trip as much as I have."

It was too much. I cried, "I love you, Skip. You are not my buddy. I love you. Somebody has got to know. I know it's the end, but I have to tell you how I feel about you. This trip with you has been the high point of my life. All I can say is, I love you, I really love you."

After a long silence he said, "I wish you hadn't said it. It makes all the difference."

We drove through the hurricaned streets of New England, and I left him at Ephraim College. At Lewiston I sold the car to the same dealer I bought it from for the same price—$200.

Amy was rebelling against her domineering mother and sister and looked on me as offer-

"Taj Mahal," Agra, India

The one perfect poem
is Taj Mahal
without blemish
except a few scars
scratched by time
and human vanity;
I can almost forgive
the social parasite
who could produce
a serene unfeeling
work of art
out of spiritual
anguish and physical
depletion of tenacious
human beings

(From *Double Vision*)

ing a refuge in genuine affection. On the way to Easter vacation, I didn't stop in Boston or Northfield on the way to Bennington. It had all been arranged that, the first night after supper, before doing dishes, Mrs. Niles would go into their bedroom and Amy and Olive into the front sitting room.

Mr. Niles and I sat at the table. I got right down to business: "Mr. Niles, I've asked Amy to marry me, and she wants me to ask permission from you."

I could see it was an important occasion for him. He said, "Amy appears to think a good deal of you. Do you think she and you can make a go of it financially? I know you have your brother to support."

"Amy and I have given a good deal of thought to it. Larry will be working somewhere this summer. I try to pay his board and room and tuition. Amy is going to try to find some kind of teaching job in Lewiston. I know for a fact that Lewiston High School is not going to hire an English teacher this coming year, but I don't know about Auburn. Larry says that if he can make it through this year, he will take a year off and go to live with Clayton and work in the factory. That way, when he goes back to college, he will pretty much take care of his junior year the same way I did when I went there as a freshman."

"What about this coming year?"

"If Amy and I can find a small apartment, we think that what I now pay for room and board will come close to supporting us."

"Do you have any reason to think you have a steady job there?"

"I talked to my chairman. He has already met Amy. He knows I'm thinking of getting married."

"Well, Lyle, as far as I know, you are a hard worker and a man of good character. Mrs. Niles and I have talked this over, and I guess I can speak for us both. If Amy wants you, you have my consent."

On the morning of July 15, 1939, I was staying out to Gramp's. Melvin in Greenfield was supposed to pick up my powder-blue jacket and white flannels from the dry cleaner.

He phoned me. "Were there supposed to be some pants, too? I got only a jacket. They said that was all there was."

"Look, tell them, find my britches. I'm an hour late already. I'm sitting here in my underwear."

A half-hour later: "They found your pants in sludge at the bottom of the vat. Had to wring them out and press them."

"You got them?"

"Yes. Bernice and I'll be there in three-quarters of an hour."

"You're already two and a half hours late. I'm supposed to be in Bennington, to call Amy. I have to pick up Larry at Mount Hermon."

"He called me. Clayt can't come. Had to work. Larry will come with Rena."

At my feet I had the boxed orange kitten from Gramp. I thought we would name him Junior to make people talk.

Mel and Larry held us up more at the Bennington Blue Diner. I was pacing the spaces between tables.

Amy's voice over the phone was sweet and short; she didn't mention that my call came three hours late.

"I still have to dress. I spent the morning at the hairdresser's. Dad planted two hemlock on the back lawn. Dug in east pasture. He heard a 'Huff!' and a cub bear made off in the blueberry brush. Dad shouldered the saplings out of there."

White dress, white roses, pink such pink cheeks, on Olive's arm she came around the corner of the ancient house to where we waited, Larry and Rollin and I.

Lyle Glazier and his daughter Laura, "coming down our back stairs in the rain," 1942

On the way into the parlor, Rawl jumped ahead of Mother, puffing toward the screen door. "Congratulations on your new son."

As if put on ice with the chicken and egg sandwiches, "That remains to be seen!"

Even after the two hundred miles to Lake Elmore, what Mother said was not enough to dampen my spirits.

At the lake cottage at midnight, in the upstairs unfinished bedroom, I crawled in, bare naked, beside my wife, and helped her out of Olive's wedding present, my mind on her contentment.

A half-hour later on the path uphill to the shithouse, I paused, naked, the night vibrating. After taking my pee, I hurried back downhill and upstairs to crawl into bed beside my naked and fragrant wife.

Coda: Two days later, in the mail, the *Bennington Banner* announced: "Big doings out at Nileses' yesterday. Walter lost his best heifer broke out of pasture, lost his daughter, and saw a bear."

Amy became the planner and organizer of our life, and I the beneficiary and, therefore, the governor by her consent. Her plan was not to have children for at least five years until I had security, either through tenure, my writing, or an advanced degree, the last of which hardly interested me. I had a chance to take over a course called "Six Poets" (Robinson, Milton, and Tennyson the first semester; Wordsworth, Keats, and Shelley the second semester), and that became the focus of my teaching. My method was the opposite of academic scholarship. I believed it was more important to learn to read poetry through an analysis of texture and argument than through reading critical analyses. I was especially interested in poetry as verbal music (metrical point and counterpoint), in poetic imagery, and in the flow of a sentence through the poem. I read Ransom's *The World's Body*, a book that became my ars poetica.

Amy got a job teaching creative writing at Bliss Business School downtown. When, in October, three months after we were married, she became pregnant, it was for her a great blow. I was secretly delighted. Our first daughter, Laura (for Amy's mother) Mary (for my mother's mother and any number of friends), was born July 30, 1940, two weeks after our first anniversary.

In the summer of 1941 Amy's mother became ill with the beginning of terminal cancer. Amy and Laura spent six weeks on the farm while I went to Bread Loaf to study under Ransom—a course in British seventeenth-century lyric—and, with Ransom and Theodore Meyer Greene of Princeton, a seminar in the arts and the art of criticism. I took also a course in Spenser with Donald Stauffer, chairman of English at Princeton. The seminar was preregistered with graduate students from Ivy League universities, and Greene thought that I, with an M.A. from Bread Loaf, did not qualify, but Mr. Ransom became my champion and prevailed. At the end of the summer I had become the star of all three courses—fortunately, because I needed their recommendations. To give tenure to their Rhodes scholar, the Bates administration and my chairman had fired me to make room for him.

On January 1, I received from Stauffer an offer of a full fellowship at Princeton—and a week later a note saying that all fellowships in the humanities had been canceled to provide for work in departments making a direct contribution to the war effort. On the strength of recommendations from all three summer 1941 Bread Loaf professors, I had offers from Tufts, Connecticut Wesleyan, and Swarthmore and chose to go to Tufts, from where, in the fall of 1942, I enrolled in one graduate course at Harvard, a course in neoclassical criticism with George Sherburn, who—to my astonishment—had me read my paper at his apartment on Commonwealth Avenue and gave me an A-minus.

From fall 1942 through the spring, summer, and fall of 1943, I earned an A-minus in four courses and passed the matriculation examination for the Ph.D. Then Sherburn (with whom I also took a course on Swift and Pope) met me on a crosswalk with bad news: "Glazier, we had a meeting of the department where it was decided that it's unfair for you to take one course a semester and get an A-minus in all of them when you are competing with students taking a full load of four courses. The decision has been made to allow you credit for an M.A. but not for a Ph.D."

"Dr. Sherburn, I teach four courses of freshman English a semester at Tufts, reading papers for 120 students, who write five hundred words a week (sixty thousand words a week, week in and week out). I doubt if your full-time students are working harder than I am.

Besides, I have an M.A. from Middlebury, and I won't take one from Harvard."

"What *will* you do?"

"I'll try to see if I can change my major to American studies, where I can perhaps use English literature as a minor."

So in the spring of 1944 I took the best course I ever took anywhere, Arthur Meyer Schlesinger's "American Social and Intellectual Literature," whose theme was exactly my meat—that the New Deal had changed American life by putting it on the road to a grassroots, U.S.-brand secular socialism.

Somewhere along about April I got my draft notice and was classified 4-F because of my parents' double suicide. Our second daughter, Susan, was born in the Lying-in Hospital in Boston. And I had an offer from Theodore Spencer to assist in his Shakespeare seminar for exactly the same salary I was getting at Tufts—$1,800 a year.

Shortly afterward I met Dr. Sherburn again, and this time he told me, "Glazier, you may be interested. We have decided that if you will come full-time, we will accept you as a doctoral candidate on trial." So in the fall of 1944 I took four courses and got two A's and two A-minuses.

By the end of the fall semester of 1945, I had passed the reading examination in German as well as those for French and Latin. Mentioning this to Dr. Sherburn, he informed me I'd also have to take reading exams in Old French, Old High German, and Icelandic.

"Dr. Sherburn, I'm a candidate in literature, not in linguistics. I won't take those examinations."

"It's pretty late to decide that. What will you do?"

"Shift back to American studies, if they'll take me."

The upshot was that the department dropped the requirement for those three language exams—and about time, because by then most candidates were in literature.

After two years of teaching English as a teaching fellow under Ted Morrison, I received an offer to become an assistant professor at the University of Buffalo.

During my last year at Bates I wrote more poems as well as a story called "Fisherman's Day" about a small boy in Northfield Farms getting up early to go up Four Mile Brook to

"Stonehenge," England

Enormous spindles
squat on Salisbury Plain
waiting the prick of dawn
to twist the skein of the sun

(From *Double Vision*)

fish for trout and seeing the day shift into midday and afternoon and into evening, when he was lying in bed waiting for the night train to pass on the track west of his house and put him to sleep. A fabric of imagery and mood shift, it seemed appropriate for the *New Yorker*. After a month I got a letter: "Send us something shorter soon." At Tufts, too busy for much writing except for a few poems I hardly had time to market, I did have stories published in the *Tuftonian* through a new poet friend, John Holmes, and in the spring of 1945 "Fisherman's Day" was printed in *Story* and listed in the Foley Index of the American Short Story as a distinctive story of the year.

I also won second prize in an international poetry contest judged by Ted Spencer and F. O. Matthiessen and served on the board of the literary magazine *Foreground*, funded by Reynal and Hitchcock as an investment for wartime excess profits.

When Ted Spencer called to tell me the pittance I had gleaned from the contest, he told me, "Mattie was especially taken with your poem 'The Adolescent,' and we both liked your ten lyrics and wonder if you are thinking of a volume." I didn't tell him that in 1942, in that last semester at Bates, I had read about the poetry publisher of *New Directions* and sent twenty

or so poems to James Laughlin. He sent them back just before we left Lewiston with a note saying that he had carried them around for several weeks and couldn't make up his mind, and wondered (too late) if I'd like to be his agent for Maine.

A follow up on Ted Spencer's remark that "Mattie was . . . taken with your poem": at the very end of 1947, on the eve of leaving Somerville/Cambridge, I went to hear Matthiessen speak to the Harvard English Club and afterward, talking to Henry Popkin, another editor of *Foreground*, was surprised when Matthiessen came directly up to us and asked if I had time to walk along with him to Harvard Square. On our way, he not only mentioned my lyric but quoted it in full:

The Adolescent

Hurt and dismayed, he will regret
each guilty spending of his life,
he will endorse the bitterest threat
against his passion's barbarous knife,

He walks with anguish in his feet
and in his breast the fire of hell,
what is this force, malign and sweet,
unbidden and unquenchable?

He will search out a secret place
within his vexed and narrow wood
where he will run and hide his face
from who would help him if they could.

"I particularly like the last line's twist of language." We parted at the entrance to the MBTA station, after I excused myself from his "Could we go for coffee? Do you have the time?" I was scheduled for a second orals the next day, after failing the first time because I froze on Perry Miller's "Discuss Wordsworth's 'Preface.'"

I knew the "Preface" well from having taught it in great detail over three years of my Bates "Six Poets" class. "Do you want me to discuss the date, the relation to the *Lyrical Ballads,* the relation between Coleridge and Wordsworth, Wordsworth's theory of the origin of poetry, his definition of the proper language for poetry, his conception of the poet as seer . . . ?"

I said this confidently, believing I had demonstrated considerable knowledge of the essay, but Miller said, with consummate acidity, *"Discuss Wordsworth's 'Preface!'"* And I clammed up in an emotional block. Dr. Sherburn, the committee chairman, for some reason had excused himself just before the exchange and came back into that harsh climate of absolute deadlock. I supposed that everybody assumed I knew nothing about Wordsworth.

Unfortunately, F. P. Magoun, the medievalist, was late for the second exam, and they put Miller first, and we tangled again, this time on Emerson's "Idealism." Again, I knew Emerson from five years of teaching American literature at Bates, but I couldn't put myself in sync with Miller's tone of voice. My mind jumped to Samuel Johnson's remark on the idealism of George Berkeley: "I confute him with this"—whereupon, lifting his gouty foot, he nearly killed himself by kicking against a rock. I said that when I thought of Emerson's belief that truth is something fed out through the mind and having no other existence, I was reminded of groping downstairs in the dark and tottering off balance because I was sure there was another step beyond the last step on the stair. The stupidity of my answer vexed me more than him, and I knew I would never pass an exam if he was on my committee and said so later to Sherburn, who said, "You haven't a ghost of a chance."

In the fall of 1947, in Buffalo, our third daughter, Alis Louise, was born in a clinic at the County Hospital on Grider Avenue. Six months later, after returning to Cambridge in the spring of 1948, I did well with the first question, from Magoun: "Discuss 'The Knight's Tale.'" I'd taken his course and knew he hadn't included that tale, but I had just read it with a tutorial student at Buffalo as an example of decadent courtly love.

I had a break also in the very last question in the exam. Harry Levin asked me to "define Joycian epiphany," and *Dubliners* was one of the books I included for freshmen at Harvard. I defined "epiphany" as a "revelation" and went on to declare that there are subjective and objective revelations in Joyce's fiction. Subjective epiphanies appear in "The Sister," "Araby," and "An Encounter," where the narrator reveals an epiphanic episode drawn from his experience; the stream-of-consciousness narrations of Stephen Daedalus (alter ego for Joyce) in *Ulysses* could also be called large-scale epiphanies. Objective epiphanies are found in "Ivy Day in the Committee Room," "Clay," and "The Dead," while in *Ulysses* the stream of conscious

of Poldy or Molly could be called objective. Somewhat naively, I said that this was all my own idea, that I had never read it anywhere. Levin said, "You needn't apologize. I think you are perfectly right." Adding this approval to Magoun's earlier comment, "Mr. Glazier has done very well. I have no further questions"—repeated twice when the chairman somewhat testily said, "You have five more minutes"—I was confident I had passed the examination.

"Blue Mosque," Istanbul, Turkey

In northern Ireland
Catholics and Protestants
blast each other's balls,
in Lebanon
Christians and Moslems
circumcize
and circum-circumcize
each other, my
Turkish friends
with a wicked glint
in their eyes
tell me steeples
are weapons aimed
to bring down God,
"But our minarets
are ethereal
stairs to climb to heaven,"
I agree with them
about steeples, with-
hold my judgment
on minarets, boxing
the compass, crouched
missile launching pads

(From *Double Vision*)

Two years later, at the end of April, I passed my final orals on a thesis written under Douglas Bush, "Spenser's Imagery: Imagery of Good and Evil in *The Faerie Queene*." Except for the first chapter on book 1, written as a term paper for Ted Spencer, the thesis was written in one summer when Bush was on vacation in New Hampshire; I sent it to him complete except he had suggested a final chapter on Spenser's imagery evaluated in the light of New Criticism.

I am telling this Harvard story as an example of academic absurdity. I nearly flunked out of the doctoral program, and yet, when I had the curiosity for the first time to write asking for a copy of my transcript about a year ago, I found no mention there of the second failed orals and at the conclusion of the record for the English Department was written, in parenthesis, "English 400," seeming to indicate that for my three semesters of graduate courses I had a four-point average. I am also sure that almost any other professor than Douglas Bush would have spurned a dissertation submitted with so little conference with the professor.

At Buffalo I started teaching an evening school course in American immigrant literature in 1948. Under a new chancellor, this course developed into an interdepartmental major in American studies, of which I became first chairman and on whose strength also I became the first Fulbright chairman of American studies at the University of Istanbul (1961–63). This appointment led in 1968 to a second Fulbright, this time at the new University Hacettepe (*Hacet* [shrine] and *tepe* [hill]). With Turkish economy of language, *Hacet* also means "shithouse," and indeed, there was an ancient and still-frequented *tuvalet* on a hill across from the university.

From Ankara I was invited to India for the summers of 1970 and 1971 to teach American literature to young teachers at branches of the University of Madras, and in 1971 to a U.S. Information Service all-India tour of six weeks lecturing on such subjects as "Mailer's *Why Are We in Vietnam?*" and "Cooper's *Leatherstocking Tales,*" or, "The American Decline of the West," "Martin Luther King and Malcolm X," and "Billy Budd and Bigger Thomas: Justifiable Sacrifices or Victims of Society?"

In the summer of 1967 I volunteered to teach remedial English at Miles College in Birmingham, Alabama, under the supervision of

The Glazier girls: (from left) Alis (two), Susan (five), and Laura (nine), 1949

John Munro, former dean of students at Harvard, and in 1980 was invited by the government of North Yemen to teach at Sana'a University with funds donated by Kuwait.

These trips abroad enriched my political, social, and literary horizons and provided new range for my poetry, as exhibited in such books as *Orchard Park and Istanbul* (Swallow, 1965); *The Dervishes* and *VD* (Istanbul Maatbasi, 1971), and the second half of *Two Continents* (Stinehour Press for the Vermont Council on the Arts, 1976), as well as my first novel, *Stills from a Moving Picture* (Paunch, 1974). I drew on my early life for my novel *Summer for Joey* (Millers River, 1987) and two books of autobiographical poetry, *Prefatory Lyrics* (Origin, 1980; Longhouse, 1986; Coffee House, 1991) and *Azubah Nye* (Origin, 1984; White Pine Press, 1988). *Searching for Amy* (part 1, Longhouse, 1991; part 2, tel let, 1993; parts 3 and 4, Shadow/Play, 1994; part 5, Shadow/Play, 1992) is collage (early life and foreign travel).

My book on the American novel, *American Decadence and Rebirth,* was published by Hacettepe

University Press in 1971, and another book of criticism, on the black experience in white America, *Great Day Coming,* was published in New Delhi by Raaj Prakashan (1987). In 1986 Bennington Colonial Press published my book on local history, *Bennington Politics and the Schools.* I am currently at work on a multivolume lyric (prose) autobiography, "WICKED . . . and Spotless as the Lamb."

The title is from Melville's 1841 letter to Hawthorne after finishing *Moby-Dick:* "I have written a wicked book, and feel spotless as the Lamb."

At University of Buffalo in the late '50s, John Crowe Ransom came to visit his fellow Oxonian friend Charles Abbott, Creator of the Poetry/Rare Book Collection, and to speak to the English faculty. In his lecture he spoke of the moral climate of *Moby-Dick,* sparking a response from a young professor of literature and psychology who shouted, "Melville said he had written an *evil* book!" A visitor from the University of Rochester and I were moved to protest at the same instant: *"Wicked!" "Wicked!"*

It is Ahab who has a vision of an evil universe governed by an all-powerful God who derives pleasure from putting mankind on the rack. This is Gloucester's vision and Lear's after they have lost their innocence: "As flies to wanton boys are we to the gods. They kill us for their sport." Ishmael's vision, like Melville's, is more subtle, making mankind responsible for their own suffering at the hands of often good men like Starbuck, or the lawyer in "Bartleby," whose view of the universe is dominated by manmade political correctness, especially by the principle that money and power are all-important. Even when they seem to get off scot-free, those who don't subscribe to this view are subtly punished.

With naivety and courage and high good humor and more risk than he could have fully comprehended, Melville revealed in his early books (*Typee, Omoo, White Jacket*) a proclivity for homosexuality and political iconoclasm that become basic threads in the fabric of his stories, and throughout his writing (*Moby-Dick, Pierre, Clarel, Billy-Budd*) homosexuality and political iconoclasm keep intruding in his narratives, even though timid critics deny it and would like readers to believe that the title of his posthumous novel should have been *Starry Vere* instead of *Billy-Budd, Sailor.* When he called *Moby-Dick* "wicked and spotless," he was stating a Thoreauvian protest against absolutist political correctness and proclaiming the innocence of people whose nonviolent nonconformity makes them victims of a predatory society.

In writing my book, I have tried to go back into my life and rid myself of present political biases and become the person having the experience. The method is lyric in the Wordsworthian sense: "poetry is the spontaneous overflow of powerful feelings: it takes its origin from emotion recollected in tranquillity." From this base, Wordsworth goes on to claim that the powerful feeling, or emotion, finds incidents, characters, images, language, bits of remembered conversation, to flesh out the moment described. "[I am] well pleased to recognize in Nature and the language of the sense the anchor of my purest thought, the nurse, the guide, the guardian of my heart, and soul of all my moral being." This is an apt description of his method in *The Lyrical Ballads,* where he created Joycian epiphanies unencumbered with the platonic vocabulary that corrupts later poems like *The Excursion,* in which scholars have traced instances of the older poet going back over his lines to substitute *God* for *Nature.*

I have aimed at an absolute honesty uncorrupted by a temptation to strike out whatever may offend in order to appease the sensibilities of people governed by institutionalized religion or ambition for money and power. Too much of current society is colored by a moral and social vision quite obsolete in the light of what is common knowledge about our physical universe. Scientists and political scientists are among the worst offenders and are guiltier even than politicians and religious fundamentalists of whatever faith, for the scientists are compromising the results of their own research. Equally guilty are postmodernist poets who believe any kind of political activism to be wrong. By withdrawing from altruism, they become conspirers with politicians and corporate executives who believe the most important thing is money. The ultimate falsehood, I believe, is to define democracy as identical with free-enterprise capitalism unbridled. No creed has ever been more ruthlessly materialistic and antisocial than the present-day corporate dictatorships that sacrifice the potential community of capital and labor. They will use any means for their own profit, and it is no accident that today the so-called U.S. democracy, proclaimed

The author's wife, Amy Louise Niles Glazier, about 1973

as the "most powerful nation on earth," could not survive without the Pentagon. I am proud that for twenty years in Bennington I have had the reputation of being "Mr. Negative" because I have spoken out against corruption locally, nationally, and internationally.

I could not for a moment write my poems and lyric fiction if I kept my mouth shut about corruption. However, at eighty-five, I am finding that the expense of spirit from speaking out does exact a toll. Writing my book sometimes seems to be a matter of writing a record not only of intense feeling but of paying a price. I rationalize that it would be easy to go through a manuscript and red-pencil out any passage that might offend a Victorian sensibility, but to do that would be fundamentally dishonest to the vision of life I am trying to create. When I am attacked and my feelings are hurt, that is part of the price I pay.

Amy used to get a quarterly alumni magazine from Brown University, and in one there was an article about research on the human brain's memory bank. A team of psychologists

and pathologists discovered through microscopic inspection that there are infinitesimally small, threadlike filaments, on which there are tiny follicles that seem to store the record of experience. They pondered what prompted such a record, and it occurred to me that Wordsworth's "spontaneous overflow of powerful feeling" might explain why some people seem to have the ability to go back and remember so many moments of ecstatic response or intense anxiety: "I hurt therefore I am."

This thought gives me a strange comfort. If I have this gift, I'm immensely grateful. It satisfies my desire for immortality. I don't need anything more. Whether or not anybody ever reads my record is not so important as that I should make it.

Beside a great block of granite in Bennington's Park Lawn Cemetery, my wife's grave is marked with an unobtrusive stone hardly a foot long and eight inches wide. On it is printed her name and the dates of her life: "Amy Niles Glazier. 1911–1987." My own name is printed under hers. When the Massachusetts Medical School in Worcester, Massachusetts, has finished with its experiments, what remains of my body will be cremated and the loose ashes scattered somewhere on the acre and a half of our Bennington property. The box with what ashes remain in it will be buried in a shallow slit in the ground opened in front of the stone. Then the earth will be filled in. I am indifferent as to whether or not the dates for my life are filled in. I leave that to the satisfaction of my three daughters and three sons-in-law. In time what will be planted there will be earth, good enough for anybody.

The author would like to thank his daughter Susan Glazier Swartz and his niece Linda Glazier Taylor for providing the family photographs which accompany this essay.

SELECTED POETRY

The Fisher

At half past four mornings in June
he met the sliding, slippery sound
of Four Mile Brook and liked the tune,
and liked the logroad morning hushed,
his bare feet liked the dew soaked ground

At half past ten he was headed for home
having fished his last last-hole for luck
the heat and noise of the day had come
but his bones kept the cool of the brookside
  shade
and his ears kept the whirlpool's silvery suck.

(From *Reflections on a Gift of Watermelon Pickle*)

*

7.

Morning air
is so clear here
and today so still
a herd of cows
four sheep
are pasted
like a child's cutout
white against green
on the opposite hill

(From "Vermont" in *Two Continents*)

*

17.

I walked in heaven
last night
from Dikem Evi
to Kizilay, Ankara's
streets star
bright a flute
ruffled trees
heavy with June
leaves trilling tunes
from Anatolian villages,
this boy full tilt
bumps me full on
twining till
we clasp
and on my way
amused
remembering
smiles, a room
with two ripe plums
and plum pits on a plate
orange crates crammed
with textbooks
and salaams
"My house is yours."

(From "Asia" in *Two Continents*)

*

The Shanties

1.

West window looks to the river
beyond houses
strung on a valley road
east window looks to the mountain

We hear the drag of the saw
a long time before
we see the dustcloud

A team is unloading in the bay
Perry snags logs with a canthook,
Maurice is sawing

Pop brings Mayflowers in April
swamp pinks in June
wild honeysuckle in July. . . .

(From *Prefatory Lyrics*)

*

Excerpts from *Azubah Nye*

I.

What does it mean
for my neuroticism
if I trace back
to Brushy Mountain
an Indian tiptoeing
from her father's tepee?
(I hear Jonathan's
whisper "Azubah! Azubah!"
and she came.) . . .

Under the neighboring sky
Jonathan, felling timber,
burned treestumps
under heaped-high brush
with you Azubah helping,
pitching in, quick
as a twittering catbird,
you liked
your golden boy.

Did you pick blackberries
for your family
on that high hill?
I'm sure you did,
surprising Jonathan
well pleased
with his bride

"Good!" he said
"good!" You glowed.
My mother was small
enough to walk
under my lifted arm,
a shy dark woman, so
dark Chester Goodwin
(my Black friend)
seeing her picture
liked her for Black,
a red Indian blowback, great
great grandchild, both sides
of my family spring
from you, Azubah, doubling
the Indian in me.
You gave the baby
berries, red juice
splashing his chin, you
laughed, Jonathan laughed
"Azubah, you did good."
The two of you,
—the black-haired black-eyed girl,
the boy with shining hair
and blue eyes, dry ice—
met first by chance
one afternoon on opposite sides
of a highbush blueberry
looking through.
Did he offer a handful
or did you court him? . . .

I fancy them standing
in a skirt of trees
till they fell
on a cushion of branches
balsam or hemlock or pine,
her small body
already moving
opening to admit him
too eager at first
but held inside and
growing again,
this time patient,
wondering at his power
and her will to submit,
now moving slowly
because of her. . . .

"An Indian girl . . ."
I read it first
in that memo
of Uncle Forrest's
"Jonathan Glazier
came to Brushy Mountain
in 1790.
He married Azubah Nye,
an Indian girl . . ."

III.

Two weeks ago
driving to Moores Corner
for Uncle Forrest's
Historical Society meeting
in the restored schoolhouse
I passed the valley house
its ridgepole sagging,
and, in uncropped hay,
a center beam
bought to replace rotten timber
and straighten walls
to be shored up.
You'd have to jack sills
ready to tumble
into that shallow cellar—
I hear the click
of trennel in the hand-forged latch
of the flimsy door
on the stairs
between pantry and kitchen
and smell mould
of aged earth down there,
gone with Gramp to fetch
apples from the bin
scooped under floorboards,
a kerosene lamp in his hand
held high to see
northern Spies, Wagners,
blue Pearmains, russets,
then upstairs at table
beneath the stinking lamp,
the *Youth's Companion* flat
under my eyes,
some yarn by C. A. Stephens
of Way Down East,
Gramp reading the *Recorder*
peeling, quartering, passing
a chunk on a shining blade,
"Here, Bunny,"
Gram hunched over mending
biting the thread off short,
Gramp's throat-rasp as he read,
my handthrust automatic
for each new offering,
eyes never lifted,
evening lengthening
in front of the bowlegged range
puggled in winter,
banked in summer,
hiding the fireplace, screened
to keep out drafts
sucked down the greasy chimney
into the soothole
concaving the length of the wall
between sitting room
and northwest bedroom, Gramp's
     and Gram's,

mine the small chamber
by the side entry
morning glories at the window
a hunting print on the wall,
red setter, white setter at point
the print visible at sunset
when we went early to bed
to the purl of water
piped from a mountain spring
into a chest-high barrel
flowing through sink
to back-kitchen
watering trough,
woodland gurgle
inside the house,
plumbing improved by Gramp
in the tremendous 'twenties
when he dismantled the trough
diverted the stream
to a tin funnel
in a closet tucked
behind pantry
and emptied by grumbling drainpipe
into chickenhouse runnel
ditched under road
to the river.

    That was a banner day
they ripped out
the three-holer inside backhouse
and tore out the corridor
masked from backdoor callers
by upright unplaned boards
along the length of the woodshed.
Their hifalutin living
scarcely outlasted
rebuilding the east ell
and opening the slanting roof
for a third upstairs bedroom
never finished off—
money ran out
when Gramp signed a note
for Caldwell
—"a fool and his money
soon parted"
—rather, "a good honest man
can always be fleeced
by a scoundrel. . . ."

    From time to time
he cut another pine
and, once fleeced,
never ventured again,
a glum old man at seventy,
at eighty resigned,
Gram dead from hawking her lungs
  out
in the northwest bedroom,
I gave her a clean rag

to spit into,
helped her turn over,
she never wanted
not even milktoast
I brought for lunch
"Don't bother."
She was dying,
Gramp at the mill,
I spending June vacation
between school teaching
and summer school,
nowhere else to go,
blotting from memory
my folks' death
how they died, . . .

    That was after
Pop had his job
in the stockroom
of Millers Falls Tool Company.
A calculus whiz,
he kept books for the foreman.
When he was dead Gramp realized
"I should've mortgaged
the place to get him
an education, I
never did know nawthin."
Anti-union
Pop thought himself
potential management
not a laborer.
Promoted when his boss retired
he was so grateful
he never got the raise
that should have come with the job,
went on working
at $30 a week
nine hours a day
& Saturday mornings
he worked along with his men,
never dressed to be foreman.
He must have gone stark crazy
the morning he was called in
(October '33)
"We have to let you go."
He was stealing
sacks of woodscrap
and oil for the Model A,
the true reason coming out later,
the job needed
for a nephew of one of the bosses.
The engine burned red hot
under his ten mile dash
back home where he was raised,
no time for thoughts of Mertie
or the boys, one still
at college, bell-hopping,
peeling spuds, anything
to keep going,

one still in school,
one graduated, jobless,
Mel jobless with his girl.
He passed the mill,
Gramp and Perry waving
above the idling saw,
on past the sandbank,
into the yard,
past Gram in the kitchen
"I need the shotgun
to kill a skunk out back"
ramming shells,
legging it to the barn
finger on trigger
what it had he got,
Gram rushing, Gramp
and Perry brought by cranky phone,
Mom told long distance
at a neighbor's,
remembering "I
don't know where
the money's coming from."

    That afternoon
she managed an apple for her sister
then hurried
to the barn privy, scuttled
down henyard stairs
across to the river road.
At the ferry landing
water rose to her knees,
her groin, her
waist, her mouth, her breath,
she floated,
there was nothing for artificial
    respiration
in sackclothes wedged
under oak roots a half mile on

BIBLIOGRAPHY

Poetry:

Orchard Park and Istanbul, Alan Swallow/Big Mountain Press, 1965.

You Too, Istanbul Maatbasi, 1969.

The Dervishes, Istanbul Maatbasi, 1971.

VD or Voices of the Dead, Istanbul Maatbasi, 1971.

Two Continents, Vermont Council on the Arts, 1976.

Azubah Nye, Origin, 1984, White Pine Press, 1988.

Recalls, Longhouse, 1986.

Prefatory Lyrics, Coffee House, 1991.

Searching for Amy (part 1), Longhouse, 1991, (part 2), tel let, 1993, (parts 3 and 4), Shadow/Play, 1994, and (part 5), Shadow/Play, 1992.

Fiction:

Stills from a Moving Picture, Paunch/State University of New York at Buffalo, 1974.

Summer for Joey, Millers River, 1987.

Nonfiction:

American Decadence and Rebirth: Representative American Novels (criticism), Hacettepe University Press, 1971.

Bennington Politics and the Schools, Bennington Colonial Press, 1986.

Great Day Coming: African American Experience as Recorded by Black Americans and White Americans, Raaj Prakashan (New Delhi), 1987.

Other:

(Contributor) *Reflections on a Gift of Watermelon Pickle,* Scott, Foresman, 1995.

Author of *Double Vision,* a collection of original poetry and photographs held in the Poetry/Rare Books collection at the State University of New York at Buffalo.

Poetry has been published in *American Prefaces, Beloit Poetry Journal, Country Journal, Golden Horn, Longhouse, Mouth of the Dragon, New University Thought, New Yorker, Origin, Partisan Review, Shadow/Play, tel let,* and other magazines; fiction has appeared in the *Alternate, Gay Sunshine,* and *Story Magazine;* scholarly articles in *Aligarh Journal of English Studies* (Aligarh Muslim University), *American Quarterly, College English, Fag Rag, Kansas City Review, Litera* (University of Istanbul), *Modern Language Studies,* and *University College Quarterly;* and general interest articles and reviews in *American Schoolboard Journal, Bennington Daily Banner, Free Inquiry, The Humanist, The Iconoclast,* and other publications. Represented in *Asian Response to American Literature,* 1971.

Ernest Hebert

1941-

Ernest Hebert, 1993

Since I first learned the alphabet, my efforts to write and be understood have been frustrated by darn near unreadable penmanship. Why this is so, I cannot say. As a boy, I learned to whittle, throw a fluttery knuckle ball, eat with a knife and fork, flip a coin and catch it behind my back, and pick my nose until the blood ran; by the time I was seventeen I could drive a car, smoke a Camel cigarette, shift gears, and keep my arm around the shoulders of my girl—all at the same time. So there's nothing wrong with my eye-hand coordination and dexterity. But even the Sisters of Mercy, who taught the Palmer method of penmanship at St. Joseph's School in Keene, New Hampshire, could not teach me to write legibly. Eventually, I lost interest in the entire business of setting down words.

From elementary school at St. Joe's I went on to Keene Junior and then Senior High School, where I (just barely) graduated in 1959. My junior year I received two D's and two F's in English, mainly because I wouldn't pass in written work; I graduated in the lower third of my class. I took the still-used ACT test required for application at Keene State College, and ended up with a sixth-percentile score in English. Ninety-four percent of the people taking the test did better than I, and accordingly I was denied admission to the state college in my hometown.

"My mother, Jeannette Vaccarest Hebert," 1940

I remember the words of the dean of admission, Fred Barry (who later went on to become a good friend): "Some people are cut out to go to college, some aren't."

I joined the army reserves, did six months' active duty, where I was trained as a supply clerk. Something very important happened during that training period: I was taught to touch type. I remember the instructor, the roughest, toughest son-of-a-gun the army could find. I think the brass must have thought that anybody can teach/persuade a young kid to shoot a gun, stick a bayonet into somebody, but it took a real man to make him type. Not that learning Q W E R T Y changed my attitude toward writing. It didn't occur to me that I could use the skill for myself; typing was for army paper work only.

Upon completing my six months of active duty, I went back into civilian life, and, with the recommendation of my maternal uncle, George Vaccarest, I was hired by the New England Telephone and Telegraph Company, as a central office equipment installer. Guys in that branch of what was then known as Mother

Bell used to joke, "I was a spy for C.O.E.I." All of northern New England was in the throes of a conversion from manual telephone offices (number puh-lease) to dial. I traveled with gangs of men in Massachusetts, New Hampshire, Vermont, and Maine installing relays, running cables, and wiring bays of relays. The color code of the wires remains in memory to this day tinged with an esthetic awareness the way another person might remember the flowers in a garden. As a telephone man, I thought of the colored wires departing from my solder connections as art; voicing the names of the colors in the proper sequence was my poetry: blue, orange, green, brown, slate; blue-white, blue-orange, blue-green, blue-brown, blue-slate; orange-white, orange-green, orange-brown, orange-slate; green-white, green-brown, green-slate; brown-white, brown-slate; slate-white.

My model of a telephone man was Harold Archer, a quiet fellow from Maine who took enormous pleasure in his work. Harold not only could wire a bay swiftly and accurately, but he could do it artistically. We used to tie the bundles of skinny colored wires with twine (called twelve-cord). Harold created sweeping bends, made beautiful stitches and solder joints; and he worked with passion, often getting so wrapped up in the job that he labored right through coffee breaks. When he was finished, guys would come over and admire his work. Harold Archer taught me to do as well as I could, to work with passion and commitment—that everything that can be made can be approached in its creation as a work of art. The thing itself, when it's finished, no longer belongs to the artist. It belongs to whoever can appreciate it, whether that's the vast public for a painter such as Vincent van Gogh or a bunch of telephone guys admiring a Harold Archer wiring job. The artist musn't dwell on his performance—he has to go on to the next piece. Harold Archer was such a soul, a maker. I'm sure that all those bays that Harold wired have been shipped off to salvage yards, replaced by electronic parts, but Harold's works will stand in my mind as great sculptures.

Like the rest of the fellows I worked with, I appreciated Harold for his skill, but at the time I never thought to emulate him. I couldn't see myself as an artist, as a maker of anything of esthetic value, and certainly not as a writer; I wrote no letters, no diary notes, no anything. But I was feeling restless. I didn't want to spend the rest of my work life with the phone company. In the world I came from, ambition ended with a job. You had a good job, you stayed with it, like my dad who worked as a weaver in a textile mill from the time he was sixteen until the mill shut down forty-five years later. I didn't discover how to go about finding what I needed until I went into the army for the second time. The year was 1961—I had just turned twenty-one.

We reservists were activated in the regular army for what was then called the "Berlin crisis." But a good deal of our training related to fighting in jungles and tropical regions. Nobody understood what was going on, but we knew that Berlin was not the top priority. Vietnam was years away, but somebody in the military was already gearing up for a conflict in Southeast Asia.

Though I was trained as a supply clerk I ended up a cannoneer on an eight-inch howitzer at Fort Bragg, North Carolina. Every morning units for the Eighty-second Airborne Division used to double-time by our barracks waking us up with a song that went something like this, "Hey, Legs, dirty Legs, fat Legs, ugly Legs." I don't know why they called us Legs; they were the ones on foot. We got to ride in the backs of the five-ton trucks that pulled the howitzers. These accurate, riffled bored weapons were fun for young guys to play with, at least in peace time. We used old World War II ammo. The 225-pound projectiles made big booms leaving the muzzle and picturesque explosions in the impact zones. The sounds left me with a slight middle-range hearing loss and a noise in my left ear—a sort of voiced hush sound—that lingers to this day.

I was lonely, mainly for the sight of women, but if I wrote letters I can't remember. What I do remember vividly are two incidents, one that led me to question just who I was and the other that served as a clarion call to give college another try.

One hot summer weekend, I took off with two other buddies to Myrtle Beach, South Carolina. We spent two days on the beach getting tans and (unsuccessfully) attempting to pick up girls. My dark skin and superb tanning genes, courtesy of my French-Canadian and Italian heritage, sucked up the rays very nicely. I already had gotten some sun, so I didn't burn at all, just got darker. On the way back to

base we stopped at a bar for a drink in a small town in South Carolina. The bartender looked me over; I thought he was going to ask me for an I.D. to check my age. Then he said, "Boy, unless you show me your ass is white, I ain't going to serve you." I didn't know what to say or even what to feel. All I knew was I wanted to get out of there, which I did.

With my dark skin, dark eyes, I've been mistaken for a lot of different ethnic groups. People have talked to me in Italian, Spanish, and Arabic, and expected a response. Some people think I'm part Native American. (Could be. My Acadian ancestors were said to be very friendly with the Mic Macs in Nova Scotia.) Every time I go near the Mexican border, I get stopped by the border patrol. When I speak in my New Hampshire accent, they let me go. Once I went to a party in New Orleans (where the son of a black friend was being confirmed in the Catholic church), and one of the guests assumed I was "a big ole Creole boy." I have a brother who is slightly darker than I. When he was thirteen, someone remarked on his tan. For years afterward, he wore a big hat and stayed out of the sun. My parents never voiced any prejudices against anybody, except once when my mother slurred her own people. "Ah, the French," she said contemptuously. "When I was a little girl they used to say, you're dark, but you're not dark like a Frenchman, you're dark like an Italian." I didn't know what to make of these incidents based on skin color. All the

Ernest with his mother,
in Keene, New Hampshire, 1943

debate was over big ideas, big biases, big racial crimes. Nobody talked about the little day-to-day slurs, jokes, innuendoes, and sly omissions that really determine how we treat other. I found myself a little wary, and a little envious of people who were obviously and demonstrably white, and ashamed for that feeling.

The incident in the South Carolina bar made me realize that even though I was brought up in one of the "whitest" parts of the country, the issue of skin in America is never far away. Growing up in New Hampshire with no black friends (or enemies), I should be free of racial biases. On the conscious, intellectual level I'm a standard PC liberal. Underneath, in matters of race, I find my feelings strange, paranoid, irrational, often paradoxical. I like it better this way, the ambivalence, the inability to create certainties: there's no hate in a feeling like this, no threat implied, no uneasy peace; it's just a recognition of a mystery and, in the full awareness of that recognition, without harm.

The second incident also revolves around a trip from Fort Bragg to South Carolina. This time I went with two guys with college degrees, Chuck Gilson and Eddie Grimason. We were in Charleston, and they were marveling at the architecture, in particular a Christopher Wren church. I had no idea who Christopher Wren was or what my friends were talking about, but I wanted in on the conversation. I said some kind of bull about a church I happened to spot. And Chuck said, "It's a neo-Gothic monstrosity." I thought, Wow!

That "wow" was the start of my education. From that moment, I was determined to improve myself. I wasn't after wisdom, or a better job, so much as the ability to wow my friends as I had been wowed. But I fell into an old pattern: I thought about it but didn't do anything. It wasn't until I was released from the military (the Berlin crisis blew over), and returned to civilian life and the telephone company, that I began to change. I realized that I hated my job.

Meanwhile, two of my friends went to work on me. Bill Sullivan and I had been pals since first grade at St. Joseph's. Like myself he was not a great student in high school. His avenue to college was a football scholarship at the University of New Hampshire. There, he quit football, eventually becoming captain of the track team and a serious student. The other friend was Margaret Ware. Maggie was a student at

Grandmother Elise Vaccarest, mother, Jeannette, and uncle, the Reverend Joseph Ernest Vaccarest, who was known as "Father Vac"

Elmira College in New York. We dated when she was in town; when she was at school we often talked long hours over Mother Bell's telephone lines. Bill and Maggie would give me their books to read. I didn't think I was smart enough to go college, and I felt sick at the thought of being rejected again. But they badgered me, gave me confidence. Nights, instead of going out drinking with my fellow telephone men, which was what I used to do, I would read. For about a year, all I did with my spare time was read. I was really repeating the habit of my boyhood years, which I'd let slip in my teens. Without being aware of it, I was preparing myself for more formal higher education.

Keene State College accepted me the second time around. Once that happened I had a new fear, that my handwriting would hold me back. At the suggestion of my old pal, Bill, I hired a private tutor, Mrs. Isabelle Streeter, who made me read *The History of Henry Esmond* by William Makepeace Thackeray, and write a paper about it. My parents were a little upset when they learned I was giving up a good job with the phone company to return to school. From their perspective—children of the depression—it was a move that didn't make sense. Still, my mother revealed to me that her brother, who had died when I was a teenager, had had a dream that I would go on with my education; it was a revelation that had great meaning for me.

The Reverend Monsignor Joseph Ernest Vaccarest was the great man of our family. I was named after him, so my full name is Joseph Ernest Vaccarest Hebert. My family from both sides came down from French Canada during this century to work in the mills. In those days, the French Canadians along the St. Lawrence Valley often named their first sons Joseph. Since that would make for too many Joes in the world, they gave the boys another name. Hence, Ernest. My great-grandfather Giovanni Vaccaressi migrated to Canada from Las Spezia, Italy. Vaccaressi was given a French ending, Vaccarest, the "t" at the end unvoiced. When Giovanni's son, Jean Baptiste, came to the United States, the "t" was sounded. (My grandfather Vaccarest emigrated from Canada by train, arriving in Suncook, New Hampshire. He was eleven, his brother nine. The boys were living in an orphanage, and nobody in the family quite knows how they happened to get on that train. A Franco-American cobbler took them in. One of my brothers today has my grandfather's cobbler's bench.)

On the Hebert side of the family, I can trace my roots through Quebec all the way back to 1719 in Acadian Nova Scotia. After the "grand derangement" of 1755, when the English deported the Acadians to various points south, one branch of Heberts wound up in Massachusetts, another in Quebec. They eventually reconnected in French Canada. Both my grandfather, Arthur, and grandmother, Regina, were Heberts. When I lived in New Orleans in 1967, people mistook me for a Cajun. "Hebert," they would say, pronouncing the name Abare, "that's a *fahn* South Louisiana name." But in New England, Hebert is sounded out Anglo style, "Hee-bert." Some local people with heavy regional New England accents say "Hee-bit," as in, "Ehnie Hee-bit, he's a writah." Some American Heberts kept the pronunciation, but changed the spelling. That's why you'll find Abares in

telephone books all over New England. My philosophy regarding the correct pronunciation of names is that there is no such thing as "correct." Hebert or any other name surely has been pronounced many different ways, not only on this continent but over the centuries in Europe, too. Which pronunciation is correct? In my book, local custom and personal whim prevail.

It wasn't until I was almost forty that I learned from my parents that not only was French my first language, but that until I was five and started kindergarten it was my only language. My mother told me that I had such a difficult time in school, partly struggling to learn English and partly in response to other kids and some adults making fun of my accent, that my parents decided to stop speaking French in the household. The upshot of this situation is that I lost my French. That's the phrase Franco-Americans use—"That Ernest, he lost his French." I took French in high school but it never took in me. And I have no memory of ever speaking French. Perhaps because of this peculiar memory loss, and corresponding block, I often find myself creating characters who have forgotten some important, usually traumatic event from childhood.

The Reverend Vaccarest, Father Vac as he was known, was an energetic man with whom I greatly identified. He was deeply devout in his faith, a linguist (he spoke French, English, Italian, Latin, some Spanish, and sign language for the deaf), and a powerful and moving speaker who attracted big crowds when he said mass at St. Edmonds and later at St. Marie's in Manchester, the biggest parish in the state. He was the only adult I can remember who never condescended to me and who always listened to my opinion. When I was twelve years old he took me aside and asked me if I had a vocation for the priesthood. I said no with some shame, because I didn't want to disappoint him. He reassured me, telling me that a vocation for the priesthood was not something that could be forced. It was a gift from God. He told me that eventually God would send me a sign to tell me just what my vocation was, and that he would support me in that quest.

Even though he was a man of the cloth with a rectory full of books, Father Vac was also very much a man's man in his habits. He hunted, fished, collected guns, loved boxing matches, smoked too much, drove too fast, drank too much, ate too well, and in his spare time hung around with good ole boy types. As an intellectual and sportsman, he was the kind of role model I was looking for as a kid. I remember well him going out fishing in his boat with his pal Vic Bresett. I remember being at my uncle's cottage on Granite Lake. I can see him and Vic going in Father Vac's Penn Yann runabout and can hear their voices, arguing and joking, drifting in on the early evening air. They would come back with a couple of small-mouthed bass and many empty beer bottles.

I was thirteen when Father Vac at age sixty-three was found dead of a heart attack praying at his kneeler in his room. I went into a kind of daze that lasted, well, maybe until I was twenty-one, or maybe his death had nothing to do with the daze. Maybe I was one of those people who matures late. Anyway after he died, my grades in school went down; I got into a number of fist fights; and I have these memories of the world being a vague, surreal place, myself moving through it ghost-like.

A personal tragedy also befell my natural father when he was thirteen. His mother died giving birth to her fifth child. Years later, he told me that he missed her terribly; it was no accident that he would marry my mother, a nurse four years his senior. After my grandmother's death, my grandfather Hebert remarried a Yankee woman and French disappeared around the house.

My parents met at a mansion owned by the Cabot and Pierce families in Dublin, New Hampshire. My mother was a nurse for one of the Cabot children. When the boyfriend of one of the maids showed up on a motorcycle with a friend, my mom was recruited to fill out the foursome. She recalled that they went to a night club, and they were the only two people in the place who didn't drink. My father got his French back when he married my mother, who carried the language culturally from the west side of Manchester, New Hampshire—a place where French is still spoken—to the Yankee town of Keene where I was raised.

My father must have felt in an oblique way abandoned when his mother died, a feeling that he later left me with. It wasn't his fault. He was certainly a good husband, as my mother often testified to, and "a good provider," which is the seal of approval for Franco-American men. (It's no coincidence that first-born boys are called

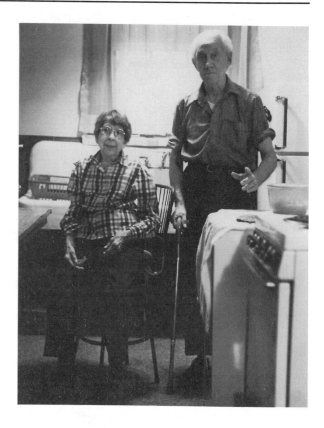

The author's parents, Jeannette and Elphege, 1990

Joseph, after Jesus's stepfather, a good provider for the Holy Family.) My father had no interest in the things I was interested in as a boy—sports, hunting, fishing, reading. In fact, as I learned later, he was just trying to survive. He worked fifty-five hours a week in a textile mill, one week days, one week nights, for forty-five years. He avoided his kids just so he could rest. My mother graduated from high school and nursing school; my father barely reached the eighth grade. My mother managed the household.

Today, at this writing, my father is eighty-three, a happy, emotionally healthy man, but for a long time he lived in the shadow of a trauma. My mother once confided that when he returned from the navy my dad would dress in a suit and tie every morning and just stare out the window all day. This went on for months, before gradually he returned to work. Over the next decades his mental health slowly improved. By the time he reached his fifties, he was once again the cheerful, fun-loving man my mother married in his twenties. And so he remains to this day. But when I was growing up, I remember him as distant, troubled.

But what happened to him in the navy? As a married man of thirty-three with two sons at the time, he wasn't drafted until toward the end of the war, and he was only in nine months before the war ended and he was discharged; he saw no combat. Yet clearly he suffered from what today is called post-traumatic stress syndrome. In turn, his sons endured a double absence, the months lost when he was away in the service and the years lost when he was preoccupied after he'd returned home. When I talk to my friends whose dads also served in World War II, it turns out that all those old soldiers had been stricken with some form of battle fatigue, which later affected in some way their children. I'm convinced that the personal traumas of the veterans of World War II were among the great character-shaping mechanisms of the generation we call baby boomers.

About six months ago, my father revealed to me the incident that caused his trauma. The story just kind of spilled out, for he'd long put it to rest. Once I heard the story, I was able to put into perspective much of my own childhood.

My father was a seaman who worked in the engine room of a small transport vessel. Somewhere in the Pacific near the Philippine Islands the ship hit some shoals and got hung up. When the ship was dragged off the rocks, one man was needed below the decks in the engine room. That man was my father. What the ship's officers didn't tell him and what he discovered during the crisis moment of this operation was that they had locked him in. I suppose there was good reason to batten down those hatches. After all, if the ship's hull had been ripped open while it was being pulled off and the water had started rushing in, my father probably would have wanted to get out of there. If he had opened a hatch, the act might have endangered the entire ship. In addition, if he had known they were going to lock him in, he might not have volunteered for the job. So they didn't tell him, and he was down there, locked in—in effect, betrayed by his fellow seamen. I imagine him thinking about that betrayal as he listened to the scraping of the hull as the ship was pulled free. During those months when my father, dressed in a suit and tie, sat by the window, he had some things to ponder.

My father was quiet, not very articulate. He did not share my interests. It's only in the last couple years, since my mother's death, that I have gotten to know him. It was natural that I should adopt my uncle as a father figure. To this day, I think of myself as a man who had two fathers, one who left him too soon, and the other who stayed long enough so that I could finally get to know him. I am grateful.

In my suspicious mind, a shadow hung over my uncle—his cottage on Granite Lake. How could a priest afford a place, albeit small, on pricey lakefront property? My mother told me that his parishioners donated the materials and time to build the three-room cottage my parents inherited. But how did Father Vac acquire the land? The question nagged at me for years. When my mother died, I went through her papers and found the original deed of the lakeshore property. Father Vac's fishing buddy, Vic Bresett, sold him the lot for one dollar.

I learned from my mother that Father Vac was a closet writer all his life. Whenever he could get away, he would drive to his place on Granite Lake and write. He never told anybody what he wrote, but she was aware that he had produced more than one book-length manuscript. When he died suddenly, the manuscripts were forgotten or overlooked. To this day, I have no idea what happened to them. I don't even know what language he wrote in.

When I started college at age twenty-three, my mother dug through the attic and came up with Father Vac's typewriter, the instrument on which he wrote the now-lost tales. It was a standard office-size black-body Underwood manual typewriter. The machine had a solid feel when I hit the keys. I knew that this was the sign that he had told me about that would come from heaven. I was going to be a writer. But what kind of writer? The answer to that question was still in the future. At this point, I'm tempted to rearrange my narrative to make my story flow better. But the fact is I didn't use the typewriter right away. I continued the pattern of revelation followed by delay. I used a smaller, newer, unromantic (during its time) Smith-Corona portable all the way through college. What happened was I experienced a moment of awe in discovering my uncle's typewriter, so overwhelming in that it reminded me of the man that I could not bear it. I returned the typewriter to my parents' attic. It wasn't until years later in my early thirties that I rediscovered the machine and with it a method of writing that allowed me to complete my first published novel.

Influenced by my friend Bill Sullivan, I started Keene State College as a history major. Everything changed when I read some lines of poetry. There's a moment in every young writer when he or she is ready for a particular work. For me that moment came when I was a sophomore at Keene State College, taking a course in contemporary American literature from David Battenfeld. I read a poem by T. S. Eliot—"Preludes." This poem of the twisted streets of Old Boston touched me deeply. A strange feeling came over me. For few minutes I was at peace with myself and the world. That poem helped me become not only a more relaxed person but a better person. To this day, that is my standard for literature. After one has finished reading a great work of literature, one is not only a better person but a happier, more able person. I thought, and these words actually came to mind, "If I could for other people what T. S. Eliot just did for me, my life would have meaning."

I switched my major to English and decided to become a poet. Later, I was accepted into the Stanford University master of arts program in creative writing by British poet Donald Davie. I washed out of Stanford, lasting only a year, and never earned the advanced degree. I reached a point where nothing in academia seemed new. It was time to get out, so I did. Even so, I credit Stanford with helping me find my way as a writer. Donald Davie, a man I liked personally and admired professionally, made me see that my talent was more for narration than prosody. I decided to give up poetry and become a fiction writer. The late Wallace Stegner, who founded the creative writing program at Stanford, let me into his advanced fiction writing class. For the life of me, I can't say why, for I was certainly no whiz-bang graduate-school writer.

When I left Stanford, I had the kind of confidence you can only have before you've actually done anything. All my work was in the future, and therefore I had no past record to demonstrate my limitations, reveal my flaws. I was almost thirty years old, had never written a novel, had no clue how to write one, and yet for some crazy reason I believed it would happen. I was arrogant, but not particularly

Ernest and Medora, on their wedding day, Dover, New Hampshire, March 22, 1969

ambitious. My goal was to publish one good book, quit, and go on to something else, maybe oil painting. (Even today I have moments when I dream of quitting writing, and becoming a painter or a sculptor.) Too stubborn—or perhaps in my unique way, too dim—to learn how to write a conventional or genre novel, I spent the next four years inventing my own version of the novel, producing two failed manuscripts whose only virtue was teaching me a few skills and producing in me the habit of writing. Eventually, at age thirty-four, I started writing the book that would become my first published novel, *The Dogs of March.*

I can credit three things with helping me achieve a breakthrough in my writing: (1) my Franco-American heritage (2) marriage, and (3) a method of composition that worked for me.

My father, with his long hours in the mill, my mother, who worked full-time as a nurse, fought off physical disabilities, and managed the household, typify my heritage as a Franco-American, a culture that values service to family over individual achievement, labor over leisure, doggedness over talent, submissiveness over assertiveness.

This background helped me establish good work habits. Many of the French Canadians who moved to New England had something of an inferiority complex, believing themselves less able or even less intelligent than other ethnic groups, their competitors for jobs. But the Frenchmen always believed they could out work anybody. I remember reading George Orwell's *Animal Farm,* and identifying with the horse, whose philosophy was: I will work harder. I think the nature of my confidence was more a belief in the value of my ability to persist and labor than in my talent.

I met my wife-to-be in college. I was a twenty-six-year-old aging junior, she an eighteen-year-old freshman. At the time I was embroiled with two other women, so I did not need one more romance, but I certainly noticed the tall, statuesque brunette with the high cheekbones and the carriage of a fashion model. By the end of the year I found myself suddenly disembroiled from both of the previous relationships. How Medora and I finally got together and fell in love is part of a longer story that began in the summer of 1968. I'd had a bad year. Confused and upset over love and other matters, I went on an odyssey with one of my apartment mates, Jack Brouse.

Brouse was a Beatle look-alike, a musician, a singer, a poet, a *bon vivant.* He used to call me Ernesto—in fact, he still calls me Ernesto.

Jack Brouse, 1968

We were a compatible pair as we headed south on our way to Albuquerque, New Mexico. Our plan was to pass the summer with my friend Bill Sullivan, by now a Ph.D. candidate at the University of New Mexico.

On the way, Jack and I stopped in at Resurrection City, where I was involved in yet another incident with a racial component. Resurrection City was a shanty town built on the great lawn in front of the Lincoln Memorial. The idea was to show symbolically the hidden poverty in America. None of us at the time could have guessed that two decades later poverty would be all too obvious with hordes of homeless people who didn't even have a shanty to call their own.

I was one of those veterans who had opposed the Vietnam War and signed onto the liberal ship of the times. But I got off the boat after a rally where I heard many of my friends chanting, "Ho Ho Ho Chi Minh." I was sympathetic to liberal causes, but found the movement had gone too far, was suffering from group and cultural hubris. But I actively disliked and disagreed with conservative causes. I was beginning to form a dislike of all strong beliefs, which seemed to me to pollute one's ability to think clearly. Jack, too, was retreating from the politics of the time. He was shaping his philosophy, which was "life's a carnival" (a variation of the Franco-American proverb of *joie de vivre*). We were a sort of pre-slacker duo who recognized that politically we had no place to go. One reason we were taking this trip was to get away from politics and try to find some kind of personal commitment that might lead to fulfillment.

I guess what I'm trying to say is that we were going to Resurrection City for frivolous reasons. We just wanted to eyeball the place, not get involved. Our mood was jovial as I drove my 1963 Chevrolet (pulling a homemade trailer hauling my 441 cc single-cylinder Victor BSA motorcycle), and much to my surprise found a place to park.

We shambled through the narrow "streets" of the shanty town that was Resurrection City. Even the metaphors that came to my mind were frivolous. The shanties on the lawn reminded me of ice fishing huts on New Hampshire lakes. The sight of these plywood shacks triggered a familiar fantasy: building a cabin in the woods. I hardly noticed the people, who today probably would be called "inner-city blacks."

Dramatically, suddenly everything changed. Jack and I found ourselves surrounded by a score or two of young black men. There was no racial ambiguity here. Those guys knew that Jack and I were not one of them. In great anger, a young man said to me, "You think this is a zoo?" He'd seen right to the core of my frivolity. I was surprised, shocked, numbed, and clueless, as if I'd been suddenly awakened in the dead of night by armed soldiers.

Out of the corner of my eye, I spotted another white man. Somebody yelled, "He's got a gun!" In an instant the young stranger was on the ground. I never saw a gun. I saw a man getting kicked. I made a halfhearted move to help the man. The next thing I remember was being punched by a short, powerfully built black youth, maybe seventeen or eighteen. The blow landed on the top of my cheekbone under the eye and knocked me backwards but not down. Everything began to slow down. It was as if I was seeing the world as a slow-motion film. I'd had the experience before—during fists fights back in high school. The feeling is not unpleasant; indeed, it contains an element of intoxication. Pain sensors turn off. The body becomes a machine in service to warring.

Out of the corner of my eye, I saw Jack struck and felled. Did I go to the defense of my friend? Nope. My only thought was to save my own skin. I started to retreat, stepping backwards, but keeping my eyes on the melee in front. Jack disappeared in the confusion of black bodies, shouts. Meanwhile, I was being stalked by my attacker.

I kept backing. He would throw these ponderous left jabs, which I would avoid by pulling my head back. I watched his eyes. They were light brown with dark dots for pupils in yellowish orbs. He wore a white T-shirt. His arms were very muscular, the color of raw leather. I have no memory of his face; my memory is of a change in my emotion, from shock to a growing hatred. I wanted to kill him. I wished I had a gun. It even went through my mind that I couldn't for first-degree murder. Maybe only manslaughter. Maybe I'd even get away with the act. There is no doubt in my mind that if I'd been armed I would have shot and killed that young man.

By now I'd backed all the way down to the reflecting pool. The view opened up. I could see Abe Lincoln in white marble looking at

the shanty town, at these young black men trying to make a point about poverty, at these New Hampshire guys and their frivolous attitude. That image in my memory will always remain one of my images of America. My adversary now could see that I could no longer back up—unless I wanted to get my feet wet. As for myself, I was now ready to fight. I doubled my fists and held them up before me. A second later the altercation was over. The young black man melted back into the crowd. Jack showed up, a lot more bruised than I was, but not seriously injured.

I have no idea what happened to the other young white man. I'd had my moment of murderous anger. It had passed, replaced by clammy fear. I wanted to get out of there. Jack was boiling with rage. In retrospect I can see that we got off easy. Those young blacks could have easily killed us or hurt us seriously. But at the time, we reacted not intellectually but emotionally. This was translated into instant bigotry. For the next couple days, I hated and feared all young black men. A sullen black face, a glance of hostility from a young black man would bring out in me a cold fury, a desire to hurt, to punish, to get even. I didn't lose that feeling until Jack and I arrived in New Orleans a few days later. (A year earlier, I'd taken a semester off from college, and ended up living seven months in New Orleans.) We visited old friends, including Joan Cotton, a black woman I worked with when I was an attendant at a psychiatric hospital. When I saw Joan and her family, I realized that I had gone temporarily insane.

That's the whole shameful event as I remember it. The incident taught me that tolerance for others is not necessarily a natural condition. It must be cultivated. It taught me that racism is often hidden in the beast, just waiting to emerge given the right conditions. The memory of my desire to kill that young man who punched me lightly is the main reason that today I've developed into a strong gun control advocate. I believe in societal mechanisms—legal, cultural, and religious—to suppress the individual's urge for vengeance.

Jack and I pushed on to New Mexico. We lived in Bill's adobe apartment in the university district in Albuquerque. Our time was very pleasant that summer. In August, I received a pleasant, newsy letter from that tall brunette back at Keene State. Her name was Medora Lavoie. Her home town was Dover, New Hampshire. About the only thing I knew for sure about her was that we had in common a Franco-American heritage. She enclosed in her letter a piece of fabric from a dress she'd made. For reasons that today still remain mysterious to me, I was touched by the gesture. The feel of the fabric in my hands made me think about Medora. I thought about her often all that summer, although I had no real plans to contact her.

On the way back to New Hampshire, Jack announced out of the blue that we had to go to Canada. He too had been doing some thinking. Why Canada, I asked. Because Carol was there was Jack's answer. Carol had been Jack's high school sweetheart back in Salem, New Hampshire. They'd split up three years earlier. Jack knew Carol was staying with her brother in Ontario. So Jack and I headed for Canada, where he and Carol behaved like the long-lost lovers they were. I left Jack and Canada and returned to New Hampshire alone.

I was so low on dough that I couldn't afford to pay the toll on the New York Thruway. I drove all night on Route 20, a road that runs parallel to the divided highway . . . thinking . . . thinking . . . thinking. At dawn I reached the pass near the summit of Hogback Mountain in Vermont. The view of the Green Mountains with the early sun on them was spectacular. I pulled over, got out, to take it all in. Something came over me, a glimpse of the future, a confidence and serious-mindedness I'd never felt before. Later that morning, after reaching home in Keene, I telephoned Medora in Dover, New Hampshire. It was an old-fashioned courtship. I was solicitous toward her parents, even her (then) obnoxious high school–age brothers. We were married the following spring. Around the same time, Jack and Carol married. Today, after twenty-seven years, they have two daughters, and Medora and I have two daughters.

M arriage was the best thing for my writing. Before, I had done more talking about writing than writing. I hadn't realized that the romantic side of writing, long discussions of literary works with friends, the contemplation of huge projects that would bring great honors (not once does the true literary romantic think of monetary reward), was in fact the day-dreaming life of a reader, not a writer. A lot of people see writing as a commitment to an

Medora Lavoie Hebert, 1987

ideal, or a means toward gaining some meaning in one's life, or a vocation to make money, or an outgate for one's personal demons, or an avenue toward fame. Writing is none of those things; writing is not a value judgment. Writing is a description of an activity. Writers write, period. After marrying Medora, instead of just talking about writing, I started to apply my Franco-American work ethic and actually do it. Marriage to Medora settled me down to good living habits. Marriage to Medora made me realize that my normal state of being was cheerfulness, a condition that, with the exception of two bad years, has persisted; her love brought me serenity, freed me to work.

One reason I decided in college to be a poet was that I couldn't face the idea of writing anything long, because my handwriting was illegible, my hunt-and-peck method on the Smith-Corona typewriter slow and tedious. When I turned to fiction in graduate school, struggling (not very successfully), I knew something was missing. Upon returning to New Hampshire, I went to my parents' house and dug up my uncle's old Underwood. That typewriter, because it had belonged to my beloved uncle, because it was beautiful and well made, because it felt good to pound on the keys, helped me make the connection between thoughts and paper.

In a felt if not a reasoned way, I knew I was ready for an instrument that would bring me to a higher level as a writer. Through some alchemy of memory I do not understand, I recalled the touch-typing system I had learned in the army. Almost immediately I went from being a two-fingered typist on the Smith-Corona to a fast touch typist on the Underwood. To this day, I can't tell you where the "p" is or any other letter on a standard keyboard without stopping to think, but my hands know. Becoming inspired by means of a device makes no sense, but that's what happened.

Over the next few years with an assist from writer/teacher John Gardner, I developed a method that worked for me. I would write in longhand on white-lined paper to the end of the page, then transcribe the work on the typewriter double-spaced. The act of typing released my creativity. As I would start typing, new ideas and arrangements of words would come to mind. Unlike handwriting or computer keyboarding, typing on a manual typewriter is unforgiving. I'd start to write a sentence, not knowing where it was going to go, and then have to fight my way through to make it work. Usually I failed, but once in a while I'd actually write something I didn't know I was capable of. The Underwood forced me to do my best work.

My method was slow but had in it the seeds of inevitability. I would copy my work on the typewriter, remove the paper, pencil edit it, and then retype the whole thing, again making changes, discovering new ideas and arrangements of words. I'd often type the same page ten times or more. I wouldn't go on to the next page until the current page was as good as I could make it. This is a good method for novel writing; it is based on the principle that in a long race the tortoise beats the bunny. The trouble with the bunny system—spewing out a first draft on a word processor as fast as possible—is that one writes a bad scene, which becomes the departure point for the next bad scene. For an analogy, imagine a man lost in the woods running a hundred yards in any direction, stopping to take a deep breath, then

With brothers, Paul (left) and Omen, 1989

running another hundred yards. By day's end the man is not only more lost than ever, but tired. For the writer, the bunny system produces huge manuscripts so unwieldy that they cannot be brought into any kind of shape. I have four or five such manuscripts tucked away in a drawer some place. By working page by page, produced slowly and painstakingly, I was able to create a half way good scene in the first draft, which then became the departure point for the next scene. My method served me like a compass.

During this period I worked for the *Keene Sentinel* newspaper, first as a sports writer, then as a general assignment reporter, and later as a copy editor. My job was demanding, but I found the time I needed. I worked two hours a day, six days a week, for four years. At the end of that period I had produced my first publishable novel, *The Dogs of March*. It was accepted in early May of 1978, the same week that our first daughter was born. Writer Lael Wertenbaker helped find me an agent, who was able to place *The Dogs of March* very quickly. The agent was Rita Scott. Medora and I named our first child Lael Scott Hebert. I was thirty-seven. For more than a decade I'd courted the idea of literary success. I'd never wanted to be a father—that had been Medora's idea, and I'd gone along for the sake of the marriage. But the thrill of my daughter's birth was far greater than the thrill of seeing my publishing dreams come true.

I never expected or desired to publish more than one book. So far I've published seven books. That's the condensed version of my writing career thus far. Actually, the issue is more complicated than that. My ambition was to write one good book that would be published. I didn't realize that the "one" book would actually be five novels, part of what was called "The Darby Series." In my own mind, they've always been one book. Partly for practical reasons (tricking the publisher) and partly for some kind of psychological reasons that I have no insight into, I kept this idea a secret until I actually published *Live Free or Die,* the last volume, in 1990.

I got the work done that I had set out to do—though the effort took me about a decade more than I thought it would. I never expected or desired to be a family man—and find myself today married twenty-seven years with two children and obligations concerning other family members. (Our second daughter, Nicole, was born in February of 1984.) I used to dream of living with a subservient wife in the woods in a log cabin—and have settled into a small-town neighborhood with a wife who is a dynamo and leader of the family. I left college with an idea of never going back to academia—today I teach at Dartmouth. My dreams of literary success were very modest, and I fulfilled my goals and then some—but achievement never brought me happiness. The common lifestyle I'd occasionally scorned and believed was not for me—conventional home, stable marriage, children, responsibility, respectability, doing for others—is what brought me happiness.

After some time in the newspaper business I learned, like most reporters, to spew out a passable first draft of a news story in a very short time (sometimes minutes), which then was fixed up by a skilled editor, set in type, proof-read, and put in the paper. We at the *Keene Sentinel* knocked out copy on IBM Selectric typewriters.

The machine, though it had an annoying hum, was not that far removed from the Underwood; the newspaper-writing method of

With author Thomas Williams and poet Debra Allbery, Canaan, New Hampshire, 1990

producing copy did not affect my method for fiction writing. Then, in 1980, the paper converted to a computer-driven editorial system. I was a brand-new copyeditor at the time. Reporters typed copy on keyboards, their words appeared on a video display terminal, and they could manipulate the words as they desired—add new ones, delete old ones, move blocks of text, all the stuff we're familiar with these days in the now ubiquitous computers. The first hour I was exposed to this system I knew I was in trouble. Sure enough, within a month, my old writing method no longer worked for me.

A year went by when I produced a good deal of journalistic writing on the company terminals, but no fiction of note at home. I could no longer compose on the Underwood. If I'd had the courage and the foresight, I would have quit my job, never looked at a computer again, and gradually settled back into my comfortable method. But I was seduced by the dark side of the force. I wanted my own word processor.

Thanks to a grant from the National Endowment for the Arts, I got my wish. It was odd how this grant came about. When my first novel was accepted for publication, another writer—one of my mentors, in fact, John Morressy of Sullivan, New Hampshire—happened to mention that I was now eligible to apply for an NEA grant. I sent in the form along with my writing sample, the first chapter to a novel about a priest. That project never got off the ground; in trying to put the failed work behind me I managed to forget my NEA application. A year later I got a check in the mail—$10,000. No doubt, I didn't deserve this money. That was probably why it felt so good. I was giddy as a burglar. I quit my job, and bought my first word processor, a Radio Shack Model I, at the time a pretty hot machine.

Grants for individual artists make me cringe today, though as a recipient of one I should be the last one to complain. I sometimes think that writing is such a selfish and self-gratifying act, whose personal rewards are in the doing, that nobody ought to get paid for it; money and prestige corrupt a writer's talent. The more professional a writer is in his skills and outlook the less apt he is to produce work that does something meaningful for other people or that advances our literature. Let all writers be amateurs, I say. Let the work stand in the marketplace without the author's name on it. Let everything be by anonymous.

The computer helped me write a book. When I had trouble getting going on the next book, I blamed my computer: not powerful enough. I bought another computer, this time a Model III. Computer mania set in. I couldn't seem to get going on a project without an expensive new piece of equipment. After the Model III Radio Shack came the Model 100 Radio Shack, one of the first serviceable portable models; the Atari ST; an XT IBM clone; a DOS-based laptop; and three different kinds of Macintoshes. Over the years I augmented the CPUs with hard disks, big monitors, a scanner, a couple of modems, and various other gismos, such as electronic note pads; the more unnecessary the equipment, the more I wanted it. I also spent a small fortune on software, the more complicated the better. Mastering new software became a sort of side mania, producing euphoria and then a corresponding depression after there was nothing new to learn; I was beginning to exhibit the symptoms of a drug addict. Hooked on the chip.

Perhaps nostalgic for my old writing life, I made a pitiful attempt to reform. But I was long past working on a manual typewriter. I bought an IBM electronic typewriter, with a memory, delete and insert modes. Such typewriters are common today—you can buy a good one for a couple hundred bucks at K-Mart. But at the time I bought mine, only IBM produced an electronic typewriter and it cost a couple thousand bucks. A huge thing about as heavy as a washing machine, that first IBM electronic typewriter turned out to be one of the great dogs of writing machines ever made. The thing was always busted. Luckily, I'd paid for an expensive service contract, and the IBM repairman and I became buddies.

My equipment madness culminated when I was hired on the faculty of Dartmouth College in the creative writing program of the English Department. I was surprised to learn that I was given a $15,000 start-up grant to be used for "research" or for some aspect of my discipline. At the time I was not working on a writing project that required research. What to spend the money on? My head was spinning. I blew it all on computer equipment. I bought a Mac II, top of the line for its time with two monitors, one color and one black and white. I still had money left over, and I bought all

"With Jan Kerouac, canoeing 'on the road' in flood waters on Route 43 between Alton and Orono, Maine, April 3, 1987"

the word processing programs then available for the Macintosh—MacWrite, WriteNow, Microsoft Word, Nisus, Mindwrite, WordPerfect, and half a dozen other smaller programs designed to help writers organize their material and time.

During the period I was writing *Live Free or Die,* the fifth and last of my Darby series novels about a town in New Hampshire, I would work for a while in one word processor, save it as a text file, and then work on the novel in another word processor. By the time *Live Free or Die* was finished, I have no doubt that it was the most word-processed novel ever written.

The "book" I'd set out in the 1970s to write and publish was now finished, even if the work took five volumes. In another year I'd exhausted my mania. I sold the Mac II and settled down with only necessary equipment. Currently I work on a Macintosh SE in my home office and a MacPlus at my Dartmouth office, both older machines that can be bought

for less than two hundred dollars used. In addition I use three manual typewriters, one each in my home and college offices and one in the house, which I move around to wherever I might be tempted to write something. One of those is the ancient Underwood I inherited from my uncle. I also carry note cards with me for notes penned with a Pilot brand extra-fine rolling ball pen, and I leave full-sized note pads lying around the house and office. To the casual observer this may seem like a lot of equipment, but by my standards it's quite a cutback. I'm getting better, aren't I doctor—aren't I?

So many writers I know, especially writers just starting out with no dough, think they need a new computer. After whistling every whistle and ringing every bell, I can say with authority that writers ought to go low-tech every time when picking a computer and word processor. For writers who have yet been untouched by word processing, my advice is stay away. Stick with handwriting and a manual typewriter.

The trouble with composing on a computer is that it's not writing, it's editing. I mean that the creative part of the writer is wild and crazy and at times, perhaps most times, infuriatingly unproductive. It's also stressful—fighting to make a good sentence. Handwriting and typewriting are compatible to this kind of thinking, handwriting because it's so visceral, the hand an extension of the brain, typewriting because it forces one to create on the fly. The computer, because it allows for quick fixing of mistakes, interposes the writer's mental editor in the process. The editor is plodding, unimaginative, simple-minded. None of the equipment I bought allowed me to write any better, or to reach for some kind of meaning unavailable in other, less expensive ways. I knew that all along. I was hooked on the kick, the pleasures of playing with a software, of partaking in the speed of one's chip.

While word processing has affected composition habits—the writer's process—it has also affected the world, and this effect in the long run is more profound.

Before the *Keene Sentinel* switched over to computers, reporters wrote "hard copy," that is, they wrote on paper. That paper was edited by an editor. If the copy was so poorly organized that it couldn't be edited, the editor would kick it back to the reporter and make him/her do it all over again. After, deadline reporters often met with the editors, who were older and more experienced, of course. The reporter could see what he had written and what the editor had done to his copy. Long discussions about writing ensued. A reporters had a mentor, a base for improvement (the edited copy). There was real free-flow between reporters and editors. We all sat more or less in a bunch; we all dressed more or less the same, in dress shirts with ties pulled down the neck. Just like in the movies. About the only way a visitor could tell a reporter from an editor was by age.

The computers changed the relationship between editor and reporter, the very sociology of the newsroom. I was an editor when the computers arrived and I saw it all developing in front of my eyes. Under the new system, a reporter would type his story into the computer system and save it under a file name. The editor would call up the file with his own monitor and edit the copy. Except that we editors

didn't really edit, we rewrote. If a sentence didn't look right, or a sequence was not well organized, it was easier and faster for the editor simply to redo the work. Editors in effect became rewrite men and women. Also, the position of proofreader disappeared. The editor/rewriter became the proofreader.

The new system gave more power to the editorial desk and took power away from the writers, the very kind of thing that leads to mediocrity that the powers that be like so much. Reporters now wrote copy and they read the revised copy in the newspaper. They couldn't remember exactly what they wrote, only that it wasn't what was in the paper. The basis for an reporter/editor relationship was removed. Needless to say, bad feelings developed between the editorial and reporting staffs.

When I returned to the *Sentinel* a decade later, the editorial desk had been separated from the reporters' desks. Male editors wore tight ties up against their throats, women dresses; the reporters looked as they'd always had, young slobs, but their demeanor was of an oppressed people. They were sullen, resentful, scornful. Who could blame them?—the editors had taken over.

This is just one change in the writing world. Who knows how many others, and what they mean? On the whole, I think the switch-over has been bad for writing, especially for so-called literary writing. Computers with their editing functions, spell checkers, and formatting functions make writing too easy, allowing bad writers to produce huge manuscripts, which have swamped publishers, who have responded by hiding behind agents. (In fact, the biggest change in the publishing world in the last decade is the emergence of the middle person, the agent, as now the most important element. Blame computers.) Writers—and I'm a prime example—have let computers dominate their thinking; writers in groups rarely talk about literature anymore. They talk about their latest hard disk or monitor or connection to the Internet. Computers have undermined the readers, too. People who used to curl up with a book at night now surf the Internet. Many of my students can't compose without a computer. It's a shame that somebody needs a device that requires a plug or a battery to write, but that's what it has come to. I try to encourage my students to take some interest in the manual typewriter. I say, "It's a word processor that saves right to the paper." But even as I deliver my plea, I

The author with Medora, and their daughters,
Nicole (left) and Lael, 1990

know that to the students it's only an eccentric professor's nostalgia.

At this writing, the latest computer innovation is e-mail. At Dartmouth College where I work, everyone—from students to faculty—is connected to everyone everywhere. I see a hopeful sign in e-mail that computers can help writing and writers. E-mail writing tends to be sloppy, but at times wildly creative. E-mail writers, because they're in a rush, don't let the editor in themselves take charge. It's the kind of method that Jack Kerouac (another Franco-American) would have liked because he believed in the integrity of the first draft. It's too early to tell how e-mail will affect writing for the long run, but it is intimate; it's what people do these days instead of writing letters. I'd like to end with an e-mail message.

A student, Ryan Molde, asked me over e-mail if I'd ever had an out-of-body experience. As one will over e-mail, I just started typing off the top of my head. When I was finished, I realized I'd tapped into some thoughts about my mother.

Hey, Ryan, I've had a couple of strange and rather thrilling experiences that might be categorized as "out of body," but under it all I'm a hard core realist. The first time it happened was when I was hospitalized briefly with a kidney stone. Very very painful. They gave me some kind of pain killing drug, and the next thing I knew (this all happened in less than a minute), the pain was gone and I felt as if I was floating above the room, watching the pitiful wreck of a body that was me on the bed.

The second experience was much more deeply profound. I was with my mother, holding her hand, when she died two years ago. Her hand was icy cold. I sensed when she was about to die. She kind of shook a little, and her breaths were more spaced apart. About five minutes later, she took her last breath. What amazed me was how final and sudden actual death was. She went from being kind of rigid, her body shimmering with tension, to absolutely stone still. At that moment, the moment of death, her icy cold hand that I was still holding warmed my hand. I guess that when her heart stopped the warmed blood rushed to her extremities. Anyway the feeling of warmth from my mother sent a rush of deep emotion (I don't have a name for this feeling) right to my spinal cord.

The out-of-body experience, if that's what it was, occurred later. I drove twenty miles from the nursing home to Keene to tell my father and brother about my mother's death, and then I called home and told my wife. On the drive from Keene to my home in West Lebanon, around 3 AM on I–91, I saw what I thought was the moon rising over Mount Ascutney. From this "moon," rays of light shot upward. I was seeing the Northern Lights. In minutes the entire sky was a symphony of light. I saw these lights until I turned off the interstate into White River Junction, and then they had vanished entirely. The only other time I've seen the Northern Lights was the day before the birth of my first daughter. But what makes this a strange experience is that the next day I heard nothing about anybody else seeing the Northern Lights—no radio or TV or newspaper reports, nothing. So I don't know what happened, but the experience was very exciting, even ennobling. The upshot is that since my mother died, my own fear of death and the unknown has been greatly diminished; indeed, I felt myself grow more serene, better able to face life's difficulties.

BIBLIOGRAPHY

Fiction:

Mad Boys: A Novel, University Press of New England, 1993.

The "Darby" series:

The Dogs of March, Viking, 1979, University Press of New England, 1995.

A Little More Than Kin, Viking, 1982.

Whisper My Name, Viking, 1984.

The Passion of Estelle Jordan, Viking, 1987.

Live Free or Die, Viking, 1990, University Press of New England, 1995.

The Kinship (includes "People of the Kinship," *A Little More Than Kin,* and *The Passion of Estelle Jordan*), University Press of New England, 1993.

Nonfiction:

Greetings from New England, Graphic Arts Center Publishing, 1988.

Alicia (Suskin) Ostriker

1937-

FIVE UNEASY PIECES

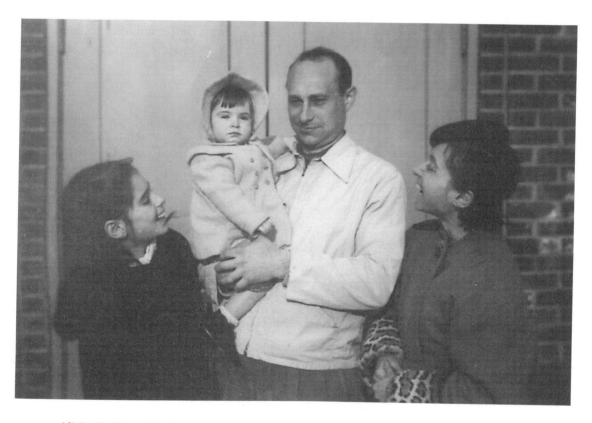

Alicia Suskin with sister, Amy, father, David, and mother, Beatrice, New York, 1948

I. Eating the Tomato

In the beginning, what I remember is being loved. Unconditionally, absolutely, and without boundaries. I remember being loved and loving. Drinking it, touching it.

There was a cement stoop, big people talking, blackish-green bushes standing around creating shadows. A little ant rushing across the cement. There was the face of my grandfather leaning over me singing very quietly. There was an apartment, a wide rumpled bed, a radio playing, my mother and father laughing. And food, licking a mound of pudding slowly from the spoon. Apples more crisp. Then coming home from shopping with her, sweaty, who moved from the paper bag globes more intensely red than apples, skin more sleek. What did I expect when I went to bite? There was a membrane breaking, then pulpy slippery awful spurting sour red wetness and seeds. Then in the afternoon outside she sitting on a playground bench while I made sand pies in the sandbox, then while I climbed the monkey bars. She watching me adoringly. She reading poems to me. He dancing. She hugging. Kissing passionately. He pushing me on the swing, he doing a headstand, a handstand, he balancing me in midair

261

on his feet while I became an airplane, he bringing home chalk from the shipyard for me to draw on the pavement. He playing a harmonica. She speaking with a voice like music, looking into my eyes with her deeper eyes, putting iodine on my cut, squirting an eyedropper full of codliver oil into my mouth, making a newspaper funnel of steam for me to breathe when I had croup. She teaching me to read. She playing connect the dots with me. He teaching me to swim and ride a bicycle. The three of us during blackouts, for it was wartime, watching Mickey Mouse movies on the wall so that I would not be afraid. All of us singing Union songs at the formica table when he was going to meetings. We shouted the chorus:

> Oh you can't scare me,
> I'm sticking to the Union
> I'm sticking to the Union
> Till the day I die.

She saying poetry. Shakespeare, Tennyson, Browning: "I sprang to the saddle, and Joris and he—I galloped, Dirk galloped, we galloped all three!" The name of that was "How We Brought the Good News from Ghent to Aix." Another time, it was "Let me not to the marriage of true minds / Admit impediment." Her eyes filling with tears. Tears of joy spilling down her cheeks because of poetry.

I was a Depression baby, born in Brooklyn on November 11, 1937. The date then was Armistice Day, celebrating the end of World War One. Since then the holiday has been changed to Veterans Day, an alteration which I resent. As if we needed yet another holiday to honor war, when we have not even one to honor peace. My young parents, David Suskin and Beatrice (born Linnick) Suskin, were second-generation atheist socialist Jews whose parents came from eastern Europe during the pogroms of the 1880s. They were two of what Irwin Shaw calls "the gentle people," who failed to outgrow being poor and proud. Down with the bosses, up with the working classes. They met in college, both English majors, both hoping to be writers, but nothing came of that. What jobs did my father have? Work in a shipyard. Work as a prison guard. A prisoner jumped him once to kill him, but because he was known for his kindness, other prisoners pulled the man off. Work teaching English to immigrants. Work,

finally, for the New York City Department of Parks, as a playground director. He was the man who gave out the checkers and the paddles for paddle tennis, and called the ambulance if a kid fell off a swing. He did that for twenty-five years.

When I began my first job as a college teacher, I made the same salary as my father was still making, seven thousand dollars a year. He had been offered a promotion to supervisor once but turned it down. He liked wearing chinos, giving out the checkers, playing basketball with the colored boys. He rejected being a boss.

I do too.

None of the men in my family were dominant personalities. Neither my father, his brothers, or my two grandfathers. The women were in charge of dominance. After we moved from Red Hook Houses in Brooklyn to East River Drive Houses in Manhattan, when I was six, so that I could attend Hunter College Elementary School—because somebody had given me an IQ test and the Board of Ed. told my parents to send me to Hunter, an experimental public school where all the students were "geniuses"—it took an hour and a half to get to my father's parents by subway. We went each Saturday. Climbed a tenement stairway, entered a living room where the walls were cream-colored, the plaster was textured in bumpy swirls, and the furniture hardly left space to move. My grandfather Heschl, who was called Harry in America, would be sitting on a wooden chair next to an upright piano nobody ever played. He would

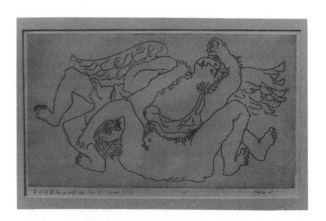

"I will not let thee go except thou bless me," the author's etching from Genesis 32:27

rise and take my hands in his calloused hands, smiling into my face with such radiance that it was like looking through the windows of a mansion aflame with lights. If he spoke, my grandmother waved her hand angrily, and he stopped. Grandma gave orders in a raw voice. She cooked. We had to sit and eat everything, although nobody ever saw her eat.

My mother's father, Simon, was a pharmacist. These tender-hearted Yiddish-speaking men, do they still exist? Compassionate sons of compassionate fathers, as Talmud calls them, do they still believe in universal brotherhood? Are they still convinced that to be a Jew means, above all, the imperatives of study and kindness? Do they still await a world of peace and dignity for all working people—comes the revolution?

Because this grandfather remembers hunger in Russia, and because he nearly starved to death during his first months in America and had to eat his landlady's cat food in the alley, he cannot bring himself to collect the overdue bills at the pharmacy. When my grandmother scolds, because it is she who pays the bills as well as she who cooks, cleans, writes poetry in English and Yiddish, and sews all the family clothes with her "golden hands," he shrugs in shame. It is this grandfather who sits me on his lap when I am in first grade in 1944 and uses the phrase "the Jews in Europe," which I simultaneously do not understand and—I cannot say how—understand utterly. As if looking downward through fathoms of dark yet transparent water. He strokes my hair so that neither of us will cry, he says *shayne maydel* but otherwise speaks English as I press against his chest and feel the buttons of his cardigan, smell his pipe tobacco, hear my mother and my grandmother talking in the kitchen.

It is I who am the *shayne maydel,* the beautiful little girl. It is I who sit on his lap, listening to the story of The Man Who Traveled from Place to Place, which he has invented to entertain me, and whose adventures with Rabbit, Fox, and Bear are a softened version of his own odyssey. It is I who curl in the wing chair when he plays chess, the pharmacist playing with the doctor, two grey-headed men in cardigans, their heads wreathed in pipe smoke. It is I to whom he turns and winks after a good move.

Frank, the freckled Irish gardener who trims the bushes around the Project where we live,

bows to me as if I were a princess. The old gentlemen on the park benches playing checkers fuss over me when I come around to watch them play; they teach me and let me win. I am going to be a checkers champ. Because old men simply love me, and never give me orders, I never learn to fear and obey them. How unusual, how lucky. Teachers, too, are my friends. I love to read and write, crayons are kingdoms—those orange and green Crayola boxes. Those notebooks with speckled black-and-white composition covers and pages, when they are new, like milk. Pages, blue-lined, to run the hand over. Books containing, from the very beginning, the other, the more true reality. "O how I love to go up in the swing, Up in the air so blue! For I do think it the pleasantest thing, Ever a child can do!" I am not sure whether this was what I learned first, or this: "Whether 'tis nobler in the mind to suffer / The slings and arrows of outrageous fortune / Or to take arms against a sea of troubles / And by opposing end 'em." She tells me that I recited Hamlet's soliloquy back to her when I was three, word for word, except that instead of "Ah, there's the rub" I said, "Ah, there's the rub-in," because she used to rub my chest with mustard plaster when I had a cough. She tells me that I composed my first poem at the same age.

The thing about people in books is that they are more real than people around you because you know them better. Also, you can *be* them. It would never occur to you to be your mother and father, or your teachers, or other children. Later when you want to *be* some man you hold in your arms, it doesn't work. It never does. But you can be brave Greta in "The Snow Queen." You can be Rebecca of Sunnybrook Farm, who has braids and brains like yours. You can be fierce Jo March, plus a bit of Meg, Beth, and Amy. You can be Tom Sawyer. Robin Hood. You can be Hamlet. You *are* Hamlet. You *are* Cleopatra, King Lear, Stephen Dedalus, Cassandra, Raskolnikov, and Kafka's K. You are Jacob wrestling with the angel, saying "I will not let thee go except thou bless me." But that is getting ahead.

The other thing is drawing. Growing from crayon to pencil. In margins and endpapers of books, in notebooks, on scraps of paper and on the labels from cans. Especially the labels from half-gallon juice cans. Copying comics, or illustrations from my books, or drawing pretty girls posing or having adventures, or drawing trees, or real people, what I was going to be was an artist. When you are drawing, time and space cease to control you. Nothing exists beyond your eyes, the pencil, the label from a can of tomato juice flattened onto a book on your lap, and a tree over there.

What then is the problem? For one cannot become a writer without some inextricable thorn in the heart.

The problem is other children. In East River Houses, they are mostly Irish and Italian Catholics, and we are Jews. *Jew, Jew, how do you do?* My mother explains to me about prejudice. She explains superstition. Her ideas about such things are very clear, along with her ideas about money, germs, despising clothing and other appearances, being a good mother (it is frequently pointed out to me that the neighbor women are bad mothers), and the importance of intelligence, kindness to others, and grammatically correct English. My father has a funny song about how religion is used to exploit working people:

> There'll be pie in the sky,
> In that glorious land way up so high,
> Work and pray, live on hay,
> You'll get pie in the sky when you die.
>   IT'S A LIE!

You are supposed to shout the ending. IT'S A LIE! I can already figure out for myself that if you are good just in order not to go to hell, that isn't real goodness. Also, a God who just wants people to worship him, and sends them to hell if they don't, does not deserve to be worshiped. When children in my building say their catechism, it doesn't make them better. They fight and curse just the same. They tell on each other. *Mama!* Tommy will yell up to his window. *George said a B!* And their mother will fill the window with her body and the air with her screaming. The Heywood children get beaten with a strap if they curse. (But when Tommy and George come home with a stolen bicycle, their mother hides it in the basement and screams at a woman who comes to claim it.) When I read books that tell me childhood is a time of innocence, I know better. Childhood is a time of malice, meanness, and violence.

A boy in the next building is what my mother calls a Mongoloid. He stumbles when he walks, and tries to get in our games, smil-ing with his lip hanging down. Everyone but me yells at him, *Stupid Joey! Stupid Joey!* At me, because my name is funny, some boys yell, *Alicia no capisha! Alicia no capisha!* I have no idea what this means but it is supposed to make me despise myself, and it does. I hate my name. When they see me reading or drawing they say, *Who do you think you are, Einstein?* Or, *Who do you think you are, Rembrandt?* They surround me and make me spell Mississippi, and laugh when I say i-p-p-i. My mother says sticks and stones will break my bones but names will never hurt me. This is untrue. She says they are jealous of me because of my high IQ. For a while I believe this but then my classmates in Hunter also discover what fun it is to tease and mock me; they do it with more wit because they have high IQs too. Why can I never tell beforehand when someone will hurt me? In the middle of a game of jacks: *Let's not play with Alicia.* Jump-rope, can I have a turn now? *No,* and a gale of giggles. Stoop ball, ringoleevio, hide-and-seek, patsy on the chalked squares, somebody would always cheat. Never listened when I explained they should stick to the rules. Why this incomprehensible spoiling the fun? And why the hitting? I never hit back because I knew hitting was wrong.

The blizzard of 1947 fell when I was nine. A tremendous calm. Sculptured shapes simplified what used to be bushes and benches. Into my snowsuit and boots, and out in the blue-and-white morning before anyone else, I made the first snowman of my life. The snow creaked as I rolled the heavy lumpy spheres. He was as big as I was. Patting him, I saw two kids approaching from behind a building across the courtyard, a boy and girl. Didn't recognize them. They came up to me and without a word kicked my snowman to pieces. I asked them why. The boy said, Somebody busted ours so we busted yours. But that's *wrong,* I said. If somebody does something bad to you it should make you *sympathetic.*

I actually said this. I was being reasonable. I was trying to explain what my mother had explained to me. At the same time the universe opened up—split into two simultaneous spaces. It was like that moment on my grandfather's lap years earlier when I knew something, saw something, which I could not possibly have known, something of a vast sorrowful emptiness. In one world I stood in the snow, gesticulating with snow-caked mittens. In the other, a depth gaped. Into it something was falling—falling like snow, but without an earth. Limitless, bottomless, infinitely downward in space, endless in time, irretrievable. Evil. It was a word I had heard. Now for the first time I saw and understood: evil is logical, inevitable, like a law of motion.

Is goodness substance, and is evil absence? Is one real and the other unreal? Years later, the two principles became clothed in language for me. You know the heart of the stranger, God tells the children of Israel, because you were strangers in Egypt. Having suffered, you wish to heal the suffering of others. That is what it means to be a Jew. A simple logic. On the other side stands the other logic, in the tidy words of W. H. Auden: "Those to whom evil is done / Do evil in return."

Absent from both these formulations is the way innocence yearns toward knowledge—the awful bloody seedy spurt of it. And another thing. Whatever I personally suffered in my shy and vulnerable childhood, and however much I saw the world through my mother's moralizing eyes, there was always a part of me for which everything—everything, the brick buildings of public housing, cracked sidewalks, delivery trucks, subways, luminous sky of clouds, wicked people—was spectacle. Glorious theater. The vitality of those hard streets, poverty and ignorance bawling through our lives, was a sight to behold. The swing and punch of the bad language I was told not to imitate was live music to my ears, far more interesting than proper English. Literature—any art—exists to embody such perception. Exists to praise what is. For nothing.

II. Stepping Out

Thank God for the exodus from childhood. Not that you ever do leave, I suppose. But there are those wonderful moments when you think that now, at last, you are out of that womb, that prison cell, that dream-and-nightmare. The bud climbs blindly through the stem.

Sex is a big part of it. Lucky for me, there were all those non-domineering men in my family, so I never thought to identify sex with submission. Lucky too, my mother was so far inside her own bubble that she never taught me what every woman should know: that men just want what they can get from you, that I should be ashamed of my body—that sort of thing.

When I was ten and Tommy wanted me to go in the elevator with him to kiss, along with my friend Annie and Annie's boyfriend, I asked my mother if I could. She had some very long speech to make, which I didn't understand, but the end of it was that she told me to use my judgment. My judgment told me it would be romantic to kiss Tommy, and I spent a winter doing that. Actually, it was more romantic watching Annie—two years older—kissing her boyfriend. What they were doing was real. They said they were in love. I was only rehearsing.

Then there was a boy at summer camp. Next year another boy. In high school I was thoroughly unpopular with both sexes. A brain, a geek, a scholarship kid at Fieldston School in bargain-basement clothes surrounded by acres of cashmere sweaters, without a clue about how to be sophisticated and ironic. I would trail after one or another group of girls, trying to laugh when they laughed. Once or twice I endured the torment of wallflowering at school dances. But in the neighborhood—by then we were in another housing project, Dyckman Houses, up in the north of Manhattan—I joined the Y, and successfully pursued Eddie. Tall, dark, very handsome, Eddie had a beautiful smile, a future as a printer in his father's union shop, and a car. A forest green Chevrolet with bits of mica-like sparkle afloat in its enamel. How many long evenings of parking, how many thousand kisses, embraces, how hot, how sweet—it buoyed me up, it tided me over, it convinced me that this was what I was born for. I never changed my mind. As Sharon Olds says, I signed on for the duration. The smell of Eddie's flannel shirt alone could fill me with happiness. His smile, like my grandfather's, held nothing back. He could recite the whole of *The Rubaiyat* of Omar Khayyam. And he was a fine dancer. When I lay in my virginal bed at night, aroused as a horse, his form appeared to hover near the ceiling like a cluster of glowing stars. Somehow it was both a body and a constellation. Later, when I was reading *Romeo and Juliet,* the professor singled out the passage where Juliet awaits her wedding night and Romeo's arrival:

Come, gentle night, come, loving black-brow'd
   night,
Give me my Romeo; and, when he shall die,
Take him and cut him out in little stars,
And he will make the face of heaven so fine
That all the world will be in love with night,
And pay no worship to the garish sun.

*Newlyweds Alicia Suskin and
Jeremiah P. Ostriker, 1958*

That conceit about the stars, said Miss Doran, was an instance of bad writing because it corresponded to nothing in reality. Oh, Miss Doran, how wrong you were.

What else sprung me? Two years of ballet classes at the old Metropolitan Ballet School with my classmate Susan, whose father, an art dealer with a Miró the size of the Alhambra in his foyer, decided that I was a diamond in the rough. They told me the teacher was letting me take the class for free, and I believed it. After each class Susan and I went to a drugstore for black-and-white ice-cream sodas, and she regaled me with ballet lore. Thank you, Susan. Thank you, Susan's father. Two years of lessons, with the consequence that I love dance for the rest of my life. Then Saturday morning life-drawing classes at the Art Students' League, on scholarship, and attending the tiny Amato Opera in the afternoon with James, a fellow student who was gay, but I didn't know that. The discovery of poets on my own: Whitman! Blake! Hopkins! Keats! John Donne! W. H. Auden! The great heterodox visionaries

with their fusions of passion and intelligence. Each of them confirmed, in one way or another, the connection of the soul to the body. The music of language in its many registers. The sacred energy within myself, that was the same energy within a stone or a star. The sublime moment when I first came eyeball to eyeball with a Van Gogh. The summer when I was sixteen and spent a week of afternoons in the Cloisters, high above the Hudson River, reading William James's *Varieties of Religious Experience*, recognizing the moments of vision in my own life. No, not illusion. Reality. If the doors of perception were cleansed, as Blake says, we would see everything as it really is, infinite.

To learn was freedom. I had one gifted teacher after another. Miss Murphy, under whose massive dowager wing I glimpsed the clean beauty of geometry. Mr. Heyman, a refugee from Eastern Europe, who brought European history to life by his tenacious attachment to the Reformation. Was everyone as thrilled as I when Martin Luther nailed his Ninety-five Theses to the door of Wittenburg Cathedral, in defiance of the Pope? Here I stand; I can do no other, said Luther. Mr. Lenrow in Fifth Form English, who snarled Hamlet's "one can smile and smile and be a villain" speech magnificently, capping it with a crescendo "O vengeance!" ending in a long bellow. Miss French, a lady dry as sand, who once uncharacteristically played *Threepenny Opera* in class. Oh, the shark had pretty teeth, dear, and Lotte Lenya's voice was like the rasp of my own adolescent contempt for society and propriety. Over my shoulder I scanned the classroom, certain that none of my privileged classmates could understand. The wry and twinkling Mr. Brown in Sixth Form, as advisor to the high school yearbook, chose the quotations for each student's senior portrait. The quote for me was "Liberty of thought is the life of the soul." The quote for Jerry Ostriker, whom I did not yet know I was going to marry, was "I thought of questions which have no reply."

By the time I went to college, I wanted more than anything to leave home. My mother was always telling my sister Amy—a distant ten years younger—to be more like me. My father had grown increasingly silent, like his father. Increasingly my mother raged at my father and sister, feuded with neighbors, disputed the honesty of shopkeepers, poured one or another grievance into my captive ear. She was sliding into the role of child, making me her mother. I felt guilty for hating this. How could I pull away from the person who cared for me more than anything, who was so proud of me? How could I flinch from her kisses?

I attended Brandeis because they offered me a full scholarship. Poverty, like the prospect of hanging, can clarify one's mind. At Brandeis, between 1955 and 1959, I studied with an array of extraordinary professors, including Irving Howe, Philip Rahv, J. V. Cunningham, Herbert Marcuse, Philip Rieff, and Paul Vigée. I sank deep into English literature, wrote poetry, edited a literary magazine, moved off campus, attended folk music concerts, and felt either inferior or superior to the rest of the world in confusing swings. It was becoming clear that I would never be a visual artist; every studio art course I took, I could see students around me doing with ease what I could never do with color, composition, verisimilitude. My oils were mud. I have loved art all my life, and continue to draw and do graphics, while grinding my teeth at the inadequacy of my gifts. On the other hand, nobody could make me feel ashamed of my poems.

In the one poetry writing course I took, Professor Cunningham—splendidly organ-voiced, sharp, alcoholic, cruel, a disciple of Yvor Winters and a despiser of "damp" poetry—wished us all to write epigrams. Having produced some verses of appropriate aridity, I resumed my native lyric moisture. At semester's end, each of Cunningham's students was permitted a single conference with the great dragon. Mine was a turning point. Returning my packet of work he informed me that I was going to apprentice myself to a major poet, then rebel and become a minor poet. I had entered the conference timidly; I departed infuriated. Smoke was coming out of my nostrils. Minor poet? How dare he? He was describing himself! I never spoke to him again. I resolved on the spot never to be anyone's follower. (To be sure, I fell in love with William Blake years later, but I had braced myself only to beware of living masters, not dead ones.) Decades later it struck me that J. V. Cunningham had actually perhaps identified with me. With this thought sprang a curious tentative gratitude. Had he half-consciously intended to provoke the rage necessary to any poet? But by then Cunningham was dead.

The summer of my freshman year I worked in a playground—my dad got me the job—and bicycled through Pennsylvania Dutch country. After sophomore year I went to Mexico with a roommate, and fell in love with a boy from Texas. The summer of junior year I traveled through Europe on the Vespa of a Danish boy who thought he was in love with me. By the middle of my senior year I was married to Jerry Ostriker, Harvard physics major. He was the only boy I knew who could defeat me in an argument. He was wild, funny, athletic, fiercely intelligent, irreverent, arrogant. He taught me to drink wine and love Mozart. He teased me out of my normal solemnity. He loved my writing, my mind, my independence, my breasts. I was not too brainy or too artistic for him. Finally there was someone with whom I could speak without caution. We went to Fresh Pond and read Thoreau. We secretly lived together in an apartment that cost us, if I recall, fifty dollars a month. Icy wind blew through its many cracks. The shower was one he rigged up over the big laundry sink in the kitchen, draped around

With daughter Eve, 1965

with a grass-green plastic shower curtain, into which friends climbed to bathe during parties. He helped me revise my term papers and threatened to divorce me if I ever dwindled into a housewife. We had two weddings: one on December 1, 1958, for ourselves and our friends before a justice of the peace in Somerville, Massachusetts, another on December 27 at the Park Avenue Synagogue. This was a concession to Jerry's family; we free spirits of course despised the whole notion of ceremony. I wore a blue-green chiffon dress, since virginal white would have violated my principles. We have lived intimately and bumpily ever after—two difficult workaholics, a poet and a scientist, united by the knowledge that anyone else as a mate would be hideously boring.

III. The Rules of the Game

Unlike those of mathematics and science, athletics, or war, and certainly unlike those of any legal code, the laws of art are invisible and incommunicable. To the artist, all human experience is raw material. But how to shape it? The sound must seem an echo of the sense, says Pope. A poem is that species of production in which the perfection of each aspect is consistent with the perfection of the whole, says Coleridge. Capable of being in uncertainties, mysteries, doubts, without any irritable reaching after fact and reason, says Keats. To break the pentameter, that was the first heave, says Pound. Ecstasy affords the occasion, says Moore, and expedience determines the form. No ideas but in things, says Williams.

You play tennis *with* a net, as Frost says, or you hack through the dark forest. The imagined net, the imagined forest—but these things are real. Form is the extension of content, say Creeley and Olsen. We break our heads working to get the poem right, dropping an adverb here, changing an assonance there, typing the damn thing over every time we put in or remove a comma. If the poem cannot ride on its music, if it ain't got that swing, it might as well be junked. What you want to express

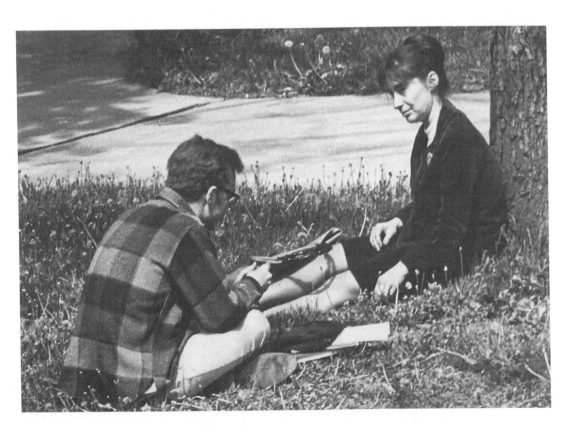

The author and a poetry student at Rutgers, late 1960s

The backyard at Princeton, 1972

is worthless. You hold the poem up to its unrealized Platonic form. Closer, closer.

I had always written formal poetry. My first masters were Keats, Hopkins, Auden. In graduate school I wrote a string of term papers on prosody—Campion, Tennyson, Herbert—each poet a new set of technical and emotional problems. My doctoral dissertation tracked the prosodic experiments of William Blake, rulebreaker and revolutionary, from the nursery rhyme cadences of the *Songs of Innocence and Experience* to the roar of his late prophecies. The year in which I wrote it was heavenly and hellish. I was happily pregnant, but the writing was difficult beyond my wildest dreams of difficulty. Determined to give birth to the dissertation before the baby, I did nothing but work. I swore I would never write another book. Our first daughter was born a week after I submitted the dissertation, in August 1963; she was a week late. *Vision and Verse in William Blake* was published eighteen months later, and has become the standard text on Blakean metrics. Blake would remain my guru in matters spiritual, psychological, and political for ten years. (The essay "The Road of Excess: My William Blake" in *The Romantics and Us* describes this romance, its breakup, and its residue.) Meanwhile, in my own poetry, I was gingerly step-

ping into open form. A foot in the water, a knee, a plunge.

After the dissertation, a year playing with Rebecca while Jerry finished his Ph.D. in astrophysics at Yerkes Observatory in Williams Bay, Wisconsin. Then a postdoctoral year in Cambridge, England, where Eve was born (this is called family planning) on Valentine's Day of 1965 in a nursing home run by starched nuns, and I worked on my first long poem, "Once More Out of Darkness," which Elaine Showalter later called "a poem in nine parts and a postpartum." "Once More" gave me my first conscious taste of rule-breaking. At that time I had never read anything written by a woman about pregnancy and birth, for the subject was, in mixed company, taboo.

When I began teaching at Rutgers University in 1965, my models for a living art almost immediately became Whitman, Williams, Ginsberg. We were in Vietnam time, an era of heartbreak and shame. If you paid your taxes, you were burning South Vietnamese babies alive. Everyone I knew marched and sang in antiwar demonstrations. It was also an era of sex and drugs and rock and roll. People younger than myself inventing utopia and smashing themselves against the stone heart of what Ginsberg calls Moloch. To be angry at America was right and justified. Yet there was an American poetry that stood, in quite precise ways, for hope. And to sustain an American poetics of inclusion you needed open form, a language able to ride the elevator from vernacular basement to Latinate penthouse, and a refusal to divide the sacred from the profane. Open form is to traditional form as democracy to autocracy. Open form, the art of improvisation, stands for the artist's faith that the past need not wholly determine the future. It is a gamble on freedom. My own freedoms were, of course, modest. No beatnik or Black Mountaineer I, but a struggling wife, mommy, teacher. By the mid-seventies, as I lifted my head after editing Blake's complete poems for Penguin and writing two hundred pages of notes to those poems, I began reading women poets. Reading? No, rather devouring.

I belonged to a generation of educated women who enjoyed a degree of good fortune unprecedented in history. We could read and write. We could work alongside men and control our own earnings and property. No longer required to spend our adult lives pregnant and lactating, we stood a very good chance of not dying in childbirth if we did have children. On the other hand, as critics like Elaine Showalter, Sandra Gilbert, and Susan Gubar were soon to demonstrate, an overtly ambitious woman is a monster; and she is especially monstrous if she obtrudes her sexuality upon the world. A woman who supposes her personal experience might mean something to others is "confessional" (always a term of opprobrium when applied to women, though not when applied to Robert Lowell) and embarrassing. An angry woman is strident, a visionary woman is escapist, and a woman who since childhood has hoped to "change the laws of history," as Adrienne Rich says, is obviously a mere propagandist. "I am large, I contain multitudes," announces Whitman. "I'm nobody," whispered Emily Dickinson in 1862, and not that much had changed a century later.

My husband and I job-hunted in 1964. I had a Ph.D. in hand and a book in press at a time when assistant professors were hired before their dissertations were finished. We both applied for positions at Princeton. He received an offer. I received a letter which addressed me as "Miss Ostriker." When you read that salutation, you know the news will be disagreeable. It read: "As a glance at our catalogue might have informed you, our faculty here at Princeton is entirely male. My reply to your query must therefore be in the negative." Very truly mine, signed, The Chairman. When I accepted an assistant professorship at Rutgers University, and we began living in Princeton's junior faculty housing, I found no other woman who was both mother and teacher (or who worked at any other profession). Nor was there another woman like me in my department. Nor were women writers taught in our classrooms, except for the obligatory Jane Austen, Emily Dickinson, George Eliot, none of whom was married or had children. My tenured colleagues were charming and clever men who behaved as if they had never in their lives gazed upon a diaper.

During my first year as a teacher my father-in-law died, my father died, and eight-month-old Eve nearly died. Between classes I sat in the hospital watching her tiny chest inside the oxygen tent gasping for breath. When she recovered I held her and sang the same lullaby, over and over, each night for a month. For two years I thought obsessively of death. Of such matters I did not dare, in our jolly academic lunches, to say a word.

As wife, graduate student, mother, teacher, scholar, I possessed an acceptable array of identities and an impossible set of burdens and obligations. Mostly, like countless others, I felt at the crumbling edge of depression, insanity, utter exhaustion, murderous rage. Like a generation of women, I read Sylvia Plath's *Ariel* with awe. Yet I was living a life I had myself chosen. Not for anything would I consider giving up a husband to love and quarrel with, children to adore and be driven crazy by, students whose thoughts I could observe crystallizing around fresh perceptions. My daily life included surges of joy, floods of eros, and the awareness that this odd existence was an experiment being performed by history.

When my first book of poems, *Songs,* was published by Holt, Rinehart in 1969, I encountered the fascinating silence of my colleagues. It was as if I had produced an illegitimate child. They had already tenured me for my academic work, and they were enlightened enough not to sew a scarlet letter onto my breast, but then again they would not embarrass me by mentioning my mishap. Rule of the game: "creative writing," in a scholarly English Department, was the equivalent of basket weaving. And then of course the book failed to sell and was pulped within a year. Rule of the game: poetry, to a commercial press, is a tax break. (Actually, there is little in that first book I can bear to read now; "juvenalia" seems too kind a term.) Small presses were more human, more countercultural. Over the next decade I published a string of small-press chapbooks climaxing in *The Mother/Child Papers.* That work was begun in 1970, when my son Gabe was born, a few days after President Nixon invaded Cambodia and National Guardsmen shot and killed four protesting students at Kent State University in Ohio. It was completed in 1980. Bill Mohr, the noble fool who ran Momentum Press in Los Angeles, had told me he would publish the book if I could finish it. To do so required understanding maternity in the light of a death-worshipping civilization. It also required facing my own potential for violence. And finding a poetic music capable of dealing with such things at the same time as the quotidian texture of family life. (See "A Wild Surmise: Motherhood and Poetry" in *Writing Like a Woman.)* Madmen like Bill, and the series of community-based poets' co-ops I belonged to, including US 1, which I helped found, probably saved my sanity. Rule of the game: no young writer should have to survive without a group of similarly haunted friends. I was also learning to read in public, and not simply to whisper into my collarbone but to perform. Semesters in California taught me. Watching Allen Ginsberg read and chant Blake with shameless abandon. Watching my ex-labor leader friend Jack Micheline stride up and down Telegraph Avenue shouting his broadside poems and selling them for a buck apiece. Rule of the game: write what you fear to write. Write what embarrasses and shames you. Write what you believe. Then say it loud. Be a fool for poetry.

There was also a road not taken, the road of journalism. For awhile I wrote book reviews for *Partisan Review* and ephemera for *Esquire*. Rule of the game for *Esquire:* be witty, be trivial, and they'll pay you well. My first assignment was on the chic New York restaurant Elaine's. I polished that piece of cotton candy as if it were bronze. A more entertaining assignment was a piece on Norman Mailer, who had appeared on the Johnny Carson show announcing that he had inherited Hemingway's mantle

as the Champion Novelist of America. This one I did as a mock-heroic poem in the style of Alexander Pope, called "The Rape of the C__K." It took me four hilarious days to write, and then four months to obtain permission to publish, from Mailer and the other literary celebrities the poem traduced. My last assignment was a profile of Yoko Ono, whom I interviewed in the cavern of the Dakota apartment. I swooned at the sight of her cheekbones and dancer's body. Alas, every word from her mouth was a cliché. She was the Sensitive Artist, the Avant-Garde Artist, the Misunderstood Outsider. Since everyone else hated Yoko I had been determined to like her, but all I could think of doing was splicing this banal monologue with quotations from Kafka's mean story about pretentious art, "Josephine the Mouse Singer." Impossible; for to do so would have been unkind to another woman.

Which brings me to feminism. Or my own version of it, which starts up where Blake leaves off. "If one woman told the truth about her life," Muriel Rukeyser once said, "the world would split open." What poets was I reading, begin-

Reading at the Dodge Foundation Poetry Festival, Waterloo, New Jersey, 1986

ning in the mid-seventies? White women: Plath, Piercy, Atwood, Sexton, Rich, Kumin, Kizer, Levertov, Wakoski, Swenson. Black women: Brooks, Giovanni, Lorde, Jordan, Walker, Shange, Clifton. Dirt-poor street-talking women: Ai, Alta, Grahn. They went directly to my bloodstream. And H.D., to whom I was introduced by my student Joe Boles, who wanted to write a dissertation on Auden and H.D. Auden and who? I asked. So Joe gave me *Trilogy, Helen in Egypt,* and *Tribute to Freud.* Unbelievable. Reading *Helen in Egypt* was like reading Blake's prophecies for the first time; I experienced the same sense of utter bafflement, and the same certainty that when I succeeded in understanding these books I would have a priceless treasure for the remainder of my life. There was at this time no guide to H.D.—nothing but the condescension of Hugh Kenner, to whom H.D. was an insignificant pebble in the Ezra Pound torrent, and a few other gentlemen critics explaining that H.D.'s poems represented the quest for the phallus she didn't have. Susan Stanford Friedman's pathbreaking *Psyche Reborn,* which I read in manuscript, changed all that, and offered a model of feminist criticism: minutely scrupulous in its scholarship, eloquent in its interpretation of H.D.'s "spiritual reality," unswerving in its insistence on a woman writer's capacity both to honor and to transform the heritage of her culture.

My views on individual women's poetry and the women's poetry movement in America are in *Writing Like a Woman* and *Stealing the Language,* plus several subsequent essays. I think I have demonstrated quite clearly that women poets are speaking some unprecedented truths about the self, the body, anger and violence, love and community, tradition and myth. I try to show how their need produces stylistic and formal experiment, and how they tend to transgress the dualisms that govern our thinking. These ideas are attacked, naturally, by traditionalist critics who fear that the barbarians at the gates are destroying the citadel of poetry. Current critical theory, on the other hand, even when it means to be feminist, tends to flatten poetry into abstraction, losing the flesh and blood of it. It pains me to see quantities of acute and adventurous writing by women poets ignored by the critical establishment. But in the long run the academy cannot matter very much. To be or not to be brave enough to say the unsayable: that is the question. The contours of American poetry have been altered by the

The author's portrait of her daughter Rebecca, 1991

explosion of women's voices; my own poetry has gained immeasurably. What a time to be alive, what a time to be a woman writer, up in the air so blue. Turning silence into speech. Changing the rules.

While *Stealing the Language* was being revised and *The Imaginary Lover* was in press, in the fall of 1985, I experienced the episode of automatic writing described in the preface to *The Nakedness of the Fathers.* I found myself speculating about Job's wife—that nameless woman whose ten children God permits Satan to kill on a sort of bet. I felt a scream six thousand years old in my throat. It was Job's wife screaming to high heaven. I could hear her demanding justice from the God of patriarchy. From that time to the present, I have been obsessed with religion, and especially with the Bible. From this obsession have come poems, essays, classes, lectures, workshops, and (so far) two books. The sequence of poems called "A Meditation in Seven Days," in *Green Age,* began itself while

I was reading Adrienne Rich's "Sources," Merlin Stone's *When God Was a Woman,* and Raphael Patai's *The Hebrew Goddess.* Brooding over the exclusions of females and femaleness within Judaism, the sequence ends with a dream of a woman's hand on a latch, "about to enter." *Feminist Revision and the Bible* looks at the burial of women in Biblical narrative and at the way women poets rewrite some of those stories. *The Nakedness of the Fathers: Biblical Visions and Revisions* records my own wrestling with the Hebrew Bible. These rewritings are in the high tradition of Jewish argument, which always challenges authority, and in the tradition of midrash, which encourages the free play of imagination. Rule of the game: there is always another interpretation. So says Talmud, though the Talmudists did not take into account the possibility that the interpreter might be a woman. Or, even worse, that the woman might tear down the *mechitza* that divides a man's prayer from a woman's prayer. Whose covenant is it? Whose stories are they? I find myself in Sarah, Rebecca, Rachel, and Leah. But also myself in Abraham, Isaac, Jacob. Jacob the sneak-thief, Jacob the visionary, who one night is assailed by a mysterious being, and wrestles with that being all night until the dawn. "Let me go," says the strange man. "I will not let thee go except thou bless me," responds Jacob.

Nakedness pursues a Biblical trajectory from the Adam and Eve who are the image of Elohim—evidently an androgynous divine being—to David, Solomon, Job, and beyond. When I began this writing, it seemed like falling off a cliff. But I had been preparing for it all my life. When I first read the Bible, fortunately on my own rather than for a class, the stories and poetry enthralled me, and I skipped Leviticus. An etching hangs on my foyer wall, done when I was still in school, of a frowning Jacob wrestling a smiling angel. "I Will Not Let Thee Go Except Thou Bless Me" is its title. When I first read *Paradise Lost,* I rooted for Eve and the apple. Yes, girl, get us out of that sleepy obedient Eden, that womb, that tomb. I had been enamored with the Blake who embraced Jesus but loathed every form of orthodoxy. The final chapter of *Stealing the Language* had celebrated what I called revisionist mythmaking in other women's poetry. A tradition either grows and changes, or it dies, I argued. To steal the language is to appropriate what we need. To be the growing tip. When Gabriel

was studying for his Bar Mitzvah, I thoroughly enjoyed going to the Princeton Hillel and discussing the weekly Torah portion. In *The Imaginary Lover,* a poem called "Every Woman Her Own Theology" proposes my "requirements" for the sacred, and concludes in a half-jesting expectation of revelation. I was ripe.

Writing *The Nakedness of the Fathers* over a period of nearly ten years has been the most exciting work of my life. Discovering others doing similar work made it the more thrilling. Books and essays, poetry and fiction by women (and some men) engaged in transforming the meaning of religion are today surging from the presses. Lilith returns from exile, the Shekhinah materializes in women's new rituals, goddesses borrowed from Pagan, Hindu, Native American, and African traditions reappear in feminist theology. Liturgy is changing for Jews and Christians. Despite the frightening exuberance of militant fundamentalism everywhere on the planet, some of us believe in what H.D. called "the unwritten volume of the new." We cannot separate ourselves from the past; but the past

A drawing of son Gabe, 1991

does not wholly determine the future. Rule of the game: improvise. Be open.

IV. Twelve Common Questions

*W*hy do you write? Here I stand; I can do no other.

Whom do you write for? Myself and strangers, Gertrude Stein said. A nice answer. To write is to walk in fog flinging seed from your hand in the knowledge that you will never see it hit the ground. I might also say that I write for the noble dead whose beauty and courage and love of art have inspired me. It is my timid fantasy that I might join them. "And I shall dine at journey's end / With Landor and with Donne," says Yeats. I share with Yeats, and T. S. Eliot, and James Merrill, the fantasy that a sort of large, shifting party is going on in the great beyond, populated by the artists one loves. Imagine arriving at the entrance. Imagine being allowed to enter.

Do you have any other strange fantasies? Yes, many. Every major work I have undertaken has attempted to solve some problem or understand something that confused me. Most have also involved some absurd imagined goal. Writing a set of autobiographical poems in the early '70s, I thought the poems would show me where it all went wrong in my childhood. The result would be purgation; I would be free at last, a grown-up. Naturally the poems came out differently from what I expected, and the purgation did not quite occur.

In order to annotate Blake's poetry, I vowed that I would read through the poems systematically, stopping whenever I encountered something I didn't understand, working until I could explain that phrase or line somehow, and then writing a clarifying note. I had agreed to do this because Harold Bloom's notes to the Erdman-

Rebecca, Alicia, Jerry, Eve, and Gabe hiking in Colorado, 1988

Bloom edition seemed designed not to illuminate Blake but to show how erudite Harold Bloom was. My students wanted something more helpful. My plan was to make William Blake so clear that cats and dogs in the street could understand him. When that happened, obviously, tyranny and oppression would yield to universal peace and freedom.

Writing *Stealing the Language,* and the poems in *The Mother/Child Papers, A Woman under the Surface,* and *The Imaginary Lover,* I fantasized that I belonged to a sisterhood of women writers. Allied across the boundaries of race and class, lesbianism and heterosexuality, we were about to change the paradigms of American poetry and criticism. "Pull down thy vanity, I say pull down!" Pound said that, but didn't mean it. We would mean it. The collective poetic voice of woman was going to help end gender stereotypes and transform our conceptions of the body, the passions, the mind. Oh yes, and it would improve men's behavior.

And what was my fantasy while composing *Nakedness?* At the close of the Book of Job, God rebukes Job's false comforters—the pious friends who insist that God would never afflict a virtuous man. "Ye have not spoken of me the thing that is right, as my servant Job hath," he declares. Writing *The Nakedness of the Fathers,* I hoped to discover what the Bible signified to me, and I to it; to unravel what I admired and hated in Judaism, its men and women, its principles, its God; to see what illumination its ancient stories shed on current history and politics. Soon after commencing, I recognized that there was something in my manuscript to offend everyone. To orthodox Jews it would be heresy, while to Christians it would be altogether too Jewish. Men would find it irritating as a feminist tract. Feminists would disapprove of its enthusiastic heterosexuality. Biblical scholars would see it as the work of someone without credentials. Goddess worshippers would be disgusted at my refusal to walk out of Jahweh's ancient patriarchal house, slamming the door like Nora. The common reader, that mythical animal, would be confused by the mixed genres. So what did I think I was doing? The absurd truth is that I thought I was writing the book for God. After whom I panted as the hart panteth after the water-brook. Whom I seek as the Shulamite seeks the beloved through the streets of the city. As if the book were an extended prayer, a window, a mirror held to

the sky. As if God would glance over some heavenly ramparts at the armies of fundamentalists and murmur, "They have not said the thing about me that is right, as my servant Alicia has."

If you were raised an atheist, what is all this nonsense about God? A good question. A good question.

What is the difference between critical writing and poetry? Left brain, right brain. When I write a critical essay I design the argument beforehand, know my audience, and know what others have to say about my topic. When I write a poem I never plan. The poem finds me, interrupts whatever else I am doing, throws me some words and demands that I start writing. Then I crawl forward in the dark. Or I am assailed by emotions or images I cannot understand unless I write. The poem is a translation, always inadequate, of nonverbal experience into language. Some postmodernists tell us that no reality exists outside of language, but poets know that, as e. e. cummings said, "feeling is first" and language limps afterward. Whereas when you write criticism you feel masterly and in control—which is, of course, an illusion.

Since I hate compartments and boundaries, I have tried to make my criticism and poetry feed each other. To write intelligent poems and passionate criticism. Shifting my critical writing from dead white males (whom I loved) to twentieth-century women poets (from whom I learned courage) helped considerably. I continued and continue to write critical essays on male poets, however. Shifting into gear for *The Nakedness of the Fathers* meant, further, that no border was sacred; everything I knew could be poured into that vessel, and every category could leap into every other. Sacred, profane, sublime, ridiculous, private, public, prose, poetry. The copulation of past with present, commentary with autobiography, anger with joy.

How did you manage to raise three children, teach full-time, and write all those books? The short answer: I didn't get the housework done and I didn't have a social life. To young women foolish enough to want to marry, raise families, and write, I tentatively proffer a longer answer. First, choose the mate carefully. If your heart misgives you regarding his (or her) support of your work, find another partner. Second, find a community and make sure you have adequate child care. The nuclear family seems designed to maximize stress and guilt, and its envelope should be stretched. They say it takes a village to raise a child. We had au pair girls for ten years, and they became friends, and it helped some. Third, be prepared to kiss your liberty goodbye for a couple of decades. Fourth, remember that your family is raw material. Whoever they are, whoever you are, they will inevitably put you through hell, purgatory, and heaven; they will teach you truths you can learn in no other way; they represent absolute hope and absolute despair, like the world itself, of which they are each a microcosm. Study them. Each of them is a different cosmos. Bring them into language. Trust.

How does your family feel about being put into language? Variously. My mother is a true sport. She overlooks poems in which I represent her as crazy lady; she bursts with pride at my citation of her as the first woman poet in my life, and as beloved wise woman in *Nakedness*. Jerry, who has had to put up with colleagues asking him how he feels about having a poet for a wife, says things like "It's a package deal," which I suppose is code for "none of your business." Although we talk about nearly everything, I was for a long time reluctant to inquire about this. Finally—this is now years ago—after a couple of stiff bourbons I screwed my courage to the sticking point, and asked him how he really felt. He replied that writing poetry was my job, and that when I write about marriage I am writing for all those who do not have the language. I nearly fell off my chair with gratitude, since I can tell the difference between my husband saying "okay" with a whole heart, and "okay" with small print; this was the real thing. Gabriel was an early enthusiast, getting his teachers to invite his mother the poet to classes. He likes *The Mother/Child Papers*, which feature him, and doesn't like some other things. Eve, who has become a young scientist, approves of the "Birthday Suite" in *Green Age*. Rebecca I fear to have offended. I raised that girl to be a free and independent spirit—and when she actually became one, surprise! I felt devastated. During a period when she was on leave of absence from college, living in San Francisco and not writing or calling very frequently, I wrote a set of mother-daughter poems describing her as "Hacking away at this iron umbilicus / Having sensibly put three thousand miles between us." That she had to separate herself from me I understood intellectu-

ally; the poems explored my own painful and rueful emotions at the loss of her. They were good poems. Generic. For two years I performed "Listen" and "A Question of Time" at readings, and audience members would invariably come up afterward saying "I'd like a copy of those mother-daughter poems for my mother" or "I wish my daughter could see those poems." But I felt increasingly uncomfortable sharing this material with strangers when my daughter herself had never read it. Finally I bit the bullet; as the manuscript of *The Imaginary Lover* was in preparation, I hinted of the existence of these poems. The next time Rebecca was home—August of '84 I think it was—she demanded to see the manuscript the minute she walked in the door. I handed it to her; she closed herself in her bedroom and I waited with sweaty palms. When she emerged, she said coolly that three of the four poems were acceptable. The fourth, "The Unsaid, or, What She Thinks When She Gets My Letter," was unacceptable. I imagined, in that poem, that she might tear the mother's missive up or forget to open it, and Rebecca umbraged: "I would never do that!" My dear, dearest, my princess, my queen, no problem. I'll take it right out of the manuscript. A few days later she informed me haughtily that I might put the poem back in the manuscript.

What is it like being married to a scientist? A profile of the two of us in *Scientific American* tells all.

Do you enjoy teaching? For years, because I cared so much about doing a good job and was so convinced of my inadequacies, I had stomach cramps before every single class. But the truth is 'that I adore teaching. Incredible good fortune that I can do this work I love and get paid for it. Rutgers undergraduates in particular are so gratifying because they tend to come from lower middle-class or working-class homes. Often theirs is the first generation to attend college. They run the gamut from semiliterate to brilliant. Some, it is true, seem to major in beer-drinking. The best of them are charged with energy, irrepressible, ambitious, idealistic, unintimidated, ready to experiment intellectually and emotionally. Our graduate students are splendid. Over the years I have taught whatever interested me: Blake and Milton, Contemporary Poetry, Prosody, Poetry by Women, The Bible and Feminist Imagination, Boundary Crossing (this was a course where we read twentieth-century male and female writers in pairs—my favorite segments were Momaday and Silko, Zora Neale Hurston and Ishmael Reed). Students of mine have become poets, novelists, writers of children's books, scholars, teachers, political activists, underground publishers, musicians, artists, photographers, actors. When I think that a little of what I gave them has shaped what they do, that my life ripples into theirs as a metaphor ripples into its many meanings—no thought gives me greater pleasure. Oh how I like to go up in the swing. There is also the knowledge that I have changed and expanded people's lives, quite apart from what they may or may not have done professionally. Helped some through insane stretches, trauma, grief. Numerous students have come out as gay to me, in preparation for telling their parents. Then there is the knowledge of those I could not reach. Or could not save. One of my loveliest students was dealing drugs the last I heard from him. Two have killed themselves. Two were destroyed by mental illness, one a Vietnam vet, one a folksinger whose wild gifts ended in a lobotomy. These memories are torments.

Do you enjoy doing readings? When I stand before an audience I shed my shyness and perform. Causing people to laugh and cry makes me feel alive. Helping them hear messages from their own minds makes me feel immortal.

Do you have any advice for young poets? Kill the censor. Write what you are afraid to write. Do it for yourself and strangers.

Are you satisfied with the work you have done? Of course not. Dissatisfaction goes with the territory.

V. These Are the Words

There is a promised land one is never permitted to enter. From the crest of middle age, I see it spread to the horizon like a mirage. Never to be given to me. Never. All I can do is imagine it, a place in which swords have been beaten into plowshares, spears into computer chips, and alabaster cities rise undimmed by human tears. In my husband's field, astrophysics, they are attempting to understanding the material origin of the universe. They can speak a global language about this. In my field, nobody knows what the soul is or what God is, but some think they do. And those who think they know, speak the ancient language of division and exclusion, of God-is-on-our-side, of death-to-the-infidel. The rigidly righteous are full of passionate intensity, not to mention stupidity, and they can choose their weapons.

How long will hate-saturated orthodoxies, claiming to be God's word, hold the high ground? How long before we wrestle, from the sacred traditions of the earth, an adequate blessing? If I believe anything, I believe that poets should contribute their wildest dreams to the ongoing life of the spirit. We know that the being we in the West call God the Father swallowed God the Mother in prehistory, some six thousand years ago, at the advent of monotheism. I believe that he is pregnant with her—perhaps our sufferings are God's labor pains—and that she will inevitably be reborn. Jewish mystics might call her the Shekhinah, Christians might call her Sophia. What this repressed being will be like when she returns, I cannot begin to guess. My own vision is far too weak.

I hold my life up to its unrealized Platonic model, the life it was meant to be. Forget it, I think. The eyes fade. The teeth wobble and begin to wave farewell. A breast surrenders to the surgeon's knife. An arm that laid bricks for a house in the country gets tiny arthritic twinges. A knee, with which one walked, danced,

With sculptor Sheila Solomon, 1990

Doing an interview at Bucknell University for
Feminist Revision and the Bible, *1991*

the day I die. Meanwhile, the world is what it is. Blood and bullets leak from the TV screen. The rich prey on the poor as they have always done. The irredeemably damned human race goes to the mall. The humanities self-destruct. Everywhere on the planet, women are still either angels or whores. Our teacher Moses, on this side of Jordan, gathered his people together and ranted the entire Torah at them, begging them to remember God's commandments while raging at them for their inevitable future apostasy. Increasingly I too feel the weary impulse to hand off whatever I have learned or done, so little as it is, such failure as I see it to be, to the young runners. Young men, young women. Here, I want to say. Take this. Look there. Scan the horizon. Go on. You go ahead. Carry it on. All of you who are able, use your imaginations. Open yourselves. Remember when you were loved. Carry it on. Please.

BIBLIOGRAPHY

Criticism:

Vision and Verse in William Blake, University of Wisconsin Press, 1965.

(Editor) *William Blake: The Complete Poems,* Penguin, 1977.

Writing Like a Woman ("Poets on Poetry" series), University of Michigan Press, 1983.

Stealing the Language: The Emergence of Women's Poetry in America, Beacon, 1986.

Feminist Revision and the Bible: The Bucknell Lectures on Literary Theory, Blackwell, 1993.

Poetry:

Songs: A Book of Poems, Holt, Rinehart, & Winston, 1969.

Once More Out of Darkness and Other Poems, Berkeley Poets' Press (Berkeley, California), 1974.

A Dream of Springtime: Poems, 1970–78, Smith/Horizon Press (New York), 1979.

The Mother/Child Papers, Momentum Press (Los Angeles, California), 1980, Beacon Press, 1986.

rode a bicycle, hiked mountain trails, signals at last that we were never intended to be upright creatures. The loss of these would be tolerable, perhaps, if it were not for the eraser wiping away streaks of one's mind.

Never trust anyone over thirty, they used to say. When I became thirty, I stopped thinking of myself as girl, and began calling myself woman. Thirty-five was excellent. When we reach heaven and are permitted to decide what age we want to be (if we cannot do that, it is not heaven), I will be thirty-five and go dancing every night and hiking on weekends. The approach of forty signalled that I needed to get on the horse, make my move, do whatever I meant to do with my life. Fifty was difficult. The prospect of sixty, unreasonably, feels like Ecclesiastes, the golden bowl broken, the silver cord snapped, the wheel broken at the cistern.

Whatever one has not accomplished now will never be done. So it seems when a person is tired. It is only a mood, I remind myself. I have promised to stick to the union till

A Woman under the Surface, Princeton University Press, 1982.

The Imaginary Lover, University of Pittsburgh Press, 1986.

Green Age, University of Pittsburgh Press, 1989.

The Nakedness of the Fathers: Biblical Visions and Revisions, Rutgers University Press, 1994.

The Crack in Everything, University of Pittsburgh Press, 1996.

Contributor of numerous articles to anthologies, including *Blake and the Moderns,* edited by Robert Berthoff and Annette Leavitt, State University of New York Press, 1982; *Politics and Poetic Value,* edited by Robert Von Hallberg, University of Chicago Press, 1987; *Sexton: Selected Criticism,* edited by Diana Hume George, University of Illinois Press, 1988; *Signets: Reading H.D.,* edited by Susan Stanford Friedman and Rachel Blau DuPlessis, University of Wisconsin Press, 1990; *Marianne Moore: The Art of a Modernist,* edited by Joseph Parisi, University of Michigan Press, 1990; *The Romantics and Us: Essays on Romantic and Modern Culture,* edited by Gene W. Ruoff, Rutgers University Press, 1990; *The Poetry of Irving Feldman,* edited by Harold Schweizer, Bucknell University Press, 1991; *The Continuing Presence of Walt Whitman: The Life after the Life,* edited by Robert K. Martin, University of Iowa Press, 1992; *Literary Influence and African-American Writers,* edited by Tracy Mishkin, Garland Publishing, 1996; *People of the Book: Thirty Scholars Reflect on Their Jewish Identity,* edited by Jeffrey Rubin-Dorsky and Shelley Fisher Fishkin, University of Wisconsin Press, 1996; *Maxine Kumin,* edited by Emily Grosholz, University Press of New England, 1996; and to periodicals, including *American Poetry Review, Blake: An Illustrated Quarterly, Contemporary Literature, Cream City Review, The Emily Dickinson Newsletter, Poetry East,* and the *Wallace Stevens Journal.*

Louis Owens

1948-

Mississippi was thick and deep in the heat of a cotton field. I remember well the prickly cotton bolls, the long rows, the big wire-mesh cotton trailers at the end by the road, the scales where bags were weighed, the brittle shadows cast along the droning furrows. I recall the easy talk of the Black pickers who loomed above me, laughing often, sometimes singing long stories whose words I couldn't make out as I dragged my own minuscule cotton bag behind me and pretended to do what they did.

That was fun. At my pleading, my grandma had sewn the bag out of a flour sack just like the ones that made my shirts, and I was allowed to go into the fields to do play-work. But when the wet heat was too much, unlike the others I could retire to the shade of the big pecan tree by our cabin to play stretch with my older brother, Gene, at age seven two years older than me. The trick was to throw one's pocketknife so that it stuck in the earth. The opponent had to keep one foot next to his rival's foot and stretch his other leg far enough to step in the spot where the knife had stuck. Sometimes the trick was to see how close to a bare foot a knife would stick. Once my knife stood quivering upright a half inch above my brother's big toe and about an inch in toward the center of his right foot, with surprisingly little blood showing where the blade had entered his skin. When we tired of that we could sneak into the cotton trailers and jump in the great soft mounds of cotton until an adult shouted us out.

Some days we would ride in the tarpaulin-covered back of our grampa's big truck to take sandwiches and Nehi Punch to cotton pickers in distant fields. No one ever said what was in the sandwiches, but whatever it was came from our father's hunting trips in the swampy forest along the river each night. We knew it wasn't coon because Black and Indian neighbors came out of the woods to take away the skinless raccoon bodies every morning. There were hints

Louis Owens

of alligator sandwiches, but as we lounged in the shadowy interior of the truck on those wet-hot days, drinking illicit sodas, no one was interested enough to look between the slices of white bread.

Across the dirt road from our two-room cabin were dense woods with vines to swing on, and not much farther was the great Yazoo River, as fearsome and thrilling a body of water as the world has ever seen. Along its banks the Yazoo spawned squadrons of poisonous snakes with names like cottonmouth and water moccasin, and in the brown water lived snapping turtles, alligators, needle-toothed gars, and catfish big enough to eat a rowboat. A photograph in my mother's trunk showed my uncle and grampa posed with a trot-line catfish from the river so big that with its head tied to a horse's saddle pommel the tail dragged the ground behind the horse's rear hooves. Once my father gave a beloved, half-grown pup to a man across the river, and the next day the pup was back, having swum that awful river to play with us, bearing no grudge for the mistake that had taken him to the other side. When our father took the dog back again, even my older brother—the toughest person I've ever known and, for years, my hero—cried.

When people ask me where we lived in Mississippi, all I can say is next to the Yazoo someplace north of Vicksburg. There was no town that I can remember, only a tiny, falling-down store a few miles up the dirt road in one direction close to the ferry and a grim-looking gas station more miles down the same road in the other direction. For a year we went to school a long, long bus ride somewhere beyond the gas station, where each day I watched the round, glass-topped pumps as we passed by and tried to stare into the dark, cavernous garage. Invariably two or three overalled white men sat on a bench outside the garage staring back at our bus and spitting mean brown arcs into the greasy dirt. My oldest sister, who was nine, and my brother and I felt pretty rich on that bus, for we had shoes and once we even had a nickel each to buy peanuts that someone on the bus sold. Forty years later I cringe at a memory of selfishly denying my last peanut to a boy from across the river who, shoeless himself, worked up the courage to ask. My brother, I recall, turned his head away in embarrassment for me. At the school, I also recall, other people turned their heads away from all of us who came on that bus.

Mississippi was my father's birthplace, the black earth of his Choctaw roots and the sweaty paradise his Irish and French ancestors had invaded, undoubtedly a cast-off people much poorer than the Indian families they married into. He'd taken us—my mother, brother, and three sisters—there with him when he left the army in the early fifties. We had all been born in California, though my older sister and brother had different fathers and I was my father's first child, and after a few short years in Mississippi we would all be back in California, where the family would eventually grow to nine children and our poverty would inconceivably grow even more desperate. We made a couple of experimental moves back and forth between Mississippi and California before my mother—

Parents, Ida Brown and Hoey Owens, 1947

tired of a plank-walled cabin with no electricity or plumbing—won the argument and we stayed near the Pacific Ocean.

First we lived in a tent along with many other farm workers on the outskirts of Delano in California's Central Valley, a nicer version of the Okie camps I'd later read about in *The Grapes of Wrath*. Though only one room, our A-frame tent had a wooden floor and was clean. There was a spigot for running water outside, and after a while we were allowed to move into one of the little white houses on the "ranch" where my father worked. A little while later he was fired and in the process, either before or after the firing, called a "goddamned Indian" by the boss. That I heard while eavesdropping on my parents' conversation from the kitchen. From Delano we camped up and down the Central Valley for a time before being accepted in the low-income county "housing project" in Paso Robles, a wonderful place full of wild brown and black kids.

Somewhere during this time, there was a summer in Oklahoma, too, where my mother's

Cherokee and Irish family were rooted. On a farm where my mother's father lived alone, tenanting for an absentee landlord, my brother and I teamed up with boys our age from a Black shantytown nearby to steal my grampa's watermelons. We'd swing across a dry creekbed with a watermelon under one arm and one hand and both feet wrapped around a rope, hoping to reach the shantytown side with our spoils. At least half the melons died explosive pink deaths in the creekbed, but the other half were even greater sources of exultation and joy. When not stealing melons, we rode in the back of our grampa's rattling Jeep, alert to dodge the tobacco juice that would whip our way without warning. We went with him to buy blocks of ice for the icebox, and we helped pluck the headless chickens after they were dipped in boiling water. I realize now that my mother barely knew that man, her father, who had deserted his children many years before, and the summer was a tenuous reaching out that didn't work. I can't remember ever seeing him again.

Autobiography must be the story of family and place. For me there are two primary places that frame my life in black and white: Mississippi and California. No two worlds could have been more different in deep, soul-carving ways. Whereas today I have a strange nostalgia for and shadowy half-memories of that Yazoo country, a sense of something lost there that cannot be regained, about California I feel a fine, clean sense of love. Not for the crowded, humanity-impacted place I see when I return today, but for the California of my childhood and adolescence. That was a world of sun and warmth where my brother and I wandered through the coastal mountains and amidst the tangled growth of the dry Salinas River, armed with slingshot, shotgun, or rifle. When our family left the county housing project, we took up residence deep in the coast range, the beautiful Santa Lucia mountains, where whole hillsides would erupt in orange-gold poppies and shimmering blue lupines each spring. The oaks rose in wondrous gleaming branches or drooped canopies right to the earth. We climbed them and hid ourselves in their shaded interiors while our father rode a bicycle fifteen miles to work in a laundry, standing all day in water that rotted both shoes and feet because he couldn't afford rubber boots. At night I'd watch him

take off the decaying shoes and socks and see the ulcerated skin falling away from his feet and the controlled expression on his face. That is the only memory to darken the time in the Santa Lucias.

From the coast range we moved to the verge of the Salinas River, and that, too, was a world of light and life, the river coming to raging life during the winter rains and drying to white sand every summer. At that time my father had a job as a water witch for a man who drilled wells, using a forked willow stick to locate water in the sun-beaten oat hills east of the Salinas. I like to think of him now walking those dry, golden hills in boots that never touched the water he found.

In the course of those growing years—and to my wonderment today as I look back—we killed everything that moved and breathed, from sparrows to rabbits, squirrels, quail, and deer. We made jerky out of blue-jay and thrush breasts and practiced tanning mouse skins, activities that caused much hilariousness among a Lakota friend and his Yurok wife when I confessed many years later. "Must be a Choctaw thing," he said, as they held their sides and rocked with badly repressed mirth. Having forsaken hunting more than twenty-five years ago, I remember those countless days of carnage as though they are part of someone else's story. We ate everything we shot, of course, except the sparrows. And certainly we could not have lived, the eleven of us, without the many deer and innumerable rabbits and quail. But today I have difficulty imagining myself putting a bullet through any animal. I recall with some pain the moment I quit hunting with a bow. It was the day I pinned a rabbit to a tree with an arrow through the skin of his chest and he spun in crying circles around the arrow shaft. I also know the wrenching cry of a wounded deer, a sound that doesn't go away.

It seems a terrible thing, all of that killing of animals, but it seemed the most natural thing in the world at the time, and it was a necessity. More than that, however, hunting taught me about the natural world with an intensity and depth I could have found no other way. It isn't just a cliché to say that the true hunter becomes one with his prey. Hunting taught me the way a rabbit or deer or quail responds to its world, the habits and patterns, the comfortable or nervous reactions of large and small. Stalking the dry riverbed or the oak-and-pine coast range on cold fall mornings, I learned to discern the difference in shading between a still cottontail's hunched form and the grass and brush around it. I knew that if flushed it would bound away and, always, stop just within eyesight to look back. That pause was inevitably its end. And I learned the differing textures of shade that told me a deer was browsing in the drooping canopy of an oak or in tall grain in the half-dark just before dawn. I knew how far a quail would run before exploding into flight. I watched the intricate courting of doves and many other creatures. To successfully stalk and kill these animals one must come very close to them. Today, after so many years away from the hunt, I can still detect the differing textures and hues of color that tell me a coyote or deer or rabbit is motionless within a cluster of oak or creosote bush. I can differentiate the angular motion of a rabbit caught just out of the corner of my eye from the jerky race of a fleeing squirrel or the slide of a fox, without actually seeing any of them fully.

Living in a house in the dry New Mexico mountains now, I put out bird feeders and sunken troughs of water, and I watch with great pleasure the rabbits and tassel-eared squirrels come to eat the spilled feed and drink the water. Both squirrels and rabbits, in fact, have become so familiar that they simply move a few feet out of the way when one of our family appears, not to be stepped on, and continue whatever they are doing. At times I find myself politely asking cottontails to move from the doorstep so that I can enter my house, or I am awakened by the chattering of a squirrel peering through my upstairs window, angry because the sunflower seeds haven't been replenished in the second-story squirrel feeder. But amidst this peaceable kingdom I now inhabit, I confess that I still cannot watch a fat cottontail grazing beneath the bird feeder without almost tasting the aroma of lightly floured rabbit breast frying in butter. Someday, I think—and tease my children with the thought—I might yet weaken and eat my wild neighbors just as my neighbors do to one another. When I run the forest trails near my home, I watch for the deer, fox and coyote, bobcat and badger, porcupine and skunk tracks that appear every morning. And on the very best mornings, my strides become faster and lighter as I find myself gliding over the almost dainty tracks of a black bear who has ambled along the same trail some time during the night.

My first job, besides the play-work of cotton-picking, was in the bean fields when I was nine. For sixty-five cents an hour, along with my brother, I hoed weeds, undoubtedly hoeing as many pinto bean plants as weeds. All around us in that part of central coastal California were fields bursting with growing things in long, tidy, heavily sprayed rows. Every summer we headed for those fields: beans, sugar beets, strawberries, celery, tomatoes, lettuce. In the morning the plants would be heavy with the night's irrigation, soaking us to the skin and chilling us brutally in the first ten minutes of work, but by afternoon the sun would feel like death and I'd keep my eyes down not merely to see the weeds which were the enemy but to avoid seeing the interminable stretch of each row that lay ahead. We used *el cortito*, the accurate, short-handled hoe that has since been made illegal because of the back problems it caused field workers. Planes would come and spray lines of herbicides and pesticides over the fields, and we would half-heartedly wander out of the way, confident that no spray could dent the armor of our youth. Often we worked with the people then called *braceros*, the workers who came up from Mexico every year for the crops and taught us to say delicious words or phrases like *chingada*, *pendejo*, and *hijo de la puta*. We learned that in the right circumstances it wasn't even necessary to say *tu madre* to get into a fight; with the right intonation *tuyo* or even *tu* alone would do the trick. Today I still sometimes feel a painful twitch just to the right of my dorsal spine where a very large sugar beet swung by its stem by a wiry young man laid me out between the rows. I thought I had won that fight until I stupidly turned my back.

For a couple of years we lived on a chicken ranch that my father managed in a canyon of the coast range. It was a beautiful setting despite the constant presence of mountains of chicken manure outside each long chicken house. At twelve and fourteen, my brother and I did almost all of the work before and after school, on days of being ordered to play hooky, and during summers: hoisting the huge sacks of chicken feed into the automated hoppers and pulling mutilated chickens out of the chain-driven feeding trough. When one of the automatic waterers would break, the foot or so of dry chicken droppings in a house would magically be transformed into instant, real, maggot-infested shit, and we would get the job of shoveling and wheelbarrowing that out also. At night raccoons would come and reach their hands through the wire to grasp whatever chicken part was handy, often beginning their meal with chicken toes and leaving legless hens for us to find in the morning. Not too differently than the raccoons, our family barbecued the "culls" on weekends, those chickens who had lost some cosmic dice throw and been born with legs on backwards or some such unmarketable disfigurement. All chickens look alike on the barbecue.

It was on the chicken ranch when I was in fifth grade that my father gave me my first real gun, a single-shot .22 so ancient and fragile that once it was cocked it would go off if I rapped my knuckles against the stock. Rabbits and squirrels and many birds suffered from that gun.

When the chicken ranch corporation manager showed up once too often to discover children doing adult work and the proper adult nowhere to be found, our father was fired and we moved ten miles east to the banks of the Salinas River. Meanwhile, however, armed with our extensive training, my brother and I hit upon the clever scheme of forming our own two-person company for cleaning out chicken houses, of which there were scores at our end of the Salinas Valley. At fourteen and sixteen years old, we would contract for a fixed rate to remove tons of chicken shit, often two feet deep, from houses as long as football fields, leaving in the end nothing but gleaming white concrete floors. We were good at it and the pay was better than field work. I saved enough to buy a five-speed bike the first summer. My brother bought a green '51 Chevy which later, when he went to Vietnam for the first time, became mine. The chickenshit cleaning company died when, in my sophomore year of high school, I elected to go to Merced to work in the tomato fields.

It began as a project to get poor Black kids out of California's cities. There had been riots and burnings in Los Angeles the summer before, and the politicians were desperate to prevent the same thing again. Coincidentally, the *bracero* program that allowed for imported Mexican field labor had just been declared null and void. Politicians and corporate agriculture,

usually close bedfellows if not Siamese twins in California, hit upon what must have seemed a brilliant idea: they would take African-American youths from the innercities and put them to work in the fields, thus solving the labor crisis while also preventing summer riots. They must have leaned back in their chairs and grinned themselves silly when the idea came to them. But of course it couldn't be that simple. They knew they couldn't get away with a program that glaringly took Black boys from the cities and stuck them in fields recently emptied of brown laborers. So they hit upon a politically correct definition: it would be a summer work program for financially underprivileged teens. And guess who qualified?

Our busload of riff-raff from our little ranching and farming region (doctors' and engineers' children were *not* on the bus) contained one Black person. His nickname was Doc, and he was from Paso Robles, the next town over. Seventeen-year-old Doc was, according to accounts not of his own telling, the greatest lover ever to strike our part of the state. Tall and lean, with a millionth-degree black belt in karate or judo (which none of us could tell apart, of course, but had seen in James Bond films), full of jokes and smiles, while still on the bus Doc was saying that when he got back he was going to "lay more pipe than a plumber." We were in awe of Doc despite the fact that some among us were not predisposed to like people with very dark skin.

When the bus took us through the guarded gate of our farm labor camp outside of Merced, and we saw ourselves surrounded not merely by ten-foot chain link fences topped with barbed wire but, more shockingly, by hundreds of the toughest and meanest-looking Black people any of us had ever imagined, Doc became an even more invaluable asset. I think each one of the thirty of us knew instinctively that Doc would save our collective asses, and on our second day in the camp he did just that.

It happened exactly as we knew it would. We walked out of the mess hall, where the food was inedible, and found a wall of very dark individuals from foreign places like Watts and East Palo Alto waiting for us, people very different from the friendly "colored" neighbors I'd known in Mississippi. Very calmly one of them announced that they thought they might just stomp our white butts into the dirt. I remember looking around at our group, probably the toughest bunch our county had to offer, and knowing we were done for. I considered confessing that I was not really entirely white, but realized it probably would do more harm than good. And then Doc stepped forward, picked up the speaker, twirled him around a few times, and deposited him on the ground in an odd assortment of shapes. Everyone on both sides was impressed and delighted by the novelty, including the one on the ground. It was decided then that we should all be friends, just like that. From that day forward we played basketball together and dug our way out of the back of the compound together to buy edible food in town and threw up together when we smelled the rotten slop they tried to feed us for lunch and dinner.

It was a three-week adventure. At the end of those three weeks the good citizens of Merced could no longer tolerate a bunch of "niggers" on the edge of their town, so a mob attacked the camp. Though a line of police vehicles surrounded the camp to protect us innocents, one person outside the camp was killed and we were all, including the toughest from deepest L.A., scared shitless. The next morning we all awoke to discover the camp's office closed and no white adults to be found. We learned in short order that we would not be paid and that we were on our own to get home. They had charged us exorbitant fees for lodging in the lice-infested barracks, for the powdered eggs and watered orange drink and foul cauldrons of soup at breakfast, lunch, and dinner, and for transportation to the tomato fields on the backs of flatbed trucks in the freezing pre-dawn darkness. Plus insurance, of course. Though some had enough money for bus tickets or could phone someone for help, most of us were broke and on our own, so we began hitchhiking the several hundred miles toward home. In the end I lost twelve dollars on the whole deal but learned a valuable assortment of lessons, most importantly that if at five-feet-eight-inches I wished to be able to dunk a basketball like the even shorter kid from Stockton I would have to do a lot of leg work with weights, both of which I accomplished.

My mother was a waitress in small cafes occasionally, but as our family expanded to nine children plus three cousins informally adopted for several years, it became impossible for her to work outside the home. The fact that our house usually resembled a refugee camp or homeless shelter, with a revolving population of cousins, friends, and even strangers, made her job of mothering still tougher. We had no curfews, no limits on when we could leave the house or return, no rules. It certainly would have been impossible for anyone to keep track of us anyway. I can't remember a time when someone wasn't sleeping on the couch and several others on pallets on the floor. Beds often had between two and four occupants, kids sometimes sleeping with heads in opposite directions so that you'd wake up with someone else's stinking feet next to your face. Once a woman stayed nearly two weeks before we all sort of realized that no one really knew who the woman was. Perhaps she'd been invited by my older brother or sister, or maybe an aunt, but no one would confess. After she left, the knowledge surfaced that she was a prostitute who'd decided our house was a good place to hide for a while. Today I admire that woman's brazen wit—who'd notice her in the maelstrom of our household, indeed? I also recall a certain unusual interest she had taken in me, but my seventeen-year-old consciousness had enough sense to become very nervous and cause me to flee when that happened. Thus my virtue was preserved.

With deteriorating health, eventually including tuberculosis, double radical mastectomies, and the emphysema that would kill her, my mother struggled to keep the constant pot of beans cooking and to peel enough potatoes for every dinner. Because my mother's sister had married an Italian-American bean farmer, we always had a hundred-pound sack of pinto beans or baby limas reclining in a corner of the kitchen. Because probably fifteen or twenty deer a year found their way into our freezer and we either gleaned potatoes from harvested fields or bought them by the hundred-weight, there were always frying meat and frying potatoes. Everything was fried, even the okra. (Once I fried a grasshopper, which turned out to be bitter but nicely crisp.) Lard came with the commodities from the county, so there was always plenty of grease for the frying. My strongest memory of my mother is of her standing at a stove turning over potatoes in a sputtering pan, the bones of her frail body sticking through her clothes and her graying black hair escaping in wisps from behind her ears. She always seemed far older than her age. As a young woman she had been very beautiful, black-haired and brown-eyed with an incredible perfect smile. Photographs tell me that. She was born in Texas, just across the border from Oklahoma, to a three-quarters Cherokee mother who was thirteen years old at the time. The stories of my mother's childhood were fragmented, always incomplete, involving different men—temporary fathers—in various parts of Oklahoma, Texas, and Arkansas. In one story as a child she caught an alligator gar longer than she was, and dragged the thrashing monster up onto the riverbank. In another story she went into the woods with a Cherokee stepfather to search out a lightning-struck tree for some purpose she didn't understand. In another she had a pet flying squirrel. In one particularly sharp fragment, told to me from what we both knew was her deathbed, she and her little brother and toddler sister walked what in the telling seemed all of one long winter, barefoot, across Texas with their mother. They were trying to reach Oklahoma. She couldn't

remember why. In the most painful story, at age eleven she was given away by her mother at a country dance. A sharecropper admired my grandmother's children, and my grandmother simply said, "Well, you can have them," and disappeared. I heard that story when I was eleven or twelve, and since the hearing I have held in my mind a dark image of that country dance, a summer evening with a crowd of farming people—Indians and whites—moving in and out of a well-lit barn, cornfields and blurred hardwood forests outside, and my mother and aunt and uncle as children comprehending the terror of abandonment.

In part of that story, the sharecropper kept my mother, aunt, and uncle for two years, a violent drunk who abused his wife as well as the children he'd been given. One night my mother dreamed of three little people who stood on the steps of the screened-in porch where she slept and watched her with dark, silent eyes. When she awoke from the nightmare, the little people were still there, and they stayed

The Owens home in Mississippi. Louis Owens, age two, has his back to the camera,
while his older brother Gene, age four, is on the porch steps.

with her until daybreak. Terrified, she told the sharecropper's Indian wife, who interpreted the vision: the little people had come to tell her that in three days her stepfather would be dead. Three days later the man was bitten by a snake while plowing. After he died, my grandmother appeared at the farm to take her children away with her to share her nomadic life. From that story I gained a great respect for and fear of what the Cherokee call Little People. My mother had other stories about them, but none so huge as that one. My father had frugal stories of little people, too, from Choctaw tradition, but his little people were tricksters, hide-behinds who stayed just out of view when you walked in the woods, throwing sticks and acorns at a person, delighting in pestering.

Once we had left Mississippi for good, we moved about a great deal, never living in the same house longer than two years and often as briefly as a few months before the rent couldn't be paid or a new job beckoned my father. Sometimes we moved just a few miles from where we had been, always staying in the country where we could hunt right outside the backyard. My father labored on farms and ranches driving tractors, working cattle, building fences, fixing machinery, and generally doing whatever could be done. A man of extraordinarily broad skills, he could do or fix anything, it seemed. The only thing he couldn't do was support his too-numerous family, no matter how hard or long he worked. Looking back now, I realize that he was a man with a third-grade education (like my mother) who had three kids and a wife to support by the time he was nineteen, and seven by the time he was thirty. Compared to other fathers who might be successful ranchers or doctors or engineers for the county, he seemed lacking. I am saddened to admit now that I was painfully ashamed of my family. When we drove through town in one of our junked automobiles he'd probably put together from parts in the front yard, I ducked in acute embarrassment at his tobacco spitting and our general squalor. When people asked where I lived, I lied if possible, hoping they wouldn't associate me with the shack fronted by empty automobile hulks, overturned washing machines, transmissions, differentials, axles, blocks, heads, stray carburetors, manifolds, and just about any other large or small grease-caked automobile part that might someday, somehow,

somewhere come in handy. I wanted with a desperate childish intensity to live in a colorless tract home and have my family drive a station wagon like respectable families. For a while, in seventh grade, I dreamed of being an architect, and I'd spend hours drawing up plans for modest, *Leave It to Beaver* kinds of houses, showing the plans to my mother, who would always gently say that maybe we'd have that very house sometime. The reality, of course, was that we never owned a house at all, except for a brief spell of five or six months one time. But today I also realize that through all those difficult years, when he worked twelve- and fourteen-hour days to bring home a check that wouldn't even buy enough food, he never stopped working and he never left us the way so many fathers would have. The thought must have tempted him the way it could never have tempted my mother, as buried as she was under the mass of our demanding lives. He was a flawed man to be sure, as even at age seven or eight I could tell, and I can never remember him touching me in either love or anger, but the unavoidable fact is that he never quit and he never left.

For a while he became a long-haul truck driver and we moved to the Bay Area not too far from San Francisco, settling in San Leandro, where I attended third grade and became part of a street gang and burglary ring. Because I was small, the bigger guys would boost me through an open, or opened, window and I would tiptoe to unlock a door for them. We stole many things that I'm sure somebody made a good profit on. I was never given or paid anything, and it never occurred to me that I should be. I was in it for the fun, and the greatest fun of all was the time we burglarized the boys' reformatory and almost got caught. The authorities spotted us and logically thought we were trying to break out. We made our escape through a storm drain, and as we already knew the map of the city's storm drain system by heart, we had no trouble getting away and plopping like rats out a narrow pipe a mile or so distant. I wondered afterwards, and still wonder today, why the boys in the "juvey," as we called it, didn't take the same route out we had taken. Shortly after that, amidst ominous rumblings from neighbors and just before our first officially scheduled gang fight was to take place, our family moved a few miles away to the town of Irvington, where my parents used my father's GI Bill to buy a small tract home exactly like all the other dream-homes in our tract. All of us were in heaven, except my father, who was on the road constantly. We worked hard to plant a smooth lawn and make the house look as much like all the others as possible. We studied all the houses around us, trying to figure out and imitate this new culture. There was even a small creek nearby where we could catch stickleback fish and frogs. But the heavenly reward was short-lived, and within a few months the electricity was turned off, the phone gone, and on the last miserable night in the house neighbors brought a large pot of soup to us after my younger sister accidentally admitted we hadn't eaten in two days. I don't remember which of us hid in a back room, but I recall it was more than just myself.

In a long, hallucinatory night-ride we got from the dark, repossessed house in California to the desert outside of Las Vegas, Nevada, where my grandmother—the same who had given her children away—lived with her current husband, a very fine and patient man with a crooked back whom we quickly learned to love and call Grandfather. In the desert we children had time to catch scorpions, find a pet tortoise, watch the wild burros in the distance, and marvel at the Las Vegas "Strip," where our new grandfather worked in the Silver Slipper and Golden Nugget as a light-man, the person who kept the spotlight on the stage performers. We also discovered that it was a fad for people to cement silver dollars into the steps of their swimming pools in the developments not too far away. We learned at once that a screwdriver could pop the coins out of the concrete with little trouble. But Nevada was even more short-term than the Bay Area, and fifth grade found me with my family back in California, in a town called Atascadero just ten miles south of Paso Robles, where we'd lived for a while in the county housing project. The locals said Atascadero meant "place of standing waters" in Spanish, but a Chicano friend told me it really meant "mud hole," a name that certainly fit better.

As an adolescent and teen in Atascadero life didn't seem too hard, though the time my rubber shoes came apart at recess in the rain was awkward, and to this day I feel badly that my sisters could not go to school as well dressed as other girls.

The school-clothes problem was cleverly solved by each of my siblings in turn as they dropped out of school, usually by ninth or tenth grade. If it was physically possible, they became pregnant. Only my brother Gene made it through, the first in our extended family to graduate from high school. He had forged a path for me as usual and proudly stood to receive his diploma in the very same suit I would wear two years later to receive mine. Even the white dinner jacket he had saved money to buy for the senior prom became mine when I wore it to the Girls' League Formal with Becky Hogue. Very gamely, she did not comment on the fact that the two-year-old jacket was slightly large and a bit yellowed, and when we went out for a chicken dinner I somehow got her to hurry out of the restaurant with me when, after we'd eaten, I discovered I didn't have enough money to pay. I remember with gratitude that though she had invited me to the dance she didn't complain once about what a raw deal she got, even when during our dash she lost a heel on one shoe and had to two-step that night in stocking feet with a greasy-haired guy in a baggy, off-white jacket, a guy who couldn't dance too well to begin with. Becky was a cheerleader and could have done better than me, but she bravely acted as though everything was the cat's meow.

By the time I was embarrassing my date in his tainted dinner jacket and driving his '51 Chevy, my brother was serving his second tour of duty on a Swift boat in Vietnam, where he would eventually be the only survivor of three straight crews. Like everyone else in our little town, he had been gung ho, not only enlisting in the Navy but volunteering to go to Vietnam to save our agrarian paradise from Communists. (There were rumors that he'd been caught *in flagrante* by the local deputy sheriff crew and given a choice of jail or military, but he'd been planning to enlist anyway, so if the story is true he probably felt he got a good deal.) I, too, planned my life around Vietnam. My plan was to enlist on what the military called the "buddy system," but my buddy was a year younger than I, so I had a year to kill, so to speak. The week I graduated from high school, my buddy—who was also a mixedblood, being part Osage—and I embarked on a celebratory week-long backpacking trip up the coast range, a meandering route that took us ironically from a camp called The Indians to the campgrounds at Big Sur. Badly equipped to begin with, me in borrowed boots two sizes too large and the two of us sharing a wooden pack frame with one-inch shoulder straps and a frameless Yucca pack that was utter torture to carry, we soon ran into trouble. Because we forgot half of our food at his house and on the first day threw away stuff like bread, which we did not care for, we ran out of all food halfway through the trip and emerged at Big Sur very hungry and irritated. His father picked us up and drove us home, except that my home was gone when we got there. My family had moved while I was hiking and starving, fleeing town abruptly to avoid creditors and, quite naturally under such circumstances, leaving no forwarding address. Luckily, I had an aunt living in town and was able to stay with her for a month until I learned that my family was now living in Hayward, again close to San Francisco.

I hitchhiked to Hayward, where I found work in a can factory and attended riotous Teamsters Union meetings all summer until my mother and old high school friends convinced me to go to junior college in San Luis Obispo. Not being college material, having taken a great deal of wood shop, metal shop, and so on in high school, I enrolled reluctantly and walked between the old army barracks of our brand-new campus with reverence. College was scary. There were still cattle wandering between the barracks that made up our campus, leaving dangerous things to step in if one's head was deep in intellectual thought, and there was also the incomparably beautiful Adela Camacho, with whom I fell hopelessly—very hopelessly and rather stupidly it turned out—in love.

After two years there my journalism advisor convinced me to apply for admission to the University of California at Santa Barbara and helped me fill out the forms. Apparently when the officials saw that I had eight brothers and sisters and my father's income for the previous year was about three thousand dollars, they jumped for joy. I was a poster boy, probably the finest specimen they could find for the relatively new Equal Opportunity Program that sent underprivileged or under-somethinged kids to college. When I received a letter telling me they were going to give me a whole bunch of money to go to college, I instinctively threw the letter and accompanying forms away. I'd seen my parents have to leave town in the middle of the night to escape credi-

tors, and I wasn't going to be boondoggled like that. It was my journalism advisor who choked when he heard what I'd done, called the university to request new forms, and made me fill them out. And that's how I ended up enrolled at a University of California campus living in a student apartment that was so luxurious I felt guilty.

I took my first semester at the university very seriously, nearly tiptoeing down the hallowed halls, so much in awe was I. I studied hard because I knew that now I was among the really smart people of the world, and consequently I received all A's that year and made the Dean's List for the only time in my career. When I went home for a visit at the end of that first triumphal university year, however, I found that my family had abruptly moved again. Our hometown newspaper had printed a little piece about my being on the Dean's List at the university, and rather than inspiring the pride Beaver Cleaver's family would certainly have felt, the article was quite upsetting to my family since it gave away their whereabouts to creditors they'd been dodging. So they'd had to flee once more.

At the university I learned to take hallucinogenic drugs and began to protest the very war I had two years before been hot to join. I was also drafted three times. I had tried to be exempted as a conscientious objector, but I naively told the truth: I did not believe in a Christian god and was, in fact, what my draft board considered a pagan. I also did not entirely disbelieve in war as a means of defending one's family and nation; I just disbelieved in this particular immoral war. I even got an understanding priest to write a letter explaining what he termed my "Native American" religion. The argument didn't cut any ice with the Protestant ranchers and car dealers on my home-county draft board, and I was quickly bussed to L.A. to bend over so military doctors could look up my ass and then just as quickly drafted—having, it seemed, a totally adequate ass to be shot off. The first two times I was drafted, I wriggled off the government hook because I was close to graduation and then firefighting for the U.S. Forest Service and doing other things that somehow caused them to cancel the induction notices. The third time, however, both my local draft board and I knew I was a goner. By that point my brother and friends who'd been there—including my room-

With Chelly, cross-country skiing above Lake Tahoe, 1982

mate at the time, who had been in Special Forces in Nam as early as 1960—had fully convinced me that we were doing an unconscionably bad thing. My brother already had, in fact, come back from the war only to disappear into the Ozark Mountains for the next twenty years, one of the war's psychological casualties. A number of friends had simply been killed there, including Eric Bosch, the most gentle and frail human being I have ever known. I knew I couldn't go kill those people in Vietnam. My only choices were Canada or a federal prison. Because I feared I might never be able to come home again if I crossed the Canadian border, I opted for prison and prepared to undergo "going-to-prison" counseling offered at the university. One week before I was to report for either Vietnam or a federal penitentiary, however, as a political gesture my good friend Richard Nixon canceled the draft for that quarter and along with many others I was free.

While the riots in Isla Vista and UCSB were going on, the Bank of America being burned,

a fraternity boy shot through the heart by a sheriff's department sniper, and the war being featured like *Apocalypse Now* on nightly news framed by Walter Cronkite's terse lips, Adela Camacho married Billy Fell, the ex-marine whom I grew to like and with whom I played intramural basketball. About that time also our family learned of the strangely synchronous murders of my only two uncles: my father's brother, quiet and likable Uncle Bill, found floating in Lake Charleston one morning; and my mother's brother, high-stepping and smooth-talking Uncle Bob, bludgeoned to death in a Texas oil field—both unsolved homicides like those of so many Indian, or mixedblood people.

I avoided joining the Native American Students Association at UCSB despite numerous invitations because I did not trust the blond-bearded hustler who claimed to be Flathead Indian and was president of the association. Instead, I hung out with friends from the Asian American Students Association and MECHA, one of two Chicano groups on campus. I marched, petitioned, yelled, one night made Molotov cocktails which were never used, and learned to love the poetry of William Butler Yeats and to think of the world as an Eliotic wasteland. Most importantly, I met the Kiowa author N. Scott Momaday, who had just won a Pulitzer Prize for a book called *House Made of Dawn* and who was at that moment ending his brief teaching career at UCSB.

Meeting Momaday was a turning point. All of my life I had thought of myself as "part-Indian," something like a psychological centaur, perhaps. I had listened to my mother's stories about growing up in Oklahoma and Texas, about what she and my uncle, aunt, and grandmother still referred to as the "Nation," meaning Cherokee Nation. She told us stories about little people and lightning, and she knew wild plants that one could eat or use for medicine, even in California. Above all, she was fiercely proud of her Cherokee heritage and made us feel the same. About her Irish ancestry she seemed to neither know nor care, perhaps the result of her own white father's disappearance from the scene for most of her life. My father, on the other hand, who was descended from Choctaw, Irish, and Cajun people of Mississippi and Louisiana, seldom said anything at all about his ancestors. Of course he seldom said anything at all, period, and to this day he remains nearly mute on all subjects but hunting. But I had lived in Mississippi and had known my Choctaw grandmother. I felt deeply connected with that heritage by earth and blood if not story. In California, however, we didn't live in any essential "Indian" way—unless one counts hunting every day and having a house full of relatives and strange guests as peculiarly "Indian" things to do. We just lived.

When I saw in a Santa Barbara newspaper that a Kiowa professor at my university had won a prize for an Indian novel, I went out and got the book and read it. Then I went and met the man in his campus office, an act that took uncommon courage for me, for I was a student who sat in the back of the class and never, ever spoke to professors. Momaday was gracious, courteous, understanding, and very awe-inspiring, as he remains today. We spoke of his novel, *House Made of Dawn*, and of being mixedbloods. I recall that he confided that it was "our" generation that had the luxury of remembering, of seeking out a cultural identity that our parents had had to just live unquestionably within or even put aside to sur-

vive. To this day I am flattered and perplexed by having been included in "our" generation, but the conversation itself turned me into the path I am still taking. After leaving Professor Momaday's office—and because his novel had spoken to me in a way none other had—I set out to learn what else had been written by Native American authors, full- or mixedbloods, especially novels, because the novel form was my great literary love.

Gradually I began to uncover strange and forgotten texts that my teachers had certainly never mentioned—not that any of my teachers had ever mentioned *any* Native American text. I came across John Rollin Ridge, John Milton Oskison, Mourning Dove, John Joseph Mathews, D'Arcy McNickle, and eventually a multitude of other even more forgotten writers. Joaquín Murietta, whom I'd heard about most of my life, I found to be the invention of the half-Cherokee Ridge. As a child I'd been taken by my father, with my mother, brothers, and sisters, to see an actual cave where Joaquín and his bloody partner Three-Fingered Jack had hidden from the law. Now I found that a halfblood refugee from Indian Territory had invented the swashbuckling story of the Spanish-California outlaw.

But aside from this one fascination, I was not an enthusiastic student. I took an extra year to finish the B.A., enjoying such taxing courses as sailing and weight-training, music appreciation and soccer, and as a fifth-year senior I managed to be staring out the door of a French I class filled with freshmen when the most beautiful young woman in the world came coasting up late to class barefoot on a bicycle. Before she had swung her long, blue-jeaned legs from the bike and brushed back her waist-length blonde hair, I was in love. Within a week I had overcome her appropriate suspicions and convinced her to go for a drive in my old but sleek Sunbeam Alpine sports car. Since my Sunbeam hadn't run for quite a while, however, I borrowed a friend's that looked exactly like mine and even ran. That first night, in the starlit darkness of San Marcos Pass high above Santa Barbara, I proposed marriage, thereby justifying all of her suspicions, frightening her thoroughly, and undoubtedly disgusting her a bit as well. It would take four more years and great agony before I would win the argument and we would be married, as we are still today, twenty-five years since that French class. Her name was, and is, Polly, and she had, and has, green eyes and an extraordinarily beautiful face. Most importantly, she was and remains much smarter than I, a fact fortunate for our two daughters, who like all children have had to play genetic roulette with their inheritance. They are the children of ancestors who signed the Declaration of Independence and of other ancestors for whom that declaration meant merely two hundred more years of oppression, exploitation, and life in the trash diaspora of America.

From that French class, I learned how to say, in French, "Help, help, I'm drowning," a phrase I have tried unsuccessfully to work into conversations in Paris more than once. When embarrassed by my horrible French, however, I fall back on my few phrases of Choctaw, such as "Hello. How are you, Great Horned Owl? I would like some meat." This invariably impresses the hell out of Parisians, who listen patiently as I teach them this commonplace Choctaw greeting and subsequently go around saying it to one another.

During those college years I not only met my future wife but also began my treasured association with the U.S. Forest Service, first working on a trail crew in the Glacier Peak Wilderness of the North Cascades and then switching to wilderness rangering for a while and finally firefighting as a sawyer on a Hotshot crew in Arizona. For seven glorious years I opened trails, backpacked the alpine region of the Cascades alone, and chainsawed firelines through blazing Southwestern ponderosa and lodgepole pine forests. Meanwhile, lured back by the presence of my true love and certainly not educational goals, I had scraped together enough credits for a master's degree in English at UCSB, managing to publish a couple of critical essays along the way and still remain entirely undistinguished. After getting married and working on the Hotshot crew out of Prescott, Arizona, for a season, I began to feel the weight of being a married man and so started looking around for a career. Arizona State University on the outskirts of Phoenix looked like fun, so I enrolled in a Ph.D. program in English, which had always been easy at least. It remained easy, too, so much so that in my first year I earned a total of around three credit hours but made some very good friends before I gave up, dropped out, and

Louis Owens with his wife, Polly, and daughters Elizabeth and Alexandra (in Louis's arms), 1987

returned to the Forest Service determined to make wilderness rangering my life's ambition. My new wife and I put all we owned in and on our VW Rabbit and headed for northern Washington, where I had a job waiting as Supervisory Wilderness Ranger. I loved every moment of it, but my new wife did not. While I designated myself the North Country Ranger and backpacked through the trail-less primitive area at the northern edge of the wilderness, Polly took graduate courses in physics at Western Washington State University and waited. Meanwhile, it rained—every day and night all spring, summer, and fall until the snow began. Sleeping bags mildewed in one day when hung against a wall. Hiking boots turned into balls of lovely blue-green fungus if left untended for a week. Slugs made slime trails across kitchen counters. King Boletus mushrooms grew as large as pumpkin pies. My wife rebelled, and we headed for Arizona sun.

The second time I enrolled at ASU, I lasted a week before I quit again and decided to be

With his daughters Elizabeth (center) and Alexandra,
about to embark on a backpacking trip, 1995

a writer. Here, we fast-forward this essay past a romantic, starving-writer year with unemployment insurance, a delightful new English setter pup, six-packs of the cheapest beer, a young wife riding my bicycle to work each day at a local department store in Phoenix, increasing desperation, and a brief job for me as assistant manager of a backpacking and climbing store. For complex reasons, the next year found us with our dog in Davis, California, and three years later I had a Ph.D. from the University of California at Davis, with a quick dissertation on John Steinbeck, and I was teaching as a Fulbright Scholar in Pisa, Italy, where everyone thought I was Hungarian or some kind of East European stranger and where we had such a fine time that it was difficult to come home.

But we had to come home at year's end, and after applying for a hundred jobs, receiving a blurry purple mimeographed rejection from a small state college and even more humiliating rejections from others (the University of Chicago didn't deign to reply), and despite

swearing that the only place in the world I would not teach was Southern California, I accepted an assistant professor position at California State University, Northridge, in the San Fernando Valley, where my first daughter, Elizabeth, was born on the first day of classes. Because she wisely preferred to stay where she was, it took thirty-six hours to coax Elizabeth into the world, and thus I missed the first classes of my official tenure-track teaching career. But at Northridge, my colleagues were wonderful, generous, and often hilarious human beings, and most of my students were the products of several generations of experimental Hollywood breeding programs designed to produce the most attractive (white) physical specimens possible. The air was so polluted that in a closed room our apple-crate furniture gathered a daily layer of black soot, and the cost of living was more than startling. The Native American Students group on campus, for whom I served as faculty advisor, was delightful for a year before falling prey to the usual politics of Indian country and splintering into bitter factions. During my second week on campus two members of the Indian student group interviewed me for their newspaper. When I casually mentioned that I had grown up hunting, they casually asked if I ever hunted with a bow. The ensuing article in the student paper pointed to my extensive bow-hunting as evidence of my authentic Indian identity, which was both amusing and bemusing. While things went well, I helped make and sell frybread, served as ringmaster at powwows, counseled urban Indian students, and was reported to a dean for teaching *Bearheart*, a novel by the notorious Chippewa author Gerald Vizenor, in one of my courses. Every morning before daylight the dog and I did our six-mile run through darkened San Fernando Valley neighborhoods, enjoying the quiet, the relatively clean pre-dawn air, and the strange things one sees in lighted suburban windows before sunrise. By the end of two years, however, both Polly and I had given up on L.A. living, and I had decided to bag teaching. I'd applied and been accepted into a master's degree program in forestry at Utah State University. To my surprise they did not hold a Ph.D. in English against me, but were very friendly and inviting, rather the way evangelical missionaries welcome sinners back into the fold. I'd also discovered the works of Gerald Vizenor, whose fracturing of every cliché I'd ever encountered and whose brilliant prose expeditions toward truth exhilarated me like no other writer had.

Just before it was time to leave for Utah, a phone call came from New Mexico and I flew to Albuquerque and almost instantaneously accepted a position at the University of New Mexico, where with the exception of five years on the faculty of the University of California at Santa Cruz (as bizarrely insane a place as the U.S. has managed to produce) I remain today.

In the meantime I have written and edited a number of books, among them four novels dealing with mixedblood Native Americans. The search that began after my conversation with N. Scott Momaday resulted in a critical bibliography of Indian novels published in 1985, co-authored with Tom Colonnese, who taught me to play racquetball at Arizona State University when I was doing everything but studying. My fascination with the fiction of John Steinbeck, whom I consider the most underrated and misread author in America, resulted in two books. My obsession with novels by Native American authors gave birth in 1992 to *Other Destinies*, a study of such novels and the capstone at that point to twenty years of searching and reading.

My first novel, *Wolfsong*, was born from a filing cabinet in the District Ranger Station where I worked as a wilderness ranger. In that cabinet one day I discovered a copper company's plans to put an open-pit mine in the heart of the Glacier Peak Wilderness. The plans laid out in careful, precise detail the construction of a road more than twenty miles into the wilderness, the dimensions of the pit, the clearcutting necessary for a mill site and town site and tailings dump. If carried out the plan would tear the very heart from one of the most beautiful and sacred places in the world. For short-term profit. The wilderness and surrounding forests were sacred to the Suiattle Indian people who lived in the area as well as to a number of other

With Chippewa author Gerald Vizenor at the Annual 3rd World Conference, Chicago, Illinois, 1996

tribes. The Suiattle people knew that they had been born from the great white peak for which the wilderness was named; they called it the Great Mother. I had spent countless days and weeks alone wandering the high country around that peak, and the copper company's plans left me depressed and horrified. At first I tried to interest environmental magazines in doing an exposé about the coming crisis, but the price of copper had taken a worldwide plunge, and the magazines didn't want to do anything until it looked like danger was imminent.

So I began in 1976 to write a novel that would try to illuminate this disaster from the point of view of a young Indian man whose ancestors had always lived there—a character modeled upon someone I worked with in the Forest Service. I thought of it as a novel about ecology, a whole ecosystem in which human beings were an integral part. Wilderness, I understood, was a European invention. The natural world was a natural habitat for Native people, who belonged there as surely as the trees and rivers. However, I wanted to make the real protagonist of the novel the so-called wilderness itself, that is the great rain forests, the glacier-fed rivers and high, snow-covered ridges and peaks, the uncountable streams, the bears, eagles, ravens, and, maybe, the wolves whose existence everyone debated. Within that matrix I placed a great deal of my own personal anxieties and concerns about mixed and relational identity, past and present, and the forces of language and dream.

I put that novel aside for more than a decade, while I finished a Ph.D., became the father of two magical little girls, and wrote the academic papers and books that matter for tenure in a university. I picked up *Wolfsong* again, revised it, and published it at the tail end of 1991. The National Endowment for the Arts had given me a grant in 1990 to work on another novel, *The Sharpest Sight,* but I felt the unfinished business of *Wolfsong* hanging over me. So I rewrote it and published it as quickly as possible with a small press, West End Press,

Owens with his daughters—Elizabeth is "The Lone Ranger" and Alexandra, "Pocahontas," 1995

in Albuquerque, a publishing event no one in the whole world seemed to notice.

The following year, in 1992, I published *The Sharpest Sight*, a novel that had also been years in the making. Though I used both my father's and grandfather's real names and a great deal of our family history in that book, and though it is above all a work of fiction, it is a novel written largely for my older brother, who had returned from a third tour of duty in Vietnam only to vanish. He had come to see me when he got back, at a cabin I shared with a friend in Morro Bay, California. I was working nights, and the friend—the same Osage mixedblood I'd once planned to enlist with—was home alone when he heard my brother coming in through the back window of the cabin. Doors couldn't be trusted because of booby-traps, but he explained that he'd come to say good-bye. Because I wasn't home, I didn't see him, and I never saw him again. It was as if, like Attis McCurtain in the novel, he had never really come back at all. Only years later, after *The Sharpest Sight* was published, did we reestablish contact. He'd seen the book in a store in Arkansas, bought and read it, and realized it was to a great extent about him. So he called my sister to find out where I was. That's how we learned he had disappeared into the Ozark Mountains for two decades. Today he is clearly still afraid of family, of anyone who knew him before he became whatever it is that he is now. He has vanished again, but like so many other surviving casualties of that awful war, especially the ones from small towns or with dark skins, he isn't a statistic or a name on the black wall in Washington.

I've written and published two other novels since *The Sharpest Sight*. *Bone Game*, published in 1994, is a sequel to *The Sharpest Sight*, featuring Attis's brother, Cole McCurtain, and most of the cast of the previous book. I think of it as a novel about the dangers of forgetting responsibility, of removing ourselves from history, of not recognizing the crucial relationship we have not merely with each other but with the very earth. It is a novel about an America haunted by its bloody past and its refusal to acknowledge that past. A similar theme rises up in *Nightland*, published in 1996, but in that novel I moved away from the Choctaw roots of the previous two—my father's roots—and focused on two mixedblood Cherokee men trying to survive in a harsh New Mexico land-

Louis Owens, above Juneau

scape. That novel grew out of a telephone call in 1992, when my Aunt Betty phoned to ask if I would do some research to find out who she is. The last surviving member of my mother's family, she knows she's Cherokee and Irish, but she has no paperwork to prove her existence. No one in her family had birth certificates, enrollment cards, nothing at all to testify to their earthly lives, nothing but stories passed from one generation to another. So I did the research, found my aunt's (and mother's) grandfather on the tribal rolls and 1910 census, discovered some other interesting things about that part of our family, and realized with guilt that I never wrote a book for my mother before she died. I resolved then to write a book about Cherokee mixedbloods for my aunt before it was too late. *Nightland* is dedicated to my aunt and mother, as strange a story as it is.

Recently a friend asked me if I ever thought about writing a novel that has nothing to do with Indians; after all, she pointed out, I'm more than half white myself. Because of my name, in fact, I keep being invited to join

Celtic associations, an idea that intrigues me. I thought about it and replied that everything I'm interested in, every problem I want to explore or question or try to resolve, revolves around being of mixed ancestry, crossedblood, in-between. When I begin to write, it seems that my words always move in that direction. Maybe sometime I'll try to write a mystery novel about a white detective or professor—maybe an uproarious academic novel about the complete, unbelievable absurdity of my profession—but my imagination doesn't seem to want to bend around such an idea or task. Perhaps it's the uncertainty, self-doubt, fear of inauthenticity that drives me to words, sentences, pages, and stories. So I'll probably keep writing about myself and my family in one fashion or another. My brothers and sisters, at least, like what I write. "That's true," they say, adding, "Boy, no wonder you don't talk like that. You use all the bad words in your writing."

Today I'm going to finish the horse fence around our two-acre place in the Manzano Mountains. This morning during my run in the National Forest next to the house I saw fresh bear tracks, and a coyote stopped just up the trail to watch me for a moment. A beautiful red tanager sits on the side mirror of my old Land Cruiser, looking at himself and then jumping to the top of the mirror to look for the bird on the other side and then going back to look in the mirror again. Later, I'll have to clean the birdshit off the mirror, but I worry about the bird who is looking so hard for another in his own reflection. I hope he finds a friend. Next week I'll take my daughters, nine and fourteen years old, backpacking on the White Mountain Apache reservation, to a special place on a river where no one else goes. Meanwhile, I'm working on a novel about a mixedblood Choctaw ranger and a young Indian man who sells vision quests to Europeans. Writing novels is the most exciting thing in the world, an exploration into the unknowable, each one a new world.

BIBLIOGRAPHY

Novels:

Wolfsong, West End Press, 1991, reprinted by University of Oklahoma Press, 1995.

The Sharpest Sight, University of Oklahoma Press, 1992.

Bone Game, University of Oklahoma Press, 1994.

Nightland, Dutton Signet, 1996.

Criticism:

John Steinbeck's Re-Vision of America, University of Georgia Press, 1985.

(With Tom Colonnese) *American Indian Novelists: An Annotated Critical Bibliography*, Garland Press, 1985.

The Grapes of Wrath: Trouble in the Promised Land, G. K. Hall, 1989.

Other Destinies: Understanding the American Indian Novel, University of Oklahoma Press, 1992.

Other:

Work represented in anthologies, including *Narrative Chance: Postmodern Discourse on Native American Indian Literatures*, University of New Mexico Press, 1989; *Rediscovering Steinbeck: Revisionist Views of His Art, Politics, and Intellect*, edited by Cliff Lewis and Carroll Britch, Edwin Mellen Press, 1989; *Writing American Classics*, edited by James Barbour and Tom Quirk, University of North Carolina Press, 1990; *The Steinbeck Question: New Essays in Criticism*, edited by Donald R. Noble, Whitson Publishing, 1993; and *Native American Literature*, edited by Gerald Vizenor, HarperCollins, 1995.

Contributor of numerous stories, articles, and reviews to periodicals, including *Albuquerque Journal, America West, American Book Review, American Indian Quarterly, Arizona Quarterly, Icarus, Los Angeles Times Book Review, Northeast Indian Quarterly, San Jose Studies, South Dakota Review, USA Today*, and *Western American Literature*. Member of editorial board, *Steinbeck Quarterly*, 1982—, and *New America*, 1985–88; associate editor, *American Literary Realism*, 1986–88; co-editor, *American Literary Scholarship: An Annual*, 1989–90.

Alma Luz Villanueva

1944-

Alma Luz Villanueva, 1994

Because dreams, and then poetry, have always guided my life, I begin this glimpse of my life with a poem, a dream of my birth:

Indian Summer Ritual

I was born in Indian Summer,
by the sea, at sun set—

I slid from my mother's womb,
face to the sea—

I felt a dolphin leap
from the sea for joy—

I cried in agony because
I was naked, cold, beached—

It was Indian Summer
and the clouds were purple—

It was Indian Summer
and Venus glowed in the west—

It was Indian Summer
and the moon rose, a ripe, gold melon—

It was Indian Summer
and fire was in the ascendant—

It was Indian Summer
and I danced and danced with dolphins

all the first night of my birth,
until the eagle's cry brought the sun—

It was Indian Summer;
light wolves and dark wolves howled through
   the day—

It was Indian Summer
and a snake shed its skin—

Then, and only then, was I properly
human.

I was born to Lydia Villanueva Sims and Leon Russell Sims on October 4, 1944, in Santa Barbara, California. She was twenty-seven; he was twenty-six. My father was stationed in the army there, and my mother worked as a medical secretary on the army base. My father was German and English (blonde, blue-eyed, tall, handsome); I never met him. My mother is first-generation from Mexico, barely making it over the border to Tucson, Arizona, to be born. Her father, Pablo Villanueva, was Mexican (mes-

Grandparents—Jesus Luján de Villanueva and Pablo Villanueva—in Hermosillo, Mexico, 1906

tizo, mixed-blood, Spanish and Yaqui), and her mother, Jesus Luján de Villanueva, was a full-blood Yaqui Indian. (It's not common to name a girl-child Jesus in Mexico, but her mother, Ysidra, insisted on the name.)

My father was a farm boy from Monroe, Louisiana, where his people owned a large, working farm. The entire family (brothers, sisters, grandparents, uncles, aunts) lived on the farm in separate houses within walking distance to each other. My mother went to live on the farm for a little over a year when I was two, leaving my grandmother, Jesus, who had taken care of me since birth, in California with my aunt, Ruth (my mother's younger sister).

I grew up hearing their stories (my mother and aunt), their versions of themselves, each other, and me. Lydia, my mother, was the favorite child of her father, a Baptist minister (who earned his doctorate in philosophy in

Mexico). Though both sisters took piano lessons, and both could play, Lydia was considered to be the "gifted one" and was chosen by their father to play in his East Los Angeles church every Sunday, starting when she was twelve. Ruth helped in the domestic chores with her mother, and Lydia was told to concentrate on her music, to prepare for public recitals (which meant dressing up, looking poised, and talking to the congregation afterward), as well as accompany her father to people's houses and other churches. Lydia was chosen to go to a Christian boarding school for a better education, and she attended two years of college. An interesting comparison between the two sisters was that Lydia was very light-skinned with Spanish features, while Ruth was dark-skinned with Indian features, which I'm sure in that color-caste Mexican society, coupled with the dominant Anglo (white) society, must have fed the confidence of one sister and starved the other.

My aunt Ruth played for Sunday services only rarely, if Lydia was sick. Her great dream was to be a registered nurse, and she worked as a nurse's aide for quite a few years. It's not a coincidence that Lydia became a medical secretary and Ruth worked as a nurse's aide; their mother was a healer (as had been her mother). However, their father forbade his wife to treat people that began to come to her for healing in East Los Angeles. The word in church was spreading: Bruja (witch, sorcery). I often think that was an excuse—his ministry, his church—and that he was jealous of her healing skills, her gifts. He had a doctorate in philosophy, he was a minister, but he couldn't heal; the people came to her. And I'm sure he forbade her to teach her children *dreaming* (as she later taught me), though I know my aunt Ruth had been chosen to learn, secretly, since she was with her mother daily.

As I grew up Ruth told me many of her incredible dreams and waking visions; they sustained and tormented her almost equally. They were her deepest self, her soul, but they had no outer value, no worth. My aunt was to spend six years, in her twenties, in a TB ward in San Francisco General Hospital. Her younger brother, Reuben, a gifted violinist, was to die at twenty-one from pneumonia, banned from the family home by his minister father for cross-dressing. My mother never spoke of her dreams, ever, to me.

One of the central truths of my childhood, beginning at my birth, was that my mother did not enjoy taking care of babies, children. Motherhood, for Lydia, was *only* a prison, taking time meant for herself, as well as her best energies, which she thought should be focused on looking her attractive best, drawing male attention, and going out of the house to work (reminiscent of her childhood training to perform for her father). And so, my real mother, the one who took joy in my infancy and childhood (and the daily care) was my grandmother, Jesus Villanueva. She mothered me until I was taken to my father's farm in Louisiana at the age of two.

When his family expected my mother to work in the fields, she promptly found a job in town as a medical secretary. She told me, "They didn't see any difference between a Mexican and a nigger" (their words), and so she was definitely an "uppity nigger." It was the late forties in Monroe, Louisiana, and I must admire her raw, blatant, irrational courage to refuse her role or to compensate for the "disgrace" of being a Mexican. From her stories of that time it's clear she thought she'd landed on Mars: she was supposed to wear only one dress all week, no makeup, no fingernail polish, and when she went to town only white people walked on the wooden planks that served as sidewalks. Black people walked in the mud, she told me, and she saw men slap women right in the street.

Lydia got dressed every day in a different outfit, put on her makeup, took the bus to town, held herself erect as she walked the wooden sidewalk, keeping her eyes straight ahead as one of the men forced his wife to walk in the mud, obviously as an example of his white, masculine authority and what he really wanted to do to her. Lydia left me with my German grandmother for that year, and by the time we returned to California (and to Jesus), I had a southern accent in my baby talk which would disappear into my first fluent language, Spanish.

I don't even have a shadow of a memory of that man named Leon Russell Sims, although I do have a *feeling*; he meant me no harm. Period. I'm told he was easygoing, very gentle, somewhat lazy, and had to be pushed to work. And so, I still see him as a tall, awkward, young soldier, completely dazzled by the exotic beauty and (I'm sure) overwhelming confidence, in-

telligence, and seductiveness of my mother which led them to walk through a row of raised swords (I'm told), their marriage. My birth that year. In Indian Summer.

Two years later, when Lydia came home from work she found her bags packed on the front porch. Supposedly, they wanted to keep me, and Leon wasn't to be seen. She said they never had even one fight; I gather his style of conflict was to go silent. But the outward disapproval of his family (except for one sister-in-law who also wanted to work in town) was an everyday pressure and fact. Every day that Lydia went to work meant that Leon couldn't handle his own wife, an uppity Mexican who belonged in the fields, at that.

Lydia cleared out her secret savings, and we escaped back to California by train, to the Pacific Ocean that I love like my own tidal blood. My grandmother, whom I called "Mamacita," and Aunt Ruth joined Lydia in San Francisco in 1948. Lydia worked as a medical secretary during the day and a cashier at a theatre at night. Ruth continued to work as a nurse's aide until she had to be hospitalized with TB. I was my grandmother's child, watching with a certain longing and fascination as the beautiful lady, Lydia, prepared herself for work or to see one of her many boyfriends.

There were times my grandmother and I lived alone, and I know now how difficult it must have been for her. I never heard her speak English; she refused to. Though I'd notice the most subtle change of expression on her face from time to time when English was spoken (she understood it). By the time I was seven I was Mamacita's official translator to the English-speaking Gringo World (she referred to most white people as Los Gringos). I realize, now, she suffered more because she looked like an Indian. She experienced prejudice from some Mexican, mestizo people, as well, in church and in public; but her spirit was indomitable, and her sense of humor, in private, was outrageous.

Jesus was only forty-three when Pablo died. She never married again in order to protect her daughters, she said, from men who weren't their fathers. Her mother, Ysidra, married five times. "Each time a better man," she'd been known to say. (I believe her second husband was cruel to Jesus, burning her feet with coals once for trying to run away—Ysidra threw him out.) A year after Pablo's death a handsome doctor, my aunt told me, proposed, but Jesus refused saying, "He just wants my daughters."

The second half of her life was a test of her spirit; she spent it basically poor, with little protection. She had been a minister's wife whose house had been filled with good furniture, who cooked and cared for her family and her husband's guests (socially and those he was helping find housing and a job), who came to this country in her early thirties when her husband's politics forced them out of her country, Mexico. (Pablo had been a young minister, running a newspaper in Sonora, publishing articles and poetry contrary to those in power. They threatened his life and then escorted him to the border, the story goes. Later, he was given the church in East Los Angeles.) And so, though her two brothers begged her to return to Mexico after Pablo's death, to be completely taken care of, they said—one was a teacher, the other a judge; they had been sent to school; she had been taught to read—she refused to return to a country which had, she felt, thrown her family out.

When I close my eyes I see her: fragile, ferocious.

> *To Jesus Villanueva, with Love*
>
> My first vivid memory of you,
> Mamacita,
> we made tortillas together—
> yours, perfect and round—
> mine, irregular and fat—
> we laughed
> and named them: oso, pajarito, gatito.
> My last vivid memory of you
> (except for the very last
> sacred memory
> I won't share)
> Mamacita,
> beautiful, thick, long, grey hair,
> the eyes gone sad
> with flashes of fury
> when they wouldn't let you
> have your chilis, your onions, your peppers
> "What do these damned gringos
> know of MY stomach?"*
> So when I came to comb
> your beautiful, thick, long, grey hair
> as we sat for hours
> (it soothed you

---

*Translated from Spanish.

> my hand
> on your hair)
> I brought you your chilis, your onions, your
>   peppers.
> And they'd always catch you
> because you'd forget
> and leave it lying open.
> They'd scold you like a child
> and be embarrassed like a child,
> silent, repentant, angry
> and secretly waiting for my visit, the new
> supplies.
> We laughed at our secret,
> we always laughed
> you and I.
>
> You never could understand
> the rules
> at the clinics, welfare offices, schools,
> any of it.
> I did.
> You lie. You push. You get.
> I learned to do all this by
> the third clinic day of being persistently
> sent to the back of the line by 5 in the
>   afternoon
> and being so close to done by 8 in the
>   morning.
> So my lungs grew larger
> and my voice got louder
> and a doctor consented
> to see an old lady,
> and the welfare would give you the money
> and the landlady would remember to spray
>   for cockroaches
> and the store would charge the food till
>   the check came
> and the bank might cash the check if I got
>   the nice man this
> time
> and I'd order hot dogs and cokes for us
> at the old Crystal Palace on Market Street
> and we'd sit on the steps
> by the rear exit, laughing
> you and I.
>
> Mamacita,
> I remember you proudly at Christmas
> time, church at midnight services;
> you wear a plain black dress,
> your hair down, straight and silver,
> (you always wore it up
> tied in a kerchief,
> knotted to the side)
> your face shining, your eyes clear,
> your vision intact.
> You play Death.
> You are Death.
> You quote long stanzas from a poem I've

long forgotten;
even fitful babies hush
such is the power of your voice,
your presence
fills us all.
The special, pregnant
silence.
Eyes and hands lifted up,
imploringly and passionately,
the vision and power
offered to us.
Eyes and hands cast down,
it flows through you
to us,
a gift.

Your daughter, my aunt,
told me a story I'd never
heard before:
You were leaving Mexico
with your husband and two
older children, pregnant
with my mother.
The U.S. customs officer
undid everything you so
preciously packed, you
took a sack, blew it up
and when he asked about
the contents of the sack,
well, you popped it with
your hand and shouted
MEXICAN AIR!*

aiiiiiiiiii Mamacita, Jesus,
I won't forget my visions and reality.
To lie, to push, to get
just isn't
enough.

(From *Blood Root*)

I went to Catholic school until the second grade, learning English from a Spanish/English-speaking nun. (I briefly went to public school, but they put me in the "retarded class" because I couldn't speak English.) One day, as I was walking home from lunch on a beautiful spring day (I remember the slant of light from the sun, a newness), I stopped to watch a line of ants disappear into a tiny hole surrounded by bunches of sweet-smelling flowers. I noticed they were entering the hole, as well as leaving it, in a long, dark, living line. I remember the perfect warmth of that day (on my back as I bent over); I lost track of time. I was seven.

By the time I got to school, class had started, and I was sent to Sister Superior, a very stern woman whom everyone feared. She asked to see my hands, and I thought she wanted to admire them. (Mamacita admired my hands; she often rubbed rose water on them.) A ruler came down on my outstretched hands. The pain was unthinkable. I grabbed the ruler from her, swung at her dark, thick skirt, and ran all the way home (too shocked to cry). Large, raised, blood-red welts rose on my hands, making Mamacita furious.

I stayed home from school until the fourth grade, travelling with her to China (town) to shop for live fish and chickens, Golden Gate Park to feed the squirrels, the street car to the end of the line: the Pacific Ocean. We even went during storms, once at night, and though I was afraid I only had to look at Mamacita's eyes; she thought it was wonderful. I went with her to Valentino movies, Spanish-speaking movies where all the women in the audience wept when the heroine always seemed

*"With my grandmother, Jesus Villanueva,
'Mamacita,'" San Francisco, California, 1948*

---

*Translated from Spanish.

to die of love. I'd look at Mamacita to see if she was crying; sometimes her eyes were sad, and sometimes her eyes were laughing.

This time with her probably set the tone of my entire life: fugitive, outlaw, obstinate seeker of freedom, take-no-wooden-nickels tomboy kid who could fly in her dreams, and when she paid attention her dreams often came true. It was in the attention. Mamacita never said it, but she reminded me, daily.

When I was nine I began to go to school again, sporadically, and I discovered the library on a field trip. These were the years I began to read voraciously, from about nine to twelve (and then for the rest of my life). My favorite books at that time were *The Island Stallion* series by Walter Farley, about a boy who discovers an island and finds a way in through tunnels to a paradise with wild horses. I loved these books. I think I felt like the boy, the island, *and* the horse he loved; and it (the island) was the boy's secret. That's when I began to write poetry, small poems I'd stuff in my pocket, read once or twice, and forget. Mamacita had taught me to memorize poetry for church recitals, but these I could write down like a secret, tell no one, and forget.

After Mamacita died (transformed), I rode the 22 Fillmore from one end of the line to the other, from the waterfront by the Bay Bridge to the marina by the Golden Gate Bridge, passing through the Fillmore District, a tough, black neighborhood (like the Mission District was a tough, Latin neighborhood, where we lived). I rode the bus from one end to the other for about a week or so, writing poems in a notebook I'd stolen; not about Mamacita, but about the people I saw on the bus. The ones that made me sad. Especially those people. The poor, the old, the desperate. I felt them, their desperation, and so I wrote poems about them, describing what I saw and felt. That's how I was able to mourn her absence from my life.

I was eleven, the year my menstrual began. I'd climbed a building scaffold to the top after sunset by myself. I was living with a woman who'd taken me in; Demerce was her name. Lydia was living with her second husband, Jack, and my baby brother, John. Jack was a cruel and violent man, especially when he drank. I'd knocked him out with an ashtray once as he was strangling her (she was pregnant with John). And so, Jack couldn't tolerate my presence, nor I his.

Mother, Lydia Villanueva, and Alma,
San Francisco, 1955

Usually I climbed and rode bikes all over the city with my friend, Judy, who looked more like a boy than a girl. This night I was alone and terrified as I climbed to the top. But the sunset, I remember, was so beautiful, and it was close to my twelfth birthday, so it was Indian Summer, that rare coastal warmth in fall. As I sat on the highest beam of that building's skeleton looking out at the lights of the city and the emerging lights in the sky I felt something warm and strange gather and spill: blood. Down my leg. Blood.

This was the year I'd meet a man who would become my father: Lewis McSpadden, nicknamed "Whitey" as a boy because of his white-blonde hair. Lydia had separated from my stepfather, Jack, so I'd gone back to live with her in an apartment where the bathroom was shared by an apartment next door. However, she still took my baby brother to see Jack, and often she'd be gone for days. Whitey was my next-door neighbor, and I was very wary of him (as a man and co-occupant of the bathroom). He noticed I was alone most of the time and probably wondered if I ever ate (I was so skinny). Every time I'd see him he'd say, "How ya doin'?" and I'd bolt into the apartment or down the stairs to see if I could eat dinner at a friend's or if Demerce was at home.

One night his door was open (facing our door), and the most delicious smells stopped me in my tracks. Before I could open the door to my apartment and run inside, he appeared and asked in a gruff, matter-of-fact voice: "You hungry? Got more'n I can handle, some fried chicken, mashed potatoes, what'd you drink, soda?" Before I could answer he walked away and reappeared with a plate loaded with steaming food in one hand and a soda in the other. I was rooted to the spot. He motioned with his head toward a table in his front room, walking toward it with the plate of food.

"I'll eat it right here," I said in a too loud voice. I couldn't believe I was saying it, but I was hungry, and that food smelled *so good*. He laughed loudly and brought the plate and soda to the door, waiting for me to take it.

"Just put it down, I'll eat it right here," I ordered without a please or thank you. I remember just a flicker of anger in his eyes, then his loud, careless laugh.

"Have it your way, kid. So, what's your name?" He stared at me, vastly amused. I didn't answer him. Quickly, he put the food down outside his door, saying as he went back to the kitchen, "Just give a yell if ya want s'more, Pocahontas," with another loud laugh.

I ate it at the top of the stairs, ready to run or throw the plate at him (after my violent stepfather and other negative male experiences, I was cautious and street-smart, to say the least). I ate this way for at least two months, finally venturing inside his apartment, an inch at a time. The first time he shut the front door it took all my self-control not to run, but to trust. And he never betrayed my trust.

Whitey and my mother met during the same year we lived in that apartment next to his. They never married but were together for thirty-nine years. Whitey died/transformed January 22, 1996, at eighty-five. I realize that I missed my grandmother (mi Mamacita) the first half of my life, and that my task was to become my own mother. Now, I see I must become my own father. In the forty years I knew him, he

never said the words "I love you" (though to his great embarrassment, and pleasure, I told him straight out in his last few months).

In the following excerpt of a poem I wrote to him, I realize he did tell me ("I love you") in his own way.

Weighing My Father's Soul

To Whitey, born January 21, 1911

1.
You come to me at sunset, on your birth day;
you, my father, 80 miles away, leaving, oh
    leaving,
your body (you are not the father of my
    body,
you are the father of my soul). Your soul
    comes to

me, I feel it floating in the air, I breathe it
    in,
tell stories: He fed me when I was 12 and
    hungry,
a wild tomboy kid, called me Pocahontas
    when I refused
to say my name, my grandmother gone, now
    it was his

turn. He gave me all his money when he
    drank on
payday (he worked the manholes of San
    Francisco),
told me not to give it back, even if he asked,
begged, demanded, until Monday morning, so

I hid it in a can, in the dark, in the
    cobwebbed
basement. Monday, I gave every dollar back.
    In
return, $20 for the movies, Playland at the
    Beach,
new tennis shoes, white socks, my first AAA
    bra.

I stole his Kools, smoked them one by one in
    the
back row of the movies on Mission Street with
friends, and when boys tried to sit next to
    me
I'd threaten them with my fists or a burning

cigarette. He gave me his old wool army
    jackets
(which I loved), loaned me his
fishing tackle, pole and reel.
This stranger who sometimes drank

"My father, Claire Lewis McSpadden,"
San Francisco, 1956

too much and told me stories of his life
(how he ran away from home at 12,
hopped the rails from Texas to Los Angeles,
leaving his younger brothers and sisters

behind to be beaten; he threw rations to the
hungry children that ran after the jeeps in
World War 2: "I ain't never seen kids that
hungry, that kind a hunger's a crime, some

a them carryin' a baby as big as themselves . . ."
Worked in a burlesque house, the women
let him sleep there, safe, each woman
his dead mother, sold papers on the

corner, ran errands for everyone, the
lively, smart-talking, wiry, towheaded
kid nick-named Whitey).
this generous whiskey in the stomach,

tears in the eyes never falling,
maker of stews, spaghetti, deep-fried
chicken with frozen carrots and peas,
baker of cherry cakes and too sweet

pink cherry frosting, with sweeter yet
blood-red cherries on top, their stems
teasing the air: he was,
oh yes, he was

my father. . . .

8.
Once, when you were drinking,
you told me (at least 20 years
ago): "You always brought me
water in the desert."

You were born in the desert.
Your mother's name was Claire
(a piece of paper tells me).
You were born: Claire Lewis

McSpadden. Claire. Clara.
Clarity. A feminine light.
How well you hid it. But not
from me. This summer

I'll take a measure of your
ashes (a measure I'll keep)
to a sacred granite lake
in my mountains, where my eagles

know my voice and shadow,
my feminine light.
when I call,
when they come,

I will give this last measure
to the mountain, to the lake.
You loved these places as a young
man, and you always wanted to return,

I know. A dream: *You're young,*
in your army uniform, you're so very
handsome, your spirit entirely intact,
you're standing on a field, smiling,

arms waving with excitement, waving
in your plane. "You always brought me
water in the desert."
These are the words

I'll say to the eagles,
to the lake, to the sun.
Now I understand, father.
You always loved me

in that desert, Claire.

Reborn January 22, 1996

He had cancer of the pancreas, and in spite
of the advanced stage and pain, he was still
getting up to go to the bathroom until that
morning, after his eighty-fifth birthday, when
he fell, slipping into a semiconscious state. When
I walked into his room he was lying on his

side, one arm waving, firmly, back and forth (for his plane).

It's early March right now, a beautiful morning in early spring after a series of storms (which were also beautiful—wind, rain, rainbows arching suddenly through patches of sunlight). I'm sitting in a beach chair under an umbrella, writing in the open, listening to the ocean approach and recede. I take a quick walk to stretch my body, feel the soft sand and hard rocks under my feet, the cold, sharp clarity of the sea whispering: "Life, death, life, death, journey without end." I gather my thoughts to write here, today. Two stones, with bands of white crystal completely circling them, are my allies in this discipline of focus and flow. They tell me: "Circle yourself, circle yourself with silence, with silence and the sea, and listen only to your secret heart, your own truth." I pause here, for the present, to say that whenever I'm in need I come to the Earth, and I'm given what I need (the answer, the poem, the words, these stones). . . .

When I realized I was pregnant with my daughter at fourteen, at first I wanted to die. I met her father (my first boyfriend and later my first husband) on the corner of Sixteenth and Guerrero (in the Mission District) at our usual time, 6 P.M. Ed was sixteen; I was fourteen. He was French and Lithuanian, and his parents didn't like what the Mexicans were doing to their once "good working-class neighborhood." Therefore, I was taboo, off-limits, and pregnant. I was having morning sickness and, when it finally dawned on me, I counted my missed menstruals: five.

When we saw each other at a distance we waved. Ed was smoking a cigarette and stamped it out as I approached. We held hands and began to walk. I burst into tears, told him I was pregnant. He cried, said we'd get married. "I love you," Ed said.

One phone call: "My parents won't let me marry you, they say you'll have ten kids by the time you're twenty, I'm sorry. . . ." That night I went to the roof of the apartment building (where we'd made love under the stars, in the cold fog, where he had loved me), and I walked to the very edge of the roof overlooking the tiny yard below. There was a small tree that bloomed sometimes down there, but I couldn't see it. All I could see was the darkness everywhere I looked, and I knew how impossible this was, being pregnant at fifteen now, all alone. I knew my mother didn't (really) love me, wouldn't take care of me (and a baby). I had no money. I was alone with that life in my body, and I could jump. Just a few years earlier I used to jump roofs (roof to roof) for adventure, joy, freedom. This jump was not for joy, or freedom (I wondered).

I leaned into the darkness, over the roof's edge. A voice welled up from the darkness, from the yard, perhaps from the small tree that blossomed sometimes. It filled the night with one commanding word: LIVE.

My daughter, Antoinette, was born that year, 1960. The nuns at the hospital bound my breasts in cloth because I wasn't breast-feeding; they talked about "sin" in my presence (I was unmarried). Lydia tried to give Antoinette away; she couldn't stand her crying. And so, I had to move out on my own with a roommate (a sixteen-year-old friend also on her own). I did babysitting, cleaned houses, and Whitey helped me make ends meet financially. When I was pregnant two years later with Antoinette's brother, Ed, Jr., I wrote to Ed, telling him I was pregnant with his son (I dreamt my daughter's sex also). He was in the marines and got special permission to come home to marry me. Me in a black suit (the one I'm wearing in the photo with Antoinette at three on the next page), he in his marine uniform; we went to San Francisco City Hall, barely making closing time. The judge, seeing his uniform, let us in, his last marriage of the day. Ed stayed two nights and then was shipped to Okinawa for two years.

I moved into low-income housing called the Sunnydale Projects when I was about four months pregnant with my son and Antoinette was not quite two. These projects were extremely dangerous, so they put me in a vacant unit facing the office, which was open in the day. I was on my own at night. I rigged an alarm system of empty cans that I set up every night facing the front room and kitchen windows (which were downstairs). I slept upstairs with a large butcher knife under the bed, and Antoinette slept with me. We slept together until Ed came back. I can still remember her sweet baby smell, fresh from her long toy-filled bath, and how we laughed and played before sleep. Once she was asleep, I stayed awake a while longer, dozing and waking, listening all night for danger.

One night the cans crashed to the floor. I could hear the struggle with the window (Whitey had wired the handles to open only halfway). I grabbed the knife (Antoinette was sleeping), crept silently down the stairs, and stabbed the hand in my house. A scream, swearing, blood on the broken window, the wall, the floor. I called the police. After they took the report one came back and wanted me to let him in to talk. I refused and threatened to complain if he didn't leave me alone. (I wonder, now, where I got such wisdom and courage at seventeen.)

A woman was raped in the back where I hung the diapers, someone was shot in the building across the way, a small child was kidnapped, people beaten, mugged, burglaries . . . all fairly common. One of my neighbors, a Jamaican woman named Donna (with five children, twins who were blind and a daughter named Madonna who was Antoinette's best friend), kept me in the know. She was the neighborhood drum: "Girl, you keep yourself locked up tight, you hear? Mrs. Meyers been robbed *and* raped, and just over in building ten, uh-uh, girl, over by those damned trees, I wouldn't live next to those trees for free, girl, if they paid me. . . ." She laughed, and laughed often, giving me a portion of her mysterious strength.

And then a neighbor moved in next door: the biggest drug dealer in the projects, Sonny. His wife had just given birth (they were in their late teens, maybe), and she'd left after a loud, violent fight. That night his music was so loud I could feel it in my body (you could hear a raised voice through the walls). And then I heard the baby cry upstairs in the bedroom, a thin, pitiful, newborn cry. I couldn't believe she hadn't taken her baby.

I lay in the bed with Antoinette listening to the music, loud male voices downstairs, and the baby crying upstairs for over an hour. It was becoming a single, thin scream, then silence (the music shook the entire building). Then the single, thin scream. Enough. I jumped up, grabbed a coat, went barefoot next door, didn't knock, walked in to see about six very large, very tough-looking, black men sitting and drinking. They just stared at me. I yelled over the music, "I'm going to get the baby! You should be ashamed! That baby's been crying for over an hour!" It was the tiniest thing and worn out with clenched fists, entirely soaked with urine. I grabbed some clothing, a small stack of diapers, wrapped the baby in a dry blanket that lay at his tiny feet.

With her daughter, Antoinette, San Francisco, 1962

I stomped down the stairs carrying the now silent baby. Still no one spoke. "And turn down that damned music, right now!" I yelled to the mesmerized, probably stoned, group as I returned to my apartment. The music went down, I changed the baby into clean clothes, sponge bathing him quickly, fed him a bottle of formula I fed baby Ed. Then I put him in a drawer lined with blankets. We slept (my ears tuned to the empty cans).

The next day, Sonny (who was at least six foot four) shyly came to my door asking for his baby. "If that music ever too loud, you let me know right off, you hear? Don't tell his mama, she'll kick my ass she know you come get him like that. You let me know anyone mess wich ya, I'll take care 'a it, ya hear?"

And no one ever did mess with me again during the entire time I lived there. Even the catcalls I used to get going to the store and the laundry, four blocks away, stopped. And Sonny took my garbage can to the curb with his.

A year after Ed was born, I got extremely restless being home all day (I was only eighteen), so on a lark I called a modeling agency in downtown San Francisco. Luckily, the director himself answered the phone, and I think he was amused that I'd call and ask about the possibility of modeling. We set up an appointment for the following week after he asked my age, height, weight, and such. The agency accepted me and trained me for runway work, luncheons, salon work, and took a series of photos, putting me to work at least once or twice a week. It was very good money, and I only had to be gone from the children minimally. It was exciting work, but I also learned I had to take care of myself in tricky situations. Once at the Fairmont Hotel, in a room dominated by a bed, I was asked by the man who would hire me to model furs to take off my *thin* dress, alone with him in the room. I refused, saying, "I'm not that hungry," and left. It was wonderful (at eighteen) to be acknowledged for my "beauty" (and be paid), but the predatory sexual pressures kept me on my toes.

I saved enough money to get a Victorian flat, living under a family who would become my extended family—a Central American family with four children of their own. The husband and wife (Irma and Fred) were also painters, as well as delightful, supportive, wonderful people. We borrowed everything from each other, from butter to Tampax, and kept an eye out for each other's children, who were like siblings after about six months.

When Ed returned from the marines he was angry and violent, drinking, sometimes breaking things, and leaving for days. So, this extended family of friends (as well as others) was crucial to my survival. Ed began to do ironwork—walking the beams on skyscrapers, working on the Golden Gate Bridge. It paid well, and it was death-defying work, which seemed to satisfy him, but nothing ever seemed to truly make him happy.

His father had been an ironworker (and taken part in the thirties' struggle to unionize, becoming president of the union for a while). He too had been an unhappy man who drank, and was a cold, distant father. Ed's mother was a stern disciplinarian (tying him up in chairs, gagged, for hours as a child). I realize now how much of Ed's behavior was almost purely self-hatred, and how tragic that was for such a potentially brilliant person.

A part of the gentle boy who was bright, loved to read and talk, and was very funny (people loved Ed for his humor) remained, but the violent drinking episodes made my life almost unbearable at times, especially when he spent the entire paycheck.

Then, at twenty-one I had a third child, Marc. When Marc was a year old, I enrolled in City College of San Francisco. Since I hadn't graduated from high school (leaving in the tenth grade to have my daughter), I was surprised they allowed me to attend. I began to learn the process of reading and *thinking* again, and I loved it. I earned an Early Childhood Education certificate, took a lot of psychology courses, and got straight A's.

I worked as a nursery school teacher for about two years and then as a bank secretary for a year. (I got tired of child care and wanted to dress up for work.) During this time, the mid-sixties, I took part in anti-Vietnam demonstrations, signed petitions, and wrote letters of protest to stop the war in Vietnam. A friend (a filmmaker who worked with KQED, Channel 9, San Francisco) brought shocking war photos to our dinner get-togethers; photos of dead women, children, the old. What kind of war was this, I wondered. I wrote poems at this time, but kept them to myself.

During the time I was working as a bank secretary, Ed had a nervous breakdown and had to be hospitalized for a month. He'd taken the three children (they were ten, eight and two) on a wild car ride, almost crashing it, come home and smashed the engine to pieces with a mallet while they watched. Ed was out of work with a back problem, so he was taking care of the children. I had to admit him. The doctors wanted to do electroshock therapy. I refused, worrying it would cause damage to his brain, and I didn't believe he was really *crazy.* However, I never left the children in his care again.

We tried living together another year, and for the first time Ed hit me, punching me in the face. A week later, when he returned, I took him into the front room, alone, and told him, in a calm, even voice, that if he ever hit me again I'd stab him to death as he slept. He believed me.

I went into therapy with a wonderful woman who would eventually become a good friend. Many times she'd sit with me, saying, "You don't have to say a thing if you don't want to." And

I'd cry, speak a little, cry. I experienced unconditional acceptance, perhaps love, from her.

When Ed told me the truth one night I suppose I was ready: he was seeing men. Then one day he went to the store and didn't return. (I give myself credit, even then, for laughing at this cliché exit.) He called from Oregon, asking me and the children to join him. At last, I'd had enough, but it wasn't easy to refuse him, to say NO.

In that final year together he'd painted a huge sunburst over our front door with a rainbow arching away from it, stretched over the entire side wall of the house. It was like a promise he'd made to the children and me but couldn't keep, and so I had to keep the promise for both of us. That rainbow. That sun.

22.
When she left this man she thought
she'd die.
But she didn't. She thought
the sun would go out.
But it didn't.
And she heard a voice, distant
and small, but
she heard it.
And her mouth opened slightly
and a word spilled out. The word
was 'I'.

Inside
I am here. (do
you hear me?) hear
me. hear me.
I am here. Birthing
(yourself) is
no easy task.
I am here. (pleading)
I am here. (teasing)
I am here. (taunting)
I am here. (simply)
I am here.

(From "Mother, May I?")

After my refusal to join him, he would see the children twice and then disappear from their lives. He gave me no financial support and never dropped them a birthday card. I was always *the parent* (mother and father) and continue to be. I didn't tell them about their father's homosexuality until their late teens, when they were old enough to understand, and I never spoke badly of him (for their psychological health). If Ed had openly loved and lived with a man and supported his children, I would have respected him. He didn't do any of the above.

I was twenty-six and alone with three children under the age of eleven. At this time a friend of mine, Leslie, was dying of cancer. We had met the year before in a strange way. I was driving, with my three children in the car, when I noticed an extremely handsome black man in a colorful dashiki. He began to run and, to my astonished eyes, grabbed a woman by the arm, pulling her down the street while she was holding a baby, and a child was left, wailing, behind her. Without really thinking, following instinct and anger, I aimed my car at him. I could hear her screaming, "Let go of me, you fucker!" He'd tried to snatch her purse, but it was wound around her wrist.

Now it was his turn to be astonished. He saw me coming and tried to run, but I pinned him against a wall. I had a choice: to kill him (or really injure him) if I slammed him harder, or let him go. I stopped, and that beautiful man limped away, fast.

Leslie and her husband, David, were from Palm Springs, an upper-class world I knew nothing about. When Leslie and I went shopping together she had a command that left no doubt that she *owned* the place. She spoke French and Spanish fluently and had been to Europe. She was extremely beautiful, intelligent, and articulate. David was a longshoreman and a talented poet (who hadn't published, but I read his manuscript). He came from an artistic, middle-class family, and he drank too much beer. Supposedly, he'd tested in the genius level as a child, but he refused to go to Harvard, finish college, go to law school as he promised his father (who sounded like Jehovah on the phone with his booming, authoritative, overbearing voice). Leslie had grown up in a fair amount of luxury in an upper-middle-class home in Palm Springs. David's family lived close to an Indian reservation in middle-class comfort, but David was drawn, secretly, to play with his friends on the reservation. He had close ties to the desert (as a sacred place), whereas Leslie was more comfortable in Saks Fifth Avenue.

In Leslie's last months I took her to doctor appointments and had long talks about what it was like to die at twenty-seven (in great pain from cancer) and leave her two young children (Jacob and Eric), two and four. To say she had courage is an understatement; she was heroic. Though her doses of morphine to dull the pain were enormous, she was always conscious and clear.

After her death David would leave the children with a sitter and drink himself beyond his own pain. Often he would be at my door at 3 A.M., and I'd let him in, to the couch until the next day. We became friends as I encouraged him to stop drinking and take better care of his children and full responsibility for his life to come. Then, we became lovers, but I backed out of an intimate relationship, telling him I cared for him but didn't love him. In truth, his drinking was the problem, and I didn't love him as I had Ed. I continued to help him with his children, went food shopping with him (he hated supermarkets).

After a huge supermarket splurge that would hopefully last David a few weeks (we stored most of it in a back porch freezer), the building he lived in caught fire, wiping out the back porch, his kitchen, and ruining most of his belongings. His renters insurance had lapsed by three days; he'd forgotten to pay it. The next morning, barely dawn, revealed David at my door, in shock. Eric and Jacob sat in the car, looking lost and terrified. And looking right at me.

"Come on in, bring the kids," I found myself saying. David fell into my arms, and the children came into the house like two small shadows. Who could blame them; first their mother, then their house, all their toys, most of their clothing, gone.

David's son Eric and my son Marc were the same age (five) and had previously been friends, going to the same nursery school, so Eric's transition was a little easier, but it was hard for both Eric and Jacob. And for me. I had *five* children ranging in ages from three to twelve.

We lived in San Francisco for another year. During the first few months Eric began having mysterious pains in his right arm. David took him for X-rays, but nothing was broken. His pain increased so that he couldn't even stand. I took him to the University of California Hospital (the hospital Leslie died in just months before). After being examined by numerous doctors, an older one recognized Eric's problem: osteomyelitis. He could have lost his arm if it had progressed; osteomyelitis is a bone disease that literally kills the tissue internally

(Eric was mourning Leslie deep in his body). After two surgeries the doctors said his arm would probably not develop normally.

At the same time Jacob would suddenly start screaming in terror, unable to move. Antoinette was especially wonderful with him, holding him for hours, even sleeping with him some nights. She and Leslie had also become very close (Leslie called Antoinette "my little butterfly"), so comforting Jacob was a natural extension of her love for Leslie, as well as her own sense of loss of such a vital, loving person.

I had been longing for a while to move out of the city, to the country. The house I had lived in with Demerce (who took me in, in Bolinas, California—she'd moved from San Francisco) for about six months when I was twelve was just steps from the ocean, with no visible neighbors. I loved the silence, peace, and sense of safety. The feeling of constant danger and lurking men, in the streets, was absent (though I had to learn to trust it). I loved the dark nights and the stars that seemed to explode overhead with light. In Bolinas I wrote stories, which I'd read to Demerce, and she'd listen with careful attention. She'd say words I didn't know; I'd write them down, look them up in the dictionary, then add them to my stories.

A neighbor let me exercise his old mare, Cinnamon, in the afternoons, so almost every sunset found me roaming the coastline, each day with less fear. Eventually, returning in the dark, letting Cinnamon take us home, was part of my daily life.

This trust I learned in Bolinas, with Demerce, was very crucial and healing for me at twelve. When I was seven I had been sexually molested (thankfully, not raped) by a seventeen-year-old boy. He threatened to kill me with a gun, which he showed me, if I told anyone. I walked (I distinctly remember walking, not running) home and promptly told my aunt Ruth, who called the police. I found his photograph in a series of mug shots; I can still remember finding his tiny face in the row of all the other faces. They picked him up at school and found the gun in his locker. I remember riding in the police car, in back; him in front, turning once to glare at me. Now, I imagine he was probably molested, maybe raped, and he passed it on to other children. I still remember what he looked like; a frightened boy with a terrified child. I had to tell; it was a matter of my soul (which had been violated). I also remember lying next to my mother after the ordeal of identifying him, the physical exam they gave me to see if I'd been raped. I remember her words: "He's going to jail because of you, because you told." I continued to love her, but I would never trust her again.

Now when students (women, some men) share their horror stories, in their poems and prose, about years of sexual abuse from fathers, grandfathers, stepfathers, I have knowledge of that horror.

To this day I sleep with my large, sharp buck knife when alone or backpacking. I've taken kung fu and know some good defense moves and killing blows. I listen to my dreams, the wind as it shifts. I'm compassionate (and I think kind), but I'm not willing to suffer anyone's stupidity or cruelty. Learning to trust the Earth, the natural (native) goodness of most people (all people are born with it—I don't believe in "original sin"—I believe in "original innocence"), has made me a fierce warrior and lover of my life, and all life.

Riding Cinnamon home in the dark allowed me to hear the ocean, the chorus of birds at sunset, over my frightened, pounding heart, to see the darkening shapes of trees as beautiful against the gentle and blazing sunset sky, to smell the delicate aromas that enveloped me, and to trust my instincts in a universe that wished me well, as I trusted Cinnamon (her strong, horsy smell, her muscles, her legs, her big, yellow, square teeth, her existence separate from mine, yet touching mine) to know the way—a little bit darker, a little more trust— home.

I loved the smell of the oils Demerce used to paint her flowers and animals, even me; and that she cooked dinner every day for us. She enjoyed my stories and laughed at my jokes. Her husband (an engineer on a ship) was gone for months at a time, so I had her all to myself. I even loved the times she left me by myself for three nights at the most. She made sure I had enough food, and she called me at night to check in on me. She was in the city with friends (and a lover, I knew even then). Then it was my job to put out deer food and cat food, water all the plants, play music as loud as I wanted, swim in the ocean, finish a story to show Demerce upon her return. And ride Cinnamon until darkness brought us home.

I just remembered this, a memory (though I've thought of it, off and on, for years, but have never written of it): once while swimming in the ocean by myself and going out a little further than usual (I could swim a mile easily, having been on a swim team for a year), an undertow caught me. Though I'd been trained not to, I struggled with it until I realized it was taking me out (maybe) further than I could swim back to shore. When I stopped struggling— that very instant—the undertow let me go. By then I was exhausted from the struggle, and land looked so far away. I knew, right then, at that very moment, I was going to die. Waves of terror rippled through my body, and then, still floating on that treacherous ocean, I saw the lights (from the sun) on every wave envelope me, leave me, surrounding me. Suddenly, I was calm, and as I slowly began to swim toward shore (feeling too tired to reach it), this is what I felt: a large, cupped hand scooped my tiny body up (the light-filled wave) and, without any break or pause, brought me riding, floating, flying to shore. I knew this was a miracle, but I didn't want to repeat it, so I never swam out that far again on the open ocean. (Now I swim and kayak in Monterey Bay, which has canyons deeper than the Grand Canyon—imagine.)

Looking back, thirty-nine years later, I see the importance of this memory: trust, limitation, revelation, *trust with knowledge.* I see that death (transformation) has always been my teacher; that when death and life *meet* miracles occur. As a writer, I treasure this truth, for without it: nothing.

When Demerce wanted to adopt me, my mother refused to allow it. She couldn't/wouldn't take proper care of me, but she wouldn't let me go. As I drove over the Golden Gate Bridge, coming into the city with Demerce to return to Lydia (a perpetually empty house with no food), I cried silently. I hated the bright lights of the bridge, the city in the distance, the noise of cars all around me. I knew I was losing so much that I loved (Cinnamon, the Black Stallion on the island: freedom). And someone that loved my stories, laughed at my jokes and gave me new words every day. Someone I admired.

And so, back to my life with five children in 1971. After some violent incidents in the neighborhood: someone tried to break into the house; ten-year-old Ed was being chased home by older gang kids (for which he credits his later interest in track); Antoinette, twelve, was surrounded by an envious group of girls on the last day of junior high. I'd made the dress she was wearing; I called it her "coming of age" dress. It had a sunburst design I'd embroidered on her solar plexus, and it was long and flowing. I'd made it to honor her first menstrual.

The group of girls held hand hatchets and knives. I'd told her repeatedly if anything like that ever happened to never "go into a ball," but to yell and fight back. She broke through the ring of girls, knocking one down, and ran to a door just as a man who'd been watching was opening it to help her. To top it all off, teenagers had adopted the vacant lot behind our yard to sniff glue.

A childhood friend, Judy, had moved to Sebastopol, California, and I decided to look there. We were fortunate to find a wonderful human being as a realtor (we had a tiny down payment). He saw our huge family and decided to help us with a personal loan(!) I found a farmhouse on two acres with a creek running through it. The farm had two huge barns, almost every imaginable tree (walnut, pear, fig, apple) growing on it, including a stand of redwoods (that held eternity in their circle), an old grape arbor that produced rich, purple grapes that my daughter and I made into semi-decent wine, and willow trees so old they spoke freely in the wind, night or day. And blackberry bushes. So many blackberries that even when the boys ate their fill picking them, we had more than enough for pies, cobblers, jams.

> 23.
> It began
> with the death of
> her friend
> and she took
> her friend's husband
> and she took
> her friend's children
> and her own
> and they all
> moved

In Sebastopol, California, 1978

to the country
to the trees
to the grass
to the hay
to the honeysuckle
to the daffodils
in spring
to the naked ladies
in fall
to the full creek
in winter
to the tall corn
in summer
to the fresh lettuce
to the red tomato, apple
to the plump chickens
to their fresh eggs
to the turkey vulture
to the red-tailed hawk
to the great blue heron
under the bridge
to the steer in the field (we
ate him)
to the pigs in the pen (we
ate them
too)
to the frogs in the creek
that drown out
the night
to the wild turkey
my son never
caught
to the plump quail
we've never
tasted
to the frost on the bridge
on the leaves
on the trough
on the spider's web
with its millions
of stars
to the blossoming trees
that scatter
like snow
to the dying leaves
that warm
the ground
to the pruning of trees
to the plowing of earth
to the turn
to the turn

of the seasons.
24.
And she went in, carefully.
She went, cautiously.
She went in, trembling.
She went in,

alone.

(From "Mother, May I?")

It was here that Eric's arm healed, completely, and was normal in every way. He climbed trees, built forts, played baseball, swam, and we never reminded him of his "bad arm." Jacob and I talked about his mother a lot (he had baby pictures of himself and her to look at anytime, as did Eric), and then he talked about her less, but I know she was always with him. One night Eric turned to me with tears on his face: "I just want to see her one more time!" "Me too, Eric, me too," I said, crying with him.

And it was here I began to write poetry in a sustained fashion. Every morning after the kids were gone to school, I sat to write. The poems swept over me like fire and erupted with such force they sometimes frightened me, yet delighted me. They were mine. In the beauty, silence, and safety of that farm, I was able (free) to open my self to a channel, to a voice that was me, yet greater than me. I asked, it answered, I knew. The cycle of renewal. The *real* magic of poetry. Its power: transformation.

David introduced me to the poetry of Robinson Jeffers, Jack Spicer, Sylvia Plath, Jean Toomer, and more. I found others: Pablo Neruda, Walt Whitman, Anne Sexton, Denise Levertov. . . . How I loved these poets (and so many more), and I still do. I began to show my poetry to David (as he shared his with me). I remember sharing a just-finished poem, a rather short one, and he read it slowly and carefully. He looked up at me and said, "Take it further." Those were the words I needed, and I did.

I'd bought a typewriter for David at Christmas and put it on his desk. I began borrowing the typewriter, the desk. I found his small press publishing book and opened it up to find hundreds of small presses calling for poems to publish. I couldn't believe my eyes. I had at least eighty or so poems, so I asked David what he thought about the possibility of submitting work for publication. He told me he'd tried and met with repeated rejection, so he'd come to the conclusion that the presses published only friends or friends of friends. I knew his poetry was very good, so I was discouraged for a while. But I just couldn't resist the temptation to try.

My hands were shaking and my heart was in my throat as I chose ten poems to send. I decided to send to two presses that sounded fairly friendly. As I handed the envelope to the postal clerk I thought I'd pass out. The first press returned my poems with a sarcastic note. I found myself responding, telling them not only did they lack basic human manners, they also lacked taste in poetry (and from me, an unpublished poet). The second press was Place of Herons Press in Austin, Texas, whose editor was Jim Cody.

Jim wrote me a two-page letter heralding me as a "great new universal poet in the tradition of Walt Whitman," no less. What was crucial, and most important to me, was that Jim Cody believed in my work, in my voice, and he published my first poems in his magazine. He published my first book of poems, *Blood Root*, in 1977, the year I won the Third Chicano Literary Prize at the University of California, Irvine. In 1984 he published *Life Span*, my third book of poems.

Before the publication of *Blood Root* he hitchhiked out to my farm in Sebastopol, stopping to give readings along the way (he's also a poet). He fit right in with the family, playing jacks with the kids and fighting with them when he thought they were cheating. Doing archery with the boys in back and swearing very loudly when he missed the target on the haystack. Sleeping in the boy's fort in the willow by the creek and laughing when they pelted him in the morning with walnuts to wake him up. Helping me with dinner and the dishes. I gather he had a difficult childhood, but it only made him a compassionate, wonder-seeking man.

One night after a barbecue on the Sonoma Coast—we'd sat by the fire as Jim told us Trickster stories, making the kids howl (the Trickster farted a lot and got into endless trouble)—we'd packed everything into the van, and as I counted heads (necessary in a group that large), Jacob said, "Jim's not here."

The boys went down to the beach, yelling for him. Nothing. We waited. Nothing. After thirty minutes or so, I was about to leave, concluding that maybe he hitched a ride. I was angry by then, when Jim appeared. He was full of good spirits and beaming (I was livid). The kids were silent, taking my cue. Jim launched into a story, how he'd become a bear when he walked off by himself in the dark; he'd forgotten, apparently, about us humans.

"You were a bear?" I echoed.

Jim began to describe the experience, and the kids began to growl, loud, loud, louder. I joined in. Jim gave up the story, got into the van, and had to tolerate growls and bear swipes from their paws all the way home. I secretly think Jim hid in a good, dark place and bathed in the glow of our concern as six people shrieked his name, over and over, in the warm August night.

In the meantime, David didn't care for Jim, or the fact that I was getting published. Jim did publish two of David's poems, but he wasn't interested in publishing a book of his. I also was published in a magazine at Sonoma State, where I went for a year until a psychology class focusing on dreams made me realize I didn't belong there. The teacher spoke of dreams, interpreting them in a pathological fashion, whereas I'd been taught by Mamacita that dreams are guides, wisdom, prophecy. I was very close to receiving my bachelor's degree in psychology (my former therapist had encouraged me to consider counseling others), but at this point I lost interest in the formal, academic study of psychology. I still read many books in that field, especially in-depth writing connected to the spiritual (mind, body, spirit).

In 1976 David and I separated as he began to drink heavily again. It was decided I'd keep his children; they were more like mine anyway. During this time I dreamt I gave birth to a child, but couldn't imagine whose it would be. Plus, I had *no* desire to have any more children. Once when I was driving away in the van, my daughter told me she saw a dark-haired little boy standing next to me.

After *Blood Root* was published and I won the prize at University of California, Irvine, my friends in Sebastopol and some friends in San Francisco plotted a celebration at Cesar's Latin Palace in San Francisco for dancing and getting together. I'd just gotten back from a trip to Baja California with my old friend, Judy, and her son, plus my three children. (Eric and Jacob's grandparents—Leslie's parents—took them to Disneyland, and they visited their Palm Springs home.) It was a horrible *and* wonderful journey. We went to see the whales; we were too late. But we did see an eclipse of the moon over a deserted mountain road at midnight (and uniformed soldiers shooting at dogs for target practice at San Ignacio Lagoon, as well as a group of young men who sat on the lagoon's bank to watch my daughter swim until I asked them, in Spanish, what their mothers would think of their rudeness). An old man in a restaurant looked at me and asked, "A donde van, hija?" ("Where are you going, daughter?") A good question. A wonderful question. I felt my grandmother's spirit rise in me as I crossed the border into Mexico, and it was her spirit I saw in his dark, tired, wise eyes. I was feeling strangely free, floating like a dandelion in the wind, yet in possession of myself, rooted in the daily life of my family.

For some reason I was not in the mood to go to San Francisco, but both sets of friends got me there. Then I didn't feel like dancing, rare for me. A couple of men asked me to dance, and in a Latin club it's done rather formally. I refused with a smile, saying perhaps later. As I watched my friends dance to some great salsa, I heard a guarded voice, "Would you like to dance?" I felt him before I saw him. His energy felt massive, dark, and I almost said no; but then I saw his face. I saw a certain vulnerability, not the usual, smooth mask. Sighing, I said, "Sure."

The salsa turned into a slow song, and we began to talk. He asked if my friends and I were celebrating, and I told him we were celebrating a poetry prize I'd just won. His eyes opened in surprise and he stood still, saying, "Poetry?" He was also a poet.

We talked like old friends until we realized (yes) that the music had stopped. Then I told him I had five children . . . "Five children?" And that I lived on a farm in Sebastopol . . . "On a farm?"

This is how I met my second husband, Wilfredo Q. Castaño. Later, he confessed to being in a slight state of shock (the five children—he had a son who lived in Arizona with his mother), but he didn't want to scare me away or offend me.

I wasn't quite sure about him until he sent me some poems; I loved them. He was also a photographer and a Vietnam War veteran. (He now teaches photography full-time.) When he came to the farm (after a walk on the beach and our first kiss), he met the children, one by one, as they came in from school (brave man). Antoinette, who was sixteen, liked Wilfredo right away. It took the boys longer, Marc (ten at the time) the longest. "I don't like that guy," he'd say, glaring at him.

We married on the Sonoma coast at sunset, standing at the edge of a cliff, on Veterans Day, 1977, a fitting day. Both of us veterans of the man/woman war; both of us warriors. He'd been through a war, a marriage,

Wilfredo Q. Castaño, 1986

relationships, and I'd been through mine. For the second time, I wore black (my way of saying, I agree but not to everything).

Later, we built a fire on the beach, ate and drank, and did Greek line dancing on the tideline with friends and family. We found that when we stamped the wet sand, little white lights followed our feet.

The next morning we had a huge argument, so I left for a walk. This was to become a pattern in our relationship; much passion, but a royal battle of wills. There was a part of him that wanted a traditional "Mexican wife," and I wasn't about to do that role. Wilfredo is Mexican American from Arizona (and Yaqui Indian like myself). He was brought up by his stern but doting grandmother, as well as her daughters, who tended to indulge him (he never cooked or washed a dish).

For our honeymoon we went to Mexico City and the ancient city of Teotihuacán (which is close by), climbing to the top of the Pyramid of the Sun and the Pyramid of the Moon. Wilfredo took many photos; I wrote poetry. We took a speeding, death-defying bus ride through the jungles of the Yucatán, then a ferry ride (after hurricane-like winds died down) to Isla Mujeres. We got so drunk at a hotel pool (facing the turquoise ocean) that we had to crawl across the sand, laughing. The bartender liked us and must have given us triple shots in our delicious margaritas.

When I landed on the shore of Isla Mujeres I felt a flash of recognition (as I had at the pyramids). The ancient cultures of Mexico spoke loudly to me, which translated into poetry. The first Spaniards landing there named it "Women's Island" because of the goddess statues poised in the sand, facing the turquoise sea.

Returning home, I sold my farm in Sebastopol and bought a house in Pacifica, down the coast from San Francisco. It was a beautiful house with a clear view to the ocean and some wonderful cliffs, thanks to a vacant lot across the street. Wilfredo had a darkroom downstairs, and my work area was in the garage, which was fairly peaceful. But after the farm's serenity and safety, I felt like I was back in

In Pacifica, California, 1980

the city; and with a husband who was jealous and possessive. There was (is) much love and passion between us, but this was new to me: jealousy. Questions about my whereabouts, who I was seeing, was I hiding something . . . It was like one of the bad Mexican movies I went to see with Mamacita as a child, only I wasn't going to die of love (he was).

A friend and fellow poet, Ron Hale Thatcher, set up my first poetry reading in Albion (Mendocino, California), and it was wonderful. There was a fire behind us in a fireplace, and as I gathered up my courage to read after Ron, I felt its warmth on my back. The reading was successful (no one believed it was my first time), and afterwards we all, including the audience, went to a local bar. They made me feel like a bride; the bride of poetry.

During my time in Pacifica, about three years, Wilfredo and I did some poetry readings together. He coordinated two benefit readings for the Native American "The Longest Walk" (a march to Washington, D.C., bringing attention to Native American rights and broken treaties). The readings were held at Grace Cathedral and Glide Memorial Church in San Francisco. I also did readings by myself at bookstores, museums, colleges, and once at the Berkeley Flea Market, where I just planted myself in the space provided (poetry books for sale), some chairs in a circle, a mob of people, not an audience, and started yelling my poetry, not once looking up for at least twenty minutes. When I finally did, I had an audience. One man even had *Blood Root* for me to sign. Wilfredo and a friend (the sculptor/painter Horace Washington) also did a poetry video which included me and other poets. And in the almost twenty years I've known Wilfredo, he's continued to photograph our lives, as well as his own ongoing work.

In the spring of 1980 I sold the house in Pacifica (our battles had become a siege) and followed a message from a dream. In the dream I had to take a small, black dot and stretch it open with my hands (which was very painful, all the way up my arms to my shoulders). The black dot revealed a meadow, a stretch of sky that seemed closer to the sun, and a small cabin. That June I drove up to Plumas County, in the Sierras, passing through a formidable canyon swept with granite walls, sheer drops to the Feather River, and mountains that made me forget to breathe. Sheer, utter, ruthless beauty.

My engine caught fire on the way up. Two men leaped from their cars with fire extinguishers, saving my car. All hoses were replaced on the engine, and I continued my drive through the beautiful, ruthless, granite canyon, steadily climbing to five thousand feet. I was silent with awe and terror (waiting for my engine to catch fire again—it didn't).

The first cabin I was shown was the one in the "black dot dream." I bought it, moving up that summer with my fourteen-year-old, Marc. Eric and Jacob had gone to live with Leslie's parents (their grandparents) after much pressure from them, the grandparents. I gave them up with the stipulation that they could return, if they chose to.

Marc wasn't especially thrilled to be moving to The Boonies, The Sticks, The Woods (as he put it), and with no TV. In other words, The Middle of Nowhere; I used to say under my breath, "the middle of everywhere." (Zooming ahead to the present, sixteen years later, Marc now lives in the mountains in Boulder, Colorado, with NO TV by choice.)

Two months later, I realized I was pregnant with my husband's child (the one I'd dreamt about in Sebastopol). I had a job in town, Quincy (twenty miles away from my cabin in Spring Garden, population 80), training as a typesetter. I'd bought a Land Cruiser to get in and out during the winter, which started in early October and lasted until late April. (I didn't know this at the time.) The Land Cruiser had snow tires and four-wheel drive, and I was assured the dirt road that led to my cabin would be plowed after heavy snowfalls. Marc and I had gathered downed wood and, on the advice of a neighbor, I ordered five cords of wood, enough to fill a large room, floor to ceiling. "You're going to be cold up there," he warned. He lived in the village of Spring Garden. I lived up the dirt road, further into the heart of the mountain.

But a child? A fourth child? Here? Now? In this cabin? And alone? In the chaos of moving and separating from Wilfredo I hadn't noticed my missed menstrual.

I prepared, at the age of thirty-five, for an abortion (and I believe having a choice is absolutely crucial). Then one morning as I began to write a poem I heard: "I'm here, Mother." Clearly.

. . . Child,
you come among
dreams, tides,
stones and
dark blood—
but you come,
like the earth,
perfect and pure
at the center
of the
heart.

(From "Dark Roots" in *Life Span*)

I told Wilfredo and of course he wanted me to return. I couldn't return. I just couldn't. Now even my friends, I knew, were beginning to wonder if I'd gone "off the deep end." Staying felt slightly suicidal, but going back felt like murder: of my self. I stayed for over four years. The first month or so, Marc and I slept in the front room together; it was so *dark* at night. The first snowfall we ran outside screaming and laughing; then we sat under a pine tree in silence, together, as white, soft, melting miracles fell from the hard, black sky all around us. In cold, cold silence.

Eventually, Marc got used to not having a TV, and the fire during the winter became our TV. We both read voraciously; he got straight A's in school. Many times Marc's playfulness and humor were exactly the medicine I needed; we counted on each other for a lot (friendship, survival, entertainment). One of the hallmarks of my relationship with Marc is our friendship, which I think stems from those extraordinary and challenging years together. (Antoinette was living on her own, and Ed lived with Wilfredo, by choice, and went to college.) Next year Marc, at fifteen, would go out with a chainsaw and cut most of our winter wood. He also learned to ski (quite well) at the local ski run, and he continued to train as a runner, breaking his high school's record in the mile. (In his early twenties he toured Europe, running in major races.)

I continued to write poetry, and stories from time to time. The power of the mountain (in the Native sense of sacred presence), especially the peak behind my cabin, became my "dreaded ally." Wondrous, terrible, but without it (that key to the universe), I was not alive. I was at work on many levels, to say the least, and though I had a list of human worries, I knew I was where I was supposed to be (where death and life met, daily).

I think this poem conveys the meaning of this time most accurately.

"I've told you that the true art of a warrior is to balance terror and wonder."

—Don Juan

The Balance

The mark of the Merlin
Hawk is on my window—
its clear substance that
looks like a bird
in flight. Stunned,

I picked you up, wings
stilled, black talons
dug into my hand, your
fierce love—you
look at me with one
red eye, burning.

I held you, hawk—

you speak to me of
nothing less than life—
nothing less than death—
nothing less than this
will do. I

placed you on a tree
stump, to make your
choice. My son said,
"What isn't balanced,
in nature, must
die." "Sometimes
that balance must be found," I say.

I held you, wild love,

in my hands, with
a terror and a wonder.

(From *Life Span*)

A year after my fourth child, Jules, was born prematurely (at seven months), I was accepted into a masters of fine arts program on the East Coast. It was a low-residency program requiring two weeks each semester in Vermont, then study and writing at home with teacher contact by mail and phone. I received my MFA in writing in 1984. During the two-week residencies Jules stayed with Wilfredo in San Francisco. We were definitely separated, with both

Pregnant in Spring Garden, California, 1980

of us seeing other people, and I had no desire to return to him.

During this period of being in Spring Garden (on my mountain), then flying to my MFA program on the East Coast, I was acutely aware of going to school in my dreams (in the universe) and going to school in my waking hours (in the world). It was a profound and necessary time for me; a time that allowed my "spiritual antennae" to fully sprout. I was safe (from the daily onslaught of patriarchal culture, the negative masculine—as in the constant threat of rape; I did carry a buck knife and take my wolf-mix dog, Zeke, with me on solitary walks) in this unpopulated, wild place, surrounded by silence and beauty, as well as blizzards that bent trees to the ground, the creek that broke its dam and tried to flood my cabin (it was rerouted by a bulldozer to run by my cabin), eight foot snows by morning (shovelling to the road), a tall, dark figure that dwarfed my seven-foot bedroom window (that I left curtainless to see the diamond stars) as it stood, just staring in.

The first time it happened I nearly picked up and ran, but my wise voice said, "Be still, be calm, be still . . ." So, I stayed. During the winter months, when it snowed, I'd wake up around 1 or 2 A.M. to see this dark, massive, tall figure standing there. And the feeling was gentleness—huge but gentle—and that, most strangely, it was taking care of me and my family. I picked up a book by Peter Matthiessen, *The Snow Leopard,* in which I acquired the word *yeti* (also known in Nepal as "guardian of the goddess"). So, this was Yeti? I accepted his (the creature felt male) presence, and his presence gave me immense comfort.

I experienced other "spiritual and mystical" phenomena on my mountain, which to me are sheer gifts from the Earth and the universe. I will not detail them here, but instead offer this poem as proof.

Spectrum

I journey to joy, it's
my landmark now—
invisible, full

and flowing.
The wing beats of
an eagle are

slow and sure.
The air caresses
them, old lovers

that have flown
and know the
tangible joy of

flight. The wind,
slim crystal, guides
you to the edge

that holds the
rainbow, its quickening
shadow. That

spectrum of
light that blinds
you as you climb

to the sun.
That lover
that surrounds

you: light, dark,
light, and all
you will never

see. As
real as
an eagle,

or a fish
gulping air:
joy, love,

joy, love
has found
me. Now

I travel through
the crystal of
my eye, in

the heart of
an eagle, with
no proof,

whatsoever.

(From *Life Span*)

Today, March 25, 1996, I'm back at the beach (a beautiful, clear day after high winds yesterday). The comet Hyakutake is passing overhead, only ten million miles away. They say the last time it passed this way was 18,400 years ago, during the time humans were crossing the then-glaciated Bering Strait into North America. Last night Jules (who's fifteen now) and I went outside to see it through the binoculars. As I stared at the comet, its wide splash of light tail, it seemed I could see it move. I imagine my (our) ancestors crossing the Bering Strait, the immense, most incredible leap of faith to push forward. I imagine they dreamt their destination. They *knew* this continent was here. I imagined myself, 18,400 years ago, standing on ice; ice behind me, ice in front of me. I shuddered. How amazing we are, we humans.

I handed the binoculars to Jules. We were silent. Later, his father, Wilfredo, would come home late from teaching his class. Jules and I moved to Santa Cruz, California, in the fall of 1984 to be with his father (my partner and husband). This took a comparatively tiny leap of faith, but here we are. We rediscovered each other, with new boundaries, new territory, with some familiar expectations we had to resist (possessiveness, male/female roles, old, but ingrained, patriarchal roles), or we'd lose the together, again. We still have to resist, of course, and create (dream) our paths separately, and trust they will continue to meet and converge.

Today I sit on the sand, facing a cliff with eucalyptus trees growing on the edge of it. The largest one has roots extending all the way down the steep cliff: gnarled, twining, *exposed*. Its other roots extend into the ground behind it, *hidden*. This, I think, is the ongoing task of the writer, and as I look at this tree, I see it's not an awkward sight. Not at all. It affords me a view of its life. There's beauty and grace in that.

During the time I've lived here in Santa Cruz, I've written three novels, a short story collection, and two books of poetry. When I began my first novel, *The Ultraviolet Sky*, it was with blind panic and seizures of terror; another leap of faith. I'd told family and friends I was going to write a novel (I told myself I was going to write a novel), and so not to was to admit defeat. Failure. So, I wrote the first fifty pages blind (yet dreaming), my heart in my throat.

My main character, Rosa, was a painter, and I had plans for her (until page one hundred or so). One morning when I sat down to write I just couldn't. Not a thing. I had no link. To the novel, to the plot, to any of the characters, and especially not to Rosa. It was as though everything and everyone, in the novel's world, had died; they refused to speak to me, much less appear. Though Rosa's character had sprung from me, my life, I could already see what she looked like, and she didn't look like me or walk like me or talk like me. She looked, walked, talked like *herself*. That morning I couldn't even glimpse Rosa. She was dead, everything was dead. And I was absolutely devastated, to my surprise; this had never happened to me before. All I could do was mourn, though I told no one at this point. I assumed this was the end of novels for me.

About two weeks later I was in the shower listlessly washing my hair, feeling pretty damned depressed, as though my usual sense of purpose and will were absent. I was just washing my hair. Suddenly, large as life (more vividly than I'd ever seen her), Rosa strode, and I mean *strode*, right into me. It was electrifying, orgasmic.

Son Jules and Alma, 1993

"My family (from left): Ashley, Antoinette, Cody, Alma, Barbara (Marc's girlfriend), Marc, Ed, Maureen (Ed's girlfriend); (kneeling) Wilfredo and Jules

Quickly, I towel-dried, found the notebook I'd hidden from view, a pen, and sat to write. Anything. I got a fix on Rosa; or rather she had a fix on me. There she was, looking right at me. Sternly. She had some things to say about *her life,* and she set me straight. About the number of children she had—one; I'd given her two. How she felt about her lover, her work, her friends, the painting *she* envisioned and had to create, the world as she perceived it. On and on. I sat there and listened. To my character, Rosa.

And that's how the novel was written; that's how I was allowed to write the novel, by allowing Rosa, and all the other characters, to reveal themselves to me, bit by bit, in their own time, in their own voice. Yet the vision, the central theme, was mine, and that's what I had to stay true to while struggling with the truth of the characters. As I look back on it now (and forward to future novels), I see a kind of passion play of self and ego(s). Self (eternal, wise, knowing) and ego (temporary, innocent/guilty, learning).

I learned a lot. There was magic in the writing process for me, the usual terror and wonder. Many times I would dream an especially difficult sequence—an outline, a piece of dialogue, a character's presence—making it possible to continue with fluidity.

The next novel, *Naked Ladies,* wasn't quite as terrifying. The process was similar, but certainly not the same. Each novel, each short story, each poem takes that leap of faith—that I ask (from my deepest longing) and that I'll be answered (from an endless, mysterious source: creation).

When I teach I try to convey this process to my students. I attempt to teach writing (creation) as the waking dream, dreaming awake, transformation of energy into matter. Imagine: it's the faith of a woman who's just learned she's pregnant. She imagines the darkness of her womb, the size of her womb, so small. She imagines the tiniest creature, a seahorse-child, a spiral-shaped creature, nestled in her womb. Invaded. Penetrated. Chosen. Blessed. Cursed. Captured. She imagines her life, whether it's possible. To create (this child, this novel, this poem, this painting, this equation). She imagines its birth (form, words, color, song, the unknown face). And she leaps. She allows. She struggles. She dreams. Until it is complete. Unto itself.

And then she lets go. She will create again. She will love again. If her faith is intact. If she is willing to leap, again and again, into the unknown. The undiscovered. The uncreated source.

As I sit here in the sweet spring sun, I think of my daughter, Antoinette, now thirty-five and a critical care registered nurse, with two children of her own: Ashley, fourteen—born in the same year as Jules, and Cody, eleven. My grandchildren are intelligent, beautiful, and very humorous. My son Ed, now thirty-three, is a professional bike racer and also attends college. Marc, who's twenty-nine, teaches high school biology (and is track coach) in Boulder, Colorado, and is also a writer. And Jules (fifteen) is a handsome, sensitive, boy-man who also has a gift for writing, and he's a bodyboarder and a surfer. All of them continue to complete themselves, unto themselves. They are their own creations.

As I sit here, dolphins surface to breathe revealing their fins, their black, shiny bodies. I read that dolphins arrived in the Monterey Bay about ten years ago, about the time I did. Last summer when I was swimming I saw a flash of darkness in the water; I nearly screamed as I registered SHARK. Then, a silky, smooth body brushed alongside my own: a dolphin. It was like being brushed by a jolt of joy. At fifty-one, I can truly say that my joy outweighs my sorrow, and I'm *grateful* to know this.

As I sit here a group of teenagers with a small boy are building a fort with washed-up driftwood. I wonder if the boy is their son or brother (people often thought Antoinette was my sister). I can see the boy is loved; the way they play with him, touch him, include him. And I think: Wherever there's love, there's innocence. There's a beautiful innocence about this group. I feast my eyes.

There's a juggler a few feet away. He's very good, juggling three, then four frisbees.

And then there's the world, beyond what I can see, but I can *feel* it: Bosnia, China, Africa, Tibet, Mexico, Nicaragua, Russia, Turkey, Korea, Cambodia, India . . . The

Earth as we're faced with a new, uncreated century.

As I sit here I pray that innocence survives, that the Earth survives (us), that we survive (as compassionate human beings), that the juggler be truly skilled. And I pray (to the Goddess and the God) that I may write for the rest of this lifetime, and dream always.

I wrote this poem yesterday ("Dear World" is a series of poems I started two years ago):

March 24, 1996

Dear World,

18,400 years ago, this comet
we call (in 1996) Hyakutake,
came close to the Earth (10 million
miles away, 10 million), but we

can see it with the naked
eye, floating in the sky like
a tail of light. The last
time it came within 10 million

miles, humans were just crossing
the terrible, icy glaciers,
the Bering Strait, into this
land mass, North America, one

of the floating, enduring Turtles.
The Turtles whispered, "Leap of
faith, dream, leap of faith, dream,"
as the comet edged its way

10 million miles, so close. 18,400
years later, the Turtles whisper,
"Leap of faith, one planet, leap
of faith, one people." This planet

floating through the stars, comets
coming home to sing to the Turtles:
"Cross the terrible, icy glaciers,
the human heart, leap."

It's mid-April. I've completed typing this essay, the poems, into my word processor. On my desk are two photographs, close together, that catch my eye. I realize I've never looked at them together. One is a photo of my grandmother, Jesus, at eighteen or nineteen, sitting with a friend. They're sitting in chairs next to each other; a large, white, fur rug extends from the floor to the back of their chairs. My grandmother's friend strikes an intellectual pose, placing her left hand to the side of her face as though considering something important; the other's in her lap. My grandmother has her left hand in her lap, while her right hand caresses the soft, sensual fur. Her face is sensual, intuitive, beautiful, a little sad. She is my ancestor.

The other photo is of me at nineteen with four-year-old Antoinette. I can't see my hands, but I remember. They washed diapers and sheets by hand when the children (Antoinette and Ed) had measles one after the other for a month, and I couldn't go to the laundry. I imagine my right hand is curled around my daughter's soft, slightly chubby baby's leg, exposed because of her dress. My face is sensual, intuitive, beautiful, a little sad. I imagine my left hand rests nervously in my lap (with nothing to do). My daughter's head eclipses the right side of my face; the left side is just me at nineteen.

I had no idea I would ever really write (and publish). In fact, I often thought I might not even survive. But I did. And I realize, now, that to survive I had to be transformed (reborn). I had to die. I have to do this dying cyclically in order to be reborn (a small, green snake slithered in front of me on a trail yesterday, reminding me of this truth, my new skin). But first, one must learn to die.

I am my ancestor. Thanks to the nineteen-year-old (twenty, thirty, forty-year-old) woman I was, I am the fifty-one-year-old woman I am now. Thanks to the dead and the living I have known (and not known), I am able to write these words. I write to remember the dead, all that is no more. I write to remember to love, all that yearns to be. Created.

BIBLIOGRAPHY

Poetry:

Blood Root, Place of Herons Press (Austin, Texas), 1977, reprinted 1982.

Mother, May I?, Motheroot Publications (Pittsburgh, Pennsylvania), 1977.

Life Span, Place of Herons Press, 1984.

(With Alfonso Rodriguez, Gary D. Keller, Leroy V. Quintana, and Carmen Tafolla) *Five Poets of Aztlan* (Villanueva's poem "La Chingada" appears in English and Spanish translation), Bilingual Press (Tempe, Arizona), 1985.

Planet with *Mother, May I?*, Bilingual Press, 1993.

Fiction:

The Ultraviolet Sky, Bilingual Press, 1988, Doubleday, 1993.

Naked Ladies, Bilingual Press, 1994.

Weeping Woman: La Llorona and Other Stories, Bilingual Press, 1994.

Other:

Letters to My Mother, Pocket Books, 1997.

Author of essays published in *Ms. Magazine* and the anthology *Hot Flashes*, Faber and Faber, 1995. Contributor of poetry and fiction to numerous anthologies.

ruth weiss

1928-

ruth weiss with DOUG O'CONNOR *on acoustic bass at El Rio,*
San Francisco, 1993

EXCERPTS

black don't crack she said & called me girlfriend when i told her i was 64. her elegant
hand brushed my face. . . .

i was back in 1928. in berlin. i had just been
born. the nurse asked MUTTI if PAPA was black.
it was the '20s & jazz musicians were made
most welcome in europe. what do you mean
MUTTI cried. your baby is quite dark but she
has light eyes . . . maybe green maybe blue.
what do you mean let me see her MUTTI said.
this is my baby she looks just like OSCAR. and
he's dark she said. and his mother even darker.

she didn't say any more. like his mother is
from budapest & maybe even gypsy & a jew
through & through.

1938. i'm in vienna since 1933. one day i'm
in school. in fourth grade. same teacher same
classmates since first grade. one day i'm in school.
the next day it's JEWS OUT.

the TORAH that holy scroll is rolling in the
street. MUTTI starts to pick it up. don't FRAU
WEISS. please. it's the cop on the beat. who
helped us school-kids cross the street. don't
FRAU WEISS. please. your life. MUTTI & i
walk away hand in hand. slow. and do not look
back.

INCIDENT

october 1938 we had to flee vienna.
my grandmother hungarian boarding house
was wanted by a nazi official.
hungary was still out of nazi clutch & my
    grandmother hungarian.
we were austrian citizens —
my father, his mother's only son.

we left quickly in the night for the swiss border.
the border had closed one night before our
    arrival.
rain —
dizzy alp trails —
we climbed to slide muddy back to the
    border village.
another try —
now a desperate 20 (mostly young men)
with hired guide across the flooded rhine.
one woman slips in the mud . . .
shotssinging above our heads
not really meant to hit us (the swiss
    sharpshooters) —
the warning realenough —
go back we can't take any more.
we couldn't either.
the three of us penniless in the innsbruck
    trainstation —
obvious unaryan.

what now ?

any moment the question —
the only answer !

a young woman brushed by —
a whisper the follow-me.
what could we lose ?

wet night
narrow streets —
we kept a block behind
until she vanished into a doorway.
a slit of light —
we entered.

are you hungry ? she said.
i'll show you your bed.

all night the venetian blinds caught light.
once there was a knock.

the sun rayed through the blinds
when she called us for breakfast.
a young man with unslept eyes was sipping coffee.
where are you headed ?
vienna.
the man nodded, kissed the woman, left.
her hands put money & tickets into ours.
she directed us to the station —
first checking the street.

PAPA & MUTTI, Oscar and Fani Zlata Weiss,
in Cannes, 1926

at the station an official gleaming a huge
    swastika neared us.

what now ?

then we saw his face.
it was the young man who hadn't slept.
there had only been one bed in the flat.

in vienna our visa from new york awaited us.
there was still time to leave.
december 31st, 1938 —
midnight —
the last possible moment.

we boarded a train for holland.

in switzerland we would have spent the war
in an internment camp.

1938. december 31. the train enters holland. our tunnel through the night. our tunnel into light. the last train allowed out.

the ship WESTERNLAND. from the port of vlissingen. taking us to america. to the land of the west. to the new world.

but i know it is the old world. of copper-sheen skin.

i know new york is a city. still it is a shock when i arrive. where is the welcome of painted red skin. where are the feathers. where are the drums.

i have always known cities. berlin & budapest. zagreb & prague. and of course vienna. so new york the city engulfs me. i walk easy on cement. and forget what i know.

1939. home in harlem. a children's home in harlem. a lone white jewish children's home in harlem. so who's new in the neighborhood. she new in the neighborhood. why was i now in harlem. maybe that bronx children's home where no one was to be after age 9 they'd found out i was going on 11 not 8 like PAPA & MUTTI said. once i know english out comes that i know algebra. and then oops it was fast from class 2 to 4 to 5.

in the bronx all the streets so even & clean & no green. no one on the street. the houses straight up & down.

oh vienna my hand still on your grillwork. on your balustrades.

harlem streets are narrow. houses lean one to the other. sideways & frontways. steps up & down. and other streets oh so wide. smiling. and everybody is out there at one time or another. or from the window. and there's skipping & jumping & clapping. and stopping. and sitting & talking. and always the dance.

school. the only white girl in the class. and i don't speak yet too much english. and this one & that one takes me home to show mama & sister & brother.

don't you have a mama. yes i have a mama & a papa too. but where are they. i see them on sunday. and where are your sisters. and where are your brothers. i don't have a sister. i don't have a brother. you do now. yes i do.

but i miss SUSI. i miss SUSI. SUSI ROSNER. my close close friend for 5 years in vienna. and sometimes see her brown eyes see her dark hair & white skin reflected in the black.

*   *   *

looming above its neighbors. half as wide as its neighbors. this house of eyes shut & open. this house of small & large windows. this light or that light on always. rents its small or large rooms basement to attic $7 a week. to artists & poets. this is the ART CIRCLE on deming place. near north side chicago. 1949. my first home in bohemia. in the basement.

painted it black. from floor to ceiling. did the floor first. had to do it again.

ruth in Berlin, 1930

ruth, Iowa City, 1940

my just-bought not-new turntable. under a blue bulb. i hear

    BIRD
    PREZ
    LADY DAY
    BUD
    MONK
    VILLA LOBOS
    DJANGO
    SARAH
    SCHOENBERG
    SHOSTAKOVICH
    BARTOK

i go to the bars. not to talk. to write. i look. i listen.

i never hear the scratching of the needle. i never hear the rats scratching outside my window from the empty lot next-door. patches of sky. come rain come shine.

i visit STUFF SMITH. his south-side chicago kitchenette apartment. stuffed with music. his violin wild jazz opens the ceiling. brings back the firmament.

i write on park-benches. at night. under the one light. words make wings. protect.

i write on the "L." it shudders through the city. some lines hard to read later. a 24-hour cafe. i write.

i work as a dice-girl at the CAPITOL LOUNGE. on state street. that great street. DIZ is there with PERCY & MILT & the rest of the to-be MODERN JAZZ QUARTET. it is 3:45 a.m. DIZ trumpet in hand leaps on the bar from the stage behind. through the greyhound station next-door. around. re-enters the LOUNGE from the street. closes the show. sez HOOPAKTECAH HOOPAKTECAH WHO PARKED THE CAR.

walk home the 20 blocks or so. saves fare. forty some years later am still riffing HOOPAK-TECAH. . . .

KEN is blue-black. we walk. talk. logic. facts. mathematics. i love mathematics. went through solid geometry in high school. all A's. the only girl in the class. teacher MRS. McILVAIN. when asked what to study to write. i say mathematics. no i mean really. yes i mean really.

oh there is literature at the ART CIRCLE. living literature. WILLARD MOTLEY comes to visit. *KNOCK ON ANY DOOR.* GWENDOLYN BROOKS comes to visit. *A STREET IN BRONZEVILLE.* a fine tooth-comb. WILLARD's lover is lovely BILL. BILL in my class at sullivan high. BILL dies young. "i want to die young & have a beautiful corpse."

drawing sessions at the ART CIRCLE. i model in the nude. other classes. other schools.

i teach myself not to move. my leg is asleep. i teach myself. let no one know. i teach myself. how to move. not moving. i teach myself. how to move. every 20 seconds another pose. i played statues in vienna. my head is without a thought. at the break the thoughts tidal-wave in. into words. on paper.

i pay my rent.

jam sessions at the ART CIRCLE. from south chicago the musicians. from north chicago the musicians. it's jazz black & white. in the clubs it is either black or white.

and poetry aloud.

ERNEST ALEXANDER long & brown listens to my poem. in my black blue-bulb room. pulls me upstairs. sez now read to these folks. they gotta hear this.

my first own home. my first turntable. my first modeling nude. my first poetry aloud. someone blows a horn. someone brushes a drum. i'm reading to jazz man.

oh ALEX lover of my first woman-lover JERI WANTAJA. your paintings of birds. your studio bright & wild with their flight. your studio a three-cornered touchstone where i write in a corner. look out at warehouses trucks dawn. come rain come shine.

a streetcar brakes to a stop. JERI & i break from ALEX's hug. barely land on the step as it moves on. break the big apple he shouts. his long figure recedes. his wave lingers on. our first ride out of town to new york.

oh ALEX. is it 1955 or 6 or 7. THE CELLAR. san francisco north beach. where i had started poetry & jazz. you walk in. i carry glasses & bottles. almost drop them. we hug. your wife with you. your first-born soon after. it's all a blur. your wife & boy dead. mexico.

you become a legend. it's the beat-time. day after day.

in & out of the CO-EXISTENCE BAGEL. you stand outside. you sit inside. you walk up & down. you talk at. you talk at. you talk at. you hold my eye in your hand. it slips from your hand. it is wet with tears.

tears clear. years i wouldn't cry. years i couldn't cry. PAPA liked that. he taught me kilometers of walking. cold showers. also leaves & flowers. erica. my 2 & 3 & 4-year-old berlin fragrant with erica. heather. i am searching fragrant heather in america. erica in america. the last time i saw PAPA. tied to his bed. in the hospital. a stroke. he couldn't speak. i didn't either. our eyes locked. filled with tears.

tears clear. i'm in new york again. new york new york. JERI back in chicago. long ago.

ruth & MUTTI, at Mount Tamalpais, 1953

i find my room on 11th street between 5th & 6th avenue. it found me. a month after my arrival.

i model in the nude in manhattan. the smell of charcoal. the smell of oil-paint.

in one class. one black man. what do you do when you leave here he asks. i write. poetry. may i see sometime. it's . . . i read his face. why not.

we meet next day in washington square. to this day i have kept his note.

> please bill me for the price of your first book. i have enjoyed the deliciousness of your thoughts and felt them part of myself. continue to give of yourself your intimate self and your success shall know no bounds. how strange it is that you have found what i am also seeking. i can feel it in your writing. it is more of a conversation with *true self* than i have ever read. success *is* yours. you have only to realize this to crystalize the gems of truth into reality. what is really reality.
>
> WILLIAM PARKER

my first book *STEPS* out in 1958. never knew his address.

summer 1950. hand to mouth. month to month. i pay my $45 rent. a room with a shower. a room with a view. facing the back of the new school for social research. narrow window from floor to ceiling. its wall-lined shelves open-arm to a growing stack of books. gathered from the new york treasure-trove of second-hand bookstores.

the whisper of ghosts. this old house. unlike any of its newer neighbors. two old ladies in gossip. this house & the tree in front. the landlady a once-famous lawyer. championed the poor. called a radical.

breakfast is a spud-nut. a kind of donut. lunch is a 13-cent hot-dog with sauerkraut bought in the subway station. supper well maybe a candybar or better yet a 10-cent beer on macdougall street.

i'm 22.

don't think i'll make it to 30. don't think. write. words are my friends. words are wings. protect. i have a room of my own. i shall always have a room of my own. that i will. this cancer girl gotta have a room of her own.

summer heat. heavy man. few classes. few schools. how pay the rent. gotta pay the rent.

i walk through washington square. a voice familiar sez hey . . . you speak german. you speak french. there's a convention in atlantic city. they need interpreters. here's the number. hurry.

it's a job for a week. to a breath of sea-air. pays fare hotel meals & $12 a day. a miracle. my life a crazy-quilt of miracles.

the boardwalk. atlantic city. monopoly the game. translate technical terms i don't understand. the words are the same. it's all on the accent.

the night is my own. i listen to the surf. order room-service for one. a sandwich & a beer. then head away from the sea to the dark part of town.

am i blue. the notes of a sax arrow through. oh lordy. on hermes wings. street after street. my feet in front of a neighborhood bar. bye bye blues. no more a stranger in the city. MISS D they're doing your songs. for seven days. night after night. the only white face in the place. they treat me so fine.

back in new york city. not so light in august. a knock on my door. it's JERI. not heard from in a year. with a bag of grapes & a fiver in her hand. let's go to new orleans. my palms turn up. nothing you see. she waves her 5-spot her 5-dollar bill. flashes a diamond engagement ring. we can hock this when we get there. she's got a fever all right. it's catching. i've got to store all that. i point to the books.

R.J. has a studio. on third avenue. near houston street. we step over empty wine bottles & someone asleep in the doorway. climb up to the loft.

a big black cat R.J. he really is. he's on his mattress. fully clothed. a chessy smile. sketches all over the floor. the "L" rattles by. the sketches lift & settle. what's up. who's your friend. going to new orleans. need to store my stuff. in august. you crazy — girl. got nothing in new york. you can always move in here. a friend's a friend. and there's always a pot on the stove. help me bring my boxes over. get someone else for that. i ain't movin'. you the laziest mutha in town. right. but who gets the commissions. you dream 'em up huh. you got it girl.

eight months later. april 1951. i fly back only to ship it all to chicago. the boxes are where i left them. R.J. is on his mattress. fully clothed. a chessy smile. sketches all over the floor. not the same ones.

where's your friend. back in chicago. and you. i like new orleans. my rent is $15 a month.

how come green hair. that's another story. what do you do in new orleans. i ride in the back of the streetcar. the one named desire.

i always thought you black.

1952. light waves in august. heat makes mirage. august on the road again. the road going west. san francisco rises out of the fog. a city in gauze.

my last ride drops me on broadway & columbus. north beach. sez, this is where you belong. right on.

up a few steps from broadway on montgomery a hand-scrawled sign. room for rent. my room is in there. i can hear it whisper my name. no doorbell. i knock. no answer. i knock again. i hear it resounding down a long hall. now what.

the corner grocery. of course. the corner grocery always knows the neighborhood. it does. i leave with the landlord's phone number ringing in my hand.

a few days later my typewriter & i move in. a corner fireplace in an empty room. my first fireplace. $25 a month. i have exactly $25. started with $30 from chicago. $30 & a waitress union traveling card. in chicago membership cost $15. in california $100. which i didn't know at the time. it's always that way. i always find out later what i didn't know i know.

i find a mattress. unused. boxes from chinatown — a desk. boxes from chinatown — shelves. a chair. burlap bags — curtains. the large window faces the street.

san francisco. i'm home. a walking city. up & down steps. vienna. not quite. a pang here & there. enough. this is not a travelogue.

crash. it's 5 a.m. the garbage truck. oh no. i'm right on the alley. the garbage truck twice a week. enough.

i call the landlord. any other room. we–ell there's one upstairs. you'd better take a look at it. it's a closet with a lightwell. $10 a month. great. that fits my finances. a shower on the roof. yeah. size of a phone-booth. steam of the shower. night-fog. the ferry-building-clock is my timepiece. a fine view of the bay bridge. this is the time before the freeway years later an earthquake crashed.

TEN TEN

TEN TEN
cometh the dragon
skims on ten thousand feet
drumming remember
along the street of applause
pauses —

it was 1952
a dragon-year
at broadway & columbus
my last hitch from chicago
said this is where you belong

found my room on montgomery
1010 montgomery
10 dollars a month
with a light-well
and a shower steaming on the roof
through the fog

across the hall
professor FOON
kept music in a room

tongue click against tooth
a nervous habit
from near-miss of bomb
on his home in hong kong

butterfly harp
i danced he played
kept us both
from being afraid

we spoke no english
i wrote in it though
and ate with chopsticks

but not pizza
ten fingers for that

one late-night-walk
uphill on kearny from pacific
the man stopped his black & white
and asked what are you doing
out at night ?
just then FRANKIE LUPO
(another up-all-night-freak)
stepped through the gate
of his kearny palace
told the man
(since i didn't speak)
she just likes to walk
then invited me in
to share pizza reheated on coal
with a glass of red
to warm the soul

talked of MAMA upstairs
through glass-clink & fog-blink
regaled me with tales
i'll never forget nor remember

my first book STEPS 1959
41 dragon-steps
up the steps of kearny casbah
where for years we smoked
joint to the east
made a point in the west
ONE MORE STEP WEST IS THE SEA

on pacific THE INTERNATIONAL
    SETTLEMENT
where i worked the tables
in THE HOUSE OF BLUE LIGHTS
the girls dark & grace
how i loved that place
the music was so fine

lullabye of broadway
garbage-truck smash-crash at dawn
fuck ! — can't sleep
climb to coit tower
ONE MORE STEP UP SEE SUN RISE

TEN TEN
cometh the dragon
skims on ten thousand feet
drumming remember
along the street of applause
pauses —

CHINA GONG
1990
where's that monkey KAISIK WONG ?
his floats a saga
the crowd going gaga
while he scampers away
floated away
in his robe of atlantis

CHI CHI
CHI CHI

is that you ?

TEN TEN
cometh the dragon
skims on ten thousand feet
drumming remember
along the street of applause
pauses —

the dragon arrives

typewriter rattling on the boxes. writing the blues. and other colors. where's the jazz.

night-walk from north beach to the fillmore. i wear black. i always wear black. melt into the night.

bright-light JIMBO's BOP CITY. jazz 2–6 a.m. what a jam.

JIMBO i don't have a dollar. you don't have one dollar. i'm running a business. all right. go on in. but next time . . . next time. JIMBO i . . . listen girl. grab a tray. no wages. but there's tips. only near beer. you hear.

STAN WILLIS *THE WILD MAN* & *GENIUS IS A RARE THING JONES* on keys & singing. COW-BOY on trumpet picking a note here & there. at the back of the stage always. STEVEN rocking in on his limp. fingers cradle the bass. these are. these are my touch-points. smoking buddies.

STAN knows where pianos live. enters the homes where pianos wait for him. a soft smile hello. not another word. sits down & plays & plays. leaves. no door is ever locked to him where a piano lives.

oh that first time i heard STAN. the night all night at PHILIP LAMANTIA's & GOGO's pad. a victorian on the west side of van ness. we three are all around twenty-five & about five-foot-two. wear black. the poems verbal & spark.

GOGO is in her dark-room. had apprenticed to ED WESTON in monterey. i look at her photos of rock emerging through the solution.

GOGO comes out of her dark-room. sez let's go to BOP CITY. PHILIP's hands stop in mid-air. keeps on talking.

GOGO & i at BOP CITY. it is mid-week & quiet. STAN on piano. solo. we listen & scribble.

and we both see birds. mine going upward. GOGO's flying into a yellowswollen sun.

STAN gives me his record. maybe his first. writes on it. "for ruth who is in time to tame the universe." COWBOY looks the same forty years later as he blows behind me at an oak street session. it is in STEVEN's pad i first hear *NIGHT IN TUNISIA.*

well-known names drop in from gigs at THE BLACKHAWK. from other clubs. 2 a.m. soulfood. a rib here. a riff there. the joint is jumpin'. there are girlfriends & paid girlfriends. the paid girlfriends with more manners. sparkles. the wheel round & round. the dealing. it's a scene man. yet every so often a quiet face. tuned in.

6 a.m. BOP CITY closes. half a block away JACKSON's NOOK. a counter. a room small & dark in the back. the wonton soup delicate. the coffee strong. delicate & strong. MR. JACKSON. tall. light-skinned. his hair grey & curly. an ageless face. his children behave here. this is a listening place.

one by one the ones who *must* play — enter. the search for that note — that only one. it's a jam for the heartbeat. no feet tapping. no hands clapping.

i walk slow through daybreak-blue. back to north beach. my lids fold around my whole being.

one night i'm walking the dark streets. looking for a light. i meet this big black cat. and take him to my $10 a month pad. few friends have ever seen. and show him my writings. few friends have ever seen. his eyes get big. and he sez. you're really on to the blues.

with TAYLOR MEAD, North Beach, San Francisco, late '50s

my typewriter is in hock. had to pay the rent. so he brings me one. probably a stolen one. sez go type away. write me more blues & we'll get you out there.

and what do i do. i say take back your typewriter. get out of here. i'm getting my own out of hock. and taking my time to do it right. my time will be my time.

i lived in the SUTRO mansion on pine street in the '50s. wood from around the cape. my room on the second floor. $25 a month. marble sink & fireplace. a balcony semi-circle with balustrades. looking over lawn & garden. the mansion torn apart in the shark-building-frenzy of the '60s. boxes now squat on its grave.

1953. MEL WEITSMAN my lover & later my first husband takes me to meet HAYWARD KING. in his north beach basement apartment. in an alley just off broadway. CLYFFORD STILL their teacher at art school.

abstract expressionism. unwittingly funded by the GI bill. buckets of housepaint. jars of tar. pas-

ruth on Grant Avenue, North Beach Street Fair, late '50s

sion. revolt. then points to the zen. enough. this is not a trip through art history.

HAYWARD KING. the man is his name. this huge black man. always the only black man. sparked the 6 GALLERY in the '50s. then off on a fulbright to sorbonne.

walk into a gallery. there's HAYWARD KING. walk into an art museum. there's HAYWARD KING.

1976. i walk into SPECS. north beach. we haven't seen each other in years. i know he's there before i enter. he's there. a drink in his hand. and in mine the moment he sees me.

he visits me & my lover artist PAUL BLAKE. in our nob hill basement garden apartment. we lunch inside. allergies. allergies. his laughter shakes the walls. we are rolling with laughter. tears stream down our faces. become rivers of pain. i panic. he is so frail. so vulnerable. this huge black man.

we ask him to help hang a show for PAUL. in a restaurant on polk street. so many pieces. such a small space. he walks in. the space expands. all the pieces fit singing to each other.

1977. i work as cashier at the art museum. it's not artists who get the money. i worry about things like that.

HAYWARD is walking through the art palace gates. you here he sez. meet you for lunch.

we drink our lunch at the corner bar. he is shaking his head. don't think so much. have another drink. but those new chairs upstairs. they cost $30,000 each. i know. have another drink.

are you writing. am i breathing. how about *DESERT JOURNAL*. ever finish it. long ago. 1968. just got published this year. had a book-party in april. in north beach of course. at the SAVOY TIVOLI. i missed that. april in paris. no that was another year. where was i.

you also missed the one for *LIGHT and other poems*. in '76. never had a book-party before that. not for any of my four books before that. *LIGHT and other poems* was my first. my first celebration for a book out.

i remember you writing during light-shows. in the dark. that was '59 or was it '60. man you have a memory. one of my heavies. have another drink. i used to tease you about writing in the dark. a beer in one hand. a pen in the other. eyes of a cat.

and you don't work in the dark.

i have white walls.

four months later. july 1977. last day in july. a sunday afternoon. we're at his studio. his home on rincon hill. wall-to-wall people. his friends.

white walls alive with art. his own & others. PAUL's *VIGIL* red-dragon-dog among them. the sun shines through glasses filled & refilled. it's a book-signing party for both of my books. HAYWARD is pouring champagne into my glass. from his height. doesn't miss a drop. you see i didn't miss the party did i he laughs.

he lost his rincon hill place. maybe it was torn down. was homeless for years. stayed with this or that friend. moved into a tenderloin hotel. one day he moves across the street. his own studio again. white walls in the tenderloin. alive with art. his own & others.

you see him. there he goes. a black star in a blue sky. he's gone. 1990.

slide back a few years. 1958. MEL & i are married. one year. home is a seven-room apartment. $60 a month. 1207 south van ness. heart of the mission. san francisco. BREW MOORE lived there just before. blew his horn there. that apartment is many stories. many ghosts.

1955. a party at BREW's. in that seven-room apartment. a san francisco jazz-party. maybe over 200 people. from in-town. from out-of-town.

i get there about 3 a.m. after work at THE CELLAR. others are arriving after gigs.

i climb the long stairway up. never guessing how many times i would climb those same stairs later from '57 to '64.

i'm peopled out after work. what am i doing here.

no need to head for the kitchen. i carry my own beer. as always.

thrum. thrum.

the sound draws me to the front room. dark & quiet.

thrum. thrum.

i see the bass. i see the fingers upon the strings. and the bass & the man are one.

the sound stops. the sky is pale with day-come-slow. a poem in my hand. something about panthers & the sea.

ruth thanks you i whisper. i hand him the poem. i'm LEROY he sez.

when i see LEROY VINEGAR again it is thirteen years later. in a club in los angeles.

1963. i'm in the village of mendocino. on little lake road. in a $25-a-month cabin. husband home san francisco far away.

i'm here to clear. to be with MOTHER EARTH. to find the next step. barefoot.

swim naked. in a red-mud pond. red dragon-flies abound. sun naked on portuguese beach. nestled between logs. back to the cabin. sand between toes. oh earth i walk you.

it is day & gray. no horizon. my head in the fog. my feet in the sand. crash of waves i cannot see. head down i walk back to the cabin. and look up.

a car parked by my door. is that my husband MEL on the step. just sitting there. MEL WEITSMAN not seen in weeks.

and why today.

since he had stopped doing art. the silence between us. the silence so long.

our eyes meet. beads of tears. we both know the next step.

someone left you a fish.

i've made good friends here. i'll make lunch. before i pack.

in the city i pack again. i move back to north beach. and he to the zen.

1966. i'm in my pad in north beach. for three years now. on my lily-pad. just right for this little frog. except that I'm sharing it for a year now. with my second husband. the sculptor. the junkie. the ex-con. ROY ISBELL.

high times. low times. fun times. deep times. getting rid of garbage. and he off junk.

tonight it is dark. i see darkness stretching a long way ahead. ROY is away. in my gut i know where he is. back to his former love. junk.

i don't want to look. i don't want to think. just clean my pad. i'm sweeping.

it's 2 or 3 a.m. i'm sweeping.

i'm awake through the night. next morning i see NASS. a shaman of the barbershop who usually feathers my crown with a few deft cuts. but not today. i want you to cut all my hair off. my short hair drifts to the floor. NASS poises his scissors. you want more. yes all of it.

she returns home. ROY is back. she opens the door. his back to her. he turns. it looms before him. his past. pimps shave the heads of their whores when they cop out. his voice a hiss. his fist flings out.

she does not move. does not make a sound. the fist drops.

a door slams.

a cut from the dark.

i live through my concentration camp guilt. that i got away. will i ever dare to put roots down. i see my relatives with shaved heads. and all the others. in the gas-chambers.

*   *   *

i work for the post office. fourth-class mail. the only woman in the four-story ferry annex. near the ferry building. the first steady job in years. 4 hours starting late afternoons.

time for myself through the night & part day. MALCOLM supervisor likes the way i work. all there & hard. the crew mostly hippie-hair-long jibe — got caught in a lawn-mower.

"ruth taken by PAUL BEATTIE in San Francisco," 1960

leave her alone MALCOLM sez. if you guys can wear your hair down your ass she can have it off if she wants.

and they leave me alone.

one day two women show up on our crew. from another branch of the post office. one of them is SILVER. now there are three women at ferry annex. SILVER sees my bald head and insists on becoming my friend.

walk in north beach. in the '60s. in the '70s. along diagonal columbus. up grant avenue.

at one of the storefronts or one of the bars. CALVIN is washing windows. CALVIN GILBERT. a small black man in jeans & sweater. a woolen cap over his ears. all year around. a smile from inside out. reflecting in the window.

now he sits on a step with his tiny dog DUKE. small enough to keep in a hotel room.

then it started to happen. DUKE would disappear. the smile would disappear. the dog & the smile would reappear. only it was another dog. this would happen again. no one could tell who stole the dog. dog after dog. all named DUKE.

one more time.

CALVIN let go. he let go of the world. of this life at 68. on the 6th of january 1975.

poets & musicians gathered at his wake. JACK HIRSCHMAN. WAYNE MILLER. EUGENE RUGGLES. myself. others. and BOB KAUFMAN.

BOB KAUFMAN shuffles in. faces the audience. there is silence. and he is silent.

it is the late '50s. he is standing on grant & green. in front of the CO-EXISTENCE BAGEL SHOP. he is watching a shadow-play. his shadow in the noon-day sun. another shadow. the cop on the beat. and a stick as it strikes the skull. the same cop again & again. stars & angel-wings. beaten & beaten. never beaten. black & a jew. or is he.

he sez someone who i am is no one. in france known as the black RIMBAUD. beat the system. beatitude. attitude beatific. oh terrific battle-field of demons & angels. vowed into silence to stop the war.

1960. i'm walking past the BAGEL. a poster in the window. screaming CARYL CHESSMAN. a long list of poets below that name. mine too. for a reading scheduled there the next day. to help save CHESSMAN. to stop capital punishment.

who put this together. who included me. BOBBY of course. just as he had sparked *BEATITUDE* in '59. that rag done on a mimeograph. hit & miss. sold in bar & bookstore. i helped sell to fund my daily beer. decades later to become a collector's item.

i had 24 hours to write the appropriate. and i did.

13 SENRYU

seed of every crime
is in our dreams to blossom
water well with blood

revenge is fertile
look how only one such act
brings one many more

monsters in the clouds
all devouring each other
yet become yet more

hate begets more hate
hate just once passionately
learn the churn delight

shock well with all crime
the one that will shock you most
is yours to nourish

don't forgive ever
you might find you on the road
of forgiving self

talk sweetly always
you will see that all your words
bitter in your mouth

if no one guilty
can be found to take the blame
best yet one guiltless

killing is release
so they've said for centuries
why not a few more

what's a human life
razored by all the others
blood alone will tell

trap trip trample thrice
who will shake the devil's dice
i will you will he

such fun to play god
after all he really ain't
kill kill kill kill kill

have stone rope gas shock
will do in name of the law
to protect revenge

seed of every crime
is in our dreams to blossom
water well with blood

looks like a rerun. now in 1996.

winter of '72. PAUL & i are on grant avenue. on our way to FIGONI the hardware store. for paint. to re-do the room FREDDIE KUH has given us. in the OLD SPAGHETTI FACTORY. for our *SURPRISE VOYAGE*. a thursday venture into the sphere of the word. to open the day after valentine's day. for the love of poetry.

BOB is moving toward us. the words float by as he passes.

JOHN HOFFMAN

you spoke of sea
of flight
of wind
sand-wheeling
to the sun

you marked your time
in blue
greened
to the sun

did you hear that. he spoke. the closing lines of my 1960 book *BLUE IN GREEN*.

he just blessed *SURPRISE VOYAGE* PAUL whispered. but we haven't let anyone know about it yet i said.

CALVIN's wake. BOB moves away from center stage. without a word. and looks at me. and looks at me. so i go on with a poem for CALVIN

GILBERT. closing line: CAL went with a clean window.

CAL went with a clean window BOB echoes. and out comes his poem as it forms. a one-man jam. from angel-breath of holy flame. one has to strain to hear. and then we're all inside the poem. and there is no need to hear.

he died in '86 going on 61.

FOR BOBBY KAUFMAN

crossed your bridge
with your big word
and your huge silence

*   *   *

years before BEATNIK exploded through the media i arrive in north beach. 1952. thumbing from chicago. within hours i'm in THE BLACK CAT. a bar that is legend. marbles of memory pinged me there. mention san francisco and someone would say THE BLACK CAT. in chicago. in new orleans. even in new york.

once a watering-hole for the literati. SAROYAN. STEINBECK. now a gay bar. same sawdust & black walls. rampant with paintings. the faces in the paintings at the tables & on bar-stools.

it's 2 a.m. you don't have to go home but you can't stay here the bartender shouts over the last drink.

i'm in the street. with the crowd. someone sez let's go to THE GOURMET.

i'm sitting on someone's lap in a taxi. we pour out of the cab — 8 or 9 of us — a MARX BROTHERS movie. we're at THE GOURMET. a gay after-hours in the fillmore. a dance-place.

i never stop dancing. the bottle passes under the table to fill our soda-setups.

that first night in san francisco i never stopped dancing. across my golden gate bridge from north beach to black fillmore.

my room on the same street as THE BLACK CAT. three blocks uphill on montgomery. my hermit-cave that room.

i go to the waitress union-hall. take a job from the call-board. long enough to pay the rent.

i collage boxes with intent to sell. give them instead to new-found friends.

my feet learn every crack on the side-walk of those three blocks. they walk there without a penny in the pocket. someone always buys me a beer. quiet afternoons there fill pages that continue in the room.

awake for days. asleep for days. is it day or is it night. the past comes a-haunting. in dreams she won't remember. she is head & feet. her hands hold a palpitating heart. the rest of her body has vanished.

EDMAN GORDNIER is my bridge-crossing part-ner. north beach to fillmore bridge-crossing partner.

when did we meet. was it one early evening at THE BLACK CAT. an elegant suit on his tall slim frame. just after work. looking at me through his glasses. a glass in his hand. a beer for me in the other. to the table where i am writing.

don't want to disturb you. you're not i say. i was just about to break.

or was it at JACKSON's NOOK. one early morning.

one here. one there. at the half dozen or so tables. a bass. one or two horns. a piano. the acoustic days. the ear fine-tuned to the nu-ance of the jam.

EDMAN lives on ash street. an alley a few blocks away. in the heart of the black fillmore. an upright piano against the wall of his narrow apartment.

his long pale fingers are flying over the keys. DEBUSSY. SATIE. the room expands. disappears. colors of dawn. of dusk.

nightfall. we're in a chinese restaurant. his long pale fingers hold chopsticks. as do mine. the click of the sticks punctuates our repartee.

his arch & special humor. sharpens my wit. dislodges my ennui. my weltschmerz. a gift he brings to my wedding to MEL WEITSMAN in 1957. where he even flirts with the father of the bride. my father. european. a scholar & a gentleman. takes it in his stride. considers himself flattered.

sundays. sundays chez EDMAN. EDMAN & i & sometimes NEAL with flute bob white in a sea of black faces.

jazz & laughter. much laughter. a joint passed 'round. to some who do. and some who don't. EDMAN's broccoli & tuna souffle. and gin.

and me with my beer.

it spills on someone who's just entered. his head sharp-angles toward me. a cigarette wav-ing in his left hand.

ah done took mah showah this monin'.

and sees my face a slow blush rising. and purrs. cat got yo tongue. ahm JAIME. yo ruth. yo know a lot. got lots ta larn. but yo got music in yo soul.

and off he sails camping through the crowd.

1991. EDMAN back home to buffalo more than 30 years before. i'm in the COLUMBUS. a north beach bar. down the street is GINO & CARLO's. a more well-known hangout. but now noisy with video-games.

JAIME enters.

evah heah from EDMAN. ah'll nevah forget thah boy. and yo sweet chile. yo lookin' goo-od!

you too!

. . . oh honey. ahm a mee–en black queen. ah knows ta take caa-re of mahself. they caa–an't kill me . . .

*   *   *

1955. HILL-HAVEN. several buildings & many rooms. between 19th street & cumberland. MILLIE is the landlady. married to JOHNNY

ruth & filmmaker STEVEN ARNOLD, San Francisco, 1972

ELGIN. a piano-player i knew in new orleans in 1950. HILL-HAVEN becomes haven for jazz.

jamming in the boiler-room. JOHNNY ELGIN on piano. SONNY NELSON or WIL CARLSON on drums. actor JOHN ADKINS. just listening in. all then living at HILL-HAVEN.

maybe JACK MINGER or DICKIE MILLS drop in with trumpet. or MAX HARTSTEIN with bass. or BREW MOORE on tenor.

white skin. black & blue sounds.

i live at THE WENTLEY. on polk & sutter. other voices. other rooms. but often cross san francisco to join in the jam.

words into smoke. notes into fire.

1956. WIL & SONNY & JACK open THE CEL-LAR. a jazz-joint on green street. in north beach.

a wednesday. first night of poetry & jazz at THE CELLAR. my first time in public with poetry & jazz. other nights i carry beer & wine to the tables. but this is wednesday.

an hour or so before the show. i'm at the bar. my glass shaking in my hand.

JOHN ADKINS comes in. ready to work the door. his arm is around my shoulder. don't ever put yourself down. don't ever allow anyone to put you down he sez in his grand shakespearian voice.

another wednesday. i walk in. ready to gig. someone is on piano. not the soft-blue of BILL WIESJOHN. it's blue all right. electric blue. sparks into blue flames.

who are you i whisper. BOO PLEASANT she laughs never missing a note. i jump in & off we go. the drum & the bass thrum behind us. and little MALCOLM on trombone. and another horn. what a set. what a night.

BOO PLEASANT was on the scene for a short time only. lean & tall & black. hovering over the keys that talked before she touched them. how she unlocked those sounds.

the keys to her life were a different story. her lover at the time a married man. whose wife was not about to let him go. BOO in an auto-crash. scarred her goddess face. never saw her again. she left for new york. many years later she played in oakland. i only heard about it a few weeks after she left. never saw her again.

a sun-break-through-the-cloud smile on his earth-colored face. JOHN HANDY. he puts his lips to his alto sax. wings soar beyond human perception. then all becomes visible.

JOHN first thought to be a painter. realized his media in music instead. is that why his sounds hit me so deep. most of those close to me are sculptors, painters. my words carry pictures.

our eyes meet. quicken into a smile. in a club. on the street. san francisco in the late '50s. through the early '60s.

and one day in '65. JOHN is in my north beach pad. talk through the night. about the sheer cliff. the slippery rock. how to go on.

1967. whirling good-bye san francisco. PAUL & i stop at the BOTH/AND on divisadero. to hear JOHN. at the break he joins our table.

i'm moving to los angeles to live with PAUL i tell him. he's into jazz & he's an artist. JOHN opens the next set with a tune meant for us.

we meet again in '71. we've been back 2 years. and yes PAUL & i are together. and doing art. in los angeles i worked with a bass-player. BENFARAL MATTHEWS. a friend of PAUL's. lives in topanga canyon.

now i'm playing with a koto-player. MICHIKO KIMURA. moved here from japan. started the koto when she was four. they begin early in japan. we were at the arts festival this year. and later at the EXPLORATORIUM. the arts festival featured oriental performers.

there was quite a crowd. and my mother was there. with PAUL. he was wandering around looking at exhibits when he saw her. she had no idea i was performing that day.

i didn't know you had such a voice she said.

1979. PAUL & i in mexico. 6 months at a time for 3 years. PAUL shows art there. i read poems to people who speak no english. they hear. we even thought of moving to mexico. art & poetry. poetry & art. working together. working apart.

not seen JOHN in years. '84 or '85. we see he's at MILESTONES. a new club on 5th near harrison. billed with FRANK MORGAN. also on alto sax.

FRANK MORGAN. his recent comeback. from years behind walls. but the music never stopped. the muse keeping the walls from closing in.

we park. the wheels just miss broken glass. garbage here. garbage there. no one in sight. we walk a block down the dim street. and go in.

it's between sets. soft lights. tan walls. black wood. the hum of conversation & warm laughter. clink of ice in glasses. men in suit & tie. the women's jewelry reflecting light. black & tan & white.

a couple rises to leave & we get their table. an eye-contact. JOHN HANDY. a smile. a hug. few words. the next set is about to start.

soft into a tune. the rhythm is steady. one horn starts. then the other. tagging. up & up. playing free. a scent of the past. a streak of sad. breaks into rainbows. no more walls. glint of feathers in the sun. a tickle of feathers. i fall into laughter through tears.

the set is over. but not quite. JOHN is introducing the band. talks about FRANK MORGAN. who smiles. gracious & shy in the long applause. then i hear our names. something about celebrities. PAUL & i rise. more applause. we sit. but my ear is in the sound of brother saxophones. playing free.

august 1990. JOHN HANDY with CLASS appears at the mendocino music festival. comes to lunch at our place in the redwoods. gives us his most recent record. writes —

> **ruth** & PAUL — my dear soulmates
> bless you and your creative energies
> please continue in your artistic pursuits
>
>   love — JOHN HANDY

1992. one afternoon at JOHN's home. dusk. our talk turns to the past.

remember BOO PLEASANT. she's gone he sez. a year or so ago. back home in texas.

i break the sad silence. in 1959. in a book of mine. *GALLERY OF WOMEN*. i have a poem for her.

BOO

a bird
wing-sure
red-wing-tipped
to the sun

flying low
flying high
in the sun

storm

not a single leaf
on a single tree

a bird
flying
wing-singed
INTO
the sun

*   *   *

march 1981. we are leaving mexico. one gate after another clangs shut behind us.

in san francisco the landlord tells us we have to leave. after 12 years.

2 years before. PAUL wakes from a nightmare. the landlord's son will move into our place. and so it comes to pass.

how will we move all that work. and where.

time to leave the city. but not too far. inverness. north of san francisco. shell beach. our favorite beach to swim.

at sunset. between inverness park & inverness. a screeching of huge birds. a rare nesting-tree. a-flutter with blue heron. by this old house.

SARAH owns the house. the first one built here. over a century ago. she could rent us the back. an addition from the '50s by a millionaire. french windows. high ceiling. oak floor. a marble fireplace. from italy.

and 2 years of neglect. chickens are nesting there now.

june through october. in lieu of rent. the hammer never stops. the chisel. the skilsaw. we live on sawdust & sardine. and we clean. and we clean. move truckloads from the city. our art. material for more art. 12 years of a garden.

PAUL unearths a brick-walk from our door & around. and a curving stone-wall.

october. the work is done. we have a home. we have a palace. we have a place to do our art.

our first visitor. PAT MORRISON. we know each other over a decade. PAT whose dreams are precognition. my dream shows you in mendocino. a golden book the roof of your house.

i'm glad you'd like us near you. (she lives in mendocino.) but we're not about to move.

october. falling leaves. i feed pippins from an ancient tree to the two huge mares. who live in the classic barn up the hill. near the stream.

winter of '82. the fourth of january. it's been pouring for days. we've just returned from mendocino. driving inch by inch through a sheet of rain. spent the holidays with PAT. around 4 that morning we collapse into bed.

the fourth of january. not yet dawn. crash! a gallop of hooves. PAUL & i scramble from a 2-hour sleep. and watch the two mares streak down the road. this is not a dream. it is real. and a nightmare.

the stream so gentle. turned to river raging. uprooted the tree that split the barn. swallowed the wheelbarrow. swallowed the shovels. left by SARAH's teenagers in the path. the path that is now all water.

a colander. 18 inches across & rusty. from out of nowhere. never seen before.

it's the perfect tool for trenching PAUL shouts. he trenches. around the house. mudful by mudful. in the pouring rain.

the river is pouring into the bay. still feet away from the house. maybe it won't widen.

i'm inside. with a sponge & a bucket. mud seeps in at the baseboard.

with artist SUTTER MARIN at the Old Spaghetti Factory, North Beach, 1977

you think we'll make it i ask. keep bailing PAUL
sez. we haven't been put here to die & lose
our life's work.

i open the *I CHING*. book of changes. no time
for coins. the words jump out. the bird must
stay in its nest.

SARAH has a battery radio. more storms on
the way she tells us. i'm going up the hill
with the kids. the house is going to go.

trees are falling. one of the canyons has col-
lapsed.

the bird must stay in its nest i shout. she goes
back upstairs.

i write a haiku. between buckets of mud.

> five is like changes
> after a visit from hell
> with day break clear day

fifth of january. at dawn. the rain stops.

36 hours. trenching. bailing. keeping the stream
from a log-jam. no sleep. no food. numb.

fifth of january. the sky is golden at sunrise.
for 17 days the sun. night-sky of stars.

the phone rings. the phone! it's been out for
days. PAT. are you all right. i'm crying. the
tears won't stop.

seems we can get calls in. not out. give her a
list of people to call. to call us.

eerie the lights from point reyes station across
the bay. electricity there never went out. ours
still is. take showers there.

squatters. live like squatters. for months. no
idea what's ahead. day by day. out of the mud.

the phone rings. SILVER. we've kept in close
contact. her daughter our god-daughter. she's
been in mendocino for years.

i think i have a house for you. in albion. near
me. i know the people moving out.

we call the owners. you lived in one place 12
years. we don't need references. albion it is.

the caravan starts. last of all the garden brought
from the city.

summer '82. august. i wake to the sound of hammers. PAUL & carpenter DAVID are on the deck. making a closet & other storage space.

the south wall is all windows. the redwood just beyond. my hand on the glass. my eye on the trees.

suddenly in the clearing. a semi-circle of dancers. feathers in motion. feet drumming the earth. the rhythm two words.

WELCOME HOME

they rise up. lifted by a golden thread. an arc. and reflect a full circle.

and are gone.

i go out. the circle inside me. feel the red bark. find one feather.

walk to the deck. the hammers are pounding. echo my heart. hand PAUL the feather. that's from a golden eagle DAVID sez.

ADDENDA

up to this point, the essay is a collage from current work of synchronistic reminiscence — pieces from my stories, *I AL- WAYS THOUGHT YOU BLACK* and *FULL CIRCLE. INCIDENT* was lifted from my 1958 story *SINGLE OUT,* published in *MATRIX #2,* 1970, and again in my book *SINGLE OUT,* published in 1978. excerpts from the poems *ANAÏS* and *THE BRINK,* which appear in the following sections, are also in *SINGLE OUT.*

BILL McNEILL & ruth *with his portrait of her, San Francisco, 1977*

PROJECTED WORK

and what of all the decades, those inner and outer dances with: SUTTER MARIN, poems to his paintings, the lead in my plays, my movie, *THE BRINK,* his paintings in my book *GALLERY OF WOMEN,* and all that says nothing of what doors burst open. DIANE VARSI directs my play *THE 61st YEAR TO HEAVEN* after breaking with hollywood. SEVERN DARDEN in chicago, in new orleans, in san francisco, his cape and capers flying. PAUL BEATTIE paints and buys a 16mm movie camera. write a script, he said. i had just finished a narrative poem. let's do that. puts me into a director chair. i love movies. don't know a thing about cameras. but i did learn the editing machine. the moviola. dog ZIMZUM watches me write, goes with me to mexico, travels the nights to THE CELLAR with me, listening to jazz. his favorite instrument, the bass, ears straight up and smiling. NADALINI covers the side of buses with his silkscreen poster of our show at LUCIEN LABAUDT GALLERY. *THE COLOR OF PAINT AND WORDS AT ONE.* BILL SPENCER creates with sounds. what he does with my play *THE 61st YEAR TO HEAVEN* one only realizes when the music stops. then there is my film, *THE BRINK.* he rolls a chain across a wooden floor. and ocean-waves crash on the shore. ANAÏS NIN — i quote from the poem to her.

    i didn't know ANAÏS
    some cards, some presence
    but never the real touch-point

    a queen has to be
    too careful to touch

    ANAÏS
    purple-cloaked
    european
    and proud of decadent heritage
    proud to display it
    proud to play it
    in full

    and saying
    i'm in america
    now
    show me
    show me
    if you dare
    your subtlety
    as strong as mine !

BENFARAL MATTHEWS and i are improvising. poetry and bass. the night is storm in topanga. the electricity goes out. the recording stops. but not the music. STEVEN ARNOLD, his eye mesmerizes me, once camera-shy, into his films. MADELINE GLEASON, MADDIE, asks me, "do your poems haunt you," as she reads with me at a women's bar, WILD SIDE WEST, onto the last reading of her life. writer TODD LAWSON brings out my book *LIGHT and other poems* through PEACE & PIECES FOUNDATION in 1976. my first book in print since 1960. BILL MCNEILL is painting. a series of poets. WALT WHITMAN with MARILYN MONROE. EMILY DICKINSON with JAMES DEAN. one of me. with a blue rose. while sitting for him, he asked for stories. the blue rose is one of them. LARRY PIET, the camera brush and palette. flowers erotic. my title-poems. his photo-garden. his favorite is old lady rose. the petals about to drop. RON TOWE lives music, writes music, teaches voice. i learn to breathe. i learn to take my stage. CLAUDE DUVALL does everything himself with 1000 helpers. he puts on my play that way. in 1001 nights. his NOH ORATORIO SOCIETY, my *THE THIRTEENTH WITCH,* at STUDIO EREMOS in PROJECT ARTAUD.

there have been other cats in my life, but CARLOTTA BLANCA is high priestess. she lived next door to our garden-apartment on nob hill in san francisco. on jones street, our home for almost thirteen years. became our over-night guest. we would leave for mexico, six months at a time. PAUL was having art exhibits in galleries and museums there. opening the door on our return, there was CARLOTTA, waiting at the window. when our landlord's son wanted our place, we left for inverness, fifty miles north. a year later, in 1982, after surviving the flood, we were packing to move to albion. the phone rang. it was our former neighbor saying, "you've always loved my cat. i'm leaving the city and she's too old to go on a plane." CARLOTTA was thirteen then. an hour later she was on her way with us to inverness. the next day on to albion. she stepped out of the car where she'd been sleeping between my feet, stretched, yawned, and let us know that she was home. seven years later, on her last night, i read her my poems till dawn. promised her i'd keep on writing.

those are just a few from my past. now gone. through poems i find my way to say good-bye.

ruth & *PAUL BLAKE "in our garden on Jones Street, San Francisco."*
photo of ruth *by INGEBORG GERDES, 1972, photo of PAUL*
by LISA WUENNENBERG, 1980, collage by PAUL BLAKE.

and maybe see them again. my mother, FANI ZLATA WEISS, neé GLÜCK, born in daruvar, yugoslavia, november 24, 1900, in 1985. my father, OSCAR WEISS, born in vienna, july 19, 1897, in 1984. they died exactly a year apart on the jewish calendar.

others from my past still strong in the present. others of more recent times. GERHARD SAMUEL sets my *FORTIETH DAY* from *DESERT JOURNAL* to music for soprano, spoken voice, oboe, alto saxophone, violin, cello, keyboard and percussion — premiered at the MONDAY EVENING CONCERTS at the LOS ANGELES COUNTY MUSEUM OF ART in 1976, with me, who does not read music, on stage with spoken voice. a year later, he surprised us with another premiere, a composition for PAUL's work. PAUL BLAKE, *IKON-MAKER.* and there's more on the horizon. on a visit to our home in albion, the electricity went out for days. and we shared stories from our past, never told in all the years of our friendship.

a branch of my extended family. MOSS BUTLER, met at the SAN FRANCISCO ART INSTITUTE where i was modeling, connects me to PATRICIA MORRISON, to LISA WUENNENBERG (what a singing voice), just arrived from madison, wisconsin, to mother CAROL WUENNENBERG on her visit to the west coast. close in birth year, with the same astrological sign, it was amazing (that's one of MOSS's words) how often we would be wearing the same colors.

then the youngest daughter, SUSI, same name as my close childhood friend, resembling her in face and ways and age when i last saw her.

MINNIE BAKER, her MINNIE's CAN-DO CLUB in the fillmore. a neighborhood bar, all colors, in the early '70s. MINNIE asks me to run a weekly poetry reading. PAUL does the poster. *COME TO HEAR POETS READ THEIR HEARTS OUT.* and they did. publications birthed. my play *NO DANCING ALOUD* performed several sunday afternoons. friends from then, still now. MICHAEL DUFF. others. MICHAEL sits there. again and again. doesn't say a word. i ask if he has any poems. and he reads. for the first time. JACK MICHELINE in from new york. PAUL and i expand the scene. start *SURPRISE VOYAGE*, a weekly poetry theater at the OLD SPAGHETTI FACTORY in north beach. today it's NANCY KEANE who runs a bi-monthly open reading at her 3300 CLUB in the mission district. the same and not the same.

the year following the publication of *LIGHT and other poems*, CHARLEY SHIVELY, poet, teacher and editor of GOOD GAY POETS, publishes *DESERT JOURNAL,* a work from 1961–1968, after hearing me at WILD SIDE WEST, on his visit to san francisco from boston. the two-hundred pages of *DESERT JOURNAL*, a book of forty poems, is an inner journey of forty days whose energy still propels me in current performances with the audience calling the numbers. PAUL BLAKE, whose drawings appear in the book, did them before we ever met. PAUL writes, "the drawings are moments — places — rememberings parallel with (but not illustrative of) *DESERT JOURNAL* connected from the core." in 1978, again a year later, DOREEN STOCK, poet and publisher, puts out my book, *SINGLE OUT,* the title-story, a recall of my escape from the nazis and arrival in new york.

INGEBORG GERDES at STEVEN ARNOLD's studio taking photos during the filming. it's a long time since i've spoken german. and then there's that session with me as PIAF. her focus so potent, i had to stop her from finishing the roll. TAYLOR MEAD. i cried when i first heard him read in north beach in the late '50s. did a role with him in RON RICE's film, *THE FLOWER THIEF,* that was edited out. i write a play, *M & M,* a fantasy of him on the road. most recent contact. january 1996 in new york city, when i was there for my film, *THE BRINK,* showing at THE WHITNEY. GUSTAVO RIVERA gifts us with a painting. wants to exchange it for a recent one, twenty years later. no way, i tell him. you put our names on the back. GUSTAVO gives PAUL contacts in mexico, resulting in museum and gallery shows, meeting artists and collectors. it was tempting to move there. but the arrow pointed north. CINDY SAPP from my WILD SIDE WEST bartending days in the '70s. ten years later, she sez, you've been looking for a bass-player. my landlord, DOUG O'CONNOR, plays acoustic bass. has jam-sessions at his house. check it out. we got together. got bookings. at times performed with poet EARL LeCLAIRE and bassist STEVE SHAIN. today i do a monthly *POETRY & ALLTHATJAZZ* show in fort bragg, near my home. another one with DOUG and other musicians at THE GATHERING CAFFÉ in north beach. that place was THE CAPRI, where PAUL and i met in 1967, "summer of love." the next rung on the spiral. and who knows what the next bend has in store.

march, 1996. PAUL picks up a copy of *PHOTO METRO* magazine. C. R. SNYDER with photos of the beat era. i'm sure he has some of you from that time, PAUL sez. i doubt it. was camera-shy in those days. we call and yes he does — reading at the grant avenue street fair, reading at a bookstore-gallery, others. i also still have a poem you gave me then, he tells us.

what perfect timing for those photos to appear and be included in the BANCROFT LIBRARY's beat publication exhibit from april through november, in an anthology *WOMEN OF THE BEAT,* due out in october, in the M. H. De YOUNG MEMORIAL MUSEUM during its BEAT CULTURE show from THE WHITNEY. BILL WESTWICK, his camera, my shows. 1980 at a theater-bar in polk-gulch (i'm in a tuxedo with MONA MANDRAKE, painter MICHAEL SHAIN's other persona), at EL RIO in the mission district, at THE GATHERING CAFFÉ, at the mid-june 1996 grant avenue street fair in north beach, where i have not performed since 1958. (what happened to the poet's stage there all these years ?) an exhibit at LEVI STRAUSS & CO., also mid-june — DANNY NICOLETTA, his photos of drag queens, drag kings, of HARVEY MILK as clown. (DANNY had worked for HARVEY in his camera store on castro street.) "did you see the one of you" DANNY sez. and there, reminiscent of a photo PAUL BEATTIE took in '60, is my profile, the smoke of a cigarette curling upwards. ROBERT J. STEWART, a photo session at THE WHITNEY. i am with cigarette in hand, unlit, next to the *NO SMOKING* sign. how could they've made movies in the '30s, in the '40s, in the '50s, without that cigarette ! JOCK MCDONALD, another camera, another exhibit in '96 at GALLERY 16, included images of PAUL and me. in one, taken during a session at our home, i'm running nude into the forest. it was the Y on your back, JOCK said. 1994, a three-month joint exhibit with PAUL at the SAN FRANCISCO MAIN PUBLIC LIBRARY in the civic center, chronicling twenty-five years of our work. at the reception, DORRWIN BUCK JONES, founder of MEALS ON WHEELS, FAMILY LINK, civic awards ad infinitum, appears in tuxedo, cane in hand. no matter how busy, he shows up at my performances, PAUL's art openings, visits us in the redwoods. DORR and i go back in time. he still chuckles when he mentions me taking my clothes off, that day more than thirty years ago, on the main street in locke (an old chinese settlement), to swim in the river.

after a performance in 1993 at KIMBALL's EAST, a jazz club, i needed to have my audio cassette engineered and met LOU JUDSON, one of those we've-known-each-other-forever connections. LOU insists on recording all my current readings and all those tapes from long-ago jams, some of them still on reel-to-reel. don't touch those, he warns, they have to be saved. it turns out that he records for BOB KRIEGEL, author of *if it ain't broke . . . BREAK IT!* BOB is married to MARILYN. they met in big sur at ESALEN. SUTTER MARIN had introduced me to MARILYN HARRIS. in the '60s, she volunteered to type eleven of my plays. later, helped me through my bout with hepatitis as did SILVER. now writing a book, *CONFESSIONS OF A MARRIAGE COUNSELOR.* their muir beach home is often a haven for PAUL and me on our trips to san francisco.

in 1959, *GALLERY OF WOMEN* was published. it was an homage to women with whom i felt a sisterhood. poets LAURA ULEWICZ and IDELL TARLOW were included in those poem-portraits. LAURA moved me from my tiny $10-a-month room to share her spacious apartment in 1953 — for the same rent. IDELL, who since has changed her name to AYA, was married to ELIAS ROMERO. my 1976 book, *LIGHT and other poems,* features the long poem *LIGHT* done in response to ELIAS's light-shows in the '50s. when CONARI PRESS contacted me for an interview for their forth-coming book *WOMEN OF THE BEAT GENERATION: THE WRITERS, ARTISTS AND MUSES AT THE HEART OF A REVOLUTION,* i was able to connect them with several women from that era, including IDELL. as far as i know, it's the first publication to focus on the women working in the arts then. about the same time, SERPENT's TAIL, a london-based press, contacted me for their book *A DIFFERENT BEAT,* due out in 1997. again i was able to connect them with others, including LAURA. that anthology will only have reprints of poems published in those years. however, the commitment is to show that the literature done by the women during the break-through of the BEAT held its own in quality and output, even though they were usually pushed into the background or even completely ignored.

when SUTTER MARIN visited PAUL and me in los angeles in 1968, we decided to do an updated version of *GALLERY OF WOMEN,* titled *GALLERY OF WOMEN REVISITED,* since that book was out of print. in 1961, there had been a show of the original paintings with the book at the SAN FRANCISCO MUSEUM OF ART. SUTTER did a series of new *sumi*-ink paintings to accompany the new work, which includes the portrait of MARILYN, as well as others. the book is still waiting in the wings.

i wrote my first poem at age five in berlin. my first painting, at age eight, was in vienna, a class-assignment of a farm-yard — all of us city-bred. my first tools were faber colored pencils dipped in water, a technique i thought i invented. i carefully rendered a red barn, set in a field of green grass. the teacher held up the piece, demanding, "what about the animals." "inside the barn," i replied, baffled by the laughter that followed. as a refugee in new york in 1939 in a children's home, i spent nights doing watercolors in the well-lit bathroom. at school, not yet speaking english, i made friends with my classmates, giving them my drawings.

in the '50s, JACK KEROUAC and i spent nights writing haiku. i lived in THE WENTLEY, whose residents were artists, poets, and old-timers on limited pensions, attracted by the low rent. you write better haiku than i do, he'd say. but then you're the novelist, i'd answer. watercolor-haiku became one of my mediums. taking the poem as a reference point, i would give it my visual interpretation, then put the words into the painting. throughout the years, they've appeared in group-shows. in 1980 was my first solo show of twenty-five pieces, entitled *BANZAI!,* a japanese word i interpret as *ALL-THE-WAY!* in 1994, another solo show i named *A FOOL'S JOURNEY.*

some of my work, not always haiku, has been produced as serigraphs in limited editions by PAUL BLAKE. "when the spirit so moved me," i would gift myself with a birthday poem. they too have appeared as poem-prints. PAUL insisted that i do the images for them myself. JANET de BAR of LION's DEN PRESS, using an albion press from 1862 (no connection to albion where i live), handset and printed my poem *THIS IS REALLY REAL* and PAUL created and screened that image. that project took a year, choosing with care the correct paper, the correct type-face. JANET and ROGER live on the coast, an hour from us.

in the spring of 1995, the electricity went out in northern california for some as long as two weeks, including us in albion, preparing for an exhibit in san francisco. JANET and ROGER's home had its lights back on after three days.

at ruth & PAUL's art opening (from left) TUREEDA MIKELL,
JOHN HANDY, ruth weiss, PAUL BLAKE, JANET DE BAR &
(back row) LOU JUDSON, San Francisco, 1995

and we were invited, stayed more than a week. champagne (which has become a ritual for us), great dinners (JANET is a superb cook and a poet), conversation and laughter. and, of course, dog KALI. and all the space we needed to continue our project. champagne is my favorite beverage. then beer. never wine. CATHRYN HEART at home with her four black cats — ISIS, SPIRIT, MEERA, and MOONLIGHT. CATHRYN is the sister i never had. as different from me as only a sister can be. we toast life with champagne, explore new and ancient vistas of healing ourselves and the planet.

in the summer of '92, when WARREN FRENCH, traveling from the east coast, stepped off the bus in albion for a visit and an interview, PAUL and i were delighted to meet this leprechaun in bright colors, his silver hair, his warm embrace. researching my work for his book, *SAN FRANCISCO POETRY RENAISSANCE, 1955–1960,* WARREN had tried to locate me earlier. by the time he reached me, the book, which includes a few references to me, had already been published in 1991. in the following days, our conversation was interrupted only by the high-pitched sound of high-flying osprey, the wind

through the redwoods, the rustle of birds in the huckleberry bush. we shared candlelight dinners, days in fog and sun, and decades of stories that resulted in an article published in the winter of '92 in the then scotland-based *THE KEROUAC CONNECTION* magazine. as honorary professor of american studies at the UNIVERSITY COLLEGE in swansea, wales, and author of critical biographies (SALINGER, KEROUAC and currently STEINBECK), WARREN once told me he dreamt one night he was writing my biography.

*　　*　　*

living in the country makes having a vehicle a necessity. i don't drive. with my temperament, a bicycle is enough wheel for me to handle. PAUL, though born in new york city, grew up in los angeles and has been driving since he was sixteen. our 1964 karmann ghia we bought almost new in '72, named SILVER CLOUD, is now waiting for a renewed body. the rust started during the 1982 inverness flood, with mud up to her headlights. the man with the backhoe was needed in more urgent situations. he showed up six weeks later. as we held our breath, he dug her out. this little car. this huge machine. the man with such skill, there was not a scratch, not a dent.

JANET drives me to my monthly gig in san francisco. vows to write a story, *DRIVING MISS ruth.* CATHRYN brings us to appointments in mendocino and fort bragg. then there's ANNA MARIE STENBERG, who lends us her car whenever possible. ANNA MARIE, born a gypsy, her life on the line again and again to save MOTHER EARTH — the trees, the ocean, the children. i show her a poem, *THE BRINK,* i had written in 1960, then made into a film. some of the lines are —

> arrest the trees
> chop 'em all down
> stop !
> they've cut the trees
> the flood the flood
>
> all around the town
> blow the men & women down
> make 'em into sticks
> stop all their tricks
> put 'em into rows & rows of boxes
> where the trees once were
> they'll be of some use then

i also quote a refrain from my play *THE THIR-TEENTH WITCH,* later lifted into the poem *TURNABOUT* i read that day, february 3, 1988, in fort bragg, california, when 4000 people came to protest the plan to dot the coast with oil rigs.

> a new view of matter
> or an ancient one regained
> only a new view of what matters
> will break the trapped pattern

and yes, she sez, write for this and for that. and i do.

my not-yet-finished book of prose-poems, *MY NAME IS WOMAN.* JANET, CATHRYN, ANNA MARIE, WENDY DALTON aka COUGAR-WOMAN, BEVERLY ANN WILSON, BONNIE SANGER, SYLVIA KOZAK-BUDD, RITA CRANE, CAROL O'NEAL, ELAINE KIRKPATRICK, ZIDA BORCICH, KAREN SCHUMACHER, ALENE VICTORIA, FLAME (i first knew as ACORN), she has left us — you'll meet them and more, later, first name only, when that book is ready for the market-place.

ruth weiss, 1994

now we have a 1984 saab we call SAABINA, a safe car and luxurious, that appeared as if by magic with the help of PAUL's parents. LILLIAN (LIL) and PAUL BLAKE, my family. my mother and father (MUTTI and PAPA) now gone. the others lost long ago in the holocaust.

*   *   *

january '96 blizzard in new york city. the runway was still being cleared when PAUL and i arrived at JFK. more than twenty years had passed since our last trip to the east coast. my 1961 film, *THE BRINK,* was to be screened at THE WHITNEY MUSEUM during its *BEAT CULTURE and the NEW AMERICA (1950–1965)* exhibit. connie mayer (who also spells her name in lower-case), another friend from the san francisco WILD SIDE WEST days, had invited us to stay with her for this month-long visit. connie, now living in manhattan with her "kids" — dogs STASH and DUE and cat MOUSER — is now writing her plays in an apartment on the top-floor of a twenty-story building with a panoramic view of the city. with several bookings in different locations, i was looking for a bassist to accompany me. i had decided to focus on finding a woman bass-player and was put into contact with JUSHI. phoning her, i started to explain the situation, see if she was interested. she asked me if i had a place to stay, told me she called herself an interpressionist, did both solo and group-performances, and said to come to her place after midnight. i walk up the icy steps of a brownstone. she opens the door, sez, boots in the hall, picks up the bass, starts running some chords, as i shed gloves, scarf, hat, coat — and jamming we went. so, girlfriend, she grins, what do you think.

another midnight. july in albion. the phone rings. from venice, italy. a woman's voice from the office of LA BIENNALE, the international film festival, invites my movie, *THE BRINK*, to its 1996 RETROSPECTIVE, devoted to the BEAT GENERATION. in the background, the bells of san marco are ringing.

SUMMING UP

all those stories, their strands woven into themes, looking for a publisher (one or more volumes), spinning faster and faster — all demanding their space. yes. i'll tell them all — one — and then another — time is not a line. . . .

BIBLIOGRAPHY

Poetry:

STEPS, Ellis Press (San Francisco), 1958.

GALLERY OF WOMEN, Adler Press (San Francisco), 1959.

SOUTH PACIFIC, Adler Press, 1959.

BLUE IN GREEN, Adler Press, 1960.

LIGHT and other poems, Peace & Pieces Foundation (San Francisco), 1976.

DESERT JOURNAL, Good Gay Poets (Boston), 1977.

SINGLE OUT (includes prose), D'Aurora Press (Mill Valley, California), 1978.

13 HAIKU, Attic Press (Mendocino, California), 1986.

Anthologies:

Beatitude Anthology, City Lights Press (San Francisco), 1960.

Outburst #2, Matrix Press (London), 1962.

Mark in Time, Glide Publications (San Francisco), 1971.

Peace & Pieces: An Anthology of Contemporary American Poetry, Peace & Pieces Foundation, 1973.

Panjandrum Poetry #2 & #3, Panjandrum Press (San Francisco), 1973.

185, Mongrel Press (San Francisco), 1973.

This Is Women's Work, Panjandrum Press, 1974.

Contemporary Fiction: Today's Outstanding Writers, Peace & Pieces Foundation, 1976.

Contemporary Women Poets, An Anthology of California Poets, Merlin Press Foundation (San Jose, California), 1977.

Anthology — Women's Poetry Festival, New World Press Collective (San Francisco), 1977.

19+1: An Anthology of San Francisco Poetry, Second Coming Press (San Francisco), 1978.

Second Coming Anthology, Second Coming Press, 1984.

Beatitude 33, Beatitude Collective (San Francisco), 1986.

Beatitude 34, Beatitude Collective, 1987.

Would You Wear My Eyes ?, Bob Kaufman Collective (San Francisco), 1989.

Illuminations Reader, Illuminations Press (Berkeley), 1990.

Minnie's Can-Do-Club: Memories of Fillmore Street, Ayers (San Francisco), 1991.

Poetry at the 33, Tomcat Press (San Francisco). 1994.

Poetry at the 33, 3300 Press (San Francisco), 1995.

Poetry at the 33, 3300 Press, 1996.

Beatitude 35, Beatitude Collective, 1996.

Women of the Beat Generation: The Writers, Artists & Muses at the Heart of a Revolution, by Brenda Knight, Conari Press (Berkeley, California), 1996.

A Different Beat: Early Work by Women of the Beat Generation, edited by Richard Peabody, Serpent's Tail (London and New York), 1997.

Poem-prints:

ENTER FROM THE CENTER, serigraph by Paul Blake, 1975.

BANZAI !, image by the poet, offset, 1980.

IN-COME, image by the poet, offset, 1981.

SING STRONG YOUR CLEAR SONG, serigraph by Paul Blake, 1985.

THE POND, serigraph by Paul Blake, 1986.

IN MY 60th YEAR, image by the poet, serigraph, 1988.

TWO OSPREY FLY HIGH, image by the poet, serigraph, 1991.

BEFORE COMPLETION, image by the poet, serigraph, 1992.

THIS IS REALLY REAL, serigraph by Paul Blake, letterpress by Lion's Pen Press, 1994.

68, image by the poet, offset, 1996.

Plays:

THE 61st YEAR TO HEAVEN, first produced in Sausalito, California, by the Diane Varsi Theater Group at the Gate Theater, 1961.

B NATURAL, first produced in San Francisco at the Monday Blues Theater Coffee Gallery, 1961.

M & M, first produced in San Francisco at the Monday Blues Theater Coffee Gallery, 1961.

MISPRINTS, first produced at the Sausalito Little Theater, Sausalito, California, 1962.

NO DANCING ALOUD, first produced at the Sausalito Little Theater, 1962, published in *Contemporary Fiction: Today's Outstanding Writers,* Peace & Pieces Foundation, 1976.

FIGS, first produced at the Orb of Arts, San Francisco, 1965.

THE THIRTEENTH WITCH, first produced by the Noh Oratorio Society, Project Artaud, San Francisco, 1983.

Other:

FORTIETH DAY (a poem from *DESERT JOURNAL*), set to music by GERHARD SAMUEL for instruments, soprano, and spoken voice, first produced for the Monday Evening Concert Series at the Los Angeles County Museum of Art, December 13, 1976, with composer conducting and poet voicing.

Contributor of poems exhibited with works by artists SUTTER MARIN, LOUIS NADALINI, and PAUL BLAKE at San Francisco galleries and museums, including Brunn Gallery, San Francisco Legion of Honor, Lucien Labaudt Gallery, San Francisco Museum of Modern Art, Cadmium Gallery, and San Francisco Ecology Center. Has exhibited own paintings, watercolor-haiku, at various galleries including Joker's Flux Gallery, Gallery Become, Bay Gallery, Mendocino Moulding, 111 Minna Street Gallery, and Belcher Studios Gallery. Also exhibited a 25-year retrospective of independent and joint work with PAUL BLAKE that included books, broadsides, photos, posters, haiku-paintings, audio and video tapes at the San Francisco Main Public Library, 1994.

Videos, audio and film include *THE BRINK,* 16mm, black and white, 1961, video cassette, 1986; *POETRY & ALLTHATJAZZ, Volume 1,* audio and video, live performance with acoustic bass accompaniment, 1990; *POETRY & ALLTHATJAZZ, Volume 2,* audio, live performance with jazz trio, 1993; *INTERVIEW: HOLOCAUST ORAL HISTORY PROJECT,* video, 1993.

Other plays include *STOP THAT FLOWER !, SHOES, LATE ONE EARLY, TWO PLAYERS & FIVE CLUBS,* and *MEDIA — MEDIUM.*

Has had major roles in films produced by STEVEN ARNOLD, including *LIBERATION OF MANNIQUE MECHANIQUE,* 1967, *THE VARIOUS INCARNATIONS OF A TIBETAN SEAMSTRESS,* 1967, *MESSAGES MESSAGES,* 1968, and *LUMINOUS PROCURESS,* 1971. Also played major role in MICHAEL WIESE's film *PYRAMID,* 1972.

Contributor to more than 100 magazines since 1950, including *BEATITUDE, BOUILLABAISSE, FILM CULTURE, THE GALLEY SAIL REVIEW, LOVE LIGHTS, MISCELLANEOUS MAN, POETRY SCORE,* and *SEMINA.*

Lisa Zeidner

1955-

A SHORT SUBURBAN LIFE IN ART

A pale, rich little boy is dying in a secret garden. His wheelchair is oversized as a throne, and the garden is so vivid that it almost hurts the eyes. A girl—maybe the scullery-maid's daughter—finds the garden. She and the boy fall in love.

I don't remember if love cures the boy, or how the entrance to the garden is concealed, but since reading that children's story, there has been a trapdoor or revolving bookcase in my brain which opens onto the hot-hued foliage, the cool shade of that garden. If I believed in reincarnation I'd say that sometime before our flat, suburban backyard with its chain-link fence and swing set, I was that girl.

The book was much better in my imagination than it was when I rediscovered it as an adult. Rereading it was like revisiting my elementary school: it was hard to believe that ceilings and desks that low could have contained me, no less terrified me so, and terror is the root of art, at least of my art.

As a child I was afraid of everything—not just lightning, sirens, dark, and spiders, but loss of limb, Auschwitz, leprosy, atomic warfare, my own dreams. I was afraid of tuberculosis, the molecular structure of which I was convinced was visible, swimming toward me as dust in the night-light. For a full six months after *How the West Was Won,* I lay on my back with eyes open until I passed out, watching the window, afraid that an Indian would enter through the window and lodge an arrow in my spine.

The Indian problem was solved by sleeping under the blankets, with a kind of ant-farm-shaped tunnel carved on the side for the nose, for breathing purposes. Under my blanket, breathing quietly, I was Anne Frank, or the von Trapp kids. As I matured I modified the method to allow for an "eye googy," *googy* being the name of my toddler security blanket; this was a washcloth folded and placed precisely over the eyes.

Lisa Zeidner, "pouting, three-ish. This photo is from a legendary day, often retold. I insisted that my father take me on the roller coaster behind me. Afterward, weeping, I demanded, 'What kind of parent would take a kid my age on a ride like that?'"

The theory here was that what I couldn't see couldn't hurt me.

I used an eye googy until college, when a therapist must have had some measurable positive effect, because I only cracked out the googy for special occasions: after *The Exorcist,* or the scene in *Fellini's Satyricon* where the slave's arm is cut off without anesthetic. (Rumor had it that the amputation was real, that a real actor with bone cancer had let it be done in this rough way, for art's sake.)

Crucifixes, too. They were another childhood obsession. Because I was Jewish, I learned about Christ late, by way of art. I must have been six or seven. My father calmly explained

355

"With my parents, Joseph and Dorothy Zeidner. The suburban house and car belong to my Aunt Ruth," 1956.

that whatever your religious convictions, Christ was a real person, and that crucifixion was a standard method of execution at the time. Our art book shot him from a low angle lying on a slab, so you got a close-up right into the rough holes in his marble feet. By way of reassurance, my father pointed out that most victims would have died of asphyxiation, not the puncture wounds.

At art museums I'd hyperventilate through all of the dank Medieval rooms. Special arrangements had to be made for me on school field trips. At the New York World's Fair, I waited outside while the rest of my family shuffled by to view the Pietà.

I've always been inclined to blame my parents for my fears. Explaining Christ to me is one thing. Auschwitz, too, was an inevitable topic of conversation; I lived in a neighborhood full of concentration camp survivors and heard their stories from an early age. But why did I know about tuberculosis and polio? Does a seven-year-old really need to watch the documentary *Let My People Go,* with its stacks of dead bodies at Buchenwald? Certainly it was not a good idea to take a child like me to see the matinee of *Mondo Bizarro,* with its cannibals and strange Incan rites.

I shouldn't have been hit, either. My parents and I argued for years about the nature of what I characterize as cruel beatings and

they insist was perfectly ordinary, mild corporal punishment (see the poem "Gypsy Moths," which follows this essay). As well as having an explosive temper, my father was—is—a terrible tease, and a tenacious critic once he gets his claws into a flaw.

"Wait until you have children yourself," my mother liked to foretell. "Then you'll see." On one level she's right. Becoming a mother myself renewed some bitterness about my childhood, after many years of having put it behind me. In the hospital after the delivery, when my son had jaundice and my mother covered her eyes, wailed, had to leave the room as his feet were punctured for blood tests, I was furious at her hypocrisy: why hadn't she protected me from my father, from the hurled food and abuse? Four years later I watched, amazed, as my father taunted my son, who exploded into tears, confused and betrayed. I had never understood how very close to rage my father's teasing was—was so *used* to it, in fact, that I'd never even thought to log it in as a complaint.

My son, who is beaten neither verbally nor physically, can witness flesh being slashed on *Mortal Kombat* without much in the way of reaction. He must trust it isn't going to happen to him. "I'm not going to die, not ever," he regularly declares. He hungers for those dark images—skulls, ghosts, masked invaders. Some sense of mastery must be involved. He'll karate-chop the sharks, scream louder than the attacking lions. So far, the only thing that has given him nightmares are witches. Mean Moms. *Sleeping Beauty, Cinderella.*

Yet I was even afraid of *The Three Stooges.* One of the boys got bopped and lost a tooth. I was scared of lost teeth. My mother, in an attempt to console me, chewed a piece of black gum—where did she get black gum?—and placed it over the tooth. "You see?" she said, baring the teeth. "The hole's not real." I cried even harder.

This episode sticks in memory because of the children's book I read in bed that night, to avoid sleep. God deposits a team of angels in front of drafting tables and bids them to invent the animals. The angels come up with some intensely ornate and unacceptable models—fish with fur, dogs with rhinoceros horns. God says, "Back to the drawing board." Simplify, God suggests. Think teeth and feet, form and function. I loved the picture of the angels hunched over their little desks, their wings tucked back, trying to make things right.

For years I thought that book was imaginary. No librarian had ever heard of it. Perhaps, I thought, I should write it myself—my own feverish childhood fantasy. Then a book curator dug it up for me. It was a fifties book with outdated illustrations and awful graphics. Like *The Secret Garden,* the book was much sharper and more magical in memory.

Since rereading the actual book two years ago I've already forgotten the title and author, but I remember the imaginary book as well as I remember most of my disastrous childhood, which at least had the courtesy to happen fast.

I started kindergarten on the early side, then skipped second grade. The day I entered the second-grade class, already in session, they were reading *Stuart Little;* I knew it well. My parents say I was a hot potato that the teachers kept passing. Possible: early reading was in vogue; I read before I was potty-trained, and a child who could read, if not comprehend, the front page of the *Washington Post*—my father's chosen teaching text—was not going to sit still through a year of the alphabet.

I missed dinosaurs and Egyptology. My math skills, never stellar, suffered permanently. These days I'd test as learning disabled; certain spatial concepts were—still are—hopelessly beyond me. The problem is mixed dominance (I write with my left hand, catch a ball with my right). My brain flips and/or jumbles left and right. To this day I cannot read a map or look in a mirror to braid hair on the left side of my head. To assemble a bookshelf from instructions, I have to hold the directions up beside me, so the instructions and I are facing the same way. Presumably, more attentive early education could have addressed some of these problems.

The more critical problem of the lost grades remains my somewhat jumpy sense of self. Because of skipping those grades I will always have a double sense of being both younger than everyone else—and thus having a comfortable lead—and of being in immediate danger of falling behind. I have always been the hare: because the tortoise is always gaining ground, I'm always looking over my shoulder. On top of the predictable problems of the wunderkind turning middle-aged, you miss a great deal of scenery when you speed towards a des-

tination. My memory is bad and I'm a pathological exaggerator, so my own past often seems like a landmark I saw hastily, or neglected to see at all, on a whirlwind many-city European tour. Even the childhood traumas have been streamlined until they might as well be the gritty, two-inch human interest stories in the back of the "Metropolitan" section.

It is true, for instance, that Bill Lucy followed me around for weeks in seventh grade threatening to kill me. He claimed I'd called him a nigger, but it's a lie, since I didn't know the meaning of the word when the accusation was leveled; among my parents' Jewish circle of friends in Silver Spring, Maryland, the derogatory word of choice would have been *schwartze.* But whether the incident that finally made my mother storm to the Lucy house in my defense was Bill slitting my dress down the back with a pocket knife while I bent over a water fountain in the hall of the junior high, I can't say. Clearly as I remember the feel of the blade, I may have invented the cartoonish details.

My brother and I have a saying: "Memory disqualified." We invented it for any recollection provided by our riotously unreliable cousin Lenore, but it applies equally to most of us in an extended family of jokesters and storytellers. Because practically each member lies or trumps in his or her own way, it is very hard to confirm any memory, although I've tried.

I told my mother a story I'd related to my therapist, about a childhood ear infection being neglected for so long that I almost went deaf, how clearly I remember the cold of the doctor's long instrument. My mother gasped. The ear problem was my brother's. I hadn't even *seen* the instrument in question; I'd waited in the lobby. And it wasn't an infection. My brother had a habit of dropping things into his ears, and the item that had to be so painfully extracted was one of her pearls.

Some therapists would claim that the accuracy of the memory is irrelevant, if I remember the neglect. I disagree. To me there's a difference between a child whose health problems are ignored, and a child with a sickly brother and a case of sibling rivalry so severe that she internalizes it, claims the health problems as her own.

No doubt, though, I was fearful and unhappy. And these memories of seventh grade I stand by with certainty. Most involve breast size, the area in which—younger to begin with and a late bloomer to boot—I most visibly lagged behind my peers. I had to leave the Girl Scouts in disgrace because on a camping trip, during a game of strip poker, I lost and, rather than reveal the contents of my 28AAA bra, screamed, called the counselor to our tent, and got us all in trouble. At summer camp, the older boy counselors would pass and whisper in my ear, "We're going to crucify you tonight." (How did they know?) At a slumber party, Sharon Triplett put my bra in the freezer, then she and some other girls pinned me down to force it on. In homeroom, five boys wrestled me to the linoleum and investigated the padded contents of that bra. "If you don't like it, sit at the front of the class," suggested Mr. Ray when I wept. This may be the best advice I ever got.

Obviously, the two-year difference between me and my peers did not help in the social adjustment department, especially since the classmates I wanted to befriend were consistently the raciest and most sought-after. While I was applying hot washcloths to my breasts to make them grow (my cousin Alice suggested the technique), the other girls at that slumber party were, I learned decades later, having sex on the back of the school bus.

My first novel, completed in the sixth grade, was about me being shipwrecked on an island with all of the most popular boys in the class. I carried the book to the part of the playground where they congregated to smoke cigarettes. "This is my new novel!" I said. "You're in it! Do you want to see?"

They didn't. Writing novels is not, for those who have considered it, the most cost-effective method for capturing the attention of the opposite sex.

Shipwrecked was my first novel, but not my first book. My first book was called *The World Aroud Us* [sic] and was an unabashedly inaccurate primer on the solar system, basically crimped from my father's memorable lesson on one of our dusk walks. (When he was nice, he was very, very nice.) The text itself was about ten pages, followed by ten pages of ads and order forms:

Did You Learn Something From This Book?
Then Read The Other Books In This Series!
    The World Of Plants
      The World Of Birds
        The World Of Fish
          AND MANY MORE! *BUY THEM!!!!!*

Such carnival-barker self-promotion is rather typical of writers. Clearly, most of us write for approval, adoration.

I'm afraid that one of my early efforts was about a rag-clad Mexican girl (an orphan, of course) who sings to herself as she weaves the baskets she sells to crass American tourists. One tourist is a Hollywood producer who brings her home, gets her recording and movie contracts, and introduces her to the handsome, kind, and devoted rock star she will marry. *Everyone* is jealous.

There appear to be published works of fiction by adults for adults that follow a similar formula. The less sophisticated the fiction, the more simply sympathetic the heroes.

Another early effort, a period piece, no doubt inspired by Zola or de Maupassant: A lonely prostitute tries to pick up a man strolling by. He's a widower, dignified and mournful. They become friends. Soon he introduces her to his dignified, lonely daughter. She needs a mother. That much is clear. Friendship turns into love. . . .

Freud contends that the writer, like a child at play, "rearranges the things of his world and orders it in a new way that pleases him better." The wish, he says, is at the heart of the creational process, and I couldn't argue based on my early efforts. Clearly I identified with Johnny, the hero of "The Kite of Freedom," a story I self-published in *Belle: A Teen Magazine.* Like all of my protagonists, Johnny was motherless and friendless. When his alcoholic father came home from the gas station, he always found energy to beat Johnny with a belt. In what sense, exactly, does this constitute a "wish"? Probably in the clarity of the deprivation. I have suffered, the work says. Don't I deserve fame and fortune?

For more sophisticated writers, the wish is always to tell the truth, to be believed. In *Survival in Auschwitz,* Primo Levi talks about how all the inmates shared the same nightmare, as pervasive as dreams of food: "They are all listening to me and it is this very story that I am telling . . . It is an intense pleasure, physical, inexpressible, to be at home, among friendly people, and to have so many things to recount: but I cannot help but noticing that my listeners do not follow me. In fact, they are completely indifferent."

Obviously, an unhappy childhood is not a concentration camp. I suspect that children who are brutally, severely abused, starved, or raped or abandoned in alleys, do not grow up to become writers. It's those of us who live on the cusp: officially comfortable enough to know we could be far more so.

Many of us, I have noticed, had parents who were storytellers themselves—and whose versions of truth did not necessarily accord with our own. My father is a psychologist, witty and wise; my mother is notoriously generous. Weeping multitudes showed up for both of their retirement parties. No one would believe them guilty of any wrongdoing.

What power, then, to grow up and set the record straight. My poem "Gypsy Moths" is hardly *Mommie Dearest,* but it caused some havoc in my family. One aunt did not speak to me for years, and my parents were deeply irritated. I suggested that if they didn't want their friends to read the poem, they would just have to forego the pleasure of thrusting the book upon everyone who entered the house. "Just wait until I write my poem about you," my mother grimly forewarned. "Then you'll be sorry."

Maternal grandparents, Ann and Frank Gould, with Lisa, 1956

All of that is behind us now. I'm forty-one; they are grandparents. They are as deeply invested in my welfare, in the happiness of my husband and son, as anyone in the world. Yet my memories of childhood fear still inform all the writing I do.

I never saw a corpse as a child. No relatives died. I never attended a funeral, or a wake. From the beginning, art was how I knew about death. But art was also my hedge against death, against the fear of death. There was a deep security in opening a book, in the way that the mere act of turning the pages carried you forward. Plot was the garden path, the way out.

When I write, I'm like the girl who has come upon the secret garden by intricate, devious means. Since after Adam and Eve all of us were ejected from the garden as we were all ejected from the womb, the only way to that garden is through memory, by which I don't mean the pat stories we tell at dinner parties or in the first weeks of a love affair. I mean those momentarily open brain-doors through which you glimpse something that makes you wonder, *Why was I thinking of that?* and then, though the impression lingers, you barely remember what you were thinking about.

How can you write about such fleeting sensations without stripping them of their wonder? Memories, after all, are not fresh but dank; they need to be dredged up like buried treasures, and often, after all that time underground or in a sunken galleon, they don't glitter in the sun; they oxidize or rust when they hit the air and don't seem so valuable after all.

Take Vito.

Vito Passante (his real name) was the alpha-wolf greaser in my high school. The slicked-back hair, souped-up car, leather jacket, and chinos were regulation, but Vito had a neurasthenic, rather regal face. I've been thinking about Vito lately for reasons that seem musky and mysterious, and that also shed some light on my writing process.

High school liberated me, and as usual, freedom came from writing. I was the editor of the school newspaper and had not one but two boyfriends. Steve mountain-climbed, played rock songs by ear on four instruments, and got into Yale but cared so little about his report cards that he routinely threw them out unopened. Marc, the other boy, earned enough

Zeidner family portrait: (from left) Julie, Joseph, Lisa, Dorothy, and Russell, mid-1970s

money doing children's magic shows on weekends to have his own new car. He could entertain girls as late as he wanted in his neon bedroom.

Both boys hated their fathers, as I hated mine. Steve's father was a physicist for NASA, eccentric and so cheap that, rumor had it, he continued to drive his ancient Rambler even when it ceased to go in reverse. Marc's father was unemployed and depressed. Since my boyfriend was the household's major wage earner, he could actually tell his father, "Go to your room."

Steve's friends, the official school intellectuals, knew me for a fraud. Steve was our valedictorian. He got 800's on both of his SATs. I was 96th in a class of four or five hundred, barely passed chemistry, and could never—even in repeated attempts—get my verbal score on the SAT over 600. Steve's friends mocked me and "Marc the Magic Clown" while Steve hung staunch in my defense against both my peer critics and my father. In a famous face-down on our front lawn, Steve deflected one of my

father's fists and threatened legal action if I was ever touched again. (My tellings of this story usually involved my father ripping my shirt off and my hurling his watch, a treasured Omega, to the ground. I suspect that he ripped my shirt, but not *off,* and that the watch got shattered in the fray, but not exactly hurled.)

So why was I cheating on Steve with Marc? I don't remember. I made a big deal about being torn between them; the luxury of actually being picked twice was probably irresistible. But they also represented two poles of response to the culture-at-large, which was already torn between spiritual freedom and financial security. I was at home with both credos, and having never been at home with anything, my life was blessed. I went to a moratorium in Washington, found a fifty-dollar bill on the sidewalk, sang for peace, then ate a candlelit French meal.

By 1972, Vito Passante was already past his prime. His power was waning. There were too many factions. There were the hippies (the word as cloyingly dated now as poodle skirts) and the intellectuals competing for Ivy League acceptances. By then no one was afraid of Vito, though my story would be better if they had been.

I'd found out (probably through Miss Ruddle, the newspaper's advisor) that Vito was an epileptic. His mother was dead, and his father was an unemployed alcoholic. I used to follow Vito around. "How does it feel to go home after school?" I'd ask. "Bad? Is that why you hang out at the shopping mall? Does Marcy [his greaser-girl] worry about your children's health? Do you want children? How do you envision your future? You're obviously smarter than most greasers. Did you make a conscious decision to limit the scope of your intellectual inquiry?"

When Vito saw me padding his way, ducktoed, he'd turn to his smoking buddies and say, "It's that crazy bitch. Let's split."

I saw him once again, in the shopping mall, maybe five years out of high school. My parents had moved to a better neighborhood. I was away at college. Vito looked older. He didn't recognize me.

That's the whole story.

So why have I been thinking about him?

And why does Vito make me think of the little boy dying in the secret garden?

Why, in turn, do Vito and the sick boy in the garden lead to thoughts of a student in my graduate class about whom I had a dirty dream last week? I would not consider such an interaction awake, and even asleep I had my doubts (his hair was full of cigarette smoke), but in between doubts I sinned mightily, merrily.

Vito, the boy in the garden, and the lusty student make me think of Boursault, which I miss. Since raw milk products have been banned for import, Boursault is no longer widely available in this country.

These are the kinds of things I think about, when I write.

Vito, secret gardens, sexy students, the fifty-dollar bill on the curb, fragrant Boursault: for the moment at least, my whole childhood can be reduced to these images. The point of the free association is very different in writing than it is in psychoanalysis, since the patient merely hopes to learn something about himself from the juxtaposition, whereas the writer needs to both understand the train of thought and keep

it tangled, which is the only way it feels strange, lush, unexpected. The images must seem obvious and elusive at once, like a mosquito or butterfly on your arm, which you must capture without it getting chased away, or smashed.

If I think too hard about the train of thought I just outlined, for example, it seems too obvious. Vito and I, me and the student, the boy and the girl in the garden: all are romances across socioeconomic boundaries. The oldest plot in the book and not a bad one, since the most exciting kind of love is the kind that won't keep—as with Boursault, the richness of the cheese is in direct proportion to its perishability. The little boy dies before his time, even before the flowers in the garden wilt; Vito Passante is unseated from his high school throne and relegated to a shopping mall in a neighborhood that, like Vito himself, is past its prime.

Unless he's mayor now, or a millionaire . . .

But I will not write about Vito.

What could I say? I couldn't write a Raymond Carver-type piece of realism revealing the existential, inarticulate sadness of a lower-middle-

Lisa with her sister, Julie (left), and brother, Russell

class man in a shopping mall, because that isn't my subject. I prefer to write about talkers, thinkers, ambitious people who are aware to some extent of their foibles and talents. Maybe my relatively cushy suburban childhood has rendered me insensitive to other lives, but at this point I don't think it's a limitation that psychoanalysis will cure. Besides, while I admire Carver's work, it is not the only kind of story. Let Vito marry a rich woman who loves him to death or go back to law school. Let there be some magic. Let Vito at least find a fifty-dollar bill on the street and spend it happily.

Or let him meet a woman he knew in high school, now a writer, not rich or famous, but happy, comfortable—I won't write that story either. With the exception of my third, most personal novel, *Limited Partnerships,* I have avoided autobiography, even autobiography as tangential as my slight connection to Vito, because "writing what you know" makes you accountable to the truth, and the truth, as a rule, is tedious. *I am not destined to be with Vito but I wonder if, sometimes, he thinks of me, as I think of him:* this is not material to keep a reader on the edge of a seat.

Even with the true plots and characters that are mesmerizing, writing from life is a little like choosing colors from paint chips. The color never looks on the wall the way it looked on the chip. The intensity of the color changes with the size of the painted surface, the light, the context. Vito Passante has an aura for me because I know his scale and surroundings: how he fits with my maturation, my decade, the metropolis in which I grew up. In the amount of time it would take to establish that much background in a piece of fiction, Vito would shrink too much, not seem worth the effort, and I couldn't bear to do him further damage.

And, as I learned from *Limited Partnerships,* every change for tone or dramatic effect produces a distortion, which leads to another distortion. Once I make my heroine a painter rather than a writer, because I hate books about writers, shouldn't she *speak* like a painter and not a writer? Once I give her a large family, to make her visits home interesting, shouldn't she *act* like someone from a large family? With a work of fiction that is wholly imagined, following those roads to whatever clearings or dead ends they provide is the fun of the process. It's fine to meander. But one doesn't want to feel like a liar, or a fraud.

*Lisa and John Pierre Lafont
on their wedding day*

The best fictional possibility for Vito, I believe, is the simplest. Just tell the story. The smart greaser, power waning, in the shopping mall, trailed by the duck-toed Lois Lane, interviewing. It might attain the wistful, bittersweet feeling that high school material so often gets, and it is vaguely a nice twist to have the ugly duckling, emerging from the abuse of junior high, suddenly aggressing on the aggressor.

I will never write about Vito, however. And the nicest thing about being a writer is that at least in the relatively free West, you don't have to write about anything. Or you can choose a subject, fiddle with it for weeks, shove the pages in the trash with the coffee grounds, and no one has to know. In days or weeks where all plots lead to the trash, I try to think about things like a 1906 photograph of five thousand uniformed women shoved together in a big, hot room, bent under lamps to hand-cut felt for Stetson hats.

As for the sick little boy, the garden, the fifty-dollar bill, Boursault: they're all still there, behind closed but unlocked brain-doors, in the apparently infinite storage space of the brain-labyrinth. The brain-Rolodex shifts gears, flies open—while making love, while teaching or grocery-shopping, or, best of all, in the middle of a work of fiction—and there the image is, ready for use. A lawyer who was a greaser in high school in his garden, eating Boursault. The cheese is delicious, but it doesn't cheer him. His son is sick. . . .

The word *garden* just produced a flash of the patch of grass in the neighbor's backyard, in my parents' old neighborhood, near the swing set, where only four-leaf clovers grew. Hundreds of perfect, bright-green four-leaf mutant clovers—it was magnificent. The smell of just-mown grass cuts through Boursault.

When I first met my husband, John, I treated him as if he *was* Vito. "I'm not lower middle class," he kept reminding me, sourly amused. "I'm just not Jewish." It's true that our families had very different priorities about education. While mine kept warning, "You can't make a living as a poet," and encouraged my academic pursuits, his wanted him to give up the luxury of meaningless knowledge and get a good-paying government job. Cutting off college was an historic thing in his family: his father, a policeman, had been denied tuition money unless he agreed to become a priest. He did not agree.

Although I suppose that both John and I are officially baby boomers, I definitely got the better end of the stick of the sixties cultural revolution. While I went off to college, experimenting with sex and drugs as I got my degree—albeit with some cheating on the math and science requirements—my husband, eight years older, agonized about avoiding the draft and suffered rifts with his devoutly religious, Nixon-loving parents. He hung out with poets and filmmakers, and for a moment it looked as if he could be recognized for his talents, make his place in an artistic culture without being weighed down with the formality of accreditation. When the recession hit, he was unemployed, and I had tenure.

I should point out that John is not a rapist. Though many people assume that the sexually irresponsible architect in my second novel, *Alexandra Freed,* was modeled on John, I met John while cleaning up the second draft of the novel. A copy editor pointed out that you don't *lay* Sheetrock, and that it wouldn't hurt

for me to step foot onto a work site, to get my facts straight. Then John presented himself at a party.

My first boyfriend Steve, incidentally, lasted a little over one semester at Yale before he dropped out. He found the competition insufferable. Now he is a union organizer in the Pacific Northwest.

Clearly I need these risktakers around me. At this point in his life, John's sense of self is totally independent of anyone else's evaluation of him. My son, age five, seems to have gotten the renegade genes. "I can do whatever I want to do," he announces, almost daily. Whereas even still, I experience that kind of exhilarated confidence, of freedom, mainly when I write.

And to this day, though I live in and write about cities, my thoughts of writing are strangely pastoral. A repeated transcendental dream which I first had in high school: I am sitting on a rock in a forest, near a waterfall, totally alone, a pad on my knee. I write, and as the words come, I begin to whirl, as you would from drunkenness but without the lurching sense of imbalance, until I am spun out of myself. Yet I'm right there, writing, by the waterfall.

The best-kept secret of my childhood, and my writing: I was happy. I am happy still.

Gypsy Moths

Some friends can't understand
how I can be close to my parents
when my father beat me
and my mother stood by, letting it happen
or intervened out of fear for him, not me
("Stop it, Joe—you're going
to have a heart attack").

Of course Dot and Joe insisted
back when I beat on the topic, when they
(as they liked to point out) were paying
for psychotherapy as well as tuition,
that *beat* was wanton hyperbole
and even then I was inclined
to believe them, not only

because victims often take the blame
(raped women "have it coming")
but because even now I am
an unreliable witness who woefully
exaggerates, all statistics trumped.
Still, it is a fact that I left
for summer camp one year—the year

that my bunkmates planted under my pillow
a bullfrog, which was supposed
to leap out, but it suffocated—
with a black eye.
My brother and sister both remember hiding
under tables in tears
while I was knocked about,

and if I was a "difficult child,"
the obvious question is why.
Why, at nine years old, did I suffer
from psychosomatic blindnesses
during Math class that forced me
to be led to the school nurse
then dragged every Saturday morning

to a child psychiatrist near the zoo?
After these sessions, my father always
took me to a Hot Shoppe for hash browns.
The diagnosis: classical Electra Complex.
Hard to argue when my stories at the time
were about a bird family
in which the mother bird fell from the nest

but the father and daughter bird
(no siblings in the sublimated version)
got on fine without her.
A later psychiatrist suggested
that maybe I just didn't like Math.
She believed that my harangues
against my violent father were a smokescreen

for the real problem: Mom.
How could I think my mother loved me
when I knew, from the Bill Lucy incident
(Bill had taken to tormenting me at school
and when he finally ripped my dress
down the back with a pocket knife
while I was bent over a water fountain

my mother marched to his house,
grabbed him by the collar, and threatened
murder if he ever touched me again),
my mother's power, yet she would not
wield it for me against my father?
In a quaint restaurant with a lover
in Perugia, Italy, in 1985, decades after

my parents were anything but charming,
I could still cry discussing this,
as if motherlove were a wash of sunlight
and I the frail, stunted houseplant.
If the Freudians are right, then everything
can be traced to that primal neglect.
"You can feel that," my companion said,

"but in your more grown-up head
you must realize it's not so simple;
if you were your child, you'd beat you too."
As we know from concentration camp inmates
stealing a homeland from the Palestinians
and affirmative action decisions
making it sticky for white males

with seniority, two rights can often
make a wrong. It could have been worse:
I was always fed, never molested;
I was not raised in an orphanage
by angry nuns with rulers; while my father
had been known to hurl
a plate of spaghetti at my head

when I spilled a drink,
he also took me to museums and zoos
and was proud of me, in some sense;
while some psychologists insist
a random reinforcement of praise and blame
is a worse fate for a child, the people
I most like now all had trying childhoods.

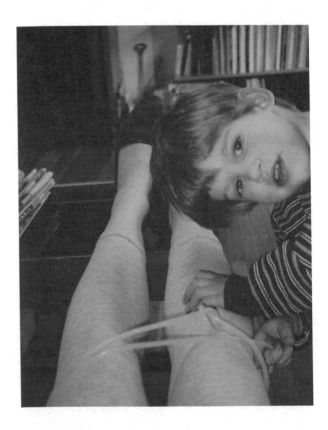

*"My son, Nicolas Roman Lafont, tying Mom up
a la 'Gulliver's Travels'"*

The fundamental tenet of psychoanalysis,
so Judeo-Christian: suffering strengthens.
My mother's father died when she was two
and she was abandoned to an old granny
so her mother could pursue a new man;
when Dot was reclaimed, she already had
a stepbrother, much preferred.

Her shoes never fit, thus her misshapen feet.
My father slept four to a bedbuggy mattress—
head, foot, head, foot, often a toe
in his nose—with four siblings,
the oldest of whom, Harry,
was institutionalized for schizophrenia
after he ran naked in winter across

the Brooklyn Bridge reciting Communist verse;
every Sunday for almost forty years
a sibling has visited him in the loony bin.
To us, Harry is nothing more
than a threatening, slightly cross-eyed
ancestor in the scrapbook
we've looked at so often

we know the pictures by heart:
my mother at fourteen, the buttons of her
    blouse
pulled slightly apart (how badly
she wanted a bra and her freckles gone);
us as infants, bland and blond,
anonymous, yet some tension in our posture
prefiguring future personality

as my father's swagger in the sailor uniform
suggests his sneaky wit tonight,
at this family gathering.
Aunt Ruth is complaining about children
who write spiteful autobiographies
biting the hands of celebrities
who fed them—the ingrates!

Don't you believe, my brother asks,
that Joan Crawford beat her daughter?
No, Ruth says, and even if it's true
how disgusting to tell the world so.
Baiting his sister, Dad asks who Ruth thinks
has the power, the parent or the child?
"The parent always does," he says,

"for years and years, so if the child finally
strikes back, who's to blame?"
Ruth retorts with statistics
on child molestation—she thinks
all that's invented to spite the parents.
We smile at each other: no way
to win an argument with Ruth.

Lisa Zeidner

Strange how rarely I argue with my parents.
They are witty, generous, their refrigerator
stuffed to the gills with delicacies
(I'd always assumed they stocked
for our visits, but my brother remarked
that a five-pound jar of ketchup
indicates otherwise).

"You need to put on some weight,"
my mother always says, as mothers will,
with her cool hand on my cheek or arm:
"How lovely to see you." My father,
cigar in mouth, asks us to join him
on "the grounds"—a wry description
of his suburban quarter-acre,

though we children cannot match
our parents' standard of living
in food stock or real estate,
our dwellings never as clean or inviting;
even our television reception is poorer.
Outside, my father frets about gypsy moths.
They are devouring his huge pin oaks.

The oaks wear skirts, and he has sprayed
the leaves as high as he could reach,
but the insects are plentiful and hardy.
We watch one caterpillar (they are not
moths yet, their whole cycle just
ten days—"they eat, lay eggs, and die,"
my father says, shaking his head,

"what a life")—crawl painstakingly
around the burlap skirt to find the bark.
All along the house's aluminum siding,
caterpillars make their obstinate ascent.
My father is killing them one by one
with the tip of the key to his Japanese car.
"I don't think that's going to do it,"

my sister observes, but Dad, coughing
from the cigar, says every bit helps.
Later that night, after a glut of movies
on the VCR (nothing at our house
in moderation), he brings us outside.
The gypsy moths are munching in the dark:
an otherworldly racket, like the crunch

of breakfast cereals in commercials.
You can hear the insects' excrement
hitting the pavement in the driveway,
a chorus of delicate pellets.
"By the morning," my father says sadly,
"the whole driveway will be covered
with shit, the leaves shot full of holes;

in three days the leaves will be gone."
The exterminator is supposed to come
tomorrow, but the forecast predicts rain
to wash away the spray. "How did the trees
get to be this old?" he asks.
"How did they survive this long?"
My mother smiles: "your father,"

she confides, "must always have something
to worry about." Remarkable how much
she loves him, for how long:
we can't touch such devotion
with our own mates, at least not yet.
We had always assumed my father
would die first; now we're not so sure.

My mother has complained
about a pain in her chest.
She falls asleep on the couch, TV on,
as if she doesn't deserve the luxury
of bed and darkness,
as during family dinners
she eats standing up while serving us.

We tiptoe past to the upstairs room
with the scrapbooks where, at 3 A.M.,
we huddle by a window to watch
our lone father
like a mad scientist or Martian
on the lawn in the dark with a flashlight,
still going at caterpillars with his key.

(From *Pocket Sundial*)

BIBLIOGRAPHY

Fiction:

Customs, Knopf, 1981, Jonathan Cape, London, 1981.

Alexandra Freed, Knopf, 1983, Jonathan Cape, 1983.

Limited Partnerships, North Point, San Francisco, 1989.

Serial Monogamy, in press.

Poetry:

Talking Cure, Texas Tech Press, Lubbock, 1982.

Pocket Sundial, University of Wisconsin Press, Madison, 1988.

Nonfiction:

Brandywine: A Legacy of Tradition in du Pont-Wyeth Country, photographed by Anthony Edgeworth, Thomasson-Grant, Charlottesville, Virginia, 1995.

Contributor of poems, short stories, articles, and essays to periodicals, including *Gentleman's Quarterly, The Mississippi Review,* and *New York Times Book Review.*

Cumulative Index

CUMULATIVE INDEX

The names of essayists who appear in the series are in boldface type. Subject references are followed by volume and page number(s). When a subject reference appears in more than one essay, names of the essayists are also provided.

INDEX

INDEX

INDEX